LIBRARY   043
BURBANK MIDDLE
DISCARD

W9-BHR-619

DISCARD

LIBRARY   043
BURBANK MIDDLE

INTERNATIONAL LIBRARY OF
AFRO-AMERICAN LIFE AND HISTORY

1

2

3

4

1. Frederick Douglass

2. The trial of John Brown

3. John Lawson, sailor

4. The Battle of Fort Wagner

5. Emancipation

6. Education

7. Suffrage

5

EMANCIPATION

6

7

301, A51
A
Vol 2
e. 1

INTERNATIONAL LIBRARY OF
AFRO-AMERICAN LIFE
AND HISTORY

AFRO-AMERICANS IN THE CIVIL WAR

From Slavery to Citizenship

BY

CHARLES H. WESLEY

AND

PATRICIA W. ROMERO

LIBRARY 043
BURBANK MIDDLE

THE PUBLISHERS AGENCY, INC.
CORNWELLS HEIGHTS, PENNSYLVANIA
under the auspices of
THE ASSOCIATION FOR THE STUDY OF AFRO-AMERICAN LIFE AND HISTORY

Copyright ©1978

THE ASSOCIATION FOR THE STUDY OF AFRO-AMERICAN LIFE AND HISTORY

Copyright ©1967, 1968, 1969

THE ASSOCIATION FOR THE STUDY OF NEGRO LIFE AND HISTORY

A NON-PROFIT ORGANIZATION

All rights reserved; except for brief excerpts used in connection with reviews, no portion of this book may be reproduced without permission from the publisher.

LIBRARY OF CONGRESS CATALOG CARD NO. 68-2634

INTERNATIONAL STANDARD BOOK NUMBER 0-87781-201-2

PRINTED IN THE UNITED STATES OF AMERICA

REVISED EDITION

In

loving memory

of

MATILDA HARRIS WESLEY

and

ROSE McCLURKIN BEATTY

Editor-in-Chief, CHARLES H. WESLEY

Research Editor, PATRICIA W. ROMERO

Production Editor, ALLAN S. KULLEN

Art Director, ARCHIE MIDDLETON

Copy Editor, MARY NEELY ELDRIDGE

Editorial Coordinator, EMILY EVERSHED

THE EXECUTIVE COUNCIL OF

THE ASSOCIATION FOR THE STUDY OF AFRO-AMERICAN LIFE AND HISTORY

ADVISORY COUNCIL MEMBERS

MR. EDWARD BEASLEY
Kansas City, Kansas

MRS. JEANETTE L. CASCONE
Instructor of Teachers,
Seaton Hall University,
South Orange, New Jersey

DR. HELEN G. EDMONDS
Distinguished Professor of History,
North Carolina Central University
Durham, North Carolina

MRS. DOROTHY C. ELAM
Director of Elamcon Interprises
(Promoting Records of Spirituals)
Retired New Jersey Teacher
Berlin, New Jersey

MR. WALTER FISHER
Professor of History, Director,
Soper Library, Morgan State College
Baltimore, Maryland

MR. WILLIM B. FRANCIS
New York City Building Inspector

DR. THEODORE D. HARRIS
Professor of History,
Arizona State College,
Tucson, Arizona

MRS. MARGARET G. HOLLOMAN
Instructor, Philadelphia Public Schools,
Philadelphia, Pennsylvania

DR. RALPH LATIMER
Dentist
Lima, Ohio

DR. HOLLIS R. LYNCH
New York, New York

MISS GERTRUDE P. McBROWN
President
Heritage Inc.
Jamaica, New York

MR. RICHARD B. MOORE
President, Afro-American Institute
New York, New York

MR. ERWIN SALK
President
Salk, Ward & Salk, Inc.
Chicago, Illinois

DR. ARTHUR M. SCHLESINGER, JR.
Professor, City University of New York,
New York, New York

DR. JOHN W. DAVIS
Consultant, The Herbert Lehman
Education Fund, New York City

MR. ROBERT E. EDWARDS
Instructor, New York Public
Schools, Brooklyn

DR. JOHN HOPE FRANKLIN
Professor of History,
University of Chicago,
Illinois

DR. KENNETH G. GOODE
Professor of History,
University of California,
Berkeley

DR. LORENZO J. GREENE
Visiting Professor of History,
Lincoln University,
Jefferson City, Missouri

DR. ADELAIDE C. GULLIVER
Chairman, Afro-American Studies
Center, Boston University
Brookline, Massachusetts

MR. JOHN H. HARMON
Director, Afro-American Center
White Plains, New York

DR. NATHAN I. HUGGINS
Professor of History,
Columbia University,
New York City

MR. LUTHER P. JACKSON, JR.
Instructor,
Columbia University
New York City

DR. FELIX JAMES
Professor of History,
Southern University,
New Orleans, Louisiana

DR. CHARLES WALKER THOMAS
Dean of Students,
D.C. Teachers College,
Washington, D.C.

DR. EDGAR A. TOPPIN
Professor of History,
Virginia State College,
Petersburg, Virginia

MR. IRVEN WASHINGTON
Assistant Principal,
D.C. Public Schools,
Washington, D.C.

DR. CHARLES H. WESLEY
Former College President; Director
Philadelphia Afro-American
Bicentennial Museum, Pennsylvania

DR. PRINCE E. WILSON
Professor of History,
Atlanta University,
Georgia

MR. ANDERSON THOMPSON
Instructor, Chicago Public Schools,
Chicago, Illinois

DR. EARL THORPE
Professor of History,
North Carolina Central University,
Durham, North Carolina

MISS DORIS WARD
Instructor,
San Francisco State College,
San Francisco, California

DR. LORRAINE A. WILLIAMS
Acting Vice President
for Academic Affairs,
Howard University,
Washington, D.C.

DR. GEORGE R. WOOLFOLK
Professor of History,
Prairie View A&M College,
Prairie View, Texas

MRS. VASSIE D. WRIGHT
Director, Region 9, ASALH
Los Angeles, California

MRS. SUE BAILEY THURMAN
San Francisco, California

Class of 1975-76

DR. MARY F. BERRY
Provost,
University of Maryland,
College Park

DR. ROBERT H. BRISBANE
Professor of History,
Morehouse College,
Atlanta, Georgia

DR. SAMUEL D. COOK
Professor of Political Science,
Duke University,
Durham, North Carolina

DR. RAYFORD W. LOGAN
Emeritus Professor of History,
Howard University
Washington, D.C.

MR. HERBERT MARSHALL
Norfolk State College,
Virginia

Class of 1976-77

MR. LERONE BENNETT, JR.
Senior Editor,
Johnson Publishing Company,
Chicago, Illinois

DR. JOHN W. BLASSINGAME
Professor of History,
Yale University
New Haven, Connecticut

DR. LOUIS HARLAN
Professor of History,
University of Maryland,
College Park

DR. GOSSIE HAROLD HUDSON
Professor of History,
Lincoln University,
Jefferson City, Missouri

DR. ELIZABETH PARKER
Instructor,
Department of Ethnic Studies,
University of San Francisco,
California

Ex Officio Members

DR. CLARENCE A. BACOTE
Atlanta University,
Georgia

DR. ANDREW F. BRIMMER
Visiting Professor of Economics,
Harvard University,
Cambridge, Massachusetts

MR. CHARLES A. BROWN
Principal,
Birmingham High School
Birmingham, Alabama

MISS WILHELMINA M. CROSSON
Retired Former President of
Palmer Memorial Institute,
Sedalia, North Carolina

Preface

THE Association for the Study of Afro-American Life and History joins with Pubco Corporation in presenting this new series of volumes which treat in detail the cultural and historical backgrounds of black Americans. This Association, a pioneer in the area of Afro-American History, was founded on September 9, 1915, by Dr. Carter G. Woodson, who remained its director of research and publications until his death in 1950.

In 1916 Dr. Woodson began publishing the quarterly *Journal of Negro History*. In 1926 Negro History Week was launched, and since that time it has been held annually in February, encompassing the birth dates of Abraham Lincoln and Frederick Douglass. The *Negro History Bulletin* was first published in 1937 to serve both schools and families by making available to them little-known facts about black life and history.

During its sixty-one years of existence, the Association for the Study of Afro-American Life and History has supported many publications dealing with the contributions of Afro-Americans to the growth and development of this country. Its activities have contributed to the increasing interest in the dissemination of factual studies which are placing the Afro-American in true perspective in the mainstream of American history.

We gratefully acknowledge the contributions of previous scholars, which have aided us in the preparation of this *International Library of Afro-American Life and History*.

Our grateful acknowledgment is also expressed to Charles W. Lockyer, president of Pubco Corporation, whose challenging approach has made possible this library.

Though each of the volumes in this set can stand as an autonomous unit, and although each author has brought his own interpretation to the area with which he is dealing, together these books form a comprehensive picture of the Afro-American experience in America. The three history volumes give a factual record of a people who were brought from Africa in chains and who today are struggling to cast off the last vestiges of these bonds. The anthologies covering music, art, the theatre and literature provide a detailed account of the black American's contributions to these fields—including those contributions which are largely forgotten today. Achievement in the sports world is covered in another volume. The volume on the Afro-American in medicine is a history of the black American's struggle for equality as a medical practitioner and as a patient. The selected black leaders in the biography book represent the contributions and achievements of many times their number. The documentary history sums up the above-mentioned material in the words of men and women who were themselves a part of black history.

CHARLES H. WESLEY

Washington, D.C.

Table of Contents

INTRODUCTION xi

CHAPTER

ONE   Prelude to War 1

TWO   Civil War and Emancipation 25

THREE   Admission to the Armed Forces 55

FOUR   In the Battles for Freedom 79

FIVE   The Aftermath of War 115

SIX   Negro Life during the War 143

SEVEN   The Period of Transition 177

SELECTED IMPORTANT DATES 212

PICTURE ALBUM 215

BIBLIOGRAPHY 263

PICTURE CREDITS 277

INDEX 279

Introduction

THIS study of Afro-American life and cultural achievements in the Civil War presents a relatively unknown story. The struggle which Afro-Americans faced in obtaining the transition from bondage to enfranchisement is dramatic and enlightening. It was not the Emancipation Proclamation alone, nor the Thirteenth Amendment, nor the triumph of the faith of the abolitionists—as important as they were—which changed Afro-Americans from property into free persons. It was the united efforts of a people who sought freedom through participation in the War and on the home front by joining their fellow Americans in the cause of peace.

The facts contained in this study will indicate that slavery was the underlying cause of the War, despite the economic and political questions which were involved. The North contended that its fight was to preserve the Union, while the South rested its defense on states' rights. Each section declined to recognize slavery publicly as a cause of the War—until the issuance of the Emancipation Proclamation.

In the first year of the War, the additional evidence of slavery as a cause was manifested in Lincoln's desire to keep the black man—as an issue—out of the War and thereby settle the conflict as quickly as possible. In the second year, the refusal to use Afro-Americans as soldiers was dominant; and yet, when given the opportunity in the later period, Afro-Americans proved to be brave and true.

Following the War, obtaining land and the ballot was important, and help in securing these rights came through the Freedmen's Bureau. The reply of the ruling elements in the South when they regained control was in the form of the Black Codes, which would provide another more subtle type of tyranny over the Afro-Americans.

The display of hatred, force, fraud and treachery did not succeed in pushing the Afro-American people backward. Instead, through the Fourteenth and Fifteenth Amendments, which came through the initiative of an interested Congress, the states acted in behalf of the democratic principles on which this country was founded. The Afro-American was an active participant in the efforts to attain those inalienable rights expressed in our Declaration of Independence.

Afro-Americans were on the march to goals, they prayed, they sang, and they worked. They fought, they were wounded, and they died, but they never lost faith in the principle of freedom for all Americans.

CHARLES H. WESLEY
PATRICIA W. ROMERO

Washington, D.C.

CHAPTER ONE

Prelude to War

Slavery as an Issue

A fundamental cause of the War.

IN the past century, there has been considerable disagreement among historians as to the fundamental causes of the Civil War. Was slavery the sole issue, or were there many associated causes? There can be no doubt that attempts to simplify the problem will lead one up blind alleys. The issues and causes of the War were not simple. They were very complex then and remain so today.

It is extremely difficult to discern now the many points of view that existed in 1860. The leaders in both the North and the South may not have reflected the majority opinion of the people they served, but they did reflect the social, economic and political issues of their day. In the North, there were citizens who believed that the Southern states should be allowed to depart in peace. Others berated the abolitionists for their contribution to the hostilities that arose between the states.

The Republican Party's platform of 1860 stated that each state had the right to control its own "domestic institutions." Slavery was regarded as one of these institutions. In spite of this, many Southern leaders pursued the cause of Southern independence based upon "immediate, absolute, eternal separation." In order to achieve separation, a convention of delegates from six of the cotton-growing states met at Montgomery, Alabama, February 4, 1861, and established a government under the title of "The Confederate States of America."

The attitude of some Southern leaders, with reference to Negro slavery, was expressed by Alexander H. Stephens, Vice-President of the Confederacy. Speaking at Savannah, Georgia, on March 21, 1861, he declared:

> The Confederacy's foundations are laid, its cornerstone rests upon the great truth, that the Negro is not equal to the white man; that slavery subordination to the superior race is his natural and moral condition. This, our new government, is the first, in the history of the world, based upon this great physical, philosophical, and moral truth.

It was evident that this meeting for secession expressed the attitudes of many in the South. They wanted independence based upon states' rights, and they championed slavery. The leaders of the movement were from the cotton-growing states and were joined later by those in the rice, sugar and tobacco states. There were, however, many Southerners who opposed secession.

The Civil War (1861–1865) has been called the Second American Revolution, the War of the Rebellion, the War between the States, the War for Southern Independence, the Rich Man's War and the Poor Man's Fight, the War to Save the Union, and the War for Freedom. It was also called a struggle between national sovereignty and states' rights. It has been referred to as a contest between profiteers, North and South. We know that it was a revolution in which both slaves and owners were freed, for both were enslaved by the system of forced labor.

James Ford Rhodes, Civil War historian, stated in 1913, "of the American Civil War

it may safely be asserted that there was a single cause, slavery." Other historians disagreed. Charles Beard stated that the economic development of the nation had created a second American Revolution with the "Capitalists, laborers and farmers of the North and West on one side and the planting aristocracy of the South on the other."

Historians have written that disagreement over states' rights, or the supremacy of the individual state over the Federal government, was the primary cause of the Civil War. Usually the belief in the doctrine of states' rights and support of the institution of slavery have gone hand in hand, in a somewhat subtle manner. This doctrine was often advanced by Southern writers, one of whom was Alexander H. Stephens.

Still another view of the Civil War was held by the school of historians known as the revisionists. A spokesman for this group, James G. Randall, concluded that the Civil War was a "repressible conflict." By this he meant that the War could have been avoided had emotional issues not colored the thinking of both Northern and Southern leaders. On May 4, 1861, *Harper's Weekly* had given evidence of the strong feelings of many in the North when it heatedly declared:

> It was not even a question of union or disunion. The question simply is whether Northern men will fight Southerners who have rebelled and dragged our flag in the dirt in the belief that because we won't fight duels or engage in street brawls, therefore we are cowards. The question now is whether or not they are right.

The *New York Times,* April 6, 1861, reported, "the issue is between anarchy and order—government and lawlessness—between the authority of the Constitution and the recklessness of those who seek its destruction." The *New York Tribune,* July 7, 1861, stated: "Some speak as if abolition of slavery were the object. But putting down the gigantic conspiracy against the government is it. That and nothing else is it."

Today historians generally agree that a combination of factors—social, economic and political—was responsible for the division of the nation. There is no doubt that the importance of the slavery issue was demonstrated when the Confederacy was formed. Because there were fifteen slave states, the Confederacy chose fifteen stripes for its flag, although at that time only seven states had seceded.

Slavery had been an active and acute issue in the decade 1850–1860. Outbreaks of emotional expression had been witnessed in the Compromise of 1850, the vivid and dramatic presentation in 1852 of *Uncle Tom's Cabin,* by Harriet Beecher Stowe, and the Kansas-Nebraska Act of 1854. The last led to the issuance of an "Appeal of the Independent Democrats," which called for the rejection of the program of slavery extension in the Territories. This split in the ranks of the Democratic Party was widened and, combined with widespread dissatisfaction with the Kansas-Nebraska Act, led to the formation of the Republican Party at Jackson, Michigan, July 6, 1854.

The Dred Scott case provides additional evidence that slavery was a fundamental cause of the War. In 1834, Scott, a Negro slave, was taken by his master, Dr. John Emerson, a surgeon in the United States Army, from the slave state of Missouri to Rock Island, Illinois, then a free state. In 1836, Dred Scott was taken to Fort Snelling, Minnesota, a free territory, where he married Harriet, a slave of Major Taliaferro. Soon after Scott's return to Missouri, Dr. Emerson died. In 1846, Scott sued Mrs. Emerson, the physician's widow, for his freedom on the basis of his residence in a free state and territory. He was granted a judgment in his favor in the lower court, but this was later reversed on appeal by the state's supreme court.

In the meantime, Mrs. Emerson had married Dr. C. C. Chaffee, a member of Congress and an antislavery leader. Because of this, the ownership of Dred Scott was then transferred to Mrs. Chaffee's brother, J. F. A. Sanford, of New York. The case then became *Scott* v. *Sanford* in the U.S. Circuit Court of Missouri, despite the allegation that the court in Missouri did not have the proper jurisdiction. Because citizenship was not granted to Negroes in Missouri, the court decided in favor of Sanford. The case was then appealed to the United States Supreme Court.

Scott v. *Sanford* was argued before the Court in 1855 and 1856, with the Court rendering its decision on March 6, 1857. President Buchanan had said in his Inaugural Address that the Court would deliver a decision giving a final judicial settlement of the question of slavery in the Territories. Each of the nine justices offered a separate deci-

HARRIET BEECHER STOWE

HARRIET SCOTT

DRED SCOTT

sion, with Chief Justice Roger B. Taney delivering the opinion of the Court. Three major questions were involved: (1) whether Scott was a citizen of Missouri; (2) whether he was free as a result of residence in free territory; and (3) whether the Missouri Compromise prohibiting slavery in Territories was constitutional. The decision on these questions was that a Negro whose ancestors were slaves could not become entitled to Federal citizenship, since Negroes were not citizens of the states at the time of the Declaration of Independence and the adoption of the Constitution. Said Justice Taney:

> They had for more than a century before been regarded as beings of an inferior order, and altogether unfit to associate with the white race, either in social or political relations; and so far inferior that they had no rights which the white man was bound to respect; and that the Negro might justly and lawfully be reduced to slavery for his benefit.
>
> . . . Dred Scott was not a citizen of Missouri within the meaning of the Constitution of the United States and not entitled as such to sue in its courts; and consequently, the Circuit Court had no jurisdiction of the case.

Taney further stated that even if Scott and his family had been carried into free territory for permanent residence they were not made free by these acts. Scott was not entitled to freedom, and the implication was that the slave masters were entitled to their slave property anywhere in the Federal domain.

Six justices—Wayne, Nelson, Grier, Daniel, Campbell and Catron—concurred in the denial of citizenship and the affirmation of the unconstitutionality of the Missouri Compromise. Justices McLean and Curtis dissented. The opinion of the latter was quoted widely. Curtis declared that some Negroes, although descended from African slaves, were already citizens and, meeting these qualifications, had the franchise as electors in the states of New Hampshire, Massachusetts, New Jersey, New York and North Carolina. He concluded by dissenting from the opinion that a person of African descent could not be a citizen of the United States.

The Taney decision was both defended and criticized. Many newspapers in the South voiced approval, but Republican opposition was vehement and without restraint. It was said that seven of the nine judges were Democrats and five of these were from slave states. To citizens of states practicing slavery, the Dred Scott decision was a basis for defense—if not for war. The *New York Tribune* in an editorial comment reported that Taney's decision "will be found to exhibit all the characteristics that have mocked his career. It is subtle, ingenious, sophistical and false. It is the plea of a tricky lawyer and not the decree of an upright judge."

The main question in the Dred Scott case was the status of slaves who had lived in free territory and had later returned to the states of their former masters. This question had been decided in 1851 by the Supreme Court case *Strader* v. *Graham*. The decision, rendered by Taney, was that the status of a slave depended on the law of the state of his residence, and if the law of the state considered him as a slave, he was a slave. If the doctrine of *Strader* v. *Graham,* which was a unani-mous decision, had been followed, the controversy over the Dred Scott case might have been avoided. It was evident that the purpose of the Scott case was to pass upon the constitutionality of the Missouri Compromise, which barred slavery from the Territories. Ironically, the Compromise had already been annulled by Congress in 1854, when the Kansas-Nebraska Act was passed.

Frederick Douglass, Negro abolitionist, referred to the Dred Scott decision in May, 1859, as the

> lying decision in favor of slavery and come what will, I hold it to be morally certain that sooner or later, by fair means or foul means, in quiet or in tumult, in peace or in blood, in judgment or in money, slavery is doomed to cease out of this otherwise goodly land, and liberty is destined to become the settled law of this Republic.

REOPENING THE SLAVE TRADE

The problem of obtaining additional labor for the industrial development of the Southern states usually ended with the importation of more slaves from Africa. While the slave trade had been abolished legally in 1808 by the Congress of the United States, the illegitimate trade, especially along the coast, had continued. It was generally accepted that free Negroes were troublesome and that they should be colonized in other lands. It was argued too that white workers would not work with Negro workers. As a result, the only solution was to increase the quantity of African workers. This was among the arguments presented in the Southern commercial conventions during the late 1850's. In 1856, a program for reopening the slave trade was proposed at a Southern commercial convention at Savannah, Georgia. Similar proposals were made in Knoxville, Tennessee, in 1857 and Montgomery, Alabama, in 1858.

Governor James H. Adams presented a message to the South Carolina legislature recommending that the state withdraw its

CHIEF JUSTICE ROGER B. TANEY

An artist's conception of the slave deck of the "Wildfire" when it arrived in Key West on April 30, 1860.

consent to the law making the trading of slaves an act of piracy. Governor Adams argued that the full development of the South would come by repealing this law and that the South would then reach a plane of equality in the national government. But it was stated in the U.S. House of Representatives that, at this time, the reopening of the slave trade "would shock the moral sentiment of the enlightened portion of mankind."

Despite the position of the U.S. Government on this matter, there was continued sentiment for renewal of the slave trade. The house of representatives of the state of Louisiana passed a bill to import 2,500 Africans to be indentured for fifteen years or more, but the bill was defeated by two votes in the senate. In 1858, a similar bill, authorizing the importation of 2,500 Africans as indentured servants for not less than fifteen years,

The execution of Nathaniel Gordon.

was adopted by the lower house of Georgia. This measure was postponed indefinitely by a majority of only two votes in the upper house. An effort was made in Mississippi to resume legal slave trade when a bill was introduced in the lower house requesting "a supply of African laborers." This bill was passed by the house, but was defeated in the senate. Similar action took place in South Carolina.

A Southern commercial convention met at Vicksburg, Mississippi, May 9, 1859, and passed a resolution concerning the slave trade. It decided that all laws prohibiting the African slave trade should be repealed. The delegates from Alabama, Arkansas, Georgia, Louisiana, Mississippi and Texas supported this resolution. The vote of the South Carolina delegation was divided, and Tennessee and Florida were opposed to the resolution.

This sentiment was accompanied by actual participation in the trade during the decade prior to the Civil War. W. E. B. Du Bois, in his *Suppression of the African Slave Trade to the United States of America,* reports that

eighty-five ships were engaged in the slave trade between 1851 and 1860. Despite these endeavors, however, slavery and the slave trade had run their course in American history, and free labor was in the offing.

The courts' desire to uphold the law was clearly shown by the imprisonment of Nathaniel Gordon. He was indicted under the act of May 15, 1820, which made slave importation "piracy on the high seas" and therefore punishable by death. No one had been punished under this act in the forty years of its existence until the case of *U.S.* v. *Gordon,* 1861. The piracy consisted of the shipping of eight hundred Negroes who had been taken on board at the Congo River, West Africa. Gordon was on the ship, the *Erie,* when it was captured. He was found guilty. President Lincoln refused to interfere in any way, so Gordon was sentenced to death. He was executed on February 21, 1862. In the other cases tried under this act, disagreement among the jurors or legal technicalities prevented the parties from being found guilty.

ABRAHAM LINCOLN

THE EMERGENCE OF LINCOLN

While the controversy over slavery and re-opening the slave trade raged in Congress, another event occurred, in the state of Illinois, that was to have an influence on these matters: Abraham Lincoln and Stephen A. Douglas became embroiled in a series of debates concerning these issues. It was 1858, and each man was challenging the other for the same Senate seat. Both had become prominent leaders of their respective parties in Illinois, and the major factor that divided them was the extension of slavery into the Territories.

Representing the Republican Party, which had been formed in 1854, Lincoln spoke out against the spread of slavery. Douglas, who had authored the Kansas-Nebraska Act of 1854, which provided for the extension of slavery, stated that each state had the right to decide for itself whether or not slavery would be allowed within its borders.

Prior to the campaign of 1858, Lincoln had earned a reputation of some standing as a competent attorney in Illinois. He had begun his career as a small-town lawyer handling minor individual claims. Moving later to the capital, Springfield, he had become prominent there for the manner in which he argued and won cases for some of the major railroads.

Lincoln, whose ancestors had been poor pioneers, was imbued with ambition and drive. Although he had received no formal education, his determination and his logical and quick mind helped him forge ahead in spite of this handicap. Probably his greatest asset in a Western state like Illinois was his warm, affable personality, his "belonging" to the common people and his complete lack of pretence or affectation. He was known as an honest man, not merely for the way in which he handled his clients' money, but also for the manner in which he sincerely and candidly stated his convictions.

Lincoln earlier had been elected as a Whig to four terms in the Illinois legislature. He also had served one term in the United States House of Representatives. While serving in Congress, Lincoln had introduced a bill to abolish slavery in the District of Columbia. Negroes were bought and sold in the nation's capital, according to Lincoln, "like a sort of Negro-livery stable"; and he found this practice "offensive in the nostrils of all good men, Southerners as well as Northerners." At the conclusion of his term, Lincoln had returned to Illinois and to his law practice, but he had maintained an active interest in politics.

A study of Lincoln's life in these years as it relates to the slavery issue becomes a matter of interpretation. His background and his personal make-up reveal him to have been basically conservative. He was not an outstanding reformer but rather was personally revolted by the concept of enslaving human beings to the will and domination of a master class.

It might be safe to assume that Lincoln did not know exactly how he felt about Negroes and slavery. Although he always agreed in principle that it was an evil and horrendous practice, his writings reveal an ambiguity of thought and approach to the issue. In 1841, while traveling with his friend Joshua Speed down the Mississippi River, Lincoln had encountered a group of enchained slaves on board ship. Soon after this experience, he had related it to a friend, by letter, stating that the Negroes were being sold away from family and friends, were chained together in groups of six, and were sailing into unknown and undoubtedly unhappy circumstances. However, he had continued with the observation that the slaves "were the most cheerful and apparently happy creatures on board." Then, philosophically, Lincoln had paraphrased the Bible by stating that "He renders the worst of human conditions tolerable, while He permits the best to be nothing better than tolerable."

Fourteen years later, in 1855, again by letter, Lincoln had reminisced on the event with his sailing companion of the earlier trip. Looking back upon the scene, he had stated:

> You may remember, as I well do, that from Louisville to the mouth of the Ohio, there were on board ten or a dozen slaves shackled with iron. That sight was a continual torment to me, and I see something like it every time I touch the Ohio or any other slave border. It is not fair for you to assume that I have no interest in the thing which has, and continually exercises, the power of making me miserable. You ought rather to appreciate how much the great body of the Northern people do crucify their feelings in order to maintain their loyalty to the Constitution and the Union. I do oppose the extension of slavery because my judgments and feelings so prompt me; and I am under no obligations to the contrary. If for this, you and I must differ, differ we must.

This second letter seems to illustrate that his feelings had become stronger with the passage of time than they had been when the event had occurred.

Whether Lincoln was politically opposed to slavery remains unclear. Most of his early remarks on the subject had been confined to the issues of citizenship and the extension of slavery. His personal correspondence reflects opposition to the institution of slavery but a willingness to abide by the laws that sustained it. Nevertheless, following his early activities in politics and his return to the practice of law, it was the slavery issue that brought Lincoln back into the political arena and eventually to the White House.

In 1854, Congress had passed the Kansas-Nebraska Act, which provided for the extension of slavery into the Territories. And Lincoln, for either political or moral reasons, or both, had voiced his opposition to the act in a manner that had been noticed by the leaders of the newly formed Republican Party.

The Republican Party had antislavery origins reaching back into the 1840's, and for this reason the party leaders were anxious to cultivate men who were willing to oppose slavery. In 1856, when the party held its first national convention to select a presidential candidate, Lincoln barely missed the vice-presidential nomination. The Republicans lost the election, but Lincoln retained his support in Illinois.

The following year, when the Supreme Court handed down the Dred Scott decision, Lincoln became more vocal about the question of slavery. He took the stand that the Taney Court had erred in declaring that a slave had no power to sue in the courts; and he said that the implications of the case went far beyond Dred Scott. On June 16, 1858, Lincoln decried the decision with the statement that "Such a decision is all that slavery now lacks of being alike lawful in all the States. . . . We shall *lie down* pleasantly dreaming that the people of *Missouri* are on the verge of making their state *free;* and we

STEPHEN A. DOUGLAS

In his outspoken opposition to the Dred Scott case, his further declarations against the Democratic administration and his debates with Stephen Douglas, Lincoln used his ability to logically argue the antislavery position, effectively if not conclusively. As the debates ranged from the spring of 1858 until the fall election of that year, they became heated and attracted nationwide attention. As the author of the Kansas-Nebraska Act, Douglas was forced to uphold his position and that of his party. And Lincoln relentlessly pursued his opponent by declaring that "A house divided against itself cannot stand. I believe that this government cannot endure permanently half-slave and half-free." He was accurately predicting what the nation might be forced to face as a result of the question of slavery—the Civil War.

Douglas, who defeated Lincoln in the election, argued that "this government was established on the white basis. It was made by white men, for the benefit of white men and their posterity forever. . . ." The fact that Douglas could make this statement and then be elected to represent Illinois in the United States Senate reveals the prevailing attitudes in the state at the time. It also illustrates what may have influenced Lincoln in his attitude toward slavery. Coming as he did from the border state of Kentucky to Illinois, which was part of the original Northwest Territory, Lincoln did not have the abolition background possessed by many of the leaders in the East.

In the presidential primary of 1859, this served to his benefit: he was not identified with the more radical wing of the Republican Party, and he was chosen by the Republicans to be their presidential candidate.

Thus, although it is clear that Lincoln was not always an uncompromising and outspoken opponent of slavery, it is important to realize that his basic sentiments as he approached the presidency were his antipathy toward slavery and his dedication to freedom.

shall *awake* to the *reality,* instead, that the *Supreme Court* has made Illinois a *slave* state."

Again, however, it is difficult to evaluate Lincoln's attitude because, although he opposed the Dred Scott decision, he qualified his opposition with the statement that he was not in favor of Negro citizenship. Since he was not in favor of slavery but did not sanction Negro citizenship, it is doubtful that he actually considered the Negroes' problem in light of its true solution.

THE JOHN BROWN RAID

By 1859, the disagreements between the defenders and the opponents of slavery had grown more acute. State governments in the North had legislated to prevent the recovery of fugitive slaves. These states included Maine, Vermont, New Hampshire, Connecticut, Rhode Island, Massachusetts, Pennsylvania, Ohio, Michigan and Wisconsin. Their actions were naturally denounced by many Southerners. Then, in 1859, in the case of *Ableman* v. *Booth*, Chief Justice Taney announced the decision that Federal law was supreme and that this supremacy had to be maintained against state interference. While the echoes of this decision and the Dred Scott case were reverberating, and rumors of antislavery activity were coming out of Kansas, there arose the mystic figure of John Brown, the precursor of emancipation.

Brown was born in Connecticut in 1800 and had worked at tanning, raising sheep, and selling land. He had devoted much time to reading and meditating on the Bible while moving to Ohio, Pennsylvania (where he aided the Underground Railroad), Massachusetts and New York. In 1855, he moved to Osawatomie, Kansas, with six of his sons and joined with the Free Soilers there. Proslavery families were attacked at Pottawatomie Creek and five men were slain. Brown's complicity was not proved, but he and his adherents were attacked. Brown's son Frederick was killed and the village was burned. Shortly thereafter, Brown left Kansas and returned to the East, where he planned to establish a post for freedom within slave territory.

Brown had formulated a plan to overthrow slavery, and his scheme was daring and quixotic. He planned to establish one post in the mountain areas of Virginia then extend his plans to Tennessee and North Carolina. He would attract slaves to these spots of freedom, arm them and instruct them for de-

JOHN BROWN

A view of Harpers Ferry, West Virginia, where John Brown's raid took place in 1859.

fense. He had gained cooperation from several extreme antislavery leaders, among them Gerrit Smith, and had secured two thousand dollars, several hundred Sharps rifles, and bundles of pikes. It is evident that the means and personnel at his command were small in terms of the project and the opposition which he faced.

The headquarters for his project was established at Chatham, in Canada. On May 8, 1858, Brown called a convention to draft a constitution for his new republic, and he proposed to create a state by appropriating portions of land located in the South. His ultimate plan was to form a government in this new area and then to secede from the United States.

In July, 1859, Brown took a few followers, including five Negroes, and settled in a farmhouse five miles from Harpers Ferry, Virginia. Later, on October 16, Brown and a band of twenty-one marched to Harpers Ferry, crossed the Potomac River, held the bridge, and then seized possession of the United States Arsenal. One of the Negroes

was Osborn Perry Anderson, who came from Canada to join Brown. Anderson escaped, wrote *A Voice from Harpers Ferry* in 1861, and later served with distinction in the Civil War. Another Negro in Brown's band was Lewis Sheridan Leary, a free mulatto living in Oberlin, Ohio, who was a saddle and harness maker. Shields Green, a sailor, was a fugitive slave from Charleston, South Carolina, and a protégé of Frederick Douglass. The remaining two Negroes were John Anthony Copeland, a North Carolinian who had studied in Oberlin, Ohio, and Dangerfield Newby, formerly a slave from Fauquier County, Virginia, who had been living in Oberlin.

On the evening of the attack, the first of Brown's little group to fall in battle was Dangerfield Newby, who was shot near the armory gate. Brown might have escaped with his band after daybreak to the mountains, if he had so decided. But he remained to fight and was later caught in a trap, forcing him to withdraw his men into the engine house. By the time Colonel Robert E. Lee arrived

TOP: *The John Brown Fort.*
RIGHT: *The engine house used in the raid.*
BOTTOM: *The interior of the engine house during the raid.*

OSBORN
PERRY
ANDERSON
DANGERFIELD
NEWBY
JOHN
ANTHONY
COPELAND
LEWIS
SHERIDAN
LEARY
SHIELDS
GREEN

with Federal troops, the telegraph had spread the news of the raid across the countryside. Brown left under cover of darkness, taking six of his followers with him, two of whom were wounded. But early next morning, Brown and his surviving followers were taken into custody.

The judge at first suggested that Brown should be examined for insanity, an idea which Brown met with scorn. Seemingly, it had suddenly occurred to Brown that every hour's delay until the execution came would diminish the tide of Northern feeling against slavery. A brief trial followed, and on December 2, 1859, John Brown was hanged in the public square of Charlestown.

The last note written by Brown, which was handed to his jailer on the morning of his execution, read:

> I, John Brown, am now quite *certain* that the crimes of this *guilty* land will be judged away but with blood. I had, do I now think, vainly flattered myself that without much bloodshed it might be done.

Brown's fate was shared by the courageous John A. Copeland, a member of Brown's original band. Copeland is quoted by the *Baltimore Sun* as saying on his way to the gallows, "If I am dying for freedom, I could not die for a better cause—I had rather die than be a slave." Reverence for John Brown among free Negroes in the North was widespread, because the general feeling was that Brown was chosen to lead the nation down the road to freedom.

Frances Ellen Watkins Harper, gifted Negro author and teacher, had written a letter to John Brown, while he was imprisoned at Harpers Ferry:

> . . . I thank you that you have been brave enough to reach out your hands to the crushed and blighted of my race. You have reached the bloody Bastille; and I hope that from your sad fate great good may arise to the cause of freedom. Already from your prison has come a shout of triumph against the giant sin of our country. The hemlock is distilled with victory when it is pressed to the lips of Socrates. The cross becomes a glorious ensign when Calvary's page-browed sufferer yields up his life on it; and if universal freedom is ever to be the dominant power of the land, your bodies may be only her first stepping stones to dominion.

Brown had also received a note on behalf of the colored women of Brooklyn, New York: "We consider you a model of true patriotism, and one whom our common country will yet regard as the greatest it has produced, because you have sacrificed all for its sake." A New Bedford, Massachusetts, meeting of free Negroes, December 16, 1859, resolved that "the memory of John Brown shall be indelibly written upon the tablets of our hearts, and when tyrants cease to oppress the enslaved, we will teach our children to revere his name and transmit it to the latest posterity as being the greatest man of the 19th Century."

John Brown was a hero of freedom. His devotion as an American to direct action was without precedent in the history of American slavery. Brown displayed dignity and courage at the time of his capture and at his execution. He stated in his last speech before the court that his purpose and design were to free the slaves. Brown insisted: "That was all I intended. I never did intend murder, or treason, or destruction of property, or to incite slaves to rebellion as to make insurrection."

John Brown was not insane because he wanted to establish a center in the mountains to which slaves would come for freedom. Nor was he insane because his project became an adventure which did not achieve its goal of liberty for the slaves. The historian Edward Channing, in his *History of the United States*, dramatically draws a parallel between the brave Greeks at Thermopylae and the American patriots at Lexington. They were outnumbered and were without available materials, but they reached their goals through blood, tears and death. Similarly, John Brown was a man devoted and dedicated to the cause of freedom. Yet historians and writers have made him appear as a desperate, foolhardy leader of a small band with an erratic hope of obtaining his objective through the shedding of blood. His bravery and sense of martyrdom are demonstrated not only in the way he went to the gallows but in his last message before his death:

> Now, if it is deemed necessary that I should forfeit my life for the furtherance of the ends of justice, and mingle my blood further with the blood of my children and with the blood of millions in this slave country whose rights are disregarded by the wicked, cruel and unjust enactments—I submit; so let it be done.

John Anthony Copeland and Shields Green followed their leader to the gallows. Copeland, who at an earlier date had helped a fugitive slave to escape, was a resident of Oberlin. Lewis Sheridan Leary, who was killed in Brown's raid, was also from Oberlin and was Copeland's uncle.

A monument was erected by the people of Oberlin to the memory of Copeland and Leary.

During his lifetime, John Brown had contacts with many abolitionist leaders. Among them were Gerrit Smith, Joshua R. Giddings, G. L. Stearns, Frank Sanborn and Frederick Douglass. Governor Wise of Virginia and President Buchanan had sought to have Douglass brought to Harpers Ferry during Brown's trial. Douglass continuously asserted

The trial of John Brown.

that he was innocent of any connection with Brown. However, on the advice of friends, he left Rochester, New York, and went to Canada. From there he traveled to England for a visit which he had planned prior to John Brown's raid on Harpers Ferry. More than two decades later, Frederick Douglass went to the shrine in Oberlin and delivered an address on "John Brown and West Virginia." He stated:

> I wish however to say, just here that there is no foundation whatever for the charge that I in any way urged or instigated John Brown to his dangerous work. . . . If John Brown did not end the War that ended slavery he did at least begin the War that ended slavery. If we look over the dates, places and men for which this honor is claimed, we shall find not Carolina but Virginia —not Fort Sumter, but Harpers Ferry and the arsenal—not Colonel Anderson, but John Brown began the War that ended slavery and made this a free Republic.

John Brown's invasion of Harpers Ferry produced emotional reactions throughout the nation. Southerners saw in it a sense of crisis, and the belief was widespread that the abolitionists were seeking to instigate insurrections in Southern areas. Vigilante committees and volunteer military companies were organized as a result of this excitement. Southerners had visions of Negro insurrections similar to the uprisings in Haiti. Many Northerners also were critical of the Brown raid, and the Republican platform of 1860 denounced it as a "lawless invasion," and as "among the gravest of crimes." However, the episode was of the stuff that heroes are made; and Brown was venerated by many in the North.

SLAVE INSURRECTIONS

Successful slave outbreaks, organized and well planned, have been few at any time in history, whether the slaves were white or black. The Haitian Revolution led by Toussaint L'Ouverture in the 1790's was one of the rare instances of a general slave insurrection, but in this effort there were patriotic motivations which carried it beyond the single endeavor of slaves to strike for their freedom.

There were sporadic and minor outbreaks in the South, but these were discovered and brought under control. Although the rumors of slave revolts were widespread, the South wanted to think of its slaves as being loyal. This is best expressed in a statement made by Governor William S. Walker of Florida in 1865:

> Where, in all the records of the past, does history present such an instance of steadfast devotion, unwavering attachment and constancy as was exhibited by the slaves of the South throughout the fearful contest that has just ended? The country invaded, homes desolated, the master absent in the army or forced to seek safety in flight and leave the mistress and her helpless infants unprotected, with every incitement to insubordination and instigation, to rapine and murder, no instance of insurrection and scarcely one of voluntary desertion had been recorded.

Speeches have been made many times on the same theme; but facts partly disprove these assertions. There were slaves who revolted, slaves who stayed at home, and slaves who ran away. Insurrections were reported in Virginia, South Carolina and Louisiana. The danger of other revolts was greatly lessened by the escape of the bolder spirits to the Union lines. Larger and larger numbers deserted the Southern areas and took refuge within the Union lines. Planters were advised to move their slaves into the interior so that they would be beyond contact with the Union armies. The arrival of these armies was the signal for the exodus of the slaves. This road to freedom was easier than any other. It was possible to wreak vengeance on the masters' homes and their unprotected families, but the slaves chose the more humane method of flight in obtaining their freedom. They could have resorted to violent revolution; but, instead, most of the slaves found their way to freedom without shedding the blood of their oppressors.

General Thomas F. Drayton, a native of the South, but serving as a Union officer at Beaufort, South Carolina, wrote:

> So far from there being any insurrectory feelings among the Negroes, I have never heard nor seen any act of pillaging, incendiarism or violence in any direction.

There was a small number of Negroes who were claimed to have expressed sympathy for the Confederacy at the opening of the War. This attitude could have been expected when the issues of the War were as unclear to them as to others in the South. The *Vicksburg Whig* of 1861 was reported as stating that a free Negro, Jordan, who was too old for active service, but had served in the War of 1812, had given his horse to a Confederate cavalry company and agreed to have the Confederate agent call on him for five hundred dollars. The headlines of this report bore the title, "Patriotic Loyalty of a Colored Man." The *Charleston Mercury* of 1861 reported that the free Negroes of this city had contributed four hundred and fifty dollars to the Confederate cause. The news item stated:

> The zealous and unfailing alacrity with which this class of our population had always devoted their labor and their means to promote the safety of the state is alike honorable to themselves and gratifying to the community.

Similar actions were reported in New Orleans and in Norfolk. Such reports are isolated ones and are greatly overshadowed by the numerous occasions of support given to the Union armies. These instances increased as the War continued, particularly as the information concerning emancipation became more general and the attitude of the Union generals and armies was directed by a definite government policy.

Insurrections, runaways and defiance grew more widespread with the progress of the War. There were approximately twenty-five important plots and insurrections during the War and a larger number of lesser disturbances, with rumors of others. The fear of slave rebellion was an important factor in the defeat of the movement for the South's independence. Negro civilians aided the contrabands as they passed through the Confederate lines. The women made flags for the Union troops and served as nurses, spies and guides. Among this group were Harriet Tubman, Sojourner Truth, Susie K. Taylor, Elizabeth Keckley and Mary Elizabeth Bowser, all dedicated and courageous Negro women.

THE NEGRO PEOPLE IN 1860

The Negro population in 1860 had risen to 4,441,830. About 90 per cent were born in the United States; over 10 per cent of these were of mixed descent, white, Indian and African. The Census of 1860 showed that most of the Negroes were living as slaves in the Southern states. In this section, there were 3,838,765 Negro slaves. In the border states and sections of the Northern states, there were 114,966 Negro slaves, with only 29 Negro slaves being reported living in the Western states. This represented a total slave population of 3,953,760. The free Negro population had increased by 23,736 in the slave states and by 29,838 in the free states between 1850 and 1860. There were 258,346 free Negroes in the Southern states, 225,274 in the Northern states and 4,450 in the Western states.

These colored Americans had secured their freedom before the issuance of the Emancipation Proclamation in 1863. They comprised about 2 per cent of the Northern population and about 1.5 per cent of the entire population of the country in 1860.

The Negroes' attitude and participation in the Civil War and their desired freedom from slavery were significant factors in this great struggle between the people of the United States. Their adjustment to the changed polit-

The United States Census of 1860, Showing the Number of Free and Enslaved Negroes in Each State

STATES	TOTAL NEGROES	TOTAL WHITES	NEGRO SLAVES	FREE NEGROES
Alabama	437,770	526,271	435,080	2,690
Arkansas	111,259	324,143	111,115	144
California	4,086	323,177	—	4,086
Colorado	46	34,231	—	46
Connecticut	8,627	451,504	—	8,627
Delaware	21,627	90,589	1,798	19,829
District of Columbia	14,316	60,763	3,185	11,131
Florida	62,677	77,746	61,745	932
Georgia	465,698	591,550	462,198	3,500
Illinois	7,628	1,704,291	—	7,628
Indiana	11,428	1,338,710	—	11,428
Iowa	1,069	673,779	—	1,069
Kansas	627	106,390	2	625
Kentucky	236,167	919,484	225,483	10,684
Louisiana	350,373	357,456	331,726	18,647
Maine	1,327	626,947	—	1,327
Maryland	171,131	515,918	87,189	83,942
Massachusetts	9,602	1,221,432	—	9,602
Michigan	6,799	736,142	—	6,799
Minnesota	259	169,395	—	259
Mississippi	437,404	353,899	436,631	773
Missouri	118,503	1,063,489	114,931	3,572
Nebraska	82	28,696	15	67
Nevada	45	6,812	—	45
New Hampshire	494	325,579	—	494
New Jersey	25,336	646,699	18	25,318
New Mexico	85	82,924	—	85
New York	49,005	3,831,590	—	49,005
North Carolina	361,522	629,942	331,059	30,463
North Dakota	*	2,576	—	—
Ohio	36,673	2,302,808	—	36,673
Oregon	128	52,160	—	128
Pennsylvania	56,949	2,849,259	—	56,949
Rhode Island	3,952	170,649	—	3,952
South Carolina	412,320	291,300	402,406	9,914
South Dakota	*	*	—	—
Tennessee	283,019	826,722	275,719	7,300
Texas	182,921	420,891	182,566	355
Utah	59	40,125	29	30
Vermont	709	314,369	—	709
Virginia	548,907	1,047,299	490,865	58,042
Washington	30	11,138	—	30
Wisconsin	1,171	773,693	—	1,171
TOTAL	**4,441,830**	**26,922,537**	**3,953,760**	**488,070**

Source: U.S. Bureau of Census, 1860
* Dakota Territory

ical, economic and social conditions occasioned by the War marked one of the most dramatic episodes in the history of the nation.

The free Negroes were regarded from one point of view as being "a valuable class of citizens." However, they were also regarded as a "degraded" people and as such were excluded from church membership, theaters, streetcars, and public buildings in many places in Ohio, Pennsylvania, Indiana, Illinois and New York. There were those among them who were refined and very well educated, and large numbers had good sense and sound morals. A minority report to the Convention of Slaveholders in Baltimore, Maryland, in 1859, stated that free Negroes were monopolizing the labor market in hotels, and that they were serving as barbers, coachmen, draymen, steamboat waiters and sailors. They were reported as causing considerable concern because they lessened the opportunities of the white mechanics to obtain work. It was said that if emancipation continued,

others, such as doctors, lawyers, merchants, clerks, newspaper editors and publishers, would begin to feel the effects of free Negro competition.

The occupations of free Negroes in Boston, Charleston, St. Louis, Philadelphia, Cincinnati, New Orleans and Washington showed comparable reports of skilled and unskilled labor. The value of property owned by free Negroes in New Orleans in 1860 was estimated to be $15,000,000. In Philadelphia in 1855, they were reported as having $800,000 in real property and $2,655,000 in real and personal property. They had 108 incorporated mutual-benefit societies with 9,762 members, and an invested fund of $28,366 in Philadelphia banks. A national convention of colored Americans in Philadelphia in 1856 reported that the colored people of New England had accumulated about $2,000,000 in business exclusive of agriculture; in Ohio, Illinois and Michigan, $1,500,000; in New York and Pennsylvania, $3,000,000; and in California, $200,000. In Charleston, South Carolina, there were 352 Negroes who had paid taxes on $778,423 worth of real estate, and 108 of them owned 277 slaves and had paid $12,342 in taxes on them.

A new era in the publication of newspapers by Negro Americans was begun in the period prior to 1860. Newpapers had been published by them since the launching of John Russwurm's *Freedom's Journal* in 1827, the first weekly newspaper produced by Negroes. Beginning with *Freedom's Journal,* many papers were edited, printed and owned by Negroes. The *North Star*, 1847, which changed in 1851 to *Frederick Douglass' Paper*, was established "to attack slavery in all its forms and aspects; advocate universal emancipation; exact the standard of morality; promote the moral and intellectual improvement of the colored people; and hasten the day of freedom to over three million enslaved fellow-countrymen." Other

JOHN B. RUSSWURM

Negro papers and some of their editors were: *The Colored Man's Journal,* New York, 1851, editor, L. H. Putnam; *The Alienated American,* Cleveland, Ohio, editor, W. H. Day; *The Mirror of the Times,* San Francisco; *The Herald of Freedom,* Cincinnati, Ohio, 1855, Peter H. Clark, editor; *The Christian Record,* 1856, Jabez Campbell, editor; and *The Anglo-African,* New York, 1859, Thomas Hamilton, editor.

Whether they were from the North, South, East or West, there were Negroes at work in America in the pursuit of their own individual interests and those of their particular ethnic group. Certain individuals were occupying important places in occupational and community life, while the masses did not have this opportunity. These persons were not satisfied with having the masses proscribed and restricted as they were. The industry of many communities, North and South, was dependent upon the labor of free Negroes. The assumption is not true that Negroes were unable to care for themselves as other Americans until after the Civil War and that their progress had begun with their emancipation. To the contrary, individual Negroes had freed themselves or had been freed by various means from human slavery and economic want many years prior to the Civil War.

THE CAMPAIGN OF 1860

In 1860, there were remnants of scattered political parties in the United States—Whigs, Free Soilers and Know-Nothings. Because of internal divisions, none of these parties would have the opportunity of participating in the national election as a separate entity. The Democratic Party, however, assembled at Charleston, South Carolina, April 23, 1860, to select its candidate for the presidency. A platform was presented affirming Stephen Douglas' doctrine that "control of slavery in the territories was the decision of each territory." When this platform was adopted, the delegations from South Carolina, Georgia, Arkansas and the Gulf States departed from the auditorium.

A second session at Baltimore, Maryland, on June 18, selected Douglas as its presidential candidate and H. V. Johnson of Georgia as the vice-presidential candidate. The bolting delegates held a convention at Baltimore on June 21 and adopted a platform, selecting as candidates John C. Breckinridge of Kentucky and Joseph Lane of Oregon.

The Republican Party held its second presidential convention at Chicago in May, 1860. The platform was designed to attract voters to the new party. It declared that the exclusion of slavery from the Territories was necessary and denounced the doctrine that the Constitution was responsible for carrying slavery into the Territories. It also advocated free homesteads in the West, and urged that "the Union of the States must and shall be preserved."

William H. Seward, formerly Governor of and then United States Senator from New York, led on the first two ballots at the Republican convention. On the third ballot, the presidential nomination went to Abraham Lincoln. Lincoln was less of an antislavery radical than Seward, and this was a prime factor in his nomination. Because he was the son of poor parents and a self-educated man, he would have special appeal to the large groups of laboring people in the North. For its vice-presidential candidate, the convention chose Hannibal Hamlin of Maine, who was prominent in the antislavery movement.

The Constitutional Union Party, which included remnants of the Know-Nothing Party, assembled at Baltimore, Maryland, on the 9th of May. Its platform pledged to uphold "the Constitution of the country, the Union of the States and the enforcing of the laws." The candidates nominated were John Bell of Tennessee and Edward Everett of Massachusetts.

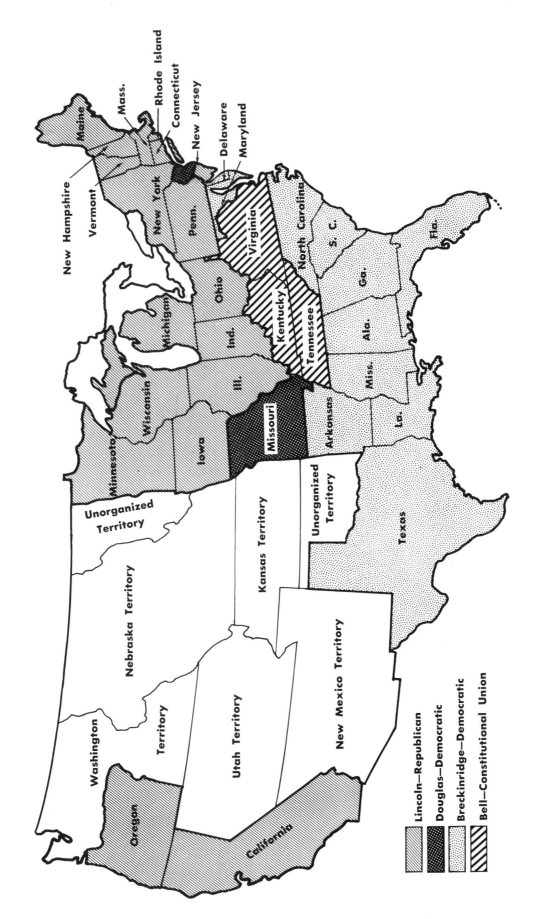

PRESIDENTIAL ELECTION OF 1860

Lincoln—Republican
Douglas—Democratic
Breckinridge—Democratic
Bell—Constitutional Union

HANNIBAL HAMLIN

The campaign of the Republican Party was conducted on two planes. One was preservation of the Union and Western expansion. The other was based on antislavery and was exemplified by the speeches of Carl Schurz. Schurz, an eloquent orator, later to gain distinction as a statesman, soldier and historian, was in great demand as a speaker for Negro freedom and campaigned with dedicated fervor for abolition.

The Democrats took pains to magnify such evidences of opposition to slavery. Southerners charged that the Republican ticket had its racial implications. R. Barnwell Rhett, South Carolina legislator and ardent secessionist, declared, "If the Black Republicans succeed in electing Lincoln and Hamlin, then we shall have to look to ourselves. Hamlin is what we call a mulatto. He has black blood in him. They put a renegade Southerner on one side for President, and they put a man of colored blood on the other side of the ticket for Vice-President." Such statements were untrue, but they may have influenced many Negroes to vote Republican.

The stature of Lincoln grew as he received Northern recognition during the campaign. To Negroes, he was not an ideal candidate, because of what they referred to as "his proslavery character and principles." On the other hand, they were not attracted in any way to Stephen Douglas because of the Democratic Party's decision that slavery in the Territories should be decided by the Supreme Court. As a result, the party of Abraham Lincoln was the least antagonistic, and most Negroes who were permitted to vote gave their votes to the Republicans.

Not all Negroes in the Northern states could vote. In the majority of the New England states, Negroes were allowed to vote on the same basis as whites. In New York, however, there was a restriction which stated that a colored man should possess a freehold, with a value of at least $250, in order to be allowed to vote. A special election in 1860 to change this requirement was defeated. Ohio, Indiana and Illinois had similar provisions that restricted Negro voting.

Special efforts were made in Ohio by Negroes to secure the vote. In 1859, the General Assembly of Ohio had adopted the following authorization:

> The judge or judges of any election held under the authority of any laws of this state shall reject the vote of any person offering to vote at such elections, and claiming to be a white male citizen of the United States, whenever it shall appear to such judge or judges that the person so offering has a distinct and visible admixture of African blood.

This statement was later viewed as the "Visible Admixture Law," and was declared unconstitutional in 1860. The Unionists recognized this decision, but the Democrats opposed it. Sections of the state of Ohio differed in their election participation. In some places, even "full-blooded" Negroes were allowed to vote. In Illinois, Pennsylvania and Indiana, constitutional provisions invited suffrage and, therefore, entry into these states.

Despite all the obstacles and restrictions in their way, Negroes who were able made a

FREDERICK DOUGLASS

his readers that ten thousand votes for Smith would do more for the abolition of slavery than two million for Lincoln or any other candidate "who stands pledged before the world against all interference with slavery in the slave states and who is not opposed to making free states a hunting ground for men under the Fugitive Slave Law." In being selected as one of two electors-at-large, Douglass became the first Negro to be chosen for such a party position.

Another great Negro American, the lawyer, educator and diplomat John Mercer Langston, in his own words concerning the support of the Republican Party in the campaign, said that he ". . . gave prompt support in every national and local contest and showed himself [*sic*] its sincere and determined advocate and supporter."

The importance of the election of 1860 was stressed by the *Atlantic Monthly* in the following statement, "We believe this election is a turning-point in our history." Negro Americans regarded it as one of their great moments.

The election reports of the votes cast on November 6 were: for Lincoln, 180 electoral votes; for Breckinridge, 72; Bell, 39; and Douglas, 12. A simple majority of electoral votes was enough to elect Lincoln as President. The popular vote revealed that Lincoln had received 1,866,352; Douglas, 1,375,157; Breckinridge, 847,514; and Bell, 587,830. Lincoln's vote was greater than any one of his opponents, but he had a smaller total vote than all others combined—1,866,352 to 2,810,501; and, accordingly, he was elected as a minority president. Lincoln's voting power was confined to the North and far West, thus was sectional in this respect. He received not a single popular vote from ten Southern states.

Reaction to Lincoln's victory was immediate; and on December 20, 1860, by unanimous vote, the South Carolina legislature, meeting at Charleston, declared that the

great, concerted effort in this critical period. No special attempt was made to attract Negro voters to the Republican Party. Yet in some large cities, such as Pittsburgh, they formed political marching clubs and paraded with capes and hats. The prominent Negro statesman Frederick Douglass said that he threw himself into the Republican campaign "with firmer faith and more ardent hope than ever before," and went on to say that what he could do with his pen or tongue, he did with a will. Douglass campaigned actively in Michigan, Wisconsin, Iowa and New York. This may have been because Gerrit Smith had said earlier that he was more inclined to Lincoln than to Seward, and that he expected greater good from Lincoln's election than from a victory for his Democratic opponent.

Later, however, Frederick Douglass, in editorials, letters and speeches, advocated the election of Gerrit Smith, a candidate of the radical antislavery party. Douglass advised "union between South Carolina and the other states under the name of 'United States of America' is hereby dissolved." Georgia chose secession by a vote of 84–15. Alabama seceded by a vote of 61–39; Florida, by a vote of 62–7; Louisiana, by a vote of 113–17; Texas, by a vote of 166–8. Mississippi seceded by a vote of 84–15 and followed with mass meetings, parades, speeches and fireworks.

By making the following statement in his Inaugural Address, March 4, 1861, Lincoln expressed his desire to conciliate the South while preserving the Union. "I have no purpose, directly or indirectly, to interfere with the institution of slavery in the states where it now exists. I believe I have no lawful right to do so, and I have no inclination to do so." Negroes had waited with expectation for this message, and were disappointed. As the *Anglo-African* commented, "We gather no comfort from the inauguration of Abraham Lincoln."

A month after Lincoln's inauguration, seven states of the lower South had voted for secession, and eleven states finally joined together to form the Confederate States of America. The prelude to War had come to an end, and the War had begun with slavery and the Negro deep in its midst.

CHAPTER TWO

Civil War and Emancipation

The Transition to Freedom

Negroes entering Union lines to sell food and seek aid.

WHEN the Civil War began with the Confederate attack on Fort Sumter, April 12, 1861, the leaders of both North and South failed to recognize that the Negro and slavery were important underlying causes of the War. The Congress of the United States had resolved:

> The War's purpose was not the overthrowing or interfering with the rights of established institutions . . . [but] to preserve the Union with all the dignity, equality and rights of the several states unimpaired; and that as soon as these objects are accomplished, the War ought to cease.

The North had no official plan to free the Southern slaves, for this was solely a war to preserve the Union. And yet, with 3,838,765 slaves and 258,346 free Negroes in the South, many people, both North and South, realized that in the final analysis the threat to the Union was in the contest between slavery and freedom.

Although Southern Negroes initially were cut off from nearly all news of the War, they managed to keep informed. They had for years in the past devised ways of communicating without speaking. When the telegraph wires conveyed reports of the advancing Federal armies deep into the Confederacy, house slaves often were able to overhear enough to

LIBRARY 043
BURBANK MIDDLE

Negroes unloading boats for the Union Army.

relay the messages to others on the plantation. These people, in turn, passed them on to neighboring slave populations. Signals such as a tip of the hat, a left-hand greeting or a cough were used to pass on the much-desired information about the location of Union troops.

Long before the leaders of the North admitted that they were fighting a war to end slavery, the slaves themselves held this conviction. Almost with the first shot at Fort Sumter, word had gone out that freedom was not far behind. As the slaves grew more restless in their anticipation of being released from their bonds, the plantation owners became more stringent in their attitudes toward the Negroes. Passes were revoked and longer hours were called for in the field. These measures served the dual purpose of keeping the slaves confined while also producing more for the growing needs of the Confederate Army.

Masters who had previously been somewhat permissive with their slaves often became harsh and cruel. Their intention was to frighten the slaves into remaining on the plantations and to keep them submissive to the will of the master. But they were unsuc-

cessful in many cases, and the issue of slavery was brought openly into question in the U.S. Congress and in the armies of the North by the appearance of hundreds of Negroes coming into Union lines to sell food and seek aid.

The Negroes who first came within the Union lines were either taken into custody as fugitives or sent back to their masters. However, on May 24, 1861, General Benjamin F. Butler declined to return three Negroes who had come into Fort Monroe, declaring that workers were needed by his army, and that the Fugitive Slave Act did not apply to Virginia, which was, after secession, "a foreign country." General Butler declared these slaves to be "contraband of war." But he was concerned about the newcomers and, as he said, "in utmost doubt what to do with this species of property." A Virginian appeared at Fort Monroe and demanded the return of his slaves. He was received by General Butler, who informed him that, if he would take the oath of allegiance to the United States, the slaves would be returned. But the slaveowner refused to comply. Postmaster General Montgomery Blair wrote General Butler on May 29, 1861, that he was right in declaring secession Negroes as "contraband of war." Thus, "contraband" became a word generally used for escaping slaves.

In 1861, Negroes who were former slaves worked under General Sherman in South Carolina, General Banks in Louisiana, General Butler in New Orleans, and General Grant around Vicksburg. They labored on the fortifications, loaded and unloaded boats and performed other work required by the armies. This use of Negroes by the Union armies had been preceded by the Confederate armies' use of slaves in the construction of their military defenses.

As the Federal forces moved into the areas of rebellion, the Negro slaves in search of freedom continued to come into the camps. Many Negroes left their work on the plantations and flocked toward the approaching armies; but, for every one who left, there were five who remained. General Grant appointed John Eaton, Jr., one of the chaplains of the 27th Ohio Infantry, as general superintendent of Negro affairs. Eaton was promoted to colonel of the 63rd U.S. Colored Troops and authorized to aid the increasing number of contrabands throughout the Departments of Tennessee and Arkansas. He established special camp areas, organized the slaves as military laborers, fixed wages and kept accounts. He directed government subsistence for some and gave others the opportunity to contribute their labor for their own support. For many, this was the first time in their lives that they received payment for the services they performed.

As their numbers increased within the Union lines, it became necessary to construct additional camps. Picket lines were set up by the Confederates to prevent the escape of their slaves to the Federal forces. But despite these precautions, it was soon said that a flag of truce in the hands of a Negro became a welcome sight to the advancing Federal troops.

FIRST EXPERIMENTS WITH FREE LABOR

Public efforts for the relief of Negroes made free by their entrance into Union lines were undertaken in February, 1862. Initially the Union commanders planned relief, and then work, for the freedmen. But on February 6, 1862, General W. T. Sherman issued an order describing the conditions of the freedmen and inviting the assistance of the public. Meetings were held in local areas, and on February 22 the National Freedmen's Relief Association was formed in New York. Shortly thereafter, the Contraband Relief Association, which later became the Western Freedmen's Aid Commission, was organized in Cincinnati, and in 1863, the Northwestern Freedmen's Aid Commission was started in Chicago. The Western Sanitary Commission of St. Louis and the United States Sanitary Commission at Washington were also organized to relieve distress among the freedmen. The American Freedmen's Aid Commission, with offices in Washington, New York and Chicago, was formed later to centralize the work of these organizations. The freedmen were placed in camps, where schools were established for them, and projects for productive labor were started through these various societies.

The first organized experiment with free labor began at Port Royal in 1861. It was soon discovered that the freedmen wanted to work, especially when the returns from their labor came to them. The freedmen picked, baled and rolled cotton and were paid at the rate of one dollar for every hundred pounds delivered. These bags of cotton were marked with the owner's name; and when the owners proved their loyalty to the Federal government, they were credited with the compensation.

In 1862, a similar system of supervised labor was planned in New Orleans under General Butler, who had established a Department of Negro Affairs. Butler insisted that the Negroes could be as well governed and as economically profitable in freedom as they were in slavery and urged the Negroes to buy land, form villages and build homes for their families. It is very possible that he was correct because his government agents reported that with free labor they were able to make a hogshead and a half more of sugar per day than was made with slave labor. The first barrel of sugar made in this area with free labor was sent to President Lincoln. Other experiments were tried in several different places and proved to be successful both in terms of monetary gains and in the introduction of the Negro slave worker into the wage system.

After the fall of Vicksburg, it was reported that there were 113,650 Negroes under supervision and 41,150 in service as soldiers, laundresses, cooks, officers, servants and laborers. There were 62,300 reported as being self-supporting. These were employed as plantation workers, mechanics, barbers, hackmen, draymen and conductors of small enterprises. Their wages were five dollars a

month for common laborers, eight dollars a month for ordinary mechanics and twelve to fifteen dollars a month for skilled laborers. It was reported that the value of contraband labor amounted to over a million dollars in 1861.

LINCOLN AND THE GENERALS AS EMANCIPATORS

The events of the War soon brought the issue of slavery into the open and aroused greater interest in the freedom of the slaves. It will be remembered that the abolitionists were instrumental in designating slavery as the cause of the War. Through the year 1861, they had continued to seek the abolition of slavery, and they were joined in their effort by the vigorous *New York Tribune* editor Horace Greeley. Even in Lincoln's Cabinet there were those who had strong antislavery beliefs, such as Salmon P. Chase, Secretary of the Treasury; Edwin M. Stanton, Secretary of War; and William H. Seward, Secretary of State.

Abolitionist feeling grew stronger as the War continued, and Congress was sent hundreds of petitions calling for emancipation. One of these petitions was signed by Susan B. Anthony, noted crusader for women's rights. Another contained the signatures of Henry T. Cheever, Congregationalist minister, and Lee Claflin, who later founded a college for Negroes in South Carolina.

Lincoln was a man of great moral strength and had much warmth and affection for his fellow men. He personally did not believe in slavery, and as early as 1831 it was reported that he stated in New Orleans, "If I ever get a chance to hit that thing, I'll hit it hard." A few years later, when speaking in Cincinnati, Lincoln had remarked that slavery and oppression must cease or American liberty would perish. However, Abraham Lincoln, as President of the United States, was not his own master in reference to this issue. He was

Free Negroes picking cotton.

forced to put aside his personal convictions and to act for the good of the country and its people as a whole. During the first year of conflict between North and South, the President refused to allow the issue of slavery to have a dominant role in the affairs of the rebellion. Instead, he treated the seceded states like children who had gone astray and sought to reconcile their differences rather than provide a deeper division, particularly in the border states, which a direct confrontation with the question of slavery would certainly have done.

On August 6, 1861, Congress passed a Confiscation Act which declared that, when slaves were used in the military service of those in rebellion, the claims of the owners to such slaves were forfeited. While the interpretation of this act was uncertain, it marked the first step in a changing policy towards emancipation. Congress itself was divided over the issue of slavery, with Congressman Thaddeus Stevens of Pennsylvania and Senator Charles Sumner of Massachusetts serving as leaders in the antislavery movement.

General John Charles Frémont had been given command of the Western division of the War and established headquarters in St. Louis. Frémont had been an antislavery man prior to the War and was still active in this cause at the time of his appointment. In 1856, he had been the Republican Party's first candidate for President, running on a program for the non-extension of slavery. Upon assuming his command, Frémont found that conditions in the West were in a turmoil. There was division among the people of Missouri. Many sympathized with the South, while others were loyal supporters of the North. And the Union armies in the West were faring about the same as those in the East: they were not winning battles.

The conflicting views regarding the War and slavery, coupled with Frémont's isolation from Washington, caused him to believe that drastic action was called for on the

GENERAL JOHN CHARLES FRÉMONT

Western front. With this view in mind, he issued a proclamation declaring martial law in the state of Missouri.

Frémont declared that all persons engaged in activities against the government of the United States were guilty of treason. As a result, their property was to be confiscated, and any slaves they held were to be freed. He then set up a commission to issue deeds of manumission to the former slaves. This was the first act performed by a government official which offered emancipation as a means of punishing persons in rebellion. A furor arose in Washington over Frémont's action. There had been no authorization for such a measure; indeed, Lincoln had tried to avoid the issue of slavery as a cause of the War.

The Union was on shaky ground with sentiment on the issue of slavery divided. Especially important to Lincoln were the border states which were loyal to the Union despite their practice of slavery. Frémont's proclamation served to sow seeds of discord im-

PROCLAMATION
Headquarters Western Department
St. Louis
August 30, 1861

Circumstances in my judgment are of sufficient urgency to render it necessary that the commanding General of this department should assume the administrative powers of the State. Its disorganized condition, helplessness of civil authority and the total insecurity of life, and devastation of property by bands of murderers and marauders, who infest nearly every county in the State, and avail themselves of public misfortunes, in the vicinity of a hostile force, to gratify private and neighborhood vengeance, and who find an enemy wherever they find plunder, finally demand the severest measures to repress the daily increasing crimes and outrages, which are driving off the inhabitants and ruining the State.

In this condition, the public safety and success of our arms require unity of purpose, without let or hindrance to the prompt administration of affairs. In order, therefore, to suppress disorders, maintain the public peace, and give security to the persons and property of loyal citizens, I do hereby extend and declare established martial law throughout the State of Missouri. The lines of the army occupation in this State are for the present declared to extend from Leavenworth, by way of posts of Jefferson City, Rolla, and Ironton, to Cape Girardeau on the Mississippi River. All persons who shall be taken with arms in their hands within these lines shall be tried by court-martial, and if found guilty, will be shot. Real and personal property of those who shall take up arms against the United States, or who shall be directly proven to have taken an active part with their enemies in the field, is declared confiscated to public use, and their slaves, if any they have, are hereby declared free men.

All persons who shall be proven to have destroyed, after the publication of this order, railroad tracks, bridges, or telegraph lines, shall suffer the extreme penalty of the law. All persons engaged in treasonable correspondence, in giving or procuring aid to the enemy, in fermenting turmoil, and disturbing public tranquility, by creating or circulating false reports, or incendiary documents, are warned that they are exposing themselves.

All persons who have been led away from allegiance, are required to return to their homes forthwith. Any such absence without sufficient cause, will be held to be presumptive evidence against them. The object of this declaration is to place in the hands of military authorities power to give instantaneous effect to the existing laws, and supply such deficiencies as the conditions of the war demand; but it is not intended to suspend the ordinary tribunals of the country, where law will be administered by civil officers in the usual manner, and with their customary authority, while the same can be peaceably administered. The commanding General will labor vigilantly for the public welfare, and, by his efforts for their safety, hopes to obtain not only acquiescence, but the active support of the people of the country.

J. C. FRÉMONT,
Major General, Commanding

mediately. Among those states hanging in the balance, Kentucky was very important, and Lincoln could not afford any rash actions which would lose that state to the Confederacy. His full-scale defense of Fort Sumter in April, 1861, had cost him four slave states, and he could not afford another loss of this type. Because of this, he immediately wired Frémont to revoke his order before it created further opposition. This the General refused to do, stating that the only way he would withdraw the proclamation would be if Lincoln publicly ordered him to do so. He then dispatched his wife, Jessie Benton Frémont, to Washington to argue the case with President Lincoln. Upon her arrival at the capital, Mrs. Frémont only succeeded in making matters worse. In her determination to aid her husband, she was neither tactful nor considerate of the President. Lincoln later stated that he did not even bother to explain the reasons for his action to her. His letter in reply to General Frémont modified that portion of the proclamation dealing with slaves.

THE NATION DIVIDED

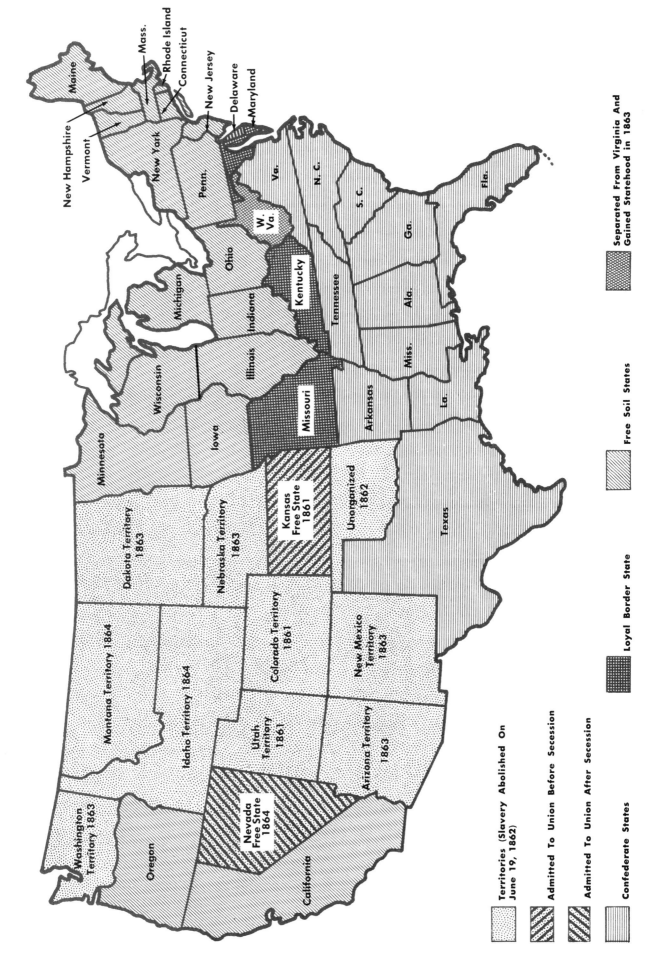

New Hampshire
Vermont
Maine
Mass.
Rhode Island
Connecticut
New Jersey
Delaware
Maryland

New York
Penn.
Va.
W. Va.
N. C.
S. C.
Fla.
Ga.
Ala.
Miss.

Ohio
Michigan
Wisconsin
Indiana
Illinois
Kentucky
Tennessee
Arkansas
La.

Minnesota
Iowa
Missouri

Washington Territory 1863
Oregon
Montana Territory 1864
Idaho Territory 1864
Dakota Territory 1863
Nebraska Territory 1863
Kansas Free State 1861
Unorganized 1862

California
Nevada Free State 1864
Utah Territory 1861
Colorado Territory 1861
New Mexico Territory 1863
Arizona Territory 1863
Texas

Separated From Virginia And Gained Statehood in 1863

Free Soil States

Loyal Border State

Territories (Slavery Abolished On June 19, 1862)

Admitted To Union Before Secession

Admitted To Union After Secession

Confederate States

September 11, 1861
Major General John C. Frémont:

Sir:

Yours of the 8th, in answer to mine of the 2nd inst., is just received. Assured that, you upon the ground, could better judge of the necessities of your position than I could at this distance, on seeing your proclamation of August 30th, I perceived no general objection to it; the particular clause, however, in relation to the confiscation of property and the liberation of slaves, appeared to me to be objectionable in its non-conformity to the Act of Congress, passed the 6th of last August, upon the same subject; and hence I wrote you, expressing my wish that that clause should be modified accordingly. Your answer, just received, expresses the preference on your part that I should make an open order for the modification, which I very cheerfully do. It is therefore, ordered that the said clause of said proclamation be so modified, held, and construed, as to conform with, and not to transcend, the provisions on the same subject contained in the Acts of Congress entitled "An Act to Confiscate Property Used for Insurrectionary Purposes," approved August 6, 1861; and that the said Act be published at length with this order.

Your obedient servant,
A. LINCOLN

If Frémont had managed to raise the ire of the President, he also had succeeded in raising the hopes of the abolitionists with this first step toward emancipation. The significance of Frémont's proclamation was immediately apparent. Harriet Beecher Stowe, author of *Uncle Tom's Cabin,* wrote: "The hour had come and the man! The hero of the golden gate who opened the doors of that splendid new California has long been predestined in the traditions of the slave as their coming Liberator." Frances Ellen Watkins Harper, talented Negro poetess, hoped that Frémont's stand would "inspire others to look the real cause of War in the face and inspire the Government with uncompromising earnestness to remove the festering cause." Following Lincoln's public rejection of the proclamation, John Greenleaf Whittier assured Hunter he had acted "a brave man's part."

Frémont's precipitous action caused him to lose his command of the Western division

soon after the issuance of the proclamation. He was followed by General David Hunter, who, ironically, became the second person to issue a proclamation of freedom for slaves, in 1862. This took place after Hunter had moved south and was in command of the Federal troops along the South Atlantic Coast. On May 9, Hunter felt it to be his duty to issue a proclamation freeing the slaves in his district. Without consulting the President or the Department of the Army, Hunter announced that all slaves in Georgia, Florida and South Carolina were freed by the following general order:

Hdqrs. Dept. of the South,
Hilton Head, Port Royal, S. C.
May 9, 1862

GENERAL ORDER NO. 11

The three States of Georgia, Florida and South Carolina, comprising the Military Department of the South, having deliberately declared themselves no longer under the protection of the United States of America, and having taken up arms against said United States, it became a military necessity to declare martial law. This was accordingly done on the 25th day of April, 1862. Slavery and martial law in a free country are altogether incompatible; the persons in these three States, Georgia, Florida, and South Carolina, heretofore held as slaves, are therefore declared forever free.

By Command of Major General D. Hunter:
(Ed. W. Smith)
Acting Assistant Adjutant General

When this news reached the White House, President Lincoln was engaged in patiently persuading the leaders of the border states to accept gradual emancipation based upon compensation. Hunter's proclamation not only thwarted his efforts in dealing with those states, but caused Lincoln to make a public announcement to the effect that the order was "null and void." To prevent further precipitous action on this subject, Lincoln firmly declared that no general anywhere had been or ever would be authorized to end slavery by proclamation. He then went on

FRANCES ELLEN WATKINS HARPER

MAJOR GENERAL DAVID HUNTER

to use his rebuke of Hunter as an appeal to slaveholders, and stated that "problems of military emancipation are questions which, under my responsibility, I reserve to myself."

AND WHEREAS, the same [Hunter's Proclamation] is producing some excitement and misunderstanding.

Therefore, I, Abraham Lincoln, President of the United States, proclaim and declare that the Government of the United States had no knowledge or belief of an intention on the part of General Hunter to issue such a proclamation, nor has it yet any authentic information that the document is genuine; and, further, that neither General Hunter nor any other commander or person have been authorized by the Government of the United States to make proclamation declaring the slaves of any State free; and that the supposed proclamation now in question, whether genuine or false, is altogether void, so far as respects such declaration. I further make known that, whether it be competent for me, as Commander-in-Chief of the Army and Navy, to declare the slaves of any State or States free; and whether at any time, or in any case, it shall have become a necessity indispensable to the maintenance of the Government to exercise such supposed power, are questions which, under my responsibility, I reserve to myself, and which I cannot feel justified in leaving to the decision of commanders in the field.

Those are totally different questions from those of police regulations in armies or in camps.

On the sixth day of March last, by a special Message, I recommended to Congress the adoption of a joint resolution, to be substantially as follows:

RESOLVED, That the United States ought to cooperate with any State which may adopt gradual abolishment of slavery, giving to such State pecuniary aid, to be used by such State in its discretion, to compensate for the inconvenience, public and private, produced by such change of system.

The resolution, in the language above quoted, was adopted by large majorities in both branches of Congress, and now stands an authentic, definite, and solemn proposal of the nation to the states and people most interested in the subject-matter. To the people of these States now I mostly appeal. I do not argue—I beseech you to make the arguments for yourselves. You cannot, if you would, be blind to the signs of the times.

I beg of you a calm and enlarged consideration of them, ranging if it may be, far above partisan and personal politics.

This proposal makes a common cause for a common object, casting no reproaches upon any. It acts not the Pharisee. The change it contemplates would come gently as the dews of Heaven, not rending or wrecking anything. Will you not embrace it? So much good has not been done by one effort in all pastime, as in the Providence of God, it is now your high privilege to do. May the vast future not have to lament that you have neglected it!

In witness whereof I have hereunto set my hand and caused the seal of the United States to be hereunto affixed.

Done at the city of Washington this 19th day of May, in the year of our Lord 1862, and of the independence of the United States the eighty-sixth.

                    ABRAHAM LINCOLN
By the President:
W. H. Seward, Secretary of State

In the meantime, Congress was making progress with an emancipation program, in spite of the conservative and hesitant policy of the President. The Annual Message to Congress of President Lincoln, December 3, 1861, stated that some slaves would be freed as a result of the War and others would probably be freed by the action of states. Therefore, action should be considered looking toward the adoption of some plan of compensation for cases of voluntary emancipation. He also proposed that consideration be given to the colonization of the freed slaves in a congenial place, outside the United States. Congress delayed action on all these proposals. But on July 17, 1862, an act was passed by Congress prohibiting the return of slaves from within Union lines. Congress was moving forward on slavery more rapidly than the President.

In July, 1862, in talking about compensation to congressmen from the border states, Lincoln stated:

> If the war continues long, as it must, if the object be not sooner attained, the institution in your States will be extinguished by mere friction and abrasion—by the mere incidents of War. It will be gone, and you will have nothing valuable in lieu of it. I do not speak of emancipation at once, but of a decision at once to emancipate gradually.

Lincoln was of the opinion that, if slave-owners were compensated for relinquishing their slaves, this would give recognition to states' rights and property rights. He proposed a plan of compensation to the slave-holders of Delaware at $400 a slave, but this did not prove to be acceptable. He then talked with leaders of the border states concerning a similar scheme as a solution to the slave question, but these conferences ended in failure. Lincoln had estimated the cost of compensated emancipation to be about $173,000,000 for the combined slaves held in Kentucky, Missouri, Maryland, Delaware and the District of Columbia. There was considerable criticism voiced in the Congress as to the financial strain such a policy would place on the government in addition to the large expenditures that were necessary to pay for the War. However, despite these setbacks, a plan of compensation for the freedom of the slaves in the District of Columbia was passed April 16, 1862, and it immediately received the President's signature.

In December, 1861, Secretary of War Simon Cameron had urged the use of Negro troops by the United States Army. This was probably a move to gain support of the abolitionists for himself, as he was both ineffective in his leadership and incapable as an administrator. In fact, he was soon released from his post, and nothing was achieved through his efforts. Lincoln remained determined to keep the Negro out of the War, both as an issue and as a soldier.

NEGRO ATTITUDES AT THE BEGINNING OF THE WAR

The Negroes in the Northern states soon realized the significance of the War, and their patriotism began to manifest itself. One of them, a citizen of Boston, wrote in the *Daily Atlas and Bee,* April 19, 1861:

> Though the colored American has had but little inducement, so far as the National Government is concerned, to be patriotic, he is, nevertheless, patriotic; he loves his native land; he feels for "the glory and the shame" of his country; his blood, as in revolutionary times—in the time of Old Sam Adams and Crispus Attucks the black —boils, ready to flow in the defense; not as a black man, but as an American—he will fight for his country's defense . . . and asks only for his rights as an equal fellow-countryman.

CHARLES LENOX REMOND

WILLIAM WELLS BROWN

Charles Lenox Remond, Negro abolitionist, speaking in Boston, January 20, 1862, used as his subject "The People of Color—Their Relation to the Country and Their Duties in the Present Crisis." William Wells Brown toured New York State using as his subject "The War and Its Connection with Slavery."

These expressions were given practical significance by the actions of the Negro people toward the War. They were among the first groups to seek to defend the nation in 1861. It is recorded that the first casualty of the War was Nicholas Biddle, a Negro militiaman. A tablet was erected in his honor at Pottsville, Pennsylvania, bearing the words, "His was the Proud Distinction of Shedding the First Blood in the Late War for the Union, Being Wounded while Marching through Baltimore with the First Volunteers from Schuylkill County, April, 1861."

In June, 1861, a Confederate privateer, *Jeff Davis*, captured the schooner *S. J. Waring* and its crew of captain, mate and four seamen. Three of the original crew were kept on board: the German pilot; a Northerner who was placed in irons; and a colored man, William Tillman, who had served as steward and cook. Tillman was told that on his arrival at Charleston, South Carolina, he would be sold as a slave. As night came on, Tillman began to plan a way to take charge of the vessel. He entered the captain's room and struck him a fatal blow while he slept; he then struck the mate a similar blow. A third met the same fate with a revolver. He drove the crew below deck, put them in irons and headed the ship for New York with the Stars and Stripes flying at the masthead. Five days later, the vessel arrived at the port of New York. The *New York Tribune* commented, "To this colored man was the nation indebted for the first vindication of its honor at sea." Tillman was awarded six thousand dollars as prize money for his capture and return of the schooner.

William Tillman recapturing the S. J. Waring.

Companies of Negroes were formed, anticipating the use of their services in the War effort. Such companies were formed in New York City and Cleveland, Ohio. In the latter, a resolution was adopted at the time of the company's organization stating, "Today, as in the time of '76 and the days of 1812, we are ready to go forth and do battle in the common cause of the country." The Negro citizens of Boston at a meeting in April, 1861, resolved "to defend the government and the flag of the country"; and they declared that "they were ready to raise an army of 50,000 men if the laws can be altered to allow them to enlist."

There was no law which prohibited the War Department from enlisting Negro volunteers in either the army or navy. Paragraph 1299 of the United States Army Regulations provided for the enlistment of "any free white male person"; and, prior to 1861, the regular army was composed only of white troops. This fact did not prevent Negroes from seeking to enlist as soldiers after the opening of the War.

Several days after the fall of Fort Sumter, Jacob Dodson, a Negro who had crossed the Rocky Mountains and had been with Frémont in his Western journey, wrote to the War Department stating that he could interest three hundred Negroes in the District of Columbia in the defense of this territory. On April 29, Secretary Cameron replied that the War Department had no intention, at the time of his letter, "to call into the service of the Government any colored soldiers."

During the remainder of 1861, Secretary Cameron issued orders to General Sherman instructing him to return fugitive slaves to their owners and to put able-bodied Negroes to work by organizing them into squads or companies for service. By the Act of July 17,

1862, Congress authorized the enlistment of persons of African descent. Under this act, Negroes were employed in constructing entrenchments and performing camp services. Other acts gave legislative authority for limited employment of Negroes in connection with military service.

In the fall of 1861, Dr. G. P. Miller, a Negro physician of Battle Creek, Michigan, had written to Secretary of War Cameron requesting that he grant the doctor permission to raise a brigade of Negro soldiers to serve especially as sharpshooters. The reply on November 8, 1861, was that the War Department's orders to General Sherman had authorized "the arming of colored persons only in cases of great emergency and not under regular enrollment for military purposes."

These various statements represented an indefinite attitude on the part of the Secretary of War, although it seemed certain that Negroes could be used for military purposes, but not as soldiers. In the meantime, Northern Negroes in various centers were asking for the privilege of fighting for their country and defending their flag.

PROPOSED USE AS SOLDIERS

From the opening of the War, there was opposition to the enlistment of Negroes in the Union Army. Differences of opinion concerning the use of Negroes as soldiers continued until it was generally known that the Confederacy was making use of them as laborers, workers and servants.

The first enlistment of Negroes in the Union was undertaken by General David Hunter, who announced in May, 1862, that he would form a Negro regiment under a detail of white officers, in order to reinforce his troops which were holding portions of South Carolina, Georgia and Florida. He assumed the authority to enlist Negroes as soldiers, to issue arms, equipment and rations

Negroes working as laborers for the Confederacy.

to them, and ordered Sergeant C. T. Trowbridge to recruit a Negro regiment. This order resulted in the formation of the 1st South Carolina Volunteers, with white commissioned officers, and brought the issue of Negro enlistments before the public. This was a courageous move on the part of General Hunter, and it greatly influenced the acceptance of Negro enlistments.

When the report reached Washington, inquiry was raised in Congress through a resolution introduced by Congressman Wickliffe of Kentucky. In reply to this inquiry, General Hunter reported:

> . . . No regiment of fugitive slaves has been or is being organized in this department. There is, however, a fine regiment of loyal persons whose late masters are "fugitive rebels," men who everywhere fly before the appearance of the national flag, leaving their servants behind to shift as best they can for themselves.

He wrote that General Sherman had been authorized to make use of loyal persons in the defense of the Union and that, when these orders were turned over to him for his guidance, no distinction had been made as to character or color or the nature of the employment. These orders had been transmitted to him and he had organized from forty-eight to fifty thousand of these soldiers. General Hunter added:

> The experiment of arming the blacks, so far as I have made it, has been a complete and even marvelous success. They are sober, docile, attentive, and enthusiastic; displaying great natural capacities for acquiring the duties of the soldier. They are eager, beyond all things, to take the field and be led into action; and it is the unanimous opinion of the officers who have had charge of them, that in the peculiarities of this climate and country, they will prove valuable auxiliaries—fully equal to the similar regiments so long and successfully used by the British authorities in the West Indies Islands.

General Hunter had won the confidence of the Negroes in his department. Slaves who enlisted were given "freedom papers," such as the one below:

> Headquarters, Dept. of the South
> Port Royal, South Carolina
> August 1, 1862
>
> The bearer, Prince Rivers, a sergeant in the First Regiment South Carolina Volunteers, lately claimed a slave, having been employed in hostility to the United States, is hereby, agreeably to the law of the 6th of August, 1861, declared *free forever*. His wife and children are also free.
>
> D. HUNTER
> Major-General Commanding

This policy to place arms in the hands of former slaves was not supported by the administration, and because of this, General Hunter asked to be relieved of his command.

The discussion of arming Negroes continued in Congress during the summer of 1862. A motion was made by Senator Henry Wilson of Massachusetts on July 9, 1862, authorizing the President to call out the militia to suppress insurrection. Senator J. W. Grimes of Iowa then offered an amendment that all able-bodied male persons of the usual military ages should be used and that no exception should be made on account of lineage or color. Objections were raised to this amendment, mainly by senators from the border states. Senator Preston King of New York presented an amendment to authorize the President to receive into the military service persons of African descent for the construction of entrenchments or to perform camp service or any service for which they were found competent. In addition, the mothers, wives and children of these persons were to be granted their freedom.

A similar bill had been introduced in the House under the leadership of Thaddeus Stevens. Section 15 of the bill provided "that persons of African descent, who under this law shall be employed, shall receive ten dollars per month and one ration, three dollars of which monthly pay may be in clothing." This bill was passed on July 17, 1862, and signed by President Lincoln despite his hesitant attitude on the employment of colored soldiers. This action meant a discrimination in pay, as Negro soldiers were to be paid three dollars less than white soldiers. They vigorously protested this action until it was changed.

The issuance of the preliminary emancipation proclamation on September 22, 1862, giving notice that the freedom of the slaves in disloyal areas was one of the aims of the War, was encouraging to those desiring the use of Negroes as soldiers. The need of soldiers by the Union Army in the summer of 1862, and the need for weakening the Confederacy, were factors in accomplishing the successful fulfillment of the proposal.

In pursuance of this act, and acting upon his interpretation of it, General James H. Lane, on August 6, 1862, began the enlistment of two regiments of Negroes as home guards in Kansas. He was informed by Secretary of War Stanton that these regiments could be raised only on the express authority of the President, and that this had not been given to him.

Many objections were made to the enlistment of Negroes as soldiers. One was that it would lay the basis for a slave insurrection, and the horrors of the Nat Turner and Haitian insurrections were described to the Congress by Senator Davis of Kentucky. Others said that the Negro would not fight because of his inferior race and long bondage, and that white troops would not fight with him.

The first authorization for the enlistment of Negroes as soldiers was sent on August 25, 1862, by Secretary Cameron to General Rufus Saxton, who had succeeded General Hunter. He was authorized to enlist Negro soldiers not to exceed five thousand and Negro laborers not to exceed fifty thousand. With the one remaining company of the 1st South Carolina Regiment enlisted by General Hunter, General Saxton began his recruiting, and in January, 1863, the 1st Regiment of the South Carolina Volunteers was mustered.

GENERAL RUFUS SAXTON

However, the first authorized muster-in of a Negro regiment was that of the 1st Regiment Louisiana Native Guards on September 27, 1862. These colored troops, of which there were three battalions, originally referred to themselves as the Corps d'Afrique, but their name was later changed to the Louisiana Native Guards by General Benjamin F. Butler.

In the meantime, there were other smaller areas in Louisiana in which Negro soldiers, under state authority, were unofficially associated with the Confederate Army. Some of these Negroes had been slaveowners who were willing to fight for the protection of their slave property. A parade of Confederate soldiers was held in New Orleans on November 23, 1861, with a regiment of free Negroes participating. The *New Orleans Picayune,* February 9, 1862, described this regiment as follows:

> We must pay deserved compliment to the companies of free men of color, all well-dressed, well-drilled and comfortably uniformed. Most of these companies have provided themselves with arms unaided by the administration.

This outstanding regiment of Negroes not only declined to leave the city of New

Negroes serving as teamsters, laundresses and cooks for the Union Army.

Orleans when General Butler entered there in 1862, but volunteered its services to him. General Butler did not accept these troops, although he was in need of reinforcements, because the Federal government had not as yet made a decision concerning the use of Negro troops.

Butler's need became so pressing, however, that, on August 22, 1862, he issued a proclamation and "called upon Africans to defend the flag of their native country as their fathers did under Jackson at Chalmette against Pakenham and his myrmidons." This reference was to Jackson's employment of Negro soldiers in the Battle of New Orleans in 1814. Jackson issued a proclamation inviting them to join in the battle and later praised them for their courage. Within two weeks, a regiment of one thousand Negro soldiers was organized, with colored line officers and white field officers. Throughout 1862, while

the issue was being argued between the President, Congress and military commanders, Negroes continued to be used as laborers, scouts, teamsters and cooks in the Federal armies and for similar duties in the Navy. When the Confederate government learned of these activities, and particularly of the actions of General Hunter and his staff, it declared them to be "hereafter outlaws not covered by the laws of war; but to be executed as felons for the crime of 'inciting Negro insurrection' wherever caught."

LINCOLN JOINS COMPENSATION AND COLONIZATION WITH EMANCIPATION

What influence did President Lincoln's family background and his experiences prior to the Civil War have on his feelings about Negroes and his reactions to the problem of slavery? His career was similar to that of many rural and small-town Southern politicians. He was the child of pioneer parents in early rural Kentucky and had married into a slaveholding family. He broke openly with the abolitionists and even declined to go along with the Free Soil Party. The influence of environment had considerable effect upon his career, for he shared with Southerners many of their views concerning the Negro.

The environmental influence played a dramatic role in the lives of the two leaders of Civil War history, Abraham Lincoln and Jefferson Davis. They were born within one hundred miles of each other, with one year separating their birth dates, 1808 and 1809. One moved in childhood to the Southwest and the other to the Northwest. Both were in the Black Hawk War. Both served as presidential electors in 1844, Davis voting for Polk and Lincoln for Clay. They were both elected to Congress within one year of each other, Davis in 1845 and Lincoln in 1846. Davis became President of the Confederacy on February 18, 1861, and Lincoln became President of the United States on March 4, 1861. The fact that Lincoln was born in Kentucky, moved to Indiana at the age of seven years and from there went to Illinois had a definite and pronounced influence on his attitudes toward slavery and Negro Americans.

In his Inaugural Address of 1861, Lincoln disclaimed any purpose, directly or indirectly, of interfering with the institution of slavery in the states where it existed, and specified that there was no design to violate the rights of the states with slavery. And, yet, in the same speech he also remarked that he would be exceedingly glad to see slavery abolished in the District of Columbia. He associated with this policy the projects of compensation

ABRAHAM LINCOLN

JEFFERSON DAVIS

and colonization. Compensation, emancipation and colonization went hand in hand in his thinking and, therefore, into his proposals to Congress. In his message to Congress in December, 1861, he directed attention to the Confiscation Act of August 6, stating that "The United States ought to cooperate with any state which would adopt a gradual abolishment of slavery." He also added, "The Union must be preserved; and hence all indispensable means must be employed." Even William Lloyd Garrison, while proposing the freedom of slaves, had advocated that "a fair pecuniary award" be paid to loyal owners.

Lincoln also suggested that consideration be given to the colonization of the freed slaves, but Congress delayed action on these proposals. Finally, on April 16, 1862, slavery was abolished in the District of Columbia with compensation; and on June 19, 1862, in the Territories emancipation without compensation was adopted. This action reversed the Dred Scott decision, and as a result, three thousand slaves living in the District of Columbia were freed. These former slaves were reported as working harder than before and earning more money for their new employers than they had for their previous owners. The congressional acts prior to Lincoln's Proclamation are often disregarded in the consideration of emancipation's development. It is well, however, to observe that Congress had made considerable progress prior to the action of the President.

In his Annual Message to Congress, December, 1862, Lincoln proposed that each state should have the opportunity of devising its own plan of gradual, compensated emancipation to be completed before January 1, 1900. Under this plan Federal assistance would be provided. This procedure, said Lincoln, "spares both races from the evils of sudden derangement; . . . most of those whose habitual course of thought will be disturbed by the measure will have passed away before its consummation. They will never see it."

Even after the Emancipation Proclamation, Lincoln was ready to receive any peace proposals "embracing the restoration of the Union and abandonment of slavery." Meeting with Confederate Vice-President Alexander Stephens in 1865, Lincoln was asked what the meaning of the Emancipation Proclamation would be if the Southern states returned to the Union. Stephens reported what Lincoln said:

> His own opinion was that as the Proclamation was a War measure, and would have effect only from its being an exercise of War power, as soon as the War ceased, it would be inoperative for the future. It would be held to apply only to such slaves as had come under its operation while it was in active exercise.

Lincoln, it can be seen, was determined to restore the Union at any cost.

As the War became increasingly severe, Lincoln often visited the telegraph room in the White House in order to keep better informed of happenings around the nation, as well as to receive his messages more promptly. While there one day in June, 1861, he asked Thomas T. Eckert, who was in charge of the office, for a sheet of paper. Lincoln had made this request on other occasions and had frequently made notes on the papers, at times placing question marks after sections that he had written. Eckert did not know then what had been accomplished, but Lincoln later told him that he had drafted a paper which would free the slaves in the South and bring about an earlier end to the War.

On August 14, 1862, President Lincoln met with a group of Negro leaders who had come to the White House seeking the President's support for the abolition of slavery. In response to their plea, Lincoln admitted that slavery was in fact responsible for the War. He stated, "But for your race among us there could not be War . . . without the institution of slavery, the colored race as basis, the War could not have an existence."

HORACE GREELEY

President Lincoln followed a policy of watchful waiting and caution, in spite of the pressure placed upon him, especially by the abolitionists. Horace Greeley's editorial, "Prayer of Twenty Millions," in the *New York Tribune,* August 20, 1862, called upon the President to execute the Confiscation Acts of Congress and free the slaves as a blow against the rebellion. Greeley wrote:

On the face of this wide earth, Mr. President, there is not one disinterested, determined, intelligent champion of the Union cause who does not feel that all attempts to put down the Rebellion, and at the same time uphold its inciting cause, are preposterous and futile—that the Rebellion, if crushed out tomorrow, would be renewed within a year if slavery were left in full vigor—that Army officers, who remain to this day devoted to slavery, can at best be but half-way loyal to the Union—and that every hour of deference to slavery is an hour of added and deepened peril to the Union. I appeal to the testimony of your Ambassadors in Europe. It is freely at your service, not mine. Ask them to tell you candidly whether the seeming subserviency of your policy

to the slave-holding, slavery-upholding interest, is not the perplexity, the despair of statesmen of all parties; and be admonished by the general answer!

I close, as I began, with the statement that what an immense majority of the loyal millions of your countrymen require of you is a frank, declared, unqualified, ungrudging execution of the laws of the land, more especially of the Confiscation Act. That Act gives freedom to the slaves of rebels coming within our lines, or whom those lines may at any time enclose,—we ask you to render it due obedience by publicly requiring all your subordinates to recognize and obey it. The rebels are everywhere using the late anti-Negro riots in the North—as they have long used your officer's treatment of Negroes in the South—to convince the slaves that they have nothing to hope from a Union success—that we mean in that case to sell them into a bitter bondage to defray the cost of the War. Let them impress this as a truth on the great mass of their ignorant and credulous bondmen, and the Union will never be restored—never. We can not conquer ten millions of people united in solid phalanx against us, powerfully aided by Northern sympathizers and European allies. We must have scouts, guides, spies, cooks, teamsters, diggers and choppers, from the blacks of the South—whether we allow them to fight for us or not—or we shall be baffled and repelled. As one of the millions who would gladly have avoided this struggle at any sacrifice but that of principle and honor, but who now feels that the triumph of the Union is indispensable not only to the existence of our country, but to the well-being of man-kind, I entreate you to render a hearty and unequivocal obedience to the law of the land.

Yours,
HORACE GREELEY

Although he had read a preliminary draft of the Emancipation Proclamation to his Cabinet on July 22, Lincoln did not reveal his proposed intentions when replying to Mr. Greeley:

Executive Mansion, Washington
August 22, 1862

Hon. Horace Greeley:

Dear Sir, I have just read yours of the 19th instant, addressed to myself through the New York Tribune.

If there be in it statements of assumptions of fact which I may know to be erroneous, I do not know and here controvert them.

If there be any inferences which I may believe to be falsely drawn, I do not know and here argue against them.

If there be perceptible in it an impatient and dictatorial tone, I waive it in deference to an old friend whose heart I have always supposed to be right.

As to the policy "I seem to be pursuing," as you say, I have not meant to leave any one in doubt. I would save the Union. I would save it in the shortest way under the Constitution.

The sooner the national authority can be restored, the nearer the Union will be the Union as it was.

If there be those who would not save the Union unless they could at the same time save slavery, I do not agree with them.

If there be those who would not save the Union unless they could at the same time destroy slavery, I do not agree with them.

My paramount object is to save the Union, and not either to save or destroy slavery.

If I could save the Union without freeing any slave, I would do it; if I could save it by freeing all the slaves, I would do it; and if I could do it by freeing some and leaving others alone, I would also do that.

What I do about slavery and the Colored race, I do because I believe it helps to save this Union; and what I forbear, I forbear because I do not believe it would help to save the Union.

I shall do less whenever I shall believe what I am doing hurts the cause; and I shall do more whenever I believe doing more will help the cause.

I shall try to correct errors when shown to be errors; and I shall adopt new views so fast as they shall appear to be true views.

I have here stated my purpose according to my views of official duty; and I intend no modification of my oft-expressed *personal* wish that all men, everywhere, could be free.

Yours,
A. LINCOLN

The opponents of slavery were steadily gaining in number and continued to send letters, petitions and memorials to President Lincoln. A group of representatives from Protestant churches sought a conference with the President on September 13, 1862, urging the adoption of an emancipation policy. President Lincoln gave the delegation this answer:

Now, then, tell me, if you please, what possible result of good would follow the issuing of such a proclamation as you desire? Understand: I raise no objection against it on legal or constitutional grounds; for, as Commander-in-Chief for the Army and Navy in time of war, I suppose I have a right to take any measure which may best subdue the enemy; nor do I urge objections of a moral nature, in view of possible consequences of insurrection and massacre at the South. I view this matter as a practical war measure, to be decided on according to the advantages it may offer to the Suppression of the Rebellion.

. . . .

I will also concede that emancipation would help us in Europe and convince them that we are incited by something more than ambition. I grant, further, that it would help; somewhat at the North, though not so much, I fear, as you and those you represent imagine, still, some additional strength would be added in that way to the war; and then, unquestionably, it would weaken the Rebels by drawing off their laborers, which is of great importance; but I am not so sure we could do much with the blacks. If we were to arm them, I fear that in a few weeks the arms would be in the hands of the Rebels; and, indeed, thus far, we have not had arms enough to equip our white troops. I will mention another thing, though it meet only your scorn and contempt. There are fifty-thousand bayonets in the Union Army from the Border Slave States. It would be a serious matter if, in consequence of a proclamation such as you desire, they should go over to the Rebels. I do not think they all would— not so many, indeed, as a year ago, or as six months ago—not so many, today as yesterday. Every day increases their Union feeling. They are also getting their pride enlisted, and want to beat the Rebels. Let me say one thing more: I think you should admit that we already have an important principle to rally and unite the people, in the fact that constitutional government is at stake. This is a fundamental idea, going down about as deep as anything.

The idea and plan for an emancipation proclamation had been under consideration by President Lincoln for some time. When

"It is the beginning of the end of the Rebellion; the beginning of the new life of the Nation."—TRIBUNE.

A PROCLAMATION

By the President of the United States.

I, ABRAHAM LINCOLN, President of the United States of America, and Commander-in-Chief of the Army and Navy thereof, do hereby PROCLAIM and DECLARE that hereafter, as heretofore, the war will be prosecuted for the object of practically restoring the Constitutional relation between the United States and the people thereof, in which States that relation is, or may be, suspended or disturbed; that it is my purpose upon the next meeting of Congress, to again recommend the adoption of a practical measure tendering pecuniary aid to the free acceptance or rejection of all the Slave States so called, the people whereof may not then be in rebellion against the United States, and which States may then have voluntarily adopted or thereafter may voluntarily adopt the immediate or gradual abolishment of Slavery within their respective limits; and that the effort to colonize persons of African descent with their consent upon this continent or elsewhere with the previously obtained consent of the Governments existing there, will be continued; that on the first day of January, in the year of our Lord one thousand eight hundred and sixty-three, all persons held as slaves within any State, or any designated part of a State, the people whereof shall then be in rebellion against the United States, shall be thenceforward and forever free, and the Executive Government of the United States, including the military and naval authority thereof, will recognize and maintain the freedom of such persons, and will do no act or acts to repress such persons, or any of them, in any efforts they may make for their actual freedom; that the Executive will, on the first day of January aforesaid, by proclamation, designate the States and parts of States, if any, in which the people thereof respectively shall then be in rebellion against the United States, and the fact that any State, or the people thereof shall on that day be in good faith represented in the Congress of the United States by members chosen thereto at elections wherein a majority of the qualified voters of such State shall have participated, shall, in the absence of strong countervailing testimony, be deemed conclusive evidence that such State and the people thereof have not been in rebellion against the United States.

That attention is hereby called to an act of Congress entitled "An act to make an additional article of war," approved March 13, 1862, and which act is in the words and figures following:

Be it enacted by the Senate and House of Representatives of the United States of America in Congress assembled: That hereafter the following shall be promulgated as an additional article of war, for the government of the army of the United States, and shall be obeyed and observed as such:

Article. All officers or persons in the military or naval service of the United States are prohibited from employing any of the forces under their respective commands for the purpose of returning fugitives from service or labor, who may have escaped from any persons to whom such labor is claimed to be due, and any officer who shall be found guilty by a court-martial of violating this article, shall be dismissed from service.

SEC. 2. *And be it further enacted,* That this act shall take effect from and after its passage.

Also, to the ninth and tenth sections of an act entitled "An act to suppress insurrection, to punish treason and rebellion, to seize and confiscate the property of Rebels, and for other purposes," approved July 17, 1862, and which sections are in the words and figures following:

SEC. 9. *And be it further enacted,* That all slaves of persons who shall hereafter be engaged in rebellion against the Government of the United States, or who shall in any way give aid or comfort thereto, escaping from such persons and taking refuge within the lines of the army; and all slaves captured from such persons or deserted by them and coming under the control of the Government of the United States; and all slaves of such persons found on (or being within) any place occupied by Rebel forces and afterward occupied by the forces of the United States, shall be deemed captures of war, and shall be forever free of their servitude and not again held as slaves.

SEC. 10. *And be it further enacted,* That no slaves escaping into any State, Territory, or the District of Columbia, from any of the States, shall be delivered up, or in any way impeded or hindered of his liberty, except for crime or some offence against the laws, unless the person claming said fugitive shall first make oath that the person to whom the labor or service of such fugitive is alleged to be due, is his lawful owner, and has not been in arms against the United States in the present Rebellion, nor in any way given aid and comfort thereto; and no person engaged in the military or naval service of the United States shall, under any pretence whatever, assume to decide on the validity of the claim of any person to the service or labor of any other person, or surrender up any such person to the claimant, on pain of being dismissed from the service.

And I do hereby enjoin upon and order all persons engaged in the military and naval service of the United States to observe, obey, and enforce, within their respective spheres of service, the act and sections above recited.

And the Executive will in due time recommend that all citizens of the United States who shall have remained loyal thereto throughout the Rebellion, shall (upon the restoration of the constitutional relation between the United States, and their respective States and people, if the relation shall have been suspended or disturbed) be compensated for all losses by acts of the United States, including the loss of slaves.

In witness whereof I have hereunto set my hand and caused the seal of the United States to be affixed.

Done at the City of Washington this twenty-second day of September, in the year of our Lord one thousand eight hundred and sixty-two, and of the Independence of the United States the eighty-seventh.

ABRAHAM LINCOLN.

By the PRESIDENT,

WM. H. SEWARD, *Secretary of State.*

The preliminary emancipation proclamation issued by President Lincoln on September 22, 1862.

PRESIDENT LINCOLN AND HIS CABINET SIGNING THE EMANCIPATION PROCLAMATION
Standing from left to right are Salmon P. Chase, Secretary of the Treasury; Caleb B. Smith, Secretary of the Interior; Montgomery Blair, Postmaster General. Seated left to right are Edwin M. Stanton, Secretary of War; Abraham Lincoln, President; Gideon Welles, Secretary of the Navy; William H. Seward, Secretary of State; and Edward Bates, Attorney General.

the preliminary draft was read on July 22, Secretary Seward suggested that such a proclamation should be issued only after a decisive military victory, since the issuance of such a statement now would be ludicrous. The Union forces had been unsuccessful in defeating the enemy in every major encounter and had been fighting a war of containment, not one of successful aggression. By waiting for a military triumph, Seward felt that public opinion and support of emancipation would be greater and interest on the international scene would be more intense.

On September 22, after the Battle of Antietam, a second draft of the proclamation was read to the Cabinet. This became known as the preliminary emancipation proclamation, announcing that the War would be continued for the restoration of the Union. It warned the rebellious states that if they did not lay down their arms by January 1, their slaves would be freed. It further stated that voluntary emancipation with compensation for states which were loyal was recommended and that the plan of colonization would continue. Lincoln commented, "I may advance slowly, but I don't walk backwards."

Continuing his reference to the high character of the emancipation proposal, President Lincoln stated in his Second Annual Message to Congress, December 1, 1862:

> The dogmas of the quiet past are inadequate to the stormy present. . . . In giving freedom to the slaves we assure freedom to the free—honorable alike in what we give and what we preserve. We shall nobly save or meanly lose, the last best hope of earth. Other means may succeed; this could not fail.

Finally, on January 1, 1863, President Lincoln issued the long-awaited Emancipation Proclamation, which he had promised in September.

By the President of the United States of America:

A Proclamation.

Whereas, on the twenty-second day, of September, in the year of our Lord one thousand eight hundred and sixty-two, a proclamation was issued by the President of the United States, containing, among other things, the following, to wit:

"That on the first day of January, in the "year of our Lord one thousand eight hundred "and sixty-three, all persons held as slaves within "any State or designated part of a State, the people "whereof shall then be in rebellion against the "United States, shall be then, thenceforward, and "forever free; and the Executive Government of the "United States, including the military and naval "authority thereof, will recognize and maintain "the freedom of such persons, and will do no act "or acts to repress such persons, or any of them, "in any efforts they may make for their actual "freedom.

"That the Executive will, on the first day

"of January aforesaid, by proclamation, designate
"the States and parts of States, if any, in which the
"people thereof, respectively, shall then be in rebellion
"against the United States; and the fact that any
"State, or the people thereof, shall on that day be, in
"good faith, represented in the Congress of the United
"States by members chosen thereto at elections
"wherein a majority of the qualified voters of such
"State shall have participated, shall, in the absence
"of strong countervailing testimony, be deemed con—
"clusive evidence that such State, and the people
"thereof, are not then in rebellion against the
"United States."

    Now, therefore, I, Abraham
Lincoln, President of the United States, by virtue
of the power in me vested as Commander-in-
Chief, of the Army and Navy, of the United
States in time of actual armed rebellion against the
authority, and government of the United States,
and as a fit and necessary war measure for suppressing said rebellion, do, on this first day of
January, in the year of our Lord one thousand
eight hundred and sixty-three, and in accordance
with my purpose so to do publicly proclaimed
for the full period of one hundred days, from the

day first above mentioned, order and designate as the States and parts of States wherein the people thereof respectively, are this day in rebellion against the United States, the following, to wit:

Arkansas, Texas, Louisiana, (except the Parishes of St. Bernard, Plaquemines, Jefferson, St. John, St. Charles, St. James Ascension, Assumption, Terrebonne, Lafourche, St. Mary, St. Martin, and Orleans, including the City of New Orleans) Mississippi, Alabama, Florida, Georgia, South Carolina, North Carolina, and Virginia, (except the forty-eight counties designated as West Virginia, and also the counties of Berkley, Accomac, Northampton, Elizabeth City, York, Princess Ann, and Norfolk, including the cities of Norfolk and Portsmouth, and which excepted parts are, for the present, left precisely as if this proclamation were not issued.

And by virtue of the power, and for the purpose aforesaid, I do order and declare that all persons held as slaves within said designated States, and parts of States, are, and henceforward shall be free; and that the Executive government of the United States, including the military, and naval authorities thereof, will recognize and maintain the freedom of said persons.

And I hereby enjoin upon the people so declared to be free to abstain from all violence, unless in necessary self-defence; and I recommend to them that, in all cases when allowed, they labor faithfully for reasonable wages.

And I further declare and make known, that such persons of suitable condition, will be received into the armed service of the United States to garrison forts, positions, stations, and other places, and to man vessels of all sorts in said service.

And upon this act, sincerely believed to be an act of justice, warranted by the Constitution, upon military necessity, I invoke the considerate judgment of mankind, and the gracious favor of Almighty God.

In witness whereof, I have hereunto set my hand and caused the seal of the United States to be affixed.

Done at the city of Washington, this first day of January, in the year of our Lord

one thousand eight hun
and sixty three; and of t
Independence of the Unit
States of America the eig
seventh.

Abraham Lincoln

By the President:

William H Seward
Secretary of State.

This document now stands in the National Archives in Washington, D.C. It is written on two large sheets of paper, folded to make four leaves, or eight pages. The last three are blank. Most of the original red and blue ribbon which tied the document remains, but only part of the wax seal is still decipherable.

On the eve of this issuance, Negroes and their friends held scores of meetings across the country. One such gathering was held in Boston, where a line of messengers was established between the telegraph office and the platform of Tremont Temple awaiting the announcement. Frederick Douglass, who was present at this meeting, described it in his memoirs as being an evening of tense excitement. In recounting his experience, Douglass wrote:

> The effect of this announcement was startling beyond description, and the scene was wild and grand. Joy and gladness exhausted all forms of expression, from shouts of praise to sobs and tears. My old friend, Rue; a Negro preacher, a man of wonderful vocal power expressed the heartfelt emotion of the hour, when he led all voices in the anthem, "Sound the loud timbrel O'er Egypt's dark sea, Jehovah hath triumphed, his people are free."

Douglass later summed up the effect of the Emancipation Proclamation on the War in these few words: "Now the War was invested with sanctity." William C. Nell, Negro author and historian, was also present at the Tremont Temple on this providential occasion, and declared:

> New Year's Day—proverbially known throughout the South as "Heartbreak-Day" from the trials and honors peculiar to souls and separations of parents and children, wives and husbands—by this Proclamation is henceforth invested with new significance and unperishable glory in the calendar of time.

Numerous celebrations took place in the South after word spread of the issuance of the Proclamation. Slaves hearing the news were ecstatic with joy and overwhelmed at the concept of freedom which had at last come to them. Booker T. Washington, born a slave on a plantation near Hale's Ford, Virginia, April 5, 1856, described a scene from memory following the reading of the Proclamation:

> For some minutes there was great rejoicing, and thanksgiving, and wild scenes of ecstasy. But there was no feeling of bitterness. In fact, there was pity among the slaves for our former owners. The wild rejoicing on the part of the emancipated colored people lasted but for a brief period, for I noticed that by the time they returned to their cabins there was a change in their feelings. The great responsibility of being free, of having charge of themselves, of having to think and plan for themselves and their children, seemed to take possession of them.

However, not all of the news out of the South was similar to Booker T. Washington's experience. In a neighborhood near Amesville, Virginia, seventeen Negroes were found together with a copy of a newspaper bearing Lincoln's Proclamation. These slaves were taken to Amesville and lynched because the white planters were fearful that the news of the Emancipation Proclamation would cause a major slave uprising.

The Proclamation was a war measure and, as such, was issued by Lincoln as Commander-in-Chief of the Army and Navy, rather than in his capacity as President. Army officers in some places did not take kindly to the Proclamation, and some resigned because they now saw the conflict as one freeing the slaves rather than preserving the Union. There were those Southern Unionist leaders who chose to lend support to the Confederacy rather than to the abolition of slavery. One such person was an important East Tennessee Union leader, T. A. R. Nelson, who became an announced supporter of the Confederacy.

Although not directly responsible, the Proclamation was instrumental in bringing about the dismissal of General George B. McClellan. McClellan was opposed to the Proclamation and had threatened to resign rather than support it. His reluctance was paradoxical because it was his success at Antietam that had created the military victory Lincoln so desired. It was not until October 7, 1863, that McClellan finally issued the Proclamation, and he issued it without his own endorsement.

REACTIONS TO THE PROCLAMATION

There was considerable discussion concerning the power of the President to issue such a proclamation freeing slaves. His right to do so was acknowledged by several authorities. One of these was the solicitor general in the War Department, William Whiting, who stated that:

> The ordinary way of depriving the enemy of slaves is by declaring emancipation. . . . The Constitution confers on the Executive, when in actual war, full belligerent powers. The emancipation of enemy's slaves is a belligerent right. It belongs exclusively to the President, as Commander-in-Chief, to judge whether he shall exercise his belligerent right to emancipate slaves in those parts of the country which are in rebellion. If exercised in fact, and while the war lasts, his act of emancipation is conclusive and binding forever on all the departments of government, and on all persons whatsoever.

There was division of opinion concerning the Proclamation itself. After the preliminary proclamation had been issued, it was stated that foreign workers and native ones "of the white race must feel enraptured at the prospect of hordes of darkeys overrunning the Northern states and working for half wages, and thus ousting them from employment." On the other hand, the colored people of the North accepted with acclaim the announcement that the slaves were to be freed. They were inspired by joy and thanksgiving; they assembled in churches to sing and pray—and to give thanks to God and Abraham Lincoln.

All over the South, there was restrained happiness on the part of the slaves. This new development caused slaveholders to have ad-

The great emancipation meeting held in Exeter Hall, London.

ditional fears of insurrections, and they urged that steps be taken to prevent such insurrections from occurring. However, the Negroes, the abolitionists, and a growing number of white people believed that this was a major step forward in the United States' War for Freedom.

Abroad, the Proclamation was both praised and denounced. The London *Times* and *La France* were the first to voice opposition. They felt that the Proclamation would be ineffective, and that it was issued too late in the War. The *Times* even considered it to be unconstitutional, possibly reflecting the opinion of England's upper class, which supported the Confederacy during the early years of the War. But the working men of England felt differently and, after holding hundreds of meetings, issued a resolution praising Lincoln's proclamation of freedom.

Nearly all of the South received the Proclamation with opposition and criticism. On January 12, 1863, Jefferson Davis said:

> We may well leave it to the instincts of that common humanity which a beneficent Creator has implanted in the breasts of our fellow men of all countries to pass judgment on a measure by which several millions of human beings of an inferior race—peaceful and contented laborers in their sphere—are doomed to extermination while at the same time they are encouraged to a general assassination of their masters by the insidious recommendation to abstain from violence unless in necessary self-defense.

Davis also declared that his government would deliver to the several state authorities all commissioned officers of the United States who were captured in any of the states embraced by the Proclamation. He ordered that they be dealt with in accordance with the laws of those states which provided for the punishment of criminals engaged in insurrection. In the case of the enlisted soldiers, he would direct their discharge and return them to their homes on parole. As to its overall impact, Davis felt that the Proclamation left only one of three possibilities: the extermination of the slaves, the exile of the white population of the Confederacy, or "the absolute and total separation of these states and the United States."

In the North, there was also opposition to the Proclamation, mainly from those opposed to a war to free the slaves. The Illinois legislature was firm in its criticism of Lincoln's action, and seven days after the Proclamation was issued, the following resolution was adopted:

> Resolved: That the Emancipation Proclamation of the President of the United States is as unwarrantable in military as in civil law; a gigantic usurpation, at once converting the War, professedly commenced by the administration for the vindication of the authority of the Constitution, into the crusade for the sudden, unconditional and violent liberation of three million Negro slaves; a result which would not only be a total subversion of the Federal Union but a revolution in the social organization of the Southern States, the immediate and remote, the present and far reaching consequences of which to both races cannot be contemplated without the most dismal foreboding of horror and dismay. The proclamation invites servile insurrection as an element in this emancipation crusade—a means of warfare, the inhumanity and diabolism of which are without example in civilized warfare, and which we denounce, and which the civilized world will denounce, as an uneffaceable disgrace to the American people.

The section of the Proclamation declaring that Negroes would be received into the armed forces was received gladly by those who had been anxious to enlist since the beginning of the War. At no period in the first two years of the War had President Lincoln acceded to this appeal by Negroes in the Northern states. The War was initially a white man's war, with Negroes not being considered as participants. But now, after two years of the War had passed, they were proudly enrolled as fighting soldiers of the United States Army.

On March 3, 1863, an act authorized the enlistment of "under-cooks of African descent"; and soon many under-cooks were employed in regiments of white soldiers. On March 23, an additional act provided that all able-bodied male colored persons between the ages of 20 and 45 should be received into the military service and that the bounty of one hundred dollars should apply also to them.

Keeping in mind that the Emancipation Proclamation was a war measure designed and planned to save the Union, careful study of it leads to some very interesting observations. It shows that slaves in some Southern states, as well as in counties of other states, were left in slavery and that the basis of the Proclamation was an intent to strike only at those parts of the Confederacy affected by its declaration. But its real greatness lies in the feelings it created in the colored people, both North and South. It seized and stirred their imaginations, converted their discouragement into strong faith, and prophesied a tomorrow containing freedom and justice.

CHAPTER THREE

Admission to the Armed Forces

The First Steps

THE differences of opinion on slavery and freedom for Negro Americans influenced the question of their participation in the War. Abolitionists were of the opinion that Negroes should be used as soldiers so that they would be able to contribute to the winning of the War and thus rise to a recognized place in American society. Others were of the belief that only the "superior" race should have the right to defend the flag and that the use of Negro troops would lead to insurrections. The question was first debated by the United States Senate in 1861, with Senator Henry Wilson and Senator Charles Sumner urging the employment of Negroes by the armed forces. Sumner declared, "I do not say carry the War into Africa, but carry Africa into the War."

The Senate debate was so active that the *New York Express* stated:

> If Senators make officers' opinions against the impolity and the folly of creating Negro regiments as soldiers to march side by side with Americans, Irishmen, and Germans in the test as proposed, there is scarcely a General in the Army who will stand it. If Senators make the test, from all that we can fear, the President of the United States will overrule them and recommission such officers as stand up for their color, their race, their breed—as the superior race of the Negro.

A view to the contrary was held by Gerrit Smith and other staunch friends of the Negro, who were advocating the use of Negro troops in 1861. They believed that Negroes should be admitted to the army for the good effects which discipline would have, and thereby to gain the respect of all Americans from this experience. The argument was made by abolitionists that Generals George Washington and Andrew Jackson had used Negroes effectively in the American Revolution and the War of 1812. It was said that they would prove to be an asset for the North when used as spies, teamsters or scouts; and furthermore, any hand which could help should be used, even though that hand was black. Toussaint L'Ouverture, the man who had foiled the plan of Napoleon to gain a foothold in Haiti and laid the foundation for its independence, was cited as an example of black courage and efficiency in war. It was also known that the Confederacy was using slaves against the Northern armies. The Southern states had undertaken the use of Negroes in support of their armies prior to the period of the War when the North was considering it. Free Negroes were used by the Confederate states first in Tennessee, Louisiana and South Carolina. This was a serious matter in Southern thinking, for the arming of these colored persons could be very dangerous, particularly in areas where Negroes outnumbered whites.

During the early days of the War, free Negro volunteers had been accepted by the Confederates in local areas. At Nashville, Tennessee, in April, 1861, a Negro company offered its members for Confederate service. At Memphis, Tennessee, a recruiting office was opened. The following notice was used:

ATTENTION VOLUNTEERS!

Resolved by the Committee of Safety, that C. Deloach, D. R. Cook, and William B. Greenlaw, be authorized to organize a volunteer company, composed of our patriotic free men of color, of the city of Memphis, for the service of our common defense. All who have not enrolled their names will call at the office of W. B. Greenlaw and Co.

F. TITUS, President
F. W. Forsythe, Secretary

On June 28, 1861, the Tennessee General Assembly became the first state assembly to adopt military service for free Negroes. This

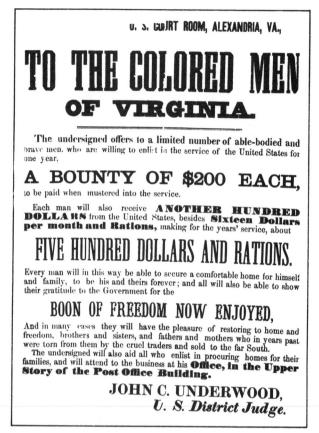

A typical Army recruiting poster.

state had a large population of free Negroes who were property owners, and some even owned slaves. The purpose of the act was not to give Negroes an opportunity to participate in military service as soldiers but rather to relieve the white volunteers of the necessity to perform menial work. It read as follows:

An Act for the Relief of Volunteers

SECTION 1. *Be it enacted by the General Assembly of the State of Tennessee,* That from and after the passage of this Act, the Governor shall be, and he is hereby authorized, at his discretion, to receive into the military service of the State all male free persons of color between the ages of fifteen (15) and fifty (50) years—of such number as may be necessary—who may be sound in mind and body, and capable of actual service.

SECTION 2. *Be it further enacted,* That all such free persons of color shall be required to do all such menial service for the relief of the volunteers as is incident to camp life, and necessary to the efficiency of the service, and of which they are capable of performing.

Sections of the act dealt with pay and rations of food and clothing for the Negroes; sheriffs were required to collect information on the movements of free persons of color, and officers were required to see that such persons did not suffer from neglect or mistreatment. If the necessary number of Negroes was not obtained, the governor was empowered to impress them. The Florida legislature gave to its governor a similar power, though it depended upon an authorization by the Confederate government, and other states adopted actions of a similar nature.

The Adjutant General's Office of the Louisiana Militia issued Order No. 426, found in the *Official Records of the Rebellion*, which stated:

> The Governor and the Commander-in-Chief relying implicitly upon the loyalty of the free colored population of the city and State, for the protection of their homes, their property and Southern rights, from the pollution of a ruthless invader, and believing that the military organization which existed prior to February 15, 1862, and excited praise and respect for the patriotic motives which prompted it, should exist for and during the War, calls upon them to maintain their organization and hold themselves prepared for such orders as may be transmitted to them.

The *Baltimore Traveler* commented on the organization of regiments of Negroes to defend Richmond if it should be attacked, stating that they were being "formed into regiments, and armed for the defenses of that city." In this connection, Horace Greeley wrote in *The American Conflict:* "For more than two years Negroes had been extensively employed in belligerent operations by the Confederacy. They had been embodied and drilled as rebel soldiers and had paraded with white troops at a time when this would not have been tolerated in the armies of the

Negroes moving a cannon for Confederate forces during the attack on Fort Monroe.

Union." It is well known that Negroes were used in piling up sandbags for fortifications at Fort Sumter and at Charleston. They were employed as teamsters, cooks and helpers in a variety of tasks. At Lynchburg, Virginia, a newspaper comment on the enlistment of seventy Negroes read, "Three cheers for the patriotic Negroes of Lynchburg." At the first Battle of Bull Run, July 21, 1861, loyal slaves were said to have fought with outstanding bravery by the sides of their masters.

Two official comments have value in this connection. One was by James A. Seddon, Secretary of the Confederate War Department, who wrote: "They the Negroes have, besides, the homes they value, the families they love, and the masters they respect and depend on to defend and protect against the savagery and devastation of the enemy." The other comment came from Governor Wallace of Florida, a former slaveholder, in a speech before the legislature:

The world had never seen such a body of slaves, for not only in peace but in War they had been faithful to us. During much of the time of the late unhappy difficulties, Florida had a greater number of men in her army than constituted her entire voting population. This, of course, stripped many districts of their arms-bearing inhabitants and left our females and infant children almost exclusively to the protection of our slaves. They proved true to their trust. Not one instance of insult, outrage, or indignity has ever come to my knowledge. They remained at home and made provisions for the army.

Further observations concerning Southern Negroes reveal that not all of them were submissive and loyal to their masters. For instance, a Mississippian who lived near Port Gibson wrote of his experience during the War as follows:

When the advanced forces of the enemy reached Nitta Tola . . . the fetters of slavery were broken instantly and the hoe and plow handle dropped from the hands of the Negroes, and I ceased to be a planter forever. It is amazing with what intuitive familiarity the Negroes recognized the moment of deliverance.

The first Battle of Bull Run.

Another comment, which provides additional evidence, comes from a North Carolinian who wrote that "Our Negroes are beginning to show they understand the state of affairs, and insolence and insubordination are quite common."

Differences of opinion on the reactions of Negroes to the War were as widely scattered as were the individuals who gave them. Each saw a group, or groups, of Negroes and drew conclusions concerning their actions, judging them too often without being acquainted with the backgrounds which influenced the attitudes and behavior of the former slaves.

Following the attack on Fort Sumter, a proclamation calling for seventy-five thousand volunteers was issued. In the Northern states, Negroes were among those answering the call—but they were rejected. Here is additional evidence of the Negro's attempt to serve his country, only to be defeated by a discriminating society.

PROPOSALS FOR NEGRO ENLISTMENTS IN UNION ARMIES

Many objections were made to the enlistment of Negroes as Union soldiers. The consensus was that the Negro could not fight because of his inferior race and his long bondage and that white troops would not fight with him. In spite of these views, the first authorization for the enlistment of Negro soldiers was sent on August 25, 1862, to General Rufus Saxton, General Hunter's successor. He was authorized to enlist Negro soldiers not to exceed five thousand and Negro laborers not to exceed fifty thousand.

In the meantime, there were local areas in Louisiana where Negroes had been slaveowners and were willing to fight for the protection of their property and their slaves. They belonged to the New Orleans free colored population and were, in the main, mulattoes who were self-reliant and of middle-class status. General Butler said of their

RICHARD HARVEY CAIN

appearance, "The darkest of them were about the complexion of the late Mr. [Daniel] Webster."

The question "Why should we fight?" was one which colored men in the North often asked. The subtle forces they encountered differed little from the hostilities they met in the South. They were not admitted generally to the public schools or to the juries; and while Massachusetts, Maine, New Jersey and Connecticut made no distinction in laws, there were separate schools for Negroes in many cities of these states. As contrabands they were not admitted into the states of Illinois and Indiana. Separate streetcars were authorized in Philadelphia, and some streetcars in New York City were denied use by colored people. Worst of all, Negroes rode in segregated cars in the nation's capital.

However, when the charter for the Washington-Alexandria Railroad came up in Congress, Senator Sumner moved to amend the bill with the addition of the provision that "No person should be excluded from the cars on account of color." This provision passed both houses without debate and was approved by the President, March 3, 1863. When a bill to amend the Metropolitan Railroad of Washington City came to the floor, Senator Sumner was its chief proponent and wanted to add a provision similar to that above. This action resulted in considerable debate, but the amendment was adopted and the company was restrained from maintaining separate cars for colored persons. Finally, Negroes had not been accepted in the armed forces, even in the call for volunteers. Living under these pressures, it was not at all strange that colored men should ask themselves, "Why should we fight?"

Nevertheless, when war came there were favorable reactions among thousands of Negro Americans. One such reaction was given by Richard H. Cain, a student at Wilberforce University, Wilberforce, Ohio. Cain, who was later to become a member of the U.S. House of Representatives and to be elected a bishop of the African Methodist Episcopal Church, stated:

I was a student at Wilberforce University in Ohio when the tocsin of war was sounded, when Fort Sumter was fired upon, and I shall never forget the thrill that ran through my soul when I thought of the coming consequences of that shot. There were one hundred and fifteen of us students at the University, who, anxious to vindicate the stars and stripes, made up a company and offered our services to the Governor of Ohio; and sir, we were told that this is a white man's war and that the Negro had nothing to do with it. Sir, we returned, docile, patient, waiting, casting our eyes to the Heavens whence help always comes. We knew that there would come a period in the history of this nation when our strong black arms would be needed. We waited patiently; we waited until Massachusetts, through her noble Governor sounded the alarm, and we hastened to hear the summons and obey it.

The threatened invasion of Cincinnati by John Morgan's Confederate army in 1862 led to action for the defense of the city. General Lewis S. Wallace, who was in command of this project, placed the city under

Negroes hiding in private cellars were seized and impressed into military service by the Army.

JUDGE WILLIAM M. DICKSON

martial law and issued a proclamation which called for "Citizens for labor: soldiers for battle." The next day, Mayor George Hatch issued a proclamation requesting all employers and employees to assemble in their respective wards at the usual places of voting and to organize themselves in such manner as was thought best for the defense of the city. He said that "Every man, of every age, be he alien or citizen, who lives under the protection of our laws, is expected to take part in this organization."

This all-inclusive proclamation could have been interpreted to include the colored population, but it was apparent that it was not so intended and they remained in their homes. In the meantime, the military authorities had decided to impress colored men for work upon fortifications, and the police notified them to report for duty. These policemen went from house to house, followed by a group of citizens who searched private cellars where Negroes had hidden, and dragged out those who were to be utilized by the army. The *Cincinnati Gazette* opposed this treatment and wrote an editorial stating:

> Let our citizens be treated civilly and not exposed to any unnecessary tyranny, nor to the insults of poor whites. We say poor whites, when none but poor spirited whites insult a race which they profess to regard as inferior. It would have been decent to have invited the colored inhabitants to turn out in the defense of the city.

The task of organizing the colored men was then turned over to Judge William M. Dickson, who was given command of these forces. They were to work on the fortifications near Newport and Covington, Kentucky. Immediately the brutality ceased, and the men who had been seized were permitted to return to their homes and prepare themselves for camp duty. For the next three weeks, the black brigade worked on the fortifications. The brigade had an enrollment of 706, but this did not represent the complete membership, which numbered over 1,000. About 300 were assigned to various duties in camps and on boats. Colonel Dickson reported that the brigade labored cheerfully and joyfully and displayed a high order of intelligence. During the first week, the brigade worked without compensation; but during the second week, each man received a dollar a day; and during the third week each received a dollar and a half a day.

By September 20, Cincinnati's fear of invasion had passed. Two years later, Colonel Dickson wrote of this experience:

> It is indeed regretted that they were not permitted to enter the service under the auspices of their own state, whose soil they had defended; but this privilege which the authorities of their state denied them, was granted them by the sagacious, patriotic and noble Governor of the ancient Commonwealth of Massachusetts.

This brigade was the first group of colored men organized in the Middle West for purposes that were even related to military matters. With three exceptions, all of the officers in this brigade were Negroes, and one regiment was commanded by a colored officer. It was reported that the one commanded by the Negro was so decidedly superior that this regiment would afterward always be commanded by colored officers.

Colored citizens in other parts of the state of Ohio attempted to volunteer for the army. But they, too, were refused during 1861 and the first part of 1862. W. T. Burt and J. T. Boston directed a letter to Secretary of War Cameron informing him that they had previously written to Salmon P. Chase, Secretary of the Treasury, who had been known in Ohio as the "attorney general for runaway slaves." Chase suggested that they should apply to the Secretary of War. Their letter stated that they were legal voters who had voted for the present administration. They wrote: "The question now, is will you allow us the poor privilege of fighting, and, if need be, dying, to support those in office who are our choice." Other appeals in this vein failed to win any approval.

By the middle of 1863, a change in attitude had taken place. Adjutant General Lorenzo Thomas wrote to Major General John M. Schofield from Cincinnati that he was on the way to organize regiments of volunteers of African descent and requested Schofield to enlist as many colored men as possible. He was to organize able-bodied men into regiments and select officers whose hearts would be in the work. This opened a new phase in Civil War history.

Among the generals in the army who proposed and fostered the use of colored troops was Brigadier General Daniel Ullmann. He wrote the Adjutant General that colored men should not be kept in the background and degraded as laborers, because their morale would be destroyed by such treatment. Brigadier General Gillmore issued General Order No. 77, stating that Negroes detailed for fatigue duty would be employed in the preparation of camps and the performance of menial duties for white troops. Ullmann ordered that this assignment was unauthorized and improper and that it was "hereafter expressly prohibited." Colored troops in some

GENERAL BENJAMIN F. BUTLER

camps and forts of the South received bad treatment. Some white officers were reported as exercising their authority in "the harshest treatment and were acting more like that of a brute than a human being." These instances were few in number, but they had their effect on the morale of both Negroes and whites.

The original legislation controlling the recruiting of colored troops had directed that white officers be placed in command. These officers were to be selected carefully on the basis of military experience and were to be chosen from those volunteering. Massachusetts' Governor Andrew wrote Secretary of War Edwin M. Stanton, who had recently replaced Cameron, and requested that the prohibition be relaxed so far as line officers, assistant surgeons and chaplains of the proposed regiments were concerned.

General J. W. Phelps, a West Point graduate, was in charge of a regiment of the Union Army at Carrollton, Louisiana, under General Butler's command. He wrote General Butler in June, 1862, declaring that it

THE LINE OFFICERS OF THE FIRST LOUISIANA NATIVE GUARDS

2nd Lieutenant V. Lavigne, Co. D.   *2nd Lieutenant J. L. Montieu, Co. A.*

Captain Charles Sentmanat, Co. D.   *1st Lieutenant L. D. Larrieu, Co. A.*   *Captain E. Davis, Co. A.*

was through the military that enfranchisement had come to the people of Europe and that slaves here might be prepared for freedom through the same source. He was of the opinion that fifty regiments of colored soldiers could be raised.

General Butler did not reply, and General Phelps wrote another letter on July 30. He said he could raise three regiments and that he had then about three hundred blacks in five companies who were willing for any test, except the submission to slavery. He wrote: "It is for the interests of the South, as well as for the North, that the African should be permitted to offer his black [*sic*] for the temple of freedom." He asked also that West Point cadets be sent into South Carolina and Louisiana to drill Negro recruits and that line officers could be selected from those in the services.

General Butler finally replied that he was not willing to accept the Negro as a soldier and advised that he should be used as a laborer. On July 31, General Phelps wrote General Butler that he was "not willing to become the mere slave driver you propose, having no qualifications that way," and offered his resignation from the army. It was after this experience, in August, 1862, that General Butler appealed to the free Negroes of New Orleans to enlist in the army. Three outstanding regiments, known as the 1st, 2nd and 3rd Louisiana Native Guards, were inducted into the Union Army as the Corps d'Afrique. General Butler's earlier refusal to use colored soldiers was based on the lack of government sanctions and did not represent his personal opinion. Prior to his departure for North Carolina, Butler had determined to test the use of these Negro troops.

The U.S. Colored Troops were used to seek out slaves and draw them into the advancing Union Army.

He assembled eighteen hundred colored men at Norfolk and placed them under the command of General Edward A. Wild, an abolitionist doctor. Two columns of cavalry and additional artillery were added to these troops, and the men left for a raid into North Carolina.

The colored men were to serve two purposes. First, they were actively to engage the enemy in combat, and second, they were to seek out slaves and draw them into their advancing lines. The fact that they were able to burn four guerrilla camps, a dozen homesteads, two distilleries and to capture four Confederate soldiers convinced Butler of their military ability. And since the unit returned with twenty-five hundred men, seven hundred more than they started with, Butler was more than pleased with the conduct of these Negro troops.

It was also in August that Secretary Stanton sent an order to General Rufus Saxton concerning the enlistment of Negroes. Stanton wrote the general that, in view of the small force under his command and the inability of the government to increase the number, he was "authorized to arm, uniform, equip, and receive into the service of the United States such number of volunteers of African descent . . . [as necessary] not exceeding 5,000; and may detail officers to instruct them in military drill, discipline and duty, and to command them." He felt that this plan would serve to reduce the laboring strength of the Confederates. Before the close of 1862, there were four Negro regiments enrolled in the Union Army by action of commanders, but without the official sanction of either the president or the United States Congress.

THE MOVEMENT GAINS HEADWAY

The movement for presidential approval of the use of Negroes as soldiers gained momentum as the Union forces met defeat at Fredericksburg and Vicksburg. With thousands scheduled for discharge during the summer and fall of 1863 and with the volunteers not producing the expected results, it became apparent that more men were needed.

Following the Emancipation Proclamation and under Lincoln's direction, Secretary of War Stanton authorized Brigadier General Ullmann to organize regiments of Negro troops. Ullmann was told to raise four regiments of infantry and a battalion composed of six companies of mounted scouts. Headquarters for recruiting were established in New York City and in New Orleans. Ullmann obtained a list of qualified soldiers who would make good officers and found more than two hundred officers from the Army of the Potomac, whom he considered capable as well as "educated gentlemen."

While this plan was under organization and Kansas and Massachusetts were enlisting Negro soldiers, the decision was made by the administration not only to accept but to bring Negroes into Union lines. As General Henry Halleck wrote to General Grant, March 31, 1863:

> It is the policy of the Government to withdraw from the enemy as much productive labor as possible. So long as the rebels retain and employ their slaves in producing grains, etc., they can employ all the whites in the field. Every slave withdrawn from the enemy is equivalent to a white put *hors de combat*.

General Halleck told Grant reports had been made to the Secretary of War that the officers of his command had discouraged Negroes from coming under the protection of his army and, by ill-treatment, had compelled them to return to their masters. He regarded this as a bad course of action, one which was directly opposed to the government's program. In reply, General Grant wrote that at least three army corps commanders had taken up the new policy of arming Negroes and using them against the Confederates. A few days later, Grant issued an order for "the completion of the Negro regiments now organizing in this department," in which he stated that all commanders were to exert themselves "not only in organizing regiments and rendering them efficient but also in removing prejudice against them."

General Grant then sent General Lorenzo Thomas to the Mississippi Valley to set the new policy in operation. On April 8, General Thomas addressed the army, saying that the administration had decided to take Negroes away from the enemy, "and compel them to send back a portion of their whites to cultivate their deserted plantations; and very poor persons they would be to fill the place of the dark-hued laborer." This meant that the Ne-

GENERAL HENRY HALLECK

gro would not be turned away, but that his aid would be enlisted for the Union. General Thomas also said that he was "authorized to raise as many regiments of blacks as I can," and to give commissions to the proper persons. The general traveled extensively—to Memphis, Tennessee; Helena, Arkansas; Vicksburg, Mississippi; and parts of Louisiana—recruiting as many men of color as possible.

General Order No. 143 established the Bureau of Colored Troops in the Adjutant General's Office for the conduct of all matters relating to the organization of these troops. Inspectors examined the problems of recruiting at the different points and reported the facts to a board of examiners for the command of colored troops which had been established. This board was made up of two Negro and three white soldiers, of whom one was a lieutenant colonel, one a surgeon and one a lieutenant. There were about 3,000 candidates examined, with 1,700 recommendations for commissions ranging from second lieutenant to colonel. However, all of these were chosen from the ranks of white men; and as a rule, the noncommissioned officers were Negroes.

These white officers were treated with contempt by Southerners because they were in command of colored troops. The Confederate War Department on April 21, 1862, issued an order proclaiming that captured commissioned officers of slaves in the armed services would not be regarded as prisoners of war but would be held in confinement for execution as felons. The Confederate Congress passed a resolution on January 12, 1863, stating that, when captured, these officers would be charged with inciting servile insur-

General Thomas addressing the Negroes of Louisiana on the duties of freedom.

The Enrollment Act of March 3, 1863, calling for the drafting of all male citizens, was interpreted to include free Negroes.

rections and would "be put to death or otherwise punished at the discretion of the court." Confederate General Kirby Smith ordered that officers in charge of colored troops and their men should be shown no quarter, meaning that they were to be killed in action. This led to the bravest of fighting by colored troops when confronted by the enemy.

Responding to this challenge, President Lincoln issued a proclamation, on July 30, 1863, declaring that for every soldier of the United States killed in violation of the laws of war, a rebel soldier also would be executed. There is no evidence that the Confederate order was ever carried out. However, there is abundant evidence of Confederate hatred and mistreatment of these white officers because they were in command of colored soldiers.

There were Negroes who resented the discriminatory manner in which white officers were selected to command them and the lack of opportunity for Negro promotions beyond the rank of noncommissioned officer. Negro commissioned officers had been used by

General Butler when the Louisiana Native Guards were first organized, but he later discontinued the practice because of difficulties between white and colored officers. A state convention of the colored people meeting in New Orleans, Louisiana, in January, 1865, appointed a committee "to inquire why we are commanded and cannot command."

The Enrollment Act of March 3, 1863, with provisions for drafting all male citizens, was interpreted to include free Negroes. There was opposition to this act in Kentucky. In view of this opposition and Kentucky's precarious position in the Union, General Ambrose E. Burnside enrolled those qualified for service but did not attempt to draft Negroes. In February, 1864, another enrollment act provided specifically that "all able-bodied male colored persons, between the ages of twenty and forty-five years, resident in the United States, shall be enrolled." This act gave protection to slaveholders in the border states by giving them one hundred dollars for each slave drafted or, if the slave volunteered with his owner's consent, a compensation not

CAPTAIN O. S. B. WALL

to exceed three hundred dollars. The Congress was, therefore, compensating the slave-owner for the services of his "property," but the man who was going into battle for his country's defense received nothing. Not only Negroes born free but former slaves were included, so that this action led to more extensive Negro enlistment and organization.

Recruiting efforts were continued in Louisiana by General Thomas, and on October 13, 1863, authorization was issued by the Adjutant General's Office for the enlistment of Negro troops in Maryland, Missouri and Tennessee; Delaware was included on October 26. Enlistments were also conducted in New York, Pennsylvania and other Northern states. A special military school to train officers commanding Negro troops was opened in Philadelphia.

Governor Seymour of New York declined to permit the enlistment of Negroes, despite petitions from such outstanding American leaders as Horace Greeley and William Cullen Bryant. On August 4, 1862, Governor Sprague of Rhode Island had issued an appeal for the enlistment of Negroes as soldiers, and it was reported that the eagerness of the

Negroes to volunteer induced more than six hundred to go from New York to Rhode Island to enlist. By December, 1863, authorization for recruiting Negroes was given in New York; and within sixty days, through the activities of the members of the Union League Club, more than 2,300 Negroes had enlisted.

THE FIFTY-FOURTH MASSACHUSETTS REGIMENT

On January 26, 1863, Secretary Stanton had authorized Governor John A. Andrew of Massachusetts to raise such numbers of volunteer companies of artillery "for duty in the forts of Massachusetts and elsewhere, and such corps of infantry for the volunteer military service as he may find convenient. Such volunteers to be enlisted for three years, unless sooner discharged, and may include persons of African descent organized into separate corps."

Governor Andrew enlisted the support of Mayor George L. Stearns of Medford, Massachusetts, who had assisted John Brown in his plan for giving freedom to the slaves. Stearns, who was appointed assistant adjutant general of volunteers and commissioner for the organization of colored troops, organized a committee to assist in raising the Massachusetts regiment. Among those selected were colored attorney John M. Langston and O. S. B. Wall—a colored boot and shoe merchant—both from Oberlin, Ohio, and Frederick Douglass of Rochester, New York. Their appearances and speeches before assemblies and their personal contacts brought an increase in the enlistments of colored men for the Massachusetts cause. Fifty colored men joined at Toledo and fifty-four went from Cincinnati. Mayor Stearns wrote to Secretary Stanton, June 26, 1863, "My regiment is progressing handsomely." And he added, "Colored men begin to understand they gain nothing by standing off but if they would gain their rights and secure protection at the hands of the government they must rally at its call."

In order to consummate the recruiting in Massachusetts, a letter was sent by Governor Andrew to Francis G. Shaw concerning the recruiting of colored troops and the choice of white officers.

COLONEL
ROBERT
GOULD
SHAW

Francis G. Shaw, Esq., Staten Island, N.Y.

Boston, Jan. 30, 1863

Dear Sir—As you may have seen by the newspapers, I am about to raise a colored regiment in Massachusetts. This I cannot but regard as perhaps the most important corps to be organized during the whole War, in view of what must be the composition of our new levies; and therefore I am very anxious to organize it judiciously, in order that it may be a model for all future colored regiments. I am desirous to have for its officers—particularly for its field officers—young men of military experience, of firm anti-slavery principles, ambitious, superior to a vote of contempt for color, and having faith in the capacity of colored men for military service. Such officers must necessarily be gentlemen of the highest tone and honor; and I shall look for them in those circles of educated anti-slavery society which, next to the colored race itself, have the greatest interest in this experiment.

Reviewing the young men of the character I have described, now in the Massachusetts service, it occurs to me to offer the Colonelcy to your son, Captain Shaw, of the Second Massachusetts Infantry, and the Lieutenant Colonelcy to Captain Hallowell of the 20th Massachusetts Infantry, the son of Mr. Morris L. Hallowell of Philadelphia. With my deep conviction of the importance of this undertaking, in view of the fact that it will be the first colored regiment to be raised in the free states, and that its success or its failure will go far to elevate or depress the estimation in which the character of the colored Americans will be held throughout the world, the command of such a regiment seems to me to be a high object of ambition for any officer. How much your son may have reflected upon such a subject I do not know, nor have I any information of his disposition for such a task except what I have derived from his general character and reputation; nor should I wish to undertake it unless he could enter upon it with a full sense of its importance, with a deep determination for its success, and with the assent and sympathy and support of the opinions of his immediate family.

I therefore enclose you the letter in which I make him the officer of this commission; and I will be obliged to you if you will forward it to him, accompanying it with any expression to him of your own views, and if you will also write to me upon the subject. My mind is drawn toward Captain Shaw by many considerations. I am sure that he would attract the support, sympathy, and active cooperation of many among his immediate family relatives. The more ardent, faithful, and true Republicans and friends of liberty would recognize in him a scion from a tree whose fruit and leaves have always contributed to the strength and healing of our generation. So it is with Captain Hallowell. His father is a Quaker gentleman of Philadelphia, two of whose sons are officers in our Army, and another is a merchant in Boston. Their house in Philadelphia is a hospital and home for Massachusetts officers; and the family are full of good works; and he was the adviser and confidant of our soldiers when sick or on duty in that city. I need not add that young Captain Hallowell is a gallant and fine fellow true as steel to the cause of humanity as well as to the flag of the country; I wish to engage the field officers, and then get their aid in selecting those of the line. I have offers from Oliver T. Beard of Brooklyn, New York, late Lieutenant Colonel of the Forty-Eighth New York Volunteers, who says he can already get six-hundred men; and from others wishing to furnish men from New York and Connecticut; but I do not wish to start the regiment under a stranger to Massachusetts. If in any way, by suggestion or otherwise, you can aid the purpose which is the burden of this letter, I shall receive your cooperation with the heartiest graditude; I do not wish the offer to go begging; and if the offer is refused, I prefer it being kept reasonably private. Hoping to hear from you immediately upon receiving this letter, I am, with great regard.

Your obedient servant and friend,
JOHN A. ANDREW

On receipt of this letter, Shaw took it to his son, Captain Robert Gould Shaw, who was at the time a commissioned officer in the Union Army. Captain Shaw immediately telegraphed his acceptance to Governor Andrew. Born in Boston on October 10, 1837, and admitted to Harvard College in 1856, Shaw had discontinued his course in the third year to join the army. He entered the 7th New York National Guard, then received a commission as second lieutenant in the 2nd Massachusetts Infantry, and was later promoted to captain. As a result of his appointment to command the 54th Massachusetts Regiment, he received the rank of colonel.

The other persons nominated to command the regiment were carefully selected by Governor Andrew—fourteen of the twenty-nine appointed were veteran soldiers, six had been previously commissioned. Several were Harvard men, and others were descendants of soldiers who had served in the American Revolution and the War of 1812.

The motives of these white soldiers in joining this experiment were of significance, due to the fact that the country, generally, was opposed to the Negroes' services, because it was thought that they would not make good soldiers. It required courage to accept such a commission in view of these conditions.

John W. M. Appleton of Boston was selected for the recruiting commission, and this call was published in the *Boston Journal*.

TO COLORED MEN

Wanted. Good men for the Fifty-Fourth Regiment of Massachusetts Volunteers of African descent, by Colonel Robert G. Shaw. One-hundred dollars bounty at expiration of term of service. Pay thirteen dollars per month, and state aid for families. All necessary information can be obtained at the office, Corner of Cambridge and North Russell Street.

Lieut. J. W. M. APPLETON
Recruiting Officer

Within five days, twenty-five men had volunteered, and fifty or sixty were recruited about the last of March from the small Negro population of Massachusetts. Recruiting was also undertaken in cities of other states. In Massachusetts and Pennsylvania, colored ministers were informed of the plans for the recruitment of Negro troops, and these plans were then announced in their churches. On February 15, Governor Andrew appointed a committee to supervise the raising of recruits. The committee consisted of George L. Stearns, Amos A. Lawrence, John M. Forbes, William I. Bowditch, LeBaron Russell and Richard P. Hallowell of Boston; Mayor Halloran and James B. Congdon of New Bedford; Ward P. Phillips of Salem; and Francis G. Shaw of New York. This committee, known also as the Black Committee, later increased its membership to one hundred persons, all of whom were prominent citizens and leading businessmen. Their first project was to collect funds; and within a short time five thousand dollars had been raised. A total of nearly one hundred thousand dollars eventually was attained.

The burden of establishing this regiment fell upon George L. Stearns, who was appointed an agent for the committee. Traveling first to Rochester, New York, Stearns sought the cooperation of Frederick Douglass; during his stay he enrolled Douglass' son as his first recruit. A line of recruiting posts was established from Boston to St. Louis. Meetings were held in churches throughout the area, with stirring appeals made to Negroes. Frederick Douglass issued an announcement under the title "Men of Color to Arms," which was intended to encourage enlistment and urgently requested that this opportunity be accepted.

William Lloyd Garrison and Wendell Phillips were among the notable guests in attendance when Governor Andrew presented the state and national flags to Colonel Robert Gould Shaw of the 54th Massachusetts Regiment at the camp located in Readville, Massachusetts. In presenting the flags,

MEN OF COLOR, TO ARMS!

A Call by Frederick Douglass.

When first the Rebel cannon shattered the walls of Sumter, and drove away its starving garrison, I predicted that the war then and there inaugurated would not be fought out entirely by white men. Every month's experience during these two dreary years has confirmed that opinion. A war undertaken and brazenly carried on for the perpetual enslavement of colored men, calls logically and loudly upon colored men to help to suppress it. Only a moderate share of sagacity was needed to see that the arm of the slave was the best defence against the arm of the slaveholder. Hence with every reverse to the National arms, with every exulting shout of victory raised by the slaveholding Rebels, I have implored the imperilled nation to unchain against her foes her powerful black hand. Slowly and reluctantly that appeal is beginning to be heeded. Stop not now to complain that it was not heeded sooner. It may, or it may not have been best—that it should not. This is not the time to discuss that question. Leave it to the future. When the war is over, the country is saved, peace is established, and the black man's rights are secured, as they will be, history with an impartial hand, will dispose of that and sundry other questions. Action! action! not criticism, is the plain duty of this hour. Words are now useful only as they stimulate to blows. The office of speech now is only to point out when, where and how to strike to the best advantage. There is no time for delay. The tide is at flood that leads on to fortune. From east to west, from north to south the sky is written all over with "now or never." Liberty won by white men would lack half its lustre. Who would be free themselves must strike the blow. Better even to die free than to live slaves. This is the sentiment of every brave colored man among us. There are weak and cowardly men in all nations. We have them among us. They will tell you that this is the "whiteman's war;" that you will be "better off after than before the war;" that the getting of you into the army is to "sacrifice you on the first opportunity." Believe them not—cowards themselves, they do not wish to have their cowardice shamed by your brave example. Leave them to their timidity, or to whatever other motive may hold them back.

I have not thought lightly of the words I am now addressing to you. The counsel I give comes of close observation of the great struggle now in progress—and of the deep conviction that this is your hour and mine.

In good earnest, then, and after the best deliberation, I, now, for the first time during the war, feel at liberty to call and counsel you to arms. By every consideration which binds you to your enslaved fellow countrymen, and the peace and welfare of your country; by every aspiration which you cherish for the freedom and equality of yourselves and your children; by all the ties of blood and identity which make us one with the brave black men now fighting our battles in Louisiana, in South Carolina, I urge you to fly to arms, and smite with death the power that would bury the Government and your liberty in the same hopeless grave. I wish I could tell you that the State of New York calls you to this high honor. For the moment her constituted authorities are silent on the subject. They will speak by and by, and doubtless on the right side; but we are not compelled to wait for her. We can get at the throat of treason and Slavery through the State of Massachusetts.

She was first in the war of Independence; first to break the chains of her slaves; first to make the black man equal before the law; first to admit colored children to her common schools, and she was the first to answer with her blood the alarm cry of the nation—when its capital was menaced by rebels. You know her patriotic Governor, and you know Charles Sumner—I need add no more.

Massachusetts now welcomes you to arms as her soldiers. She has but a small colored population from which to recruit. She has full leave of the General Government to send one regiment to the war, and she has undertaken to do it. Go quickly and help fill up this first colored regiment from the North. I am authorized to assure you that you will receive the same wages, the same rations, the same equipments, the same protection, the same treatment and the same bounty secured to white soldiers. You will be led by able and skillful officers—men who will take especial pride in your efficiency and success. They will be quick to accord to you all the honor you shall merit by your valor—and see that your rights and feelings are respected by other soldiers. I have assured myself on these points—and can speak with authority. More than twenty years unswerving devotion to our common cause, may give me some humble claim to be trusted at this momentous crisis.

I will not argue. To do so implies hesitation and doubt, and you do not hesitate. You do not doubt. The day dawns—the morning star is bright upon the horizon! The iron gate of our prison stands half open. One gallant rush from the North will fling it wide open, while four millions of our brothers and sisters shall march out into Liberty! The chance is now given you to end in a day the bondage of centuries, and to rise in one bound from social degradation to the plane of common equality with all other varieties of men. Remember Denmark Vesey of Charleston. Remember Nathaniel Turner of South Hampton; remember Shields Green, and Copeland, who followed noble John Brown, and fell as glorious martyrs for the cause of the slaves. Remember that in a contest with oppression, the Almighty has no attribute which can take sides with oppressors. The case is before you. This is our golden opportunity—let us accept it—and forever wipe out the dark reproaches unsparingly hurled against us by our enemies. Win for ourselves the gratitude of our country—and the best blessings of our prosperity through all time. The nucleus of this first regiment is now in camp at Readville, a short distance from Boston. I will undertake to forward to Boston all persons adjudged fit to be mustered into this regiment, who shall apply to me at any time within the next two weeks.

FREDERICK DOUGLASS.

Rochester, March 2, 1863.

the Cross and a special flag from the Putnam family, Governor Andrew said:

> May you, sir, and these, follow not only on the field of battle, but in all the walks and ways of life, in camp, and hereafter when on returning peace, you shall resume the more quiet and peaceful duties of citizens—may you but follow the splendid example, the sweet devotion mingled with manly, heroic character, of which the life, character, and death of Lieutenant Putnam was one example.

Colonel Shaw replied, "May we have an opportunity to show that you have not made a mistake in entrusting the honor of the state to a colored regiment;—the first state that has sent one to the War."

Ten days afterward, Governor Andrew reviewed the regiment as it marched through downtown Boston en route to its embarkation for Port Royal, South Carolina; and the men received the enthusiastic acclaim of the crowds.

REGIMENTS IN BOSTON, PHILADELPHIA AND NEW YORK

The second Negro regiment recruited in Massachusetts was the 55th Massachusetts Volunteers, organized at Camp Meigs in Readville, during May, 1863, under the command of Colonel Alfred S. Hartwell. He had been advanced in rank from first lieutenant in the 44th Massachusetts Regiment, served as a captain in the 54th Massachusetts Volunteers, and advanced to lieutenant colonel of the 55th Massachusetts Volunteers in June, 1863. Finally he was promoted to colonel of the same regiment in December, 1863.

The recruitment of colored troops in the Northern states had been so effective that the ranks of one regiment planned for Massachusetts had been filled. Another regiment was filled with men "mainly enlisted in and sent from Ohio." On July 21, the regiment took its leave for the South. Its departure was not acclaimed with a parade and decorations but was, instead, a quiet one. Rioting and other opposition to Negroes had taken place in Boston, New York and other Northern cities with large Negro populations, and another outbreak was expected in Boston. Because of this fear, there was no military dress parade. The regiment, with muskets loaded and ready for any attack, marched to its ship.

The third Negro group to be organized in Massachusetts was the 5th Regiment of Cavalry, inducted at the same camp as the first two regiments. In May, 1864, it was placed under the command of Colonel Samuel E. Chamberlain, who had a long record of military service. He was a private in 1846; a first lieutenant of the 3rd Massachusetts Militia in 1861; captain, 1st Massachusetts Cavalry in 1864; colonel of the 5th Massachusetts Cavalry, September 11, 1865; and brevet brigadier general of the United States Volunteers, February, 1865. This brave commander was wounded seven times during the Civil War and was finally captured by the enemy at Poolesville.

Philadelphia had been a city of enthusiasm and active interest in the enlistment of colored troops. On June 6, 1863, this sentiment was directed beyond the talking stage to the preparation of a petition to the Secretary of War, seeking authority to raise three regiments of colored men. The Adjutant General's Office gave an affirmative reply on June 22.

A mass meeting was called on July 6 for the purpose of giving impetus to the use of Negro troops. At this meeting, the speakers were Frederick Douglass, Judge W. D. Kelley and Miss Anna E. Dickerson; each urged Negroes to enlist as a basis for freedom, to show their courage, and to prove their bravery through their actions. Frederick Douglass, the third to speak, proposed to treat the subject in a plain and common light. Beginning with the declaration that slavery had been abolished in the District of Colum-

COME AND JOIN US BROTHERS.
PUBLISHED BY THE SUPERVISORY COMMITTEE FOR RECRUITING COLORED REGIMENTS
1210 CHESTNUT ST. PHILADELPHIA.

bia and in all of the Territories, Douglass summed up the progress made thus far in the War:

> . . . The foreign slave trade, with its ten-thousand revolting abominations, is rendered impossible; slavery in ten states of the Union abolished forever; slavery in the five remaining states is as certain to follow the same fate as the night is to follow the day. The independence of Haiti sits recognized; her Prime Minister sits beside our Prime Minister, Mr. Seward, and dines at his table in Washington, while colored men are excluded from the cause in Philadelphia; showing that a black man's complexion in Washington, in the presence of the Federal Government, is less offensive than in the City of Brotherly Love. Citizenship is no longer denied us under this Government.

> . . . Once let the black man get upon his person the brass letters U.S.; let him get an eagle on his button and a musket on his shoulder, and bullets in his pocket, and there is no power on earth or under earth which can deny that he has earned the right to citizenship in the United States. I say again, this is our chance, and woe betide us if we fail to embrace it.

Later, Douglass was concerned about the discrimination in pay for colored soldiers as contrasted with white soldiers. Douglass was urging Negroes to enlist and fight and was of the opinion that they should have the same compensation for the same services. He thus went to Washington, sought an appointment with Lincoln and informed him

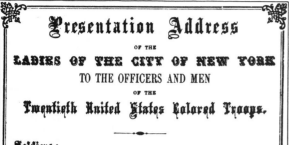

Presentation Address

OF THE

LADIES OF THE CITY OF NEW YORK

TO THE OFFICERS AND MEN

OF THE

Twentieth United States Colored Troops.

Soldiers:

WE, the Mothers, Wives, and Sisters of the members of the NEW YORK UNION LEAGUE CLUB, of whose liberality and intelligent patriotism, and under whose direct auspices, you have been organized into a body of National Troops for the defence of the Union, earnestly sympathizing in the great cause of American free nationality, and desirous of testifying, by some public memorial, our profound sense of the sacred object and the holy cause, in behalf of which you have enlisted, have prepared for you this Banner, at once the emblem of freedom and of faith, and the symbol of woman's best wishes and prayers for our common country, and especially for your devotion thereto.

When you look at this Flag and rush to battle, or stand at guard beneath its sublime motto: "GOD AND LIBERTY!" remember that it is also an emblem of love and honor from the daughters of this great metropolis, to her brave champions in the field, and that they will anxiously watch your career, glorying in your heroism, ministering to you when wounded and ill, and honoring your martyrdom with benedictions and with tears.

Names of Subscribers to the Flag.

Mrs. J. J. Astor	Mrs. M. Clarkson	Mrs. H. G. Thomson
" G. W. Blunt	" J. O. Stone	" F. C. Pendexter
" J. W. Beekman	" J. G. King, Jr.	" H. G. Chapman
" S. Wetmore	" H. Van Renselaer	" G. Bancroft
" S. B. Chittenden	" J. A. King, Jr.	" M. K. Jessup
" G. Bliss, Jr.	" J. C. Cassegee	" J. C. B. Davis
" S. J. Bacon	" J. L. Kennedy	" W. H. Scheiffelin
" R. B. Minturn	" F. Prime	" C. C. Dodge
" Charles King	" Barnwall	" John Jay
" S. W. Bridgham	" Wheelwright	" E. M. Young
" W. E. Dodge	" E. Collins	" J. T. Schultz
" R. Stebbins	" Bradish	" J. E. Brenly
" S. B. Schieffelin	" Bruce	" H. Chauncy
Miss King	" Tuckerman	" R. M. Hunt
Mrs. J. B. Johnston	" Shaw	Miss Jones
" N. D. Smith	" Williams	" J. Scheiffolin
" T. M. Cheeseman	" P. Richards	" Fish
" H. A. Coit	" R. Winthrop	" Jay
" A. P. Mann	" Weeks	" Anna Jay
" J. J. Phelps	" Jaques	" Young
" G. B. Deforest	" A. Brooks	" Schultz
" LeG. B. Cannon	" W. Felt	" Russell
" W. A. Butler	" J. W. Goddard	" J. M. King
" N. A. Murdock	" F. G. Shaw	" Cochrane
" A. Dunlap	" R. G. Shaw	Mrs. Vincent Colyer
" T. E. Howe	" G. B. Curtiss	" Catharine C. Hunt
" W. H. Lee	" R. C. Lovell	" Catharine Williams
" W. E. Dodge, Jr.	" C. G. Kirkland	" Emily H. Chauncey
" David Hoadley	" B. De Forest	" E. W. Cruger
" C. Ludington	" Boerum	" W. C. Bryant
" G. Lemist	" Hamilton Fish	" F. B. Godwin
" E. C. Cowdin	" Alfred Pell	" Emily Boerum
" J. A. Roosevelt	" Kennedy	Miss Norsworthy
" J. Sampson	" J. Johnston	
" R. B. Minturn, Jr.	" T. L. Beekman	---
" Alfred Pell, Jr.	" J. F. Gray	Mr. H. G. Chapman
" W. Hutchins	" J. Tuckeman	" Ira Brenly
" Geo. Opdyke	" F. A. Whittaker	" Peter Marié
" G. C. Ward	" J. H. Macy	" C. Berryman
" C. G. Judson	" F. H. Macy	" C. De P. Field
" S. W. Roosevelt	" J. McKaye	" C. H. Tuckerman
" E. D. Smith	" W. L. Felt	" C. A. Heckscher
" S. Gandy	" T. Haskell	" E. Scheiffelin
" R. L. Stuart	" Isaac Ames	" B. N. Field
" E. W. Stoughton	" L. F. Warner	" L. Scheiffelin
" J. W. Bigelow	" A. G. Phelps	" D. J. Clark
" M. O. Roberts	" N. Chandler	" W. H. Scheiffelin
" H. K. Bogart	" H. Potter	" Wadsworth
" E. C. Hall	" P. S. Van Renselaer	" S. A. Scheiffelin
" J. LeRoy	" Walter	" R. H. Hunt
" J. Brown	" H. Baldwin	" B. W. Griswold

that it was difficult to enlist these troops in Pennsylvania because there was a strong feeling among the Negroes that the government was not dealing fairly with them.

The state legislature of New York did not authorize a Negro regiment; nevertheless, one was raised in November, 1863. A petition was presented to President Lincoln, signed by fifteen prominent New Yorkers—including Horace Greeley and William Cullen Bryant—urging an authorization for a Negro regiment. This petition declared that three thousand Negroes had agreed to serve if Major General John C. Frémont was placed in command. President Lincoln replied that he could only act if Governor Seymour would definitely refuse to issue such an authorization. It was not until October that Governor Seymour answered by declining to authorize the enlistment of Negroes as soldiers.

A committee of colored men from New York City talked with the governor and tried unsuccessfully to influence him to authorize a regiment of colored troops. He replied that the position they would occupy in the army would be one of extreme danger and would lead to the sacrifice of life. In December, after a series of further discussions, this authorization was received from Secretary of War Stanton; and within sixty days, Negroes had been enlisted, giving New York its colored troops.

NEGRO EMPLOYMENT IN THE NORTH

At the beginning of the War, there was serious unemployment in the North. As wartime prosperity gained momentum, wages increased; but so did living costs. This meant that the real wages (wages based on purchasing power) were actually less than before the War. As production increased and the need for supplies grew, labor was forced to work longer hours. Also, due to the crisis of the War, there was less concern for the plight of the workers than would have existed under normal conditions. In the factories, laborers were subject to sweatshop conditions, long hours and, in many cases, starvation wages. Based upon these factors, resentment and discord were already present among the working classes in the North. The added fear of an influx of Negro laborers from the South, who presumably would work for less money and who were suspected of now being submissive to hard working conditions, no doubt added to this resentment.

Immigration fell off at a great rate at the beginning of the War. In 1861, there were 142,000 who migrated to this country; in 1862, there were 72,000; and in 1863, it increased to 132,000. Nevertheless, these figures were very low when compared to the arrival of 427,000 immigrants in 1854. Therefore, it was evident that any labor shortage would not be filled by an immigrant population.

The movement for organizing labor increased during the War. There were several craft unions organized in Northern cities, and all of them excluded the Negro from membership. By 1865, total union membership was estimated at 200,000. The unions were instrumental in keeping the Negro in the ranks of unskilled labor, and there can be no doubt that they contributed to the reaction against Negro labor in the years during and after the War.

This was during a period of American history when every labor gain was bitterly opposed by employers. When strikes were called, employers frequently called in Negro strikebreakers, who were in need of employment because of discriminatory hiring practices, to fill the void created by the strike. This action created more prejudice against the Negroes by white laborers. Negroes were not to be blamed for this predicament in which they found themselves—for despite the criticisms that many would level against the colored man, the need to survive is universal,

and a man fulfills this need in any way he can when he is placed outside the periphery of his society.

The working class of the North, as a body, was not favorably disposed to emancipation. This fact was illustrated by the Democratic conventions held in Northern states—particularly Pennsylvania, Ohio and Indiana—during the year 1862. The first election of any consequence since Lincoln assumed the presidency found the Democrats rallying the white working class to their standard by announcing that freeing the Southern slave would flood the labor market with Negroes. This would cause white workers to face unlimited competition, according to the Democratic Party, and these workers were therefore faced with a dilemma which could only be solved by joining ranks with the Democrats. The success of this strategy was evident from the election returns, which resulted in the Democrats gaining a majority of the seats in the U.S. Congress.

Strikes and riots were another indication of the white workers' fear of Negro competition. Interestingly, these workers were prejudiced by the opinions of others, not by the facts themselves; and they allowed their uncertainty to reach a peak of violence. In Cincinnati, Ohio, during July, 1862, a race riot occurred which joined the Irish and German laborers against free Negro workers. The riot was precipitated by an article in the *Cincinnati Gazette* claiming that Negroes escaping from the South were displacing white workers. Although there may have been an element of truth in this, the paper did not relate the whole story.

As a matter of fact, Negroes had been hired to work on boats which traveled down the Ohio River to Cairo, Illinois, then on to St. Louis. Wages had risen in the West to a higher level than those being paid in the Cincinnati area, and steamboat owners who hired white labor frequently were deserted by these men when they arrived in

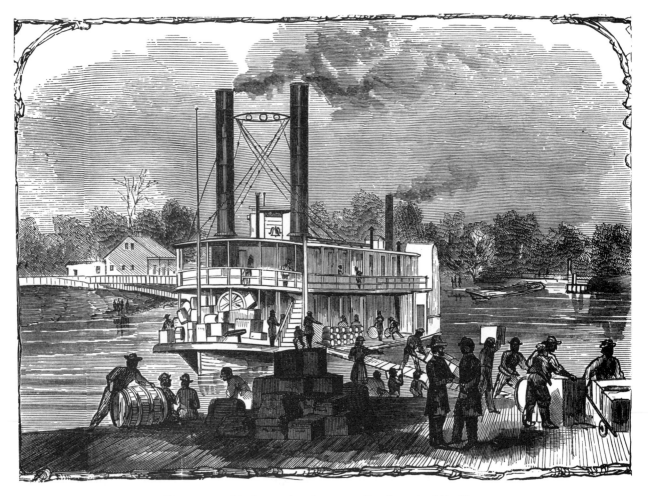

Negroes were hired to work on boats traveling down the Ohio River.

Illinois because of the wage differences. Negroes, on the other hand, were not as apt to "jump ship," having no desire to get in a position where they would again be placed in slavery. This fact accounted for the preferences given them by employers in some instances. The article in the Cincinnati paper was followed by one from a Philadelphia paper which stated that in Chester County, Pennsylvania, the hiring of Negro laborers had caused wages to drop.

These two incidents, combined with other prejudices which had accumulated in various ways, led the Irish, particularly, and a few Germans to enter the Negro section of Cincinnati and nearly destroy it. Homes were set on fire, Negroes were brutally beaten, and some were killed. The colored men did not stand by meekly while their homes were destroyed and their families mistreated but gathered in force and invaded the Irish section of town. The rioting became so violent that the police were forced to call out a posse to assist in quieting the two groups. As it was, the riots lasted five days, and a part of the colored section was completely destroyed.

In 1862, a similar riot occurred in New York initiated by Irish workers who had been displaced on the docks by Negro labor; however, the police were called in to quell the storm before real violence erupted. In Brooklyn, a group of white laborers invaded a factory where Negro women and children were working and forced them upstairs, whereupon they set fire to the lower story. The fire did not spread as rapidly as had been intended, and the people were saved by a group of colored men who assisted in their escape from the building while awaiting the arrival of the police. In December of the same year, Chicago was the scene of another outbreak against Negro labor. This time the results were mostly in the form of protests against the bringing in of Negro employees who would be in competition for jobs with white laborers.

All of these attempts to thwart employers in their efforts to use Negro labor occurred prior to the Emancipation Proclamation. The white laboring element, which was largely responsible for its own displacement in the Cincinnati affair, had not been faced with a great number of Negro migrants. And, on the whole, due to the shortage of labor, they had nothing to fear from the few Negroes who were seeking to work.

The year 1863, following the Proclamation, saw one of the bitterest and most destructive race riots in history. In the spring, Congress had passed a conscription law calling for the drafting of those who could not pay three hundred dollars. Failing to realize that the Negro was as poor, if not poorer, than he, the white worker through some tormented notion began to lay the blame for this unfortunate circumstance upon the Negro. Due to the Proclamation, there was an element of resentment created when some be-

lieved that they were no longer fighting to save the Union but to abolish slavery. However, the Negro families living in New York at the time of the draft riots were just as innocent of causation as the whites themselves. *Harper's Weekly,* July 25, 1863, re-

These two pictures reveal the fury of the New York draft riots. The mob soon turned to looting (above), and troops were forced to fire on them to maintain order (below).

ported the anti-Negro feeling involved in the riots:

> Though the draft was the original cause of the riot, it soon took the more familiar direction of an anti-Negro demonstration. . . . Toward the close of the day, the rage of the mob was exclusively directed against colored people, who had no more to do with enforcing the Conscription Act than the Pope of Rome.

The rioting lasted for some four days, and during this time blacks in the city were hunted down, beaten and slaughtered without mercy. The *New York Herald* reported that Negroes who had been caught by the raiders "were hung up to lamp posts, or beaten, jumped on, kicked and struck with iron bars and heavy wooden clubs." This violence resulted in thousands of Negroes being forced to leave their homes and flee the city. When order was restored, more than three thousand Negroes were left homeless. They were forced to either re-enter the city and once more establish homes or seek refuge in other areas. Among those persons who escaped the vicious assaults of the white rioters was Albro Lyons, a typical representative of the emerging middle class.

Mr. Lyons had been a free man all of his life. His family was one of the first to have membership in St. Philip's Episcopal Church in New York. Albro Lyons served as a vestryman in this church, as George Washington similarly had served in the Episcopal Church in Virginia. Mr. Lyons was a caterer by occupation—and that he was prosperous there can be little doubt. In 1836, he purchased a tract of land in the city, where he built his home. He apparently traveled in the best of circles and made substantial donations to many worthy causes, among them to William Lloyd Garrison's paper, the *Liberator*.

When the New York draft riots occurred, Albro Lyons and his family were forced to vacate the home they had shared for twenty-

ALBRO LYONS

three years and flee the city for their lives. Fortunately for Mr. Lyons, he was not ruined by this catastrophe as were many of his contemporaries; and he re-established himself in Rhode Island by opening a catering business and ice cream parlor.

This one example is not a true reflection of the plight of the masses of poor Negroes who were displaced and made homeless by the terrible destruction of the draft riots. Similar situations occurred in other cities as a result of the Conscription Act, but none reached the proportions of the New York outbreaks.

The rioting that occurred in the North was but a forerunner of what would transpire later, based upon fears set in motion prior to the War. The fear of the black workers and the competition which they would bring have been characteristics of the labor movement. It had not occurred to white labor, during the period of the War, to join with Negro labor and together seek improved conditions which would be mutually beneficial.

CHAPTER FOUR

In the Battles for Freedom

MUSTERING INTO SERVICE
Negro soldiers taking their oath of allegiance to the United States.

IN the Civil War, just as in the American Revolutionary War and the War of 1812, Negroes had to wait until they were needed. By July, 1862, the Union Army was stung by defeat—General McClellan's campaign against Richmond had failed—and volunteering had almost ceased. The efforts of field generals to use Negroes as soldiers had been unsupported and then denied. But with the announcement of the Emancipation Proclamation, Negroes were recruited for combat, and this led to their participation in the War.

On May 22, 1863, General Order No. 143 set up the method of recruiting colored soldiers, which was to be accomplished through the Bureau of Colored Troops in the Office of the Adjutant General. Major Charles W. Foster was appointed chief of the bureau and given the rank of assistant adjutant general. On June 30 of that year, the 1st U.S. Colored Troops were mustered into Federal service. State troops were no longer to be designated by their former names. Colored soldiers were to be "U.S. Colored Troops," and Negroes were now officially fighting for the United States. In the future, the success of these troops would not depend upon individual generals or the actions of states but upon the performance of the Negro as a soldier.

SLAVES' ATTITUDES IN THE YEAR OF EMANCIPATION

During the War, there was considerable unrest among the slaves in the South. The possibility of insurrections against the ruling class was a constant threat as slaves and former bondsmen used the War as an opportunity to rebel against the conditions to which they had been subjected.

One popular method of striking back was to start fires which would destroy the white man's property. Parts of Texas, Arkansas, Georgia and Alabama were some of the targets. More than one hundred colored men were arrested in northern Texas when it was learned they intended to burn large segments of property and then escape to Mexico. In this particular incident, white men were accused of being among the planners.

Later, another plot for insurrection was uncovered at Fort Worth, Texas, with a white man heading the operation. He was seized while distributing fifty muskets and fifty revolvers to Negroes and was promptly hanged from a nearby tree. A white abolitionist preacher connected with another revolution was also hanged, with similar fates being recorded for both whites and blacks in Alabama, Georgia, Virginia and Missouri. In Winston County, Mississippi, an insurrection was planned whereby poison was to be administered to the white families. This plot, which has reported by a slave girl, led to the hanging of a white man and one of the Negro leaders.

Insubordination, insolence and disloyalty were common occurrences during this period. On the other hand, there can be no doubt that some slaves were loyal, usually those who were on intimate terms with the members of their households. But the slaves who had been whipped, mistreated, ill-fed and ill-clothed had no sympathy for their oppressors.

A plan for a general insurrection in the Southern states was described in a letter discovered on a Federal ship off the coast of North Carolina in May, 1863. The letter was signed by Augustus Montgomery and endorsed by C. Marshall, a major and aide-de-camp of the Department of North Carolina. This letter was to have been sent to the various military posts with the intention of promoting a simultaneous insurrection on the night of August 1, 1863. The slaves, obtaining any available weapons, were to burn bridges, destroy railroads and telegraph lines, and then escape into the swamps or the mountains.

The facts show that Negroes made trouble for Confederates throughout the

South, despite laws passed to limit their effectiveness. They committed sabotage, fled to the Federal armies whenever they could, assassinated whites and burned property. There was constant fear among whites of these Negro revolts. This attitude affected the resistance of Southerners, for they not only had to fight the Yankees but also were forced to be constantly watchful of their own slaves.

The most memorable revolt initiated by Negroes occurred at Fort Jackson, Louisiana, on December 9, 1863. It concerned one of the original groups of Corps D'Afrique, the 4th Regiment, and was the only time in the War that a colored regiment reacted against the authority of its superior officers. In this instance, however, the troops were later cleared of any guilt when an investigation by the Department of the Army revealed that the treatment received by the 4th Regiment from its white commander was beyond belief. He had devised and exercised many cruel methods of punishment for little or no reason.

Therefore, the Fort Jackson mutiny was found to be an act of self-preservation rather than an actual insurrection.

THE FIRST COLORED REGIMENT IN BATTLE

The first colored regiment in battle was the 79th United States Colored Infantry, also known as the 1st Kansas Regiment. It began recruiting August, 1862, and consisted of Northern colored troops. General James Lane of Kansas had received a commission to raise troops in his state. He wrote Secretary Stanton that he was accepting Negroes under the act of Congress which had authorized the President to receive persons of African descent into military service in capacities for which they were competent. Without authority from the President, Lane began processing colored soldiers in Kansas—as General Hunter had done in South Carolina—and by November, two regiments were enlisted.

Negro recruits training for combat.

On October 28, 1862, the regiment was engaged in battle with the Rebel forces at Island Mounds in Bates County, Missouri. The objective was to clear out a Confederate force on an island in the Osage River. Upon landing, they found themselves opposed by a band of six hundred Confederates; but, fighting bravely, they eventually forced the Rebels to withdraw.

A NEGRO REGIMENT UNDER FIRE

The 1st South Carolina Volunteers were commanded by Colonel Thomas Wentworth Higginson—Harvard graduate, abolitionist, admirer of John Brown and former captain of the 51st Massachusetts Volunteer Militia. His was one of the first regiments of freed slaves enlisted in 1862, and the name of the regiment was the same as that which General Hunter had given to his Negro military organization, which had been disbanded by order of the War Department. This regiment went into action near the St. John River in Florida and the St. Mary's and Edisto Rivers in South Carolina.

Higginson, in praising these troops, stated: "It would have been madness to attempt with the bravest white troops what [was] successfully accomplished with black ones." He added, "No officer in this regiment now doubts that the successful prosecution of this War lies in the unlimited employment of black troops." In addition to a victory in battle, considerable property, a cannon and a flag were seized. A report of the battle stated:

> The bravery and good conduct of the regiment more than equalled the high anticipations of its commander. The men were repeatedly under

In this victory, the Negro troops seized a Confederate cannon.

In the Battle of Port Hudson, Negro regiments displayed great courage and valor.

fire—were opposed by infantry, cavalry and artillery—fought on board a steamer exposed to heavy musketry fire from the banks of a narrow river—were tried in all ways, and came off invariably with honor and success.

The exploits of this regiment of former slaves gave proof that Negro troops would fight. Justification was thus gained for General Hunter's earlier action in seeking to enlist troops in the state of South Carolina. Criticism by those who had advocated Negro enlistment now gave way before the brave actions of these soldiers. Colonel Higginson wrote critically of the "absurdity of distrusting the military availability of these people."

THE BATTLE OF PORT HUDSON

On May 27, 1863, Port Hudson, Louisiana, located above Baton Rouge, became the scene of another skirmish which involved colored troops. Negroes now displayed soldierly qualities characteristic of the best Union troops. The 1st and 3rd Louisiana Negro Regiments, raised in New Orleans by General Banks and stationed at Baton Rouge, received orders to join the Union troops at Port Hudson, which the Confederates had successfully defended against several assaults by Federal troops.

On May 21, General Banks had begun another attack, but the Confederates under General Gardner continued to withstand all efforts to capture the fort. Victory there would have given the Union control of the Mississippi between Port Hudson and Vicksburg. The question in the minds of the public who knew of this event was, "Will these Negro troops fight under pressure?"

The commander of the Negro regiments made a speech to the group prior to its march and, in handing the colors to the color-bearer, Sergeant Planciancois, said, "Color-guard, protect, defend, die for, but do not surrender these flags." Sergeant Planciancois replied in receiving the colors, "Colonel, I will bring back these colors to you in honor, or report to God the reason why!" On the day of the battle, with the order to march forward, the regiments moved toward the fort, situated on a high bluff with embankments along the sides of a bayou leading to it. Guns were placed in openings in the embankment, as well as on the bluff. At ten o'clock in the morning, facing the enemy's stronghold, the black regiments advanced into the field plainly in view of Rebel guns. With the explosion of each shot, the ranks of the soldiers grew thinner.

The order to charge was given by the commanders as the companies re-formed and advanced. The regiments continued their at-

tack until four o'clock in the afternoon, but their ranks were slowly being diminished in the face of terrific fire. A shell struck Sergeant Planciancois and the flag fell, wrapping itself about the body of its brave carrier. Another man, Corporal Heath, caught up the flag, only later to fall while holding it high. Still another corporal lifted the flag and bore it throughout the remainder of the battle. A Negro lieutenant mounted the Confederate works three or four times in command of his troops, but the enemy fire was too great and he fell—mortally wounded.

The two Negro regiments were composed of freedmen, one of whom was Captain André Cailloux, an outstanding officer. He was described by William Wells Brown as a black man who was "finely educated, polished in manners, a splendid horseman, a

The 1st Louisiana Native Guards disembark and march off to battle.

good boxer, bold, athletic, and daring; he never lacked admirers. His men were ready at any time to follow him to the cannon's mouth; and he was ready to lead them."

In order to provide a diversion, the two colored regiments—the 1st Louisiana under Lieutenant Colonel Bassett and the 3rd Louisiana under Colonel Nelson—had been placed on the right side of the attack. When they were fully exposed, the Confederate forces opened fire. Despite the dead and wounded, General Dwight ordered the charge to continue and to "take those guns." Captain Cailloux was struck by a shell. Another colored officer, Captain Joseph Howard, assumed command and led his troops into the enemy's rifle pits and drove them out. They held possession for three hours, but as a result of heavy artillery fire they were finally forced to withdraw to new positions.

These Negro regiments, by demonstrating heroic courage in the midst of murderous fire, proved the capabilities of colored soldiers. General Banks officially reported their conduct to General Halleck in Washington on May 30, 1863:

> It gives me pleasure to report that they answered every expectation. Their conduct was heroic. No troops could be more determined or more daring. They made, during the day, three charges upon the batteries of the enemy, suffering very heavy losses, and holding their position at nightfall with the other troops on the right of our line. The highest commendation is bestowed upon them by all the officers in command on the right. Whatever doubt may have existed before as to the efficiency of organizations of this character, the history of this day proves conclusively to those who were in a condition to observe the conduct of these regiments that the Government will find in this class of troops effective supporters and defenders.

Port Hudson was not taken on this occasion, and in spite of other attacks it was not until after the capture of Vicksburg that it surrendered, on July 9, 1863. However, the amazing fortitude of these colored soldiers, with the loss of six hundred out of nine hun-

GENERAL NATHANIEL BANKS

dred men, was an eloquent answer to those who doubted the bravery of Negro soldiers when placed under fire.

An editorial in the *New York Tribune* of June 8, 1863, eloquently declared: "That heap of six-hundred corpses, lying there dark and grim and silent and within the Rebel works, is a better proclamation of freedom than even President Lincoln's. A race ready to die thus was never yet retained in bondage and never can be."

THE BATTLE OF MILLIKEN'S BEND

Located about twenty miles upstream from Vicksburg on the Mississippi River, Milliken's Bend had served as a strategic position in General Grant's earlier attempt to capture this town, in 1863. Grant's army began to assault Vicksburg in late January and continued fighting into spring. During this campaign, Negro freedmen poured into the ranks

The Battle of Milliken's Bend proved that Negro freedmen made excellent soldiers.

of the army as they had throughout Grant's move into the South. This led to the formation of new regiments from these ex-slaves about as fast as could be undertaken. Chaplain John Eaton of the 27th Ohio Infantry referred to this development as follows:

> Their coming was like the arrival of cities. Often they met prejudices against their color, more bitter than they had left behind. There was no Moses to lead, nor plan in their exodus. The decision in their instinct or unlettered reason brought them to us. They felt that their interests were identical with the objects of our armies.

With the advancing of the Union armies, the Federal government enlisted Northern financial aid in the administration of the plantations along the Mississippi River. Those ex-slaves who ventured within the Union lines had been authorized by General Thomas to guard these plantations as well as to garrison the forts from which Grant was launching his attacks. During the late spring of 1863, Negro troops were stationed at Helena, Lake Providence, Young's Point and Milliken's Bend. It was at Milliken's Bend, however, that the colored troops were called upon to display valor and bravery beyond the call of duty.

During the assault on Vicksburg, Confederate General E. Kirby Smith cut off Grant's last line of supply from the east bank of the Mississippi River, hoping to starve out the Union Army. But Smith underestimated Grant, who, although cut off from outside supplies, was able to continue his attack by living off food from the surrounding countryside. The Negroes played an important role in directing Grant to additional supplies. While continuing the attack on Vicksburg, Grant established on May 18 a new supply post at Haynes Bluff, near the mouth of the Yazoo River, and withdrew all major forces from Milliken's Bend. The fort was thus left with three regiments of Negro troops, the 9th Louisiana, the 11th Louisiana, the 1st Mississippi; and one company composed entirely of white troops, the 23rd Regiment of Iowa, which numbered in its ranks about 160 men.

Confederate General Richard Taylor, arriving June 5 at Richmond, ten miles west of Milliken's Bend, found that the supply line south of Milliken's Bend was no longer significant. Taylor hoped that, if the Confederates could retake the west bank of the Mississippi, they could then get to Vicksburg with much-needed supplies for their troops encamped there. Taylor also reasoned that, if Grant's position on the Yazoo could be broken by General Johnston, his force west of the river would be ready to cooperate with the Vicksburg garrison. Whether Grant's hold could be broken and Taylor's purposes accomplished depended on another unknown factor: whether Negro freedmen would fight.

The Confederates drove the Union troops within sight of the earthworks at Milliken's Bend, where they took refuge during the night. Early in the morning, the Confederates attacked and, finding Negro troops opposing them, began the cry of "No Quarter." Two gunboats, *Choctaw* and *Lexington,* opened fire on the attacking force of Confederates. The Negro troops then rallied to the attack and charged the enemy heroically in a hand-to-hand bayonet fight. The Confederates withdrew and made no effort to renew the attack. The total number of Negro troops stationed at Milliken's Bend was 1,250 raw recruits, mustered into Grant's army on May 22, 1863. With little time for training or full induction as soldiers, they were forced to fight sixteen days later. Equipped only with faulty weapons and inadequately trained in the use of firearms, yet they fought. They fought with their poorly constructed weapons, they fought in hand-to-hand combat, and they fought with a determination that would have failed lesser men. The loss to the Union Army in this battle was 101 killed, 285 wounded and 264 captured or missing. The Confederate loss was reported as 44 killed, 130 wounded and 10 missing.

Negroes played an important role in obtaining supplies for General Grant.

An eyewitness whose account is recorded in *Rebellion Record* stated:

> White and black men were lying side by side, pierced by bayonets, and in some instances transfixed to the earth. In one instance, two men, one white and the other black, were found dead, side by side, each having the other's bayonet through his body. . . . one brave man took his former master prisoner, and brought him into camp with great gusto. A rebel prisoner made a particular request, that his own Negroes should not be placed over him as a guard. Dame Fortune is Capricious! His request was not granted.

Another wrote:

> Tauntingly it has been said that Negroes won't fight. Who says it, and who but a dastard and a brute will dare say it, when the battle of Milliken's Bend finds its place among the heroic deeds of this War? This battle has significance. It demonstrates the fact that the freed slaves will fight.

FORT WAGNER

Negro troops played a conspicuous part in the attempt to capture Fort Wagner on Morris Island near Charleston, South Carolina. On July 16, 1863, the 54th Massachusetts Regiment, under Colonel Robert Shaw, was attacked by Confederates on James Island and compelled to withdraw from the field of battle, but not before inflicting heavy losses in the ranks of the enemy, who outnumbered them. By this action they saved three companies of the 10th Connecticut Regiment.

An attack was then ordered on Fort Wagner. The 54th Massachusetts Regiment marched through swamps and mud for two days, then joined with the Union forces on the morning of July 18. Although wet, hungry and weary, they prepared for the assault. All afternoon the guns from the fleet and a semicircle of batteries poured cannon shot upon the fort. The battle line was formed under the command of General Strong, with the 6th Regiment from Connecticut under the command of Colonel Chatfield, the 48th Regiment from New York under the command of Colonel Barton, the 76th Regiment from Pennsylvania and the 9th Regiment from Maine.

The 54th Massachusetts was the only regiment of Negro soldiers in the line of battle. It was assigned the post at the head of the column and was to lead the charge. They marched toward the fort until they were about sixteen hundred yards from it, got into battle formation and then marched four hundred yards nearer. There was still little firing upon them. With the order to charge from Colonel Shaw, the regiment advanced in quick time and then in double-quick time. Grapeshot fell and musket fire began when they were within one or two hundred yards of the fort. Though their ranks were seared and divided by the losses of fallen men, the brave soldiers continued the march forward across the three-foot ditch of water and mounted the parapet. Sergeant Major Lewis H. Douglass, son of Frederick Douglass, reached the ramparts shortly after Colonel Shaw had shouted to his men, "Let's fight for God and Governor Andrew." The flag was planted there, after its bearer fell, by Sergeant William H. Carney, but the fire of the defenders became so intense that the attacking Union troops had to retreat.

Colonel Shaw fell wounded while waving his sword and crying out, "Onward boys." It was said of him that he was "one of the bravest and most genuine men. His soldiers loved him like a brother, and go where you would through the camps you would hear them speak of him with enthusiasm and affection." In an effort to cast insult upon this great commander, Confederate officials reported that they had buried him with his colored troops. Under a flag of truce, an effort was made to obtain the body of Colonel Shaw, but the searchers were informed, "We have buried him with his niggers." This action, although intended to be an insult, was actually a tribute to the ideals of the nation.

The 54th Massachusetts, the only Negro regiment in the line of battle, was assigned the post at the head of the column and bravely led the attack as the Union forces stormed Fort Wagner.

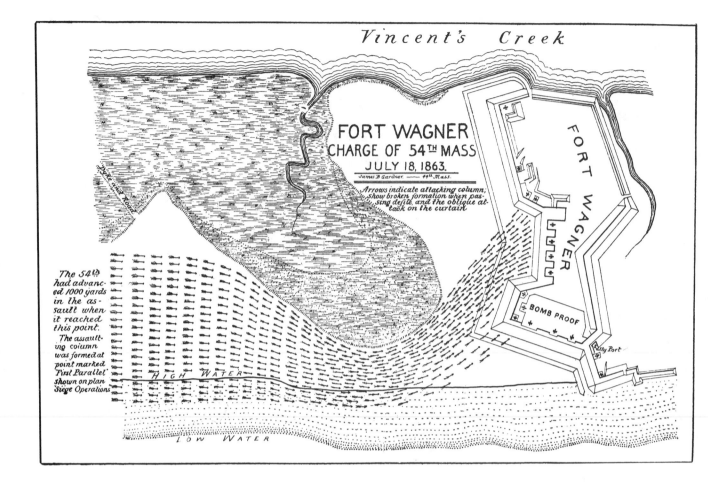

The following lines, by an unidentified poet, describe this act:

> They buried him with his niggers.
> Earth holds no prouder grave;
> There is not a mausoleum,
> In the world beyond the wave.
> That a noble tale has hallowed,
> Or a prior glory crowned,
> Than the marvelous trench where they buried
> The brave so faithful found.

Colonel Shaw's life with his soldiers seems to indicate that he would have regarded this as an honored place to be laid to rest. A monument to the memory of Shaw and his soldiers has been erected on the Boston Common; and the Gilmore Medal was awarded to the gallant soldiers of this regiment.

Many of the officers were killed and others were wounded. Sergeant Carney was wounded and fell upon his knees, but he

SERGEANT W. H. CARNEY

planted the flag upon the parapet and kept it flying as he lay on the outer slope. When reinforcements arrived with the second charge, he returned with them, still holding the flag and creeping along on one knee. When he entered the field hospital, although exhausted from the loss of blood, he said to his wounded comrades, "Boys, the old flag never touched the ground." The gallantry of these Negro troops proved again that they could be as capable in battle as any others. In the face of reports of their bravery, opposition to the employment of Negroes as soldiers continued to decline.

THE BATTLE OF OLUSTEE

The Battle of Olustee, Florida, February 20, 1864, was fought in a swampy area about fifty miles west of Jacksonville. The Union forces were commanded by General Truman Seymour. They comprised the 7th New Hampshire Regiment and the 7th Connecticut Regiment, with white soldiers, and the colored soldiers of the 8th United States Colored Troops, the 3rd United States Artillery, the 54th Massachusetts Regiment and the 1st North Carolina Regiment, known as the 35th Colored Troops.

The 8th Colored Troops had never been under fire. Their commander, Colonel Fribley, was ordered by General Seymour to take his regiment to a dangerous area near the railroad. These soldiers had neither heard nor seen the fire of a cannon; yet they marched to the selected spot and advanced toward the enemy's lines. Colonel Fribley was shot in the chest and died after being carried to the rear.

Three sergeants who carried the flag were shot down, forfeiting their lives to carry the colors forward. Finally, the men were forced to retreat, and Sergeant Taylor of Company D, with his right hand nearly severed, grabbed the flag in his left hand and brought it back to the retiring company.

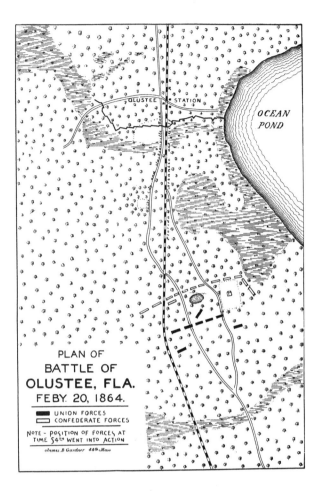

PLAN OF BATTLE OF OLUSTEE, FLA. FEBY. 20, 1864.

In the meantime, the 54th Massachusetts Regiment under Colonel E. N. Hallowell, who was now in command, had been held in the rear. The 54th quickly went into battle, followed by the 1st North Carolina Colored Regiment. The Confederate ranks broke; but, overpowered by larger numbers, the North Carolinians fell back with their colonel mortally wounded.

These two colored regiments had saved the day for the army. The *New York Herald's* correspondent stated:

The First North Carolina and the Fifty-Fourth Massachusetts, of the colored troops did admirably. The First North Carolina held the positions it was placed in with great tenacity, and inflicted heavy losses on the enemy. It was cool and steady and never flinched for a moment. The Fifty-Fourth sustained the reputation they had gained at Fort Wagner, and bore themselves like soldiers throughout the battle.

FORT PILLOW

The attack by the Confederates on Fort Pillow, Tennessee, located about fifty miles north of Memphis on the Mississippi River, April 12, 1864, resulted in one of the worst scenes of the War. This fort was under the command of Major L. F. Booth, with a garrison of 557 men, of whom 262 were Negroes, many from the 6th U.S. Heavy Artillery.

The Confederates had attacked early in the morning, and with the death of Major Booth, the Union forces retired from their outer positions to the inner fort. During a pause in the bombardment, General Nathan Forrest, under a flag of truce, demanded surrender of the fort. This was declined by Major Bradford, who had become the new commander. During the period of truce, the Confederates continued to close in on the fort, occupying the outer buildings and preparing for further assault. When the surrender was declined, the troops of General Forrest began their final advance. The fort was taken and the Federal troops began to surrender. But as rapidly as they surrendered, they were murdered. As the yell "No Quarter" rang out, they were shot down, buried alive or bayoneted to death. This massacre went on from three o'clock in the afternoon until midnight. Of the 262 colored soldiers in the fort, 238 were killed, and the total losses embraced three-fourths of the regiment. The U.S. Committee on the Conduct and Expenditures of the War conducted an investigation, and the testimony taken placed this battle on the list of the most brutal massacres of the War. Historian George W. Williams describes General For-

The massacre at Fort Pillow.

rest as "a cold-blooded murderer, a fiend in human form." The Confederate defense was that such a large number of Negroes had been slaughtered because they were resisting capture.

THE BATTLE OF THE CRATER

Negro troops became active in battles around Petersburg, Virginia, during June, 1864. Late in June, various Union commanders decided to destroy the small fort in front of the Confederate lines by constructing a mine under it. To the rear of his troops was a ravine, which could be used as an unobserved starting point. When the digging was completed, the area was under the fort and the charges of powder laid with the connecting powder trench.

Originally, this assault was to have Brigadier General Edward Ferrero's 4th Division of the 9th Corps (colored) advance as soon as the mine had been blown. However, General Grant changed the order. He later testified that, if he allowed the colored troops to lead the assault, "and if it should prove a failure, it would then be said only very properly, that we were shoving these people ahead to get them killed because we did not care anything about them. But that could not be said, if we put white troops in front."

Therefore, the three commanders of white divisions drew straws to decide who would lead the attack. General James H. Leslie, commander of the battle-weary 1st Division, drew the short straw. With this occurring on the eve of the battle, July 29, there was no time for the soldiers to survey the position before nightfall.

When the mine exploded in the morning, General Burnside sent in three divisions of white troops. The explosion left a crater about 170 feet long, 60 feet wide and about 25 feet deep. Burnside's troops advanced and the guns of the Union forces opened fire.

These troops were repulsed, being stopped in the crater, from which the surviving Confederates had fled. Then General Burnside ordered the Negro divison under General Ferrero to advance. When they reached the crater, they found the white troops there blocking the way, but some of them pushed on beyond the crater and succeeded in taking about two hundred prisoners and two standards of colors. They were compelled to fall back from under the withering fire of the Confederate lines.

A second advance was made under command of the Union officers. Some took refuge within the crater, where there were many dead and wounded. Others fell back beyond the reach of the Confederate guns. In comparing the losses, the total killed in the colored brigade was 195, as opposed to the combined deaths of 227 in the three white divisions. Colonel George L. Kilmer of the 14th New York reported that, when the colored troops poured into the crater, "pandemonium began." Not only were Negroes killed by Confederate troops, but they were slaughtered by men from their own army. After the War ended, Kilmer was to recall the scene as it had occurred that June day in Petersburg:

> The bravest lost heart [white troops] and men who distrusted Negroes vented their feelings freely. Some colored men came into the crater, and there found a worse fate than death in the charge. . . . It has been positively asserted that white men bayoneted blacks who fell back into the crater.

Despite the unsuccessful effort to secure the position, the Negro soldier had again demonstrated his bravery in the line of fire. Some of the white officers had also demonstrated their bravery. However, General Ferrero, who was in command, was found by a court of inquiry on the mine explosion to be guilty of taking refuge in a bomb-proof shelter during the attack.

TOP: *A Negro regiment making a gallant charge at the Battle of the Crater.*
RIGHT: *Union officers addressing the colored troops at Nashville.*
BOTTOM: *Negro soldiers burying their dead after one of the terrible battles at Petersburg.*

THE BATTLE OF NASHVILLE

A large number of Negro troops was engaged in the battle of Nashville, December 15–16, 1864. The brigades to which they were attached were under the command of General James B. Steedman, with the 1st Brigade under Colonel T. J. Morgan and the 2nd under Colonel C. R. Thompson. These brigades, placed on the extreme left of the Union forces, were ordered to advance so as to divert the attention of the Confederates from the main assault on the Union right. The Negro troops advanced successfully and carried out their orders, forcing the Confederates to retreat.

During the night the Confederates reformed their lines. The next day, the Union troops again engaged in the attacks and the Confederates were driven from their positions. In reporting this battle, General Steedman wrote: "I was unable to discover that color made any difference in the fighting of my troops. All, white and black, nobly did their duty as soldiers and evinced cheerfulness and resolution, such as I have never seen excelled in any campaign of the war in which I have borne a part."

THE NEGRO AS A CIVIL WAR SOLDIER

Most of the testimony on the conduct of the Negro soldiers in the War praised their endeavors, their valor and their loyalty. On August 1, 1863, the following statement appeared in the *Chicago Tribune*:

> Wherever a Negro has been tried, the courage, steadfastness, and endurance of the African race have been triumphantly vindicated. The Negro will fight for his liberty, for his place among men, for his right to develop himself in whatever direction he chooses; he will prove himself a hero, and if need be, a martyr.

General Thomas declared his faith in the ability of the Negro soldier as a result of his experience with seven thousand of them used in battles against the Confederates.

Some white officers and soldiers shared General Thomas' views. It was generally agreed that the Negro troops were not cowards in battle as many had expected they would be. Some were good fighters, some were not. Similar testimony can be produced for the activities of white soldiers. General Butler commented on the Negro as a soldier as follows:

> Of the colored soldiers of the Third Division of the 18th and 10th Army Corps and the officers who led them, the General commanding desires to make special mention. In the charges on the enemy's works by the colored division of the 18th Corps at New-Market, better officers never led better men. A few more such gallant charges and to command colored troops will be the post of honor in the American Armies. The colored soldiers, by coolness, steadiness, determined courage, and dash, have silenced every _____ of the doubters of their soldierly capacity and have brought their late masters to consider the question whether they will not employ as soldiers the hitherto despised race.

Of the Congressional Medals of Honor given to men who distinguished themselves by gallantry in action during the Civil War, twenty were awarded to Negroes. Four of these medals were presented to colored sailors, and sixteen medals were presented to colored soldiers.

OTHER BATTLE PARTICIPATION

Negro troops in the Virginia area were engaged in combat of one type or another continuously throughout late 1864 until the fighting ceased in 1865. The greatest number of colored troops in any single theater of war was involved in the time-worn strife of breaking down the Confederate Army in northern Virginia. There were numerous small encounters in which colored troops were engaged during this period.

Prior to the Battle of the Crater, Negro troops in General E. W. Hinks' Division engaged in combat with the Confederate Army on June 15. This encounter resulted in a successful attack on Petersburg, and the praise resulting therefrom helped refute later criticism of Negro troops at the Battle of the Crater.

Thirteen Negro regiments fought at Chafin's Farm on September 29 in one of the most bitter assaults that took place in that area. The fighting lasted for two days, and valor in battle became a known fact when thirteen of thirty-seven Congressional Medals of Honor given for this battle were awarded to Negro soldiers. Four of these same regiments fought again at Darbytown Road on October 13; six regiments, at Fair Oaks; five, at Hatcher's Run; and five, at Deep Bottom toward the end of October. Twenty-two regiments were engaged in the fighting which persisted around Petersburg. Fifteen regiments served in the XVIII Corps of Butler's Army of the James, eight served in the IX Corps of the Army of the Potomac.

In December, 1864, under the command of General Godfrey Weitzel, a new corps—the XXV—was created with the distinction of being the only corps composed entirely of Negro regiments. During the year 1864, its men had served with valor and distinction under General David Birney in the XVIII Corps. Birney wrote that General Grant became rather proud of their corps and sought to give them special recognition. Often they were placed on parade when such distinguished visitors as President Lincoln or Secretary of State Seward were visiting their headquarters. The regimental commanders of this corps had worked hard to condition and season their men for a prime encounter with the enemy; but, before any major offensive could be launched, the XVIII was disbanded and its troops disbursed to other commands. Many of the regiments, however, served in important battles throughout the War.

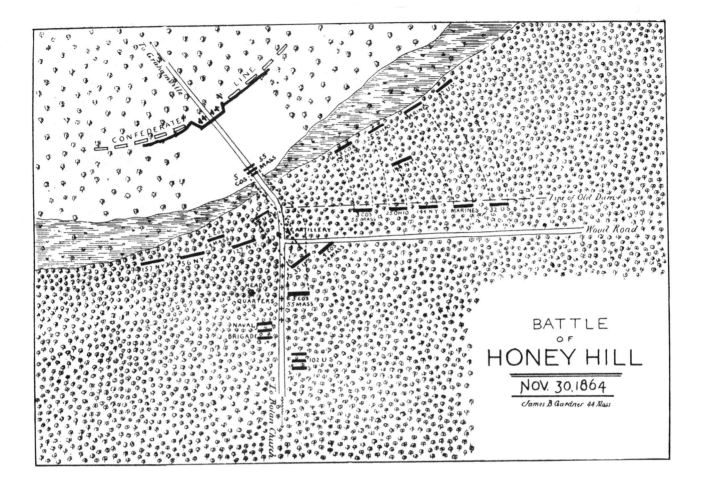

BATTLE
OF
HONEY HILL
NOV. 30, 1864
James B Gardner 44 Mass

There were other battles and military encounters in which the losses were heavy. At Overton Hill, Virginia, the 13th Regiment of Colored Troops lost 221 men, the largest regimental loss of the battle; at Honey Hill, South Carolina, the 55th Massachusetts lost 144 men; and at Fort Blakeley, Alabama, the 68th and 76th United States Colored Troops lost 192 men.

PAYMENT OF NEGRO SOLDIERS

There was continuous dissatisfaction among colored troops over discrimination in pay. Governors of states were also disturbed. Governor David Tod of Ohio on June 26, 1863, wrote to Secretary of War Stanton: "My colored regiment is progressing handsomely. They are expecting the usual pay and bounty allowed to white soldiers. Will they get it?" The white soldiers were receiving thirteen dollars per month plus three dollars for clothing, while the colored soldiers were receiving ten dollars per month with three dollars deducted for clothing. Secretary Stanton wrote to Governor Tod that, "for any additional pay or bounty, colored troops must trust to State contributions and the justice of Congress at the next session." Governor Andrew of Massachusetts wrote Colonel Shaw of the 54th Massachusetts Regiment to report that the Secretary of War "will cause right to be done as soon as the case is presented to him and, shall be fully understood."

While the Bureau of Colored Troops was being organized, Stanton requested the solicitor of the War Department, William Whiting, to give an opinion on the pay for colored soldiers. Whiting's reply was that they should be paid as laborers and not as soldiers. General Order No. 163 was then

Negro riflemen performed bravely under the fire of Confederate snipers.

issued on June 4, 1863, with the discriminatory clause making a differentiation in pay.

This was contrary to the promise given by the War Department of equal pay, according to Colonel T. W. Higginson. Subsequently, Governor Andrew went to Washington, D.C., for conferences on this subject but during his stay there he was able to secure no change in the regulation. He then asked the Massachusetts legislature to appropriate the difference in pay. The men of the regiment refused to accept this type of payment, for they felt this was equal to describing them "as holding out for money and not for principle—that we sink our manhood in consideration of a few more dollars." This meant that these colored soldiers would not accept any pay until it was made equal for white and black in similar service. They served for a year and a half and received only the fifty-dollar bounty given by the state of Massachusetts to each of its soldiers on enlistment.

Most Federal leaders felt that Negroes should be eager to serve as soldiers. And many Negroes were eager to become soldiers in the Army of Freedom, despite the difference in pay. One soldier stated that "Negroes did not come to the rescue of our country for pay. It was our duty to come, to rescue freedom which was lost."

A Negro soldier from Xenia, Ohio, wrote to the editor of the *Torch Light* from Morris Island, South Carolina, as follows:

Editor, *Torch*:

I desire to write a few words to your paper if you will allow a colored soldier the privilege of so doing. I have now been away from the city of Xenia one year and two months but have not received a cent of money from the government. Yet, Mr. Editor, I left my home for the sake of our country, to go forth and help put down this rebellion, but they have not paid the colored man anything that I can see. If they have paid them one cent of money I can't see the piece. I left home on the 8th of May for Boston, Massachusetts, and several others left from Xenia at the same time.

When three months' soldiers left Xenia for Camp Jackson, I left with them and remained until the brave and noble Colonel John C. Lowe of the old 12th Regiment was killed in the battle of Gauley in West Virginia.

Since I left home I have been in four fights, two on James Island with the assault on Fort Wagner and the Battle of Olustee. I have just come back to Morris Island from the fight that General Hatch had with the Johnnies and if I am not much mistaken, we whipped them out. The day was very hot. Several of the troops were sunstroked and died.

Yours truly,

JAMES W. BUSH
Orderly Ser't Company K
54th Mass. Inf.

Lincoln had said that the payment made to colored troops was "a necessary concession to smooth the way to their employment at all as soldiers." Secretary of State Seward said in a similar vein, "It is no time for any citizen to be hesitating about pay or place." Nevertheless, the instructions to the men recruited were that they would "receive the same pay and rations as are allowed by law to volunteers in the services." Solicitor Whiting wrote Colonel Higginson, "I have no hesitation in saying that the faith of the Government was thereby pledged to every officer and soldier enlisted under that call."

In July of 1864, the Federal government began granting aid to wives and families of Negro soldiers who had been killed or had died while in military service. This was a partial commitment, but it was after death and paid to the soldier's family. A similar distinction was made in the total amount of bounty paid white and colored soldiers. In 1862, a fifty-dollar difference was authorized by Assistant Adjutant General Thomas Vincent. However, in 1864, colored soldiers were designated to receive the bounty paid to white soldiers—one hundred dollars.

Secretary Stanton had urged Congress to correct inequalities in bounty and monthly payments to colored soldiers. He insisted: "Soldiers of the Union, fighting under its

banner, and exposing their lives in battle to uphold the government, colored troops are entitled to enjoy its justice and beneficence." Similar views had been voiced by others.

It was during the consideration of the bill to grant full pay to Negro soldiers that new pressures were brought upon government officials by Governor Andrew, Colonel Higginson, Frederick Douglass, certain generals and friendly newspapers. Attorney General Edward Bates added his influence in the decision-making effort by declaring that the Secretary of War should be directed to inform the officers of the Pay Department of the Army to equalize the pay. The *Chicago Tribune* editorialized that the colored soldier deserved "equal pay with the best" and gave the payroll of line officers and privates, showing that the colored men received only seven dollars a month, whereas the whites received from thirteen dollars for privates to twenty-one dollars for sergeant majors. This publicity was influential in bringing about a just decision by the War Department.

The Army Appropriation Act of 1864 granted equal pay, but there was still hesitation in placing it in operation. On August 18, 1864, under the direction of Secretary Stanton, the Adjutant General directed the army commanders to report colored men in their regiments who were free on April 19, 1861. By the act of Congress, these men were entitled to full pay. Colonel Hallowell, commander of the 54th Massachusetts Regiment, assembled his men and administered the following oath: "You do solemnly swear that you owed no man unrequited labor on or before the 19th of April 1861. So help you God."

This was known by the regiment as the "Quaker Oath." The rosters of the 54th and 55th Massachusetts Regiments were sent to Washington with the word "Free" after the name of every soldier who had taken this oath. Other regiments did not receive the

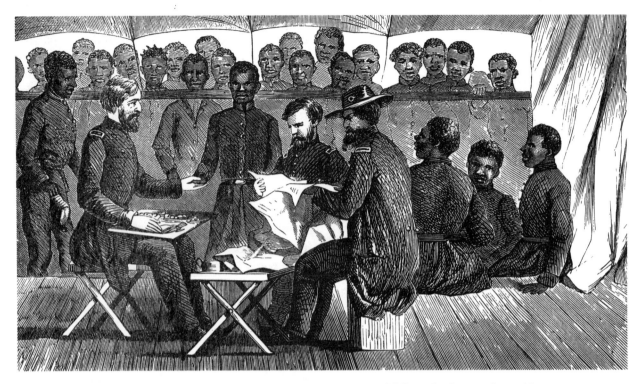

After the Enrollment Act of March 3, 1865, Negroes received full pay for their work as soldiers.

same consideration from their commanders. As Colonel Higginson wrote to the *New York Tribune*, July 10, 1864:

> There is no alternative for the South Carolina regiments but to wait for another session of Congress. If a year's discussion, however, has at length secured the arrears of pay for Northern colored regiments, possibly two years may secure it for the Southern. And meanwhile, if necessary, act as executioners for those soldiers, who like Sergeant Walker, refuse to fulfill their share of a contract where the Government has openly repudiated the other share.

This reference was to Sergeant William Walker of Company A, 3rd South Carolina Colored Troops, who declared that he would no longer serve as a soldier for seven dollars a month. Walker instructed his company to stack its arms before the captain's tent and refuse to serve duty until they received the same amount of pay—thirteen dollars—as the white troops. Sergeant Walker paid for this act of loyalty to principle, yet disloyalty to the government, by being court-martialed and shot.

On December 8, 1864, Colonel Higginson again wrote the *Tribune*, asking Congress to perform its duty and "to repeal the law which discriminates between different classes of colored soldiers, or at least so to modify it to secure the fulfillment of actual contracts. Until this is done, the nation is still disgraced."

The Enrollment Act of March 3, 1865, stated that the regiments recruited before January 1, 1864, were to receive full payment from the time of their original enlistment. It was not until the War ended, however, that colored troops were finally awarded the payments that were due them as soldiers.

THE OFFICERS OF NEGRO TROOPS

The inscription on Saint-Gaudens' monument to Shaw on the Boston Common is a statement of the contributions of white officers, black soldiers, and their work together. This inscription is as follows:

THE WHITE OFFICERS

Taking Life and Honor in their Hands—Cast in their lot with Men of a Despised Race Unproved in War—and Risked Death as Inciters of Servile Insurrection if Taken Prisoners, Besides Encouraging all the Common Perils of Camp, March and Battlefield.

THE BLACK RANK AND FILE

Volunteered when Disaster Clouded the Union Cause—Served without Pay for Eighteen Months till Given that of White Troops—Faced Threatened Enslavement if Captured—Were Brave in Action—Patient under Dangerous and Heavy Labors and Cheerful amid Hardships and Privations.

TOGETHER

They Gave to the Nation Undying Proof that Americans of African Descent Possess the Pride, Courage, and Devotion of the Patriot Soldier—One Hundred and Eighty Thousand Such Americans enlisted under the Union Flag in MDCCCLXIII–MDCCCLXV.

The white officers mentioned above had been civilians in 1861 and had achieved the positions of commanding officers through military experience. In the main, they had volunteered with their men after having raised a company of infantry. In 1861, this practice of volunteering by companies was common. The leaders would be mustered in as captains, with their rise to higher rank depending upon the expansion of their commands. However, when the time came to muster in Negro troops, a system was developed for selecting officers who had held rank in company and field units.

When the 1st South Carolina Regiment was organized by General David Hunter in May, 1862, the first major problem involved the finding of officers for the regiments. These troops were to be recruited from former slaves, and if they were to be made into soldiers, the best officers available would have to be obtained. Hunter decided that he would select men for this purpose from the most intelligent and energetic of the noncommissioned officers. He selected ten sergeants; five had been in the Engineers and five had served in the Pennsylvania Infantry Regiments. In spite of General Hunter's efforts, the plan was not approved and was never put into effect.

General Butler's attempt to obtain officers for the colored troops of Louisiana had a different result. The Louisiana Colored Troops, inducted under the Confederate Governor Thomas O. Moore, included colored commissioned officers. In the 1st Regiment some of the line officers were Negro. In the 2nd Regiment, only the two highest-ranking officers were white; while the 3rd Regiment was under the command of F. E. Dumas, who was described as a free Negro, wealthy, brave and loyal. He brought in a company of his own slaves and was commissioned as a captain immediately. Later, he was promoted to the rank of major for his gallantry in action.

General James H. Lane, recruiting a company of Negroes in Kansas, selected officers who had abolition experience and who were known to be sympathetic to the use of Negro troops. Preference was also given to officers who were known to be hard workers.

Federal interest in officers was initiated by General Daniel Ullmann, from the Bureau of Colored Troops, who issued General Order No. 7, on June 10, 1863. In this order, Ullmann reported the particular type of service and the special qualities which were needed for white officers commanding colored troops. Among these were "accurate knowledge of the drill, long experience in the field, patience, diligence, and patriotism." Then he added:

> You are brought into contact with a race, who, having lived in abnormal conditions all the days of their lives, are now suddenly elevated into being soldiers of the United States, fighting against their oppressors, as well as for their own liberties, as for the integrity of the Republic. They are to be moulded by you and drilled into disciplined troops. You cannot display too much wisdom in your conduct, both as regards to yourself and them....
>
> Let the law of kindness be your guide. Thus acting, you will soon obtain their confidence; you

will find them dazzled, impressionable, fully in-
bued with the spirit of subordination (one of the
highest attributes of a soldier), possessed of a deep
appreciation of kindly treatment and of keen per-
ception, which enables them quickly to discover
any flaw in the conduct of their superiors. . . .

You have the materials, crude though they now
may be, but perfectly malleable, to make the best
of soldiers, perform your duty conscientiously,
and our beloved and once happy country, will not
only have a body of soldiers, who will enthusi-
astically aid her in fighting her battles, but she
will also have the proud satisfaction of knowing
that she has, at last, taken a practical step toward
the elevation of a hitherto degraded and oppressed race.

The generals in the field were to select
their own officers. In the case of General
Stephen A. Hurlbut, the Adjutant General
Lorenzo Thomas informed Secretary Stanton
that Hurlbut knew of intelligent sergeants
who would make good captains. These men
were to be mustered out of their old regiments and into new companies as rapidly as
these organizations were started. The plans
were for them to have divisional examining
boards of one officer from each brigade to
examine the applications and to make a ros-
ter for the regiment. This was to be done for
those who were qualified and "whose heart
is in the work." Throughout the South, the
Federal armies used this plan extensively.

With the establishment of the Bureau of
Colored Troops, a different plan was initiated for the raising of colored troops in the
Northern states. Boards were to be convened
and posts selected by the War Department
to examine applications for commissions to
command colored troops. These boards had
authority in the selection of recruiting officers for this purpose. The boards were to sit
six days a week examining candidates who
had been authorized by the Adjutant General to appear. Despite pressures from governors and members of Congress, the boards
seem to have conducted their operations with
satisfaction.

The applicant could write directly to the
Bureau of Colored Troops, sending any rec-

An escaped slave in the Union Army.

ommendations and references with his letter. Following a positive decision by the bureau, the candidate was told to appear before the board for examination. Some persons did not accept their affirmative replies. Appearances before the board did not ensure success, since about forty per cent of all who entered the examinations were rejected. Nevertheless, rises in rank from sergeant to captain and from captain to colonel were not unheard-of results for some of the candidates who were accepted.

Martin R. Delany of Wilberforce, Ohio, was commissioned a major in the infantry and sent into the Department of the South, where he organized the 104th U.S. Colored Troops. Delany had developed a plan for the organization of what he referred to as "an Armée d'Afrique." The War ended before Delany could bring his plan to fruition, but he was successful in forming the 104th and 105th U.S. Colored Troops. Delany was the first Negro field officer in the Civil War.

With rejections and failures in examinations, the need for officers to command colored troops increased. The result was the formation of an officer candidate school to prepare the candidates for their board appearances. In Philadelphia, a free military school for applicants desiring the command of colored troops was opened on December 26. Prior to March 31, 1864, this school had sent ninety-four students to the board with recommendations for commissions, and only four were rejected. Thirty-nine of the ninety-four graduates were civilians with a minimum amount of military service. The candidates received practical experience while they were stationed at Camp William Penn near Philadelphia.

There were approximately seventy-five Negroes who served as commissioned officers, with a larger number as line officers. Among the Negro officers in the Louisiana regiment, there were one major, twenty-seven captains, eight lieutenants and nearly

MAJOR ALEXANDER T. AUGUSTA

one hundred noncommissioned officers. Outside of Louisiana, there were one lieutenant colonel, one major, two captains, two surgeons and four lieutenants. Numerous Negroes so fair in color that they appeared white served with white regiments.

The lot of the Negro physician who served in the Union Army was not an easy one. It was difficult to obtain doctors for colored troops since many white practitioners looked upon the role with disdain, and there was a serious shortage of qualified Negro physicians.

Probably one of the best-known Negro physicians during the War was Major Alexander T. Augusta, who gave up a lucrative practice in Toronto, Canada, to serve in the Union Army. Augusta was commissioned a major in the 7th U.S. Colored Troops and was stationed in Baltimore. Shortly thereafter, his white colleagues protested serving as assistants to a colored chief surgeon, and Augusta was transferred.

Although Dr. Augusta had been given the rank of major, he was paid at the same rate as colored enlistees—seven dollars per month. He continued to serve while endeavoring to receive the pay due his rank and station. After a period of more than a year, Major Augusta was finally compensated.

Seven other Negro physicians serving as surgeons during the War were given commissions as majors. In addition, complimentary commissions were given to several colored men when they were mustered out of the service in 1865. Several thousand Negroes served as noncommissioned officers in 1865.

THE NEGRO IN THE NAVY

In the Navy, Negroes served as sailors aboard vessels engaged in blockading the coast and pursuing privateers and blockade runners. They constituted nearly one-fourth of the men in the Navy, but their rate of pay was inferior. Those who had served as pilots on river and harbor boats found no difficulty in getting similar jobs on United States vessels. It was said that the Negroes were considered among the best pilots on the rivers in North Carolina. Escaping slaves made their way in small boats or by swimming to the blockading vessels, where they were put to work on board or taken to a free port for discharge. Some had served as laborers on the docks, while others had been in service on Confederate vessels in the early days of the War. The total number on the muster rolls was estimated at 29,511.

Secretary of the Navy Welles asked Secretary of War Stanton to furnish his department "with contrabands for naval service." He requested two to four thousand from any part of the country. On January 2, 1863, the Adjutant General's Office declared that colored men were "to man vessels of all sorts" in naval service. They were used on the Great

Escaping slaves made their way in small boats to the blockading vessels.

The Confederate steamer Planter was run out of Charleston harbor by Robert Smalls.

Negroes served bravely on ships such as this one during the War.

Robert Smalls (top) with fellow members of the Planter crew: William Morrison (left), A. Gradine (right) and John Smalls (bottom).

Lakes, touching at Ohio, and served on ships conducting trade along the East Coast.

One of these sailors, William B. Derrick, born in Antigua, British West Indies, was described as one to whom "the cause of the North appealed strongly." He enlisted for three years of service on the flagship *Minnesota*, of the North Atlantic Squadron. He served "as valiantly and loyally as though the Stars and Stripes were his own home banner."

The most heroic action by a Negro sailor was performed by Robert Smalls of Beaufort, South Carolina. Smalls was acting as wheelman on the Confederate steamer *Planter*. He piloted the boat out of the Charleston harbor and delivered it to one of the vessels of the Federal fleet in accordance with a previously arranged plan. Smalls was transferred to other vessels, serving as pilot on the *Crusader*, as well as the *Planter* and the monitor *Keokuk*. He was aboard a ship accompanying the fleet engaged in the attack on Fort Sumter in 1863. An official report stated that, when the captain of the vessel abandoned the pilothouse under the fire of Sumter's guns, Smalls entered the pilothouse, took command of the vessel and conducted it beyond the range of the guns. For this exploit, Smalls was made captain of the *Planter,* which was used as a supply boat throughout the War. At its close, Captain Smalls piloted his boat to Baltimore, where it was put out of commission. Other Negroes had served meritoriously as seamen, sailors and pilots on vessels of the Navy, and they were instrumental in guiding these Navy vessels in Southern waters.

Robert Brown Elliott, who was born in Massachusetts, educated at Eton College, England, and later served as a congressman from South Carolina, joined the Navy during the Civil War and was wounded during a naval engagement.

In the famous battle between the ironclads *Monitor* and *Merrimac*, on March 9, 1862, a colored seaman, Tanner Anglin, was a member of an expert gun crew. And serving on the *U.S. Hunchback*, a gunboat patrolling the James River from 1863 to 1865, there were 52 crew members, 16 of whom were colored. There were 35 vessels on which 624 colored sailors from Maryland served during the Civil War. There were probably many others, but their names are not known because the Navy Department did not require sailors to indicate their race or color.

NEGRO WOMEN IN THE WAR

Among those who served their country with distinction were women who might be called "the unsung heroines" of the Civil War. Negro women played a role which could not have been duplicated by any others. When the slaves entered the ranks of

HARRIET TUBMAN

the Union armies marching into the South, the Negro women could slip easily in and out of the lines to survey Confederate positions, camps and locations and then report their findings to the Union Army officials. These women were thought to be slaves as they moved from one plantation to another and were less likely to be suspected than Union soldiers performing the same tasks of spying. One of these women was Lucy Carter, who served courageously as a spy for the 16th New York Cavalry stationed at Vienna, Virginia. She carried a pass issued by Lieutenant Colonel George S. Hollister, Commander, entitling her to pass through the lines of the 16th New York "at pleasure."

Harriet Tubman was another woman who performed astonishing services for her country. She seemed to lead a charmed life. Despite numerous bounties on her head in many Southern states, she passed through the lines at will, giving much-needed information to the Union troops. Mrs. Tubman arrived at Hilton Head, South Carolina, in 1862, and immediately began to assume responsibilities that would aid in the war effort. She carried a pass issued by Major General David Hunter, Commander of the Department of the South, which stated: "Pass the bearer, Harriet Tubman . . . wherever she wishes to go; and give her free passage, at all times, on all government transports." As a scout, Harriet Tubman could easily deceive the enemy during her missions. Dark complexioned, short and stooped, with a bandanna wrapped around her head, she resembled a typical plantation woman. General Rufus Saxton, in charge of volunteers, wrote that she "made many a raid inside the enemy's lines, displaying remarkable courage, zeal and fidelity."

Harriet was a woman of unusual capabilities and great courage. During the years preceding the War, she had served as a "conductor" on the Underground Railroad, bringing about three hundred slaves to freedom, thus earning the name "Moses" for delivering her people from bondage.

In the war years she worked with equal zest, and her reputation became almost legendary. For two years she served as a nurse in the Sea Islands off the coast of South Carolina, caring for the sick and wounded without regard to color. Acting Assistant Surgeon Henry K. Durrant was so moved by her warmth and generous attitude that he wrote a note, addressing it "To Whom It May Concern," commending her for "kindness and attention to the sick and suffering."

In another project, Harriet Tubman served both the Union and her people. She often traveled into enemy territory with Colonel James Montgomery's Union brigade during its raids. Montgomery was a former associate of John Brown and a friend to the freedmen. While they were on these expeditions, Harriet made contact with the slaves on the plantations and informed them of the purposes of

SUSIE K. TAYLOR

her years in slavery, and she taught these basic skills to many soldiers in the company. When the hospital needed additional competent women to nurse the growing number of wounded Union troops, she quickly volunteered her services. At Beaufort in 1863, she met Clara Barton, founder of the American Red Cross, and recorded that Miss Barton was solicitous of the many Negro soldiers hospitalized there.

Sojourner Truth was another valiant Negro woman. She confined most of her activity to the Northern states during the War, and served as a spy for many Union regiments. Originally called Isabella, she adopted a new name in 1827 when she gained her freedom in New York. She felt that this new name would reveal to the world her mission—"Sojourner" because she would travel, and "Truth" because she told the truth about slavery wherever she went.

the Union forces. She was able to quiet the doubts and silence the fears of these slaves regarding stories they had heard about the "Yankees" and what they would do to the Negroes in the South; and through her efforts, many slaves were led to safety within the Union lines. After one of his raids in 1863, Colonel Montgomery wrote to General Gillmore: "I wish to commend to your attention Mrs. Harriet Tubman, a most remarkable woman, and invaluable scout." Mrs. Tubman was a living example of an old hymn which was sung by the evening campfires during the Civil War, "Rescue the Perishing, Care for the Dying."

Still another Negro woman cared for the wounded in South Carolina. She was Mrs. Susie K. Taylor, wife of a noncommissioned officer in Company E of the 1st South Carolina Volunteers. She was employed as a laundress for the company, but served as both teacher and nurse in her free time. Mrs. Taylor had learned to read and write during

SOJOURNER TRUTH

In spite of her advanced age, Sojourner Truth was an active participant in the war effort, raising money and soliciting gifts for distribution in the camps. She raised the money by singing and lecturing in various states of the North. One of the songs that she wrote was sung to the tune of "John Brown's Body":

> We are done with hoeing cotton,
> We are done with hoeing corn;
> We are colored Yankee soldiers,
> As sure as you are born.
> When Massa hears us shouting,
> He will think 'tis Gabriel's horn,
> As we go marching on.

In the fall of 1864, Sojourner Truth journeyed from Battle Creek, Michigan, to Washington, D.C., to visit President Lincoln. During their meeting, Lincoln is reported to have told her that he had heard of her activities years before being elected president. Lincoln autographed a little book in which this renowned woman kept the names of interesting people she met. In so doing, he wrote, "For Aunty Sojourner Truth, Oct. 29, 1864, A. Lincoln." Following her appointment with Lincoln, Sojourner toured the city of Washington. She became active in teaching the colored people who were new arrivals in the city and spent much of her time at Freedmen's Hospital, nursing the Negro soldiers who were patients there.

Although Mrs. Elizabeth Keckley did not serve her country on the battlefields, she was another Negro woman of prominence during the Civil War. Mrs. Keckley was Mary Todd Lincoln's seamstress in the White House, as well as her confidant. It was through Mrs. Keckley's influence that Mrs. Lincoln was said to have derived her interest in the mysticism of seances, through which she endeavored to establish contact with one of her deceased sons. Mrs. Keckley was highly regarded by the Lincolns, and undoubtedly it was through contact with this refined and gentle lady of color that Abraham Lincoln

ELIZABETH KECKLEY

began to reevaluate his position with regard to the Negro race.

A story of intrigue as fascinating as any that might be found in a novel involved Mary Elizabeth Bowser of Richmond, Virginia. Prior to the War, this young former slave had been sent to Philadelphia for schooling by her employer, Elizabeth Van Lew. After the War began, Mary Elizabeth was called back home to assist Miss Van Lew in espionage work.

Elizabeth Van Lew became the leader of the Union supporters in Richmond, engaging in activities which greatly aided Generals Grant and Butler. When Elizabeth Bowser returned to Richmond, she was placed in the Confederate White House as a servant of Jefferson Davis. While dusting furniture, Elizabeth, who pretended illiteracy, read dispatches and orders, then passed the information on to Miss Van Lew through another spy, who went to the Van Lew plantation daily to secure eggs and other farm produce.

Often while serving dinner to the Confederate President, Elizabeth Bowser was able to overhear information involving troop movements and other pertinent plans of the army. This information was relayed to Miss Van Lew, who then passed it on to General Grant.

Though her daily espionage activities placed her in a most precarious position, Elizabeth Bowser served undetected throughout the War as a Union spy in the Confederate White House.

These five women serve only as illustrations of the contributions made by many in the course of the War. Throughout the South, on untold battlefields and in many camps, Negro women worked with the Union armies as spies, scouts, nurses and teachers. They served in their way, as did their menfolk, to show the Negro's willingness to sacrifice for freedom.

EXTENT OF NEGRO PARTICIPATION IN THE UNION ARMY

Negroes supported the Union cause with 186,017 in combat troops, according to the Adjutant General's Office; and their losses were numbered at 68,178, or about one-third of the total enrolled. There were over 200,000 more in the service units. Since the figure 186,017 includes 7,122 officers, only some of whom were colored, a more accurate figure would be 178,975. Of this number, 99,337 were mustered in by authority of the Federal government and 79,638 were enlisted through the state programs.

About 8,000 Negro soldiers were raised in New England; 13,922, in New York, New Jersey and Pennsylvania; 12,711, in the Western states and Territories; 45,184, in the border states of Delaware, Kentucky, Maryland, Missouri, West Virginia and the District of Columbia; 93,346 were from the Southern states—Alabama, Arkansas, Florida, Georgia, Louisiana, Mississippi, North Carolina, South Carolina, Tennessee, Texas and Virginia.

There were 120 colored infantry regiments comprising 98,938 men; 7 cavalry regiments including 7,128 men; 12 heavy artillery regiments of 12,662 men; and 10 companies of light artillery with 1,311 men and batteries. These colored soldiers saw combat in more than two hundred engagements.

These Negro chaplains served U.S. troops during the War: Henry M. Turner, 1st Regiment U.S. Colored Troops; Samuel Harrison, 54th Massachusetts Infantry Regiment; Garland H. White (a former slave of Senator Robert Toombs of Georgia), 28th Regiment of U.S. Colored Troops; Benjamin F. Randolph, 26th Regiment of U.S. Colored Troops; Francis A. Boyd, 109th Regiment of U.S. Colored Troops; George W. Levere, 20th Regiment of U.S. Colored Troops; John R. Bowles, 55th Massachusetts Regiment; James Underdue, 39th Regiment of U.S. Colored Troops; David Stevens, 36th Regiment of U.S. Colored Troops; and William Jackson, 55th Regiment of U.S. Colored Troops. These chaplains not only succeeded in advancing the interest of the Negro soldier religiously and morally, but did so educationally as well.

The Civil War served as a school for Negro soldiers. They fought bravely, learned much of loyalty to a worthy cause, self-abnegation, discipline, authority, responsibility and the ability to work as free persons. In this connection, Colonel Oliver T. Beard of the 48th New York Infantry wrote from Beaufort, South Carolina, on November 10, 1862:

> The colored men fought with astonishing coolness and bravery. For alacrity in effective landings, for determination, and for bush fighting, I found them all that I could desire—more than I had hoped. They behaved bravely, gloriously and deserved all praise. . . . As soon as we took a slave from his claimant, and placed a musket in his hand, he began to fight for the freedom of others.

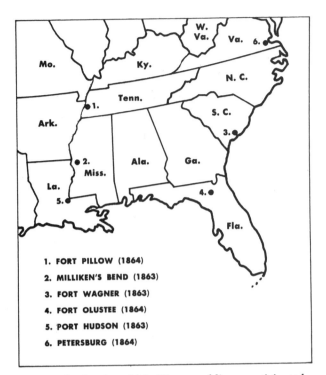

1. FORT PILLOW (1864)

2. MILLIKEN'S BEND (1863)

3. FORT WAGNER (1863)

4. FORT OLUSTEE (1864)

5. PORT HUDSON (1863)

6. PETERSBURG (1864)

Major battles in which Negro soldiers participated.

During the War, Negroes participated in about 250 engagements. They were members of the heavy artillery, the cavalry, and the Navy and, in all, obtained about 75 commissions in the Union Army. The Negro made a strong claim for citizenship and equality through his demonstration of courage and loyalty to the Union cause.

THE CIVIL WAR COLONIZATION PLAN

President Lincoln had favored a colonization plan for Negroes from an early period in his public life. In his Second Annual Message to Congress in December, 1862, President Lincoln said, "I cannot make it better known than it already is, that I strongly favor colonization." On April 16, 1862, Congress responded by passing an act providing that the slaves who had been freed in the District of Columbia might emigrate if they so desired, and were to be assisted with an appropriation of one hundred thousand dollars.

Ile-à-Vache, near Haiti in the West Indies, was chosen for this purpose. Bernard Koch, a businessman, was selected to negotiate with President Geffrard of Haiti. Late in 1862, Koch agreed to a contract: he was to colonize five thousand Negroes at fifty dollars per person and then to furnish them with comfortable homes, gardens, churches, schools, and employment for four years. Koch also sought the interest and aid of American capitalists; but when this was discovered, the government canceled the agreement. However, Koch went on with his plan; and a ship with about four hundred Negroes left Fort Monroe for the island, where life was appallingly hard and many perished. The President sent an investigator, who found the conditions deplorable, and the surviving colonists were returned to the United States.

President Lincoln conceived a similar plan to colonize Negroes in Latin America. Although it was never carried out, the possibility of such a venture aided Lincoln in convincing the border states that he was somewhat in agreement that the freed Negroes should be removed from the country.

Negroes generally were opposed to colonization prior to and during the Civil War. When Lincoln's plans for colonization were made known, groups of colored citizens met to protest such action. Resolutions asserting the right of Negroes to citizenship in this country were passed and forwarded to Washington. On July 2, 1864, Congress repealed all appropriations for Negro emigration, and these efforts for colonization were terminated.

The American Colonization Society, however, founded in 1817, colonized eleven thousand Negroes in Liberia and helped that country become recognized by the major European powers as an independent republic. The society had actively engaged in efforts to detect vessels which were engaged in the slave trade and to prevent them from clearing ports. In 1860, the capture of the slave ships *William* and *Wildfire,* with one thousand Africans aboard, presented a difficult case for the society. The society's financial secretary, William McLain, contracted with the United States Government to provide transportation and maintenance in Liberia for one year for these Africans. The government agreed to pay one hundred dollars for each African over eight years of age and fifty dollars for each one under this age, with details for their treatment outlined. In 1860 and 1861, four additional slave-trading vessels were seized. The Africans taken from these vessels were sent to Monrovia, Liberia, where the Liberian Government supervised their distribution among Liberian families. Payments to the Liberian Government were made from appropriations by action of the United States Congress, with the last payment being made in 1865.

THE CONFEDERACY'S PROPOSAL TO ARM AND FREE NEGROES

One of the last desperate measures on the part of the Confederate Government was its adoption of a plan to enlist Negroes as soldiers in the defense of its cause. Negroes had been armed and used in local areas for military activities, but they had not been officially inducted by the government.

The Emancipation Proclamation seemed to arouse interest in the subject; and in the latter part of 1863, attention was again centered upon the idea by newspapers and by a petition from the Alabama legislature submitted to President Jefferson Davis. The Confederate leadership listened patiently to arguments requesting that slaves be armed, but no action was taken until the need for manpower became more acute. By the summer of 1864, desertions had increased in larger numbers. Discouraged with the failure to attain a quick victory and by the news of increasing needs at home, men were leaving the army. The governors of North Carolina,

[Senate Bill, No. 109.]

SENATE, November 22, 1864.—Read first and second times and ordered to be placed upon the calendar and printed.

[By Mr. HENRY, from Committee on Military Affairs.]

AN ACT

To amend An Act entitled "An Act to increase the efficiency of the army by employing free negroes and slaves in certain capacities," approved February 17th, 1864.

1   SECTION 1. *The Congress of the Confederate States of America*
2   *do enact,* That the first section of said act be so amended as
3   to increase the compensation given to the free negroes and
4   other free persons of color named in said section to eighteen
5   dollars per month.

1   SEC. 2. That the second section of said act be so amended
2   as to authorize the Secretary of War to empoly, for all the
3   purposes named in the first section of said act, forty thousand
4   slaves, instead of twenty thousand, as therein provided.

1   SEC. 3. That the third section of said act be so amended
2   as to authorize the Secretary of War to impress forty thou-
3   sand slaves in case he shall be unable to procure their ser-
4   vices or hire as therein provided.

A section of the act for the employment of Negroes as laborers in the Confederate Army.

South Carolina, Alabama, Georgia and Mississippi met in October, 1864, at Augusta, Georgia, and passed a series of resolutions concerning the situation facing the South.

One of these proposed the employment of Negro soldiers. In November, 1864, President Davis recommended to the Confederate Congress that forty thousand Negro slaves be purchased and used as laborers, with the promise of freedom after the War for faithful service. Although Davis proposed using the Negro slave as a laborer, he was not thinking of arming him as a soldier. Meanwhile, in the Confederate Congress, proponents urged that, under proper leadership, the Negro would make a good soldier. The need for men was great due to the losses in Confederate ranks, and foreign sympathy and recognition might be obtained by the adoption of such a measure. Opponents said that Negroes would not make good soldiers because of their racial inferiority and their servile experiences. And yet they were accustomed to the subservience which would make possible military discipline and the obedience troops must always give to their commanding officers.

Howell Cobb of Georgia claimed, "If slaves make good soldiers, our whole theory of slavery is wrong." Others contended that, if slaves were used by the army, the white soldiers would not fight with them and they would desert to the Federals. It was also stated that, if the Confederacy armed the slaves, when slavery had been a cornerstone of its edifice, it would be announcing that the Southern leadership admitted that the abolitionists were correct in their views.

At Dalton, Georgia, General Patrick Cleburne made a proposal for the recruiting of Negroes as soldiers for the Confederate Army. This was circulated among officers commanded by General Joseph Johnston. Confederate Secretary of War Seddon urged the employment of Negroes as soldiers, as well as their complete emancipation.

Another favorable reference was made on March 17, 1865, by J. B. Jones in *A Rebel War Clerk's Diary at the Confederate States Capital.*

> We shall have a Negro army. Letters are pouring into the department from men of military skill and character asking authority to raise companies, battalions and regiments of Negro troops. It is the desperate remedy for the very desperate case—and may be successful. If 300,000 efficient soldiers can be made of this material, there is no conjecturing where the next campaign may end. . . . 100,000 troops from this source might do wonders.

A bill to enlist Negro soldiers was introduced, debated and defeated in the Confederate Congress in February, 1865. General Robert E. Lee's influence was then sought. He gave his approval, stating:

> The reasons that induce me to recommend the employment of Negro troops at all render the effect of the measures I have suggested upon slavery immaterial, and in my opinion the best means of securing the efficiency and fidelity of this auxiliary force would be to accompany the measure with a well-designed plan of gradual and general emancipation.

In his message to the Virginia legislature in 1865, Governor William Smith recommended the employment of Negroes, even though this action would result in emancipation. Shortly afterward, President Davis gave the opinion that "All arguments as to the positive advantage or disadvantage of employing them are beside the question, which is simply one of relative advantage between having their fighting element in our ranks or in those of the enemy."

On March 13, 1865, the Confederate Congress passed an act authorizing President Davis to ask slaveowners for slaves to serve in the army. If they failed to secure the required number, then they were to call on each state for a quota of Negroes, with the provision that the slaves should not exceed 25 per cent of the able-bodied male slave population. The preamble was:

> That, in order to provide additional forces to repel invasion, maintain the rightful possession of the Confederate States, secure their independence and preserve their institutions, the President be, and he is hereby authorized to ask for and accept from the owners of slaves, the services of such number of able-bodied Negro men as he may deem expedient, for and during the war, to perform military service in whatever capacity he may direct.

An additional provision, which weakened the bill, was that emancipation would take place only with the consent of the owners and the states.

The induction of Negroes for the army was begun immediately under General Lee's orders. Recruiting officers were appointed to raise these troops in South Carolina, Alabama, Florida and Virginia. Several companies were raised; but by now the Confederacy was in its death throes, and the plan did not result in any extensive action. The extent of the Confederate collapse can be seen in this plan. It is also evident that the slaves soon would have deserted and joined the Union forces; for men, whatever their color, would not have fought to keep themselves in slavery. The rising march of the forces of freedom and democracy could be witnessed throughout the Confederate states. Freedom came not only to Negro slaves in 1865, but also to whites who had been enslaved by the system.

THE WAR'S END

The great experiment of using Negro soldiers by the Confederacy did not get even to the testing stage. For shortly after the last desperate measure for Negro recruitment, General Grant was advancing toward Richmond to meet General Lee's army, and General Sherman had severed the Confederacy with his march through Georgia.

The armies of both Union generals had regiments of Negro soldiers, with thousands of Negroes as camp followers. On April 9, 1865, General Lee surrendered to General Grant at Appomattox, Virginia. A division of Negro troops under Union General Birney fought desperately and brilliantly in this campaign. General Johnston surrendered his Confederate forces to General Sherman near Durham, North Carolina, on April 26, 1865. There were thousands of Negro troops with Sherman at the time of the surrender.

The Confederate armies commanded by General Richard Taylor in Alabama and General Kirby Smith in New Orleans surrendered in May, and the people, white and black, had won the War of Freedom. The Confederacy had fallen. Jefferson Davis escaped but was captured at Irvinville, Georgia, May 10, 1865, along with James H. Jones, the Negro from Raleigh, North Carolina, who served as his messenger during the War. The battle for freedom had been won, and before the Negro stretched the long road to equality.

CHAPTER FIVE

The Aftermath of War

THE Census of 1860 showed that there were 3,953,760 Negro slaves. They were distributed as follows: 46.6 per cent were in the South Atlantic Division, made up of Delaware, Maryland, Virginia, North Carolina, South Carolina, Georgia, Florida and the District of Columbia; 34.7 per cent, in the East South Central Division, which included Kentucky, Tennessee, Alabama and Mississippi; 15.8 per cent were in the West South Central Division, which included Arkansas, Louisiana and Texas; and the remaining 2.9 per cent were located in the Northern states of New Jersey, Missouri, Nebraska, Kansas and Utah.

PROPOSALS OF APPRENTICESHIP

One of the first problems to be considered following the War was that of shifting Negroes from enslavement to the status of free men and women. In 1833, the British Empire had attempted to solve its slave problem by the institution of a five-year period of transition called the apprenticeship. This plan had proved unsuccessful, however, and before the five years had ended, complete and immediate emancipation had been adopted. In the United States, the ex-slaves were granted immediate emancipation at the end of the War. In many of the lower Southern states, it was executed through the efforts of the occupying military forces; and in December, 1865, freedom came completely and finally to all areas as a result of the Thirteenth Amendment.

Although the details of the British apprenticeship system were not well known in this country, a similar practice had been initiated in Maryland, where slavery had remained legal until a new constitution was adopted in 1864. Beginning in 1864, as a result of the prohibition of slavery, former slaveowners began applying to Negro youths a system of forced labor already in existence for white children. White orphans had long been bound out in an amended form of the British system of apprenticeship whereby they learned a trade or skill under a master. After a number of years, they were free to begin working on their own. In the process of learning their particular craft or trade, it was required that the white children be given a basic education, which included reading, writing and arithmetic.

When this concept of apprenticeship was applied to Negroes, it differed in many ways. Very few of the colored children were orphans; instead, they were snatched from their parents and placed in the program unwillingly. In addition, the required education for the white children was not offered the Negro youths. If the master of a colored child died, the child could then be transferred to any other white person in the state without his parents' knowledge or consent. If the child ran away, he could then be sold.

All of these conditions added up to slavery under a new name. Many Negroes protested, but they were powerless to take action against the ruthless and unjust system. In some cases, when appeals were made, there were threats of violence by whites who were intent upon keeping the apprentice system in operation. When the Freedmen's Bureau became active in the state of Maryland, complaints flowed into the district headquarters and finally an investigation was conducted. It revealed that approximately 10,000 Negro youths had been subjected to forced labor since 1864. In 1867, the system was banned.

THE PRESIDENT AND CONGRESS

President Lincoln regarded the rebellion as an act of disloyalty by the people within the Confederate states. He believed the relation of the states to the Union could not be destroyed; and based on the theory of this indestructibility, the problem was to create a loyal group who, with the support of the army, would reorganize the governments of these states. With this in mind, President Lincoln had appointed a military governor to each, and in 1862, he agreed to accept two congressmen from Louisiana. His policy was one of restoration as well as Reconstruction. On December 8, 1863, Lincoln issued a proclamation of his plan of Reconstruction, which called for a loyal class of persons who would swear their allegiance to the United States and inaugurate loyal state governments. These persons were not to include the civil or diplomatic officials of the Confederate Government, or the military officers above the rank of colonel in the Army and lieutenant in the Navy. However, even these persons

could apply for a pardon on an individual basis, and Lincoln indicated he would be lenient with them.

The proclamation stated that in the states of Arkansas, Texas, Louisiana, Mississippi, Tennessee, Alabama, Georgia, Florida, South Carolina and North Carolina, whenever at least one-tenth of the number of persons who had been voters in 1860 would take the oath of allegiance and re-establish the state government, this would be recognized as the legal government of the state. The President's plan also stated that provisions adopted by the state which would recognize and declare Negroes permanently free, provide them with further education and improve upon their present condition—as "a laboring, landless and homeless class"—would be approved by the national executive.

The President's plan for Reconstruction was opposed in Congress. The Wade-Davis Bill, passed July 2, 1864, reversed the original basis of Reconstruction and called for measures which were more severe. This bill insisted that the majority, rather than the minority, swear allegiance. When this had been accomplished, those people who had taken the oath could decide upon the holding of a constitutional convention and launch a state government. The Wade-Davis Bill was passed on the last day that Congress was in session; therefore, Lincoln was able to permit the bill to fail by a pocket veto, thus making possible the acceptance of his plan.

Lincoln's message of December, 1863, had placed him on the antislavery side, and he had reluctantly agreed in the same year to the use of Negro troops. On July 30, 1863, Lincoln announced that a Rebel soldier would be executed for every Union soldier killed in violation of the laws of war; and for every one enslaved, a Rebel soldier would be sentenced to hard labor. This was, primarily, a result of the practices of cruelty and death to Negro soldiers by the Confederates. In fact, Jefferson Davis' proclamation of December 3, 1862, had declared that all commissioned officers in Butler's command would be, whenever captured, reserved for execution. However, when one of the most brutal engagements, at Fort Pillow, April 12, 1864, was investigated by a United States Senate committee, the Lincoln government undertook no retaliatory action, even though the report was made that three hundred were slaughtered "in cold blood after the post was in possession of the rebels, and our men had thrown down their arms."

By 1864, Lincoln had decided that he could probably venture a suggestion for the adoption of Negro suffrage. On March 13, 1864, he wrote to Governor Michael Hahn of Louisiana concerning the possibility of extending the franchise:

> I barely suggest, for your private consideration, whether some of the colored people may not be let in, as, for instance, the very intelligent, and especially those who have fought gallantly in our ranks. They would probably help in some trying time in the future to keep the jewel of Liberty in the family of freedom. But this is only a suggestion, not to the public, but to you alone.

It was thus, with characteristic caution, that President Lincoln approached the subject of Negro suffrage.

In September, 1864, it was reported that some Negroes were permitted to vote in the election for the Louisiana state convention. When the legislature met on October 3, a petition was presented from five thousand Negroes, many of whom had served in the Union Army, requesting the right of suffrage. No action was taken upon this request. In the meantime, Arkansas had adopted its constitution with suffrage limited to whites, basing this action on the fact that neither the Lincoln plan nor that which was contemplated in the Wade-Davis Bill made any definite provision for Negro voting rights.

Lincoln's successor, Andrew Johnson, of Tennessee, did not at first change the executive policy. Within a month after his acces-

PRESIDENT ANDREW JOHNSON

sion, it became evident that Johnson's program was to follow Lincoln's principles of Reconstruction. Although this program had been in existence from 1865 to 1867, it had not been successful. Five states had accepted the presidential plan prior to Lincoln's death: Tennessee, North Carolina, Louisiana, Arkansas and Virginia. In May, June and July, 1867, President Johnson issued proclamations for the other states, appointing military governors and authorizing constitutional conventions under the 10-per-cent plan.

In May of 1866, a riot occurred in Memphis, Tennessee, which heralded the beginning of a reign of terror over the newly freed slaves. There was dissatisfaction with President Johnson's plan of Reconstruction on the part of many, and this has been cited as a contributing factor for inciting the riot. In any event, a mob of white men assisted by policemen of Memphis embarked upon a drunken campaign against the Negroes of

This scene in Memphis, Tennessee, exemplified the beginning of a reign of terror over the newly freed slaves.

that city. Murder and various other criminal acts were committed against Negroes, resulting in forty-six deaths and the burning of many Negro schools and churches. One woman, whose husband had served in the Union Army, related her experiences in a congressional investigation and disclosed that, while she was being criminally assaulted, other members of the raiding party pillaged her house searching for the money which her husband had received upon his release from the army.

Northerners were aghast at the Memphis situation, and leading newspapers carried editorials protesting the President's lenient policies toward the South. *The New York Tribune* blasted the Freedmen's Bureau as being inadequate and insisted that harsher policies be initiated to give the Negro greater protection.

THE THIRTEENTH AMENDMENT

Emancipation by presidential proclamation was a war measure affecting states and parts of states involved in rebellion and depended upon the prosecution of the War for its total, practical execution. As a result of the antislavery crusade, several proposals for a constitutional amendment providing for the termination of slavery were made in Congress during the War. But when the Civil War ended, the complete abolition of slavery was still a matter for consideration by individual states.

The original effort for an amendment was introduced in the House of Representatives on December 14, 1863, by Representative James M. Ashley of Ohio. On the same day, Representative James F. Wilson of Iowa, Chairman of the Judiciary Committee, outlining a similar amendment in a speech opening the first period of debate, stated that "slavery being incompatible with a free government is forever prohibited in the United States; that involuntary servitude should be permitted only as a punishment of crime; and that Congress should have power to enforce the same by appropriate legislation." These resolutions were referred to the Judiciary

Committee but were not brought up until May 31, 1864.

The abolitionists were firm in their conviction that an antislavery amendment to the Constitution was a necessity. Petitions had been circulated among the antislavery societies and various women's organizations, and Susan B. Anthony and Elizabeth Cady Stanton had sent petitions signed by one hundred thousand people to Senator Charles Sumner. On February 9, 1864, a dramatic event had occurred in the Senate when two tall Negro men had filed into the chamber carrying these petitions and had deposited them on Sumner's desk. Rising to speak, Sumner had said: "Here they are, a mighty army, one hundred thousand strong, without arms or banners, the advanced guard of a yet larger army." Petitions had been sent before, but never had so many signatures been presented for a single purpose as on this occasion.

The Thirteenth Amendment was introduced in the Senate on March 14, 1864, by resolutions of Senator J. B. Henderson of Missouri and Senator Sumner of Massachusetts. The Senate Judiciary Committee subsequently proposed adoption of the amendment.

Opposition to the amendment in the Senate was active and vocal, particularly from the representatives of the border states. Senator Garrett Davis of Kentucky and Senator Willard Saulsbury of Delaware presented several amendments. Senator Davis terminated one proposal with the statement that Congress should "distribute the emancipated slaves among the free states." Senator T. A. Hendricks of Indiana asked, "Are the Negroes to remain among us?" and then replied, "They will never associate with the white people of this country on terms of equality."

This view was presented by Senator Reverdy Johnson of Maryland:

> I never doubted that the day must come when human slavery would be exterminated by a convulsive effort on the part of the bondsmen, un-

SUSAN B. ANTHONY   ELIZABETH CADY STANTON

HENRY WILSON

less that other and better reason and influence which might bring it about should be successful —the strong and powerful influences of that higher and elevated morality which the Christian religion teaches.

After continued debating, on April 8, 1864, the amendment passed in the Senate 38 to 6, with the necessary two-thirds vote. Senator Henry Wilson of Massachusetts said on this occasion, "The crowning act of this series of acts for the restriction and extinction of slavery in America is this proposed amendment to the Constitution, prohibiting the existence of slavery forevermore in the Republic of the United States."

The measure met considerable opposition in the House of Representatives. Fernando Wood of New York declared that "The local jurisdiction over slavery was one of the subjects peculiarly guarded and guaranteed to the states. . . . [To negate this provision], though within the letter of the article provid-

ing for amendments, would be contrary to the spirit of the instrument and so in reality an act of gross bad faith."

Replies were given to this argument. References were made to slavery by Representative T. B. Shannon of California as "paganism refined, brutality vitiated, dishonesty corrupted; and we are asked to retain this course, to protect it after it has corrupted our sons, dishonored our daughters, subverted our institutions, and shed rivers of the best blood of our countrymen." Representative I. N. Arnold of Illinois said that "The signing of the immortal Declaration is a familiar picture in every log-cabin and residence over the land. Pass this resolution and the grand spectacle of this vote, which knocks off the fetters of a whole race, will make this scene immortal." On June 15, the House of Representatives voted 93 to 65 on the resolution, with 23 not voting. Therefore, the necessary two-thirds vote was not attained.

Prior to the second session of the 38th Congress, which was in an election year, this measure became a hotly debated campaign issue. In June, 1864, Abraham Lincoln was nominated for a second term and recommended "such an Amendment to the Constitution to be made by the people in conformity with its provisions as shall terminate and forever prohibit the existence of slavery within the limits or the jurisdiction of the United States."

The Republican victory in the election of 1864 was interpreted as a victory for freedom by the antislavery leadership. William Lloyd Garrison asked:

Was not a spectacle like that, rich compensation for more than thirty years of universal personal opprobrium, bitter persecution and murderous outlawry?—It was a full endorsement of all the abolition 'fanaticism' and 'incendiarism' with which I had stood branded for so many years.

Lincoln's Fourth Annual Message to Congress, December 6, 1864, recommended "the reconsideration and passage of the measure at the present session"; and referring to the results of the election, he said, "It is the voice of the people now for the first time heard upon the question."

On January 31, 1865, Representative Ashley called up for consideration the resolution for the Thirteenth Amendment in the House of Representatives. After congressional debates concerning the growth of Federal power, with various comments by those who had voted against the resolution at the first congressional session, the vote was taken; and the resolution was adopted 119 to 56, with 8 members not voting. A shift of 3 votes from the affirmative to the negative would have prevented its passage.

When the announcement of the vote was made in the House of Representatives, the Speaker could not preserve order. The *Congressional Globe,* January 31, 1865, described the scene:

> The announcement was received by the House and by the spectators with an outburst of enthusiasm. The members of the Republican side of the House instantly sprung to their feet and regardless of parliamentary rules, applauded with cheers and clapping of hands. The example was followed by the male spectators in the galleries, which were crowded to excess, who waved their hats and cheered loud and long while the ladies by the hundreds waved their handkerchiefs.

The House of Representatives adjourned "in honor of the immortal and sublime event." *The Independent* declared on February 2, 1865, "We thank God fervently that we have lived to witness this great deed which, when confirmed by the people, will rank as the grandest event of the century." The resolution for the proposed amendment was then submitted to President Lincoln.

There were charges that pressures and influences were exerted by President Lincoln and by at least one of the cabinet members to secure ratification. The Assistant Secretary of War, Charles Dana, reported that Lincoln had promised the three representatives of Nevada, where a positive vote was

JAMES M. ASHLEY

vitally needed, that they would have whatever they wanted if they agreed to support passage of the amendment. Dana reported that he had promised appointments in the Department of Internal Revenue and in the Custom House of New York. Nevada's citizens voted for the amendment and ratified it. Dana added in his recollections, "I have always felt that this little piece of side politics was one of the most judicious, humane, and wise uses of the executive authority that I have ever assisted in witnessing."

A second instance concerned the efforts of William H. Seward, Secretary of State, to secure the necessary votes for adoption in Congress. It has been stated that "to gain the crucial votes needed was the object of an extraordinary lobby. Organized and directed by the Republican Secretary of State, its members were predominantly Democrats." These men worked behind the scene, particularly with New York congressmen. Six of the sixteen affirmative Democratic votes came from New York.

President Andrew Johnson, who as vice-president had succeeded to the presidency following the death of Abraham Lincoln, strongly recommended in his First Annual Message to Congress, December 4, 1865, the adoption of the amendment as an "evidence of sincerity in the future maintenance of the Union, which would be put beyond any doubt by the ratification of the proposed amendment to the Constitution."

On December 18, 1865, the announcement was made by Secretary of State Seward that the requisite number of states—three-fourths—had ratified the Thirteenth Amendment. Since thirty-six states were regarded by Secretary Seward as legally composing the United States, the required three-fourths were twenty-seven, and he reported that the latter number had ratified the amendment. Several states sent notifications of approval after Secretary Seward's announcement: Florida, on December 28, 1865; New Jersey, on January 23, 1866; and Texas, on February 18, 1870.

The Liberator, December 22, 1865, hailed the adoption of this amendment with the following words:

> Henceforth, personal freedom is secured for all who dwell on the American soil, irrespective of complexion or race. It is not merely the abolition of slavery, with the old recognized right of each State to establish the system *ad libitum;* but it is the prohibition by "the Supreme law of the land," duly ratified, to enslave a human being in any part of our national domain, or to restore what has been overthrown. It is, consequently, the complete triumph as well as utter termination of the Anti-Slavery struggle, as such.

There was a sense of finality in this position of *The Liberator* because it ceased publication in 1865. Garrison, among other abolitionists, was satisfied that the Negro's goal of freedom had been achieved, but he failed to realize that this freedom presented new problems of equal magnitude for the entire nation.

OFFICIAL PROCLAMATION,
DECLARING
"Liberty throughout all the land, unto all the inhabitants thereof."

WILLIAM H. SEWARD, SECRETARY OF STATE OF THE UNITED STATES, TO ALL TO WHOM THESE PRESENTS MAY COME, GREETING:

Know ye, that whereas the Congress of the United States, on the 1st of February last, passed a Resolution, which is in the words following, viz:

" A Resolution submitting to the Legislatures of the several States a proposition to amend the Constitution of the United States:

Resolved, by the Senate and House of Representatives of the United States of America, in Congress assembled, two-thirds of both Houses concurring, that the following article be proposed to the Legislatures of the several States as an amendment to the Constitution of the United States, which, when ratified by three-fourths of said Legislatures, shall be valid to all intents and purposes as part of said Constitution, vis:

ARTICLE XIII. SECTION 1. NEITHER SLAVERY NOR INVOLUNTARY SERVITUDE, EXCEPT AS A PUNISHMENT FOR CRIME, WHEREOF THE PARTY SHALL HAVE BEEN DULY CONVICTED, SHALL EXIST WITHIN THE UNITED STATES, OR ANY PLACE SUBJECT TO THEIR JURISDICTION.

SECTION 2. Congress shall have power to enforce this article by appropriate legislation."

And whereas, it appears from official documents on file in this Department, that the amendment to the Constitution of the United States, proposed as aforesaid, HAS BEEN RATIFIED by the Legislatures of the States of Illinois, Rhode Island, Michigan, Maryland, New York, West Virginia, Ohio, Missouri, Nevada, Indiana, Louisiana, Minnesota, Wisconsin, Vermont, Tennessee, Arkansas, Connecticut, New Hampshire, Maine, Kansas, Massachusetts, Pennsylvania, Virginia, South Carolina, Alabama, North Carolina—in all, twenty-seven States;

And whereas, the whole number of States in the United States is thirty-six;

And whereas, the before specially named States, whose Legislatures have ratified the said proposed amendment, constitute three-fourths of the whole number of States in the United States:

Now, therefore, be it known that I, William H. Seward, Secretary of the United States, by virtue and in pursuance of the second section of the act of Congress, approved on the 20th of April, 1818, entitled " An act to provide for the publication of the laws of the United States, and for other purposes, do hereby certify that THE AMENDMENT AFORESAID HAS BECOME VALID, TO ALL INTENTS AND PURPOSES, AS PART OF THE CONSTITUTION OF THE UNITED STATES.

In testimony whereof I have hereunto set my hand, and caused the seal of the Department of State to be affixed.

Done at Washington, this 18th day of December, in the year of our Lord 1865, and of the Independence of the United States of America the ninetieth.

WILLIAM H. SEWARD,
Secretary of State.

NOTE. The State of Georgia should be included in the above list of States which ratified the Amendment. It chanced to be omitted by Mr. Garrison who set the type under some pressure of haste as the paper was going to press.

Abraham Lincoln arrives in Richmond after that city was evacuated by the Confederates.

With this amendment as a basis, thousands of Negro slaves who were scattered among the Indian tribes were set free. The government of the United States, however, had to treat the tribes as nations, and treaties were negotiated for this purpose in 1866. The Seminole Treaty, concluded March 21, 1866, is an example:

> The Seminole Nation covenant that henceforth in said nation slavery shall not exist, nor involuntary servitude, except for and in punishment of crime, whereof the offending party shall first have been duly convicted in accordance with law applicable to all members of said nation, and inasmuch as there are among the Seminoles many persons of African descent and blood, who have no interest or property in the soil and no recognized civil rights, it is stipulated that hereafter these persons and their descendants, and such other of the same race as shall be permitted by said nation to settle there, shall have and enjoy all the rights of native citizens and the laws of said nation shall be equally binding upon all persons of whatever race or color who may be adopted as citizens or members of said tribe.

The Choctaw and Chickasaw Nations agreed to a treaty on April 28, 1866; the Creeks, on June 14, 1866; and the Cherokees, on July 19, 1866.

Thus slavery legally faded away in the United States, and the question was settled once and for all concerning whether or not the Constitution protected slavery and its extension. It was inevitable that it would pass, because slavery was a relic of a feudal structure already decadent. A new era of industrial expansion was dawning in the United States, and the economy was becoming more dependent on the machine and less on human toil.

LINCOLN'S VISIT TO RICHMOND

The devotion and good wishes which Negroes had for President Abraham Lincoln were demonstrated during a visit which he made to Richmond after its fall in April,

1865. In the words of a contemporary, J. J. Hill, the scene is vividly described:

At 10 A.M. on the 29th inst. we moved from the breastworks on the left of Fort Harrison to the hill in the centre, where we built a tower overlooking the rebel works into Richmond. We remained there four weeks, and on the 27th of March we moved again. Part of the 29th rested in Fort Harrison and the 2nd Brigade in the white house, known as General Birney's headquarters. All was quiet here until the 1st of April, when all was in readiness, and the order was given to strike tents and move on to Richmond. During Sunday night the brigade was out in line of battle, and at three o'clock in the morning the rebels blew up three gun boats and commenced vacating their works in our front. At 5 A.M. the troops commenced to advance on the rebel works—the 29th taking the advance, the 9th U.S.C. [colored] troops next. Soon refugees from the rebels came in by hundreds. Col. W. B. Wooster passed them about, and made them go before the regiment and dig up the torpedoes that were left in the ground to prevent the progress of the Union army. They were very numerous, but to the surprise of officers and men, none of the army were injured by them.

On our march to Richmond, we captured 500 pieces of artillery, some of the largest kind, 6,000 stand of small arms, and the prisoners I was not able to number. The road was strewed with all kinds of obstacles, and men were lying all along the distance of seven miles. The main body of the army went up the New Market road. The 29th skirmished all the way, and arrived in the city at 7 A.M., and were the first infantry that entered the city; they went at double quick most of the way. When Col. Wooster came to Main St. he pointed his sword at the capitol, and said "Double quick, march," and the company charged through the main street to the capitol and halted in the square until the rest of the regiment came up. Very soon after the arrival of the white troops the colored troops were moved on the outskirts of the city, and as fast as the white troops came in the colored troops were ordered out, until we occupied the advance. The white troops remained in the city as guards. We remained on the outpost.

The 3rd instant President Lincoln visited the city. No triumphal march of a conqueror could have equalled in moral sublimity the humble manner in which he entered Richmond. I was standing on the bank of the James River viewing the scene of desolation when a boat, pulled by twelve sailors, came up the stream. It contained President Lincoln and his son . . . . In some way the colored people on the bank of the river ascertained that the tall man wearing the black hat was President Lincoln. There was a sudden shout and clapping of hands. I was very much amused at the plight of one officer who had in charge fifty colored men to put to work on the ruined buildings; he found himself alone, for they left work and crowded to see the President. As he approached I said to a woman, "Madam, there is the man that made you free." She exclaimed, "Is that President Lincoln?" My reply was in the affirmative. She gazed at him with clasped hands and said, "Glory to God. Give Him the praise for his goodness," and she shouted till her voice failed her.

When the President landed there was no carriage near, neither did he wait for one, but leading his son, they walked over a mile to Gen'l. Weitzel's headquarters at Jeff. Davis' mansion, a colored man acting as guide. Six soldiers dressed in blue, with their carbines, were their advanced guards. Next to them came President Lincoln and his son, and Admiral Porter, flanked by the other officers right and left. Then came a correspondent, and in the rear were six sailors with carbines. Then followed thousands of people, colored and white.

What a spectacle! I never witnessed such rejoicing in all my life. As the President passed along the street the colored people waved their handkerchiefs, hats and bonnets, and expressed their gratitude by shouting repeatedly, "Thank God for his goodness; we have seen his salvation."

The white soldiers caught the sound and swelled the numbers, cheering as they marched along. All could see the President, he was so tall. One woman standing in a doorway as he passed along shouted, "Thank you, dear Jesus, for this sight of the great conqueror." Another one standing by her side clasped her hands and shouted, "Bless the Lamb—Bless the Lamb." Another one threw her bonnet in the air, screaming with all her might, "Thank you, Master Lincoln." A white woman came to a window but turned away, as if it were a disgusting sight. A few white women looking out of an elegant mansion waved their handkerchiefs. President Lincoln walked in silence, acknowledging the salute of officers and soldiers, and of the citizens, colored and white.

It was a man of the people among the people. It was a great deliverer among the delivered. No wonder tears came to his eyes when he looked on the poor colored people who were once slaves, and heard the blessings uttered from thankful hearts and thanksgiving to God and Jesus. They were earnest and heartfelt expressions of gratitude to Almighty God, and thousands of colored men in Richmond would have laid down their lives for President Lincoln. After visiting Jeff. Davis' mansion he proceeded to the rebel capitol and

Lincoln's assassination took place in Ford's Theatre in Washington, D.C.

from the steps delivered a short speech, and spoke to the colored people as follows:

In reference to you, colored people, let me say God has made you free. Although you have been deprived of your God-given rights by your so-called masters, you are now as free as I am, and if those that claim to be your superiors do not know that you are free, take the sword and bayonet and teach them that you are—for God created all men free, giving to each the same rights of life, liberty and the pursuit of happiness.

The gratitude and admiration amounting almost to worship, with which the colored people of Richmond received the President must have deeply touched his heart. He came among the poor unheralded, without pomp or pride, and walked through the streets, as if he were a private citizen more than a great conqueror. He came not with bitterness in his heart, but with the olive leaf of kindness, a friend to elevate sorrow and suffering, and to rebuild what had been destroyed.

THE DEATH OF ABRAHAM LINCOLN

The assassination of President Lincoln on the night of April 14, 1865, at Ford's Theatre in Washington, D.C., by John Wilkes Booth, brought sorrow, horror and anger to the Negro people. Hundreds of them, including Negro soldiers, stood in line during the night prior to his lying in state in the Capitol so that they might take a last look at him. The funeral procession was preceded by a detachment of Negro troops. As the procession passed to the train depot from which the president's body was to be taken to Springfield, the 8th Regiment of United States Colored Artillery was drawn up in line and presented arms.

Major Rathbone Miss Harris Mrs. Lincoln President Lincoln The Assass.

THE ASSASSINATION OF PRESIDENT ABRAHAM LINCOLN

It is reported that information concerning Booth's escape on the night of the assassination and his later locations was supplied by a Negro. Major General W. S. Hancock had issued an appeal to the colored people to aid in the apprehension of the assassin. He said that, although rewards were offered, he felt that they needed no such stimulus, but would hunt down the assassin of their "best friend" as they would the murderer of their own father. The tragedy of his death increased the antagonism of many Negroes toward the Confederate leaders, who were accused of complicity in the plot.

Assemblies of Negroes expressed their grief as they gathered during the days following Lincoln's death. One of those groups assembled was the Forty-Eighth Annual Session of the Baltimore Annual Conference of the African Methodist Episcopal Church. It held its meeting, April 13–15, 1865, presided over by Bishop D. A. Payne, then president of Wilberforce University. On April 15, Bishop Payne spoke of the "terrible assassination of President Lincoln," who had fallen at the hand of "a cowardly assassin." A committee was appointed to draw up resolutions express-

ing the grief of the conference in the death of "the great and good Abraham Lincoln."

While the blood of John Brown was shed to inaugurate the meting out of justice to those who had long oppressed the Saviour in the person of the bondmen, the death of the great President will be made the occasion of continuing the work until the divine mandate which awards death to manstealers be fully and literally accomplished.

The resolutions also offered their hands and hearts to President Johnson, "together with two hundred thousand muskets in the hands of our brethren to protect the flag of our country." This action, in the passing of these resolutions, is the first known to be taken by an assembly of any kind concerning President Lincoln's death. A delegation headed by Bishop A. W. Wayman left for Washington in order to be present at the burial services.

THE BLACK CODES

The economic system of the South was entirely disrupted by the Civil War and the freeing of the Negro. The military forces of the Union prevented a state of anarchy from existing in many localities. Southern whites suffered as much from the disorganized economic conditions as did the Negroes, some of whom left their former homes in search of better opportunities. Wherever the Union armies fought, the freedmen who flocked to the areas assembled in camps. They worked for wages and shares of crops which they raised. There were twenty thousand in the District of Columbia, one hundred thousand in Virginia, fifty thousand in North Carolina and thousands more in South Carolina, Georgia and Louisiana. In these and other localities, there were those who ran away from the plantations as soon as the news of freedom was received. Others who had formed some attachment to their masters and mistresses had remained at their work. Some planters concealed freedom from their slaves, while others ordered them from their plantations since they could not pay wages. Facts indicate the former plantation owners who would not pay wages were a contributing influence in this migratory trend. Some observers looked upon the Negroes wandering in search of freedom as fleeing from work.

The general question among many Southerners was, now that the Negroes were free, would they work? Their answer to this question was one of the bases for opposition to the abolition of slavery. The Negro, they said, would only work in slavery, and only if there was a white superior in charge. The immediate result, with restraints cast off, would be an interruption of labor. It is known by historians that this condition was not descriptive of all Negroes, for there were former slaves who adjusted to their new situations as rap-

Wherever the Union armies were in action, the freedmen flocked into the army camps and began working for wages.

idly as the whites, and in many instances more rapidly, since they faced a new opportunity while the whites faced apparent frustration.

An effort was made to maintain control over the freedmen and to strictly regulate their relations with the Southern people through the so-called Black Codes of 1865–66, which were passed by eight states. They differed in each state, but their purposes were the same. The main objectives were to proscribe relations between Negroes and whites. Various statements were made to define the meaning of the terms "Negro" and "persons of color." A South Carolina law stated that "any descendant of a person of color who may have Caucasian blood, seven-eighths or more, shall be deemed a white person." Freedmen, however, were permitted to serve on juries, to hold and dispose of personal property, to sue and be sued in the courts and to marry legally.

In some states, the right of Negroes to rent or own property was proscribed in incorporated towns, the purpose being to restrict their ownership to land outside of these areas. Vagrancy laws, fines and imprisonment were adopted for riots and trespasses, and the carrying of concealed weapons was forbidden. Licenses were required of Negro mechanics, storekeepers and artisans.

Numerous other regulations were passed. In one state a Negro could be whipped, while in another he could be "moderately corrected" and held responsible for "negligence, dishonesty and bad faults." In Alabama, a Negro vagrant was required to work under the watchful eye of public overseers. In South Carolina, a shopkeeper or peddler was required to pay a license of one hundred dollars and an artisan had to pay ten dollars. The purpose of such laws was twofold: on the one hand, to intimidate the Negro workers; and, on the other, to confine them to agriculture and menial labor. Preaching was limited in some places to assemblies under white

supervision, and seven states forbade intermarriage between the races. Apprenticeship laws were adopted, through which minors whose parents were found not to be providing for them were apprenticed by the courts. Three states provided for segregation in public conveyances and thereby brought about segregation in travel. Several patterns of segregation were thus formed in this period.

These codes were justified by some writers on the ground that the Negro slaves were lazy and ignorant of how best to use their freedom. They were regarded as members of an inferior race who needed guidance and correction or else chaos and confusion would become rampant. Negroes were put in a separate class in the codes and were known as "servants," while the contractors were known as "masters"; and any contracts had to be written with white witnesses and on approval by a judge.

Competition for jobs was one of the bases for laws restricting the occupations of Negroes. These were in effect prior to the Civil War, for laws were then the only way to prevent free Negro artisans from competing equally with white mechanics and artisans. Racial inferiority was another assumption which was in the background of this legislation. This supposition is now known to be false, for slave experience and environmental conditions much more readily explain the apparent lack of capacity to perform than the concept of racial differences. It is well to remember that there were some whites who were as ignorant and poor as many Negroes.

Protests were made against these laws, especially by some Northern people who saw in them attempts to re-establish slave conditions. Charles Sumner spoke against them in the Senate; and on February 5, 1866, he urged his colleagues to "strike at the Black Codes, as you have already struck at the Slave Code. There is nothing to choose between them. You have already proclaimed emancipation; proclaim enfranchisement."

Groups of Negroes also protested. Negroes at a convention in Augusta, Georgia, on January 10, 1866, addressing themselves to these codes, declared that during the War they had remained in their homes when they knew that they had the power "to fire your houses, burn your barns, destroy railroads and discommode you in a thousand ways," but they had decided "to wait on God and trust to the instincts of your humanity." They could no longer remain indifferent to laws which would bind them in future years, and therefore they were protesting firmly and openly against them. Other meetings of intelligent Negroes protested the passing of these laws and asked for their repeal since they served only to replace legal slavery with legal serfdom and the caste system.

THE FREEDMEN'S BUREAU

The extension of freedom to the former slave population and the disruption of the Southern way of living were followed by a major effort to assist in improving these situations. On January 12, 1863, a bill was introduced in the House of Representatives to establish the Bureau of Emancipation in the War Department, but no action was taken upon this bill. A similar bill—to establish the Bureau of Freedmen's Affairs—was introduced on December 14, 1863, and was sent to the Senate on March 2, 1864. The Senate made further changes in the bill which were unaccepted by the House, and Congress adjourned without any definite action. Finally, on February 2, 1865, a conference committee of both houses agreed upon the introduction of a bill for the establishment of "a Department of Freedmen and Abandoned Lands." Opposition to this proposal continued to develop and another conference was called.

On March 3, 1865, a new bill was proposed and passed to create "a Bureau for the Relief of Freedmen and Refugees" in the War Department, with a provision for a

GENERAL OLIVER OTIS HOWARD

commissioner of the bureau and assistant commissioners, who could be army officers, for the states in rebellion. On May 12, 1865, President Johnson appointed General Oliver Otis Howard as commissioner. General Howard—a graduate of Bowdoin College and West Point and former commander of the Army of Tennessee—took charge three days later. While he was not a great administrator, he was a capable and sincere leader—a Christian gentleman who would dedicate himself wholeheartedly to the duties of his office. Congress made no appropriation of funds for the bureau, so the work had to be financed with army funds and the contributions of private freedmen's associations. However, funds had accumulated in the Treasury Department from the sale of abandoned lands and cotton, and these were transferred to the bureau by President Johnson.

General Howard stated that his purpose was not to supersede the benevolent societies already engaged in services to the South, but to systematize and facilitate them. He issued a widely distributed circular in 1865, declaring that the commissioners would "compel all able-bodied Negroes to work." Negroes were

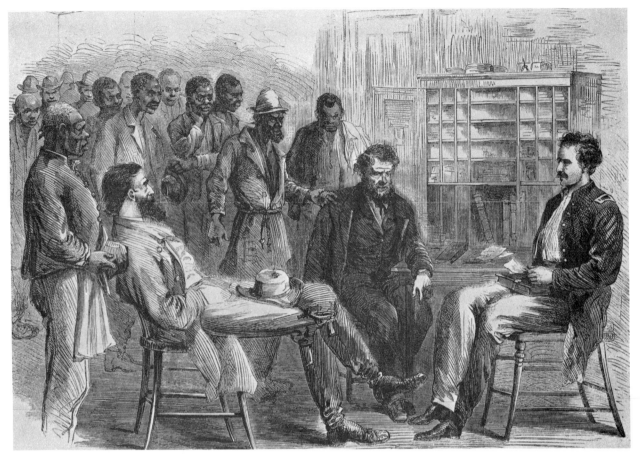

Office of the Freedmen's Bureau in Memphis, Tennessee.

to be free to accept and choose their employers, who, in turn, would submit all contracts for the approval of the bureau officers. The assistant commissioner—Major General Clinton B. Fisk—issued a circular for the states of Kentucky and Tennessee advising Negroes to enter into contracts with their former masters, with the recommendation that if "good contracts or a share of the crop" were not offered, they would have a perfect right to go where they could do better. On July 16, 1866, the bureau was continued by Congress for another two years, and funds were appropriated for its work. Its existence was again extended to January 1, 1869, and both the educational and financial operations of the Freedmen's Bureau continued until June 30, 1872.

General Howard described the conditions which first faced him in the following words:

The sudden collapse of the rebellion, making emancipation an actual, universal fact, was like an earthquake. It shook and shattered the whole previously existing social system. It broke up the old industries and threatened a reign of anarchy. Even well-poised and humane landowners were at a loss what to do or how to begin the work of reorganizing society and of rebuilding their ruined fortunes. Very few had any knowledge of free labor, or any hope that their former slaves would serve them faithfully for wages. On the other hand the freed people were in a state of great excitement and uncertainty. They could hardly believe that the liberty proclaimed was real and permanent. Many were afraid to remain on the same soil that they had tilled as slaves lest by some trick they might find themselves again in bondage. Others supposed that the government would either take the entire supervision of their labor and support or divide among them the lands of the conquered owners and furnish them with all that might be necessary to begin life as an independent farmer.

Edward L. Pierce of Boston, Massachusetts, was selected as a special agent by the

Secretary of the Treasury to assume charge in the districts which had been in rebellion. He was a graduate of both Brown and Harvard Universities and later became the official biographer of Charles Sumner.

Early in the War, Pierce had been stationed at Fort Monroe in Virginia as a private in the 3rd Massachusetts Regiment. At that time, he had been authorized to collect contrabands, keep records of them, secure tools for their use, supervise their work and procure rations for them.

Based on his experiences at Fort Monroe, Pierce wrote an article that appeared in the November, 1861, issue of the *Atlantic Monthly*. He described the plight of the freedmen, expressed confidence in their willingness and ability to meet the demands of freedom and urged that all possible steps be taken to alleviate their suffering.

In 1862, the services that Pierce had performed at Fort Monroe were recognized by Secretary of the Treasury Chase, who made him a special agent of the Union to supervise work among the contrabands at Port Royal, South Carolina.

When the Freedmen's Bureau was created in 1865, its first order was that the freed person must "earn his or her own support, . . . [and] not congregate in cities and live in idleness, but must go to the country and find homes and employment." In addition, branch offices were opened by the bureau in Northern cities to encourage the freed people who were gathering in Southern cities to migrate in search of employment as free workers.

The area that was administered by the bureau was divided into ten districts, with each supervised by an assistant commissioner. Employment was found for numerous applicants, resulting in a reduction of expenditures for the government, which was at the time providing funds for the support of many Negro families. Various officials of the bureau also set to work immediately to regulate the labor of the freedmen, to super-

Plantation workers return to their homes after a pay-day visit to the general store.

vise the dispensation of justice to the workers and to maintain schools. This program was one of military guardianship under generals of the army: General Saxton in South Carolina, General N. P. Banks in Louisiana, and General Clinton B. Fisk in Tennessee.

This policy was not only misunderstood and criticized but met opposition from most Southern white people. Their full cooperation was never received for the work of the bureau, even though its purpose was to aid in the South's recovery. Regulations providing for contractual relations between employers and employees were issued, and public meetings were held for the purpose of explaining these orders. Meanwhile, wages and terms of employment were fixed. When Negro dis-

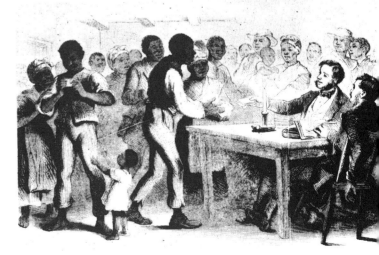

Free workers on a plantation receiving their first pay.

tricts were terrorized by marauders, bureau leaders protected them and saw that justice was maintained. Whites as well as Negroes were aided by this relief measure. In 1865, General Clinton B. Fisk reported that rations issued to white persons in Tennessee exceeded those of the freedmen. General Howard's report for 1867 showed that the number of destitute whites exceeded the number of blacks; in ten Southern states, there were 32,662 destitute whites and 24,238 destitute Negroes.

Where justice prevailed, many of these persons were rapidly put to work; and the new program of labor was reported to be successful by the assistant commissioners in Alabama, North Carolina, Mississippi, South Carolina, Tennessee and Virginia. Good crops of sugar, rice, tobacco and cotton were raised in 1866 and 1867. However, some planters found the wage system was not profitable to them and endeavored to hold back the full pay, which meant a relapse toward forced labor. The freedmen became dissatisfied, left the farms, refusing unfair contracts, and thronged to the cities, where better wages and working conditions were said to prevail. William E. Strong, the inspector general of the Freedmen's Bureau, reported in 1866 that the freedmen had been treated "universally in bad faith," and said that he could not blame them for not making contracts for another year. Conventions of freedmen continued to be held, protesting their unfair treatment as free workers.

Other work of the Freedmen's Bureau was the furnishing of transportation to both whites and Negroes who had wandered from their homes. The bureau stated that before 1867 two thousand whites and thirty thousand Negroes were provided with transportation to return to their homes. Medical aid was furnished to the sick; and by September, 1867, forty-five hospitals were under the bureau's jurisdiction. The medical department's expenditures were estimated to have been over two million dollars, while the total expenditures of the Freedmen's Bureau were estimated at between seventeen and eighteen million dollars.

There were opposition and hostility to the Freedmen's Bureau. It was claimed that it interfered with the old processes of labor, and that at least half of its agents were "wholly unfit for the positions they occupy." It was further claimed that, in their administrations of relations between freedmen and planters, "they too generally side with the former, even in cases where the right course is not difficult to choose." Many whites accused the bureau of every imaginable error, mainly because its work was misunderstood and resented as interference. Investigations disclosed some abuses, with careless administration of funds being cited. But the bureau performed services greatly needed to regulate the labor of the freedmen, the management of abandoned lands, the relief of distress, the supervision of justice and the maintenance of schools.

Education was not a stated function of the Freedmen's Bureau when it was first established; but by the amended act of July 16, 1866, this became one of its authorized purposes. Interest and activity in schools were fully expressed by General Howard and his associates. Schools were soon started for Negroes and whites, under the auspices of the bureau, comprising day, night, Sabbath and summer schools. In addition, there were industrial schools and colleges aided by bureau funds and teachers. It was reported that, from 1865 to 1871, the bureau spent $5,262,511 on these schools. The basements of churches, army barracks, barns and buildings of various kinds were used for school purposes. There were 90,589 pupils enrolled in the schools in 1860; but this number grew to 149,581 in 1870, with 3,300 teachers, as reported by John W. Alvord, who had served as an army chaplain and was the superintendent of schools for the Freedmen's Bureau.

The Abraham Lincoln School for freedmen in New Orleans.

These numbers included attendance in all types of schools which were conducted by both the Freedmen's Bureau and the freedmen's associations.

By 1869, there were 9,503 teachers in schools for freedmen, with about 5,000 of them from the Northern states. At the beginning, nearly all of the teachers were whites from the North; but in 1870, the bureau reported that there were 1,324 Negro teachers out of a total of 3,300. By 1869, thirteen higher schools or colleges had been established. In building the educational system, the Freedmen's Bureau made major contributions, while the devoted and dedicated white teachers who came from Northern states were its agents in the schools. Their work was reflected in the noteworthy lives of many thousands of educated freedmen.

RELIGIOUS AND BENEVOLENT SOCIETIES

In the development of Negro schools, General Howard cooperated with the religious and benevolent societies as well as with the state authorities. At least thirty prominent societies cooperated with the bureau and engaged in educational and relief work. The American Missionary Association was considered the most important society functioning in this field. This association originated in 1846 at Syracuse, New York, with William Jackson of Massachusetts as president; George Whipple of Ohio, corresponding secretary; and Lewis Tappan of New York, treasurer. At another meeting in Albany, New York, during September, 1847, the title of the organization was adopted. This association can be traced to four sources: the Amistad Committee, associated with the defense of revolting slaves on board the *Amistad;* the Union Missionary Committee; the Committee for West Indian Missions; and the Western Evangelical Missionary Society, for work among the American Indians. While its work was nonsectarian, its leaders were originally prominent members of Congregational churches.

From this period until the Civil War, the association became involved in various fields, among which were home and foreign missions, the amelioration of the conditions of slavery and its ultimate abolition. In 1848, its executive committee established a fund to be used for the distribution of Bibles to the slaves. With the start of the Civil War, attention was directed by the association officials to the needs of the freedmen. Three hundred and fifty-three teachers were sent into the South by the American Missionary Association in 1866, and within the next year the number was increased to five hundred and thirty-two.

Denominational boards engaged in the work of aiding and teaching the freedmen. Northern religious bodies, which included Congregationalists, Baptists, Methodists, Presbyterians, Protestant Episcopalians and Roman Catholics, devoted themselves to this cause. Denominational boards of Negro churches, including the African Methodist Episcopal Church, the African Methodist Episcopal Zion Church, the Colored Methodist Episcopal Church and the Negro Baptist

The Freedmen's Bureau played a major role in keeping the peace during the early years of Reconstruction.

Church, were engaged in a similar capacity. Since these organizations were dedicated to the purposes, methods and procedures of their work, their zeal and devotion led them to a position of leadership in education during this period of trial for Negro Americans.

Another very important society was the Freedmen's Aid Society, organized in Cincinnati in 1866 under the auspices of the Methodist Episcopal Church. Other societies for education were formed by the Society of Friends and the United Presbyterians, whose organizations began in 1862. The Baptists started the Baptist Home Mission Society in 1863; the United Brethren began activities in 1864; and the Protestant Episcopal Church, in 1865. Many freedmen's aid societies, unions and commissions—both sectional and local—were organized for educational work in the South.

These societies united in May, 1866, to form the American Freedmen's Union Commission, with the motto: "No distinction of race, caste or color in the Republic." It was stated by the commission that "It took America three-quarters of a century of agitation and four years of war to learn the meaning of the word 'liberty.' God grant to teach us by easier lessons the meaning of the words 'equal rights.' "

The courses given in the schools were shaped by the religious, humanitarian, cultural and practical backgrounds of those who attended. The teaching embraced many fields and stressed cleanliness, work habits, citizenship privileges, patriotism, singing and religious instruction. It included the higher branches of learning and the elementary subjects, with both the old and the young in the same classroom. An evaluation of the active work of these public schools would show that this educational crusade was of such proportions that it inevitably had major weaknesses, but its primary purpose was the elevation of the Negro. This was of real significance in American life. Many Southern people were generally against the schools because these purposes were misunderstood, and they became the target of adverse criticism. The Southerners thought that the North had sent in its teachers to gain control of the Negro vote for the Republican Party, and this was met with opposition from some former masters who asserted that education taxed the wrong people and interfered with labor by ruining a good Negro worker.

Some of these institutions were established as industrial schools, and by 1867, twenty-five of them were in existence. A typical school of this type—the Douglass Institute in Baltimore—taught the necessity of work and the value of thrift for both men and women. These industrial schools were the forerunners of the present technical schools for Negroes. Many intellectual persons in the South supported these educational efforts, knowing that education was necessary for the Negro in his new freedom.

NEGRO EDUCATION

An important purpose of the philanthropic and benevolent societies created during the War was the education of Negroes, which was first begun in Virginia. The first day school for freedmen was established in 1861 by Reverend L. C. Lockwood, a missionary sent by the American Missionary Association, and was taught by Mary S. Peake, a Negro woman. Other schools were established at Fort Monroe, at Norfolk, Portsmouth, Newport News and elsewhere, with the freedmen's aid societies joining in the efforts. By 1864, over three thousand pupils were in these Negro schools, with fifty-two teachers, five of whom were Negroes.

Beaufort College, South Carolina, was built in 1852 and served as a hospital for contrabands during the Civil War.

The Civil War education of the Negroes in South Carolina gained impetus on February 9, 1862. Through an order issued by General W. T. Sherman at Hilton Head, districts for work and education were established. He proposed the assignment of teachers "whose duties will consist in teaching them, both young and old, the rudiments of

CHARLOTTE FORTEN

civilization and Christianity." General Sherman stated, "Never was there a nobler or more fitting opportunity for the operation of that considerate and practical benevolence for which the Northern people have ever been distinguished."

In response to this appeal, teachers from the North began to make their way into the South. The U.S. Treasury Department became interested in the project and appointed Edward L. Pierce to supervise its management and control. Pierce, along with sixty-four others—fifteen of whom were women—set sail from New York on March 3, 1862, for the trip to Hilton Head to work among the contrabands. Among those who traveled South to teach in the South Carolina Sea Islands was Charlotte Forten. This noble woman was a member of a prominent Phila-

delphia family which had been free since pre-Revolutionary days. Charlotte Forten had been educated in Eastern schools and had served as a teacher in both Salem, Massachusetts, and Philadelphia. She became an ardent abolitionist prior to the Civil War, and when the project was established at Port Royal, she immediately offered her abilities on behalf of her people in the South.

During the years that this devoted woman taught in the Sea Islands, she kept a diary in which she recorded daily events as they occurred. Her story depicts the abject poverty of the people in these areas and reveals the real gain that was accomplished, through education, in all areas of their lives. According to estimates in 1863, there were over five thousand receiving instruction in the town and plantation schools.

Negro children in Port Royal, South Carolina, eagerly attended school despite their tattered clothing. The Northern school teachers, like the one pictured here, showed a great deal of interest and affection for their pupils.

By 1867, almost every county in the South had a school for Negroes, which was attended by both young and old.

A New England "schoolma'am" holds primary classes in Vicksburg, Mississippi.

Schools were made available to the refugees who flocked into the capital at Washington, D.C., with cooperation from the relief and aid societies, along with trustees of the Negro schools of Washington. Orders by General Nathaniel Banks on August 29, 1863, and February 3, 1864, laid the basis for education of Negroes in the Department of the Gulf. He authorized a board of education of three members, who were to direct the educational activities. By the close of 1864, there were 95 schools, 162 teachers and 9,671 pupils in the schools in the department; and by February 1, 1865, there were more than twenty thousand pupils—who ranged in age from five to twelve years—in attendance.

Throughout the various parts of the South, teachers were representing the American Missionary Association, the Society of Friends, the Western Freedmen's Aid Commission, the Western Sanitary Commission, the National Freedmen's Relief Association, the Board of Missions of the Presbyterian Church, the United Brethren in Christ and other church organizations. Negroes also began teaching in these schools. Two schools were established in Savannah, Georgia, and as a result of an examination, fifteen Negroes—five men and ten women—were certified as teachers. This was a great educational crusade, and these missionaries became, in effect, the second emancipators.

In order to centralize supervision of the school system, Adjutant General Lorenzo Thomas appointed John Eaton as its general director, with authorization to appoint other superintendents of schools. All types of buildings were used for schools: churches, barns, sheds, dwellings and cabins. One teacher, Elizabeth Bond, at Young's Point, Louisiana, described her experience in the following words in *A Report of the Executive Board of Friends Association for the Aid and Education of the Freedmen,* delivered on May 11, 1864:

I opened a school here in a rough log house, thirty feet square and so open that the crevices admitted light sufficient without the aid of windows. The furniture consisted of undressed plank benches without backs, from ten to twelve feet long, and in the center of the room stood an old steamboat stove about four feet long which had been taken out of the river.

The schools were crowded and equipment was limited. Books and slates were all too few. Bibles and tracts of the societies were used in the instruction, and religious and military influences were dominant.

An additional obstacle to the improvement of education was the attitude of many Southern people, who viewed both the pupils and the teachers with scorn, derision and contempt. There were also Northerners who were not sympathetic to these efforts; and some military officials failed to cooperate with the plans of the schools. Despite these obstacles, the education of Negroes in the South under Federal supervision made unusual progress, and significant service was rendered by this educational crusade.

There were variations in the provision of education for Negroes in the Northern states during the War. Some states made available separate schools. Illinois made such a provision in 1825, and until 1872 the state legislature regarded the public schools as schools for white pupils only. In 1841, the legislature of New York authorized any school district to establish separate schools for Negro children; and in 1864, a revised code was adopted, which continued the separation when the school authorities regarded it as expedient. Separate schools could be established in Pennsylvania, by an act in 1854, and it was not until 1881 that this act was abolished. There were private and pay schools for Negroes in Indiana, but they were not admitted to the public schools. By the Ohio Act of 1864, school boards were authorized to establish separate schools for Negroes when their number exceeded twenty. This law was not amended until 1878. The school laws of New Jersey, Massachusetts, Maine, and Connecticut made no distinction as to race or color, and yet there were separate schools established in these states. Negroes had been interested in the establishment and maintenance of these schools and had given funds and cooperated with white persons in the organization of such schools in their own church buildings.

THE RISE OF THE NEGRO COLLEGE

The Freedmen's Bureau and the benevolent societies endeavored to meet the demand for teachers in Negro schools by establishing and aiding schools of higher education for their training. An educated leadership was needed, particularly in the areas of teaching and preaching.

Ashmun Institute, named after abolitionist Jehudi Ashmun, was founded by the Presbyterian Church in 1854 in Pennsylvania; it became Lincoln University in 1866. It is the first, and oldest, institution of higher education in Negro life. Wilberforce University was founded by the Cincinnati Conference of the Methodist Episcopal Church in 1856 and was incorporated by the church with an interracial board, including Reverend Daniel A. Payne, the first Negro administrator of a college in the United States. This university was closed for a brief period during the Civil War but was reopened after being purchased by the African Methodist Episcopal Church in 1863, with Reverend Payne as its president.

Berea College was organized in Kentucky in 1858, with the motto, "God has made of one blood all nations of men"; and on this foundation, the college was for the "co-education of the races." Reverend John Gregg Fee of Kentucky, who had been an antislavery leader, was mainly responsible for its foundation.

After the close of the Civil War, Negro students were admitted to Berea. White and Negro students attended the school until 1904, when the legislature of Kentucky passed a law prohibiting the co-education of the races. Berea was the first institution to give Negroes the opportunity to attend college within a state where slavery had existed, and both white and colored youths attended in harmony.

Hampton Institute was the outgrowth of a school which was begun in 1861 at Hampton, Virginia, near Fort Monroe. General Samuel C. Armstrong, a graduate of Williams College who had commanded Negro troops and was in charge of the Freedmen's Bureau in eastern Virginia, interested the American Missionary Association in the purchase of a tract of land for this school. Hampton Institute was established in 1868 and incorporated in 1870. The charter provided for instruction in common school, academic and collegiate branches, and "the best mode of practical industry in its application to agriculture and the mechanical arts." In its earlier years, emphasis was placed upon the industrial arts and teacher training.

Howard University in Washington, D.C., named after General Oliver Otis Howard, Commissioner of the Freedmen's Bureau, was incorporated on March 2, 1867, by an act of Congress. The site was selected by General Howard and General E. Whittlesey, with a major portion of the purchase price being furnished by the bureau. After short administrations under Reverend Charles B. Boynton and Reverend Byron Sunderland, General Howard was elected president, even though he continued to serve as commissioner of the Freedmen's Bureau. In its earlier years, Howard University had the following departments: Normal, Preparatory, College, Theological, Law, Medical, Commercial and Music.

During this period, Fisk University was established at Nashville, Tennessee. Named in honor of General Clinton B. Fisk, Assistant Commissioner of the Freedmen's Bureau

Wilberforce University, near Xenia, Ohio, was founded by the Cincinnati Conference of the Methodist Episcopal Church in 1856 and was incorporated by the church with an interracial board.

Virginia Hall, one of the most beautiful and inspiring buildings of Hampton Institute, was erected chiefly through the efforts of the Hampton students.

Jubilee Hall, Fisk University, was built with money earned by the famous Jubilee Singers.

in Tennessee, and sponsored by the American Missionary Association and the Western Freedmen's Aid Commission, this institution had its formal opening on January 9, 1866. It was incorporated in 1867 for the higher education of both sexes. Its first principal was John Ogden, who served from its opening to 1870. Its departments included: Preparatory, Normal and Higher Normal courses. A model school and a night school were also conducted under its supervision.

Atlanta University at Atlanta, Georgia, was chartered in October, 1867, and its first building was completed in 1869. It resulted from the interest and activities of the American Missionary Association and various freedmen's aid societies in Georgia. Another college founded through the efforts of the American Missionary Association was Talladega College in eastern Alabama. This institution was founded in November, 1867, and received its charter on February 17, 1869.

GENERAL CLINTON B. FISK

Howard University in Washington, D.C., was incorporated on March 2, 1867, by an act of Congress.

The Freedmen's Bureau assisted in the purchase of a tract of land for the college.

Other colleges established were the St. Augustine's Normal and Industrial Institute at Raleigh, North Carolina; the Lincoln Institute at Jefferson City, Missouri, through the contributions of Negro soldiers who had formed the 62nd and 65th United States Colored Infantry; a college at Harpers Ferry, later known as Storer College; Robert College at Lookout Mountain, Tennessee; Straight College at New Orleans, Louisiana; and Tougaloo College at Tougaloo, Mississippi.

Although referred to as colleges and universities, the curriculums of these schools extended from courses in the alphabet and elementary subjects to higher education, depending upon the needs of the students. The teachers came primarily from the Northern missionary organizations. Although some were better trained than others, all of them were motivated toward the same objective: advancing the status and intelligence of the freedmen. Many of the schools founded under these circumstances and with these motivations have developed into outstanding centers of learning.

Colleges for white students were opening their doors to Negro students in this period. Among them were Lafayette College at Easton, Pennsylvania; the Normal School in Albany, New York; Jefferson College in Pennsylvania; Rutland College in Vermont; Athens College in Athens, Ohio; and Hanover College in Hanover, Indiana. Bowdoin College in Maine had the distinction of graduating John B. Russwurm as the first Negro college graduate in the United States. Schools of theology, as well as medical schools, in New York, Pittsburgh, Philadelphia and Cambridge, had admitted Negro students.

CHAPTER SIX

Negro Life during the War

WHEN the Civil War came to a close, it was estimated that about 390,000 Negroes had participated in it. (This figure does not include those who were laborers in the Union armies.) These men of color had fought for their freedom on the battlefields of the South, side by side with white men. They had learned the lessons of discipline, self-reliance, loyalty and sacrifice and had established their claims to citizenship through gallantry and service. In the North, they had arrived at this point in their history by forcing their way into the Union Army and continuing to fight in the battles for freedom. In the South, their interest in freedom was more than a passive one. Even though there were hundreds of incidents of loyalty to masters in the South, some evidences of disloyalty were reported based upon cases of insolence, refusals to work, taking refuge in the Union armies and relaying information concerning Confederate troops.

MILITARY LABOR IN THE CONFEDERACY

Most hard labor in the Confederacy was performed by Negroes. Every Negro who could wield a shovel would release a white man for the musket. The aversion which many white Southerners had for menial labor led to the use of Negroes in the Confederate military service as cooks, teamsters, ambulance drivers, hospital attendants, stretcher bearers, railroad workers, construction workers, naval and army ordnance workers, iron and mine laborers. The program of hiring them by voluntary contracts proved to be unsuccessful, so impressments were used by military officers and state governors. On March 25, 1863, the Confederate Congress authorized impressments by contracts; and in

Most of the hard labor in the Confederacy was performed by Negroes.

early 1864, the impressment of twenty thousand slaves was approved by the Congress through the states. Conflicts between the states and the Confederate Government arose, and relations between officials became strained. These conflicts developed extensively after the Emancipation Proclamation, as the slaveowners clung tenaciously to their slave property.

Life for Negroes under these conditions was restricted. Their freedom of movement was hampered; their periods of relaxation were limited; and they were continuously supervised by foremen, overseers, managers and directors. Conflicts arose between supervising agents and the slaves, most often ending to the satisfaction of the former. Food rations decreased and caused discontent among the slaves. Clothing was scarce, and it became increasingly difficult to clothe the workers properly. Sickness increased as a result of the scarcity of food, clothing and adequate shelter. The continuous rains in some sections made it necessary for slaves to work in mud and water without boots or shoes. Physicians' visits to slaves were a rarity. Life on the Confederate works was unattractive, and Negroes used every excuse to evade and desert their assignments.

In addition, Confederate soldiers brought their body servants into the army as personal attendants. Plantation life had provided their training, and the army utilized their services. The duties of the body servants included cleaning the quarters, shining shoes, washing clothes, polishing swords and guns, barbering, preparing rations, taking care of horses and foraging for food. There were usually good relations between masters and servants. As the War continued and rations became reduced, the number of body servants declined. And those who accompanied their masters to war found themselves assuming all the duties in the camps. One group of Virginia volunteers sat on a fence while supervising the work of their Negro servants.

In the meantime, on the plantations, the small farms and in the cities of the South, the masses of colored people knew the attitudes of the master class and its tendency to look upon them as inferiors. Long after slavery was repudiated as a labor system by the rest of the world, the ideology of the South stubbornly maintained justifications for slave ownership. The dominant Southern attitude was expressed in this song directed to Abraham Lincoln:

> Abraham, spare the South,
> Touch not a single slave,
> Nor e'er by word of mouth,
> Disturb the thing we crave.
>
> T'was our forefathers' hand,
> That slavery begot;
> There Abraham let it stand,
> Thine acts shall harm it not.

During the first two years of the War, most slaves were loyal to their masters in the lower South. In fact, in Alabama there was a slave population of about 435,000; and less than 10,000 slaves were employed by the Union armies. A Southern white woman wrote of the colored people on her plantation:

> In spite of the infamous proclamation our servants are still loyal, and never rendered more cheerful obedience; indeed their interest in our soldiers and anxiety for the return of peace seems as great as our own. During the Christmas week we had two thousand soldiers passing through. . . . This, of course, involved much extra cooking, and it being the servants' holiday, we were much distressed that our charity should infringe on their privileges. We, therefore, determined to remunerate them for their trouble, but when I offered them money they seemed quite hurt and said that they wanted to do their part for our soldiers and not having any money could only give their time.

After 1863, however, when the news and the meaning of freedom spread, there were many instances of disloyalty and dissatisfaction in Alabama and elsewhere. As the word revealing freedom reached the South, slaves ran away from the plantations to join the advancing Union troops.

EDUCATION IN THE UNION ARMY

The Union Army became a type of school for the freedmen who had joined as soldiers and for those who had flocked into its lines from enslaved conditions. While the able-bodied men were used in military and naval services and the women were used in hospitals, the majority—the untrained, the sick, the decrepit and the children—were left unattended. These persons were placed in camps and given rations. They were given such clothing as could be found there or was forwarded from the North for their use. Some Negroes, having served in related capacities during slavery, leased plantations and cultivated farms; and a few were able to hire other Negroes as workers.

A variety of educational programs was carried out for colored soldiers. Plans for these programs had been discussed and pre-sented publicly in the North by abolitionists, educators and relief organizations. Some of the more intelligent Union officers were the responsible agents in the schools for soldiers and freedmen.

The first such effort was made in 1862 by Secretary of the Treasury Salmon P. Chase, with the appointment of Edward Pierce of Boston as Treasury Department superintendent of the Sea Islands off the coast of South Carolina and Georgia. Pierce was to direct the labor and to procure rations for the colored workers. When the Union troops had occupied the Confederate forts of Hilton Head and Bay Point in November, 1861, they had found large cotton crops in the areas unpicked and unmarketed. Since there was a great need in the North for cotton, it was thought that, if these freedmen could farm the plantations which had been deserted by the whites, they would be aiding

There were many instances of disloyalty and dissatisfaction when the news and meaning of freedom traveled South, and slaves ran away from their plantations to join the advancing Union troops.

the Northern war effort and also be earning money for themselves. Negro workers were employed to pick, collect and load the cotton for shipping to the mainland. This was a good plan, but only a portion of the freedmen was reached by such measures.

Pierce made appeals to the relief societies for help with instruction for colored people. Fifty-three teachers and plantation managers were sent to this area of the South for the organization of schools and plantation management. Similar projects with teachers were started for schools in Virginia at Norfolk and at the freedmen's village at Arlington, under the direction of the freedmen's relief societies, the American Missionary Society and various religious agencies.

The Negro soldiers' written records of these events in education are very rare, but there is one from Joseph T. Wilson, a colored soldier of the 74th United States Colored Troops. He wrote:

Unlettered themselves, they became more and more deeply impressed through their military associations and by contact with things that required knowledge, with the necessity of having an education. Each soldier felt that but for his illiteracy he might be a sergeant, company clerk, or quartermaster, and not a few, that if educated, they might be lieutenants and captains.

. . . Generally, there was one of three things the Negro soldier could be found doing when at leisure: discussing religion, cleaning his musket accoutrements, or trying to read. His zeal frequently led him to neglect to eat for the latter. Every camp had a teacher, in fact, every company had some one to instruct the soldiers in reading, if nothing more.

Another colored soldier, Lieutenant James M. Trotter, wrote of the shortage of books in the army schools and of the Negro soldiers' eagerness to take advantage of any opportunity to learn:

. . . frequently, in an off-hand manner, schools were established and maintained not only for teaching the soldiers to read and write, but also to sing, nor were debating societies even, things

Intelligent Union officers were the responsible agents in the schools for soldiers and freedmen.

JOSEPH T. WILSON

unheard of in the camp life of these men . . . of the textbooks used there is not much to say, for these were generally few and far between. Books were used at times, of course, but quite as often the instruction given was entirely oral.

Colonel G. M. Arnold made the following observations:

In nearly every regiment a school, during the encampment, was established; in some instances female teachers from the North, impulsed by that philanthropy which induced an army of teachers South to teach the freedmen, also brought them to the barracks and the camp grounds to instruct the soldiers of the Phalanx. Their ambition to learn to read and write was as strong as their love of freedom, and no opportunity was lost by them to acquire a knowledge of letters.

These schools were possible because of the intelligent officers in the upper ranks. Lieutenant Trotter described Colonel James Beecher—a brother of Henry Ward Beecher —who was in command of the 1st North

Carolina Colored Regiment, as "a gallant fighter, an eloquent, convincing preacher and a most indefatigable and successful school teacher." And Colonel Thomas Wentworth Higginson of the 54th and 55th Massachusetts Regiments was described as "a true and tried friend of the colored race." Many colored chaplains wisely divided their time between preaching, aiding the sick and teaching.

THE BEGINNING OF FREEDOM

The freedmen recalled the days following the Emancipation Proclamation and the beginning of freedom as being of mixed blessings. One such person tells his story:

When freedom, [came] my mama said Old Master call all of 'em to his house and he said, "You all free, we ain't got nothing to do with you no more. Go on away. We don't whip you no more, go on your way." My mama said they go on off, then they come back and stand around just looking at him and Old Mistress. They given 'em something to eat and he say: "Go on away, you don't belong to us no more, you been freed!"
They go away, but they kept coming back. They didn't have no place to go and nothing to eat . . . .

A related incident involved the arrival of the Federal troops. Many slaveholders were fearful of any contact between their slaves and these soldiers because they knew the slaves would leave if they learned that they were free. However, when this man and others with whom he worked learned that they were free, they were compelled to leave the only home they had known, to forage a living for themselves.

Old Buck Adams [the master] wouldn't let us go. . . . The freedman come and read the paper and tell us not to work no more 'less us git pay for it. . . . They makes us git right off the place, just like you take a old hoss and turn it loose. That how us was. No money, no nothing . . . .

A third colored man described the coming of the Union troops:

With the various churches supplying books and teachers, schools for children began to develop rapidly.

Soldiers, all of a sudden, was everywhere—coming in bunches, crossing and walking and riding. Everyone was a singing. We was all walking on golden clouds.

> *Union forever,*
> *Hurrah boys hurrah!*
> *Although I may be poor*
> *I'll never be a slave —*
> *Shouting the battle cry of freedom.*

The necessity of leaving plantations at the request of their masters and the desire to seek new locations as free men motivated many Negroes to assemble in the Union camps, where relief, schools and work could be found. These sources of assistance were maintained through the Freedmen's Bureau, Federal troops and the relief societies. White and colored churches sent teachers and books for the schools. Fugitive Negroes were settled on the land, contracts for their labor were made, and they were paid wages.

As a result of experience they gained as wage earners, Negroes began developing initiative and buying their own businesses. Robert Smalls, the former Captain of the *Planter,* bought the large home of his former master and opened a store in Port Royal. Another man bought a large farm and hired laborers to work it. A group of Negroes collectively bought the land they had previously worked as slaves and successfully ran it as a group without the interference of whites.

When Brigadier General Rufus Saxton took command in South Carolina in 1862, he was interested in the projects for aiding the Negro because of his own abolitionist persuasion. In 1864, he reported to Secretary Stanton:

> They have shown that they can appreciate freedom as the highest boon; that they will be industrious and provident with the same incitement which stimulates the industry of other men in free societies; that they understand the values of property and are eager for its acquisition, especially of land; that they can conduct their private affairs with sagacity, prudence and suc-

cess;—that they are intelligent, eager, and apt to acquire knowledge of letters, docile and receptive pupils; that they aspire to and adopt as fast as means and opportunity admit the social forms and habits of civilization; that they quickly get rid of in freedom the faults and vices generated by slavery, and in truthfulness and fidelity and honesty may be compared favorably with men of another color, in conditions as unfavorable for the development of those qualities; that they are remarkably susceptible of religious emotions and the inspirations of music; that in short they are endowed with all the instincts, passion, affections, sensibilities, powers, aspirations and possibilities, which are the common attributes of human nature.

During his march to the sea, General William T. Sherman became aware of the extensive aid that would be needed by the newly freed Negroes. Over twenty thousand ex-slaves had followed his army, and they needed to be located on their own lands as free persons. Negroes of all types flocked in the paths of the Union armies and made a picturesque procession following the soldiers who they believed had come to set them free. It is said that Sherman, concerned about rations for them, called on an old gray-haired Negro at Covington to explain to his people the problem created by swarming crowds within the Union lines. Sherman convinced the old man that the large groups pouring into his army might deter it from the purpose of bringing freedom to the slaves. This incident is believed to have reduced the number of followers and prevented other thousands from joining in the march.

Secretary Stanton went to Savannah to confer with General Sherman, and while there, he called a group of colored ministers together for a talk. Reverend Garrison Frazier, who served as their spokesman, said that "[we] want to be placed on land until we are able to buy it and make it our own." On January 16, 1865, General Sherman issued Field Order No. 15, decreeing that the freedmen with his army should be settled on the Sea Islands and adjoining lands, with the large cotton and rice plantations divided into forty-acre homesteads.

Four hundred and eighty-five thousand acres were divided among forty thousand receivers. They cultivated the land, planted vegetables for themselves and for the market, purchased better clothing and worked daily in the fields for long hours, despite the intense heat. They had been advised to select the land owned by men who had taken up arms against the United States Government.

Negroes seeking refuge within the lines of the advancing Union forces.

After June, 1865, pardons were issued, and the planters returned to claim their land. The Negroes declined to leave the places which had proved to be so beneficial to them. One planter was told by his former slaves, "We own the land now, put it out of your head that it will ever be yours again." Others welcomed their old masters at breakfasts and dinners but registered their determination to keep the land.

The planters appealed to President Johnson in petitions which bore the signatures of prominent Sea Island white families. President Johnson ordered General Oliver O. Howard, Commissioner of the Freedmen's Bureau, to go to the islands and urge the Negroes to give up the farms and work for their former masters. When General Howard arrived and called the first meeting, two thousand Negroes were present. Howard's plea was met with cries of "No. We can't do it." He asked those who would to raise their hands and only a few did so; but when he asked how many would trust him as general and leave the decision to him, every hand was raised, for these people had confidence in United States soldiers.

General Howard's report admitted failure, for the Negroes pleaded for the opportunity of remaining there to rent or buy their homes and the land. Petitions were sent by them to President Johnson. When New Year's Day, 1866, came and passed without word concerning their possessions, the freedmen were disappointed and still refused to contract with their former masters, their overseers in slavery.

In early January, six companies of U.S. Colored Troops under the command of Major Martin R. Delany were sent as a result of a report of impending insurrection. It was reported that the Georgia Sea Islands were in a state of "anarchy and open rebellion."

On January 15, 1866, General Saxton, who had authorized the project, was relieved of his command; and the army began evicting the new owners, tearing up their title papers and compelling those who remained to sign contracts at low wages. Negroes met

Since plows were rarely used, the heavy cotton hoe was the sole means of cultivation on most Sea Island plantations.

Emancipated plantation workers gather to hear the terms of a free-labor contract.

force with force. When speculators seeking to purchase the lands for resale arrived on John's Island, they were met with guns, pitchforks and clubs in the hands of crowds of belligerent workers. Negroes on Delta Island were armed and told the officials of the bureau that they would be evicted or die rather than sign contracts.

In late February and early March, the regular military forces of the islands were ordered to restore the lands to their original owners, and the freedmen who refused to make contracts were forced to leave the property. In this case, as in all others, "forty acres and a mule" proved to be only the freedmen's dream.

Having abandoned all hope of retaining title to the land, many Negroes endeavored to obtain fair wages in place of land ownership. This solution could have aided in their transition to freedom; but, tragically, the final result of the Sea Island land experiment was a form of peonage consisting of contract labor, sharecropping, and tenant farming.

RELIGIOUS ACTIVITIES DURING THE WAR

During the Civil War, religious work among the slaves increased. The South Caro-

lina Conference of the Methodist Church issued a call for the support of missions for slaves and directed attention to the advantage of obtaining "the quiet and peaceful subordination of these people." This was one of the purposes of instruction in religion. Slaves were taught to be satisfied with the conditions in which God had placed them—to be patient and to obey their masters.

Religious instruction for slaves had emphasized subordination even before the War. When church attendance was permitted by the plantation owners, it was for the purpose of acquainting the Negroes with values which the white man wished them to acquire. By excerpting passages from the Bible that lent themselves to the philosophy of the slaveholder, the typical minister of a Southern congregation served the cause of the South more than that of his church.

Few Negroes were fooled by the false notions that God had ordained them to serve in menial capacities or that they should be thankful to their creator for their blessings on the plantation. Slavery being what it was, however, it was impossible for these people to openly contradict the religious interpretations they were taught. Many attended the church services as they were ordered to, and then secretly held their own. Often free Negroes in the South were literate and acted as ministers. These persons were allowed by the masters to hold meetings on some plantations, and on others they conducted religious services in secrecy in a cabin away from the "Big House."

The role of the Negro minister and these meetings during the Civil War period cannot be overemphasized. It was at the church services that the word of approaching freedom was often given. It was also here that plans for escape were formulated. The Negro minister passed from plantation to plantation bringing the word of God and, more important, messages from the outside. When it was impossible to hold meetings openly, the slaves resorted to an ingenious method of conducting their services. By placing a large metal pan on the floor to absorb the noises within the cabin, they were able to hold their meetings and remain undetected by the overseer or members of his patrol.

On the larger plantations, where it was impossible for the overseer personally to be aware of all the slaves' actions, other people were used to check on and observe their activities. The patrollers who stalked the cabin area at night were referred to as "pattlerollers" in the expressive dialect of the Afro-American and were often drawn from among the slave population. In places where the "pattlerollers" were used, before the religious service started someone from the group was stationed outside the cabin to warn the participants of a forthcoming check on their activities.

The ingenuity of the slave and his use of the Bible for communicating other than the "Holy Word" was remarkable. Often plans for an entire escape operation were formed by the minister and his congregation during a seemingly ordinary religious service. On some plantations where it was too risky for meetings to be held in a cabin, the faithful would gather in the woods to pray.

Religion served two primary purposes for the slaves. It made possible a sharing of practical information to be used in attaining freedom; and it gave meaning to their lives through the hope of a better life in the hereafter. Most of the slaves were superstitious and had previously had little or no exposure to Christianity. Some had been acquainted with Mohammedanism in their homeland of Africa, and others, after their capture, had interested themselves in the Christian religions. Of the several sects, the Baptists and the Methodists attracted the greatest number

The Baptists and Methodists attracted many Negro followers because of their emphasis on emotional worship.

because of their accentuation of emotional worship. The revivalistic aspects of the preaching appealed to the slave listeners. The sermons continuously voiced a heaven of bliss and happiness which would follow the burden and sorrows of their present life, and it was always the "Sweet Bye and Bye" to which they looked.

The beginning of the Civil War ushered in a new era for Negroes in the various churches. Several states, including Georgia, repealed the laws prohibiting preaching by free Negroes. This resulted in Negroes' meeting together in religious services with their own leaders and church members. One of these leaders, a slave in Virginia, after hearing of the preliminary proclamation of emancipation issued on September 22, 1862, rendered the following prayer:

> O God Almighty! Keep the engine of the rebellion going till New Years! Good Lord! pray, don't let off the steam, Lord, don't back up; Lord, don't put on the brakes! But pray . . . Good Lord put on more steam! Make it go a mile a minute! Yes, Lord, pray make it go sixty miles an hour!
>
> Lord, don't let the express train of rebellion smash up till the first of January! Don't let the rebels back down, but harden their hearts as hard as Pharaoh's, and keep all hands going till the train reaches the Depot of Emancipation.

Even before the War, it was said that there was little sympathy for the suffering of free Negroes. Some abolitionists, according to the *New York Herald* of October 27, 1859, were refusing to assist them:

> [They no longer care] for his necessities, they refuse to admit him to their houses or churches, they will not sit by his side in the cars or at tables, they reject him as a mechanic, a servant or a laborer and persecute him with neglect till he sinks to the very dregs of society and dies in misery.

HENRY HIGHLAND GARNET

This dismal note was characteristic of the attitude that the Negro was later to face, both in the North and in the South, in his search for religious opportunity after the War.

Many colored persons of mixed parentage had been sent to the North by their white relatives, and the majority of these had become self-supporting citizens. Their churches in the North were separate but were equal as places of worship. One of these was the Shiloh Presbyterian Church, organized in New York City in 1832. A New York newspaper correspondent who visited one of its morning services wrote: "The order preserved and the apparent devotion of those present were in the highest degree praiseworthy and might be advantageously imitated in many fashionable evangelical churches patronized by 'the white folks.' " At the evening service, favorable observations were made on the sermon delivered by the pastor, Reverend Henry Highland Garnet, to a congregation comprised "for the most part of colored persons, with here and there a small sprinkling of whites."

During the War, an observation of a church service on the Sea Islands, South Carolina, was written by Charlotte Forten, a colored teacher from Pennsylvania:

> About eleven they had all assembled; the church was full. Old and young were there assembled in their Sunday dresses. Clean gowns on, clean head handkerchiefs, bright colored, of course. I noticed that some had even reached the dignity of straw hats, with bright feathers. The services were very interesting. The minister, Mr. Phillips is an earnest New England man. The singing was very beautiful, I sat there in a kind of trance and listened to it, and while I listened looked through the open window into the beautiful grove of oaks with their moss drapery. . . . The sermon was quite good. But I enjoyed nothing so much as the singing—the wonderful, beautiful singing. There can be no doubt that these people have a great deal of musical talent. It was a beautiful sight—their enthusiasm. After the service two couples were married.

In most of the organized churches, Negroes were denied positions of authority prior to and during the Civil War. The Methodist Episcopal Church in the North had been requested by its colored members for separate conferences and a larger participation in church affairs. In 1858, a Negro minister, Reverend Francis Burns, was consecrated as bishop of Africa; and in 1866, Reverend John W. Roberts was consecrated to the same office. This agitation for Negro leadership in the Methodist Episcopal Church was inspired, in part, by ministers of the African Methodist Episcopal Church and the African Methodist Episcopal Zion Church, both of which already had elected and consecrated Negro Episcopal bishops. These churches were making inroads in the Negro membership of the Methodist Episcopal Church, but little action was taken by this group until after the Civil War.

The Methodist Episcopal Church in the South separated its colored members. In 1866, the New Orleans Conference of this church set apart its Negro members in separate districts and annual conferences where the election of bishops could be conducted.

REVEREND FRANCIS BURNS

It was not until 1870, however, that the first general conference was held, and the name adopted was Colored Methodist Episcopal Church.

The Baptist Church, with its policy of providing the opportunity for any ambitious novice to present his message from the pulpit, had its appeal in local centers. Individual churches sprang up in many locations, both in the North and in the South, and some were separations from a larger Baptist Church under white ministers. These churches organized and united for their mutual improvement; and state groups, such as the Negro Baptist Association of North Carolina, were formed. In 1864, the Northwestern Convention and the Southern Baptist Convention were organized, and in 1866, a United Convention was organized at Richmond, Virginia, as the Consolidated American Baptist Missionary Convention.

The Baptist Church had prominent leaders during this period, and many became politi-

REVEREND JOHN W. ROBERTS

cally active in the South. The Wood River Association was organized by Jesse Freeman Bouldon to protect the interests of the Southern Baptists, and he was instrumental in helping the Negroes of Mississippi obtain the franchise.

As the Negro church developed following the War, it served as the cornerstone for all of Negro life. It was through the church that former slaves developed their first organized efforts on their own behalf. The church served as more than a refuge for spiritual release: it was the focal point from which gradually developed much of the Negro business world in later decades.

Following the War, and throughout later years, the road to success in Negro life was paved through activities within the church. Many of the more prominent men who later developed into politicians and spokesmen for their race had their start as ministers in one of the religious denominations.

SONGS OF THE NEGRO PEOPLE

During much of the Negroes' stay in this country, especially during the years of slavery, the role of music was of special importance. In time of trial, the slaves would verbalize their feelings through song. In periods of joy, what few there might have been, Negroes again turned to music for an expression of their feelings.

As the Civil War approached, conditions for the slaves worsened in many areas of the South. New restrictions were placed upon them so that there was less opportunity for free communication. In this period, the Negro spiritual took on a special meaning. Through the use of words set to music, slaves

Whether in slavery or in freedom, there was often singing when the Negro family got together.

were able to inform each other of routes for escape and of the best times in which to seek shelter within the lines of the advancing Union forces.

Whether in slavery or in freedom, however, there was always singing. To the masses of slaves laboring on the plantations, music offered comfort, joy, inspiration and encouragement. This music lived on in spite of changing conditions, as it passed from one generation to another. A question has arisen concerning whether these religious folk songs have African or American origins. Many believe that the religious music came about as a result of the interpretation of white church hymns sung in camp meetings and revivals. But the musical form is the Negro's own. It is true that strains of music can be recognized which slaves heard as they were near the meetings attended by white persons, but such similarities can be found in the folk songs of all people. Many folk songs are the result of sadness and sorrow combined with the hope for the future, and have served as expressions of the singers' feelings and beliefs across the years.

It is well known that in many areas of Africa the African sang while performing his work. A leader would first compose a song, and the group around him would join in the strains of the chorus. This type of singing became typical of the Negro people in the land of bondage. The folk songs indigenous to the Negro people varied from spirituals to ballads and blues. They were the Negro's reaction to his American environment.

The first public recognition and analysis of this music was made by Colonel Thomas W. Higginson of the 54th Massachusetts Regiment, who heard it in the camps and on marches with colored soldiers. He wrote in the *Atlantic Monthly*, June, 1867, concerning "Negro Spirituals" and of one in particular which was sung because of the War— "Many Thousand Go." This song was first heard when a Confederate officer put the

slaves to work on the fortifications of Hilton Head. Colonel Higginson wrote: "This was composed by nobody knew whom—though it was the most recent doubtless, of all these spirituals—and had been sung in secret to avoid detection. It is certainly plaintive enough, for the peck of corn and pint of salt were slavery's rations."

MANY THOUSAND GO

No more peck o' corn for me,
No more, No more,
No more peck o' corn for me:
Many thousand go.

No more driver's lash for me,
No more, No more,
No more driver's lash for me:
Many thousand go.

No more pint o' salt for me,
No more, No more,
No more pint o' salt for me:
Many thousand go.

No more hundred lash for me,
No more, No more,
No more hundred lash for me:
Many thousand go.

No more mistress' call for me,
No more, No more,
No more mistress' call for me:
Many thousand go.

Another pioneer observer was Miss Lucy McKim, who later became the wife of Wendell Phillips Garrison, the son of William Lloyd Garrison. Lucy accompanied her father, J. Miller McKim, a Pennsylvania abolitionist who assisted in the organization of eleven Negro regiments at Camp William Penn, to Port Royal in pursuit of freedmen's relief activities. Miss McKim wrote a letter to *Dwight's Journal of Music* concerning the type of music of the colored people with whom she had contact on her journey to Port Royal:

It is difficult to express the entire character of these Negro ballads by mere musical notes and signs. The odd turns made in the throat and the curious rhythmic effect produced by single voices chiming in at different irregular intervals seems almost as impossible to place on the score as the singing of birds or the tones of an aeolian harp. The airs, however, can be reached. They are too decided not to be easily understood, and their striking originality would catch the ear of any musician. Besides this, they are valuable as an expression of the character and life of the race which is playing such a conspicuous part in our history. The wild, sad strains tell, as the sufferers themselves never could, of crushed hopes, keen sorrow, and a dull, daily misery which covered them as hopelessly as the fog from the rice-swamp. On the other hand, the words breathe a trusting faith in rest in the future—in "Canaan's Fair and Happy Land," to which their eyes seem constantly turned.

A complaint might be made against these songs on the score of monotony. It is true there is a great deal of repetition of the music, but that is to accommodate the leader, who, if he be a good one, is always an improvisator. For instance, on one occasion, the name of each of our party who was present was dexterously introduced.

. . . Perhaps the grandest singing we heard was at the Baptist Church, on St. Helena Island, when a congregation of three hundred men and women joined in a hymn: "Roll, Jordan, Roll, Jordan, Roll, Jordan, Roll." It swelled forth like a triumphant anthem. That same hymn was sung by thousands of Negroes on the Fourth of July last when they marched in procession under the Stars and Stripes, cheering them for the first time as the flag of *our* Country. . . .

There is much more in this new and curious music of which it is a temptation to write, but I must remember that it can speak for itself better than any one for it.

In the armies, the soldiers made up their own songs. One was written by an unknown member of Company A of the 54th Massachusetts Colored Troops. The tune was borrowed from Billy Holmes' "Hoist Up the Flag." Its last verse was added after the battle of Fort Wagner. The song was the regimental song of the 54th:

GIVE US A FLAG

Oh, Frémont he told them when the war it first begun,
How to save the Union and the way it should be done.
But Kentucky swore so hard and Old Abe he had his fears,
Till ev'ry hope was lost but the colored volunteers.

Chorus:

Oh, give us a flag all free without a slave;
We'll fight to defend it as our fathers did so brave;
The gallant Comp'ny "A" will make the Rebels dance,
And we'll stand by the Union if we only have a chance.

McClellan went to Richmond with two hundred thousand brave;
He said, "Keep back the niggers" and the Union he would save.
Little Mac he had his way, still the Union is in tears,
NOW they call for the help of the colored volunteers.   (Chorus)

Old Jeff says he'll hang us if we dare to meet him armed,
A very big thing, but we are not at all alarmed;
For he first has to catch us before their way is clear,
And that is "what's the matter" with the colored volunteer.   (Chorus)

So rally, boys, rally, let us never mind the past;
We had a hard road to travel, but our day is coming fast;
For God is for the right, and we have no need to fear,
The Union must be saved by the colored volunteer.
(Chorus)

Then here is to the 54th, which has been nobly tried,
They were willing, they were ready, with their bayonets by their side,
Colonel Shaw led them on and he had no cause to fear,
About the courage of the colored volunteer.
(Chorus)

A white officer, Captain Lindley Miller of the 1st Arkansas Colored Regiment, wrote these words after hearing some of them sung by his soldiers; and the music was the same as that of "John Brown's Body":

MARCHING SONG OF THE FIRST ARKANSAS COLORED REGIMENT

Oh, we're the bully soldiers of the "First of Arkansas,"
We are fighting for the Union, we are fighting for the law,
We can hit a Rebel further than a white man ever saw,
As we go marching on.

Chorus:

Glory, glory hallelujah,
Glory, glory hallelujah,
Glory, glory hallelujah,
As we go marching on.

See, there above the center, where the flag is
*   waving bright,*
We are going out of slavery; we're bound for
*   freedom's light;*
We mean to show Jeff Davis how the Africans can
*   fight,*
As we go marching on.   (Chorus)

We have done with hoeing cotton, we have done
*   with hoeing corn,*
We are colored Yankee soldiers, now, as sure as
*   you are born;*
When the masters hear us yelling, they'll think
*   it's Gabriel's horn,*
As we go marching on.   (Chorus)

They will have to pay us wages, the wages of
*   their sin,*
They will have to bow their foreheads to their
*   colored kith and kin,*
They will have to give us house-room, or the roof
*   shall tumble in!*
As we go marching on.   (Chorus)

We heard the Proclamation, master hush it as
*   he will,*
The bird he sing it to us, hoppin' on the cotton hill,
And the possum up the gum tree, he couldn't keep
*   it still,*
As he went climbing on.   (Chorus)

They said, "Now colored brethren, you shall be
*   forever free,*
From the first of January, Eighteen hundred
*   sixty-three."*
We heard it in the river going rushing to the sea,
As it went sounding on.   (Chorus)

Father Abraham has spoken and the message has
*   been sent,*
The prison doors he opened, and out the pris'ners
*   went,*
To join the sable army of the "African descent,"
As we go marching on.   (Chorus)

Then fall in, colored brethren, you'd better do
*   it soon,*
Don't you hear the drum a-beating the Yankee
*   Doodle tune?*
We are with you now this morning, we'll be far
*   away at noon,*
As we go marching on.   (Chorus)

Some Negro songs were based on specific incidents during the War. One of these was sung by the 9th Regiment United States Colored Troops at Benedict, Maryland, in the winter of 1863–64. General Armstrong called this the "Negro Battle Hymn." At Petersburg, July 29, 1864, a trooper of General Henry G. Thomas' brigade sat before the campfire singing the hymn "They Look like Men of War." General Thomas described the scene: "The dark men with their white eyes and teeth, crouching over a smoldering campfire, in dusky shadow, lit only by the feeble rays of the lanterns of the first sergeants dimly showing through the tents. After the terrible Battle of the Crater, they sang these words no more."

THEY LOOK LIKE MEN OF WAR

Hark! Listen to the trumpeters,
They call for volunteers,
On Zion's bright and flowery mount—
Behold the officers!

Chorus:

They look like men,
They look like men,
They look like men of war.

Another from the Florida plantations was:

We'll fight for liberty,
We'll fight for liberty,
We'll fight for liberty,
When de Lord will call us home.
And it won't be long,
And it won't be long,
And it won't be long,
When de Lord will call us home.

The preacher played an integral part in many of the singing services. It was he who gave the Negroes hope when all seemed lost. At times such as these they sang:

Let us cheer the weary traveler,
Cheer the weary traveler,
Let us cheer the traveler,
Along the heavenly way.

The Christmas of 1863 was a joyous event. One description of the occasion told of a prayer which gave courage even unto death to the soldiers of the 7th Regiment. A correspondent wrote home about a celebration of the 7th Louisiana Regiment Corps d'Afrique and told how they met and gave expression to their feelings on this day, their first free Christmas.

Through the years, Negro slaves had anticipated the arrival of Christmas, for it was then that they were allowed one full free day to celebrate the birth of Christ, whom many regarded as their personal savior. Their lives contained little hope, few moments of joy, yet the true Christmas spirit was felt and expressed beautifully in the following spirituals:

GO TELL IT ON THE MOUNTAIN
Go tell it on the mountain,
Over the hills and everywhere;
Go tell it on the mountain,
That Jesus Christ is born.

When I was a seeker,
I sought both night and day,
I asked the Lord to help me,
And He showed me the way.

He made me a watchman
Upon a city wall,
And if I am a Christian,
I am the least of all.

Go tell it on the mountain,
Over the hills and everywhere;
Go tell it on the mountain,
That Jesus Christ is born.

RISE UP SHEPHERD AND FOLLOW

There's a star in the East
On Christmas morn.
Rise up, shepherd, and follow!
It'll lead to the place
Where the Saviour's born.
Rise up, shepherd, and follow!
If you take good heed
To the angel's words and
Rise up, shepherd, and follow,
You'll forget your flocks,
You'll forget your herds.
Rise up, shepherd, and follow!
Leave your sheep, leave your lambs,
Rise up, shepherd, and follow!
Leave your ewes, leave your rams,
Rise up, shepherd, and follow!
Follow the Star of Bethlehem,
Rise up, shepherd, and follow!

Singing helped to make the work more pleasant.

Work songs were employed wherever companies of Negro workers assembled, in the fields or in the tobacco factories, on the levees or on the steamboats. The purpose was to increase and regulate work by the singing. The leader set the pace of the music, and the work proceeded in orderly fashion. The choruses of the boat and river songs were repeated by the workers after the leader sang each verse, as in this well-known song:

Michael, row the boat ashore.
Then you'll hear the horn they blow,
Then you'll hear the trumpet sound,
Trumpet sound the world around,
Trumpet sound for rich and poor,
Trumpet sound the Jubilee,
Trumpet sound for you and me.
Michael, row the boat ashore.

Negroes wanted to be soldiers in the army rather than only workers, and so they devised a song which combined their religious expression with this desire:

Don't you want to be a soldier, soldier, soldier?
Don't you want to be a soldier in the year of
Jubilee?
Then you must rise and shine and give God the
glory, glory,
Rise and shine and give God the glory in the year
of Jubilee.

They believed in Satan and his ability to lead one into temptation as they sang this refrain: "Old Satan wears a hypocrite shoe. If you don't mind, he'll slip it on you." Their faith in future rewards and punishment was firm and was expressed in:

My Lord, what a morning,
My Lord, what a morning,
When the stars begin to fall,
You'll hear the trumpet sound!
When the stars begin to fall,
You'll hear the sinners mourn!
My Lord, what a morning,
When the stars begin to fall.

And then they would turn to:

My Lord says there's room enough,
Room enough in the Heavens for us all,
My Lord says there's room enough,
So, don't stay away!

The victory over the enemy is well depicted in "Turn Back Pharaoh's Army":

When Moses smote the water,
The children passed over,
And turned back Pharaoh's Army, Hallelu!
And turned back Pharaoh's Army, Hallelu!

When Pharaoh's Army crossed the water,
The water came together,
And drowned ole Pharaoh's Army, Hallelu!
And drowned ole Pharaoh's Army, Hallelu!

Some Negroes had good times on the plantations, through their picnics, barbecues, cakewalks, hunting, fishing, horse racing, crap shooting and storytelling. There were clogs, jigs, charlestons, cotillions, and quilting parties. Songs were often a part of these activities.

During the Civil War and immediately afterward, Negroes began to organize minstrel troupes. Their programs included the same acts they had used to entertain their masters, mistresses and their company on the plantations—buck dancing, the pigeon wing and bone-rattling. One of the first troupes to be organized was the Georgia Minstrels, in 1865, under Charles Hicks. His successor, Charles Callender, selected only the most talented persons and trained the company for better presentations. This troupe could meet almost any musical requirement: they could perform as an orchestra or a brass band and could provide background music for singers—of solos, duets, or quartets.

They met with great success wherever they appeared. On one occasion, the *New York Sun* reported that "every song was encored some two or three times." The *New York Herald* stated, "The new melodies find in them the fittest interpretations." The *Memphis Appeal* declared, "They are good in everything they attempt." The *Cincinnati Commercial* said, "They have drawn better houses than any white troupe"; and the *Baltimore American* agreed that "All other companies are tame in comparison with them." Similar groups were organized and toured during this period and afterwards.

Many songs were the echoes of past centuries, sounding the heartbeats of the years of slavery and oppression. Through the themes of most of these songs ran the thread of hope that tomorrow would be better than today. Negroes looked forward, not backward, through the minor strains of songs combining despair and hope. There were small secret meetings held in the days of the War, but there would be a great camp meeting one of these days, and so they sang:

Oh, walk together, Children,
Don't you get a-weary.
Walk together, Children,
Don't you get a-weary.
Walk together, Children,
Don't you get a-weary.
There's a great camp meetin',
In the Promised Land.
Go'in to mourn and never tire,

Mourn an' never tire.
Mourn an' never tire,
There's a great camp meetin',
In the Promised Land.

Songs like these expressed the philosophy that no oppression, cruelty or insult could destroy the hope for the future of colored Americans, then or thereafter. How Negroes had the heart to sing through the dismal long night of slavery in the South and isolation and disparagement in the North has been the wonder of history. There was a power of expression, and a love of melody, rhythm, and harmony, which survived and developed despite the debasement of the Negro and his lack of religious instruction. Most of the colored people could not read music, but, as a people, they possessed the natural facility of catching a tune and singing along with their associates. Their synchronism in song without written or printed notes was one of the fascinating aspects of this natural ability.

The journals of Fanny Kemble, Harriet Martineau and Frederick Olmsted and the records of planters and overseers tell much of the Negro's reaction to living the strange life of slavery. A more complete picture can be obtained directly from the words of the slaves themselves. Endeavors have been made to interview slaves and record their words and thoughts. Folk music, folk literature and folklore reveal a society in slavery and Reconstruction developed by the field hand, the house servant and the artisan, who were a self-taught and group-contained people.

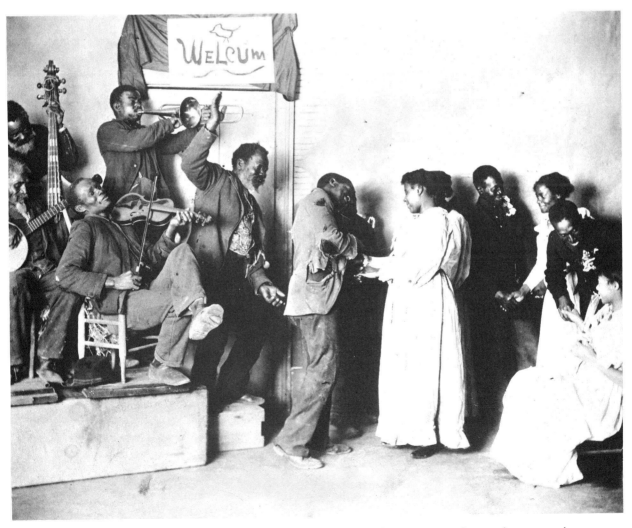

Negro bands were very popular after the Civil War and met with great success wherever they appeared.

The slaves, through laughter and song, were able to sustain themselves despite the type of life that they were forced to lead. There were many stories which demonstrated this ability. One was entitled "From Bloody Flag to White," and it quoted an ex-slave as saying:

> I was at Pamplin, and the Yankees and Rebels were fighting, and they were waving the bloody flag, and a Confederate soldier was up on a post, and they were shooting terribly. Guns were firing everywhere.
>
> All of a sudden they struck-up "Yankee Doodle" song. A soldier came along and called to me, "How far is it to the Rebels," and I, honey, was feared to tell him! So I said: "I don't know." He called me again. Scared to death, I was. I recollect gitting behind the house and pointed in the direction. You see, if the Rebels knew that I told the soldier, they would have killed me.
>
> These were the Union men going after Lee's Army, which had done been 'fore then to Appomattox.
>
> The colored regiment came up behind, and when they saw the colored regiment, they put up the white flag. You 'member 'fore this, red bloody flag was up. Now, do you know why they raised that white flag? Well, honey, that white flag was a token that Lee had surrendered. Glory! Glory! Yes, Child, the Negroes are free, and when they knew that they were free, they, oh! baby! began to sing:
>
> > *Mammy, don't you cook no more,*
> > *You are free, you are free!*
> > *Rooster, don't you crow no more,*
> > *You are free, you are free!*
> > *Old hen, don't you lay no more eggs,*
> > *You free, you free!*

LETTERS FROM SOLDIERS IN THE ARMY

Typical of many Northern Negroes who served in the Union Army were the men of the Massachusetts 54th and 55th Regiments. These "Billy Yanks" did not all hail from the Bay State but came from all over the North to join the ranks of the colored troops. One group was from Ohio; and like their comrades everywhere, these soldiers wrote letters home.

Their letters were expressive of their days in camp and in battle—of their experiences as soldiers. Quoted below are excerpts of correspondence addressed to Miss Elizabeth Woodward of Ripley, Ohio, from some of her friends in the 54th and 55th Massachusetts Regiments. These letters serve the dual purpose of acquainting the reader with the times as they actually were and of illustrating the literacy of Negroes in this period of slavery.

> Headquarters of 54th Mass Regt
> Department of South Morris Island
> South Carolina
> July the 21st, 1863
>
> Miss Woodward,
>
> Just before I wrote, I saw two battles one on James Island, South Carolina and then we were ordered to Morris Island, South Carolina, in front of Charleston. Then we made one grand charge on a Rebel fort named Fort Wagner. Our Regiment was one of the lot to make the charge. Our Regiment lost upwards to some three or four hundred men in killed, wounded and missing. But for my part, I made my escape by the hardest. Our wounded are cared for with the greatest of love in the Beaufort, Hilton Heade and Boston Hospitals....
>
> > SYLVESTER WEBBER
>
> P S: Direct your letters to
>
> > Sylvester Webber
> > Company G, 54th Mass. Regt. Volunteers
> > Hilton Heade, South Carolina
>
> and then I will get them.
>
> > S. W.

> September 6th, 1863
> Camp Delaware, Ohio
>
> Dear Miss,
> ... We have had three weddings in Camp Delaware and death has closed seven of our fellow brothers' eyes and their bodies are lying in the cold graves. Well we are left on the land among the living. Oh, I will think of Jesus and have him ever near. I'll tell him all my sorrows. I'll tell him all I fear—his ear is ever listening. He never turns away and though I can but whisper he hears when I pray. Oh, I will try to love him and serve him every day.

I suppose that we will leave before long and go to Winston [Wisenton] where *abretiam*[?] is and if so be the case, I can't tell when I will be home again but if it is the Lord's will I will see you all again on mercy's side of the grave and if we no more shall meet on earth again, I hope we will meet in Heaven where parting will be no more....

MR. JOHN ANDERSON

To Miss Eliza Woodward
Camp Delaware, Ohio,
Co. A in haste.

Camp Long Island, South Carolina
January the 25th, 1864

Dear Miss,

... I was this forenoon out with a spy glass and could see the Rebels going to and fro. It looks like a fiery path from here to Charleston to travel. The Rebels are very saucy. They hollered over to our men the other morning and said "You Lincoln hirelings we are going to our breakfast and you fellows have salt beef and hard crackers." Oh, they were mistaken that time. Well, I have said about all I know. Well it is suppertime. I will bring my letter to a close. No more at present. I remain your most affectionate one,

Corporal GEORGE D. JONES
Company E, 55 Massachusetts Regiment

Folly Island, South Carolina
May 20th, 1864

Dear Friend,

... We were in Florida two months. We ran all the Rebels out and then returned back to Folly Island near Charleston where [we] were in camp last year. I don't think we will be here on this Island very long. When we leave here, we go the Army of Potomac where there will be a little more fighting to do. I don't think this war will last much longer. The way we are whipping the Rebs. They will have to give up....

RICHARD HENDRICK
to
Miss Elizabeth Woodward

Company E
55th Regiment
Massachusetts Volunteers

Camp near Petersburg, Va.
August 12, 1864

"Miss Woodward"

Dear Friend,

You have doubtless heard of the engagement in which our Regiment has been. We lost heavily something over 100 men and three officers killed on the field. One wounded and a prisoner. Our Captain was severely wounded and has since died of his wounds. He was a good officer and we miss him very much. I am glad to say I am safe without a scratch. When I look back to where we were placed, it seems as though it was a miracle that any of us was spared. The sights I then witnessed I never shall forget. We are now about a mile to the rear of the front lines. Although not out of range of the enemie's cannon. This afternoon there has been four or five of their solid shot that fell in our camp. Although no one was hurt....

"Yours respectfully"

GRANDERSON FIELDS

The presentation of colors by John M. Langston, the recruiting agent for the U.S. Colored Troops, Oberlin, Ohio, to the 5th U.S. Colored Troops at Camp Delaware, 1863.

Savannah, Georgia
December 31, 1864

Miss Elizabeth, dear friend,

. . . .

I have written to you since we were in the Big Battle. Our Regiment fought eight hours. There were 141 killed and wounded in our Regiment. We are at Savannah doing garrison in the Rebel fort. Savannah is a nice place. Some think bigger than Ripley. . . .

Sergeant RICHARD HENDRICK
to Miss Elizabeth Woodward

Decatur, Alabama
August 13, 1864

Dear Miss,

. . . the Yankees are fetching in the colored folks from the South as fast as they can. They brought in a big lot of them yesterday and a nice lot of cattle and sheep and mules and horses so no more at present. . . .

THOMAS BARD

NEGRO HEROES OF THE WAR

Among those who gained recognition by receiving the nation's highest tribute, the Congressional Medal of Honor, were some twenty Negroes. Among them were men who served with meritorious service in the United States Navy. At the conclusion of the Civil War, a total of 118,044 men had enlisted in the Navy. About one-fourth of these—29,511—were Negroes, and four of them were awarded the Navy Medal of Honor.

There were men such as Landsman Aaron Anderson, who served on board the *Wyandank* during an expedition up Mattox Creek in March, 1865. Anderson was under heavy fire from the enemy, yet performed his duties in the face of extreme danger. Robert Blake, an escaped slave, was serving on board the steam gunboat *Marblehead* off Legareville, South Carolina, when the enemy attacked from Johns Island. Blake, a gunner, was cited for carrying out his duties in such a manner that the enemy abandoned its position.

Another naval hero was John Lawson, who served on the flagship *Hartford*. Rather than go below deck for treatment of his wounds, Lawson stayed at his station and continued to carry out his duties throughout the battle. The fourth of these Negroes who were awarded the Navy Medal of Honor was Joachim Pease, who served as a seaman on board the U.S.S. *Kearsarge* in June of 1864, when she destroyed the *Alabama* off the coast of France. As loader of the number-two gun, Pease exhibited such bravery under fire that he was awarded his country's highest military honor.

There were sixteen Negro soldiers in the Union Army who received the Army Medal of Honor. In order to be awarded this medal, a man had to exhibit bravery and courage

JOHN LAWSON

above and beyond the call of duty and, also, had to be recommended for the medal by his commanding officer. In the case of many Negro soldiers who served in divisions where the commanding officer was not sympathetic to the use of colored soldiers, it was impossible for any brave deed to receive the mention deserved. This must have been at least a factor in the manner in which medals were awarded to Negro soldiers since eleven of the citations came as a result of one battle and only five from the remaining battles in which Negroes participated.

On September 29, 1864, at Chafin's Farm, Virginia, four Negro companies of colored troops representing the XVIII Division, under the command of General David Birney, began a two-day engagement with the enemy. One man, Powhatan Beaty of the 5th U.S. Colored Troops (U.S.C.T.), assumed command of his company after all of the officers had been killed or wounded. For his gallantry in this action, Beaty received the Army Medal of Honor.

Twelve others received the medal as a result of their bravery at Chafin's Farm; they included: Private William H. Barnes, 38th U.S.C.T.; First Sergeant James H. Bronson, 5th U.S.C.T.; Private James Gardiner, 36th U.S.C.T.; Sergeant Alfred B. Hilton, 4th U.S.C.T.; Sergeant Major Milton M. Holland, 5th U.S.C.T.; Corporal Miles James, 36th U.S.C.T.; First Sergeant Alexander Kelly, 6th U.S.C.T.; First Sergeant Robert Pinn, 5th U.S.C.T.; First Sergeant Edward Ratcliff, 38th U.S.C.T.; Private Charles Veal, 4th U.S.C.T.

The Virginia campaign also brought recognition to Sergeant Decatur Dorsey, who at Petersburg carried the colors of his regiment under enemy fire and bravely rallied the men to action. Also at Chafin's Farm in September, 1864, Sergeant James H. Harris earned his nation's highest honor for bravery in assaulting the enemy. At Deep Bottom, in July, 1864, Sergeant Major Thomas

Hawkins rescued his regimental colors; he later received the Medal of Honor for his bravery.

The feats of Sergeant William H. Carney at Fort Wagner, in July, 1863, have already been mentioned; he, too, received the Medal of Honor. Christian A. Fleetwood, Sergeant Major of the 4th U.S.C.T., also earned the Medal of Honor at Chafin's Farm. Later he was dishonorably discharged from the Army due to a mistake in the muster-roll. Fleetwood was, in fact, in the hospital at the time that he was reported missing from duty, and his dishonorable discharge was later revoked. [See pages 235–243.]

All of these men of color exhibited bravery beyond the ordinary call of military duty. They were courageous in battle and steadfast in their loyalty to the United States at a time when others of their race were subjected to servitude and humiliation in the slave states. The citations which have been included illustrate the manner in which these men received their country's highest military honor. It can be noted that several of these men assumed the leadership of their regiment upon the death of the commanding officer and gallantly led the men into battle. Although wounded, many continued to fight—for the freedom which would ultimately benefit others of their race.

NEGROES IN THE NORTH

Despite the need for workers, Negro laborers met many obstacles in obtaining work in Northern cities. White workers in several industrial centers opposed emancipation and immigration to the Northern states for fear of competition from colored workers. Illinois in 1862 had re-enacted legislation against Negro immigration. Proposals were made in the legislatures of New York, New Jersey, Pennsylvania and other states for legislation against Negro immigration, However, on April 16, 1863, the *New York Tribune* opposed such action on the ground that "there was no outcry from Northern laborers of having been deprived of employment because of the influx of Negroes and that the fear of influx was wholly imaginary."

Nevertheless, New York City longshoremen were offended by the employment of Negro strikebreakers in 1862, and the police were compelled to intervene. Similar disturbances took place in Chicago, Detroit, Cincinnati, Cleveland, Toledo and Boston, resulting from the practice of employing Negroes at lower wages to take the place of white workers, thus depressing the wages of these workers. Henry Ward Beecher found the opposition so great to Negro employment in the factories, shipyards and machine shops that he said, "The only chance for the colored man North nowadays is to wait and shave, and they are being driven from that as fast as possible."

Opposition to Negro laborers was evident in other cities. A public meeting of white workers at the Chicago packing and slaughterhouses in 1862 adopted the following resolution:

> Whereas, it has come to the knowledge of the meeting, that it is the intention of one or more of the packers to bring Negro labor into competition with that of white men for the purpose of reducing the wages of the latter to the lowest possible standards; Resolved, that we the packing men of the town of South Chicago, pledge ourselves not to work for any packer who will bring Negro labor into competition with our labor and further, Resolved, that if any member of this society should demean himself as to work in a packing house where Negro labor is employed, his name shall be stricken from the rolls of this society.

A similar protest was voiced by workers in Harrisburg, Pennsylvania. One claimed that Negroes would "steal the work and bread of honest Irish and Germans." There was another who said that, because of this competition with whites in the North, Negroes should direct "their route by the Southern Cross instead of the North Star."

A country blacksmith shop.

The freedmen who came North after being in slavery were reported by some to be inefficient workers. Undoubtedly, there was some truth in this statement because of their lack of experience in industrial work. But Negroes had been engaged in some skilled activities in the South, for all types of plantation work—including the operation of the cotton gins and mills—were performed primarily by Negroes. Many of them had saved their earnings and came into the Northern areas with funds at their disposal. Others were indolent and without any thought of working. The latter had been seen by some writers who concluded that this group comprised the entire Negro population, ignoring the fact that many different types of personality exist within every group.

With the announcement of freedom made to them, thousands of Negroes fled to the cities and to the North from their homes and plantation huts. Some were influenced by the spirit of adventure; others, by the desire to try out their new freedom. Reports of wages being paid to workers and better living conditions were further inducements. There was a disposition also among some of the former slaves to rove from place to place and to move from town to town. They came in large numbers to the District of Columbia and the border states.

The population growth in cities prompted the suggestion that the freedmen should be settled in the Northwest by allowing them to take advantage of the Homestead Act. Carl Schurz, a liberal German immigrant and former ambassador to Spain, was requested by President Johnson to visit the South and send a report to him concerning the possibility of this plan. Schurz proposed that the freedmen be used in the construction of the Pacific Railroad. An agent was sent to Washington, D.C., to obtain from one thousand to five thousand workers for the job. Calls for Negro workers came from other railroad and mining companies in West Virginia, Indiana and Illinois. The National Freedmen's Relief Association established an employment office

Negroes performed some skilled activities in the South, such as getting a tobacco hogshead ready for market.

which sent over three thousand Negroes into the Northern, Eastern and Western states.

Free Negroes in the North aided their fellows from the South in their search for work. In 1864, the Rhode Island Association of Freedmen began to offer work for freedmen from the South. This association found employment for small numbers in 1864; and by 1865, there were 210 men who had formerly served in the Rhode Island Colored Troops

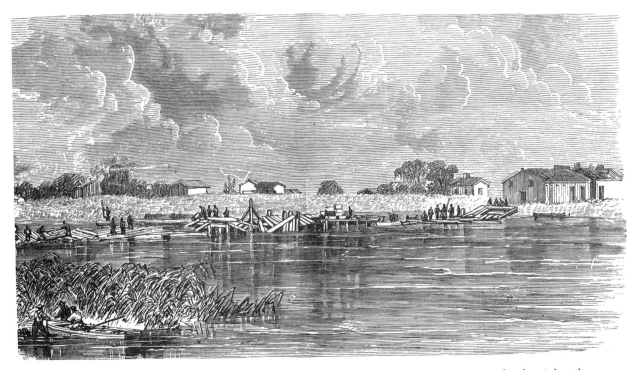

Many Negroes had to accept unskilled jobs along the rivers because of their inexperience with industrial work.

placed in employment opportunities. Contributions were received for the maintenance of the employment office from the students of Brown University, who sent fourteen dollars and fifty cents. Other individual donors sent larger amounts, so that about 900 freedmen eventually were able to obtain work and aid in Rhode Island.

INSTANCES OF SUCCESSFUL CAREERS

By 1865–66, the economic condition of the destitute part of the colored population had improved, and suffering and want had decreased markedly. Negroes worked at their trades as carpenters, masons, barbers, shoemakers and laborers. There were more than ten thousand Negro teamsters hauling supplies for the Army of the Potomac alone, and still larger numbers worked on the District of Columbia fortifications. Despite the obstacles of low wages, mistreatment and sullen indifference, there were many Negroes who were taking advantage of new opportunities to improve their lives.

Reports were made that the Negroes of Cincinnati, in 1865, owned a half-million dollars in taxable city property. There were six men among these who were worth over thirty thousand dollars each, one being worth about sixty thousand dollars. Robert Gorden, a coal merchant, had come to Cincinnati after the purchase of his freedom from slavery in Virginia. He expanded his business to include blacksmithing and the use of docks, river barges and delivery wagons for transportation. As a patriotic American, he purchased bonds and invested in real estate. Another prominent Negro was Peter H. Clark, the schoolteacher who became one of Cincinnati's most famous colored citizens during his distinguished career as a high school principal and civic leader.

In New York, Peter Vandyke, Robert Watson, J. M. Gloucester and J. Crosby were considered to be wealthy men. The Negroes

PETER H. CLARK

of New York had $775,000 invested in business which they conducted. They had invested $76,000 in Brooklyn and $5,000 in Williamsburg. They owned real estate which was unencumbered to the extent of $733,000 in New York, $276,000 in Brooklyn and $151,000 in Williamsburg.

Out of four thousand families in Philadelphia, three hundred were living in their own homes; and among them were those who were regarded as "rich men." One of these, Stephen Smith—a merchant—reportedly had assets of a half-million dollars.

George T. Downing, a wealthy caterer, was the man responsible for the abolition of segregated schools in Rhode Island. He was born in New York in 1819 and by the age of twenty-six had a successful catering business there. He conducted a summer place at Newport and moved to Providence in 1850. His business continued to succeed, so that in 1860 he financed the construction of a city block of business buildings. He continued to be an active abolitionist prior to the Civil War. At one time, he refused the offer of an introduction to President Millard Fillmore because this meant shaking hands, and he said that he was not willing to touch the hand which had signed the Fugitive Slave Act. Downing was a close friend of Senator Charles Sumner and was at Sumner's bedside at the time of his death.

On February 27, 1857, the *Providence Journal* gave notice of a movement to abolish separate schools and stated the *Journal's* opposition to any change. It was argued by the paper that white children would decline to sit beside colored children and the latter would not go where they were not wanted. Downing forthwith published a broadside stating that public schools were institutions supported by taxation and that Negroes were citizens and taxpayers. He concluded his publication with the following words:

> The colored people of today have different ideas and feelings from those they had twenty years ago. We wish our children to be educated with higher ideas, with a noble dignity. . . . We will struggle accordingly and mark our friends. This, with us, is a test matter. Politically, those for us will be our friends, those against us, we must know.

The movement was continued into 1859. A letter from colored ministers was sent to the *Journal,* but it was not published. It was then sent to another paper, the *Daily Post.* It argued against the proposal that, if colored schools were abolished, then colored churches should also be abolished; but the ministers said that all persons were welcome in their churches, which had been organized because Negroes were not welcome in the white churches.

The Committee on Education of the General Assembly of the state reported that a petition which had been signed by 388 state citizens favored no change and the majority of the committee agreed. The minority recommended that competent Negro students should be admitted to the high schools and that other schools should provide equal facilities. For the next five years, this school issue was continued, with Downing again sending petitions. In 1865, Negroes and whites submitted appeals to the Committee on Education in which they reported that the colored school at Bristol was below standard and should be abolished. The next year, 1866, colored citizens again petitioned; and the committee brought in a report declaring that segregated schools were established "by a prejudice stronger than the Constitution and stronger than justice" and that these schools should be abolished. On March 7, 1866, the General Assembly passed the following statute:

> In deciding upon application for admission to any school in the State, maintained wholly or in part at the public expense, no distinction shall be made on account of the race or color of the applicant.

This was a great victory for the colored citizens of Rhode Island. It was a victory due to the initiative and courage of George T. Downing, who began the struggle in the earlier decade. The triumph came after the Civil War and amidst postwar idealism.

Negroes were succeeding as capitalists in American society before, during and after the War. It should be evident that all Negroes did not begin their freedom in 1865 in the midst of poverty. There were nearly a half-million free Negroes in the United States in 1860, and many of these lived under fairly prosperous circumstances.

In skilled labor of the times, Negroes were maintaining their former places; and as they increased their mechanical skills and became more accomplished, prejudice against them subsided. They were blacksmiths, gunsmiths, cabinetmakers, plasterers, painters, shipbuilders, stone masons, bricklayers, pilots and engineers. In occupational skill and efficiency, they compared favorably with the best white mechanics. Barbering was one of the businesses which was a monopoly and

THE COLORED SCHOOL QUESTION.

HONORED SIR: The anxiety of a father, who loves his seven children, is my apology for personally addressing you. You are soon to decide whether the rights and feelings of my God given little ones shall be cared for in law. You are soon to decide whether they shall grow up in your midst with manly and untrammeled, or with depressed, dejected feelings. A great responsibility is involved. I know that you have it in your heart to do them justice. By the progress going on all around us in the land; by the love you cherish for your children as a parent; by the Divine law, "do unto others as ye would have others do unto you"; by your hatred of slavery; as you would have your State relieved of its last, hateful lingering relic; by the prayer to an honest heart, from an earnest heart that would be manly, that would be fully endeared to the State, allow me most friendly, most beseechingly to appeal to you; to all that is generous and just in your nature; to entreat you not to regard the unholy prejudice against color which was triumphant when slavery was triumphant,—which should die with slavery. Disregard it; do, in the matter, what your heart and head tell you is just. Fear not the hue and cry now so blatant, with a view to defeat justice; it will submit to law and order in Rhode Island as a similar blatant policy submitted in Massachusetts under like circumstances. Relieve the State of troublesome, expensive agitation.

We have stood at your legislative halls beseeching justice for ten long years. Though sorely tried all this time; though stung with the conviction of being the subjects of injustice; though unjustly accused of being immoral and otherwise obnoxious, no one can charge us with having uttered an unkind word,—with a lack of due respect to a single person. We have waited patiently for JUSTICE. We believe that it will be given unto us now; that it has been reserved unto this General Assembly to unveil to us its beautiful, elevating features.

Our case is simple. Being acknowledged by the Constitution of the State as citizens and as equals, the fact of our being colored not being allowed in the Constitution to have any weight in judging of our rights and privileges as well as our burdens, should any local authority in the State be allowed to discriminate between us and other citizens in the matter of education because of our color, simply to gratify a prejudice which existed to favor slavery? This is the question. Is not such a distinction invidious; does it not amount to a civil incapacitation?

You have two reports before you. Both of them fully concede that we have just cause of complaint; that something should be done. One gives us bread, the other a stone. We say this with no unkind feeling. Allow me to explain. The chance to enjoy superior educational facilities is within our power if we have the means and will pay for them, but it is with *you* to say whether we shall be unjustly proscribed in the State;—to be proscribed at all is, with us, the principal consideration. The majority report *legalizes any local proscription that may be forced upon us.* Hence they have given us a stone, when we ask for bread. The local authorities who proscribe us have all along declared that they give us as good schools, &c., as they do others; but they, almost with the same breath, unconsciously contradict themselves. It is strange to me how they can say so in the light of facts. But this is not material to the issue. Even if we were willing to be proscribed, which we will not, *cannot* be, and the local authorities were left free to act in the matter, there is no assurance that they will act justly by us. Any one who will reflect must conclude that the spirit which would proscribe us to satisfy prejudice, would be blind when a disregard of our rights was in question; when partiality may be shown, and the power which would have weight to perpetuate this favoritism would have power to succumb to it, or remove any Commissioner who should attempt to act impartially in our case. *You have the power to secure us against injustice.*

If local authorities should act in good faith under the law proposed by the majority report, and should establish the required schools, calculate the enormous taxation which *we* and all, whether they have or not this prejudice unknown to the law, will be subjected to, simply to gratify a prejudice. The law proposes that the teachers, and every thing else connected with these proposed schools, shall be as good as the other schools. Let us try this proposition by my city, Newport. After the city shall have erected the necessary five school houses, with recitation rooms, all the costly incidentals of the same, with all the modern regard for conveniences, for ventilation, &c., true of Newport schools, contemplating a large outlay of money; and then a costly high school which will be needed;

with many expenses which I will not stop to mention ; not speaking of assistant teachers ; we would have to be taxed annually in addition to all of the above, at least five thousand dollars for principal teachers. For the colored schools, to be as good as the others, must have as good teachers as the others, who command the highest salaries. But if the colored children go into the present schools of their district the expense will not be as great as the present expense. Notice that the present schools can accommodate all of them. We protest against this proposition as tax-payers.

The Government at Washington ; the Western States, which have been disgraced with black laws on their statute books, are repealing them rapidly. Rhode Island is free from the disgrace, shall it now, as the proposition of the majority proposes, blot her fair name by enacting *for the first time in her history, a pro-slavery, black law,* making a distinction among its citizens ?

The Constitution of the State says that " It shall be the duty of the General Assembly to SECURE to the people the advantages and opportunities of education," without regard to color. Therefore we appeal to you, in view of your constitutional obligation *"to secure"* to us, a part of the people, the advantages and opportunities of education. *We are not secured therein ; the local authorities do as they please with us.* I speak in the name of the people I am identified with, they who will in every way that may lay in their power, politically and otherwise, be grateful for justice at your hands.

GEO. T. DOWNING.

NEWPORT, February 20, 1865.

We, the undersigned, colored citizens of the city of Newport, having been appointed a Committee by the colored people to urge their petition in behalf of equal and unproscribed school rights, do endorse the above letter, and further protest against the majority report. It will not satisfy us.

SILAS DICKENSON,
JAMES PALMER,
THOS. YOUNG,
CHAS. HARRIS,
JEFFERSON MORRISON,
JONAS ELIAS,
CHAS. MELLVILLE,
ISAAC RICE,
BARNEY G. BRYANT,
BENJAMIN BURTON,
COLLINS BURRILL,
ABRAHAM RICE.

brought colored barbers into close contact with a white patronage. Some of these barbers were beyond the age for soldiers and continued to ply their trade with assurance. This situation was descriptive of the nation's capital—particularly in Willard's Hotel—and of Richmond, Atlanta and New Orleans. In Cincinnati, there was Fountain Lewis, who conducted a barber shop for a select patronage. Grant, Lincoln and other famous men were "soothed into slumber by the rhythmic music of his scissors, or the magic touch of his razor." The barber shops were places of gossip, and it was possible for white customers to keep up with the happenings in Negro life through their visits to these shops.

THE FIRST NEGRO FIELD OFFICER

Among the outstanding individuals of the colored population who made contributions of significance to the war and postwar effort was Martin R. Delany of Wilberforce, Ohio. He was an active worker in the struggle for increased opportunities for Negro Americans. Born in Charleston, Virginia, educated in private schools, a graduate of Harvard Medical School, and later a practicing physician, he became editor, in association with Frederick Douglass, of the newspaper the *North Star* in Rochester, New York. A lecturer and traveler to Africa, he was described as "a man of fine talents and unusual ability."

In 1861, Delany proposed to President Mahan of Michigan College that a Corps d'Afrique be suggested to President Lincoln. He had been acting assistant agent in recruiting for the 54th Massachusetts Regiment in association with Charles L. Remond and Charles F. Langston. On the advice of the latter, he applied for appointment as army surgeon but received no reply. He then went to Cleveland, Ohio, and continued his recruiting activities. In the meantime, he had moved his family to Wilberforce, Ohio, in

MAJOR MARTIN R. DELANY

order to provide educational opportunities for his children.

On February 6, 1865, Delany went to Washington to try to gain an audience with President Lincoln. After repeated efforts, he was successful. In describing the interview, Delany said that he referred to the late proposal of the Confederates to make soldiers of Southern Negroes and the manner in which Northern Negroes could contribute to the defeat of the proposal. He said, "And I propose, as a most effective remedy to prevent enrollment of blacks in the rebel service, and induce them to run to, instead of from, the Union forces—the commissioning and promotion of black men, now in the army, according to merit."

President Lincoln regarded this effort of the Confederacy as a desperate measure. He said that the bottom of the enemy's resources could now be seen and they had drawn upon their last branch of resources in seeking Negroes to fight for them. Delany was sent by President Lincoln to Edwin Stanton, Secretary of War, and Colonel C. W. Foster, Assistant Adjutant General of Volunteers. A letter was prepared by Secretary Stanton informing Delany that he would be commissioned a major of infantry.

The following commission was the first of this rank offered to a colored field officer:

The Secretary of War of the United States of America

To all who shall see these presents, Greetings:

Know ye, that, reposing special trust, and confidence in the patriotism, valor, fidelity, and abilities of MARTIN R. DELANY, the President does hereby appoint him Major, in the One Hundred and Fourth Regiment of the United States Colored Troops, in the service of the United States, to rank as such from the day of his muster into service, by the duly appointed commissary of musters, for the command to which said regiment belongs.

He is therefore carefully and diligently to discharge the duty of Major by doing and performing all manner of things thereunto belonging. And I do strictly charge, and require, all officers and soldiers under his command to be obedient to his orders as Major. And he is to observe and follow such orders and directions, from time to time, as he shall receive from me or the future Secretary of War, or other superior officers set over him, according to the rules and discipline of war. This appointment to continue in force during the pleasure of the President for the time being.

Given under my hand at the War Department, in the City of Washington, D.C., this twenty-sixth day of February, in the year of our Lord one thousand eight hundred and sixty-five.

EDWIN M. STANTON
Secretary of War

Other letters concerning this appointment were as follows:

War Department, A. G. Office
Washington, Feb. 27, 1865

Brevet Major General R. Saxton, Supt. Recruitment and Organization of Colored Troops, Dept. of the South, Hilton Head, S.C.

General: I am directed by the Secretary of War to inform you that the bearer, Major M. R. Delany, U.S. Colored Troops, has been appointed for the purpose of aiding and assisting you in recruiting and organizing colored troops, and to carry out this object you will assign him to duty in the city of Charleston, S.C.

You will observe that the regiment to which Major Delany is appointed is not designated, although he has been mustered into service. You will cause Major Delany to be assigned to, and his name placed upon the rolls of, the first regiment of colored troops, you may organize, with his proper rank, not, however, with a view to his duty in such regiment.

I am also directed to say, that Major Delany has the entire confidence of the Department.

I have the honor to be, very respectfully,
Your obedient servant,

C. W. FOSTER
Assistant Adjutant General Volunteers

Adjutant General's Office
Washington, Feb. 27, 1865

Sir: I forward herewith your appointment of Major in the U.S. Colored Troops; your receipt and acceptance of which you will please acknowledge without delay, reporting at the same time your age and residence, when appointed, the state where born, and your full name correctly written. Fill up, subscribe, and return as soon as possible, the accompanying oath, duly and carefully executed.

You will report in person to Brevet Major General R. Saxton, Beaufort, South Carolina.

I am, sir, very respectfully,
Your obedient servant,

C. W. FOSTER
Assistant Adjutant General Volunteers

War Department, A. G. Office
Washington, D.C., Feb. 27, 1865

Captain Henry Ketellas, 15th U.S. Infantry, Commissary of Musters:

I am directed by the Secretary of War to instruct you to muster Major Martin R. Delany, U.S. Colored Troops, _____regiment into the service of the United States, for the period of three years, or during the war, as of this date.

Very respectfully, your obedient servant,

C. W. FOSTER
Assistant Adjutant General Volunteers

The freedmen's national monument to Abraham Lincoln.

THE FREEDMEN'S NATIONAL MONUMENT TO ABRAHAM LINCOLN

The freedmen's national monument to Abraham Lincoln bears the title "Emancipation" and rests on a granite pedestal in Lincoln Park in Washington, D.C. President Lincoln stands beside a monolith upon which there is a bust of George Washington in bas-relief. Lincoln holds in his right hand the Emancipation Proclamation; and his left is held over a slave, upon whom his eyes rest. The slave is beginning to rise from the earth, and from his limbs the shackles have just been broken. The figure of the slave is that of a powerful man whose muscles are hard and firm.

The figure of this slave is not from the sculptor's imagination. It is from life and is the figure of Archer Alexander—a fugitive slave who was befriended by the Eliot family of St. Louis, Missouri. At the beginning of the Civil War, Alexander was a slave in St. Charles County, Missouri, near St. Louis. Hearing of the approach of Union troops, who would have to pass over a bridge with supports sawed through, Alexander walked five miles to warn them of this Confederate trap.

After this brave act, Alexander fled to St. Louis. He was employed there by Dr. Eliot, who later helped him escape to Illinois. In 1869, in Florence, Italy, Dr. Eliot met Boston-born sculptor Thomas Ball. Later, when Ball was commissioned to do the monument, he was instructed to use the features of a real slave. Dr. Eliot provided him with a picture of Alexander, and thus a former slave was immortalized in stone.

Charlotte Scott, a freed woman of color from Virginia who lived in Marietta, Ohio, at the time of Lincoln's assassination, initiated the movement to erect this monument. When she heard of Lincoln's assassination, she brought five dollars—the first money earned by her in freedom—to her Unionist

Major Delany began immediately to contact colored men and to urge them to be prepared for "the event of a black army being organized, to be commanded by black officers." The ending of the War prevented the achievement of this objective. However, Major Delany went both north and south in pursuit of this purpose. He was described as "a full-blooded African, and it was rather a novel sight to see him appear as he did before his audiences dressed in full uniform." Major Delany called for volunteers at his meetings, and among those to enlist was the Reverend Bryant, pastor of the Negro Baptist Church in Xenia, Ohio.

Nine other colored officers reached the rank of major. Captain F. E. Dumas, a wealthy free Negro, organized a company of his own slaves as a part of the Louisiana Native Guard. He was promoted to major and commanded two companies in Mississippi. Dr. A. T. Augusta, a medical surgeon, was promoted to brevet lieutenant colonel on March 13, 1865, for his excellent work.

employer, William R. Rucker, asking that the proposal for a monument to Abraham Lincoln be brought to the attention of those in authority. The contribution was sent to General T. C. H. Smith, in command of the military district at St. Louis, Missouri. General Smith sent to James E. Yeatman of the Western Sanitary Commission the following letter:

St. Louis, April 26th, 1865

James E. Yeatman, Esq.:

My Dear Sir: A poor negro woman, of Marietta, Ohio, one of those made free by President Lincoln's proclamation, proposes that a monument to their dead friend be erected by the colored people of the United States. She has handed to a person in Marietta five dollars as her contribution for the purpose. Such a monument would have a history more grand and touching than any of which we have account. Would it not be well to take up this suggestion and make it known to the freedmen?

Yours truly,
T. C. H. SMITH

Mr. Yeatman, in compliance with General Smith's suggestion, published the letter with a card, stating that any persons desiring to contribute to a fund for such a purpose should know that the Western Sanitary Commission would receive the money and see that it was judiciously appropriated as intended. Many of the people freed by the War, especially the colored troops, gave as freely as their resources permitted. The publication of this communication brought many responses with references to contributions from colored soldiers:

Headquarters 70th U.S. Colored Infantry,
Rodney, Miss., May 30th, 1865

Brevet Major General J. W. Davidson,
Commanding District of Natchez, Miss.

General:

I have the honor to enclose the sum of two thousand nine hundred and forty-nine dollars and fifty cents as the amount collected, under your suggestion, for the purpose of erecting a monument to the memory of President Lincoln. Every dollar of this money has been subscribed by the black enlisted men of my regiment, which has only an aggregate of six hundred and eighty-three men. Much more might have been raised, but I cautioned the officers to check the noble generosity of my men rather than stimulate it. Allow me to add that the soldiers expect that the monument is to be built by black people's money exclusively. They feel deeply that the debt of gratitude they owe is large, and any thing they can do to keep his "memory green" will be done cheerfully and promptly.

If there is a monument built proportionate to the veneration with which the black people hold his memory, then its summit will be among the clouds—the first to catch the gleam and herald the approach of coming day, even as President Lincoln himself first proclaimed the first gleam as well as glorious light of universal freedom.

I am, general, most respectfully, your obedient servant,

W. C. EARLE,
Colonel 70th United States Colored Infantry

District of Natchez, May 21st, 1865

Hon. James E. Yeatman:

Upon seeing your suggestions in the *Democrat* I wrote to my colonels of colored troops and they are responding most nobly to the call. Farrar's regiment, 6th United States Heavy Artillery, sent some $4,700. The money here spoken of has been turned over to Major W. C. Lupton, Paymaster U.S.A., for you. Please acknowledge receipt through the Missouri *Democrat*. The idea is, that the monument shall be raised to Mr. Lincoln's memory at the national capital exclusively by the race he has set free.

Very truly yours,

J. W. DAVIDSON, Brevet Major-General

The word "Emancipation" is engraved upon the base of the monument. On the front, in bronze letters, is the following:

FREEDOM'S MEMORIAL

In grateful memory of **ABRAHAM LINCOLN**, this monument was erected by the Western Sanitary Commission of St. Louis, Mo., with funds contributed solely by emancipated citizens of the United States, declared free by his proclamation, January 1, A.D. 1863.

> The first contribution of $5.00 was made by Charlotte Scott, a freed woman of Virginia, being her first earnings in freedom, and consecrated by her suggestion and request, on the day she heard of President Lincoln's death, to build a monument to his memory.

On the reverse side of the monument is this inscription:

> And upon this act, sincerely believed to be an act of justice, warranted by the Constitution upon military necessity, I invoke the considerate judgment of mankind and the gracious favor of Almighty God.

Thomas Ball was paid seventeen thousand dollars for this sculptured group. The Federal government contributed three thousand dollars for the foundation of the pedestal. In a first design, the sculptor had conceived the slave kneeling in an entirely passive attitude, accepting without effort his emancipation from the emancipator. This concept was changed in the final design, so that the slave is rising to aid in his own emancipation and straining his muscles to break his own chains. This design was nearer to historical truth. The group was cast in bronze at the Royal Foundry in Munich, Germany.

Mr. Yeatman, in dedicating the freedmen's memorial monument on April 14, 1876, directed attention to Charlotte Scott's initial participation:

> Whatever of honor, whatever of glory belongs to this work, should be given to Charlotte Scott, the poor slave woman. Her offering of gratitude and love, like that of the widow's mite, will be remembered in heaven when the gifts of those rich in this world's goods shall have passed away and been forgotten.

The financial contributions that were made by Negroes throughout the nation were evidence of the gratitude of those who worked during the War to fulfill Lincoln's goal of reunification and to bring freedom to their race.

CHAPTER SEVEN

The Period of Transition

DURING the Civil War, a unique experiment was started at Port Royal in the South Carolina Sea Islands by Edward S. Philbrick, son of the long-time abolitionist Samuel Philbrick, a friend of William Lloyd Garrison. A native of Massachusetts and a graduate of Harvard College, young Philbrick was friendly with cotton manufacturers in the North, who were of the opinion that more cotton could be produced by free men than by slaves. In addition, he had adopted his father's concept of slavery as inhumane. With this background, Philbrick resolved to prove that Negro former slaves could be employed, economically and profitably, to farm cotton.

He interested Northern investors—among them John Murray Forbes, a Boston railroad magnate, and a number of his associates— to invest in the purchase of a Southern plantation for forty thousand dollars. With lands purchased at tax sales, he became the plantation supervisor and conducted the Port Royal experiment. A major purpose of this plan was to test the Negro's ability to produce as a free laborer.

Philbrick made a profit of five thousand dollars in 1862, only one third of his expectation; but in 1863, he reported making a net profit of eighty thousand dollars. Although his plan was somewhat limited because it tested only a relatively small number of Negroes in one specific area, it proved to be valuable. By the end of the experiment, one fact was evident—that Negroes worked harder in freedom than in bondage. The Negroes on Philbrick's plantation were paid specific amounts for their labor in the field based on the number of cotton bales they picked. After the cotton went to market, they received an additional sum for every pound. These remunerations were small, amounting to around five cents per bale and two and one-half cents per pound of cotton, but they were the first payments most of the former slaves had ever received for their labor.

A further outgrowth of the Philbrick experiment was an introduction to proprietorship for the newly freed Negroes. Each family was allotted a certain amount of garden space which was theirs to use as they pleased. Many of the colored people spent long hours laboring in their own plots and increased their incomes by selling the produce at nearby markets.

Negroes in the Sea Islands proved their worth as free laborers.

After a governmental investigation of this project in 1864, Philbrick sold off parcels of the land to Negroes and whites. The land was sold at five dollars per acre, considerably more than the original cost to Philbrick of one dollar per acre but considerably less than the current market price. The lands had been cultivated, fertilized and in some places drained, so that the soil was markedly improved during the period between purchase and resale.

The *Freedman's Journal,* in 1865, commented on the Negroes who took part in Philbrick's plan: "The Negroes of Port Royal, as all the world knows, and not even enemies will deny, have made wonderful progress in knowledge and comfort, in

The home of a free Negro family.

manners and morals. They are self-support-ing; they are prosperous; they are valuable producers."

THE STRUGGLE FOR EQUAL RIGHTS

The passage of the Thirteenth Amend-ment had assured the Negroes of their free-dom from slavery. After the Civil War, the land provision section of the Freedmen's Bureau Act guaranteed Negroes access to economic opportunity by promising them free land. There were, in the South, large sections of uncultivated land which were to be opened to the former slaves for the purpose of settle-ment and farming. Those Negroes who had participated in the early experiments in the Sea Islands of South Carolina had proved themselves capable of establishing success-ful enterprises which would afford economic security. It was hoped that other freedmen in various parts of the South would follow their example.

The freedmen did not restrict themselves to economic problems as the War ap-proached its end. They lifted their united voices to reach the nation's capital with cries for the rights of citizenship and for equal opportunity in all areas of American life. They sought mutual protection and self-help through meetings, conventions and church gatherings throughout the South. Experience with slave owners had left its mark on most Negroes; and, fearful of being used as the tools of Northern groups seeking to punish Southern leaders, the ex-slaves realized they must seek allies and press for what was promised them as free men.

In the South, during the latter part of 1865, the state governments were composed of many of the same men who had piloted their states as members of the Confederacy. Negroes, therefore, felt an urgent need to organize to protect their goals as free men and to secure the reforms promised them by the Federal government. The great majority of Southern Negroes lived in rural areas and had received little or no educa-tion before their emancipation. They were not oblivious of the threats of a united aristocracy in the South, but their energies were engaged in the basic problems of sur-vival in freedom; and so the leadership of the freedmen was assumed by those men who were more urbane and better educated in the school of political life.

Among these early post-War leaders were men who would emerge later as leaders of their race on the national scene. For the present, in 1865, they were grappling with the problems of freedom while shadowbox-ing an enemy not yet in complete control of the governments of the various Southern states. The Southern aristocracy, strongly united in an attempt to regain control of Southern political life, already displayed a disdain of the Negro as a fellow country-man and a determination to destroy his new

ROBERT BROWN ELLIOTT

ROBERT C. DeLARGE

freedom. The names of Robert Brown Elliott, Robert C. DeLarge, Francis L. Cardozo, Richard H. Cain and Martin R. Delany are interwoven in the chronicles of Negro participation in American history; yet one of their most important contributions was their initial effort in this period to organize the colored people—both those who had long been free and those who had been freed by the War—for participation as American citizens.

In September, 1865, a group of Negroes met on St. Helena in the Sea Islands to protest the passage of the Black Codes which had been adopted in some Southern states as a means of subordinating the ex-bondsmen to a status not dissimilar to that which they had known in slavery. These residents of the island drew up a set of resolutions directed to the state legislature in which they referred to the Declaration of Independence as a basis for their rights.

1. *Resolved,* That we, the colored residents of St. Helena Island, do most respectfully petition the Convention about to be assembled at Columbia, on the 13th instant, to so alter and amend the present Constitution of this State as to give the right of suffrage to every man of the age of twenty-one years, without other qualifications than that required for the white citizens of this State.

2. *Resolved,* That, by the Declaration of Independence, we believe these are rights which cannot justly be denied us, and we hope the Convention will do us full justice by recognizing them.

3. *Resolved,* That we will never cease our efforts to obtain, by all just and legal means, a full recognition of our rights as citizens of the United States and this Commonwealth.

4. *Resolved,* That, having heretofore shown our devotion to the Government, as well as our willingness to defend its Constitution and laws, therefore we trust that the members of the Convention will see the justice of allowing us a voice in the election of our rulers.

5. *Resolved,* That we believe the future peace and welfare of this State depends very materially upon the protection of the interests of the colored man, and can only be secured by the adoption of the sentiments embodied in the foregoing resolutions.

In November, 1865, another convention of Negroes assembled, and this time they addressed themselves more directly to the problem of the Black Codes. In a petition submitted to the South Carolina legislature, these men and women wrote a profound and moving letter which stated their sentiments and, at the same time, appealed for recognition as individual human beings rather than as property to be dealt with accordingly.

To the Honorable Senate and House of Representatives of the State of South Carolina in General Assembly met:
Gentlemen,

We the Colored People of the State of South Carolina, do humbly appeal to you for justice. The last four years of war have made great changes in our condition and relation to each other. We were previously either Slaves or if free still under the pressure of laws made in the interest and for the perpetuation of *Slavery....*

We ask that those laws that have been enacted that apply to us on account of Color, be repealed. We do not presume to dictate, but we appeal to your own Sense of justice and generosity. Why should we suffer this, is it because of the color an All Wise Creator has given us? Is it possible that the only reason for enacting such stringent laws for us is because our color is of a darker hue?

We feel assured, Gentlemen, that no valid reason can exist for the enactments and perpetuation of laws that have peculiar application to us. We are now free. We are all free, but we are still to an extent in your power— And we need not assure you with what deep concern we are watch[ing] *all* your deliberations, but especially those which have exclusive reference to us. . . .

The petition was duly received by the legislature of South Carolina and duly ignored. Negroes were not to find the road to equal rights free of pitfalls. The story in South Carolina is an example of what was occurring in nearly every Southern state as anti-Negro forces sought to regain control and force a return to the policies of the pre-Civil War period.

PRESIDENTIAL RECONSTRUCTION AND THE NEGRO

Because of the death of President Lincoln in the final days of the Civil War, historians can only speculate as to the policy he would have pursued regarding the condition of the newly freed slaves. In his initial steps in reconstituting Southern governments, Lincoln's actions and attitudes were lenient—he proposed not to punish but to restore order and harmony in the most expeditious manner. How his approach to restoration would have affected Negroes will never be known. It is safe to assume, however, that he was opposed to any plan that would allow the Federal government to dictate policy to the individual state governments.

It is of significance that Lincoln favored colonization. The closer the end of armed conflict appeared, the more Lincoln seemed inclined to meet the problems resulting

FRANCIS L. CARDOZO

from emancipation by removing the Negroes from the United States. In February, 1865, the President had been visited by a delegation of Southerners headed by Confederate Vice-President Alexander H. Stephens. When Lincoln was approached on the question of the Emancipation Proclamation and its effects on slavery when the War was over, his answer indicated that union was more important than the Negro. He stated that the Proclamation should be regarded as a war measure and that the issue of slavery would be one for each state to solve in its own way.

There is no doubt that Lincoln hoped that slavery would be abolished because of his personal dislike for the peculiar institution; but the fact remains that in 1865 he did not consider it within the scope of Federal power to abolish it in the states.

When the Thirteenth Amendment was passed in Congress, Lincoln supported it; but it was his opinion that the transition from slavery to freedom should be a gradual procedure. After several plans to colonize the freedman had failed, he studied various means of making this transition; and he seemed to be inclined toward a type of apprenticeship such as that tried by Great Britain and later practiced in Maryland. Lincoln suggested a system in which "the two races could gradually align themselves out of their old relation to each other, and both come out better prepared for the new."

Negroes were opposed to both colonization and apprenticeship—they wanted equality now. They appealed through every means available to them for their rights, insisting that these rights had been bestowed by the Constitution and that Negroes were not chattels to be shuttled back and forth as the political winds blew. Lincoln, however, was not able to bring down the curtain on injustice in one sweep because influential forces in his own party and in the nation were unable to agree on any set of solutions to the problems of the ex-slaves.

The sudden death of Lincoln resulted in even more ambivalent policies toward the freed Negroes. Upon assuming the office of President, Andrew Johnson brought with him his early origins in Tennessee as a Jacksonian Democrat. A product of the "common people," Johnson both disliked and mistrusted the Southern aristocracy. In addition, although Johnson had originally been poor, his tailoring business flourished, and he eventually became a slave owner.

Like Lincoln, Johnson initially favored colonization for Negroes. Unlike Lincoln, Johnson did not feel that he was his brothers' keeper. Once, in offering a prayer for the common man, Johnson had stated: "I wish to God every head of a family in the United States had one slave to take the drudgery and menial service off his family."

Lincoln and Johnson both had been born in slaveholding states. Both had been relatively poor in their youths. Both were ambitious. But here the comparison wanes. While maturity and success led Lincoln toward humanitarian goals, Johnson, contemptuous of the planter class of the South yet envious of the type of culture these people enjoyed, became increasingly driven by ambition.

Upon ascending to the Presidency, at first it appeared that Johnson was closely aligned to the Republican members of Congress who wished to punish the South and at the same time aid the freedmen. For, although Johnson was a Democrat, he had been elected as a "War Democrat," or one who supported the Civil War as a means to restore the Union. It soon became evident, however, that the influence of his Southern background and old-line Democratic party ties would prevent him from carrying out the policies which had been established by the Lincoln administration.

The majority of the members of Congress, led by Thaddeus Stevens and Charles Sumner, were not only anxious to punish the South and prevent further rebellion but also felt a duty to aid the newly freed Negroes.

THADDEUS STEVENS

The lobby of the House of Representatives during passage of the Civil Rights Bill.

Johnson, however, was becoming more sympathetic to the Southerners who had regained control of their state governments and less concerned with the provision of equal rights for Negroes. Hostility developed rapidly between the President and Congress as Johnson became increasingly lenient toward the South; and Reconstruction of the South became a cause of repeated battles in the Capitol.

As the year 1865 passed, Johnson became a tool of the Southern aristocracy he had so long held in disdain. Visited by many Southern delegates, no doubt he was flattered that the very people whom he had secretly envied and disliked were now forced to come to him for favors. By the end of the year, it was evident that Johnson's attitude toward the South and the Negro had changed. Whereas before he had appeared to agree with men like Stevens and Sumner, he finally was no longer interested in their views, or those of any of the abolitionists, regarding policies to be pursued.

In his First Annual Message to Congress, in December, 1865, Johnson said he would not recommend suffrage qualifications to the Southern states since the state governments had already taken this action. An awareness in Congress of Johnson's new attitude led that body to create its Joint Committee of Fifteen to report on conditions of the former Confederate states and their right to representation in Congress.

CIVIL RIGHTS

When President Johnson allowed state governments in the South to be rebuilt on the pre-Civil War foundations, Congress, fearful that the colored people would be deprived of the full benefits of their newly gained freedom, decided to act on the question of civil rights for Negroes. The Civil Rights Act, passed by Congress in March, 1866, was designed to protect the freedmen from the state laws that sanctioned economic and social discrimination.

Johnson vetoed the bill, charging that it was an encroachment upon the powers of the state governments. On April 6, 1866, the Civil Rights Act was passed over his veto. Because the Dred Scott decision had declared that Negroes were not citizens, the Civil Rights Act was considered necessary in order to provide them with this right. Following is the first section of the act:

An Act to protect all Persons in the United States in their Civil Rights, and furnish the Means of their Vindication

SECTION 1. *Be it enacted,* That all persons born in the United States and not subject to any foreign power, excluding Indians not taxed, are hereby declared to be citizens of the United States; and such citizens, of every race and color, without regard to any previous condition of slavery or involuntary servitude, except as a punishment for crime whereof the party shall have been duly convicted, shall have the same right, in every State and Territory in the United States, to make and enforce contracts, to sue, be parties, and give evidence, to inherit, purchase, lease, sell, hold, and convey real and personal property, and to full and equal benefit of all laws and proceedings for the security of persons and property, as is enjoyed by white citizens, and shall be subject to like punishment, pains, and penalties, and to none other, any law, statute, . . . regulation, or custom, to the contrary notwithstanding.

In explaining his veto of this act, President Johnson simply stated that there were provisions which he could not "approve consistently with my sense of duty to the whole people and my obligations to the Constitution of the United States." He said: "They establish for the security of the colored race safeguards which go infinitely beyond any that the general government has ever provided for the white race. In fact, the distinction of race and color is by the bill made to operate in favor of the colored and against the white race." He noted that the bill did not give to the classes of persons it would serve any status as citizens of states and that the power to confer the right of state citizenship was with the several states, just as the

SALMON P. CHASE

right to confer Federal citizenship was in the hands of Congress.

Congress passed the act over the President's veto, with more than a two-thirds plurality. However, President Johnson took no steps to implement the act. There remained in the Congress doubts as to the constitutionality of this act, and the provision defining citizenship was later incorporated into the Fourteenth Amendment. It is of interest that not one Democratic vote was cast for this bill in either the Senate or the House. Although the act was never implemented, its passage inaugurated the concept that the civil rights of an individual or a group were to be legally protected by national legislation.

This act was upheld at U.S. Circuit Court hearings, and approval was given to its constitutionality by Justice Swayne in the case of *United States* v. *Rhodes,* which involved the right of a colored woman to testify against a white man in the courts of Kentucky; and by Chief Justice Salmon P. Chase, in *Matter of*

Elizabeth Turner, which upheld the section of the Civil Rights Act declaring for "equal benefits of all laws" and found illegal the act by the legislature of Maryland apprenticing colored children under conditions more burdensome than those imposed on white apprentices.

During the first year after the War, other rights of Negro citizens were being affirmed. The right of the Negro lawyer to argue his cases before the United States Supreme Court was definitely settled through the efforts of Senator Charles Sumner. He presented John S. Rock, a Negro, for admission to the Court. A well-educated man who had practiced medicine and dentistry before beginning the study of law, Rock waited for the retirement of Justice Taney before attempting to gain recognition by the Supreme Court. He had written to a friend, "I suppose the old man lives out of spite." On February 1, 1865, the moment arrived, and Senator Sumner arose and addressed the bench: "May it please the Court, I move that John S. Rock, a member of the Supreme Court of the State of Massachusetts, be admitted to practice as a member of this Court." Chief Justice Chase, who was presiding, nodded his head in assent, and Rock was admitted—the first of his color to practice before the highest court of the nation. The significance of Rock's admission to practice before the Supreme Court is obvious when it is recalled that, a decade before, the Taney Court had rendered the Dred Scott decision, which said that Negroes had "no rights which the white man was bound to respect."

The admission of John S. Rock to the United States Supreme Court.

The right of Negro participation in jury trials had been under question even before the Civil War because, prior to that time, no Federal constitutional provision prevented a state from excluding Negroes from jury duty. But, in 1867 in the North Carolina District Court, Chief Justice Chase instructed the marshal to summon Negroes, as well as whites, to serve on juries.

Ironically, the first interracial jury to be empanelled in a Federal court was the one selected to try Jefferson Davis. The former President of the Confederacy was arraigned in the circuit court at Richmond, with a hearing scheduled for May 10, 1867. Davis was charged with treason against the United States Government, but before actual trial proceedings were started, he was pardoned by the Federal government.

Twelve of the twenty-four jurors selected were Negroes. It would be interesting to speculate on how these Negro jurors would have decided Davis' fate. Admittedly, he was the highest governing official of the rebellious South and thus represented servitude and slavery to Negroes. However, were it not for Davis and the Southerners who provoked the War, the Negroes would not have been free in 1867 and would not have been serving on juries in Southern states.

THE RIGHT TO VOTE

The right of Negro Americans to vote had been defended by many individuals for decades. But this right had been restricted or denied by many states. In 1861, the constitutions of thirty of the thirty-four states in some way restricted voting by Negroes. Four states granted it—Vermont, New Hampshire, Massachusetts and New York. New York, however, required that Negro voters own, free and clear, property valued at a minimum of $250. Efforts to obtain the ballot for Negroes were defeated in other Northern states. During 1865, Connecticut,

Minnesota, Wisconsin and the Colorado Territory disapproved it.

Because of these prohibitions against Negro suffrage by individual states, a majority of the members in Congress favored granting suffrage through the Federal government. On December 5, 1865, two bills had been introduced in Congress granting Negro suffrage in the District of Columbia, and one of them eventually gained an affirmative vote. During its consideration, petitions were sent by white citizens of the District protesting the extension of the franchise to include colored citizens. In 1866, the mayor, Richard Wallack, sent a letter giving an opinion poll of the people of the District on Negro suffrage—6,591 were against it, and only 35 were for it.

However, a year later, on December 13, 1866, the Senate voted to approve the bill, with 32 yeas and 13 nays. The vote announcement brought heavy applause from the galleries, which had to be subdued by the presiding officer. On the following day, the House of Representatives voted its approval by 118 yeas and 46 nays, with 28 not voting. When the bill was passed in the House, there were three hundred Negroes in the galleries, whose applause added to the enthusiasm of the occasion. Many abolitionists saw this as the most significant occurrence since the ratification of the Thirteenth Amendment in January, 1865.

This bill granting the franchise to Negroes in the District of Columbia was vetoed by President Johnson but was passed over his veto on January 18, 1867, after an endeavor by Democrats to have a literacy test included was defeated. Hundreds of petitions to support the bill had been sent to the Congress by Negroes in the North and by abolitionists. A bill was also passed for Negro suffrage in the Territories.

Charles Sumner of Massachusetts and Thaddeus Stevens of Pennsylvania—both life-long champions of the cause of the oppressed—were leaders in the movement for equal rights for all citizens, regardless of color. Sumner declared in 1865 that there should be no bar of color either in the court-room or at the ballot box. He believed that "the ballot is a schoolmaster" and that through it the Negro would "be educated into the principles of government." Later that year, Congressman Stevens emphasized the need for suffrage extension, but he believed in economic opportunity as a necessary accompaniment to it. He asked, "How can republican institutions, free schools, free churches, free social intercourse exist in a mingled community of nabobs and serfs?"

In April, 1868, a Democratic convention in Charleston, South Carolina, resolved that the colored population was an "integral element of the body politic" and expressed its "willingness when we have the power to grant them, under proper qualifications, as to property and intelligence the right to vote." However, another convention, held on June 8, opposed this proposal; and it was clear that the Democrats were determined to shape their policy so as to capture the conservative vote.

Outside of Congress, public-spirited citizens like Wendell Phillips and Frederick Douglass advocated on similar grounds extending the right to vote to the nation's Negro men. Phillips stated, "Our philosophy of government since the Fourth of July, 1776, is that no class is safe, no freedom is real, no emancipation is effectual which does not place in the hands of the man himself the power to protect his own rights." Frederick Douglass, in the *New Era,* declared that practice would "lubricate the corroded hinges on which swing wide the portals of the temple of industry closed against the Northern colored man's right to labor and which can only be opened by the talismanic word of two syllables, viz: the ballot"; and he urged immediate, unconditional and universal enfranchisement of the black man in every state of the Union.

NEGRO PARTICIPATION IN GAINING SUFFRAGE

Negroes, both as individuals and in special conventions, requested suffrage by direct approaches and resolutions. They realized that the ballot would be their primary means of protecting their rights as free men. In October, 1864, a convention of colored men was held at Syracuse, New York. Those attending included Frederick Douglass, George Ruffin of Massachusetts, George T. Downing of Rhode Island, William Howard Day of New Jersey, Jonathan C. Gibbs of Florida, Peter H. Clark of Ohio, John M. Langston of Ohio and Henry Highland Garnet of New York, with a total of 140 delegates who came from eighteen states, including seven Southern ones. This national convention resolved:

> We want the elective franchise in all the States now in the Union and the same in all States as may come into the Union hereafter. We believe that the highest welfare of this great country will be found in erasing from its statute books all enactments discriminating in favor or against any class of its people, and by establishing one law for white and colored people alike . . . We claim to have fully earned the elective franchise; and that you, the American people, have virtually contracted an obligation to grant it, which has all the sanctions of justice, honor, and magnanimity, in favor of its prompt fulfillment. Are we good enough to use bullets, and not good enough to use ballots? May we defend rights in time of war, and yet be denied the exercise of those rights in time of peace? Are we citizens when the nation is in peril, and aliens when the nation is in safety? May we shed our blood under the star-spangled banner on the battlefield, and yet be debarred from marching under it to the ballot-box?

The National Equal Rights League was organized by this convention, with its objectives being severalfold: encouraging sound morality, education, temperance, frugality and industry and promoting everything that pertains to a well-ordered and dignified life. An appeal on these objectives by the executive

GEORGE RUFFIN

JOHN M. LANGSTON

board of the league appeared in the *Liberator,* December 23, 1864.

A petition from a group of Negroes in the District of Columbia declared: "Without the rights of suffrage, we are without protection, and liable to combinations of outrage. Petty officers of the law, respecting the source of power, will naturally defer to the one having a vote, and the partiality thus shown will work much to the disadvantage of the colored citizen." These colored men were capable citizens who could be expected to exercise their abilities effectively.

In 1865, numerous petitions requesting the suffrage were sent to President Johnson from meetings of Negroes in North Carolina, Virginia, Tennessee and Mississippi. A state convention of Negroes in South Carolina issued an appeal to the white inhabitants of the state urging them to grant Negroes equal rights of citizenship, the right to give testimony in courts, and recognition "as men."

Opposition to suffrage extension was strongly declared by many who felt that Ne-

groes were ignorant and unprepared to exercise the ballot and would thus be the easy prey of political masters who would use them as pawns to gain economic advantages. Their poverty was claimed to be an opportunity for corruption in politics. For such reasons, Tennessee declined in 1866 to extend the voting right to Negroes.

In the North, public opinion had to alter before Negro suffrage could be accepted. In 1867, Ohio and Kansas declined to extend to Negroes the right to vote; and in the next year, the Michigan legislature rejected its constitution because the word "white" was omitted from its suffrage clause. In New York, the limitations on Negro votes were permitted to remain, which meant only some Negroes could vote.

A delegation of prominent Negroes led by Frederick Douglass and George Downing sought an interview with President Johnson to urge his support of the plan for Negro suffrage. Johnson replied, "If I know myself, and the feelings of my own heart, they have

GEORGE DOWNING

been for the colored man." However, after stating that he had been a slaveholder and had bought slaves but had never sold one, he concluded that the freedmen with the vote would become pawns of the planters and would be used against the poor whites. He could see only one solution—the extensive movement of Negroes out of the South.

Douglass attempted to reply, but was interrupted by the President and hastened out of the office. Immediately afterward, one of Johnson's secretaries reported that the President made a rather coarse comment concerning this visit by a "darkey delegation." Douglass' reply to Johnson's impatience, which appeared in the *Washington Chronicle* on February 8, 1866, quipped that "men are whipped oftenest, who are whipped easiest" and that peace between the races could be maintained only by "a state of equal justice between all classes." Or, in other words, citizenship had to be a reality for both races

before any rapport could exist between them.

Subsequently, another position of Johnson on suffrage for Negroes, similar to the New York provision, was revealed in a private message which he sent to the provincial governor of Mississippi:

> If you could extend the elective franchise to all persons of color who can read the Constitution of the United States in English and write their names, and to all persons of color who own real estate valued at not less than two hundred and fifty dollars and pay taxes thereon, you would completely disarm the adversary and set an example the other States will follow.

THE FOURTEENTH AMENDMENT

Reports of mistreatment of Negroes, particularly in the New Orleans and Memphis riots of 1866, caused many Northerners to realize that the unrepentant South was determined to evade implementation of the Thirteenth Amendment. Congress had already expressed its doubts about the successful protection of Negro rights in the South by passing the Civil Rights Act of 1866.

Many members of Congress, however, feared that the constitutionality of this act was doubtful and believed that another Congress, at a later date, might annul the act. The Fourteenth Amendment, therefore, was an outgrowth of this civil rights legislation and was based on the necessity for defining citizenship in the Constitution.

The amendment was the result of several proposals presented to the Joint Committee of Fifteen on Reconstruction of the House of Representatives and to various committees of the Senate. On April 30, 1866, Thaddeus Stevens, as a member of the Committee on Reconstruction, introduced the joint resolution to amend the Constitution. He spoke of "a plan for rebuilding a shattered nation— not dissevered, yet shaken and riven" and of a people "educated in an error for a cen-

JOHN A. BINGHAM

tury on the subject of slavery." The joint resolution was modified and amended, and on June 8, 1866, it passed in the Senate by a vote of 37 to 11. Five days later, the House of Representatives passed the amendment by a vote of 120 to 32 and sent it to the states for ratification.

The first section of the Fourteenth Amendment—formulated by Representative John A. Bingham of Ohio, Chairman of the Judiciary Committee—included a definition of Federal citizenship and provided all citizens with equal protection of the laws. The second section dealt with the apportionment of representation so that additional representation in the Federal government could be secured by individual states through the grant of suffrage to Negroes. The third section disqualified all persons for Federal or state office who had participated in the rebellion. It was provided in the fourth section that the United States debt was valid but that the Confederate debt was void. And the fifth section gave to Congress the power of enforcement.

The Fourteenth Amendment opened the door for Negro suffrage and placed the doctrine of civil rights in the Constitution. The first part of the amendment declared its definition of citizenship in these words: "All persons born or naturalized in the United States and subject to the jurisdiction thereof, are citizens of the United States and of the State where they reside." A provision then followed forbidding a state from abridging the privileges and immunities of the United States without due process of law, or denying to any persons the equal protection of the law.

These references show that the makers of this amendment had in mind the protection of individual citizens. For a person to use the amendment for the protection of property or to uphold the right of corporations (as "legal persons") was then only a very remote consideration. But the original purpose of the Fourteenth Amendment, as conceived by John A. Bingham of Ohio and James F. Wilson of Iowa, two of its authors, was eventually submerged by subsequent Supreme Court interpretations which applied the amendment to corporations.

The Fourteenth Amendment had the purpose also of supporting the constitutionality of the Freedmen's Bureau and the Civil Rights Act, thus placing them beyond the repeal of the majorities in subsequent Congresses. The check placed upon the increase of representation by including Negroes without actually allowing their political participation was additional evidence of its intent. While suffrage was not bestowed directly, the denial of it by a state would lead to a proportionate reduction in representation in the Federal government.

Between 1866 and 1868, the Fourteenth Amendment was circulated in the various states for ratification. President Johnson had been opposed to the Fourteenth Amendment since its inception in Congress, and during the first year that it circulated the South for ratification, he advised the states not to ratify it. Whether from Presidential dictum or their own opposition to Negro citizenship, every Southern state with the exception of Tennessee was unwilling to accept the provisions and turned down the amendment.

In the main, the Northern and Western states accepted the amendment. Tennessee, after the disfranchisement of a majority of its voters, accepted it on July 19, 1866, and was restored to the Union on July 24, 1866. Congress insisted that the states ratify the amendment and, in addition, include provisions for Negro suffrage in their constitutions before being readmitted to the Union.

By 1868, the Northern states had ratified the amendment. However, New Jersey declined to delete the word "white" from its requirements; Maryland had given the suffrage only to whites; and Ohio had rejected the addition of Negroes to its group of voters.

JAMES F. WILSON

THE FOURTEENTH AMENDMENT

SECTION 1. All persons born or naturalized in the United States, and subject to the jurisdiction thereof, are citizens of the United States and of the State wherein they reside. No State shall make or enforce any law which shall abridge the privileges or immunities of citizens of the United States; nor shall any State deprive any person of life, liberty, or property, without due process of law; nor deny to any person within its jurisdiction the equal protection of the laws.

SECTION 2. Representatives shall be apportioned among the several States according to their respective numbers, counting the whole number of persons in each State, excluding Indians not taxed. But when the right to vote at any election for the choice of electors for President and Vice-President of the United States, Representatives in Congress, the executive and judicial officers of a State, or the members of the legislature thereof, is denied to any of the male inhabitants of such State, being twenty-one years of age, and citizens of the United States, or in any way abridged, except for participation in rebellion, or other crime, the basis of representation therein shall be reduced in the proportion which the number of such male citizens shall bear to the whole number of male citizens twenty-one years of age in such State.

SECTION 3. No person shall be a Senator or a Representative in Congress, or elector of President and Vice-President, or hold any office, civil or military, under the United States or under any State, who, having previously taken an oath as a member of Congress, or as an officer of the United States, or as a member of any State legislature, or as an executive or judicial officer of any State, to support the Constitution of the United States, shall have engaged in insurrection or rebellion against the same, or given aid or comfort to the enemies thereof. But Congress may, by vote of two-thirds of each house, remove such disability.

SECTION 4. The validity of the public debt of the United States, authorized by law including debts incurred for payment of pensions and bounties for services in suppressing insurrection or rebellion, shall not be questioned. But neither the United States nor any State shall assume or pay any debt or obligation incurred in aid of insurrection or rebellion against the United States, or any claim for the loss or emancipation for any slave; but all such debts, obligations, and claims shall be held illegal and void.

SECTION 5. The Congress shall have power to enforce, by appropriate legislation, the provisions of this article.

By these means, Northern states were rejecting Negro suffrage, while its advocates in Congress were insisting upon its establishment in the South. President Johnson opposed extending suffrage to Negroes, insisting they were "so utterly ignorant of public affairs that their voting can consist in nothing more than carrying a ballot to the place where they are directed to deposit it."

Nevertheless, New Jersey and Ohio rescinded their actions; Arkansas, Florida, North Carolina, Louisiana, South Carolina, Alabama and Georgia ratified the amendment between April and July, 1868, as a step toward readmission; and Massachusetts, Nebraska and Iowa also ratified it. Secretary of State Seward certified on July 28, 1868, that the required number of states (twenty-eight) had ratified the Fourteenth Amendment, "notwithstanding the subsequent resolutions of those states (New Jersey and Ohio) which purport to withdraw the consent of said states from such ratification. . . ." The next day, a concurrent resolution was adopted in the Senate without a formal vote; and the House adopted it by a vote of 136 to 31, enacting the Fourteenth Amendment to the Constitution of the United States.

In the summer of 1867, Frederick Douglass and Frances Ellen Watkins Harper spoke throughout the Southern states to further the interest of the amendment and suffrage. John M. Langston, who had been appointed an inspector of schools for the Freedmen's Bureau, also toured the South. These three were Republicans and urged the Negroes to vote for the Republican Party.

President Johnson, in July of 1867, offered to Frederick Douglass the appointment of commissioner of the Freedmen's Bureau, but his offer was rejected. Douglass said he would not "facilitate the removal of a man as just and good as General Howard and especially to place myself under any obligation to keep the peace with Andrew Johnson." This decision by Douglass was ap-

THEODORE TILTON

ROBERT PURVIS

proved by abolitionists, including Theodore Tilton, who remarked as follows: "The greatest black man in the nation did not consent to become the tool of the meanest white." The post was then offered to John M. Langston and Robert Purvis, each of whom rejected it. General Howard retained his position as the bureau's commissioner.

THE RECONSTRUCTION ACTS

During this early period of Reconstruction, internal discord developed rapidly, not only between the sections but also between the vested interests of industrial wealth and those of agricultural means, with the North seeking to establish a more binding tie with the West. In the South, the middle class and the poor whites became sharply divided. Tension was manifested in the border states as the new state administrations developed their opposition to the pre-Civil War Southern leadership.

The ability of the post-War leaders to remain in power depended upon their forming an effective alliance with the Negro voters. While they were hesitating to form such an alliance, the former Southern leadership gradually returned in the border states of Kentucky and West Virginia. As a result, Kentucky rejected both the Thirteenth and Fourteenth Amendments. West Virginia passed a law restricting the suffrage to white men; but this was later reversed.

After President Johnson had actively opposed the Fourteenth Amendment, Congress determined to curtail his authority by passing three bills that would subordinate his power to that of the legislature. The first Reconstruction Act was passed on March 2, 1867; the second on March 23, 1867; and the third, on July 19, 1867. These acts declared that, since legal governments did not exist in the Confederacy, the states concerned were to be divided into five military districts, each under military commanders. New conventions to draft state constitutions were ordered, and all Negroes over twenty-one years of age were to vote; but no white person could vote who could not pass the literacy test or who was disqualified as a former Confederate.

In this way, Confederate white disfranchisement accompanied Negro enfranchisement. After the ratification of the Fourteenth Amendment, the states would be entitled to send to Congress representatives who were to be chosen by a convention composed of delegates elected by the male citizens of "whatever race, color or previous condition."

In accordance with this legislation passed by Congress, new state conventions were held in 1867, 1868 and 1869, and constitutions were adopted conforming to the Reconstruction Acts. In 1868, seven states were admitted; and by 1870, the remaining three had also returned to the Union.

Negroes were active participants in electing representatives to the state conventions. It was estimated that in these areas there were 660,181 registered white voters and 703,459 Negro voters, as compared with a total of whites in 1860 of 721,191. Over 200,000 Southerners were disqualified to vote and hold elective office. Some Southerners were called "scalawags" because they accepted the cooperation and assistance of Negroes in their contests with the former Confederate leadership. In five states more Negroes were registered than whites, and in all of the states Southern convention representatives were elected by Negro voters.

Negroes were in the majority of voters in South Carolina, Alabama, Florida, Mississippi and Louisiana; and whites were in the majority in Virginia, North Carolina, Arkansas and Texas. In Georgia, the voting power was about equally divided between white and colored. Federal officials were appointed, along with Southerners, as registrars for the voters; and Negroes were placed on the boards of registrars in the states of Georgia, Alabama and Florida.

A Negro registrar checking voters at the poll.

THE ELECTION OF 1868

The Presidential election of 1868 gave additional victories to the Republicans. The Republican platform stated that Negro suffrage "was demanded by every consideration of public safety, of gratitude, and of justice." The Negro electorate divided its more than 500,000 votes between General Ulysses Grant, the nation's hero, and Horatio Seymour, the Democratic candidate, with about 450,000 votes for Grant and about 50,000 for Seymour. Since Grant's popular plurality was 305,456 in a vote of 3,015,071, the loss of the Negro vote would have turned him into a minority candidate. This vote was important to the Republican Party, and its leaders were aware of the Negro voters' power.

Several organizations and groups endeavored to influence the vote of the Negro electorate in 1868. Some of the former masters urged their Negroes to look to them for guidance, asserting that their best interests were in alliance with them and the Democratic Party; but the Negroes who were affected by these entreaties were too few to have any significant effect upon the election results.

The Republican Party was extolled by Union soldiers, Northern missionary teachers, abolitionists and Freedmen's Bureau officials. The freedmen listened most attentively to this small number of Northerners,

Negro voters casting their ballots.

ULYSSES GRANT

known in the South derisively as "carpet-baggers," and a smaller number of Southern whites who had supported voting rights for Negroes. Union Leagues and Royal Leagues were formed to aid the Republican Party, and rituals and sacred-rite clubs were adopted. These clubs had their origins in New York and Philadelphia and used methods in the South for influencing the Negro vote similar to those they had adopted for the same purpose with the labor vote in the North. Negroes became members and sent out their emissaries to encourage other Negroes to join the leagues.

One of the most influential and rabid organizations that came into being soon after the Civil War was the Ku Klux Klan, or the Invisible Empire, which had its beginning at Nashville, Tennessee, in 1867. In the same year, the Knights of the White Camelia were organized at New Orleans, Louisiana. These organizations were launched with the purpose of controlling Negroes and preserving white domination in the South. They increased their activities during the campaign of 1868 and spread in large numbers throughout the South.

Under designing leadership, these secret clubs began to terrorize Negroes, whipping, punishing and mutilating them, and burning schoolhouses, churches and mills. Negroes were subjected to fraud, bribery and intimidation. Armed bands roved the countryside warning Negroes who were migrating to the cities and other areas to return to their plantations and homes, as well as to remain away from the polls.

Aggressive acts were pursued by the Klan against peaceful citizens who had befriended the Negroes. Two of the purposes of these organizations were to keep Negroes away from the polls and to maintain a labor supply on the plantations through acts of coercion. Many Negroes went about their tasks unafraid; others were influenced by the garb and activities of the Klansmen, which included burning crosses during the night to threaten their victims. Many white Southerners objected to the irresponsible and criminal acts performed by the Klansmen, particularly as their terrorism grew to include other groups, such as Roman Catholics and Jews.

The South generally resented Negro participation in politics, although Negro domination was never an actual fact. The nation was thus divided, and its political leadership was unable to find a way of transition and adjustment which would restore the South, politically and economically, and succeed in giving Negroes an equal place in society.

This division led to actions of a serious nature in some places. The Georgia legislature voted to expel thirty-two colored members and replace them with whites. Similar disturbances were reported in other legislatures. In the period of transition between the end of the Civil War and the establishment of tight congressional control of Southern Reconstruction, there were several states with dual legislatures—one elected by the old-guard Southerners; a second, by the newly enfranchised freedmen. Many congressmen and abolitionists regarded this as typical of what would happen in other states if some preventive action were not taken.

THE SLAUGHTERHOUSE CASES

The Slaughterhouse cases, initiated in the courts in 1869 and heard by the Supreme Court in 1873, were major landmarks in constitutional law. In these cases, the Court for the first time rendered an interpretation of the Fourteenth Amendment. The issue in question was the constitutionality of an 1869 Louisiana statute that gave one corporation a twenty-five-year monopoly to slaughter animals. This legislation was entitled "An Act to Protect the Health of the City of New Orleans, to Locate the Stock Landings and Slaughter Houses and to Incorporate the Crescent City Livestock Landing and Slaughter House Company." Other butchers brought suits claiming that this act deprived them of equal protection, privileges and immunities as stated under the terms of the Fourteenth Amendment.

The highest tribunal in Louisiana upheld the statute, and the case was therefore appealed to the U.S. Supreme Court. By a vote of five to four, the Court decided that the Fourteenth Amendment was not intended to rob the states of their powers to define citizenship. Aside from being immediately concerned with one company's monopoly on slaughtering cattle, the Court's opinion was the first interpretation of this amendment on citizenship. What occurred as a result of this

THE UNITED STATES SUPREME COURT IN 1870
From left to right are Associate Justices D. Davis, N. H. Swayne, R. C. Grier and J. M. Wayne;
Chief Justice S. P. Chase; Associate Justices S. Nelson, N. Clifford, S. F. Miller and S. J. Field.

interpretation was a pronouncement that there were two categories of citizenship, Federal and state, with civil rights coming under state control.

NEGRO CONVENTIONS

Following the Civil War, local and state conventions of Negroes were assembled with the intent of using their collective action, through protests, to make known their requests for more democratic participation in government and equal work opportunities. There were several important conventions during 1865 and 1866. One was held at Nashville, Tennessee, in August, 1865, where resolutions were adopted requesting that Negroes be granted equal citizenship.

In a convention at Raleigh, North Carolina, in September, 1865, petitions were presented by the members asking for adequate wages in employment, better educational facilities and repeal of the Black Codes. A meeting at Charleston, South Carolina, in November, 1865, brought forth the declaration that, "If the ignorant white man is allowed to vote, then the ignorant colored man shall be allowed to vote also."

Petitions were sent to the state legislatures and to the United States Congress concerning jury trials, the suffrage, the distribution of land, the rights of free press, educational opportunities and the payment of wages for work performed. A convention in Indianapolis, Indiana, in October, 1865, extolled the part played by colored soldiers in the War and urged "equal rights with other men before the law." In 1866, a convention in Indianapolis declared:

> But while we claim that we are equally as intelligent as thousands of other citizens of the states who do vote, we hold that virtue and patriotism are more essential qualifications in the voter than intelligence. If we had virtue and intelligence enough to fight on the right side, certainly we will not vote on the wrong side.

A convention at Augusta, Georgia, on January 10, 1866, formed the Georgia Equal Rights Association, which was concerned with both political and economic rights. This convention adopted a petition to the Georgia legislature declaring:

> Notwithstanding, we are repeatedly told that the party who freed us, done so, upon the grounds of military necessity and not from philanthropic considerations. But we are not concerned about the means, we gratefully accept the result and accord the honor to God. This much however you will subscribe to our credit. We never inaugurated a servile insurrection. We stayed peacefully at our homes and labored with our usual industry. While you were absent fighting in the field, though we knew our power at the same time, and would frequently speak of it. We knew, then, it was in our power to rise, fire your houses, burn your barns, railroads and discommode you in a thousand ways. So much so that we could have swept the country, like a fearful tornado. But we preferred then, as we do now, to wait on God, and, trust to the instincts of your humanity.
>
> Though it is impossible for us to remain indifferent spectators while you are harnessing the state with laws which must affect our destiny as a people for ages to come. This privilege was not allowed us during the War. We were forced into your service to throw up breast works, forts and fortifications, and do the work of pioneers. Under the guns of your enemy, where many of us in common with yourselves were killed. We thus relieved thousands of your men for the armed services of the field.

A national convention held in Washington, D.C., in January, 1869, was attended by 130 delegates, with Henry MacNeal Turner acting as the temporary chairman. Turner later yielded the chair to Frederick Douglass, who was subsequently elected president. Resolutions adopted at this convention dealt with education, suffrage, equal rights, Western lands, industry, thrift, mechanical pursuits, the policy of Congress on Reconstruction and opposition to colonization.

Turner, a native of South Carolina, came to this convention having had varied experi-

HENRY MacNEAL TURNER

ences in the South. He was licensed to preach in 1853 and served in that capacity as chaplain of the United States Colored Troops during 1863–1865. He was pastor of the Bethel A.M.E. Church in Baltimore, Maryland, when the city was threatened by an invasion of Confederate troops.

At that time, to prepare the city for defense, the police seized all able-bodied Negroes, including Turner, and forced them to assist in building the fortifications. Upon his seizure, Turner said to his captors: "Gentlemen, all that is necessary is to let us know that you want us, and you will have five thousand of us before sundown. All I want is somebody to preach for my people tomorrow morning, and here I am." On the next day, the churches were reported as deserted, with Negro males working on the breastworks. Turner's forthright actions were mainly responsible for this result.

These conventions and many others illustrated the actions of Negroes in taking their first steps in democratic action following emancipation. Conventions which had been held by Negroes prior to and throughout the War were indicative of their consciousness that in peace they would need to organize themselves to use the processes of the new democracy which they expected to possess.

It has been stated that the Negro, during his participation in political Reconstruction, failed to use the ballot intelligently and that his bungling and mishandling of this opportunity, through corruption and ignorance, led the South ultimately to take the vote away from him. This picture was heightened further by exaggerated accounts of Negro-controlled legislatures whose delegates from the cotton fields and the plantations supposedly had engaged in such expenditures and orgies that the white South arose in indignation, forcing an end to their buffoonery and travesty on the white man's civilization.

The majority of writers of American history of the Reconstruction period have repeated the testimony of biased witnesses and upheld the accusation of Negro misgovernment. But the facts of history disprove this opinion. Historians have neglected to chronicle the large economic contribution of Negroes to the South; misrepresented their role in the Civil War; distorted their participation in Reconstruction legislatures; and expounded on the differences between North and South so that whites and Negroes are misinformed about one another.

THE FIFTEENTH AMENDMENT

The most influential and prominent of the men who advocated Negro suffrage was Charles Sumner. On September 14, 1865, in a speech at Worcester, Massachusetts, Sumner spoke out against the prohibition of the franchise on the ground of race or color. Between the close of the War and the year 1868, this subject was bitterly debated. With newspapers taking sides either pro or con, they had a great influence on the opinions of the general public.

THE FIFTEENTH AMENDMENT.

On March 7, 1867, a joint resolution on the suffrage was introduced in the Senate by J. B. Henderson of Missouri. After three years, this bill, with alterations, became the Fifteenth Amendment.

In 1868, eleven amendments were introduced in Congress for the purpose of extending the ballot to Negroes. The victory of the Republican Party in the elections of that year, along with fear of the Democrats returning to power, resulted in some favorable action upon Negro suffrage. In the 1868 elections, exclusion of the former Confederate vote in the South demonstrated the possibility of Republican domination. An increase of the Southern white vote would have threatened Republican leadership in Washington. As a result, the Republicans strengthened their political position by reconstituting Southern state governments with Negro votes.

Some Democrats were not entirely opposed to the Negro vote, as was evident in the twenty-two Democratic conventions held in 1868: eleven considered Negro suffrage; ten failed to mention it in their platforms; and one approved it. The narrowness of Grant's majority indicated to the Republican Party the importance of splitting the Southern vote and increasing Negro suffrage.

On June 11, 1868, the House Judiciary Committee reported proposals for the Fifteenth Amendment. Lengthy debates ensued as efforts were made to amend the original version, but it was finally passed in the House on January 30, 1869, and sent to the Senate for approval. After passing both houses, the final draft of the amendment was recommended to the state legislatures on February 26, 1869, after this statement by General Grant: "I never could have believed that I should favor giving Negroes the right to vote, but that seems to me the only solution of our difficulty."

This amendment provided that the right of citizens to vote should not be denied or abridged by the United States or by any state on account of race, color or previous condition of servitude. It expressly prohibited racial discrimination in casting the ballot. The second part gave Congress the authority to enforce the amendment by appropriate legislation. On March 30, 1870, in a proclamation by the Secretary of State, it was declared that the amendment had been ratified with the approval of thirty-one of the thirty-seven states.

THE FIFTEENTH AMENDMENT

SECTION 1. The right of citizens of the United States to vote shall not be denied or abridged by the United States or by any State on account of race, color, or previous condition of servitude.

SECTION 2. The Congress shall have power to enforce this article by appropriate legislation.

When the ratification of this amendment was announced, President Grant in a special message described it as follows:

> A measure which makes at once four millions of people voters, who were heretofore declared by the highest tribunal in the land not citizens of the United States, nor eligible to become so, with the assertion that, "at the time of the Declaration of Independence, the opinion was fixed, and universal in the civilized portion of the white race, regarded as an axiom in morals as well as in politics, that black men had no rights which the white man was bound to respect," is indeed a measure of grander importance than any one act of its kind from the foundation of our free government to the present day.

On the adoption of the resolution by Congress, the American Anti-Slavery Society declared that this amendment was "the capstone and completion of our movement; the fulfillment of our pledge to the Negro race; since it secures to them equal political rights with the white race, or if any single right be still doubtful, places them in such circum-

A demonstration by the colored inhabitants of New York City in honor of the adoption of the Fifteenth Amendment.

stances that they can easily achieve it." Wendell Phillips declared, however, that the work of the society, even with the passage of the Fifteenth Amendment, was not finished. When the executive committee of the society met and voted to dissolve, Phillips observed: "We may break up our ranks, but we may not yet dismiss our care nor lessen our interest; while this generation lasts, it is probable the Negro will need the special sympathy of his friends."

Efforts to prevent Negroes from exercising the right of suffrage increased, and violence in some areas was reported by Federal agents. But Northern representatives in Congress and the friends of abolition remained undaunted in the face of this challenge. At the same time, Southerners were challenged to action by legislation which disfranchised them and enfranchised their former slaves.

For the purpose of enforcing this amendment, Congress enacted the Force Bill on May 31, 1870, which provided for the protection of the civil rights of all citizens and protection of their political privileges. Punishments under the bill ranged from a five-hundred-dollar fine and one-year imprisonment to a five-thousand-dollar fine and ten-year imprisonment. The power of the government was to be brought to bear upon those who were depriving the Negroes of their rights.

The Ku Klux Klan had become so active and notorious that, in 1870 and 1871, Congress passed the Enforcement Acts, which protected the Negro's right to vote. In 1871, also, Congress appointed a committee to investigate the Klan's activities. The committee's report, embracing twelve volumes, revealed the widespread violence and disorder which had developed in many areas of the South. The Enforcement Acts gave the President the power to suspend the writ of habeas corpus when public safety required it. The chief purpose was to give force to the Fourteenth and Fifteenth Amendments and to prevent infringement of the rights of citizens. But with so few troops in the South—about nineteen thousand—it was impossible for the President to enforce these acts.

Meanwhile, Southern political leaders had succeeded in arousing opposition to the Federal officials and undermining their work; as a result, these officials found their effectiveness so impaired that they had to either unite with the Southerners or leave that section of the country.

NEGRO ECONOMIC PARTICIPATION

The problem of economic advancement for Negroes was difficult to solve. One solution proposed to relieve the problem by distributing land confiscated from the former

WENDELL PHILLIPS

slaveholders to both Negro and white workers. Land had been occupied by the Federal troops in several areas, notably, Port Royal, South Carolina; New Orleans, Louisiana; and parts of Mississippi. Negroes who came within these areas were employed as laborers and tenants. General Sherman had issued an order on January 18, 1865, authorizing Negroes to occupy abandoned plantations on the Sea Islands. An act of Congress on June 21, 1866, declared that public lands in Alabama, Mississippi, Louisiana, Arkansas and Florida were open to colonization without reference to distinction of race.

Efforts were made to encourage freedmen to settle in these sections. But the return of the Confederates to their plantations in some cases resulted in the exodus of Negroes. Tenancy, sharecropping and the crop lien system developed rapidly as Negro agricultural workers, who were by far the largest group of Negro laborers, were induced to remain on the land. They worked for low wages—reportedly, seven dollars a month for male Negro workers and five dollars for women. Others received portions of the crop for their labor under a sharecropping plan.

The presence of the Federal armies prevented only a minority of the white people from further exploitation of the Negro workers. Hostility was manifested in some places, for conclusions had already been drawn by many plantation owners that free labor was a failure, even before it had been tried. Anti-Negro violence was reported in parts of South Carolina, Louisiana, Georgia, Alabama, Tennessee, Kentucky, Texas and Mississippi.

The relation between owners and workers depended primarily upon the confidence felt between the two groups. As a result of all this, Negroes began to migrate from many rural areas to urban centers and from the Southern states to the North. During this period, several propositions were left open to Negroes. They could take advantage of the Homestead Act and settle in the West; they

Migrating to Louisiana in search of paying labor.

Newsboys in Richmond, Virginia, dividing their profits.

Working in the cotton field.

Negro dock workers at Cairo, Illinois.

The carpenter.

Negroes who migrated to urban centers found work in establishments such as this tobacco factory in Lynchburg, Virginia.

Negroes working with a huge cotton press in Galveston, Texas.

Negro longshoremen at the coal wharf in Alexandria, Virginia.

could work on the construction of the Pacific Railroad; and they could seek employment through the offices of the mining companies which were opening in several large cities. In addition, Negro workers continued to compete for jobs on the nation's wharves in spite of protests and outbreaks of violence by white longshoremen.

The National Freedmen's Relief Association established employment offices, which sent over three thousand Negroes into the Northern, Eastern and Western states. Under its guidance, the economic condition of the freedmen continued to improve, and destitution gradually decreased. While low wages, fraud and indifference were still in evidence, many persisted in their economic efforts, raised their crops, marketed them and purchased additional land.

Negro workers in the cities showed the same progress. One writer described the situation in Richmond:

They drove the teams, made the mortar, carried the hods, excavated the old cellars or dug new ones, and sitting down amid the ruins broke the mortar from the old bricks and put them up in neat piles ready for use. There were also colored masons and carpenters employed on new buildings. I could not see but that these people worked just as industriously as the white laborers.

Groups of Negroes pooled their individual resources to organize businesses. One of the important corporations owned and operated by Negroes was the Chesapeake Marine Railroad and Dry Dock Company of Baltimore, Maryland. It was organized in 1865 under the leadership of Isaac Myers—a Negro ship caulker—and was capitalized at forty thousand dollars. It employed over three hundred Negro mechanics who had felt the competition of white caulkers. A shipyard was purchased and within five years was owned outright by this company. Docks for ships were built; railroads within the dock area were laid; furnaces and workshops were built. Business flourished for several years; but in 1877 profits began to decline, and it was forced to close in 1883.

At Kinston, North Carolina, in 1865, a company was organized by Negroes on the joint stock system for the purpose of purchasing homes and encouraging thrift. This organization was typical of such group enterprises in many urban and rural areas. Out of 4,880,000 colored persons in the United States, only 9,400 were receiving aid in 1870, and nine-tenths of these were in the South.

THE RECOGNITION OF HAITI AND LIBERIA

Another permanent outgrowth of the Civil War was the recognition of Haiti and Liberia as independent republics. In November, 1864, treaties were signed between the United States and the governments of Haiti and Liberia to ensure friendship and promote

ISAAC MYERS

commerce and navigation. President Lincoln's message to the 37th Congress, in 1861, recommended the recognition of the independence and sovereignty of these two republics, with the maintenance of a chargé d'affaires in each. William Lloyd Garrison said that the President's message was feeble and rambling and that he could find nothing in it to praise except the recommendation that the United States government recognize Haiti and Liberia.

Haiti had been the second government in the Western world (following the United States) to achieve its independence, doing so in 1804. Liberia had declared its independence in 1848, and both of these republics had successfully maintained self-government. England had recognized Haiti in 1825 and Liberia in 1848; and France had followed each time, recognizing Haiti in 1828 and Liberia in 1852.

On February 4, 1862, Senator Charles Sumner introduced a bill authorizing the President to receive diplomatic representatives from these republics. Since it was assumed that Negroes would be appointed to these posts, opposition developed, especially in the border states. Senator Garrett Davis of Kentucky said: "If a full-blooded Negro were sent in that capacity from either of the two countries, by the laws of nations, he could demand that he be received precisely on the same terms of equality with the white representatives from the powers on earth composed of white people."

Senator Saulsbury of Delaware also expressed his sentiments: "How fine it will look, after emancipating the slaves in the District, to welcome here at the White House an African, full-blooded, all gilded and belaced, dressed in court style, with wig and sword and tights and shoe-buckles and ribbons and spangles and many other adornments which African vanity will suggest."

Senator Sumner replied: "I content myself with a single remark. I have more than once

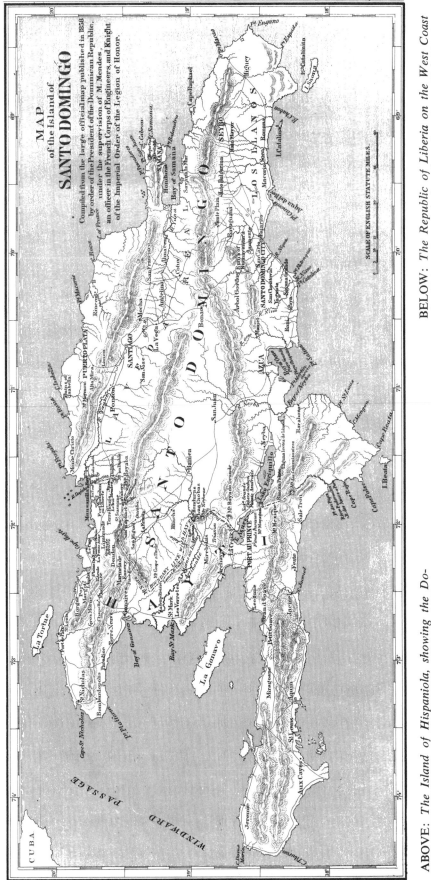

ABOVE: *The Island of Hispaniola, showing the Dominican Republic (formerly the Spanish colony Santo Domingo) and the Republic of Haiti.*

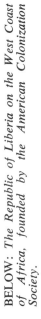

BELOW: *The Republic of Liberia on the West Coast of Africa, founded by the American Colonization Society.*

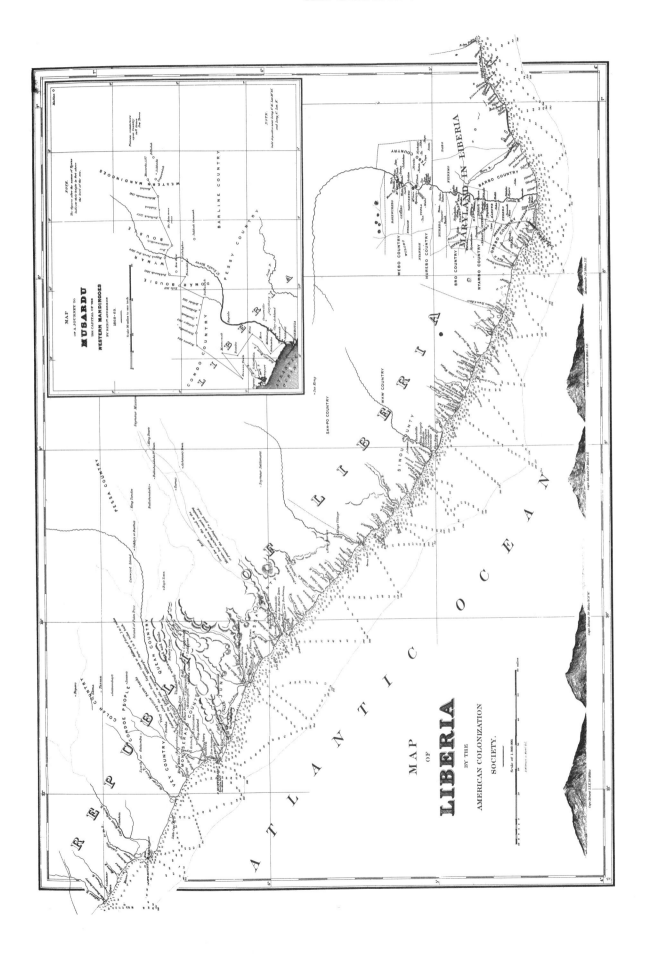

had the opportunity of meeting citizens of those republics and I say nothing more than truth when I add that I have found them so refined, and so full of self-respect that I am led to believe no one of them charged with a mission from his government will seek any society where he will not be entirely welcome." The measure passed in the Senate by a vote of thirty-two yeas to seven nays; and in the House, by a vote of eighty-six yeas to thirty-seven nays.

Although considerable turmoil had developed over the prospect of receiving Negro diplomats from these independent countries, it had not occurred to members of Congress that an American Negro would be eligible for an appointment to such a post from this country. The first three Presidential appointments made to Haiti were white men. But finally, in 1869, Ebenezer Don Carlos Bassett, a former student at Yale University, was appointed Minister to Haiti. J. Milton Turner of St. Louis, Missouri, was appointed as Minister to Liberia in 1871 after three white appointees had served short terms. In 1871, the Republic of Haiti expressed its gratitude to Senator Sumner by presenting him with a medal and authorizing the placing of his portrait in its Capitol.

Recognition was granted to these Negro countries on the eve of the termination of the slave system in the United States—sixty years after Haiti's declaration of independence and sixteen years after the Liberian declaration. Such actions had been opposed as long as the advocates of the slave system were active in determining the foreign policy of the United States. Therefore, this was one of the landmarks of the Negro's progress in the march of democracy.

A DECADE OF PROGRESS

In a ten-year period, from John Brown's raid to the appointment of a man of color as minister to a foreign country, progress for

EBENEZER DON CARLOS BASSETT

J. MILTON TURNER

Negroes in the United States became a reality. A war had been fought in which thousands gave their lives for the ultimate goal of freedom, and centuries of slavery and captivity were ended. Although the fighting ceased in 1865, the battle continued in Congress over the enactment of legislation that was the first attempt by those participating in the Federal government to secure civil rights for all Americans. The years 1866 through 1870 were as much a part of the Civil War as if the actual fighting had continued—only the scene of strife shifted, from the battlefields to the United States Congress.

During this span of years, Negroes were taking part in the political and economic struggles which occurred between North and South. Although legislation giving all citizens civil rights and the vote may have been an outgrowth of an angry North punishing the South, Negroes, through protest and resolution, were instrumental in gaining these rights. Contributions by Negroes in the struggle for freedom and gaining their inalienable rights as American citizens were immeasurable; and the stage was set for more participation by Negro Americans than at any previous time in the history of the nation.

SELECTED IMPORTANT DATES

1857—March 6	Dred Scott decision.	
1860—November 6	Abraham Lincoln elected.	
December 20	South Carolina seceded.	
1861—January 9	Mississippi seceded.	
January 10	Florida seceded.	
January 11	Alabama seceded.	
January 19	Georgia seceded.	
January 26	Louisiana seceded.	
February 1	Texas seceded.	
February 9	Convention at Montgomery adopted Confederate Constitution and elected Jefferson Davis and Alexander H. Stephens.	
February 18	Jefferson Davis inaugurated President and Alexander H. Stephens, Vice-President of the Confederacy.	
March 4	Abraham Lincoln inaugurated President of the United States.	
April 12	Fort Sumter attacked.	
April 15	President Lincoln issued proclamation for 75,000 volunteers.	
April 17	Virginia seceded.	
April 19	Proclamation by President Lincoln for a blockade of ports of the Confederacy.	
April 20	Maryland convention adopted resolutions declining to secede.	
May 6	Arkansas seceded.	
May 20	North Carolina seceded.	
May 24	General B. F. Butler declared slaves contraband of war.	
June 8	Tennessee seceded.	
July 21	First Battle of Bull Run. Union Army retreated.	
August 6	Congress passed the First Confiscation Act.	
August 30	General John C. Frémont issued proclamation of emancipation in Missouri.	
1862—January 19	Battle of Mill Springs, Kentucky.	
February 6	Fort Henry on Mississippi captured.	
February 8	General Burnside captured Roanoke Island, North Carolina.	
February 16	Fort Donelson on Cumberland River, Kentucky, captured by General Grant.	
February 22	Inauguration of Jefferson Davis as President and Alexander Stephens as Vice-President of the Confederacy.	

February 26	Union Army took Nashville, Tennessee.
March 6	President Lincoln proposed to Congress compensated emancipation.
March 9	*Merrimac* and *Monitor* in naval battle.
March 14	New Bern, North Carolina, captured by General Burnside.
April 6–7	Battle of Shiloh.
April 8	Island No. 10 on Mississippi captured.
April 10	Congress passed act offering compensated emancipation to the border slave states.
April 16	Emancipation of slaves in District of Columbia decreed by President Lincoln.
April 25	New Orleans surrendered.
May 1	General Butler occupied New Orleans.
May 3	Confederates evacuated Yorktown, Virginia.
May 5	Confederate defeat at Williamsburg, Virginia.
May 9	General David Hunter at Hilton Head, S. C., issued proclamation freeing slaves in Georgia, Florida and South Carolina.
May 9	Freedmen first armed as soldiers in the Union Army.
May 20	A treaty for the suppression of the African slave trade concluded between the United States and Great Britain was ratified.
May 25	Battle of Winchester, Virginia.
June 6	Memphis surrendered.
June 19	Congress passed an act prohibiting slavery in the Territories.
June 25–July 1	Seven Days' Battles near Richmond, Virginia.
July 17	Congress passed Second Confiscation Act, which freed the slaves of all those convicted of treason and those slaves who passed into the Union lines.
July 22	President Lincoln announced to his Cabinet his intention to issue an order "proclaiming the emancipation of all slaves within states remaining in insurrection on the First of January 1863."
August 22	General Butler called on free colored militia of Louisiana to enroll in Union Army.
August 25	War Department sanctioned recruitment of Negro soldiers by General Rufus Saxton.

SELECTED IMPORTANT DATES

August 29–30	Second Battle of Bull Run.	
September 6	General Lee invaded Maryland.	
September 17	Battle of Antietam. General Lee repulsed.	
September 22	Preliminary emancipation proclamation issued.	
October 28	1st Kansas Regiment engaged in battle in Bates County, Missouri.	
December 31	Battle of Murfreesboro, Tennessee, began.	
1863—January 1	Emancipation Proclamation issued by President Lincoln.	
May 2–5	Battle of Chancellorsville.	
May 10	The death of Stonewall Jackson, Confederate General.	
May 27	Negro troops engaged in Battle of Port Hudson, Louisiana.	
June 7	Negro troops in battle at Milliken's Bend, Mississippi.	
July 1–3	Battle of Gettysburg.	
July 4	Vicksburg surrendered.	
July 9	Port Hudson surrendered.	
July 18	54th Massachusetts Regiment stormed Fort Wagner, South Carolina.	
July 18	Colonel Robert Gould Shaw slain at Fort Wagner.	
August 21	President Davis proclaimed that Generals Hunter and Phelps should be treated as "outlaws" and "executed as felons" for their use of Negroes in battle.	
September 19–20	Battle of Chickamauga.	
November 23–25	Battle of Chattanooga.	
December 23	President Davis declared that slave soldiers and Federal officers should be turned over to the states on capture and treated according to the laws of the states.	
1864—February 20	Negro troops in Battle of Olustee, Florida.	
April 12	The Fort Pillow Massacre, where 238 Negro soldiers were killed.	
May 5–6	Battle of the Wilderness.	
May 8–19	Battle of Spotsylvania.	
June 3	Battle of Cold Harbor.	
June 13–18	General Grant made headquarters at City Point.	
June 27	Battle of Kenesaw Mountain.	

June 28	Fugitive Slave Acts of 1793 and 1850 repealed.
July 18	General Sherman at the Chattahoochee River began Atlanta march.
July 30	Battle of the Crater at Petersburg, Virginia, in which Negroes were participants.
August 5	Mobile Bay occupied by Admiral Farragut.
September 2	General Sherman occupied Atlanta.
November 7	Confederate President Davis approved employment of Negroes as soldiers.
November 8	Lincoln re-elected.
December 15–16	Battle of Nashville.
December 20	Savannah occupied by General Sherman's armies.
1865—January 11	General Robert E. Lee advised enlistment of Negroes as soldiers, with freedom at the end of the War.
February 3	Three commissioners for the Confederate States met with Lincoln and Seward at Hampton Roads.
February 18	General Sherman occupied Charleston, South Carolina.
February 20	Confederate Congress authorized Davis to raise sufficient troops "irrespective of color."
March 3	Freedmen's Bureau established.
March 23	General Sherman occupied Goldsboro, North Carolina, joining with General Schofield.
April 1	Battle of Five Forks.
April 2	General Grant entered Petersburg, Virginia.
April 3	Union Army entered Richmond.
April 9	Lee's surrender to General Grant at Appomattox Court House in Virginia.
April 14	President Lincoln assassinated.
April 26	General Sherman accepted surrender of General Johnston.
December 18	The Thirteenth Amendment to the Constitution was ratified.
1868—July 28	The Fourteenth Amendment to the Constitution was ratified.
1870—March 30	The Fifteenth Amendment to the Constitution was ratified.

PICTURE ALBUM

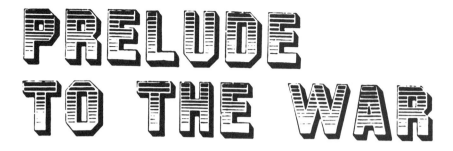

PRELUDE TO THE WAR

THE YEARS immediately prior to the Civil War were characterized by sectionalism, strife and transition. Some of the major issues during this period were the continuation of the slave trade and slavery, the John Brown raid, the election of Abraham Lincoln and threats of seccession. The War's prelude found an increasing number of Southern leaders determined to defend the institution of slavery against Northern aggression, while many Northern leaders were becoming more conscious of their commitment to equal opportunity for all Americans.

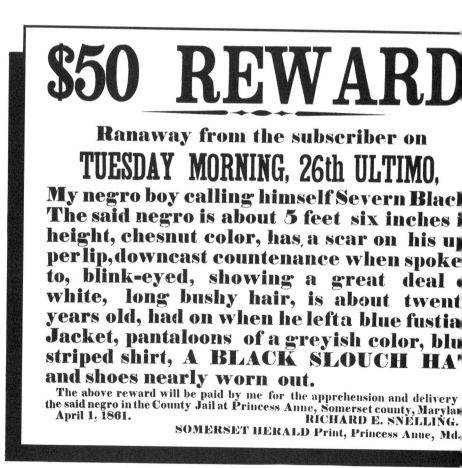

$50 REWARD

Ranaway from the subscriber on
TUESDAY MORNING, 26th ULTIMO,

My negro boy calling himself Severn Black
The said negro is about 5 feet six inches i
height, chesnut color, has, a scar on his up
per lip, downcast countenance when spoke
to, blink-eyed, showing a great deal
white, long bushy hair, is about twent
years old, had on when he left a blue fustia
Jacket, pantaloons of a greyish color, blu
striped shirt, **A BLACK SLOUCH HA**
and shoes nearly worn out.

The above reward will be paid by me for the apprehension and delivery
the said negro in the County Jail at Princess Anne, Somerset county, Maryla
April 1, 1861.   **RICHARD E. SNELLING.**
SOMERSET HERALD Print, Princess Anne, Md.

A slave pen in New Orleans before an auction.

The "Last Moments of John Brown" by Thomas Hovenden incorporates the legend that, on the way to the gallows, Brown stopped to kiss a Negro baby. John Greenleaf Whittier gives credence to this event in the following lines:

> John Brown of Ossawatomie, they led him out to die;
> And lo! a poor slave mother with her little child pressed high,
> Then the bold blue eye grew tender, and the old harsh face grew mild,
> As he stopped between the jeering ranks and kissed the Negro's child!

A portrait of John Brown as a young man.

"Last Moments of John Brown."

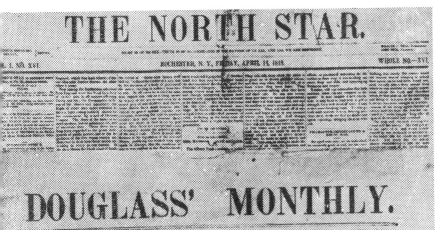

The printing and editorial office of Frederick Douglass, editor of the North Star.

The expulsion of Negroes and abolitionists from Tremont Temple in Boston, Massachusetts, on December 31, 1860.

At THE BEGINNING of the Civil War, in 1861, it was generally believed throughout the North that the War was being waged for the purpose of preserving the Union. Within a year of the attack on Fort Sumter, however, the issue of slavery had become dominant, and many who sought its abolition saw this struggle as a means to their end.

For the people of color, this conflict was their chance to prove themselves worthy of first-class citizenship. Initially, there was considerable disagreement about the use of Negro troops in the Union Army as Northern military and civilian leaders searched for a course of action that would end the War as rapidly as possible. By 1863, however, the War Department had authorized the enlistment of Negroes in the Union armies; and by the War's end, in 1865, United States Colored Troops had seen action in every theater of operation.

Negro recruits in the Union Army.

HARPER'S WEEKLY.

A JOURNAL OF CIVILIZATION

VOL. VII.—No. 324.]   NEW YORK, SATURDAY, MARCH 14, 1863.   [SINGLE COPIES SIX CENTS.
[$3.00 PER YEAR IN ADVANCE.

Entered according to Act of Congress, in the Year 1863, by Harper & Brothers, in the Clerk's Office of the District Court for the Southern District of New York.

Training Negro recruits for combat.

*Former slaves preparing to join the Union Army
at Aquia Creek, Virginia, February, 1863.*

Negro pickets on duty at Dutch Gap.

One of the "First Defenders."

The title of "First Defenders" was given to the five companies of Pennsylvania troops who marched through Baltimore, from the Bolton to the Camden Station, on the 18th of April, 1861,—a day before the mobbing of the "Sixth Massachusetts." Two companies were from Pottsville, one was from Lewistown, one from Reading and one from Allentown. Nicholas Biddle was connected with the first named. That night a pool of blood from his wound marked the spot where he lay on the Capitol floor. He was the first man wounded by a rebel in the war for the Union.

37th Congress of the United States, July 22, 1861.

RESOLVED, That the thanks of this House are due, and are hereby tendered to the five hundred and thirty soldiers from Pennsylvania, who passed through the mob of Baltimore, and reached Washington on the eighteenth of April last, for the defense of the National Capitol.

GALUSHA A. GROW,
Speaker of the House of Representatives.

The grave of Nick Biddle a Mecca should be
To pilgrims, who seek in this land of the free
The tombs of the lowly as well as the great
Who struggled for freedom in war or debate;
For there lies a brave man distinguished from all,
In that his veins furnished the first blood to fall
In war for the Union, when traitors assailed
Its brave "First Defenders," whose hearts
never quailed.

The eighteenth of April, eighteen sixty-one,
Was the day Nick Biddle his great honor won.
In Baltimore city, where riot ran high,
He stood by our banner to do or to die;
And onward, responsive to liberty's call,
The Capitol city to reach ere it fall,
Brave Biddle, with others as true and as brave,
Marched through the wild tempest the Nation to
save.

Their pathway is fearful, surrounded by foes,
Who strive in fierce madness their course to
oppose;
Who hurl threats and curses, defiant of law,
And think by such methods they may overawe
The gallant defenders, who, nevertheless,
Hold back their resentment as forward they
press,
And conscious of noble endeavor, despise
The flashing of weapons and traitorous eyes.

Behold now the crisis—the mob thirsts for
blood:—

It strikes down Nick Biddle and opens the
flood—
The torrents of crimson from hearts that are
true—
That shall deepen and widen, shall cleanse and
renew
The land of our fathers by slavery cursed;
The blood of Nick Biddle, yes, it is the first,
The patter of blood-drops presaging the storm
That will rage and destroy till the Nation reform.

How strange, too, it seems, that the Capitol floor,
Where slaveholders sat in the Congress of yore,
And forged for his kindred chains heavy to bear
To bind down the black man in endless despair,
Should be stained with his blood and thus sanctified,
Made sacred to freedom; through time to abide
A temple of justice, with every right
For all of the Nation, black, redmen and white.

The grave of Nick Biddle, though humble it be,
Is nobler by far in the sight of the free
Than tombs of those chieftains, whose sinful
crusade
Brought long years of mourning and count-
less graves made
In striving to fetter their black fellowmen,
And make of the Southland a vast prison-
pen;
Their cause was unholy but Biddle's was just,
And hosts of pure spirits watch over his
dust.

By CHAPLAIN JAS. M. GUTHRIE.

ALL RIGHTS RESERVED

The
GRAVE
of
NICK BIDDLE

IN MEMORY OF
NICHOLAS BIDDLE
died 2° Aug. 1876
AGE 80 YEARS

Nicholas Biddle, who was shot while his Pennsylvania company was on its way to defend the nation's capital, was known as the first man wounded by a Confederate in the Civil War.

Negro troops in the trenches.

Federal Negro pickets near Fernandina, Florida, defend themselves against Confederate snipers on the river banks.

The 2nd South Carolina Volunteers under the direction of Colonel Montgomery raid the rice plantations on the Combahee River in South Carolina.

The charge of a Negro regiment in battle.

General Sherman with his messenger, Thomas Laws.

In the distance a wagon train is seen leaving City Point, Virginia, General Grant's base of supplies, for the lines.

General Grant was walking on the dock at City Point, with the inevitable cigar in his mouth, when a Negro guard touched his arm, saying, "No smoking on the dock, sir." "Are these your orders?" said the General, looking up. "Yes, sir," replied the Negro, courteously but decisively. "Very good orders," said Grant, throwing the cigar into the water.

Negro scouts in action.

Negro soldiers hold Confederate Generals Edward Johnson and G. H. Stewart under guard.

Distribution of clothing to free Negroes at the headquarters of Vincent Collyer, Superintendent of the Poor, at New Bern, North Carolina.

William A. Jackson,
former coachman of Jefferson Davis.

Jeff Shields,
General Stonewall Jackson's
cook.

A medal of honor awarded to
U.S. Negro soldiers.

Presentation of colors to the 20th Regiment, United States Colored Troops, March 5, 1864.

An artist's conception of a joyous Negro regiment receiving colors.

Colored Union soldiers in a convalescent camp at Aiken's Landing.

Parade of the 20th Regiment, United States Colored Troops, in New York City.

On February 21, 1865, surrounded by a cheering crowd, the 55th Massachusetts Regiment entered Charleston, South Carolina.

Contrabands boarding a boat on the Mississippi River—going to the "promised land."

Slaves assisting the escape of Union soldiers.

Four score and seven years ago our fathers brought forth, upon this continent, a new nation, conceived in Liberty, and dedicated to the proposition that all men are created equal.

Now we are engaged in a great civil war, testing whether that nation, or any nation, so conceived, and so dedicated, can long endure. We are met here on a great battle-field of that war. We have come to dedicate a portion of it as a final resting place for those who here gave their lives that that nation might live. It is altogether fitting and proper that we should do this.

But in a larger sense we can not dedicate— we can not consecrate— we can not hallow this ground. The brave men, living and dead, who struggled here, have consecrated it far above our poor power to add or detract. The world will little note, nor long remember, what we say here, but can never forget what they did here. It is for us, the living, rather to be dedicated here to the unfinished work which they have, thus far, so nobly carried on. It is rather for us to be here dedicated to the great task remaining before us— that from these honored dead we take increased devotion to that cause for which they here gave the last full measure of devotion— that we here highly resolve that these dead shall not have died in vain; that this nation shall have a new birth of freedom; and that this government of the people, by the people, for the people, shall not perish from the earth.

The original manuscript of Abraham Lincoln's Gettysburg Address.

*General Ulysses S. Grant saluting General Robert E. Lee after the Confederate
surrender at the Court House at Appomattox, Virginia.*

Christian A. Fleetwood

*"Place on my grave a wreath
and in my hands a sword,
for I have been a soldier
in the great liberation war of humanity."*
— HEINE

Such a testimony could be written of Christian Fleetwood, Sergeant Major of the 4th United States Colored Infantry Volunteers, for he, too, fought in a war for liberation. Born in Baltimore, he graduated in 1858 from Ashmund Institute, now Lincoln University, and was inducted into the Union Army as a free citizen on or before April 19, 1861. He was appointed sergeant major on August 11, 1863.

At Chafin's Farm, Virginia, on September 29, 1864, when two color bearers had been shot down, Sergeant Fleetwood seized the colors and carried them nobly through the battle. For this valiant action, he was awarded the Medal of Honor Legion of the United States by Brevet Major General St. Clair A. Mulholland.

Card 1

A. 4. U.S.C.

Christian A. Fleetwood
Q.M.S. , Co. , 4 Reg't U.S.C. inf.

NOTATION.

Book mark: 2268. A. 1888.

Adjutant General's Office,

WAR DEPARTMENT,

Washington, Apr. 3, 1888.

Admitted to Slough gen. hosp. Alexandria, Va. Octo. 15, 1865 with intermittent fever and deserted Octo. 26, 1865 while on pass to Washington, D.C. This charge of desertion is removed. He absented himself without permission from hosp. Octo 26. 1865 and rejoined his command, date not known, and was present with it Oct. 31, 1865.

K Clogh Copyist.

(468)

Card 2

G. 4 U.S.C.T.

Christian A Fleetwood
Sgt. , Co. G, 4 Reg't U. S. Col'd Infantry.

Age 23 years.

Appears on

Company Muster-in Roll

of the organization named above. Roll dated Baltimore Md , Aug 11, 1863.

Muster-in to date Aug 11, 1863.

Joined for duty and enrolled:

When Aug 11 , 1863.*

Where Baltimore City *

Period 3 years.*

Remarks :

* Muster-in roll shows enrollment and muster-in of this company as of same date and place. See enrollment on subsequent card or cards.

Book mark: 2268-A(E13)-1888

Rose Copyist.

(356c)

Card 3

F. 4 U.S.C.T.

Christian A. Fleetwood
Rank Sergt Major 4 Reg't U. S. Col'd Infantry.

Appears on

Field and Staff Muster Roll

for May & June , 1865.

Present or absent Present

Stoppage, $ 100 for

Due Gov't, $ 100 for

Valuation of horse, $ 100

Valuation of horse equipments, $ 100

Remarks: Free on or before April 19, 1861. Appt't Sergt Major Aug 11, 1863. back pay due from date of enlistment to May 1st 1864. Charged for transportation 23 00

Book mark :

W Joiner Copyist.

(357)

Card 4

F. 4 U.S.C

Christian A Fleetwood
Rank Sgt Major, 4 Reg't U. S. Col'd In

Appears on

Field and Staff Muster-out Roll

of the organization named above. Roll Washington D.C. May 4, 18

Muster-out to date May 4, 18

Last paid to Feb 28, 18

Clothing account :

Last settled , 186 ; drawn since $

Due soldier $ 69 50 ; due U. S. $

Am't for cloth'g in kind or money adv'd $

Due U. S. for arms, equipments, &c., $

Bounty paid $ 100 ; due $ 110 100

Remarks: Free on or before April 19, 1861; Promoted from Sergt. Co. G S.O. 4th U.S.C.T. Aug 19/63 date Aug 11, 1863

Book mark: 1639. 1882. ass. Mar 15 Dec 2268.

Joiner Copyist.

(360)

Muster rolls with Sergeant Fleetwood's hospitalization, promotion and personal description.

Card 5

F. 4ᵡ U.S.C.T.

Christian A. Fleetwood
, Co. , 4ᵡ Reg't U. S. Col'd Inf.

Appears on

Regimental Descriptive Book

of the organization named above.

DESCRIPTION.

Age 23 years; height 5 feet 4 1/2 inches.

Complexion Brown

Eyes Blk ; hair Blk

Where born Baltimore Md

Occupation Clerk

ENLISTMENT.

When Aug 11 , 1863.

Where Baltimore

By whom Col. Birney ; term 3 y'rs.

Remarks: Promoted Sergeant Major by General Orders No. 17, 4th U.S.C. Birney Barracks Baltimore Md Aug 19 , 1863. Free born. Received Honorable mention in General orders No

J. Giles Copyist.

(383g)

Card 6

F. 4 U.S.C.T.

Christian A Fleetwood
Sgt. , Co. G, 4 Reg't U. S. Col'd Infantry.

Appears on

Company Muster Roll

for Aug 11 to 31 , 1863.

Joined for duty and enrolled :

When Aug 11 , 1863.*

Where Baltimore City *

Period 3 years.*

Present or absent Present

Stoppage, $ 100 for

Due Gov't $ 100 for

Remarks: Promoted Sgt Major Aug 19/63 by Regimental Order No 26.

* See enrollment on card from muster-in roll.

Book mark :

Rose Copyist.

(358c)

Card 7

F. 4 U.S.C.T.

Christian A. Fleetwood
Serg. , Co. G, 4 Reg't U. S. Col'd Infantry.

Appears on **Co. Muster-out Roll,** dated Washington D.C. May 4, 1866.

Muster-out to date , 186.

Last paid to , 186.

Clothing account :

Last settled , 186 ; drawn since $ 100

Due soldier $ 100 ; due U. S. $ 100

Am't for cloth'g in kind or money adv'd $ 100

Due U. S. for arms, equipments, &c., $ 100

Bounty paid $ 100 ; due $ 100

Remarks: Free on or before Apr 19/61 Appointed Serg Aug 11/63 Appointed Serg May Aug 19/63. Transferred

Book mark :

T A Johnson Copyist.

(361)

Card 8

F. 4 U.S.C

Christian A. Fleetwood
, Co. G, 4 Reg't U. S. Col

Appears on

Company Descriptive Book

of the organization named above.

DESCRIPTION.

Age 23 years ; height 5 feet 4 1/4

Complexion Brown

Eyes Black ; hair Black

Where born Baltimore Md

Occupation Clerk

ENLISTMENT.

When Aug 11 ,

Where Balt Md

By whom Col Birney ; term 3

Remarks: Appointed Sergt Major Aug 19/63 Regtl order No 17

E H Minnie Copyist.

(383g)

WAR DEPARTMENT,

Surgeon General's Office,

RECORD AND PENSION DIVISION,

Washington, D. C., *March 23*, 188*8*.

(TRANSCRIPT FROM RECORDS.)

It appears from the records filed in this Office that *C. A. Fleetwood, Sgt-Maj-4 U.S.C.T was admitted to Slough G.H. Alexandria, Va. Oct. 15.65 with Int. fever, and deserted Oct 26, 65 while on pass to Washington D.C.] no evidence of his return*

By order of the Surgeon General:

No. *492096.*

Chief Surgeon, U. S. Army

(108)

While hospitalized for intermittent fever, Sergeant Major Fleetwood left without official permission to return to his post, and a charge of desertion was placed on his record.

The erroneous charge of desertion was removed from his record on April 10, 1888.

2268- A- A. G. O. (E. B.), *1888.*

War Department,

ADJUTANT GENERAL'S OFFICE,

Washington, *April 10, 1888.*

To the Commissioner of Pensions.

Sir:

I have the honor to inform you that the charge of desertion of *Oct. 26, 1865*, standing against *Christian A. Fleetwood*, as *of Co. Sergeant Major, 4th U. Colt. Troops*, has been removed from his record in this office, as having been *erroneously made. He left Slough general hospital, Alexandria, Va., without permission, Oct. 26, 1865, and rejoined his regiment at Fort Slocum, D.C., on or about the same date.*

Very respectfully,

Your obedient servant,

Assistant Adjutant General.
(325)

No. of Pension Claim *unknown.*

Washington. D.C. March 12./88.

The Adjutant General U.S.A.

Washington. D.C.

Sir,

While serving as Sergeant Major of the 4th U.S.
Cold. Inft. I was stricken down by fever, on Saturday
Oct. 14./65. at "Soldier's Rest." (B. & O. R.R. Depot) Washington D.C., acquired in North Carolina, & was
sent to Hospital in Alexandria Va. Name of Hospital not now remembered, probably "L'Ouverture".
Monday Oct. 23/65. I requested the Surgeon in charge
to allow me to return to my regiment, which was
refused as he did not think me fit to be discharged.
Later in the day I managed to reach the street car, &
rode to the Ferry boat, came to Washington, and obtained
Conveyance to our Regtl. Hdgrs. then at Fort Slocum.
D.C. reporting to Lt. Col. Bournstein, then in command
and to Adjutant George Allen.

I am of the opinion that no Consolidated Mor-

ning Reports were at that time being made. Tri-monthly
reports were made however, and I am confident
that the Muster Rolls of Field & Staff for Sept. &
Oct./65. were made out by myself, and will
show me present at that time.

I have learned that the books of the Hospital
report me as a Deserter.

In view of the fact that I reported myself at
my Regtl. Hdgrs. on the same day on which I left
the hospital without leave, I respectfully beg
that the charge of desertion may be removed
to complete my military record, under the Act
of Congress, approved July 5, 84.

Very respectfully
Your Obdt. Servt.,
C.A. Fleetwood

War Dept. A.G.O.
Room 78. 4th Floor.

Fleetwood's letter to the Adjutant General explaining his absence and his application for removal of the charge of desertion.

Exy. D.

War Dept. A.G.O.
March 27, 1888.

Case of
Christian A. Fleetwood.
Sergt. Major. 4th U.S.C.T.
Application for removal of charge of
desertion
Presented by himself. [Clerk in A.G.O.]

He was enrolled and mustered in with
Co. G. Aug. 11, 1863, at Balto. Md. and is reported on rolls to Feb. 28, 1865, present.
Roll Mar. & April 1865, "absent" without remark.
Return for April. 1865 reports him "absent
sick."
On such rolls to August 31, 1865, present.
Surgeon Genl. U.S.A. reports him ad-
mitted to Slough G.H., Alexandria, Va. Oct.
15, 1865, with Int. fever, and deserted Oct.
26, 1865, while on pass to Washington, D.C.
Roll of F. & S. Sept. & Oct. 1865, "present" and so
reported on rolls to Feb. 28, 1866.
He was m.o. with H.C.L. May 4, 1866,
at Washington, D.C.
Regtl. Prescription Book shows him
treated for "Fever," Nov. 1 & 5. 1865.
No charge of desertion appears

(over)

against him on the records of his orgn.
No record of trial or order.

Under date of Washington, D.C., Mar.
12, 1888, soldier states that he was
stricken down by fever on Saturday,
Oct. 14, 1865. at Soldier's Rest, Washington,
D.C., and was sent to Hospt., Alexandria,
Va.; Monday, Oct. 23, 1865, asked the surgeon in charge to allow him to return to his regiment, which request was refused, as he did not think
him fit to be discharged; later in
the day, he managed to reach the
street cars and rode to the Ferry boat,
came to Washington, obtained a
conveyance, and reported at Head
Qrs of regiment, at Fort Slocum, D.C.,
to the Lt. Col. Comdg. & c. & c.

May charge of desertion of Oct. 26,
1865, on Hospital records be removed, and "left Hospl. without permission and rejoined his regiment" be
substituted?

Exy D.
W.G.S.   F.S.
            Lindsey, A.
                    Cl.

Letter of Sergeant Major Fleetwood to Assistant Adjutant General E. D. Townsend acknowledging receipt of the Medal of Honor.

In accordance with a congressional resolution changing the design of the Medal of Honor ribbon, Fleetwood applied for a new medal in 1907.

Application for Medal of Honor of New Design and for Rosette,

Under the provisions of the Act of Congress approved April 23, 1904, as modified by the Joint Resolution
approved February 27, 1907.

State of _District of Columbia_ } ss:
County of _Washington_

On this _twenty-fifth_ day of _March_, 1907, personally appeared before me,
a _Notary Public_ in and for the County and State aforesaid,
Christian A. Fleetwood, aged _Sixty-Six_ years, a resident
of _Washington D.C._, in the County of _____ and
State of _____, who, being duly sworn, declares that he is
Christian A. Fleetwood, the identical person of that name who was in the military service
of the United States as a member of Company _A_, in the _4th_ Regiment of _United States_
Colored Troops
[name of soldier] SERGEANT-MAJOR [If a general or staff officer, state grade or grades]
that a Congressional Medal of Honor was awarded him on or about the _Sixth_ day of _April 1865_,
at which time he was residing at _"In the Field"_, in the State of _North Carolina_;
that he received the Medal at _Goldsboro N.C._, on or about the _Fourteenth_ day
of _May 1865_; that the Medal was awarded him for _Saving the Regt'l Colors_
in action at _Chapin's Farm Va., September 29, 1864_;
[name of battle or other engagement] [date of battle of other engagement]
and is inscribed as follows: _"The Congress to Sergt Major Christian A. Fleetwood_
Fourth U.S. Colored Infy."
[here quote inscription in full, including name, organization and rank]

This declaration is made for the purpose of securing the Congressional Medal of Honor and the rosette provided for in the
Act of Congress approved April 23, 1904, as modified by the Joint Resolution approved February 27, 1907, and the applicant
desires that the new medal and the rosette be sent to him at No. _511_, _Tenth St. N.W. Tenth_
Street, in the _Branch_ of _A.G.O._, County of _War Department_,
State of _Washington D.C._

Christian A. Fleetwood
Signature of Applicant.

Also personally appeared before me _Charles R. Douglass_, aged _62_ years, now a resident
of the town of _City of Washington_, in the County of _Washington_ and State
District of Columbia, and _Hamilton S. Smith_, aged _49_ years, now a
resident of the town of _City of Washington_, in the County of _Washington_ and
State of _District of Columbia_, to me well known as credible persons, who, being duly sworn, declare that
they have been for _forty-three_ years, and _twenty-five_ years, respectively, personally acquainted
with the applicant hereinbefore named; that they _saw him sign his name_
[saw him sign his name or make his mark]
to the foregoing application; that they have every reason to believe that he is the identical person he herein represents himself to
be, and that the foregoing affidavit by him subscribed is correct and true. (1)

Signatures of witnesses: _Chas R Douglass_
Hamilton Smith
[OVER]

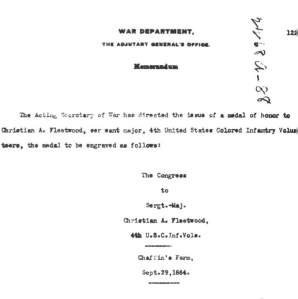

WAR DEPARTMENT,
THE ADJUTANT GENERAL'S OFFICE.

Memorandum

The Acting Secretary of War has directed the issue of a medal of honor to
Christian A. Fleetwood, sergeant major, 4th United States Colored Infantry Volunteers, the medal to be engraved as follows:

The Congress
to
Sergt.-Maj.
Christian A. Fleetwood,
4th U.S.C.Inf.Vols.

Chaffin's Farm,
Sept.29,1864.

The Adjutant General.

March 28, 1907.

*The front and back of the 1865 Medal
of Honor with the 1904 ribbon.*

2306. 6th St. N. W.
Washington. Oct. 19th 1891,

The Commissioner of Pensions,
Washington, D.C.

Sir:

I filed some time since application to be pensioned for deafness; total in left ear from gunshot concussion, & severe in right ear from Catarrh, result of disease contracted in the Army, together with all available proofs to establish same. Pension was granted for left ear and Certificate No. 481.187. issued therefor. I am advised that while Catarrh to full extent claimed & resultant deafness is clearly established, your office calls for expert testimony to connect the same with service. In my original application, I stated that I had never been treated for either deafness claimed.

The Catarrh came upon me so gradually, and I was so entirely ignorant as to the meaning of the symptoms felt, that it established itself unchecked, and is now chronic. The lapse of years, the fact that I was myself, & those about me ignorant of the disease, stealing upon me renders it impossible for me to add

anything other than my own additional statement to the testimony already filed. The fact of my perfect physical condition at enlistment is substantiated; deafness in the service and continuously since, & the disease from which and subsequent exposure the Catarrh originated proven by Hospital Records, Regt. Surgeon, Comrades and friends, & I have no further resources. Further medical testimony, or any expert testimony it is impossible for me to submit.

I was first troubled as I can now recall with the symptoms in the winter of 1865–1866, though I did not know them. The tendency to "hawk", constantly to clear the throat, the loss of purity in voice tones, and the beginning of unpleasant breath. Owing I suppose to my perfect condition otherwise and constitutional strength, the growth of the disease was slow, but it has been steady, ever since, and at no time have I been free from it, since the time mentioned above, though less troublesome at some times than at others.

When I entered the Army I had already some reputation as a singer & some note for the sweetness and purity of tone. These began to be veiled at the latter part of my service, have steadily deteriorated since, and for many years now, I have not attempted public singing, so utterly destitute of musical quality has my voice become.

I am of good reputation in this community, and wherever known, am in Government employ, and would not peril my position by false statements for the small amount to be looked for, even if otherwise disposed to do so. I have not come into this matter as to receive a favor, & desire to receive nothing but to which under the laws I am honestly entitled. I conscientiously believe myself entitled to the increase asked, and respectfully beg favorable action, & the issue of a Certificate to cover all disabilities alleged and proven before the several Boards of Physicians who have examined and reported the same.

Very respectfully
C. A. Fleetwood

Personally appeared before me this 21st day of October 1891 C. A. Fleetwood and made oath that the above statement is true according to his best belief and knowledge.
Louis H. Douglass
Notary Public

Fleetwood's letter of October 19, 1891, requesting a pension because of increasing disability.

241

[3—010 a.]

Act of June 27, 1890.

AA DECLARATION FOR INVALID PENSION. **AA**

To be executed before a Court of Record or some officer thereof having custody of its seal, a Notary Public or Justice of the Peace, whose official signature shall be verified by his official seal, and in case he has none, his signature and official character shall be certified by a Clerk of a Court of Record, or a City or County Clerk.

State of *District of Columbia*
County of *Washington* }ss.

On this *11th* day of *October*, A. D. one thousand eight hundred and ninety-___, personally appeared before me, a *Notary Public* within and for the county and State aforesaid, *Christian A. Fleetwood* aged ___ years, a resident of the *City* of *Washington* county of *Washington*, State of *District of Columbia*, who, being duly sworn according to law, declares that he is the identical *Christian A. Fleetwood* who was ENROLLED on the *11* day of *August*, 1863, in *Co. G. 4 U.S. Colld. Troops* as *Sergeant* [Here state rank, company and regiment.] in the service of the United States, in the War of the Rebellion, and served at least ninety days, and was HONORABLY DISCHARGED at *Washington D.C.*, on the *4* day of *May* 1866. That he is ___ unable to earn a support by manual labor by reason of *deafness of both ears and catarrh of head* [Here name the disease or injuries from which disabled.]

That said disabilities are not due to his vicious habits, and are to the best of his knowledge and belief of a permanent character. That he has ___ applied for pension under application No. ___

That he is a pensioner under Certificate No. *481187.* [If a pensioner, the Certificate number only need be given. If not, give the number of the former application if one was made.]

That he makes this declaration for the purpose of being placed on the pension roll of the United States under the provisions of the Act of June 27, 1890. He hereby appoints *Joseph H. Douglass #934. "F" St. N.W.* of *Washington*, State of *Dist. of Columbia* his true and lawful attorney to prosecute his claim and receive a fee of $*10⁰⁰*. That his POST-OFFICE ADDRESS is *2306 Sixth St.* county of *Washington D.C.*, State of ___

Christian A. Fleetwood
[Claimant's signature.]

Attest: (1) *John F. Cole*
(2) *H. Price Williams*

ADDITIONAL EVIDENCE.

PROOF OF DISABILITY.

CLAIM OF
Christian A. Fleetwood
Sgt. Maj. 4 U.S.C.T.

No. ___

Filed by
E. R. Begley
1914 - 11 St
Wash. D.C.

PROOF OF DISABILITY.

Declaration of Sergeant Major Fleetwood's invalid condition, as a basis for his pension request, with proof of disability.

SUDDEN DEATH OF MAJOR FLEETWOOD IN WASHINGTON

Deceased Had Completed A Useful Career In Civic and Military Life

HELD IN HIGH ESTEEM

MAJOR FLEETWOOD

Special to "Tribune.

Washington, D. C., Sept. 28.—Major C. A. Fleetwood died quite suddenly today of heart trouble, from which he has suffered for nearly two years, although able to perform his daily tasks. He was a native of Baltimore and a part of a group of young men who determined to make a mark in life.

He attended private schools and then Ashmun Institute, now Lincoln University, being a graduate of the first class in 1858.

When the call came for colored soldiers in the civil war he was among the first to enlist and was made sergeant major of the First Maryland Regiment, participating in many battles and with the crowning triumph of having saved 3000 lives, at the peril of his own, at Petersburg. For this deed Congress made him a medal man, the highest gift in the Government.

FUNERAL SERVICES HELD FOR MAJ. C. A. FLEETWOOD

Was Civil War Veteran and for More Than Thirty Years a Clerk in War Department.

Funeral services for Maj. Christian A. Fleetwood, veteran of the civil war, and for more than thirty years a clerk in the War Department, who died Monday, were held yesterday afternoon at St. Luke's Episcopal Church, Rev. Thomas J. Brown officiating. The benediction was pronounced by Rev. F. J. Grimke.

Interment was in Harmony cemetery. The 1st Separate Battalion of the District National Guard, of which Maj. Fleetwood was once the commanding officer, acted as an escort to the body and fired the usual volleys and sounded taps at the grave.

The honorary pallbearers included Wyatt Archer, Prof. George W. Cook, Lieut. Col. Arthur Brooks, William E. Bolivar, Roscoe C. Bruce, John S. Durham, Jerome Johnson, Henry Johnson, Daniel Murray, P. B. S. Pinchback, Dr. Edward D. Williston, W. McKinlay and Judge Robert H. Terrell.

The Frederick Douglass Post, G. A. R., of which the deceased was a member, was represented by the following honorary pallbearers: Alexander Oglesby, Samuel Brown, E. G. Brooks, Benjamin F. Davis and Maj. Charles R. Douglass, the present commander.

During the civil war Maj. Fleetwood served in the 4th Infantry, United States Colored Troops, and was regimental sergeant major. He was awarded a medal of honor under the act of Congress for bravery in battle at Chapin's farm September 29, 1864, where he seized the colors after two color sergeants had been shot down, and bore them through the fight.

After the war he settled in Washington and held a prominent place in the Freedman's Bank, later on being appointed to the War Department, where he remained until the end.

He was a founder of the Soldiers' and Sailors' League in Philadelphia, January, 1866, antedating that of the G. A. R. His best legacy is the large pamphlet concerning the colored soldiers in the war of the rebellion. This was made up from the records of the War Department and is one of the most valuable contributions ever written concerning that military period.

He was a useful citizen in every walk of life, and Washington already realizes the void through his death. He had a rare personality and in the closer relations of life his leave taking has caused profound sadness.

EMANCIPATION

. . . that this nation, under God, shall have a new birth of freedom;
and that government of the people, by the people, for the people,
shall not perish from the earth.

IN HIS ADDRESS at Gettysburg, Abraham Lincoln conveyed to the nation his ultimate judgment of slavery as an accepted institution in the United States of America.

From the time of his election as President, Lincoln's primary purpose had been to save the Union; and for more than a year after the Civil War began, he had resisted the influence of those citizens who demanded the abolition of slavery. Finally, however, in the Fall of 1862, he issued the preliminary emancipation proclamation. And in January, 1863, the official Emancipation Proclamation was issued as a measure to restore the Union.

In considering his decision to free the slaves, Lincoln had declared in his Second Annual Message to Congress:

. . . In giving freedom to the slave, we assure freedom to the free—
honorable alike in what we give and what we preserve. We shall
nobly save or meanly lose the last, best hope of earth. Other means
may succeed; this could not fail. The way is plain, peaceful, generous,
just—a way which, if followed, the world will forever applaud,
and God must forever bless.

A Union soldier reading the Emancipation Proclamation in a slave cabin.

ABRAHAM LINCOLN

AND HIS

Emancipation Proclamation

Whereas On the Twenty-second day of September, in the year of our Lord one thousand eight hundred and sixty-two, a Proclamation was issued by the President of the United States, containing among other things the following, to-wit:

"That on the first day of January, in the year of our Lord one thousand eight hundred and sixty-three, all persons held as slaves within any State, or designated part of a State, the people whereof shall then be in rebellion against the United States, shall be then, thenceforward and forever free, and the executive government of the United States, including the military and naval authority thereof, will recognize and maintain the freedom of such persons, and will do no act or acts to repress such persons, or any of them, in any efforts they may make for their actual freedom.

"That the executive will, on the first day of January aforesaid, by proclamation, designate the States and parts of States, if any, in which the people thereof respectively shall then be in rebellion against the United States, and the fact that any State, or the people thereof, shall on that day be in good faith represented in the Congress of the United States by members chosen thereto at elections wherein a majority of the qualified voters of such State shall have participated, shall, in the absence of strong countervailing testimony, be deemed conclusive evidence that such State and the people thereof are not then in rebellion against the United States."

Now, therefore, I, ABRAHAM LINCOLN, President of the United States, by virtue of the power in me vested as Commander-in-Chief of the Army and Navy of the United States in time of actual armed rebellion against the authority and government of the United States, and as a fit and necessary war measure for suppressing said rebellion, do, on this first day of January, in the year of our Lord one thousand eight hundred and sixty-three, and in accordance with my purpose so to do, publicly proclaim for the full period of one hundred days from the day the first above mentioned order, and designate as the States and parts of States wherein the people thereof respectively are this day in rebellion against the United States, the following, to-wit:

ARKANSAS, TEXAS, LOUISIANA (except the parishes of St. Bernard, Plaquemines, Jefferson, St. John, St. Charles, St. James, Ascension, Assumption, Terre Bonne, Lafourche, St. Mary, St. Martin, and Orleans, including the city of New Orleans), MISSISSIPPI, ALABAMA, FLORIDA, GEORGIA, SOUTH CAROLINA, NORTH CAROLINA and VIRGINIA (except the forty-eight counties designated as West Virginia, and also the counties of Berkley, Accomac, Northampton, Elizabeth City, York, Princess Ann and Norfolk, including the cities of Norfolk and Portsmouth), and which excepted parts are, for the present, left precisely as if this Proclamation were not issued.

And by virtue of the power and for the purpose aforesaid, I do order and declare that all persons held as slaves within said designated States and parts of States are and henceforward shall be free; and that the executive government of the United States, including the military and naval authorities thereof, will recognize and maintain the freedom of said persons.

And I hereby enjoin upon the people so declared to be free, to abstain from all violence, unless in necessary self-defence, and I recommend to them that in all cases, when allowed, they labor faithfully for reasonable wages.

And I further declare and make known that such persons of suitable condition, will be received into the armed service of the United States to garrison forts, positions, stations and other places, and to man vessels of all sorts in said service.

And upon this act, sincerely believed to be an act of justice, warranted by the Constitution, upon military necessity, I invoke the considerate judgment of mankind, and the gracious favor of Almighty God.

In testimony whereof, I have hereunto set my name, and caused the seal of the United States to be affixed.

Done at the City of Washington, this first day of January, in the year of our Lord one thousand eight hundred and sixty-three, and of the Independence of the United States the eighty-Seventh.

By the President: ABRAHAM LINCOLN.

WILLIAM H. SEWARD, Secretary of State.

NOTE.—The rest of the slaves were afterwards freed by Legislation and Constitutional Amendments.

President Lincoln and his son Thomas enter Richmond, Virginia, in 1865, amidst the cheers of the crowd.

President Lincoln visiting the former residence of Jefferson Davis in Richmond, Virginia, on April 4, 1865.

The emancipation of the Negro—a memory of the past and a hope for the future.

Negro emancipation found a lasting memorial in the erection of schools, churches and monuments such as these, as well as in art. Pictured here is one artist's conception of the slave—his shackles of slavery broken—paying homage to President Lincoln.

The National Emancipation Monument in Springfield, Illinois.

Sojourner Truth, valiant and courageous woman of the Civil War, is shown here with Abraham Lincoln at the White House. Her grave site is located in Battle Creek, Michigan, and on the gravestone is inscribed, "Is God Dead." This is the famous question she is reported to have asked of Frederick Douglass during the War.

ISAAC and ROSA, Emancipated Slave Children, From the Free Schools of Louisiana,
Photographed by KIMBALL, 477 Broadway. N.Y.
Entered according to Act of Congress, in the year 1863 by GEO. H. HANKS, in the Clerk's Office of the U.S. for the Sou. Dist. of N.Y.

Because of the actions of men and women such as Abraham Lincoln and Sojourner Truth, these children were able to obtain the benefits of education in 1863.

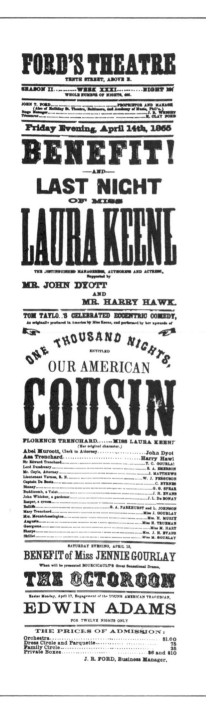

FORD'S THEATRE
TENTH STREET, ABOVE E.

SEASON II.......WEEK XXXI.......NIGHT 201
WHOLE NUMBER OF NIGHTS, 496.

JOHN T. FORD...................................PROPRIETOR AND MANAGER
(Also of Holliday St. Theatre, Baltimore, and Academy of Music, Phil'a.)
Stage Manager..J. B. WRIGHT
Treasurer..H. CLAY FORD

Friday Evening, April 14th, 1865

BENEFIT!
—AND—
LAST NIGHT
OF MISS
LAURA KEENE

THE DISTINGUISHED MANAGERESS, AUTHORESS AND ACTRESS,
Supported by
MR. JOHN DYOTT
AND
MR. HARRY HAWK.

TOM TAYLO..'S CELEBRATED ECCENTRIC COMEDY,
As originally produced in America by Miss Keene, and performed by her upwards of

ONE THOUSAND NIGHTS,
ENTITLED
OUR AMERICAN
COUSIN

FLORENCE TRENCHARD......MISS LAURA KEENE
(Her original character.)

Abel Murcott, (Clerk to Attorney.)................John Dyot
Asa Trenchard.....................................Harry Hawk
Sir Edward Trenchard...........................T. C. GOURLAY
Lord Dundreary.................................E. A. EMERSON
Mr. Coyle, Attorney..............................J. MATTHEWS
Lieutenant Vernon, R. N........................W. J. FERGUSON
Captain De Boots..................................C. BYRNES
Binney..G. G. SPEAR
Buddicomb, a Valet...............................J. H. EVANS
John Whicker, a gardener........................J. L. De BONAY
Harper, a groom
Bullis..........................G. A. PARKHURST and L. JOHNSON
Mary Trenchard..................................Miss J. GOURLAY
Mrs. Mountchessington...........................Mrs. H. MUZEY
Augusta..Miss H. TRUMAN
Georgiana..Miss M. HART
Sharpe..Mrs. J. H. EVANS
Skillet..Miss M. GOURLAY

SATURDAY EVENING, APRIL 15,
BENEFIT of Miss JENNIE GOURLAY
When will be presented BOURCICAULT'S Great Sensational Drama,

THE OCTOROON

Easter Monday, April 17, Engagement of the YOUNG AMERICAN TRAGEDIAN,

EDWIN ADAMS
FOR TWELVE NIGHTS ONLY

THE PRICES OF ADMISSION:
Orchestra...$1.00
Dress Circle and Parquette....................................75
Family Circle..25
Private Boxes...$6 and $10

J. R. FORD, Business Manager.

On FRIDAY, APRIL 14, 1865, President and Mrs. Lincoln attended the final performance of *Our American Cousin* at Ford's Theatre in Washington, D.C. During the performance, the President was mortally wounded by an assassin's bullet. Secretary of State Seward was wounded the same night by another assassin. Shortly after dawn on the following day, Lincoln died; and the nation mourned the loss of the man who had preserved the Union and freed the slaves.

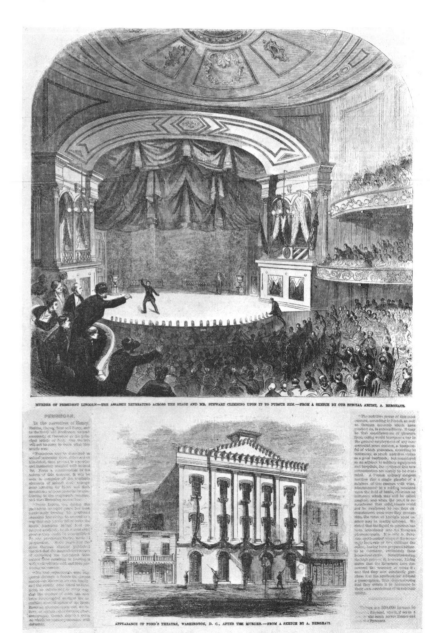

MURDER OF PRESIDENT LINCOLN—THE ASSASSIN RETREATING ACROSS THE STAGE AND MR. STEWART CLIMBING UPON IT TO PURSUE HIM.—FROM A SKETCH BY OUR SPECIAL ARTIST, A. BERGHAUS.

APPEARANCE OF FORD'S THEATRE, WASHINGTON, D. C., AFTER THE MURDER.—FROM A SKETCH BY A. BERGHAUS.

While the nation mourned its fallen leader, every effort was made to apprehend John Wilkes Booth and his accomplices.

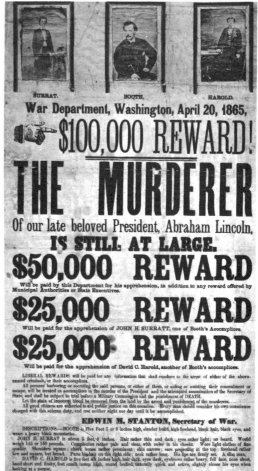

Booth did not live to face trial, but his fellow conspirators were executed on July 7, 1865, for their participation in the assassination of the President.

*The last photograph of
President Lincoln,
taken four days
before the assassination.*

*The statue of President Abraham Lincoln
in the Lincoln Memorial, Washington, D.C.*

NEGRO LIFE

THE LIVES of American Negroes before, during, and following the Civil War reflected the changing times. The adjustment of the colored people to the changed political, economic, and social conditions caused by the War marked one of the climactic episodes in the history of the nation.

Turmoil was general in Negro life for the first years following Emancipation. But the ability to live, love, and labor was not lost in spite of new anxieties; and Negroes continued to find solace in religion and began to gain new skills and confidence through education.

Going to church in the evening.

A Negro nurse taking a child for a walk.

Two boys fishing from a wharf at high tide.

253

Negroes congregate outside one of their houses on a farm in Virginia.

A Southern planter arms his slaves to defend his land.

Negroes leaving their homes on the riverbank in search of freedom.

Senator Charles Sumner pauses to give money to a Negro child.

In New Orleans, emancipated slaves joined white children in freedom schools.

A schoolboy considers a problem on his slate.

Free schoolboys.

The masthead of the Freedman newspaper, published by The American Tract Society of Boston.

A Negro policeman in New Orleans.

258

A Negro constable on the traditional mule.

The United States Government helped relocate many freed Negroes on their own land.

A wandering freedman waiting for work on a farm.

A Negro farmer hauling his tobacco to market.

A little relaxation after working in the fields.

Singing in the parlor always made the day much brighter.

Chaplain Warren of the Freedmen's Bureau performing a marriage in Vicksburg.

An artist's drawing of a Negro funeral procession.

Building a home of their own.

Bibliography

PRIMARY MATERIALS

AMES, MARY. *From a New England Woman's Diary in Dixie in 1875.* Springfield, Mass., 1906.

ANDREWS, SIDNEY. *The South since the War: As Shown by Fourteen Weeks of Travel and Observation in Georgia and the Carolinas.* Boston, 1866.

BASLER, ROY P. (ed.). *The Collected Works of Abraham Lincoln.* 8 vols. New Brunswick, N.J., 1953.

BEALE, HOWARD K. (ed.). *Diary of Edward Bates, 1859–1866.* Washington, 1933.

BEECHER, CHARLES (ed.). *Autobiographical Correspondence . . . of Lyman Beecher, D.D.* New York, 1865.

BENSON, ADOLPH B. (ed.). *America in the Fifties: Letters of Frederika Bremer.* New York, 1924.

BILLINGTON, RAY ALLEN (ed.). *The Journal of Charlotte L. Forten: A Free Negro in the Slave Era.* New York, 1961.

BLAINE, JAMES G. *Twenty Years of Congress: From Lincoln to Garfield.* 2 vols. Norwich, Conn., 1884–1886.

BOTUME, ELIZABETH H. *First Days amongst the Contrabands.* Boston, 1893.

BROWN, WILLIAM WELLS. *Narrative of William Wells Brown, a Fugitive Slave: Written by Himself.* Boston, 1847.

BROWNE, FREDERICK W. *My Service in the U.S. Colored Cavalry.* Cincinnati, 1908.

BRUCE, H. C. *The New Man: Twenty-Nine Years a Slave; Twenty-Nine Years a Free Man.* York, Pa., 1895.

BUTLER, BENJAMIN F. *Butler's Book.* Boston, 1892.

CAMPBELL, SIR GEORGE. *White and Black: The Outcome of a Visit to the United States.* London, 1879.

CARNEGIE INSTITUTION OF WASHINGTON. *Documents Illustrative of the Slave Trade to America.* 4 vols. Washington, 1930–1935.

CHASE, C. THURSTON. *A Manual on School-Houses and Cottages for the People of the South.* Washington, 1868.

CHASE, SALMON P. *Diary and Correspondence of Salmon P. Chase.* Washington, 1903.

CHESNUT, MARY B. *A Diary from Dixie.* New York, 1905.

CHILD, L. MARIA (ed.). *Incidents in the Life of a Slave Girl.* Boston, 1861.

CLARK, PETER H. *The Black Brigade of Cincinnati.* Cincinnati, 1864.

CLARKE, JAMES FREEMAN. *Anti-Slavery Days.* New York, 1883.

Congressional Globe. 35th–41st Congresses. Washington, 1858–1870.

COOPER, ANNA JULIA. *A Voice from the South, by a Black Woman of the South.* Xenia, Ohio, 1892.

DANA, CHARLES A. *Recollections of the Civil War.* New York, 1902.

DICEY, EDWARD. *Six Months in the Federal States.* 2 vols. London, 1863.

DONALD, DAVID (ed.). *Inside Lincoln's Cabinet: The Civil War Diaries of Salmon P. Chase.* New York, 1954.

DOUAI, ADOLF. *Land und Leute in der Union.* Berlin, 1864.

DOUGLASS, FREDERICK. *Life and Times of Frederick Douglass, Written by Himself.* Hartford, Conn., 1881.

————. *My Bondage and My Freedom.* New York, 1855.

————. *Narrative of the Life of Frederick Douglass, an American Slave.* Wortley, England, 1846.

EMANCIPATION LEAGUE OF BOSTON. *Facts concerning the Freedmen, Their Capacity and Their Destiny.* Boston, 1863.

Exercises at the Dedication of the Monument to Colonel Robert Gould Shaw and the Fifty-Fourth Massachusetts Infantry, May 31, 1897. Published by order of the City Council of Boston, 1897.

FISK UNIVERSITY. SOCIAL SCIENCE INSTITUTE. *Unwritten History of Slavery: Autobiographical Accounts of Negro Ex-Slaves.* Nashville, Tenn., 1945.

FLEETWOOD, CHRISTIAN A. *The Negro as a Soldier: Written by Christian A. Fleetwood, Late Sergeant Major, Fourth U.S. Colored Troops, for the Negro Congress.* Washington, 1895.

FOX, C. B. *Record of the Service of the Fifty-Fifth Massachusetts Volunteer Infantry.* Cambridge, Mass., 1868.

FRANKLIN, JOHN HOPE (ed.). *The Diary of James T. Ayers.* Springfield, Ill., 1947.

FREMANTLE, ARTHUR J. *Three Months in the Southern States.* New York, 1864.

GAY, MARY A. H. *Life in Dixie during the War: 1861–1865.* Atlanta, Ga., 1897.

GERARD, C. *Les Etats Confédérés Visités en 1863.* Paris, 1864.

HAVILAND, LAURA S. *A Woman's Life Work: Including Thirty Years' Service on the Underground Railroad and in the War.* Grand Rapids, Mich., 1881.

HIGGINSON, THOMAS WENTWORTH. *Army Life in a Black Regiment.* Boston, 1870.

HOBART, EDWIN L. *Semi-History of a Boy-Veteran of the Twenty-Eighth Regiment Illinois Infantry Volunteers, in a Black Regiment.* Denver, 1909.

HOLLAND, RUPERT SARGENT (ed.). *Letters and Diary of Laura M. Towne.* Cambridge, Mass., 1912.

HOWARD, OLIVER O. *Autobiography of Oliver Otis Howard, Major General United States Army.* 2 vols. New York, 1907.

JAQUETTE, HENRIETTA STRATTON (ed.). *South after Gettysburg: The Letters of Cornelia Hancock, 1863–1868.* New York, 1957.

JONES, J. B. *Rebel War Clerk's Diary.* Philadelphia, 1866.

KECKLEY, ELIZABETH. *Behind the Scenes.* New York, 1868.

KING, EDWARD. *The Great South: A Record of Journeys.* Hartford, Conn., 1875.

KNOX, THOMAS W. *Camp-Fire and Cotton-Field.* New York, 1865.

KOHL, J. G. *Travels in Canada, and through the States of New York and Pennsylvania.* 2 vols. London, 1861.

LANGSTON, JOHN MERCER. *From the Virginia Plantation to the National Capitol.* Hartford, Conn., 1894.

LAUGEL, AUGUSTE. *The United States during the War.* London, 1866.

LEE, WILLIAM MACK. *History of the Life of Reverend William Mack Lee, Body Servant of General Robert E. Lee through the Civil War, Cook from 1861 to 1865.* Norfolk, Va., 1918.

LOGUEN, J. W. *As a Slave and as a Freeman.* Syracuse, N.Y., 1859.

LUNT, DOLLY SUMNER. *A Woman's War-Time Journal.* New York, 1918.

McCULLOCH, HUGH. *Men and Measures of Half a Century: Sketches and Comments.* New York, 1888.

MACKAY, CHARLES. *Life and Liberty in America: Or, Sketches of a Tour in the United States and Canada, in 1857–8.* London, 1859.

MALET, REV. W. W. *Errand to the South in the Summer of 1862.* London, 1863.

Manuscript Minutes of the Founding of Wilberforce University, Wilberforce, Ohio, n.d.

MASSIE, J. W. *America: The Origin of Her Present Conflict.* London, 1864.

MAY, SAMUEL J. *Some Recollections of Our Antislavery Conflict.* Boston, 1869.

MOORE, FRANK (ed.). *The Rebellion Record.* 11 vols. New York, 1861–1868.

MORGAN, THOMAS J. *Reminiscences of Service with Colored Troops in the Army of the Cumberland, 1863–1865.* Providence, R.I., 1885.

MOSHER, ROBERT B. (comp.). *Executive Register of the United States, 1789–1902.* Baltimore, 1903.

"The Negro in the Military Service: War of the Rebellion." Manuscript in the National Archives, Washington, n.d.

NEVINS, ALLAN (ed.). *American Social History as Recorded by British Travellers.* New York, 1931.

NEW ENGLAND FREEDMEN'S AID SOCIETY. *Annual Report: 1862–1863; 1863–1864.* Boston, 1863–1864.

NORDHOFF, CHARLES. *The Freedmen of South Carolina.* New York, 1863.

OLMSTED, FREDERICK LAW. *The Cotton Kingdom.* New York, 1953.

PARSONS, C. G. *Inside View of Slavery: Or a Tour among the Planters.* Boston, 1855.

PEARSON, ELIZABETH WARE (ed.). *Letters from Port Royal, Written at the Time of the Civil War.* Boston, 1906.

PENDALL, LUCILLE H., and BETHEL, ELIZABETH (comp.). *Preliminary Inventory of the Records of the Adjutant General's Office.* Washington, 1949.

PHILLIPS, WENDELL. *Speeches, Lectures and Letters.* Boston, 1863.

POWERS, STEPHEN. *Afoot and Alone: A Walk from Sea to Sea.* Hartford, Conn., 1872.

PRINGLE, ELIZABETH W. ALLSTON. *Chronicles of Chicora Wood.* New York, 1923.

REID, WHITELAW. *After the War: A Southern Tour, May 1, 1865 to May 1, 1866.* Cincinnati, 1866.

RICHARDSON, JAMES D. (comp.). *A Compilation of the Messages and Papers of the Presidents.* 10 vols. Washington, 1896–1899.

RICKARD, JAMES H. *Services with Colored Troops in Burnside's Corps, Late Captain Nineteenth U.S. Colored Troops.* Providence, R.I., 1894.

RIDDLE, ALBERT G. *Recollections of War Times: 1860–65.* New York, 1895.

ROMEYN, HENRY. *With Colored Troops in the Army of the Cumberland.* Washington, 1904.

ROSS, ALEXANDER WILSON. *Recollections and Experiences of an Abolitionist: From 1855 to 1865.* Toronto, 1876.

RUSSELL, W. H. *My Diary North and South.* Boston, 1863.

SALA, G. A. *My Diary in America in the Midst of War.* 2 vols. London, 1865.

SCHURZ, CARL. *Intimate Letters of Carl Schurz, 1841–1869.* Madison, Wis., 1928.

————. *The Reminiscences of Carl Schurz.* 3 vols. New York, 1907–1908.

SEARS, CYRUS. *The Battle of Milliken's Bend.* Columbus, Ohio, 1909.

————. *Papers of Cyrus Sears, Late Lieutenant Colonel of the Forty-Ninth U.S. Colored Infantry Volunteers of African Descent—Originally Eleventh Louisiana Volunteers Infantry A.D. of Harpster, Ohio.* Columbus, Ohio, 1909.

SHERMAN, GEORGE R. *The Negro as a Soldier: By George R. Sherman, Captain Seventh United States Colored Infantry and Brevet Lieutenant Colonel United States Volunteers.* Providence, R.I., 1913.

SUMNER, CHARLES. *The Works of Charles Sumner.* 15 vols. Boston, 1870–1883.

TAYLOR, SUZIE KING. *Reminiscences of My Life in Camp.* Boston, 1902.

TROLLOPE, ANTHONY. *North America.* New York, 1862.

TROWBRIDGE, CHARLES T. *Six Months in the Freedmen's Bureau with a Colored Regiment.* Minneapolis, 1909.

TROWBRIDGE, JOHN TOWNSEND. *A Picture of the Desolated States, and the Work of Restoration, 1865–1868.* Hartford, Conn., 1868.

TUCKERMAN, H. T. (comp.). *America and Her Commentators.* New York, 1864.

ULLMAN, DANIEL. *Address by Daniel Ullman, before the Soldiers' and Sailors' Union of the State of New York, on the Organization of Colored Troops and the Regeneration of the South, Delivered at Albany, February 5, 1868.* Washington, 1868.

UNION LEAGUE CLUB OF NEW YORK. *Report of the Committee on Volunteering, Presented October 13th, 1864.* New York, 1864.

U.S. ARMY. DEPARTMENT OF THE GULF. *Report of the Board of Education for Freedmen, 1864.* New Orleans, 1865.

U.S. BUREAU OF THE CENSUS. *Negro Population, 1790–1915.* Washington, 1918.

U.S. BUREAU OF REFUGEES, FREEDMEN AND ABANDONED LANDS. *Semi-Annual Reports on Schools and Finances of Freedmen: 1866–1870,* by John W. Alvord. Washington, 1866–1870.

————. DEPARTMENT OF TENNESSEE AND ARKANSAS. *Report of the General Superintendent of Freedmen,* by John Eaton. Nashville, Tenn., 1865.

U.S. COMMISSION FOR COLORED TROOPS. *Orders Relating to Colored Men and Colored Troops.* Nashville, Tenn., 1863.

U.S. NAVAL WAR RECORDS OFFICE. *Official Records of the Union and Confederate Navies in the War of the Rebellion.* 27 vols. Washington, 1894–1922.

U.S. OFFICE OF EDUCATION. *Special Report of the Commissioner of Education on the Conditions and Improvements of Public Schools in the District of Columbia, Submitted to the Senate, June 13, 1870.* Washington, 1871.

————. *Special Report of the United States Commissioner of Education for 1870.* Washington, 1871.

U.S. WAR DEPARTMENT. *Register of the Volunteer Forces of the United States Army for the Years 1861, 1862, 1863, 1864, 1865.* Washington, 1865.

————. *Tactics for the Use of the Colored Troops.* New York, 1863.

The War of the Rebellion: A Compilation of the Official Records of the Union and Confederate Armies. 128 vols. Washington, 1880–1901.

WHITTIER, JOHN GREENLEAF. *The Writings of John Greenleaf Whittier.* 7 vols. Boston, 1888–1889.

WOODSON, CARTER G. (ed.). *The Mind of the Negro as Reflected in Letters Written during the Crisis, 1800–1860*. Washington, 1926.

YEATMAN, JAMES E. *A Report on the Condition of the Freedmen of the Mississippi, Presented to the Western Sanitary Commission, December 17, 1862*. St. Louis, 1864.

SECONDARY SOURCES

ABBOTT, JOHN C. *History of the Civil War in America*. Vol. II. Springfield, Ill., 1866.

ADAMS, EPHRAIM D. *Great Britain and the American Civil War*. New York, 1958.

ADAMS, JAMES TRUSLOW. *The March of Democracy*. Vol. III. New York, 1933.

ALEXANDER, WILLIAM T. *History of the Colored Race in America*. New Orleans, 1887.

American Annual Cyclopedia. 14 vols. New York, 1862–1875.

ANDERSON, OSBORNE P. *A Voice from Harper's Ferry*. Boston, 1861.

APTHEKER, HERBERT. *American Negro Slave Revolts*. New York, 1943.

———. *The Negro in the Abolitionist Movement*. New York, 1941.

———. *The Negro in the Civil War*. New York, 1938.

——— (ed.). *A Documentary History of the Negro People in the United States*. 2 vols. New York, 1951.

ARMSTRONG, MARGARET. *Fanny Kemble: A Passionate Victorian*. New York, 1939.

ARNETT, BENJAMIN W. *The Centennial Budget: A.M.E. Church*. Philadelphia, 1887.

AVARY, MYRTA. *Dixie after the War*. Boston, 1937.

BANGS, ISAAC SPARROW. *The Ullmann Brigade*. Portland, Me., 1902.

BARDOLPH, RICHARD. *The Negro Vanguard*. New York, 1959.

BARRINGER, P. B. *The American Negro: His Past and Future*. Raleigh, N.C., 1900.

BATES, DAVID H. *Lincoln in the Telegraph Office*. New York, 1907.

BEALE, HOWARD K. *The Critical Year: A Study of Andrew Johnson and Reconstruction*. New York, 1930.

BELDEN, MARVA ROBINS and THOMAS GRAHAM. *So Fell the Angels*. Boston, 1956.

BENNETT, LERONE, JR. *Before the Mayflower: A History of the Negro in America, 1619–1964*. Baltimore, 1966.

BENTLEY, GEORGE R. *A History of the Freedmen's Bureau*. Philadelphia, 1955.

BERGER, MORROE. *Equality by Statute*. New York, 1952.

BLACKFORD, L. MINOR. *Mine Eyes Have Seen the Glory: The Story of a Virginia Lady, Mary Berkeley Minor Blackford, 1802–1896, Who Taught Her Sons To Hate Slavery and To Love the Union*. Cambridge, Mass., 1954.

BLACKMAN, J. K. *The Sea Islands of South Carolina: Their Peaceful and Prosperous Condition. A Revolution in the System of Planting*. Charleston, S.C., 1880.

BLASSINGAME, JOHN WESLEY. "The Organization and Use of Negro Troops in the Union Army, 1863–1865." Unpublished Master's thesis, Howard University, Washington, 1961.

BOND, HORACE MANN. *The Education of the Negro in the American Social Order*. New York, 1934.

———. *Negro Education in Alabama*. Washington, 1939.

BOTKIN, B. A. (ed.). *Lay My Burden Down: A Folk History of Slavery*. Chicago, 1945.

BRACKETT, JEFFREY R. *The Negro in Maryland: A Study of the Institution of Slavery*. Baltimore, 1889.

BRADFORD, SARAH H. *Harriet, the Moses of Her People*. New York, 1886.

BRAWLEY, BENJAMIN. *A Short History of the American Negro*. New York, 1913.

BRAXTON, A. CAPERTON. *The Fifteenth Amendment: An Account of Its Enactment*. Lynchburg, Va., 1933.

BRODIE, FAWN M. *Thaddeus Stevens: Scourge of the South*. New York, 1959.

BROWN, INA CORRINE. *The Story of the American Negro*. New York, 1936.

BROWN, WILLIAM WELLS. *The Negro in the American Rebellion*. Boston, 1867.

———. *The Rising Son or the Antecedents and Advancements of the Colored Race*. Boston, 1874.

BRUCE, JOHN EDWARD. *A Defense of the Colored Soldiers Who Fought in the War of the Rebellion*. Yonkers, N.Y., n.d.

BRUCE, KATHLEEN. *Virginia Iron Manufactures in the Slave Era*. New York, 1931.

BURCHARD, PETER. *One Gallant Rush*. New York, 1965.

BURGESS, JOHN. *The Civil War and the Constitution: 1859–1865*. New York, 1901.

BUSWELL, J. OLIVER. *Slavery, Segregation and Scripture.* Grand Rapids, Mich., 1964.

BUTLER, BENJAMIN F. *Character and Results of the War.* Philadelphia, 1863.

CABLE, GEORGE W. *The Silent South.* New York, 1885.

CALVERTON, V. F. (ed.). *Anthology of American Negro Literature.* New York, 1929.

CAREY, HENRY C. *The Slave Trade, Domestic and Foreign: Why It Exists, and How It May Be Extinguished.* Philadelphia, 1853.

CARPENTER, MARIE E. *The Treatment of the Negro in American History School Textbooks.* Menasha, Wis., 1941.

CASH, W. J. *The Mind of the South.* Garden City, N.Y., 1954.

CATTON, BRUCE. *The Centennial History of the Civil War.* 3 vols. Garden City, N.Y., 1961–1965.

CHALMERS, DAVID MARK. *Hooded Americanism: The First Century of the Ku Klux Klan, 1865–1965.* Garden City, N.Y., 1965.

CHANNING, EDWARD. *A History of the United States.* Vol. VI. New York, 1925.

CHESNUTT, CHARLES W. *Frederick Douglass.* Boston, 1896.

Civil War Papers Read before the Commandery of the State of Massachusetts Military Order of the Loyal Legion of the United States. Boston, 1900.

CLAYTON, V. V. *White and Black under the Old Régime.* Milwaukee, 1899.

CLOWES, W. LAIRD. *Black America: A Study of the Ex-Slave and His Late Master.* London, 1891.

COAN, JOSEPHUS R. *Daniel Alexander Payne, Christian Educator.* Philadelphia, 1935.

COHN, DAVID LEWIS. *The Life and Times of King Cotton.* New York, 1956.

COLE, ARTHUR C. *The Irrepressible Conflict: 1850–1865.* New York, 1934.

COLE, CHARLES CHESTER. *The Social Ideas of the Northern Evangelists.* New York, 1954.

COLEMAN, CHARLES H. *The Election of 1868: The Democratic Effort to Regain Control.* New York, 1933.

COMMAGER, HENRY STEELE (ed.). *The Defeat of the Confederacy.* New York, 1964.

CONRAD, EARL. *Harriet Tubman.* Washington, 1943.

COOKE, DENNIS. *The White Superintendent and the Negro Schools in North Carolina.* Nashville, Tenn., 1930.

CORNISH, DUDLEY. *The Sable Arm: Negro Troops in the Union Army, 1861–1865.* New York, 1956.

COTTERILL, R. S. *The Old South.* Glendale, Calif., 1936.

COX, LA WANDA and JOHN. *Politics, Principle and Prejudice, 1865–1866: The Dilemma of Reconstruction America.* New York, 1963.

CRAVEN, AVERY. *The Coming of the Civil War.* New York, 1942.

———— *An Historian and the Civil War.* Chicago, 1964.

CROMWELL, JOHN W. *The Negro in American History.* Washington, 1914.

CURRENT, RICHARD N. (ed.). *Reconstruction, 1865–1877.* Englewood Cliffs, N.J., 1965.

CURTIS, ANNA L. *Stories of the Underground Railroad.* New York, 1941.

CURTIS, MARY. *The Black Soldiers: Or the Colored Boys of the United States Army.* Washington, 1915.

DABNEY, WENDELL P. *Cincinnati's Colored Citizens.* Cincinnati, 1926.

DANIELS, JOHN. *In Freedom's Birthplace: A Study of the Boston Negroes.* Boston, 1914.

DAVIS, WILLIAM W. *The Civil War and Reconstruction in Florida.* Gainesville, Fla., 1964.

DELANY, MARTIN R. *The Condition, Elevation, Emigration and Destiny of the Colored People of the United States.* Philadelphia, 1852.

DOLLARD, R. *United States Cavalry, Second Colored Regiment, 1863–1866.* Scotland, S.D., 1906.

DOUGLAS, WILLIAM O. *Mr. Lincoln and the Negroes.* New York, 1963.

DRAKE, THOMAS E. *Quakers and Slavery in America.* New Haven, Conn., 1950.

DREW, BENJAMIN. *A North-Side View of Slavery: The Refugees, or the Narrative of Fugitive Slaves in Canada.* Boston, 1856.

DREWRY, W. S. *Slave Insurrections in Virginia, 1830–1865.* Washington, 1900.

DU BOIS, W. E. B. *Black Folk Then and Now: An Essay in the History and Sociology of the Negro.* New York, 1939.

————. *Black Reconstruction.* New York, 1935.

DUMOND, DWIGHT L. *Anti-Slavery Origins of the Civil War in the United States.* Ann Arbor, Mich., 1939.

————. *The Secession Movement, 1860–1861.* New York, 1931.

DYER, FREDERICK H. *A Compendium of the War of the Rebellion.* Vol. III. New York, 1959.

EARLY, CALVIN. *Education of the Negro in the South, 1861–1865.* Columbus, Ohio, 1933.

EATON, CLEMENT. *A History of the Southern Confederacy.* New York, 1954.

EATON, JOHN. *Grant, Lincoln and the Freedmen: Reminiscences of the Civil War, with Special Reference to the Work for the Contrabands and Freedmen of the Mississippi Valley.* New York, 1907.

ELKINS, STANLEY M. *Slavery, a Problem in American Institutional and Intellectual Life.* Chicago, 1959.

EMILIO, LUIS F. *The Assault on Fort Wagner.* Boston, 1887.

_____. *History of the Fifty-Fourth Regiment of Massachusetts Volunteer Infantry, 1863–1865.* Boston, 1891.

FAHRNEY, RALPH RAY. *Horace Greeley and the Tribune in the Civil War.* Cedar Rapids, Iowa, 1936.

FAIRCHILD, E. H. *Berea College: An Interesting History.* Cincinnati, 1883.

FEHRENBACHER, D. E. *Abraham Lincoln: A Documentary Patriot through His Speeches and Writings.* New York, 1964.

FICKLEN, JOHN R. *History of Reconstruction in Louisiana through 1868.* Baltimore, 1910.

FILLER, LOUIS. *The Crusade against Slavery: 1830–1860.* New York, 1960.

FITE, E. D. *Social and Economic Conditions in the North during the Civil War.* New York, 1910.

FLANDERS, RALPH BETTS. *Plantation Slavery in Georgia.* Chapel Hill, N.C., 1933.

FLEMING, WALTER L. *The Sequel of Appomattox.* New Haven, Conn., 1919.

_____ (ed.). *Documentary History of Reconstruction.* 2 vols. Cleveland, 1906–1907.

FONER, PHILLIP S. *The Life and Writings of Frederick Douglass.* Vols. II and III. New York, 1950–1955.

FOOTE, SHELBY. *The Civil War.* Vol. II. New York, 1963.

FOX, WILLIAM F. *Regimental Losses in the American Civil War.* Albany, N.Y., 1889.

FRANKLIN, JOHN HOPE. *The Emancipation Proclamation.* New York, 1963.

_____. *From Slavery to Freedom.* New York, 1947.

_____. *The Militant South, 1800–1861.* Boston, 1956.

_____. *Reconstruction after the Civil War.* Chicago, 1961.

FRAZIER, E. FRANKLIN. *The Free Negro Family: A Study of Family Origins before the Civil War.* Nashville, Tenn., 1932.

_____. *The Negro Church in America.* New York, 1963.

_____. *The Negro in the United States.* New York, 1957.

FRENCH, MRS. A. M. *Slavery in South Carolina and the Ex-Slaves: Or the Port Royal Mission.* New York, 1862.

GAINES, FRANCIS P. *The Southern Plantation.* New York, 1924.

GARNER, JAMES W. *Reconstruction in Mississippi.* New York, 1901.

GINZBERG, ELI, and EICHNER, ALFRED. *The Troublesome Presence: American Democracy and the Negro.* New York, 1964.

GOLDWIN, R. A. (ed.). *One Hundred Years of Emancipation.* Chicago, 1963.

GOODELL, WILLIAM. *The American Slave Code in Theory and Practice.* New York, 1853.

GRAEBNER, NORMAN A. (ed.). *Politics and the Crisis of 1860.* Urbana, Ill., 1961.

GREG, PERCY. *History of the United States from the Foundation of Virginia to the Reconstruction of the Union.* London, 1887.

GUTHRIE, JAMES M. *Campfires of the Afro-American: Or the Colored Man as a Patriot, Soldier, Sailor and Hero in the Cause of Free America.* Philadelphia, 1899.

HAAS, BEN. *KKK.* Evanston, Ill., 1963.

HARRIS, ROBERT J. *The Quest for Equality: The Constitution, Congress and the Supreme Court.* Baton Rouge, 1960.

HART, ALBERT BUSHNELL. *Salmon Portland Chase.* Boston, 1899.

HARTSHORN, W. N., and PENNIMAN, GEORGE W. *An Era of Progress and Promise: 1863–1910.* Boston, 1910.

HAYES, MELVIN L. *Mr. Lincoln Runs for President.* New York, 1960.

HICKOK, CHARLES T. *The Negro in Ohio, 1802–1870.* Cleveland, 1896.

HINES, MARGARET McNEILL. "Northern Negroes during the Civil War." Unpublished Master's thesis, Howard University, Washington, 1940.

HINTON, RICHARD J. *John Brown and His Men.* New York, 1894.

HOLLOWELL, N. P. *The Negro as a Soldier in the War of the Rebellion.* Boston, 1897.

HOLMES, DWIGHT O. W. *The Evolution of the Negro College.* New York, 1934.

HOWARD UNIVERSITY. *The Civil War in Perspective.* Papers contributed to the 24th Annual Conference. Washington, 1961.

HUMPHREYS, A. A. *The Virginia Campaign of 1864 and 1865.* New York, 1883.

HUNDLEY, D. R. *Social Relations in Our Southern States.* New York, 1860.

HURD, JOHN CODMAN. *The Law of Freedom and Bondage in the United States.* 2 vols. Boston, 1858–1862.

INGERSOLL, L. D. *Life of Horace Greeley.* San Francisco, 1873.

INGLE, EDWARD. *The Negro in the District of Columbia.* Baltimore, 1893.

JOHNS, JOHN E. *Florida during the Civil War.* Gainesville, Fla., 1963.

JOHNSON, G. G. *A Social History of the Sea Islands.* Chapel Hill, N.C., 1930.

JOHNSON, H. U. *From Dixie to Canada: Romances and Realities of the Underground Railroad.* Buffalo, 1894.

JOHNSON, ROBERT U., and BUEL, CLARENCE C. (eds.). *Battles and Leaders of the Civil War.* 4 vols. New York, 1887–1888.

JOHNSTON, SIR HARRY HAMILTON. *The Negro in the New World.* New York, 1910.

JONES, LEWIS WADE. *Cold Rebellion: The South's Oligarchy in Revolt.* London, 1962.

KISER, CLYDE VERNON. *Sea Island to City.* New York, 1932.

KNAPP, CHARLES MERRIAM. *New Jersey Politics during the Period of the Civil War and Reconstruction.* Geneva, N.Y., 1924.

KONVITZ, MILTON R., and LESKES, THEODORE. *A Century of Civil Rights.* New York, 1961.

LEECH, MARGARET. *Reveille in Washington: 1860–1865.* New York, 1941.

LESTER, JOHN C. *The Ku Klux Klan.* New York, 1905.

LEWINSON, PAUL. *Race, Class and Party.* New York, 1932.

LITWACK, LEON F. *North of Slavery: The Negro in the Free States, 1790–1860.* Chicago, 1961.

LOGAN, RAYFORD W. *The Negro in American Life and Thought: The Nadir, 1877–1901.* New York, 1954.

LONN, ELLA. *Desertion during the Civil War.* New York, 1925.

LOVELL, CAROLINE C. *The Golden Islands of Georgia.* Boston, 1932.

LYNCH, JOHN R. *The Facts of Reconstruction.* New York, 1913.

McCONNELL, JOHN PRESTON. *Negroes and Their Treatment in Virginia from 1865 to 1867.* Ph.D. dissertation, University of Virginia, 1905. Pulaski, Va., 1910.

McKAY, MARTHA N. *When the Tide Turned in the Civil War.* Indianapolis, 1929.

McKITRICK, ERIC L. *Andrew Johnson and Reconstruction.* Chicago, 1960.

McPHERSON, EDWARD. *The Political History of the United States of America during the Period of Reconstruction: 1865–1870.* Washington, 1875.

McPHERSON, JAMES M. *The Negro's Civil War: How American Negroes Felt and Acted during the War for the Union.* New York, 1965.

————. *The Struggle for Equality: Abolitionists and the Negro in the Civil War and Reconstruction.* Princeton, N.J., 1964.

MAIN, E. M. *The Story of the Marches, Battles and Incidents of the Third United States Colored Cavalry, a Fighting Regiment in the War of the Rebellion.* Louisville, Ky., 1908.

MALLARD, R. Q. *Plantation Life before Emancipation.* Richmond, Va., 1892.

MANDEL, BERNARD. *Labor: Free and Slave.* New York, 1955.

MASSEY, MARY ELIZABETH. *Refugee Life in the Confederacy.* Baton Rouge, 1964.

MAYER, GEORGE H. *The Republican Party, 1854–1964.* New York, 1964.

MELTZER, MILTON (ed.). *In Their Own Words.* 2 vols. New York, 1964–1965.

NEVINS, ALLAN. *The Emergence of Lincoln.* 4 vols. New York, 1950.

————. *Ordeal of the Union.* New York, 1947.

————. *War Becomes Revolution.* New York, 1960.

NICOLAY, JOHN G., and HAY, JOHN. *Abraham Lincoln: A History.* 10 vols. New York, 1917.

PARRINGTON, VERNON L. *Main Currents in American Thought.* Vols. II and III. New York, 1927–1930.

PARTON, JAMES. *General Butler in New Orleans: Being a History of the Administration of the Department of the Gulf in the Year 1862.* New York, 1864.

PEIRCE, PAUL S. *The Freedmen's Bureau: A Chapter in the History of Reconstruction.* Iowa City, Iowa, 1904.

PORTER, GEORGE H. *Ohio Politics during the Civil War Period.* New York, 1911.

PRESSLY, THOMAS J. *Americans Interpret Their Civil War.* Princeton, N.J., 1954.

QUARLES, BENJAMIN. *Frederick Douglass*. Washington, 1948.

_____. *The Negro in the Civil War*. Boston, 1953.

_____. *The Negro in the Making of America*. New York, 1964.

QUILLIN, FRANK U. *The Color Line in Ohio*. Ann Arbor, Mich., 1913.

RANDALL, JAMES G. *The Civil War and Reconstruction*. New York, 1937.

_____. *Constitutional Problems under Lincoln*. New York, 1926.

RANDEL, WILLIAM PIERCE. *The Ku Klux Klan: A Century of Infamy*. Philadelphia, 1965.

REDDING, J. SAUNDERS. *They Came in Chains: Americans from Africa*. New York, 1950.

REMOND, SARAH PARKER. *The Negroes and Anglo-Americans as Freedmen and Soldiers*. London, 1864.

RHODES, JAMES FORD. *History of the United States from the Compromise of 1850*. Vols. III–V. New York, 1917.

RICE, ARNOLD S. *The Ku Klux Klan in American Politics*. Washington, 1962.

RICHIE, ANDREW. *The Soldier, the Battle and the Victory: Being a Brief Account of the Work of Rev. John Rankin in the Anti-Slavery Cause. . . .* Cincinnati, n.d.

ROBERT, JOSEPH C. *The Tobacco Kingdom: Plantation, Market and Factory in Virginia and North Carolina, 1800–1860*. Durham, N.C., 1938.

ROBERTSON, JAMES I. *The Civil War*. Washington, 1963.

ROLLIN, FRANK A. *Life and Public Services of Martin R. Delany*. Boston, 1868.

ROSE, WILLIE LEE. *Rehearsal for Reconstruction: The Port Royal Experiment*. Indianapolis, 1964.

ROSENBLOOM, EUGENE H. *The Civil War Era, 1850–1873*. Columbus, Ohio, 1944.

ROUSSÈVE, CHARLES BARTHELEMY. *The Negro in Louisiana: Aspects of His History and His Literature*. New Orleans, 1937.

RUSSELL, JOHN H. *The Free Negro in Virginia, 1619–1865*. Baltimore, 1913.

SCHEINER, SETH M. *Negro Mecca: A History of the Negro in New York City, 1865–1920*. New York, 1965.

SCHLESINGER, ARTHUR M. *The Rise of Modern America, 1865–1951*. New York, 1951.

SCHMIDT, HUBERT. *Slavery and Attitudes on Slavery in Hunterdon County, New Jersey*. Flemington, N.J., 1941.

SCOTT, MINGO. *The Negro in Tennessee Politics and Governmental Affairs, 1865–1965*. Nashville, Tenn., 1965.

SEDGWICK, CHARLES B. *Emancipation and Enrollment of Slaves in the Services of the United States*. Washington, 1862.

SELLERS, JAMES BENSON. *Slavery in Alabama*. University, Ala., 1950.

SHANNON, F. A. *The Organization and Administration of the Union Army, 1861–1865*. 2 vols. Cleveland, 1928.

SIMKINS, FRANCIS B. *A History of the South*. New York, 1953.

_____, and PATTON, JAMES W. *The Women of the Confederacy*. Richmond, Va., 1936.

_____, and WOODY, ROBERT H. *South Carolina during Reconstruction*. Chapel Hill, N.C., 1932.

SIMMONS, WILLIAM J. *Men of Mark: Eminent, Progressive and Rising*. Cleveland, 1891.

SINCLAIR, WILLIAM A. *The Aftermath of Slavery*. Boston, 1905.

SINGLETARY, OTIS A. *Negro Militia and Reconstruction*. Austin, Tex., 1927.

SMEDES, SUSAN DABNEY. *A Southern Planter*. New York, 1899.

SMEDLEY, R. C. *History of the Underground Railroad in Chester and the Neighboring Counties of Pennsylvania*. Lancaster, Pa., 1883.

SPEARS, JOHN R. *The American Slave-Trade*. New York, 1900.

SPERO, STERLING D., and HARRIS, ABRAM L. *The Black Worker*. New York, 1931.

STAMPP, KENNETH M. *And the War Came*. Baton Rouge, 1950.

_____. *The Era of Reconstruction, 1865–1877*. New York, 1965.

_____. *The Peculiar Institution: Slavery in the Ante-Bellum South*. New York, 1956.

_____ (ed.). *The Causes of the Civil War*. Englewood Cliffs, N.J., 1959.

STARR, LOUIS M. *Bohemian Brigade: Civil War Newsmen in Action*. New York, 1954.

STEWARD, THEOPHILUS GOULD. *The Colored Regulars in the United States Army*. Philadelphia, 1904.

SWINT, HENRY LEE. *The Northern Teacher in the South, 1862–1870*. Nashville, Tenn., 1941.

SYDNOR, CHARLES S. *Slavery in Mississippi*. New York, 1933.

TALBOT, EDITH ARMSTRONG. *Samuel Chapman Armstrong: A Biographical Study*. New York, 1904.

TANNENBAUM, FRANK. *Slave and Citizen: The Negro in the Americas.* New York, 1947.

TAYLOR, ALRUTHEUS AMBUSH. *The Negro in South Carolina during the Reconstruction.* Washington, 1924.

TAYLOR, R. H. *Slaveholding in North Carolina: An Economic View.* Chapel Hill, N.C., 1926.

TEN BROEK, JACOBUS. *The Anti-Slavery Origins of the Fourteenth Amendment.* Berkeley, Calif., 1951.

THOMAS, BENJAMIN P., and HYMAN, HAROLD M. *Stanton: The Life and Times of Lincoln's Secretary of War.* New York, 1962.

THOMAS, JOHN L. *The Liberator: William Lloyd Garrison, a Biography.* Boston, 1963.

TROTTER, JAMES M. *Music and Some Highly Musical People.* New York, 1878.

TURNER, EDWARD RAYMOND. *The Negro in Pennsylvania, 1639–1861.* Washington, 1911.

TURNER, HENRY M. *The Negro in Slavery, War, and Peace.* Philadelphia, 1913.

TURNER, LORENZO D. *Anti-Slavery Sentiment in American Literature Prior to 1865.* Washington, 1929.

TYLER, DENNETT (ed.). *Lincoln and the Civil War in the Diaries of John Hay.* New York, 1939.

U.S. COMMISSION ON CIVIL RIGHTS. *Freedom to the Free: Century of Emancipation, 1863–1963.* Washington, 1963.

WAMBOUGH, EUGENE. *A Selection of Cases on Constitutional Law.* Book III. Cambridge, Mass., 1915.

WARE, EDITH E. *Political Opinion in Massachusetts during the Civil War and Reconstruction.* New York, 1916.

WARMOTH, HENRY C. *War, Politics and Reconstruction.* New York, 1930.

WASHINGTON, BOOKER T. *The Story of the Negro.* Vol. II. New York, 1909.

WEBSTER, LAURA J. *The Operation of the Freedmen's Bureau in South Carolina.* Northampton, Mass., 1915–1916.

WEEKS, STEPHEN B. *Southern Quakers and Slavery: A Study in Institutional History.* Baltimore, 1896.

WESLEY, CHARLES H. *The Collapse of the Confederacy.* Washington, 1935.

————. *Negro Labor in the United States: A Study in American Economic History, 1850–1925.* New York, 1927.

————. *Ohio Negroes in the Civil War.* Columbus, Ohio, 1962.

WEST, REED W. *Contemporary French Opinion of the American Civil War.* Baltimore, 1924.

WILDER, BURT GREEN. *Fifty-Fifth Regiment of the Massachusetts Volunteer Infantry, Colored: June 1863—September 1865.* Chestnut Hill, Mass., 1919.

WILEY, BELL IRVIN. *Embattled Confederates: An Illustrated History of Southerners at War.* New York, 1964.

————. *Southern Negroes: 1861–1865.* New Haven, Conn., 1938.

WILLIAMS, ERIC. *Capitalism and Slavery.* Chapel Hill, N.C., 1938.

WILLIAMS, GEORGE W. *History of the Negro Race in America, 1619–1880.* 2 vols. New York, 1883.

————. *A History of the Negro Troops in the War of the Rebellion.* New York, 1888.

————. *Negro Troops in the Rebellion, 1861–1865.* New York, 1888.

WILSON, HENRY. *History of Anti-Slavery Measures of the Thirty-Seventh and Thirty-Eighth United States Congresses, 1861–1864.* Boston, 1864.

————. *History of the Rise and Fall of the Slave Power in America.* Vols. I–III. Boston, 1877.

WILSON, JAMES HARRISON. *The Life of Charles A. Dana.* New York, 1907.

WILSON, JOSEPH T. *The Black Phalanx: The History of the Negro Soldiers of the United States.* Hartford, Conn., 1888.

————. *Emancipation: Its Course and Progress.* Hampton, Va., 1882.

WISH, HARVEY (ed.). *The Negro since Emancipation.* Englewood Cliffs, N.J., 1964.

WOODSON, CARTER G. *The History of the Negro Church.* Washington, 1945.

WOODWARD, C. VANN. *The Burden of Southern History.* Baton Rouge, 1960.

WRIGHT, RICHARD R., JR. (ed.). *Centennial Encyclopaedia of the African Methodist Episcopal Church.* Philadelphia, 1916.

PERIODICALS AND NEWSPAPERS

ADAMS, MARY JOICE. "The History of Suffrage in Michigan," *Michigan Political Science Association Publication,* III (March 1898).

ADDINGTON, WENDELL G. "Slave Insurrections in Texas," *Journal of Negro History,* XXXV (October 1950).

ALEXANDER, RAYMOND PACE. "The Upgrading of the Negro's Status by Supreme Court Decisions," *Journal of Negro History*, XXX (April 1945).

American Freedman (New York). April 1866.

Anglo-African (New York). 1859.

Anti-Slavery Record (New York). 1863.

APTHEKER, HERBERT. "Negro Casualties in the Civil War," *Journal of Negro History*, XXXII (January 1947).

————. "The Negro in the Union Navy," *ibid.,* XXXII (April 1947).

BARDOLPH, RICHARD. "The Distinguished Negro in America, 1770–1936," *American Historical Review*, XLV (April 1955).

BAUER, RAYMOND and ALICE. "Day to Day Resistance to Slavery," *Journal of Negro History*, XXVII (October 1942).

BELL, HOWARD H. "Negro Nationalism: A Factor in Emigration Projects, 1858–1861," *Journal of Negro History*, XLVII (January 1962).

BIGELOW, MARTHA M. "The Significance of Milliken's Bend in the Civil War," *Journal of Negro History*, XLV (July 1960).

BILLINGTON, RAY ALLEN. "A Social Experiment: The Port Royal Journal of Charlotte L. Forten, 1862–1863," *Journal of Negro History*, XXXV (July 1950).

BINDER, FREDERICK M. "Pennsylvania Negro Regiments in the Civil War," *Journal of Negro History*, XXXVII (October 1952).

BLASSINGAME, JOHN WESLEY. "The Recruitment of Negro Troops in Missouri during the Civil War," *Missouri Historical Review*, LVIII (April 1964).

BOYD, WILLIS D. "The American Colonization Society and the Slave Recaptives of 1860–1861," *Journal of Negro History*, XLVII (April 1962).

BREWER, W. M. "Lincoln and the Border States," *Journal of Negro History*, XXXIV (January 1949).

BROWN, IRA V. "Pennsylvania and the Rights of the Negro, 1865–1877," *Pennsylvania History*, XXVIII (January 1961).

CARPENTER, JOHN A. "Atrocities in the Reconstruction Period," *Journal of Negro History*, XLVII (October 1962).

Cincinnati Daily Gazette. 1861–1864.

Cincinnati Enquirer. 1859, 1861, 1865.

COLE, ARTHUR C. "Lincoln's Election an Immediate Menace to Slavery in the States," *American Historical Review*, XXXVI (July 1931).

COX, JOHN and LA WANDA. "Andrew Johnson and His Ghost Writers: An Analysis of the Freedmen's Bureau and Civil Rights Veto Messages," *Mississippi Valley Historical Review*, XLVII (December 1961).

————. "General O. O. Howard and the 'Misrepresented Bureau,'" *Journal of Southern History*, XIX (November 1953).

DeBow's Southern and Western Review (New Orleans). 1846–1867.

Douglass' Monthly (Rochester, N.Y.). 1864.

DUMOND, DWIGHT L. "The Fourteenth Amendment Trilogy in Historical Perspective," *Journal of Negro History*, XLIII (July 1958).

DYER, BRAINERD. "The Treatment of Colored Union Troops by the Confederates, 1861–1865," *Journal of Negro History*, XX (July 1935).

ELIOT, CHRISTOPHER. "The Lincoln Emancipation Statute," *Journal of Negro History*, XXIX (October 1944).

FEHRENBACHER, D. E. "The Origins and Purpose of Lincoln's 'House Divided' Speech," *Mississippi Valley Historical Review,* XLVI (March 1960).

FISHEL, LESLIE H., JR. "Northern Prejudice and Negro Suffrage, 1865–1870," *Journal of Negro History*, XXXIX (January 1954).

Frank Leslie's Illustrated Weekly (New York). 1855–1866.

FRANKLIN, JOHN HOPE. "A Century of Civil War Observance," *Journal of Negro History*, XLVII (April 1962).

GANNETT, WILLIAM CHANNING, and HALE, EDWARD EVERETT. "The Freedmen at Port Royal," *North American Review*, CI (July 1865).

GEYL, PIETER. "The American Civil War and the Problem of Inevitability," *New England Quarterly*, XXIV (June 1951).

GUILD, JUNE PURCELL. "Who Is a Negro?" *Journal of Negro Education*, XXXIII (January 1964).

Harper's Weekly (New York). 1859, 1861–1865.

HENRY, JAMES O. "The United States Christian Commission in the Civil War," *Civil War History*, VI (December 1960).

HIGGINSON, THOMAS WENTWORTH. "Colored Troops under Fire," *Century Illustrated Monthly Magazine*, LIV (May 1897).

HODDER, FRANK H. "Some Phases of the Dred Scott Case," *Mississippi Valley Historical Review,* XVI (June 1929).

HOFFMAN, EDWIN D. "From Slavery to Self-Reliance," *Journal of Negro History,* XLI (January 1956).

JACKSON, LUTHER P. "The Educational Efforts of the Freedmen's Bureau and Freedmen's Aid Societies in South Carolina, 1862–1872," *Journal of Negro History,* VIII (January 1923).

JAMES, JOSEPH B. "Southern Reaction to the Proposal of the Fourteenth Amendment," *Journal of Southern History,* XXII (November 1956).

KAPLAN, SIDNEY. "The Miscegenation Issue in the Election of 1864," *Journal of Negro History,* XXXIV (July 1949).

KASSEL, C. "Educating the Slave: A Forgotten Chapter of Civil War History," *Open Court,* XLI (April 1927).

KRUG, MARK M. "The Republican Party and the Emancipation Proclamation," *Journal of Negro History,* XLVIII (April 1963).

Liberator (Boston). 1831–1865.

LOFTON, WILLISTON H. "Northern Labor and the Negro during the Civil War," *Journal of Negro History,* XXXIV (July 1949).

McCONNELL, ROLAND C. "From the Preliminary to Final Emancipation: The First Hundred Days," *Journal of Negro History,* XLVIII (October 1963).

McGORRTY, WILLIAM B. "Exploration in Mass Emancipation," *William and Mary Quarterly,* 2nd Series, XXI (July 1941).

MAN, ALBON P., JR. "Labor Competition and the New York Draft Riots of 1863," *Journal of Negro History,* XXXVI (October 1951).

Merchants' Magazine and Commercial Review (New York). 1839–1870.

National Anti-Slavery Standard (New York). 1840–1868.

National Era (Washington). 1847–1864.

National Intelligencer (Washington). 1861.

New York Times. 1861–1865.

New York Tribune. 1841.

North Star (Rochester, N.Y.). 1847–1863.

Ohio State Journal (Columbus). 1859, 1863.

OSBORN, GEORGE C. "The Atlanta Campaign, 1864," *Georgia Historical Quarterly,* XXXIV (December 1950).

PEASE, WILLIAM H. "Three Years among the Freedmen: William C. Gannett and the Port Royal Experiment," *Journal of Negro History,* XLII (April 1957).

PINKETT, HAROLD T. "Efforts to Annex Santo Domingo to the United States, 1866–1871," *Journal of Negro History,* XXVI (January 1941).

REDDICK, L. D. "The Negro Policy of the United States Army, 1775–1945," *Journal of Negro History,* XXXIV (January 1949).

REID, BILL G. "Confederate Opponents of Arming the Slaves," *Journal of Mississippi History,* XXII (October 1960).

REID, ROBERT D. "The Negro in Alabama during the Civil War," *Journal of Negro History,* XXXV (July 1950).

RICHARDSON, JOE M. "A Negro Success Story: James Dallas Burrus, 1846–1928," *Journal of Negro History,* L (October 1965).

RUCHAMES, LOUIS. "William Lloyd Garrison and the Negro Franchise," *Journal of Negro History,* L (January 1965).

ST. CLAIR, SADIE DANIEL. "Slavery as a Diplomatic Factor in Anglo-American Relations during the Civil War," *Journal of Negro History,* XXX (July 1945).

Southern Literary Messenger (Richmond, Va.). 1834–1864.

STEPHENSON, N. W. "The Question of Arming the Slaves," *American Historical Review,* XVIII (January 1913).

TEBEAU, C. W. "Some Aspects of Planter–Freedman Relations, 1865–1880," *Journal of Negro History,* XXI (April 1936).

THOMAS, HENRY GODDARD. "The Colored Troops at Petersburg," *Century Magazine,* XII (September 1887).

TOPPIN, EDGAR A. "Humbly They Served: The Black Brigade in the Defense of Cincinnati," *Journal of Negro History,* XLVIII (April 1963).

TREFOUSSE, HANS L. "Ben Wade and the Negro," *Ohio Historical Quarterly,* LXVII (April 1959).

WAGANDT, CHARLES L. "The Army versus Maryland Slavery, 1862–1864," *Civil War History,* IX (June 1964).

WEISBERGER, BERNARD A. "The Newspaper Reporter and the Kansas Imbroglio," *Mississippi Valley Historical Review,* XXXVI (March 1950).

WESLEY, CHARLES H. "The Civil War and the Negro-American," *Journal of Negro History,* XLVII (April 1962).

————. "The Employment of Negroes as Soldiers in the Confederate Army," *ibid.*, IV (July 1919).

————. "Lincoln's Plan for Colonizing the Emancipated Negroes," *ibid.*, IV (January 1919).

————. "Negro Suffrage in the Period of Constitution Making, 1787–1865," *ibid.*, XXXII (April 1947).

————. "The Struggle for Recognition of Haiti and Liberia as Independent Republics," *ibid.*, II (October 1917).

WISH, HARVEY. "Slave Disloyalty under the Confederacy," *Journal of Negro History*, XXIII (October 1938).

Xenia Torchlight (Xenia, Ohio). 1861–1866.

ZOELLNER, ROBERT H. "Negro Colonization: The Climate of Opinion Surrounding Lincoln in 1860–1865," *Mid-America*, XLII (July 1960).

BOOKS FOR CHILDREN AND YOUNG ADULTS

ARCHIBALD, HELEN A. (ed.). *Negro History and Culture: Selected Material for Use with Children.* Chicago, 1965.

BECKER, JOHN L. *The Negro in American Life.* New York, 1944.

BONTEMPS, ARNA W. *Frederick Douglass: Slave, Fighter, Freeman.* New York, 1959.

————. *100 Years of Negro Freedom.* New York, 1961.

————. *The Story of George Washington Carver.* New York, 1954.

————. *Story of the Negro.* New York, 1962.

BRAWLEY, BENJAMIN. *Negro Builders and Heroes.* Chapel Hill, N.C., 1937.

BROWN, FRANCIS WILLIAMS. *Looking for Orlando.* New York, 1961.

BUCKMASTER, HENRIETTA. *Flight to Freedom: Story of the Underground Railroad.* New York, 1958.

————. *Freedom Bound: The Real Story of the Reconstruction, 1868–1875.* New York, 1965.

CONRAD, EARL. *Harriet Tubman.* Washington, 1943.

CURTIS, CLARA K. *Fighters for Freedom.* Rochester, N.Y., 1933.

DERRICOTTE, ELSIE P., TURNER, GENEVA C., and ROY, JESSIE H. *Word Pictures of Great Negroes.* Washington, 1964.

DICK, TRELLA L. *The Island on the Border.* New York, 1963.

EDMONDS, WALTER. *Cadmus Henry.* New York, 1949.

ERDMAN, LOULA G. *The Wind Blows Free.* New York, 1952.

FAUSET, ARTHUR HUFF. *Sojourner Truth: God's Faithful Pilgrim.* Chapel Hill, N.C., 1938.

FISHER, AILEEN. *A Lantern in the Window.* New York, 1957.

FRITZ, JEAN. *Brady.* New York, 1960.

GARA, LARRY. *The Liberty Line: The Legend of the Underground Railroad.* Lexington, Ky., 1961.

GRAHAM, SHIRLEY. *Booker T. Washington.* New York, 1955.

————. *There Once Was a Slave: The Heroic Story of Frederick Douglass.* New York, 1947.

HAGLER, MARGARET. *Larry and the Freedom Man.* New York, 1959.

HENNESSY, MAURICE, and SAUTER, EDWARD., JR. *A Crown for Thomas Peters.* New York, 1964.

HOWARD, ELIZABETH. *North Winds Blow Free.* New York, 1949.

HUGHES, LANGSTON. *Famous American Negroes.* New York, 1954.

————. *Famous Negro Heroes of America.* New York, 1958.

————. *The First Book of Negroes.* New York, 1952.

————, and MELTZER, MILTON. *A Pictorial History of the Negro in America.* New York, 1963.

LEVY, MIMI COOPER. *Corrie and the Yankee.* New York, 1959.

McCARTHY, AGNES, and REDDICK, L. D. *Worth Fighting For.* New York, 1965.

McGOVERN, ANN. *Runaway Slave.* New York, 1965.

MEADOWCROFT, ENID. *By Secret Railway.* New York, 1948.

PARRISH, ANNE. *A Clouded Star.* New York, 1948.

PETRY, ANN. *Harriet Tubman, Conductor on the Underground Railroad.* New York, 1955.

RICHARDSON, BEN. *Great American Negroes.* New York, 1956.

SHACKELFORD, JANE D. *The Child's Story of the Negro.* Washington, 1956.

STEINMAN, BEATRICE. *This Railroad Disappears.* New York, 1958.

STERLING, DOROTHY. *Captain of the Planter.* Garden City, N.Y., 1958.

————. *Forever Free: The Story of the Emancipation Proclamation.* New York, 1963.

_____. *Freedom Train: The Story of Harriet Tubman.* Garden City, N.Y., 1954.

STEVENSON, AUGUSTA. *Booker T. Washington: Ambitious Boy.* Indianapolis, 1945.

SWIFT, HILDEGARDE H. *North Star Shining.* New York, 1947.

_____. *The Railroad to Freedom.* New York, 1932.

THOMAS, HENRY. *George Washington Carver.* New York, 1958.

WASHINGTON, BOOKER T. *Up from Slavery.* New York, 1901.

WOODSON, CARTER G., and WESLEY, CHARLES H. *Negro Makers of History.* Washington, 1958.

_____. *The Story of the Negro Retold.* Washington, 1959.

WRISTON, HILDRETH. *Susan's Secret.* New York, 1957.

MUSIC, PHONOGRAPH RECORDS AND FILM STRIPS

MUSIC

ALLEN, WILLIAM F., WARE, CHARLES P., and GARRISON, LUCY M. *Slave Songs of the United States.* New York, 1929.

BARTON, REV. W. E. *Old Plantation Hymns: With Historical and Descriptive Notes.* Boston, 1899.

DETT, R. NATHANIEL (ed.). *Negro Spirituals.* London, 1959.

JOHNSON, JAMES WELDON. *Books of American Negro Spirituals.* 2 vols. New York, 1940.

MOORE, FRANK. *The Civil War in Song and Story, 1860–1865.* New York, 1889.

ODUM, HOWARD W., and JOHNSON, GUY B. *The Negro and His Songs: A Study of Typical Negro Songs in the South.* Chapel Hill, N.C., 1925.

WHITE, CLARENCE C. *Forty Negro Spirituals.* Philadelphia, 1927.

WHITE, N. I. *American Negro Folk Songs.* Hatboro, Pa., 1965.

WORK, JOHN W. *American Negro Songs.* New York, 1940.

PHONOGRAPH RECORDS

Adventures in Negro History. 2 vols. New York: Pepsi-Cola Company.

American Negro Songs from Slavery Times. Sung by Michel LaRue. New York: Folkways Records.

Who Built America. New York: Folkways Records.

FILM STRIPS

Harriet Tubman and the Underground Railroad. New York: McGraw-Hill Book Company.

History of the American Negro Series. New York: McGraw-Hill Book Company.

Leading American Negroes [Mary McLeod Bethune, George Washington Carver, Robert Smalls, Benjamin Banneker, Frederick Douglass, Harriet Tubman]. Chicago: Society for Visual Education, Inc.

Legacy of Honor. [Approaches to the study and teaching of the Negro in American History.] Washington: National Education Association.

The Negro Soldier. [Contribution of the Negro soldier from Revolutionary days until World War II.] Washington: U.S. Office of Education.

Picture Credits

The authors are grateful to the following for their aid in the search for unusual and interesting photographs with which to illustrate the text. Those pictures which have not been listed are in the private collection of United Publishing Corporation, Washington, D.C.

Key: T: Top;   B: Bottom;   L: Left;   R: Right;   C: Center

American Oil Company, Chicago: iiTL, BL, 13TR, 23, 107, 108B, 174, 249BR
Cincinnati Historical Society: 61, 105T, 168
E. N. Cotter, Jr., Lake Placid, New York: 14R
Edith Fleetwood, Washington: 215BL, 235, 243
Harris and Ewing, Washington: 197
Historical Society of Pennsylvania, Philadelphia: 215CR, 232T
Historical Society of Pennsylvania–Edward Carey Gardiner Collection, Philadelphia: 153, 223
Howard University, Washington: 108T, 142, 155, 159, 183, 257BL, 260B
Library of Congress: iiC, BR, 3, 5, 6, 8, 22, 25, 26, 29, 33R, 37, 39, 41, 43, 46, 57, 66, 73, 89, 117–121, 125, 126, 129, 130, 133, 134, 137B, 141B, 145, 146, 150, 154T, 161, 179, 182, 184, 185, 190–192, 195, 196, 200, 202, 215CL, BR, 217, 219B, 229T, 233, 234, 244, 245, 246B, 247, 248TR, BR, 217, 219B, 229T, 233, 234, 244, 245, 246B, 247, 248TR, BR, 249TL, BL, 250R, 251, 252TR, 254T, 256, 259BL, 261B
Library of Congress–Map Division: 208, 209
National Archives, Washington: 47–51, 227
National Archives–Military Records Division, Washington: 236–239, 240TL, TR, 241, 242
National Park Service, Washington: 252BL
New York Historical Society, New York: 77, 215C, 222B, 254B
New York Public Library: 36, 45, 64, 71, 74, 84, 85, 100, 102, 104, 112, 122, 152, 178, 194, 204TR, 215TL, BC, 217, 218B, 220, 221, 225, 229BL, BR, 230BR, 232B, 260T, 261T, 262
New York Public Library–Schomburg Collection: iiTC, 1, 7, 12, 13TL, 15, 19, 53, 56, 63, 64, 67, 78, 82, 83, 86, 87, 148, 149, 151, 172, 181, 188R, 210B, 216, 255, 257T, 258T, 259T
Sidney S. Rider Collection, Brown University Library, Providence: 170, 171
Smithsonian Institution, Washington: 240BL, BR

Index

Page numbers in *italic type* refer to illustrations.

Ableman v. *Booth* decision, 11
Abolitionists, 1, 28, 244, *219*
  attitude toward Negroes after Civil War, 153
  and Brown, John, 15, 16
  and Frémont proclamation, 32
  and Lincoln, Abraham, 41-44
  on Negroes as soldiers, 55-56
  and programs for education of Negroes, 145
  and slavery as cause of Civil War, 28
  and Thirteenth Amendment, 119
Act for the Relief of Volunteers, 56-57
Adams, James H., 5-6
Adams, Samuel, 34
African Methodist Episcopal Church, 60
  Baltimore Annual Conference of, 126
  and Methodist Episcopal Church, 154
  and Negro education, 134
  resolution on Lincoln's assassination, 126
  and Wilberforce University, 139
African Methodist Episcopal Zion Church
  and Methodist Episcopal Church, 154
  and Negro education, 133-134
Alabama, 110, 113, 116, 132, 193, 203
  Black Codes in, 128
  and reopening of slave trade, 7
  secession of, 24
  slave insurrections in, 80
Alabama (ship), 164
Albany (New York) Normal School, 142
Alexander, Archer, 174
Alienated American, 20
Alvord, John W., 132
American Anti-Slavery Society, 201-202
American Colonization Society, 111
American Conflict, 57-58
American Freedmen's Aid Commission, 27

American Freedmen's Union Commission, 134
American Missionary Association, 133, 135, 138, 139, 141
  and Atlanta University, 141
  and Fisk University, 139, 141
  and Hampton Institute, 139
  and Negro education, 146
  and Talladega College, 141
American Red Cross, 108
American Revolution, 56, 70, 80
Amistad (ship), 133
Amistad Committee, 133
Anderson, Aaron, 164
Anderson, John, 162-163
Anderson, Osborn Perry, 12, *14*
Anderson, Robert, 16
Andrew, John A.
  and 54th Massachusetts Regiment, 68-72
  letter to Shaw, Francis G., 69-70
  and pay discrimination, 97, 98, 99
  speech to Shaw, Robert Gould, 72
  on use of Negro officers, 62
Anglin, Tanner, 106
Anglo-African, 20, 24
Anthony, Susan B., 28, 119, *119*
Antietam, Battle of, 46, 52
Antislavery movement
  during Civil War, 28
  congressional leaders in, 29
  and Lincoln's 1864 election, 120
  and Thirteenth Amendment, 119
  See also Abolitionists
"Appeal of the Independent Democrats," 3
Appleton, John W. M., 70
Appomattox, Virginia, 114, *234*
Apprenticeship, 115-116, 128
Arkansas, 20, 110, 116, 117, 203
  and Negro suffrage, 117, 192, 193
  and reopening of slave trade, 7
  slave insurrections in, 80
Arkansas Colored Regiment, 1st, 157
Arlington, Virginia, 146
Armstrong, Samuel C., 139, 158
Army Appropriation Act of 1864, 99
Army of the James, 96

Army of the Potomac, 65, 96, 163, 168
  and Negro teamsters, 168
Arnold, G. M., 147
Arnold, I. N., 120
Ashley, James M., 118, 121, *121*
Ashmun, Jehudi, 139
Ashmun Institute, 139
Athens College, 142
Atlanta, Georgia, 172
Atlanta University, 141
Atlantic Monthly, 23
  article on Negro music, 156
  article by Pierce, Edward L., 131
Attucks, Crispus, 34
Augusta, Dr. Alexander T., 103-104, 174, *103*

Ball, Thomas, 174, 176
Baltimore, Maryland, 19, 20, 22, 199
Baltimore American, 160
Baltimore Sun, 14
Baltimore Traveler, 57
Banks, Nathaniel P., 27, 131, *85*
  and Negro education, 138
  and Port Hudson, Battle of, 83, 85
  report on Negro troops, 85
Baptist Church, 134, 152, 154-155
Baptist Home Mission Society, 134
Bard, Thomas, 164
Barnes, William H., 165
Barton, Colonel, 88
Barton, Clara, 108
Bassett, Lieutenant Colonel, 85
Bassett, Ebenezer Don Carlos, 210, *210*
Bates, Edward, 99, *46*
Battles. *See individual campaigns*
Bay Point, South Carolina, 145
Beard, Charles, 2
Beard, Oliver T., 69, 110
Beaty, Powhatan, 165
Beaufort College, *135*
Beaufort Hospital, 162
Beecher, Henry Ward, 147, 166
Beecher, James, 147
Bell, John, 20, 23

Benedict, Maryland, 158
Berea College, 139
Bethel African Methodist Episcopal Church, 199
Biddle, Nicholas, 35, *223*
Bingham, John A., 190, *190*
Birney, David, 96, 114, 124, 165
Black Codes, 126-129
    justifications of, 128
    protests against, 128-129, 180-181, 198
Black Hawk War, 41
Blair, Montgomery, 26-27, *46*
Blake, Robert, 164
Bonaparte, Napoleon, 56
Bond, Elizabeth, 138
Booth, John Wilkes, 126, *126, 251*
Booth, L. F., 92-93
Border states, 38, 207, *31*
    and compensated emancipation, 34-35, 67
    and Lincoln's attitude toward emancipation, 44
    Negro migration to, 167
    and slavery issue, 29-30, 32, *31*
    and Thirteenth Amendment, 119
Boston, J. T., 62
Boston, Massachusetts, 19, 51, 90, 166
    Negro troops from, 36, 70, 72
Boston Hospital, 162
Boston Journal, 70
Bouldon, Jesse Freeman, 155
Bounties
    discrimination in, 97-100
    to Negroes enlisting in army, 54, 57, 70, 71, *56*
Bowditch, William I., 70
Bowdoin College, 142
Bowles, John R., 110
Bowser, Mary Elizabeth, 17, 109-110
Boyd, Francis A., 110
Boynton, Charles B., 139
Bradford, Major, 92
Breckinridge, John C., 20, 23
Bronson, James H., 165
Brooklyn, New York, anti-Negro riot in, 76-77
Brown, Frederick, 11
Brown, John, 68, 82, 126, *11, 218*
    and abolitionists, 15-16
    background, 11
    and Douglass, Frederick, 15-16, 71
    estimate of, 15
    execution of, 14-15
    and Free Soilers, 11
    last messages of, 14, 15
    letter from colored women of Brooklyn, 14

letter from Harper, Frances Ellen Watkins, 14
    and Montgomery, James, 107
    raid on Harpers Ferry, 12, 14-16, 210, *13*
    sanity of, 14, 15
    trial of, 14, *15*
Brown, William Wells, 35, 84, *35*
Brown University, 168
Bryant, Reverend, 174
Bryant, William Cullen, 68, 74
Buchanan, James
    and Brown, John, 15
    and Dred Scott case, 3
Bull Run, first Battle of, 58, *58*
Bureau of Colored Troops, 80, 97
    establishment of, 66
    and raising of Negro troops, 102
    selection of officers by, 66, 101, 102-103
Bureau of Freedmen's Affairs. *See* Freedmen's Bureau
Burns, Francis, 154, *154*
Burnside, Ambrose E., 67, 93
Burt, W. T., 62
Bush, James W., 98-99
Butler, Benjamin F., 59, *62*
    and Army of the James, 96
    and Confederate laws, 117
    and experiment with free Negro labor, 27-28
    and fugitive slaves, 26-27
    and Phelps, J. W., 62-63
    and use of Negro officers, 67, 101
    and use of Negro troops, 39-40, 63-64, 96

Cailloux, André, 84-85
Cain, Richard Harvey, 60, 180, *59*
California, 19
Callender, Charles, 160
Cameron, Simon, 34, 36, 37, 62
Camp Meigs, 72
Camp William Penn, 103, 156
Campbell, Jabez, 20
Campbell, John A., 4
Cardozo, Francis L., 180, *181*
Carney, William H., 88, 90-91, 165, *90*
Carter, Lucy, 107
Casualties
    at the Crater, 93
    at Fort Pillow, 92
    at Milliken's Bend, 87
    at Port Hudson, 85
    in various battles, 97
Catron, John, 4

Census of 1860, 17-19, 115
Chaffee, C. C., 3
Chaffee, Mrs. C. C. *See* Emerson, Mrs. John
Chafin's Farm, Battle of, 96, 165
Chamberlain, Samuel E., 72
Channing, Edward, 15-16
Charleston, South Carolina, 19, 20, 23, 58, 187
Charleston Mercury, 17
Charlestown, West Virginia, 14
Chase, Salmon P., 28, *46, 184, 197*
    and *Matter of Elizabeth Turner,* 184-185
    and Negro employment and education, 145
    and Negro enlistment in Union armies, 62
    and Negro jurors, 186
    and Pierce, Edward L., 131, 145
Chatfield, Colonel, 88
Cheever, Henry T., 28
Cherokee Indians, 123
Chesapeake Marine Railroad and Dry Dock Company, 206
Chicago, Illinois, 20, 166
    anti-Negro riots in, 77
Chicago Tribune
    on equal pay for Negro troops, 99
    on Negroes as soldiers, 95
Chickasaw Indians, 123
Choctaw (gunboat), 87
Choctaw Indians, 123
Christian Record, 20
Cincinnati, Ohio, 28, 68, 166
    Negroes in the defense of, 60-61
    riot in, 75-76, 77
    wealthy Negroes in, 19, 168, 172
Cincinnati Commercial, 160
Cincinnati Gazette, 61, 75, 76
Citizenship for Negroes, 4, 8
    and Civil Rights Act of 1866, 184
    and Fourteenth Amendment, 184, 189-190, 191, 197-198
    in individual states, 184, 197-198
Civil Rights Act of 1866, 183-184, 189, 190, 195
Civil War
    casualties. *See* Casualties
    important dates, 212-213
    Negro education during, 131, 135-139, 145-147
    Negro heroes of, 84-85, 88, 90-91, 96, 101, 106, 164-165, 235. *See also* Medals of Honor; Negro troops, in battle; Negroes, in the Navy

Negro life in North during, 74-78, 153, 154, 160, 165-172, 253, *253*

Negro life in South during, 17, 80-81, 143-145, 151-155, 160, 161-162, 253, *37, 143, 152, 155, 159, 253, 254, 255, 260, 261*

Negro troops in. *See* Negro regiments; Negro troops; Negroes in the armed forces; *and individual regiments*

Negro women in, 106-110

and secession of South, 1, 2, 3, *31*

and slave insurrections, 17, 80-81

and slavery issue, 2, 3, 10, 25, 34, 35, 42, 220

See also individual subject headings

Claflin, Lee, 28

Clark, Peter H., 20, 168, 187, *168*

Clay, Henry, 41

Cleburne, Patrick, 113

Cleveland, Ohio, 36, 166

Clifford, Nathan, *197*

Cobb, Howell, 113

Colonization of freedmen, 5, 111-112

and emancipation program, 34, 46, 181

and Johnson, Andrew, 182

and Lincoln, 34, 42, 46, 111, 181-182

plan for District of Columbia freedmen, 111

Colorado Territory, Negro voting rights in, 186

Colored Man's Journal, 20

Colored Methodist Episcopal Church, 133-134, 154

Committee for West Indian Missions, 133

Compensation to slaveowners, 34, 41-42, 46, 67-68

and Garrison, William Lloyd, 42

Compromise of 1850, 2, 3

Confederate armies

casualties. *See* Casualties

conditions of Negroes in, 144

desertions from, 112

use of Negroes, 27, 37, 39, 56-58, 112-114, 143-144, *37, 57, 112, 143*

See also individual battles

Confederate Congress, 66-67, 112-113, 143-144

Confederate Navy, 104

Confederate States of America, *31*

establishment of, 1-2, 3, 24

and Hunter, David, 40

Negro supporters of, 17

and Reconstruction, 116, 183, 202

Confederate War Department, 58, 66

Confiscation Acts, 29, 32, 42, 43

Congdon, James B., 70

Congregationalist Church, 133, 134

Congressional Globe, 121

Congressional Medal of Honor, 96, 164-165, *240*

Connecticut, 69

and fugitive slaves, 11

and Negro suffrage, 186

segregation in education, 59, 139

Connecticut Regiment, 6th, 88

Connecticut Regiment, 7th, 91

Connecticut Regiment, 10th, 88

Conscription Act, 77, 78

Consolidated American Baptist Missionary Convention, 154

Constitutional Union Party, 20, 22. *See also* Know-Nothing Party

Contraband Relief Association, 27

Convention of Slaveholders, Baltimore, Maryland, 19

Copeland, John Anthony, 12, 14, 15, 71, *14*

Corps d'Afrique. *See* Louisiana Negro regiments

Crater, Battle of the, 93, 96, 158, *94*

Creek Indians, 123

Crosby, J., 168

Crusader (ship), 106

Curtis, Benjamin R., 4

Daily Atlas and Bee, 34

Dana, Charles A., 121

Daniel, Justice, 4

Darbytown Road, Battle of, 96

Davidson, J. W., 175

Davis, D., *197*

Davis, Garrett, 39, 119, 207

Davis, Jefferson, *41*

and Bowser, Mary Elizabeth, 109-110

capture of, 114

compared with Lincoln, 41

on Emancipation Proclamation, 53-54

on Negroes in armies, 112-113

proclamation on treatment of Union officers, 116-117

trial of, 186

Day, W. H., 20

Day, William Howard, 187

Deep Bottom, Battle of, 96, 165

Delany, Martin R., 103, 172-173, *172*

and equal rights struggle, 180

and Sea Island freedmen, 150

DeLarge, Robert C., 180, *180*

Democratic Party, 182

and Civil Rights Act of 1866, 184

and election of 1860, 20, 22, 23

and election of 1868, 194

and Negro suffrage, 22, 186, 187, 201

split over slavery, 2-3

and white workers, 75

Department of the Army's investigation of Fort Jackson mutiny, 81

Department of Negro Affairs, 27-28

Derrick, William B., 106

Detroit, Michigan, 166

Dickerson, Anna E., 72

Dickson, William M., 61, *61*

Discrimination

and Black Codes, 127-129

in labor unions, 75

against Negro troops, 38-39, 62, 65, 73-74, 97-100, 103-104

against Negro workers, 75-77, 78, 132-133, 170-171

District of Columbia, 73

colonization plan for Negroes in, 111

emancipation in, 34, 42, 73, 207

freedmen in, 19, 127, 172

freedmen's national monument to Lincoln, 174-176, *174, 248*

Negro migration to, 168

and Negro suffrage, 186, 188

and Negro troops, 36, 110

segregation in, 59-60

slavery in, 8, 41, 72

Dodson, Jacob, 36

"Don't You Want To Be a Soldier, Soldier, Soldier?" 160

Dorsey, Decatur, 165

Douglas, Stephen A., 8, 10, 20, 22, 23, *10*

Douglass, Frederick, 12, 88, *23*

and Brown, John, 15-16, 71

and Delany, Martin R., 172

on Dred Scott decision, 5

on Emancipation Proclamation, 51

and equal pay to Negro troops, 73-74, 99

and Georgia Equal Rights Association, 198

and Johnson, Andrew, 188-189, 192-193

and Massachusetts Negro regiments, 70, 71

and Negro suffrage, 187, 188-189, 192

on Negro troops and citizenship, 72-73
and presidential campaign of 1860, 23
and recruiting of Negro troops, 68, 70, 71
and Smith, Gerrit, 23
Douglass, Lewis H., 70, 88
Douglass Institute, Baltimore, 135
Downing, George T., 168-169, *189*
and Negro suffrage, 187, 188
and segregation in education, 168-169, 170-171
Draft
and free Negroes, 67
and race riot in New York, 77-78, *77*
Drayton, Thomas F., 17
Dred Scott decision, 3-5, 11, 185
and Civil Rights Act, 184
Lincoln on, 9-10
reversal of, 42
Du Bois, W. E. B., 7
Dumas, F. E., 101, 174
Durrant, Henry K., 107
Dwight, William, 85
Dwight's Journal of Music, 156

Earle, W. C., 175
Eaton, John, Jr., 27, 86, 138
Eckert, Thomas T., 42
Edisto River, South Carolina, battle at, 82
Eliot, Dr., 174
Eliot family of St. Louis, Missouri, 174
Elliott, Robert Brown, 106, 180, *179*
Emancipation
artists on, *248*
in British Empire, 115
and compensation, 34-35, 41-43, 46, 67-68
and economic system of South, 126-128
first Christmas after, 159
and Frémont, John C., 29, 30, 32
and Hunter, David, 32-33
Lincoln's plans for, 32-34, 42, 43-44, 46, 181-182
monument in Springfield, Illinois, *248*
and Negro migration, 165, 166-167
of Negro soldiers in Confederate armies, 112, 113
opposition of white workers to, 75, 165
petitions to Congress for, 28

petitions to Lincoln for, 44
and runaway slaves, 127
and Thirteenth Amendment, 115, 118-123
and United States Congress, 33-34, 38, 42
Emancipation Proclamation, 17, 65, *47-51, 245*
drafts of, 38-39, 42, 43, 44, 46, *45*
issuance of, 46, 51-54, *244*
and race riots, 77
reaction of Davis, Jefferson, to, 53-54
reaction in England to, 53, *53*
reaction in France to, 53
reaction of Negroes to, 51-52, 54, 147-148, *244, 247*
reaction of Northern states to, 52, 54, 77-78
reaction of Seward, William H., to, 46
reaction of slaveowners to, 52-54, 144
and Stephens, Alexander H., 42, 181
steps prior to, 44, 46
and use of Negro troops, 54, 80
Whiting, William, on, 52
Emerson, John, 3
Emerson, Mrs. John, 3
Enforcement Acts, 202, 203
England
apprenticeship plan for slaves in British Empire, 115
attitudes toward Emancipation Proclamation, 53
recognition of Haiti and Liberia by, 207
Enrollment Acts, 67, 100, *67*
Episcopal Church, 134
Erie (ship), 7
Everett, Edward, 20

Fair Oaks, Battle of, 96
Federal troops. *See* Union armies
Fee, John Gregg, 139
Ferrero, Edward, 93
Field, Stephen J., *197*
Fields, Granderson, 163
Fifteenth Amendment, 199, 201-203
celebration of, *200, 202*
Fillmore, Millard, 169
Fisk, Clinton B., 130, 131, 132, 139, *141*
Fisk University, 139, 141, *141*
Fleetwood, Christian A., 165, 235, *235-243*

Florida, 32, 37, 58, 116, 122, 192, 193, 203
and recruitment of Negroes, 57, 110, 113
and reopening of slave trade, 7
secession of, 24
Forbes, John Murray, 70, 177
Force Bill, 202
Ford's Theatre, 125, 250, *125, 250*
Forrest, Nathan Bedford, 92-93
Forsythe, F. W., 56
Fort Blakely, Battle of, 97
Fort Jackson mutiny, 81
Fort Monroe, Virginia, 26, 111, 131, 135, 139, *57*
Fort Pillow, Battle of, 92-93, 117, *92*
Fort Snelling, Minnesota, 3
Fort Sumter, 25, 26, 30, 36, 59, 106, 220
Fort Wagner, Battle of, 88, 90-91, 92, 99, 157, 162, *89, 90*
Fort Worth, Texas, slave insurrection plot, 80
Forten, Charlotte, *135*
on church service at Sea Islands, 153
and Negro schools on Sea Islands, 136
Foster, Charles W., 80, 173
Fourteenth Amendment, 184, 189-192, 193
and Slaughterhouse cases, 197
Frazier, Garrison, 149
Frederick Douglass' Paper, 19
Fredericksburg, Virginia, 65
Free labor, *151*
compared with slave labor, 27-28, 148
first experiments with, 27-28
See also Freedmen's Bureau; Negro workers; Negroes
Free Negroes, *178, 229, 259, 261*
and Black Codes, 126-129
colonization of, 5, 34, 41, 42, 46, 111-112
in Confederate armies, 39, 56-57, 113-114
economic status in 1850's, 19-20
population figures, 17-18, 24
and Sea Islands experiment, 27-28, 145-146, 147, 149-151, 177-179, *136, 150, 178*
as slaveholders, 39, 174
See also Negro workers; Negroes
Free Soil Party
and Brown, John, 11
and Lincoln, 41
presidential campaign of 1860, 20

Freedman, 258
Freedman's Journal, 178
Freedmen. *See* Free Negroes
Freedmen's aid associations, 133-134, 136, 146, 148
Freedmen's Aid Society, 134
Freedmen's Bureau, 116, 129-133, 179, 192, *130, 134*
  and aid to whites, 132
  and attitude of South toward, 131-132
  and displaced slaves, 148
  and education, 131, 132-133, 139, *133*
  establishment of, 129-131
  finances of, 129
  and Fourteenth Amendment, 190
  and Howard, Oliver Otis, 129
  and Howard University, 139
  and Negro colleges, 139
  and Negro labor, 131-132, *131*
  New York Tribune on, 118
  opposition to, 132
  and Republican Party, 194
  and Talladega College, 142
  and transportation for displaced persons, 133
Freedmen's national monument to Lincoln, Washington, D.C. (Ball), 174-176, *174, 248*
Freedom's Journal, 19
Frémont, Jessie Benton, 30
Frémont, John C., 29-30, 32, 36, 74, *29*
Fribley, Colonel, 91
Friends, Society of, 134, 138
"From Bloody Flag to White," 162
Fugitive Slave Act, 23, 26, 169
Fugitive slaves, 17, *102, 104, 216, 255*
  and *Ableman* v. *Booth* decision, 11
  land for, 148
  state laws on, 11
  and treatment by Union armies, 17, 26-27
  See also Dred Scott decision

Gardiner, James, 165
Gardner, Franklin, 83
Garnet, Henry Highland, 153, 187, *153*
Garrison, Lucy McKim. *See* McKim, Lucy
Garrison, Wendell Phillips, 156
Garrison, William Lloyd, 78, 156, 177
  on compensation to slaveowners, 42
  on election of 1864, 120

  and Massachusetts Negro regiment, 70-71
  and recognition of Haiti and Liberia, 207
  on Thirteenth Amendment, 122
Geffrard, Fabré (President of Haiti), 111
Georgia, 20, 32, 37, 110, 114, 116, 127, 152, 192, 193, 203
  expulsion of Negro legislators, 196
  and indentured Negro labor, 6-7
  and reopening of slave trade, 7
  secession of, 24
  slave insurrections in, 80
Georgia Equal Rights Association, 198
Georgia Minstrels, 160
German workers, 166
  in Cincinnati riot, 75, 76
Gettysburg Address, *233*
Gibbs, Jonathan C., 187
Giddings, Joshua R., 15
Gillmore, Quincy A., 62, 108
Gilmore Medal, 90
"Give Us a Flag," 157
Gloucester, J. M., 168
"Go Tell It on the Mountain," 159
Gorden, Robert, 168
Gordon, Nathaniel, 7, *7*
Gradine, A., *106*
Grant, Ulysses S., 27, 96, 110, 172, *196, 228, 234*
  correspondence with Halleck, Henry, 65
  and Crater, Battle of the, 93
  and election of 1868, 194
  on Fifteenth Amendment, 201
  at Milliken's Bend, Battle of, 85-87
  and surrender of Lee, 114
Great Britain. *See* England
Greeley, Horace, *43*
  and abolitionists, 28
  on Confederate use of Negro troops, 57-58
  and Confiscation Acts, 42-43
  and Union enlistment of Negroes, 68, 74
Green, Shields, 12, 15, 71, *14*
Grier, Robert C., 4, *197*
Grimes, James W., 38

Hahn, Michael, 117
Haiti, 16, 39, 56, 207, *208*
  and colonization by American Negroes, 111
  English and French recognition of, 207
  U.S. recognition of, 73, 207, 210

Halleck, Henry W., 65, 85, *65*
Halloran (Mayor of New Bedford), 70
Hallowell, E. N., 69
  at Olustee, Battle of, 91
  and "Quaker Oath," 99
Hallowell, Morris L., 69
Hallowell, Richard P., 70
Hamilton, Thomas, 20
Hamlin, Hannibal, 20, *22*
Hampton Institute, 139, *140*
Hancock, Winfield Scott, 126
Hanover College, 142
Harper, Frances Ellen Watkins, *33*
  and Fourteenth Amendment, 192
  and Frémont proclamation, 32
  letter to Brown, John, 14
Harpers Ferry, West Virginia, 12, 14, 15, 16, *12*
Harper's Weekly, 2, 77-78, *221*
Harris, Miss, *126*
Harris, James H., 165
Harrisburg, Pennsylvania, 166
Harrison, Samuel, 110
Hartford (ship), 164
Hartwell, Alfred S., 72
Harvard University, 172-177
Hatch, George, 61
Hatch, John Porter, 99
Hatcher's Run, Battle of, 96
Hawkins, Thomas, 165
Haynes Bluff, Mississippi, 86
Heath, Corporal, 84
Helena, Arkansas, 66, 86
Henderson, John B., 119, 201
Hendrick, Richard, 163, 164
Hendricks, Thomas A., 119
Herald of Freedom, 20
Hicks, Charles, 160
Higginson, Thomas Wentworth, 98, 99, 100, 147
  letters to *New York Tribune,* 100
  on Negro spirituals, 156
  report on Negro troops, 82, 83
Hill, J. J., 124-125
Hilton, Alfred B., 165
Hilton Head, South Carolina, 107, 135, 136, 145, 156
Hilton Head Hospital, 162
Hinks, E. W., 96
History of the United States (Channing), 15
"Hoist Up the Flag," 157
Holland, Milton M., 165
Hollister, George S., 107
Holmes, Billy, 157
Homestead Act, 167, 203

Honey Hill, Battle of, 97, *97*
House of Representatives. *See* United States House of Representatives
Howard, Joseph, 85
Howard, Oliver Otis, *129*
    and development of Negro schools, 132, 133
    and Freedmen's Bureau, 129-130, 132, 133, 139, 192-193
    and Howard University, 139
    and Sea Islands experiment, 150
Howard University, 139, *142*
Hunchback (gunboat), 106
Hunter, David, 59, *33*
    formation of Negro regiment, 37-38, 39, 40, 81, 82, 83
    proclamation of freedom, 32-34
    selection of officers for Negro troops, 101
    and Tubman, Harriet, 107
Hurlbut, Stephen A., 102

Île-à-Vache, 111-112
Illinois, 8, 9-10, 19, 167
    attitude toward Negroes in, 19, 22, 59
    attitude toward slavery in, 3
    legislation against Negro migration, 165
    Lincoln-Douglas senatorial contest, 8
    resolution on Emancipation Proclamation, 54
    segregation in education, 138
Immigration to U.S. during Civil War, 75
Independent, 121
Indiana, 167
    attitude toward Negroes in, 19, 22, 59, 75
    segregation in education, 138
Industrial schools, 135
Iowa, 23, 192
Iowa Regiment, 23rd, 86
Irish workers
    and Cincinnati riot, 75, 76
    and New York riots, 76-77
Island Mounds, Battle of, 82

Jackson, Andrew, 40, 56
Jackson, William, 110, 133
Jackson, William A., *229*
James, Miles, 165
James Island, Battle of, 88, 99, 162
Jeff Davis (privateer), 35

Jefferson College, 142
"John Brown and West Virginia" (address by Frederick Douglass), 16
"John Brown's Body," 157
Johnson, Andrew, 126, 167, *117*
    Annual Message to Congress, 122, 183
    and Civil Rights Bill of 1866, 183-184
    and Douglass, Frederick, 188-189, 192, 193
    and Fourteenth Amendment, 190-191, 192, 193
    and Freedmen's Bureau, 129
    and Memphis riot, 117
    and Negro suffrage, 186, 188, 189
    policy during Reconstruction, 117-118, 182-183
    and Sea Islands experiment, 150-151
    and Thirteenth Amendment, 122
Johnson, Edward, *228*
Johnson, Herschel V., 20
Johnson, Reverdy, 119-120
Johnston, Joseph E., 87, 113, 114
Joint Committee of Fifteen on Reconstruction, 183, 189-190
Jones, George Daniel, 163
Jones, J. B., 113
Jones, James H., 114

Kansas, 11, 65, 81
    Negro suffrage in, 188
Kansas-Nebraska Act, 3, 5, 10
    and Lincoln-Douglas debates, 8
    and rise of Republican Party, 3
Kansas Regiment, 1st. *See* United States Colored Infantry, 79th
Kearsarge (ship), 164
Keckley, Elizabeth, 17, 109, *109*
Kelley, W. D., 72
Kelly, Alexander, 165
Kemble, Fanny, 161
Kentucky, 10, 110, 184, 203
    emancipation in, 34
    and Enrollment Act, 67
    and Freedmen's Bureau, 130
    and segregation in education, 139
    and slavery issue, 30
    and Thirteenth and Fourteenth Amendments, 193
Keokuk (ship), 106
Ketellas, Henry, 173
Kilmer, George L., 93
King, Preston, 38
Kinston, North Carolina, 207

Knights of the White Camelia, 196
Know-Nothing Party, 20. *See also* Constitutional Union Party
Knoxville, Tennessee, 5
Koch, Bernard, 111
Ku Klux Klan, 196, 202-203

Labor unions, 75
Lafayette College, 142
Lake Providence, Louisiana, 86
Land distribution, 198
    and Freedmen's Bureau Act, 179
    and Sea Islands experiment, 149-151, 177-178
Lane, James H., 39, 81, 101
Lane, Joseph, 20
Langston, Charles F., 172
Langston, John Mercer, 23, 68, 187, 192, 193, *163, 188*
Lawrence, Amos A., 70
Laws, Thomas, *226*
Lawson, John, 164, *164*
Leary, Lewis Sheridan, 12, 15, *14*
Lee, Robert E., 114, *234*
    and Brown, John, 12
    on Negroes in Confederate armies, 113
Leslie, James H., 93
Levere, George W., 110
Lewis, Fountain, 172
Lexington (gunboat), 87
Liberator
    and Lyons, Albro, 78
    on Negro suffrage, 188
    on Thirteenth Amendment, 122
Liberia, 207, *209*
    and colonization of American Negroes, 111-112
    English and French recognition of, 207
    U.S. recognition of, 207, 210
Lincoln, Abraham, 75, 85, 96, 144, 210, *8, 41, 46, 123, 126, 252*
    Annual Messages to Congress, 34, 42, 46, 111, 116, 120-121, 244
    attitude toward Negroes, 8-9, 40-41, 109, 116
    attitude of Negroes toward, 22, 24, 124-125
    background, 8-10, 41
    and colonization, 34, 41-42, 46, 111, 181-182
    compared with Davis, Jefferson, 41
    and compensation to slaveowners, 34, 41-42, 46
    and Confederate treatment of Negro Union soldiers, 66-67, 116

and Confederate use of Negro soldiers, 173
conspirators in assassination of, *251*
death of, 125-126, 182, 250, *126, 250*
and Delany, Martin R., 172-173
and Douglas, Stephen A., 8, 10
and Douglass, Frederick, 23, 73-74
on Dred Scott decision, 9-10
and Emancipation Proclamation, 42, 43, 44, 46, 52
and free labor, 28
freedmen's national monument to, 174-176, *174, 248*
and Frémont, Jessie Benton, 30
and Frémont, John C., 29, 30, 32
and Gordon, Nathaniel, 7
on Haiti and Liberia, 207
and Hunter, David, 32-34
Inaugural Address (1861), 41
and Keckley, Elizabeth, 109
letter to Greeley, Horace, 43-44
letter to Speed, Joshua, 9
and Lewis, Fountain, 172
Memorial (Washington, D.C.), *252*
and Negro suffrage, 117
on pay to Negro troops, 38, 39, 99
in presidential campaign of 1860, 20, 22, 23, 24
and Reconstruction, 116-117, 181-182
and segregation in transportation, 59
and slavery, 8-10, 20, 24, 28-29, 30, 32-34, 40-43, 181-182
on slavery as War issue, 24, 28-29, 41-42, 244
and Thirteenth Amendment, 120, 121, 122, 181
and Truth, Sojourner, 109, *249*
and use of Negro troops, 34, 38, 40, 54, 64, 81, 116, 172-173
visit to Richmond, 123-125, *123, 246*
and Wade-Davis Bill, 116
Lincoln, Mary Todd, 109, *126*
Lincoln, Thomas (Tad), 124, *246*
Lincoln-Douglas debates, 8, 10
Lincoln University, Missouri, 142
Lincoln University, Pennsylvania, 139
Lockwood, L. C., 135
Louisiana, 27, 56, 57, 59, 63, 65, 66, 68, 110, 116, 117, 127, 131, 203
and Negro suffrage, 117, 192, 193
and reopening of slave trade, 6, 7
secession of, 24
slave insurrections in, 16, 81

Louisiana Native Guards. *See* Louisiana Negro regiments
Louisiana Negro regiments, 39, 63, 81, 83-85, 86-87, 101, 103, 159, 174, *63, 84*
L'Ouverture, Toussaint. *See* Toussaint L'Ouverture, Pierre Dominique
Lowe, John C., 99
Lynchburg, Virginia, 58
Lynching, 52
Lyons, Albro, 78, *78*

McClellan, George B., 52, 80
McKim, J. Miller, 156
McKim, Lucy, 156-157
McLain, William, 112
McLean, John, 4
Mahan (President of Michigan College), 172
Maine
    and fugitive slaves, 11
    segregation in education, 59, 139
Maine Regiment, 9th, 88
"Mammy, Don't You Cook No More," 162
"Many Thousand Go," 156
Marblehead (gunboat), 164
"Marching Song of the First Arkansas Colored Regiment," 157-158
Marshall, C., 80
Martial law
    in Cincinnati, 60-61
    in Florida, Georgia and South Carolina, 32
    See also Missouri
Martineau, Harriet, 161
Maryland, 68, 110, 191
    and apprenticeship program for ex-slaves, 115-116
    emancipation in, 34
Massachusetts, 11
    and Negro suffrage, 4, 186, 192
    and pay to Negro troops, 97, 98
    recruiting of Negro troops for, 60, 61, 65, 68, 70, 72
    segregation in education, 59, 139
Massachusetts Regiment, 3rd, 131
Massachusetts Regiment, 54th, 68-70, 72, 97, 98, 156, 157, 162
    and Delany, Martin R., 172
    at Fort Wagner, 88, 90-91, *89*
    at Olustee, Battle of, 91
    and "Quaker Oath," 99
    song of, 157
Massachusetts Regiment, 55th, 72, 97, 99, 162-163, *231*

Massachusetts Volunteer Militia, 51st, 82
Matter of Elizabeth Turner, 184-185
Medals of Honor, 96, 164-165, 235, 239-240, *229, 240*
Memphis, Tennessee
    recruiting of Negro troops in, 56, 66
    riot in, 117-118, 189, *118*
Memphis Appeal, 160
Merrimac (ironclad), 106
Methodist Church, 133, 152
Methodist Episcopal Church, 154
    and Freedmen's Aid Society, 134
    Negro leadership in, 154
    and Wilberforce University, 139
    See also Colored Methodist Episcopal Church
Metropolitan Railroad of Washington City, 59-60
"Michael, Row the Boat Ashore," 159
Michigan, 19, 23, 188
    and fugitive slaves, 11
Michigan College, 172
Miller, G. P., 37
Miller, Lindley, 157
Miller, Samuel F., *197*
Milliken's Bend, Battle of, 85-88, *86*
Minnesota
    and Negro suffrage, 186
Minnesota (flagship), 106
Minstrel troupes, 160
Mirror of the Times, 20
Mississippi, 58, 110, 116, 132, 155, 188, 193, 203
    and reopening of slave trade, 7
    secession of, 24
    slave insurrection plots in, 80
Mississippi Regiment, 1st, 86-87
Missouri, 9, 68, 110
    emancipation in, 34
    martial law in, 29, 30
    slave insurrection plots in, 80
    slavery in, 3
Missouri Compromise, 4, 5
Mohammedanism, 152
Monitor (ironclad), 106
Montgomery, Augustus, 80
Montgomery, James, 107, 108
Montgomery, Alabama, 2, 5
Moore, Thomas O., 101
Morgan, John H., 60
Morgan, T. J., 95
Morrison, William, *106*
"My Lord, What a Morning," 160
Myers, Isaac, 206, *207*

Nashville, Tennessee, 56
Nashville, Battle of, 95
National Equal Rights League, 187-188
National Freedmen's Relief Association, 27, 138, 167, 206
Navy. *See* Union Navy
Nebraska
  and Negro suffrage, 192
Negro bands, 160, *161*
Negro Baptist Association of North Carolina, 154
Negro Baptist Church, 133-134
Negro barbers, 172
Negro bishops, 154
Negro businessmen, 206-207
Negro chaplains, 110
Negro colleges, 139, 141-142, *135, 140, 141, 142*
Negro conventions, 129, 198-199
Negro diplomats, 207, 210
Negro education, 132-142, *133, 136, 137, 146, 148, 249, 257*
  admission to white colleges, 142
  and American Freedmen's Union Commission, 135
  and American Missionary Association, 133-134, 135
  and apprenticeship program, 115-116
  and Freedmen's Bureau, 131, 132-133, 139
  and industrial schools, 135
  and religious organizations, 133-134, 137, 139, 142
  segregation in, 138-139, 168, 169, 170-171
  societies for, 134-135, 146
  Southern attitude toward, 135, 138
  in Union armies, 145-147, 164-165, *146*
  See also Negro colleges; Negro troops
Negro heroes. *See* Civil War, Negro heroes of; Medals of Honor; Negro troops, in battle; Negroes, in the Navy
Negro heroines. *See* Negro women in Civil War
Negro jurors, 186
Negro labor. *See* Free labor; Freedmen's Bureau; Negro workers; Negroes
Negro lawyers, 185
Negro music. *See* Songs of the Negro people.
Negro officers, 61-62, 67, 101, 102-104, 111, 173-174

Negro physicians, 103-104
Negro regiments
  all-Negro corps, 96
  in Cincinnati, 61
  of Confederate Army, 39, 56-57, 101
  first in battle, 81-82
  as home guards in Kansas, 39
  Phelps, J. W., on, 63
  and revolt at Fort Jackson, 81
  See also Negro troops; Negroes; *and individual names, e.g.* Massachusetts Regiment
Negro sailors. *See* Negroes, in the Navy
Negro schools. *See* Negro education
Negro slaveowners, 19, 39, 59, 174
Negro soldiers. *See* Negro regiments; Negro troops; Negroes in the armed forces; United States Colored Troops
Negro strikebreakers, 75, 166
Negro suffrage, 4, 22, 186-198, *194, 195*
  and Bouldon, Jesse Freeman, 155
  and Enforcement Acts, 202
  and Fifteenth Amendment, 199, 201-203
  and Fourteenth Amendment, 190-192
  and Johnson, Andrew, 188-189, 191, 192, 193
  and Lincoln, 117
  and Reconstruction Acts, 193
Negro teachers, 132-133, 135, 138
Negro teamsters, 168
Negro troops, *95, 221*
  in American Revolution and War of 1812, 40, 56
  attitude of Confederate troops toward, 66-67, 87, 92-93
  attitude toward white officers, 67
  in battle, 81-88, 90-93, 95-97, 110-111, 114, *82, 83, 84, 86, 89, 92, 94, 98, 111, 223, 224, 225*
  and Butler, Benjamin F., 39-40, 63-64, 96
  at Chafin's Farm, 96, 165
  in Confederate armies, 39, 56-58, 112-114, *57*
  Congressional Medal of Honor recipients, 96, 164-165
  in Crater, Battle of the, 93, 96, *94*
  in early days of War, 35-36
  early rejection of, 34-37, 38, 61-62
  at Edisto River, South Carolina, 82-83

education in Union armies, 145-147
  and establishment of Lincoln Institute, 142
  first authorizations for, 36, 38, 39, 59, 64, 65
  at Fort Pillow, 92-93, *92*
  at Fort Wagner, 88, 90-91, 92, 99, 157, 162, *89*
  government aid to families of, 99
  at Island Mounds, 82
  letters from, 162-164
  at Milliken's Bend, 85-88, *86*
  at Nashville, Battle of, 95
  newspaper reports of, 91, 95
  number of battles, 111
  numbers in Civil War, 110, 143
  officers' reports of, 82-83, 85, 93, 95, 96, 110
  at Olustee, 91, 99
  and pay discrimination, 38-39, 73-74, 97-100, 103-104, *100*
  at Port Hudson, 83-85, *83*
  recruitment of, 55-56, 59-65, 67-73, 74, 80, 82-83, 172-174, *60, 64, 73, 220, 222, 254*
  at St. John River, Florida, 82-83
  at St. Mary's River, South Carolina, 82-83
  white officers of, 61-62, 65, 66-67, 100-103, *63*
  See also Negro regiments; Negroes; Negroes in the armed forces; Union armies; United States Colored Troops; *and individual names, e.g.* Massachusetts Regiment
Negro women in Civil War, 106-110
Negro workers, 27, 127, 128, 148, 177, *28, 76, 131, 166, 167, 204, 205, 206, 258, 259, 260*
  employment agencies for, 167, 206
  and labor unions, 75
  opposition to employment of, 166, 203
  skilled, 168, 169, 172
  See also Free labor; Freedmen's Bureau; Negroes
Negroes
  attitudes toward Brown, John, 14-15
  attitudes toward Civil War, 16-17, 20, 25-27, 34-36, 37, 58-59
  attitudes toward Democratic Party in 1860, 22
  attitudes toward fighting in War, 59-60
  and Black Codes, 126-129, 180-181, 198
  in Census of 1860, 17-19, 115

and churches, 151-155, 169, *152, 253*

and citizenship, 4, 9, 73, 184, 189-190, 191, 198

and Civil Rights Act, 183-185

and colonization, 5, 34, 42, 46, 111-112, 181-182

and Confederate armies, 27, 37, 39, 56-58, 101, 112-114, 143-144, *37, 57, 112*

as contraband of war, 26-27, 59, 131, *232*

definitions of, 128

and equal rights struggle, 179-181, 183-186, 198-199, 201-203, 210-211

among followers of Brown, John, 12, *14*

and forced labor, 115-116

as heroes of Civil War. *See* Negro heroes

as jurors, 186

and land ownership, 148-151, 177-179, 198, 203, *259*

and Lincoln's death, 125

during Lincoln's visit to Richmond, 124-125, *123, 246*

music of. *See* Songs of the Negro people

in the Navy, 104, 106, 164, *36, 105*

and New York draft riots. *See* Riots

opposition to in Reconstruction South, 196-197

and Republican Party, 22, 23, 192, 194, 196

riots against. *See* Riots

as strikebreakers, 75, 166

and supplies to Grant at Vicksburg, 86, *87*

as supporters of Confederacy early in the War, 16, 17

during threatened invasion of Cincinnati, 60-61

and Union armies, 16, 17, 26-27, 36-40, 54, 55-56, 59-74, 80, 81-88, 90-93, 95-97, 110-111, 114, *25, 26, 40, 64, 67, 79, 81, 87, 102, 127, 145, 149, 222*

and voting rights. *See* Negro suffrage

wealthy and prominent, 168-169

in white regiments, 103

and white workers, 19, 75-78, 165-166

See also Negro troops; Slavery; Slaves

Negroes in the armed forces, 26-27, 36-40, 54, 55-56, 57-58, 59-74, 80, 81-88, 90-93, 95-97, 104, 106, 110-111, 114, 220, *222, 224, 227, 228, 229, 230, 254*

and Emancipation Proclamation, 54, 80

first authorizations for, 36, 38, 39, 59, 64, 65

and Hunter, David, 37-38, 39, 40, 82, 83, 101

officers. *See* Negro officers

and preliminary emancipation proclamation, 38-39

See also Negro regiments; Negro troops; Negroes; Union armies; United States Colored Troops; *and individual names, e.g.* Massachusetts Regiment

Nell, William C., 51

Nelson, Colonel, 85

Nelson, Samuel, 4, *197*

Nelson, T. A. R., 52

Nevada, and Thirteenth Amendment, 121

New Era, 187

New Hampshire
and fugitive slaves, 11
and Negro suffrage, 4, 186

New Hampshire Regiment, 7th, 91

New Jersey
and legislation against Negro immigration, 165
and Negro suffrage, 4, 191, 192
segregation in education, 59, 139

New Market Heights, Battle of. *See* Chafin's Farm, Battle of

New Orleans, 17, 27-28, 39, 65, 189, 203
free Negroes in, 19, 27-28, 39, 59, 63, 172

New Orleans, Battle of (1814), 40

New Orleans Picayune, 39

New York (City)
anti-Negro riots in, 76-77
draft riots in, 77-78, *77*
and Negro troops, 36, 65, 68, 72, 74
segregation in, 59
wealthy Negroes in, 168

New York (State), 19, 23
attitude toward Negroes in, 19
and legislation against Negro immigration, 165
Negro enlistments in, 68, 69, 74, 110
and Negro suffrage, 4, 186, 188
segregation in education, 138

New York Cavalry, 16th, 107

New York Regiment, 48th, 88

New York Express, 55

New York Herald, 78, 153
on minstrel shows, 160
on Olustee, Battle of, 91

New York Sun, 160

New York Times, 2

New York Tribune, 28, 43
on causes of Civil War, 2-3
on Dred Scott decision, 5
letters from Higginson, Thomas W., 100
on Memphis riot, 118
on Northern legislation against Negro immigration, 165-166
on Port Hudson, Battle of, 85
on Tillman, William, 35

Newby, Dangerfield, 12, 15, *14*

Newport News, Virginia, 135

Newspapers
and Confederate use of Negro troops, 112
on Emancipation Proclamation, 53
as instigators of race riots, 75, 76
on minstrel troupes, 160
on Negro suffrage, 199
on Negro support of Confederacy, 17
and pay to Negro troops, 99
published by Negroes, 19-20
See also individual names

Norfolk, Virginia, 17, 64, 135, 146

North Atlantic Squadron, 106

North Carolina, 11, 59, 64, 80, 110, 116, 117, 127, 132, 186
and Negro suffrage, 4, 188, 192, 193

North Carolina Regiment, 1st. *See* United States Colored Troops, 35th

North Star, 19, 172, *219*

Northwestern (Baptist) Convention, 154

Northwestern Freedmen's Aid Commission, 27

Oath of allegiance for Southern states, 116

Oberlin, Ohio, 12, 15, 16, 68

Officers
in Union armies, 52, 146, 147, *146*
white, of Negro troops, 61-62, 65, 66-67, 100-103, *63*
See also Negro officers

Official Records of the Rebellion, 57

Ogden, John, 141

Ohio, 11, 19, 75
and Negro suffrage, 22, 188, 192

and Negro volunteers, 61-62, 72, 162
segregation in education, 138
Ohio Infantry, 27th, 27, 86
Olmsted, Frederick Law, 161
Olustee, Battle of, 91, 99, *91*
Osawatomie, Kansas, 11
Overton Hill, Battle of, 97

Pacific Railroad, 167, 206
Pakenham, Edward, 40
Pamplin, Battle of, 162
Payne, Daniel A., 126, 139
Peake, Mary S., 135
Pease, Joachim, 164
Pennsylvania, 11, 19, 22, 68, 70, 72, 74, 110
legislation against Negro immigration, 165
segregation in education, 138
Pennsylvania Regiment, 76th, 88
Petersburg, Virginia, 93, 96, 158, *94*
Petitions
on Black Codes, 180-181, 198
for emancipation, 28, 44
for enlistment of Negroes, 72, 112
on Negro suffrage, 186, 188, 198
for return of lands to former slave-holders, 150
from Sea Islands Negroes to Johnson, Andrew, 150
to Secretary of War, 72
on segregated schools in Rhode Island, 169, 170-171
Phelps, J. W., 62-63
Philadelphia, Pennsylvania, 19, 103
and Negro troops, 68, 72-73
segregation in, 59
wealthy Negroes in, 19, 168
Philbrick, Edward S., 177-178
Philbrick, Samuel, 177
Phillips, Mr. (minister of Sea Islands church), 153
Phillips, Ward P., 70
Phillips, Wendell, 70, 187, 202, *203*
Physicians, Negro. *See* Negro physicians
Pierce, Edward L., 130-131
and Sea Islands experiment, 131, 136, 145, 146
Pinn, Robert, 165
Planciancois, Sergeant, 83-84
Plantations
in experiments with free Negro labor, 149-151
leased by Negroes, 145

life of slaves on, 160
See also Land distribution; Port Royal, South Carolina; Sea Islands
Planter (ship), 106, 148, *105*
Polk, James K., 41
Port Hudson, Battle of, 83-85, *83*
Port Royal, South Carolina, 27, 72, 131, 136, 148, 156, 176-178, 203, *136*
Porter, David D., 124
Portsmouth, Virginia, 135
Pottawatomie Creek, Kansas, 11
Preliminary emancipation proclamation, 39, 43, 44, 46, *45*
Presbyterian Church, 134, 138, 139
Presidential elections
of 1860, 20, 22, 23, *21*
of 1864, 120
Protestant churches and emancipation, 44
Providence Daily Post, 169
Providence Journal, 169
Purvis, Robert, 193, *192*
Putnam, L. H., 20

"Quaker Oath," 99

Race riots. *See* Riots
Randall, James G., 2
Randolph, Benjamin F., 110
Ratcliff, Edward, 165
Rathbone, Major, *126*
Rebel War Clerk's Diary at the Confederate States Capital (Jones), 113
Rebellion Record, 88
Reconstruction
and Black Codes, 128-129
and Freedmen's Bureau, 129-135, *134*
and Johnson, Andrew, 117, 182-183
Lincoln's plans for, 116-117, 181-182
Reconstruction Acts, 193
Religious music. *See* Songs of the Negro people
Remond, Charles Lenox, 35, 172, *35*
Report of the Executive Board of Friends Association for the Aid and Education of the Freedmen, 138
Republican Party, 10, 135, 182, 192, 194, 196, 201

attitude toward slavery, 1, 9, 20, 22, 23
on Brown, John, 16
convention of 1856, 9
and Dred Scott decision, 4-5
and election of 1860, 1, 16, 21-24
and election of 1868, 194, 196
and Frémont, John C., 29
rise of, 3
Rhett, R. Barnwell, 22
Rhode Island, 11, 68
segregation in education, 168-169, 170-171
Rhode Island Association of Freedmen, 167
Rhode Island Colored Troops, 167
Rhodes, James Ford, 2
Richmond, Virginia, 57, 80, 109, 114, 172, 206
fall of, 123-124
Lincoln's visit to, 123-125, *123, 246*
Riots, 189
in Boston, 72
in Chicago, 77
in Cincinnati, 75-76, 77
Greeley, Horace, on, 43
in Memphis, 117-118, 189, *118*
in New York, 72, 76-78, *77*
"Rise Up, Shepherd, and Follow," 159
Rivers, Prince, 38
Robert College, 142
Roberts, John W., 154, *154*
Rochester, New York, 70
Rock, John S., 185
Rock Island, Illinois, 3
"Roll, Jordan, Roll," 157
Roman Catholic Church, 133
Rucker, William R., 175
Ruffin, George, 187, *188*
Russell, LeBaron, 70
Russwurm, John B., 19, 142, *19*
Rutland College, 142

S. J. Waring (schooner), 35, *36*
St. Augustine's Normal and Industrial Institute, 142
Saint-Gaudens' monument to Shaw, 90, 100-101
St. John River, Florida, battle at, 82
St. Louis, Missouri, 19, 29, 70
St. Mary's River, South Carolina, battle at, 82
St. Philip's Episcopal Church, New York, 78
Sanborn, Frank, 15

Sanford, J. F. A., 3
Sanitary Commission (U.S.), 27
Saulsbury, Willard, 119, 207
Savannah, Georgia, 2, 5, 164
    schools for Negroes in, 138
Saxton, Rufus, *39*
    and Delany, Martin R., 173
    and Freedmen's Bureau, 131
    relieved of command, 150
    report on Negro labor, 148-149
    on Tubman, Harriet, 107
    and use of Negro troops, 39, 59, 64, 173
Schofield, John M., 62
Schools. *See* Negro education
Schurz, Carl, 22
    and Negro workers, 167
Scott, Charlotte, 174-175, 176
Scott, Dred, 3, 4, *4. See also* Dred Scott decision
Scott, Harriet, 3, *4*
Scott v. *Sanford. See* Dred Scott decision
Sea Islands, 136, 149-151, 179, 180, 203, *136, 150, 178*
    church service on, 153
    and Pierce, Edward L., 136, 145, 146
    See also Port Royal, South Carolina
Secession
    attitude of Northern leaders toward, 1, 2
    and election of Lincoln, 23-24
    and formation of Confederacy, 1, 2, 3, 24, *31*
Seddon, James A., 58, 113
Segregation, 59-60
    and Black Codes, 128
    in education, 138-139, 168, 169, 170-171
    in religious life, 153, 154-155, 169
Seminole Indians, 123
Seminole Treaty, 123
Seward, William H., 20, 23, 28, 73, *46*
    and Emancipation Proclamation, 46
    and Negro troops, 96
    on pay to Negro troops, 99
    and ratification of Fourteenth Amendment, 192
    and ratification of Thirteenth Amendment, 121, 122
Seymour, Horatio, 68, 74, 194
Seymour, Truman, 91
Shannon, T. B., 120
Shaw, Francis G., 69, 70

Shaw, Robert Gould, 70, *69*
    Andrew, John A., on, 69
    and 54th Massachusetts Regiment, 70, 72
    at Fort Wagner, 88, 90-91
    monument by Saint-Gaudens, 90, 100-101
    and pay discrimination, 97
    poem dedicated to, 90
Sherman, William T., 27, 36, 37, 38, 114, *226*
    and land for Negroes, 149, 203
    and Negro education, 135-136
Shields, Jeff, *229*
Shiloh Presbyterian Church, New York, 153
Slaughterhouse cases, 197
Slave insurrections, 16, 17
    aboard *Amistad,* 133
    during Civil War, 17, 80-81
    Drayton, Thomas F., on, 17
    fears of, 39, 52-53
    white supporters of, 80
Slave trade, *1, 6, 217*
    and American Colonization Society, 111-112
    reopening of, 5-7, 8, 216
Slaveholders, 33-34, 144, 147
    compensation to, 33-34, 41-42, 46, 67-68
    Indian, 123
    Negro, 19, 39, 59, 174
    Negroes on lands of, 149-151
Slavery
    attitude of Lincoln toward, 9-10, 22, 24, 28-29, 40-42, 181-182
    attitude of North toward, 1, 2
    attitude of Republican Party toward, 1, 20, 22
    attitude of South toward, 1-2, 3, 127
    and Democratic Party, 3
    in District of Columbia, 8, 41, 72
    and Dred Scott case, 3-5
    and Emancipation Proclamation, 54
    as issue in 1860 presidential campaign, 1, 2, 20, 22
    and Negro culture, 156, 160-162
    Stephens, Alexander H., on, 2
    and Thirteenth Amendment, 118-122, 123
    See also Negroes; Slave insurrections; Slave trade; Slaveholders; Slaves
Slaves
    attitudes toward masters, 16-17, 58-59, 80, 143, 144
    in British Empire, 115

    in Confederate armies, 56, 112-114, 143-144, *143*
    distribution in 1860, 115
    emancipation of. *See* Emancipation; Emancipation Proclamation
    as free laborers. *See* Free labor; Negro workers
    fugitive. *See* Fugitive slaves
    of Indians, 123
    insurrections of. *See* Slave insurrections
    music of. *See* Songs of the Negro people
    and Negro troops, 64
    and religion, 151-153, *152*
    social life of, 160, *155, 159*
    as soldiers. *See* Negro regiments; Negro troops; Negroes in the armed forces; Union armies; United States Colored Troops
    and Union armies, 16-17, 26-27, 38, 144-148, *25, 145, 149, 222, 232*
    See also Negroes; Slave insurrections; Slave trade; Slavery
Smalls, John, *106*
Smalls, Robert, 106, 148, *106*
Smith, Caleb B., *46*
Smith, Edmund Kirby, 67, 86, 114
Smith, Gerrit
    and Brown, John, 12, 15
    and Douglass, Frederick, 23
    and presidential campaign of 1860, 23
    on use of Negro troops, 55-56
Smith, Stephen, 168
Smith, T. C. H., 175
Smith, William, 113
Songs of the Negro people, 148, 155-162, *155, 159, 161, 260*
    Higginson, Thomas W., on, 156
    McKim, Lucy, on, 156-157
    Thomas, Henry G., on, 158
    and Truth, Sojourner, 109
South Carolina, 20, 27, 32, 37, 56, 63, 81, 82, 83, 113, 116, 126, 131, 132, 188, 192, 193, 203
    Black Codes in, 128, 180-181
    Negro education in, 135-136
    and reopening of slave trade, 5, 7
    secession of, 23-24
    slave insurrections in, 16
    See also Port Royal; Sea Islands
South Carolina Colored Troops, 3rd, 100
South Carolina Volunteers, 1st, 38, 39, 82-83, 101
South Carolina Volunteers, 2nd, *225*

Southern Baptist Convention, 154
Speed, Joshua, 9
Spies for the Union, 107, 109-110
Sprague, Governor, 68
Springfield, Illinois, 8
Stanton, Edwin M., 28, 62, 102, 148-149, *46*
  and authorization of Negro troops, 39, 64, 65, 68, 74
  and Delany, Martin R., 173
  and Lane, James, 81
  letter from Stearns, George L., 68-69
  letter to Tod, David, 97
  and Negroes in U.S. Navy, 104
  on pay to Negro troops, 99
  and Sea Islands experiment, 149
Stanton, Elizabeth Cady, 119, *119*
States' rights
  and *Ableman* v. *Booth* decision, 11
  and secession, 1, 2
Stearns, George L., 15, 68-69, 70
Steedman, James B., 95
Stephens, Alexander H., 2, 42, 181
Stevens, David, 110
Stevens, Thaddeus, 38, 187, 189-190, *182*
  and freedmen, 182-183
  and Negro suffrage, 186-187
  and slavery, 29
Stewart, G. H., *228*
Storer College, 142
Stowe, Harriet Beecher, 3, 32, *3*
Strader v. *Graham,* 5
Straight College, 142
Strong, General, 88
Strong, William E., 132
Sumner, Charles, *55, 256*
  on Black Codes, 129
  Douglass, Frederick, on, 71
  and Downing, George T., 169
  and freedmen, 182-183
  and Negro suffrage, 186-187, 199
  and Pierce, Edward L., 131
  and recognition of Haiti and Liberia, 207, 210
  and Rock, John S., 185
  and segregation, 59-60
  and Thirteenth Amendment, 119, 120, 121
  and use of Negro troops, *55*
Sunderland, Byron, 139
Suppression of the African Slave Trade to the United States of America (Du Bois), 7
Supreme Court, U.S. *See* United States Supreme Court
Swayne, N. H., 184, *197*

Taliaferro, Major, 3
Talladega College, 141
Taney, Roger B., *5*
  and *Ableman* v. *Booth* decision, 11
  and Dred Scott case, 4-5, 9
  and Negro lawyers, 185
Tappan, Lewis, 133
Taylor, Sergeant, 91
Taylor, Richard, 87, 114
Taylor, Susie K., 17, 108, *108*
Teachers in Negro schools, 132, 133, 136, 138, 142, 146, *136, 137, 148*
Tennessee, 11, 116, 117, 188, 191, 203
  and Freedmen's Bureau, 129-130, 131, 132
  Negro recruitment in, 56-57, 68, 110
  and reopening of slave trade, 7
Texas, 110, 116, 122, 193, 203
  and reopening of slave trade, 7
  secession of, 24
  slave insurrections in, 80
"They Look like Men of War," 158
Thirteenth Amendment, 115, 118-123, 179, 181, 186, 189, 193
  and admission of Nevada to Union, 121
  and election of 1864, 120
  and Lincoln, 102, 121, 181
  passage and ratification of, 120, 121, 122, 179, *122*
  petitions for passage, 121
  proposals for, 118-119
Thomas, Henry G., 158
Thomas, Lorenzo, *66*
  and Negro education, 138
  and use of Negro troops, 62, 65-66, 68, 96, 102
Thompson, C. R., 95
Tillman, William, 35, *36*
Tilton, Theodore, 193, *192*
Times (London), 53
Tod, David, 97
Toledo, Ohio, 68, 166
Toombs, Robert, 110
Torch Light, 98
Tougaloo College, 142
Toussaint L'Ouverture, Pierre Dominique, 16, 56
Tremont Temple, Boston, 51, *219*
Trotter, James M., 146-147
Trowbridge, C. T., 38
Truth, Sojourner, 17, 108-109, *108, 249*
Tubman, Harriet, 17, 107-108, *107*
"Turn Back Pharaoh's Army," 160
Turner, Henry MacNeal, 110, 198, 199, *199*

Turner, J. Milton, 210, *210*
Turner, Nat, 39, 71

Ullmann, Daniel, 62, 65, 101-102
Uncle Tom's Cabin, 3, 32
Underdue, James, 110
Underground Railroad, 11, 107
Union armies
  battles, 80, 81-88, 90-97, *82, 83, 84, 86, 89, 90, 91, 92, 94, 97, 111, 233*
  education of Negroes in, 145-147, *146*
  See also Negro regiments; Negro troops; Negroes in the armed forces; United States Colored Troops
Union League Club of New York, 68, 74
Union Missionary Committee, 133
Union Navy
  Negroes in, 104, 106, 164, *36, 105*
Unions. *See* Labor unions
United Brethren in Christ, 134, 138
United Presbyterian Church, 134
United States Army. *See* Union armies
United States Colored Artillery, 3rd, 91
United States Colored Artillery, 6th, 92
United States Colored Artillery, 8th, 125
United States Colored Infantry
  62nd, 142
  65th, 142
  79th, 81-82
United States Colored Troops, 80, 150, 165, *64*
  1st, 80
  5th, *163*
  7th, 103
  8th, 91
  9th, 124, 158
  13th, 97
  20th, *74, 230, 231*
  35th, 91
  63rd, 27
  68th, 97
  74th, 146
  76th, 97
  104th, 103
  105th, 103
United States Committee on the Conduct and Expenditures of the War, 92

United States Congress, 8, 59, 75, 198, 207, 210
  and Civil Rights Act of 1866, 183-184, 189
  and colonization, 42, 111, 112
  Confiscation Acts, 29, 32, 42, 43
  Conscription Act, 77
  emancipation program of, 33-34, 42
  and Enforcement Acts, 202
  and establishment of Freedmen's Bureau, 129, 130
  and Fifteenth Amendment, 201, 202
  and Force Bill, 202
  and Fourteenth Amendment, 189-190, 191, 192
  investigation into Memphis riot, 118
  and land distribution, 198, 203
  and Negro suffrage, 186
  and Negroes in armed forces, 36, 37-38, 39, 40, 67-68, 81, 102
  and pay discrimination, 99, 100
  and Reconstruction, 116, 182-183, 193, 198
  resolution on purpose of Civil War, 25
  and slavery, 5, 8, 26, 28, 29
  and Thirteenth Amendment, 118, 120-121, 122, 181
United States v. Gordon, 7
United States House of Representatives, 184, 210, 183
  and adoption of Thirteenth Amendment, 118, 120-121
  and establishment of Freedmen's Bureau, 129
  and Fifteenth Amendment, 201
  and Fourteenth Amendment, 189, 190
  and Negro suffrage, 186
  and reopening of slave trade, 6
United States Navy. See Union Navy
United States v. Rhodes, 184
United States Senate, 10, 128, 184, 210
  debate on use of Negro troops, 55
  and establishment of Freedmen's Bureau, 129
  and Fifteenth Amendment, 201
  and Fourteenth Amendment, 189-190, 192
  investigation of Fort Pillow, Battle of, 92-93, 117
  and Negro suffrage, 186
  and Thirteenth Amendment, 119, 120

United States Supreme Court, 22, 190, 197
  Ableman v. Booth decision, 11
  and Dred Scott decision, 3-5, 9-10
  and Matter of Elizabeth Turner, 184-185
  and Negro lawyers, 185, 185
  and Slaughterhouse cases, 197, 198
  and Strader v. Graham, 5
  and United States v. Gordon, 7
  and United States v. Rhodes, 184
United States Treasury Department, 129, 136

Van Lew, Elizabeth, 109-110
Vandyke, Peter, 168
Veal, Charles, 165
Vermont
  and fugitive slaves, 11
  and Negro suffrage, 186
Vesey, Denmark, 71
Vicksburg, Mississippi, 7, 27, 28, 65, 66, 85, 86, 87
Vicksburg Whig, 17
Vigilante committees, 16
Vincent, Thomas, 99
Virginia, 11, 26, 113, 117, 127, 132, 188, 193
  lynching in, 52
  Negro education in, 135
  Negro recruitment in, 57, 110, 113
  slave insurrections in, 16, 80
Voice from Harpers Ferry (Anderson), 12
Voting. See Negro suffrage

Wade-Davis Bill, 116, 117
"Walk Together, Children," 160-161
Walker, William, 100
Walker, William S., 16
Wall, O. S. B., 68, 68
Wallace, Governor, 58
Wallace, Lewis S. (Lew), 60-61
Wallack, Richard, 186
War Department, 82
  attitude toward Negroes in army, 36, 37, 220
  Bureau of Emancipation, 129
  on equal pay to Negro troops, 97, 98, 99
  and selection of officers for Negro troops, 102
War of 1812, 17, 40, 56, 70, 80
Washington, Booker T., 52

Washington, George, 56, 78, 174
Washington, D.C. See District of Columbia
Washington Chronicle, 189
Watson, Robert, 168
Wayman, A. W., 126
Wayne, James M., 4, 197
Webber, Sylvester, 162
Weitzel, Godfrey, 96, 124
Welles, Gideon, 104, 46
West Virginia, 110, 167
  and Negro suffrage, 193
Western Evangelical Missionary Society, 133
Western Freedmen's Aid Commission, 27, 138, 141
Western Sanitary Commission, 27, 138, 175
Whigs, 20
Whipple, George, 133
White, Garland H., 110
White working class
  attitudes toward Negroes, 5, 19, 52, 75-78, 127-128, 165, 166
  and Freedmen's Bureau, 132
  and organized labor, 75
  See also Negro workers
Whiting, William, 52, 97, 99
Whittier, John Greenleaf, 32, 218
Whittlesey, E., 139
Wickliffe, Congressman, 38
Wilberforce, Ohio, 103, 172
Wilberforce University, 60, 126, 139, 140
Wild, Edward A., 64
Wildfire (slave ship), 112, 6
Willard's Hotel, Washington, D.C., 172
William (slave ship), 112
Williams, George W., 92-93
Wilson, Henry, 38, 55, 120, 120
Wilson, James F., 118, 190, 191
Wilson, Joseph T., 146, 147
Wisconsin, 23
  and fugitive slaves, 11
  and Negro suffrage, 186
Wise, Henry A., 15
Wood, Fernando, 120
Wood River Association, 155
Woodward, Elizabeth, letters from soldiers, 162-164
Wooster, W. B., 124
Wyandank (ship), 164

Yeatman, James E., 175, 176
Young's Point, Louisiana, 86, 138

SERGER
Savvy™

Text by Agnes Mercik
Edited by Jeanne Stauffer

HOUSE of
WHITE
BIRCHES

PUBLISHERS
SINCE 1947

SERGER Savvy™

Copyright © 2003
House of White Birches, Berne, Indiana 46711

Editor: Jeanne Stauffer
Associate Editor: Dianne Schmidt
Technical Editor: Mary Jo Kurten
Book and Cover Design: Jessi Butler,
Ronda Bechinski
Copy Editors: Michelle Beck, Mary Martin,
Nicki Lehman

Photography: Tammy Cromer-Campbell, Tammy Christian,
Christena Green, Kelly Heydinger
Photography Assistant: Joshua J. Cromer
Photo Stylist: Tammy Nussbaum

Art Director: Brad Snow
Publishing Services Manager: Brenda Gallmeyer
Graphic Artist: Ronda Bechinski
Production Assistants: Janet Bowers, Marj Morgan
Technical Artists: Liz Morgan, Mitch Moss
Chad Summers
Traffic Coordinator: Sandra Beres

Chief Executive Officer: John Robinson
Publishing Marketing Director: David McKee
Book Marketing Director: Craig Scott
Product Development Director: Vivian Rothe
Publishing Services Director: Brenda R. Wendling

Printed in the United States of America
First Printing: 2003
Library of Congress Number: 2002108787
ISBN: 1-59217-006-4

All rights reserved. No part of this publication may be reproduced or transmitted in any form or by any means, electronic
or mechanical, including photocopying, recording, or any
other information storage and retrieval system, without the
written permission of the publisher.

Every effort has been made to ensure the accuracy and
completeness of the instructions in this book. However, we
cannot be responsible for human error or for the results when
using materials other than those specified in the instructions,
or for variations in individual work.

Welcome!

If you love to sew, then you will love using a serger! It will make your projects look better, and it will save you time. If you only use your serger for finishing seams, you are in for a real treat. In the pages of this book, you'll find projects galore and a glossary of serger stitches to try.

Don't miss out on the fun of owning a serger. It is so much more than a finishing tool. It can be highly creative as well.

Learn how to create fancy ribbons made from fabric, apply cording and beading, and how to embellish using your serger. Along with dozens of projects, we've included chapters on threads and serger accessories to make serging more pleasurable. We've also included a new technique for creating a diamond design using your serger, along with several projects that use this new technique.

Every project in this book uses a serger stitch of some kind, and some projects can be made completely on a serger. Start having fun with your serger today! You'll be amazed at what you can do!

Warm regards,

Jeanne Stauffer

Contents

Introduction 6

Machine Makeup 8

Machine Maintenance 12

Needles 13

Threads 18

Glossary of Stitches......................................24

Overlock Stitches..26

Flatlock Stitches..32

Serger Accessories 37

Serger Machines...44

Heirloom Serging..46

Heirloom Pillow 49

Creating Diamonds..52

Flatlocked Diamond Blouse...........................57

Flatlocked Diamond Fleece Pullover.............60

Diamond Leather Purse 62

Diamond Tote...64

Beaded Jewelry Bag 66

Dare-to-Be-Different Dress, Jacket &
    Purse 68

Prairie Points Purse 72

Lady of Spain Shawl......................................75

Sheer Delight Scarf 80

Double-Layer Chiffon Scarf 84

Little Miss Lace Collar 87

Rosy Fleece Robe..89

Flatlocked Oriental Tunic 92

T-shirt Twin Set..94

Opulent Abstract Elegant Jacket 96

Puffed-Braid-Closure Vest 100

Leather Beaded Vest 102

Zebra Vest 104

Seams Great 108

Flatlocked Skirt & Jacket Ensemble 110

Batik Two-Piece Outfit 114

Suede Book Cover 116

Jungle Crayon Bag 118

Sashiko Place Mat 121

Flatlocked Fringed Table Set 124

Majestic Place Mat & Napkin 126

Majestic Pillow 128

Blanket-Stitched Pillows 132

Dainty Daisy Pillow 136

Full-of-Tucks Pillow 139

Flower-Power Pillow 142

Woven Fabric Ribbon Pillows 144

Decorator Cushion Trio 148

Antique Battenburg Lace Pillow 153

Doll Bed Coverlets & Pillows 156

Chili Peppers Mini Banner 158

Butterfly Wall Quilt 160

Beaded Floral Sampler 167

Special Thanks 175

Fabrics & Supplies 176

Introduction

The overlock, or serger as it is more commonly known in this country, has been a wonderful addition to our sewing equipment. Unfortunately, there have been times when its basic function and varied applications have been misunderstood. Although there are many projects that can be done solely on a serger, more benefits and interesting variations are achieved when used in conjunction with conventional sewing machines and embroidery units. The serger then becomes a necessity, rather than just an extra accessory item.

In addition to basic functions of finishing edges and quick seaming, many features have been added to these machines in recent years to make them more versatile and user-friendly. The decorative applications are endless when combined with decorative threads and variations of basic stitches.

Accessories, similar to those available for sewing machines, further assist us in getting through troublesome situations and challenging techniques. Fortunately, serger techniques and technology have advanced rapidly over the past few years to make all this possible. It continually challenges serger enthusiasts to use this technology creatively.

Because new products and techniques are constantly being developed, we could not possibly include every new notion and thread available, as there is always one more new product to explore. The focus of this book, therefore, is to provide some fundamentals, expand upon them, show a variety of ways we have implemented these techniques and then allow creative minds to explore and develop variations.

First and foremost, every serger owner should take advantage of the class provided with the purchase of a new machine. Most reputable sewing machine companies offer these classes. Many stores will also allow you to repeat the class if necessary, as it is very important to be comfortable with the basics, such as threading, differential feed, cutting width, changing needles and pertinent functions of your particular model. Since all sergers are not created equal, it is important to know what your own machine is capable of doing.

Flatlock Oriental Tunic

Decorator Cushion Trio

Sashiko Place Mat

The information contained in this book can be applied to any manufacturer's machine. The settings are approximate, because they are generally not crucial. Settings may also vary between the various brands.

From personal experience, I have seen sergers come a long way. I was first introduced to a serger about 25 years ago, a period of time when these machines were considered "dinosaurs." They were not sold by major sewing machine companies and only cottage industry and commercial businesses used them. I can still remember accepting the challenge to teach classes on sergers. When I took my first serger home to get acquainted with it, I was surprised that there was no owner's manual to use as a guide. I unfolded a piece of paper that revealed a few instructions. This was of no benefit to me because it was written in a foreign language, although accompanied by small drawings that illustrated some of the functions. To see them better I reproduced and enlarged these tiny drawings.

There were no numbers on the tension dials, and they spun around endlessly. To make a rolled hem, I had to change a plate and presser foot and figure out the settings in order to make the fabric roll under. There were no guidelines to depend on for the settings. I truly appreciate the advances made in recent years to simplify use of these machines.

So, get these basics under your belt and serge forward. ✂

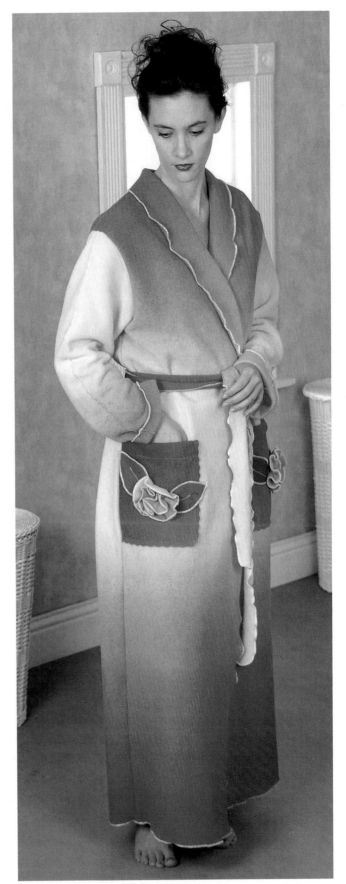

Rosy Fleece Robe

Machine Makeup

There are several variables that influence the quality of the serger stitch. The fine points of each should be examined.

Cutting Width

Cutting width is also commonly referred to as the serger stitch width. Depending on which needle you are referring to, the width is the distance between the upper knife and either the left or right needle. You may also engage the rolled hem or narrow stitch finger (Fig. 1.1), which will provide the narrowest stitch width possible.

You create this width as you cut and serge your seam. This, of course, does not include the fabric that has been trimmed off. My recommendation for the amount to be trimmed is usually defined as a "sliver" of fabric. Every machine has an area of the machine that can be used as a guideline as shown in Fig. 1.2. Another factor that influences the stitch width is the amount of fabric contained within the serged seam. You may adjust the cutting knives to allow more or less fabric for this purpose. Depending on the brand of machine you own, the cutting knives can be positioned in one of

Fig. 1.2

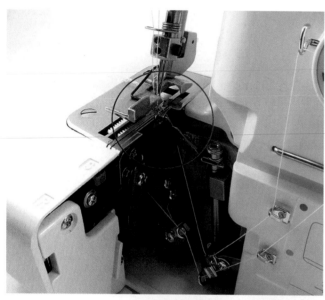

Fig. 1.1

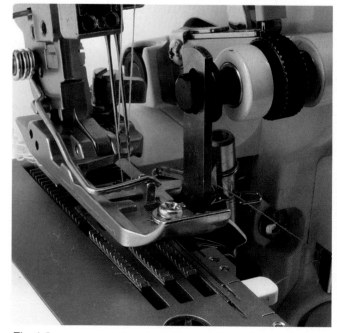

Fig. 1.3

two ways. Both can be positioned to the right and near the stitch plate controlled by a knob near this area as shown in Fig. 1.3. Or, the lower blade is near the stitch plate and the upper blade is next to the needle bar, which can be turned upward in a locked position as shown in Fig 1.4.

Fig. 1.4

Leather Beaded Vest

Depending on the fabric or technique, a good stitch can be created by simply adjusting the cutting width. This eliminates trouble-shooting the tensions. Make a test piece as shown in Fig. 1.5 to better understand this theory.

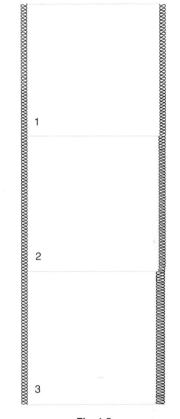

Fig. 1.5
Create a test piece as shown to determine the best stitch-width settings.

1. Cut two pieces of fabric approximately 4" x 12". Using the numbers on the cutting-width knob of your model machine, divide the fabric in equal segments. My machine numbers are 1, 2, 3, so I divided the fabric in thirds. Mark and number each segment on the lengthwise grain to correspond with the numbers on your cutting dial.

2. Set your machine for a 4-thread balanced stitch with a 2.5 stitch length.

3. Adjust the cutting width to the lowest number (1) and stitch through both layers of fabric until you reach the first line. Turn the cutting dial to the next number (2) and continue stitching to the next line. Turn the dial again (3) and continue to serge off the fabric.

4. Examine each section carefully and look for the best area of stitching. If necessary, fine-tune both looper tensions to create the best-looking, well-balanced stitch.

5. On the other side, stitch the entire length of doubled fabric with the best stitching and write down the altered settings for future reference.

Stitch Length

The stitch length, as in conventional sewing machines, is the distance created by the needle. To increase the length, turn to a higher number or to decrease, turn to a lower number. This will also affect the stitch width, as the looper thread has to cover a wider or narrower distance across the seam allowance. Typically, thicker threads will require a longer stitch length to avoid jamming or piling of threads.

Create another test piece for stitch-length settings as shown in Fig. 1.6.

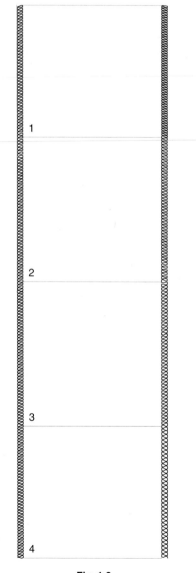

Fig. 1.6
Create a test piece as shown to determine the best stitch-length settings.

1. Cut two pieces of fabric approximately 4" x 12". Since most machines have a maximum stitch length of 4 or 5, divide the fabric into four or five equal segments and then number each section as in the above sample.

2. Use a l.5–2mm cutting width for entire test piece. Start with a 1mm stitch length and serge to the first line.

3. Change stitch length to the next number (2) and continue serging to the next line. Continue this process until you have completed the test piece.

4. Once again, analyze the sample to see where the fine-tuning adjustments have to be made. Then, on the opposite lengthwise side of the test piece, serge the entire length with the desired settings and mark the fabric with the settings for future reference.

Crosswise, lengthwise and bias grain lines may require additional fine-tuning. Make a small test piece for each grain line for future reference.

Similar test pieces are also strongly recommended for testing decorative threads. Create a notebook with the settings written directly on the fabric for future "ballpark" figures to start with. It will not only save time, but also valuable thread and some frustration. Thick-and-thin, stretchy and metallic threads require more fine-tuning than the basic serger construction threads.

Both upper and lower looper threads should hug the top and bottom of the fabric and overlock each other exactly on the cut edge for a good balanced stitch.

One or two needle threads hold the looper stitches in place. On a 4-thread stitch, the left needle stitch will resemble the top and bottom of a sewing machine stitch. The right needle, considered the mock safety stitch, will show as a straight stitch on top of the fabric and as a tiny dot on the bottom as shown in Fig. 1.7. If this dot is significantly large or loopy, then the needle tension has to be adjusted to a tighter setting.

Differential Feed System

The differential feed system consists of two sets of feed dogs—one directly in front of the other as shown in Fig. 1.8. As adjustments are made with the differential dial, the front feed dog can move forward or backward.

A higher-number setting will produce more gathering, whereas a lower number will slightly stretch the fabric.

Light- to medium-weight fabrics will produce twice the gathered fabric when set at the highest maximum differential setting along with the longest stitch length. Bias stitching frequently requires a slight fine-tuning

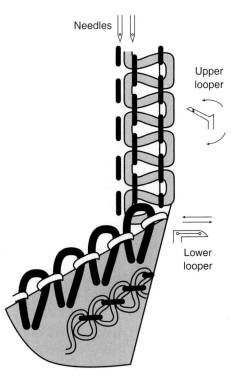

Needles

Upper looper

Lower looper

Fig. 1.7
On a 4-thread stitch, the right-hand-needle stitch should resemble a sewing machine stitch—straight on top and a tiny dot on the underside.

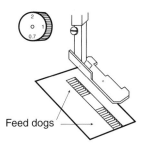

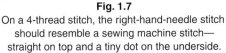

Feed dogs

Fig. 1.8
The differential feed system consists of two sets of feed dogs as shown.

toward a higher number. There are times when stubborn fabric, due to sizing or dyes, will resist gathering. Increase both needle tensions to solve this problem. Otherwise, a gathering foot or attach-ment will be necessary attachment, gathering a ruffle onto fabric

When combined with a gathering foot or attachment, gathering a ruffle onto fabric can be achieved in one operation.

To control knits from wavy seam lines, the differential is set to a higher number. A lower number is required to stretch the fabric and create a "lettuce" edge on stretchy fabrics. In most situations, only slight fine-tuning adjustments are necessary.

Presser Foot

If your machine does not have needle markings on the presser foot, add your own. Place a metal seam guide directly in front of each needle and lay it on the foot. With an indelible marking pen, mark each needle line as shown in Fig. 1.9.

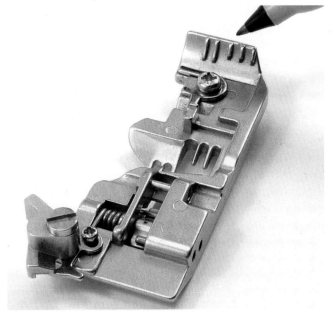

Fig. 1.9

Presser Foot Pressure

To accommodate thick and thin fabrics, the pressure on the presser foot can be adjusted as shown in Fig. 1.10. For instance, lighten the pressure for thick fabrics and increase the pressure on lighter fabrics to prevent slipping. ✂

Fig. 1.10

Machine Maintenance

Sergers need to be cleaned and oiled on a regular basis. I use a guideline of approximately every 6–8 hours of continuous serging. At this time I also replace the needle. If the machine has not been used for a period of time, it may also require some lubrication, as the oil has a tendency to drain to the bottom of some machines. Consult the manual for specific lubricating areas on your model. Typically, oiling is done on the movable joints. Use only the oil that comes with your machine. Other household oils are heavier and will probably cause problems.

Be sure the needle is in its highest position. An improperly inserted needle can cause skipped stitches. On larger needles (#90), loosen the screw slightly more to accommodate the thicker diameter. To prevent losing the screw if it accidentally falls out, place a white napkin under the presser-foot area to catch it.

Tension discs tend to accumulate lint. Floss them with a thick thread, such as topstitching thread or thick dental floss. Move the thread back and forth between the tension discs several times to remove any lint buildup.

Consult owner's manual for specific lubricating areas on your model.

The cutting knives wear out periodically, especially if you use the serger on a regular basis. Sergers are designed with a double-blade system similar to scissors. Usually the lower blade is stationary, while the upper can be moved out of working position for some techniques. The upper blade is made of a strong carbide steel and does not wear out as quickly as the lower blade, which is made of a softer steel and is also less expensive.

There is an advantage to having two different types of steel for the cutting blades and the lower one being softer than the upper blade. If a pin is accidentally hit and/or cut, the softer blade will become damaged, but it gives some, protecting the upper blade from damage. If the top and bottom blades are not aligned properly, the fabric will be ragged and perhaps jam the machine.

During normal serger use, the lower blade will require more frequent replacement. This will depend on the type of fabric you use, such as synthetics, bulky and densely woven fabric, and if you have sewn through pins. This could be a problem in itself, as it may throw the looper mechanism out of timing and require a costly repair trip. A good practice is to remove all pins before they reach the throat plate.

For general maintenance, similar to your car upkeep, take your machines to a reputable mechanic periodically for a general checkup. ✄

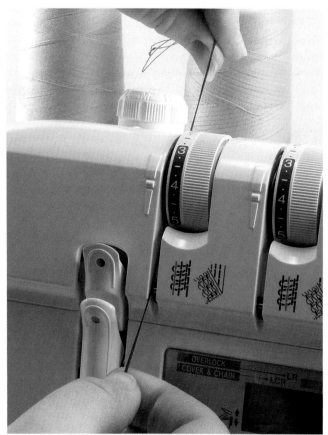

Floss your sewing machine to remove any lint buildup.

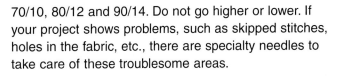

Needles

Although most sergers now use conventional sewing machine needles, be sure to check your manual to verify correct needle usage.

Quality serger and sewing machine stitching depends on appropriate needle design and size, along with a frequent replacement. As with conventional sewing machines, needles become dull from continual use. Some fabrics, such as synthetics, will dull needles faster than natural fibers. Since overlocks sew at a high speed, needles tend to wear out quickly. If you experience skipped or uneven stitches or puckered seams, change the needle. It may be dull, bent or burred. If the problem continues to occur, change the needle again. It is not unusual to find a bad needle in a new package from time to time.

Because the loopers are finely timed with the needles, it is important to stay within a size range. Use only

70/10, 80/12 and 90/14. Do not go higher or lower. If your project shows problems, such as skipped stitches, holes in the fabric, etc., there are specialty needles to take care of these troublesome areas.

Study the design of the following needle types and you will know how to make the best choice for your particular project.

A needle has two main parts—the shank and the blade. The shank is the part inserted into the machine. The blade consists of the shoulder, scarf, eye and point. The scarf is the part that is indented on the back just above the eye. There is another groove on the front that protects the thread as it is pulled through the fabric. The eye size increases with the size of the diameter of the needle. The point is made in different configurations to specifically help with special sewing and serging situations. I suggest keeping a package of each variety on hand in case you have a midnight project that requires a special needle.

An explanation of the various needle-point varieties available follows.

Universal

The universal needle (Fig. 1.11) is frequently used for easy-to-sew fabrics and is commonly referred to as an "in-between" needle. This has to do with the slightly rounded and slightly sharp point. It sews successfully on several types of knits and woven fabrics.

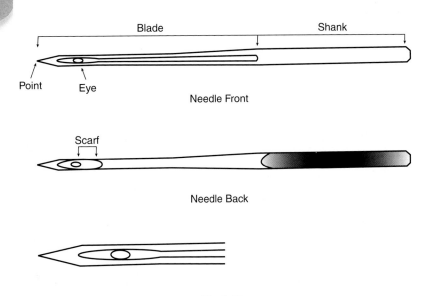

Fig. 1.11
Universal needle

A sampling of the needles available in the marketplace.

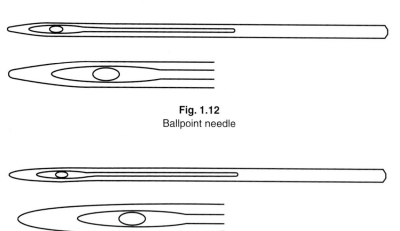

Fig. 1.12
Ballpoint needle

Fig. 1.13
Stretch needle

Butterfly Wall Quilt

Ballpoint

The ballpoint needle (Fig. 1.12) has a definite rounded point that makes it easier to stitch knits. The rounded point slips between the fibers rather than through them, thus eliminating holes in the knit fabric. This needle also prevents skipped stitches on fine and closely knitted fabrics. There are some fabrics that are not traditional knits, such as polar fleece, which benefit with use of a ballpoint needle.

Stretch

The rounded point of the stretch needle (Fig. 1.13) is somewhere between a universal and ballpoint. In addition, the eye is higher on the shaft so there is less friction on the thread. The very tiny hump between the eye and the scarf on the back provides some ease in the stitch formation by creating a larger loop on the backside of the needle. It frequently solves the problems associated with sewing braided elastic, swimwear, lingerie and some types of aerobic wear.

Jeans

The jeans needle (Fig. 1.14) has a very sharp point and is designed to penetrate very densely woven fabrics, such as denim, outerwear and fabrics used in home decorating. It is now available in a size 70 for lighter sand-washed rayon and silk fabrics. It works well on many synthetic fabrics and compares similarly to a Microtex or Microfiber needle.

Microtex and Microfiber

Both the Microtex and the Microfiber (Fig. 1.15) brand-name needles have a very sharp point similar to the jeans needle. They are made by Schmetz and Lamertz Nadelin, respectively. The point also does well on other fine fabrics and delicate laces, such as those used in heirloom work.

Heirloom Pillow

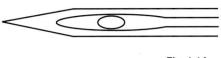

Fig. 1.14
Jeans needle

Fig. 1.15
Microtex or Microfiber needle

Suede Book Cover

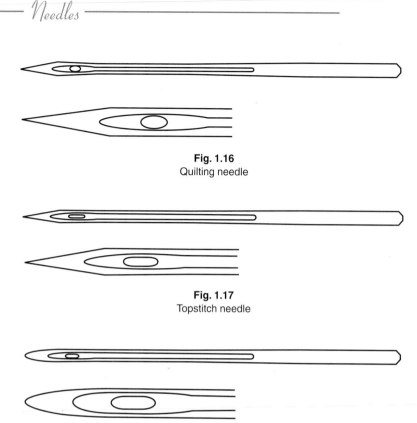

Fig. 1.16
Quilting needle

Fig. 1.17
Topstitch needle

Fig. 1.18
Embroidery needle

Chili Pepper Mini Wall Banner

Quilting

The quilting needle (Fig. 1.16) has a thin, long, tapered point to prevent skipped stitches when seaming and cross-seaming, as in quilting. Quilters are now using a variety of fabrics, some of which may be fragile, and this needle will not damage the project.

Topstitch

As the name implies, the topstitch needle (Fig. 1.17) is used for heavier threads, such as topstitching. Since the eye is twice the size of a regular needle of the same size, there is no compromise for increasing to a larger needle just to have more eye space. It is also very sharp and has a large groove to accommodate topstitching, decorative and multi-threads.

Embroidery

The embroidery needle (Fig. 1.18) is designed for delicate threads, such as those used in machine embroidery. It stands up to the higher temperatures created by the friction and speed of decorative stitching. The larger eye and groove protect the thread from fraying. The point is slightly rounded, similar to the universal.

Metallic

The metallic needle (Fig. 1.19) also has a slightly rounded point, deeper groove along the front and a much larger eye, which is coated with a synthetic layer. This prevents metallic thread, one of the most fragile threads, from shredding. It can also be used with multiple fine rayon and cotton threads.

Leather

Although rarely used, the leather needle (Fig. 1.20) has a definite chiseled point to penetrate natural skins, which are difficult to penetrate with a regular needle. During more than 25 years of serging, I have only used a leather needle in the serger one time.

JLX1

The JLX1 needle (Fig. 1.21) is used primarily for the cover stitch. It has a scarf on the back and front of the needle to hold the thread more securely while the cover stitch looper swings into the needle area. ✀

Fig. 1.19
Metallic needle

Fig. 1.20
Leather needle

Fig. 1.21
Cover-stitch needle

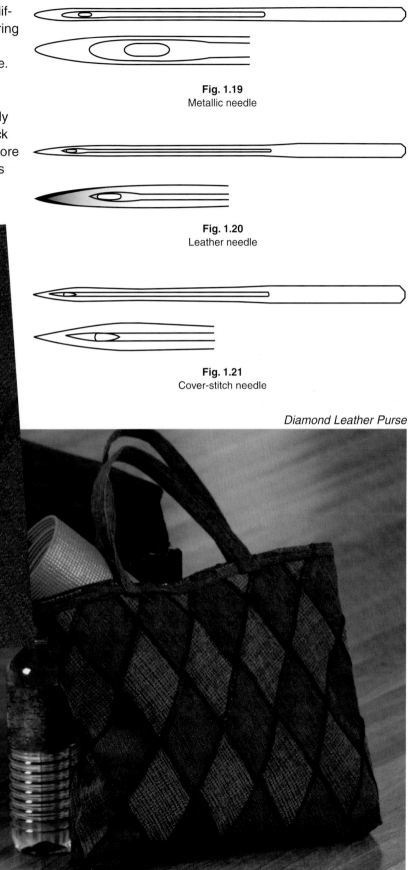

Diamond Leather Purse

Threads

There are many manufacturers and varieties of threads on the market today, and it can be confusing to try to become educated in all the possible applications. The embroidery machines have challenged thread companies to provide a variety of attractive threads. Fortunately, these threads can also be used in our sergers.

Although not all companies carry all of the varieties of fibers and textures, every decorative-thread company provides crossovers. Due to the magnitude of the inventory, most stores can only carry the threads for which they have space. Fortunately for the consumer, there are many choices.

To keep it simple, I will discuss the most user friendly threads, along with those that are interesting and fun to work with. There are basically two major categories: construction (all-purpose) and decorative, which include variations of thin, thick, slippery, fragile, rayon, silk, metallic, cotton, polyester, etc.

Construction Threads

For conventional seaming and construction, choose a good quality all-purpose thread constructed with a uniform consistency. Do not use threads that have knots, are uneven, thick-and-thin or have a hairy appearance. These threads are considered bargain-brand types and are made from the linters of good thread. We all love bargains, but if the thread continually breaks during the process of constructing a project, we really haven't saved at all. In simple terms: a high-quality thread will produce a high-quality project. The key is to look for descriptions such as long staple and/or mercerized as in cottons.

Serger construction thread is usually 100-percent polyester or cotton-core wrapped polyester and is best known for its strength and elasticity. Geared for high-speed serging, it is typically available on large cones and is cross-wound to feed uniformly. Because there is more thread in a serged seam, this lighter-weight thread reduces bulk.

You don't have to change thread color every time you start a new project. There are exceptions, however, as in all-white or all-dark garments. Choose blending colors, such as gray and beige, for medium-colored fabrics, and off-white or ivory blends for lighter shades. It is more important to match the thread color to the fabric in one or both needles. Regular sewing machine thread may be used in this case when the project requires minimum stitching.

Heavily dyed threads, such as black, navy, red, etc., will require more attention. Normal tensions will require fine-tuning.

Decorative Threads

This is a very broad category and thread manufacturers are constantly adding new varieties of threads to their lines. An entire book just on decorative threads could be written. The following explanations will help define thread characteristics and properties. Whatever its texture or thickness, decorative thread can enhance the most basic stitch to look more prominent and luxurious. Although the thicker and heavier threads are more successfully used in the loopers, occasionally they are used in a topstitch or embroidery needle.

Thin Threads

Thin threads include machine-embroidery types such as:
- #30 and #40 rayon

Construction Threads

Decorative Threads

- #30 and #60 cotton
- #35 cotton and rayon
- Silk
- Polyester, acrylic
- Fine metallic
- Flat metallic

Thick Threads

- Untwisted rayon: Designer 6—YLI; Decor 6—Madeira
- Twisted rayon: Pearl Crown—YLI
- Ribbon floss: flat and pliable
- Thick metallic: Candlelight—YLI; Glamour—Madeira

Medium-Weight Thread

There are some threads that fall into several categories, some of which can be used in the loopers as well as a needle such as the large-eyed varieties. Before you decide to

Woven Fabric Ribbon Pillows

Decorative Threads

T-shirt Twin Set

use a particular thread, first test and see if it glides smoothly through the eye of the needle.

Monofilament

Monofilament is available in both nylon and polyester and in either smoke or clear shades. It is almost invisible and works well in decorative applications and utility stitches, as it conceals part of or the whole detail of the stitch. It is strong and can help to tighten a rolled hem when used in the lower looper.

Fusible Thread

Fusible thread is a combination of polyester and a heat-activated component. It helps to temporarily stabilize areas in a wide variety of practical and decorative techniques. Do not place an iron directly on the thread. Press from the top side of the stitching. Allow this bond to cool before the fabric is moved.

Stretchy Threads

YLI was the first to introduce the Woolly Nylon type of thread. It is a textured, fuzzy type of nylon thread that fluffs out after it has been serged. Its practical use is to fill in the spaces between the stitches, such as in rolled hems and decorative edges. For aerobic active-wear, Woolly Nylon or Woolie Poly will provide the greatest stretch factor when combined with a 4-thread stretch stitch. (Two needles, lower looper and converter on the upper looper.) Other versions include Metro-flock by Mettler.

Woolly Nylon also comes in an extra-heavy weight for a more defined fill-in stitch and a metallic version that does not stretch as much. Tensions usually are set lower with any of the nylon or stretchy threads. They come in a wonderful assortment of colors and can be combined with other fine decorative threads in the same looper.

Use a lightweight cotton or a non-stick surface press sheet and set your iron on low heat when pressing over these and other decorative threads. Heat may cause melting and/or tarnishing.

Another version of this stretchy thread, Woolie Poly, is distributed by Superior Threads. It is made of polyester, is less heat sensitive, covers nicely and works in a similar fashion to the nylon version.

Resilon F

Although Resilon F is another variety of stretchy

Monfilament & Fusible Thread

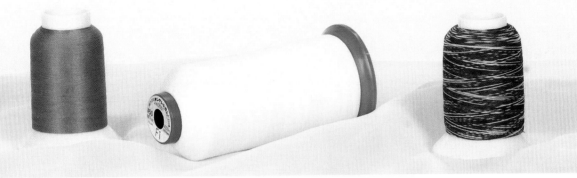

Stretchy Threads and Resilon F

thread, I am putting it in its own sub-category. It is brand-new and will be available before this book is published. It is available through Superior Thread Co. and is made of multiple-filament Nylon 66, which is semi-transparent. Because one thread color can be used to match multiple base-fabric colors, it will reduce the number of colors you need to have in your inventory and also save downtime for thread changes.

It has excellent stretchability, about 30 percent, and for that reason is primarily intended for knit fabrics—a great aid for aerobic and active-wear garments, such as leotards, swimsuits, skating outfits, etc. It is also colorfast.

Acrylic/Wool

These threads resemble fine yarn. Some consist of all-wool or all-acrylic fibers and some in combinations of acrylic and wool. Success, Monet (YLI), Burmilana (Madeira) and Renaissance (Sew Art, Int'l) are the most commonly used in this category and vary slightly in thickness. They can be used in the looper and large-eyed needle. These are good threads to use on fabrics such as wool, acrylic and polar fleece, where a fuzzy texture is desired.

Puffed-Braid Closure Vest

Acrylic/Wool Thread

Ribbon Floss & Elastic Thread

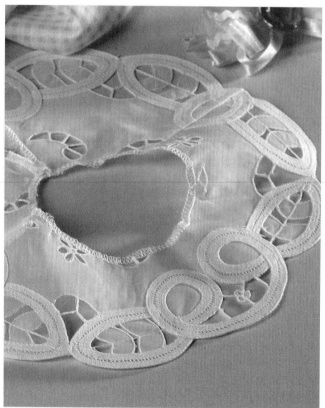

Little Miss Collar

Ribbon Floss

Ribbon floss is technically not a thread. It is a cross-woven knitting-type rayon ribbon and available in many colors, including metallic versions. It works well in the looper or in the bobbin of a sewing machine.

Elastic Thread

This type of thread is unique in that it has a thin elastic core wrapped with polyester. It comes in two weights: 1mm and 3mm. Although most thread companies carry it only in black and white, K1C2 carries it in 48 colors, including gold and silver. When used in the bobbin of a sewing machine or looper of a 2-thread straight chain stitch, it will gather fine to medium-weight fabrics. An additional shirring process takes place when the shirred fabric is steamed. When used on the right side of the fabric, the colored elastic thread adds an interesting texture. Batik-type fabrics are wonderful to shirr, as the colors in the fabric block in interesting patterns.

Variegated Threads

Variegated threads have become increasingly more popular and can be divided into two different categories. In the first category, the thread has a set of several colors or shades of one color in a definite measured

Variegated and Glowing Threads

Miscellaneous Threads

pattern. The result is that the finished edge, trim or piping takes on a color-blocked effect. Variegated threads are available in a wide assortment of fibers: stretchy, rayon, metallic, and cotton, and in several weights.

The other category is the twisted variety, which contains two different colors or shades and comes in a #35 weight. When stitched into the fabric, the combination becomes blended rather than color-blocked.

Miscellaneous

A variety of unusual yarns, such as those used in knitting and crocheting, are also delightful to use. For ease in handling, choose those that are smooth and more firmly constructed.

Baby yarns and some of the crochet-type yarns are fine for looper use, but not the needle. Because these yarns are not wound for serger use, you will find it necessary to rewind the yarn onto serger spools.

Glowing Threads

For fun and unique projects, consider using polyester neon threads or the glow-type, such as Nite Lite by Superior, Moonglow by Robinson-Anton and Glow Bug by YLI, as well as Brilliance, a metallic glow-in-the-dark thread by YLI. Solar Active produces UV threads as well as fabric, beads and buttons, all of which change colors when exposed to sunlight.

Combination Threads

You may mix threads of different textures and colors for more depth and versatility or simply use two or three lightweight threads for better coverage.

As this book goes to press there will probably be even more varieties of threads available. Do not hesitate to try them. Most decorative threads have become much easier to handle. ✂

Jungle Crayon Bag

Glossary of Stitches

Many sergers now have a combination of several stitches, but some of the older machines are limited to a very few basic stitches. Use your manual as a reference to determine which stitches are available for your particular machine. Although most of the stitches are intended for conventional sewing, decorative applications also apply.

Any stitch can look decorative simply by using a decorative thread appropriate to the project. Once you understand how thick and thin fibers affect the tension on your stitch, the experimentation process is minimal. A rule of thumb is to consider that thinner threads

will require fine-tuning tensions to a higher setting, while thick threads require a lower setting. Stitch length applies in a similar manner; thicker threads require more space to prevent crowding and jamming. Lengthen for thicker threads and shorten stitch length for fine threads.

Use the stitch width and length samples described on pages 9 and 10 as a reference. Create a card index or notebook as shown in Fig. 3.1a, 3.1b, 3.1c to note the settings for each type of thread and fabric you use. Make this an ongoing system to record techniques for future projects. ✂

**Code for
Sample Index Cards:
LN: Left Needle
MN: Middle Needle
RN: Right Needle
UL: Upper Looper
LL: Lower Looper
SW: Stitch Width
SL: Stitch Length**

Technique: 3–4-thread overlock stitch

Tension settings:

     LN: **RN:**   **UL:**   **LL:**

     SW: **SL:**

Type of thread: LN: **RN:**   **UL:**   **LL:**

Type of fabric:

Fig. 3.1a
Sample index card

Technique: Chain stitch

Tension settings:

                    Needle: Looper:

Type of thread:

Type of fabric:

Fig. 3.1b
Sample index card

Technique:

Cover Stitch tension settings:

 2-thread wide: LN: RN: L:

 2-thread narrow: LN: RN: L:

 3-thread (bottom):   LN: MN: RN: L:

 3-thread (top & bottom):
Stitch length:

Type of thread: LN: MN: RN: L:

Fig. 3.1c
Sample index card

Overlock Stitches

3–4-Thread Overlock Stitch

This stitch, as shown in Fig. 3.2, is referred to as a basic balanced stitch and is created using two looper threads that intersect at the edge of the fabric held by both right and left needle threads. It is most widely used for seaming and can be stitched on knit and woven fabrics.

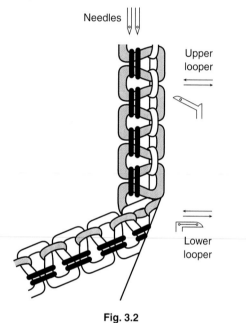

Fig. 3.2
3–4-thread overlock stitch

Variations of this stitch can be created by using either the left needle (Fig. 3.3) for a wider stitch or right needle (Fig. 3.4) for a narrow stitch.

The narrowest stitch can be created by implementing the narrow stitch finger (Fig. 3.5). This is the pin that creates a rolled hem. Whenever trims or fine seams, such as French seams, are desired, the narrow stitch finger creates the smallest space possible for a very fine seam. In this case use balanced settings.

2-Thread Over-edge Stitch

This stitch (Fig. 3.6) is formed with one needle and one looper—usually the lower looper. A converting device, shown in Fig. 3.7, is placed on the upper looper to fool the looper from being used. It is an excellent stitch to use on lightweight fabrics. Variations using this device for more techniques are described below.

5-Thread Chain Stitch

This stitch (Fig. 3.8) is formed with a separate 2-thread

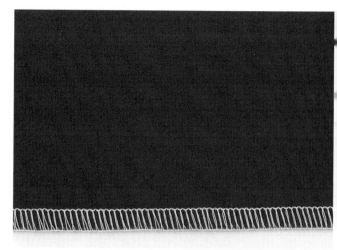

Fig. 3.3

Fig. 3.4

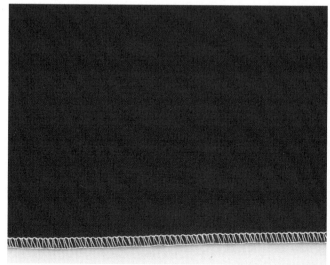

Fig. 3.5

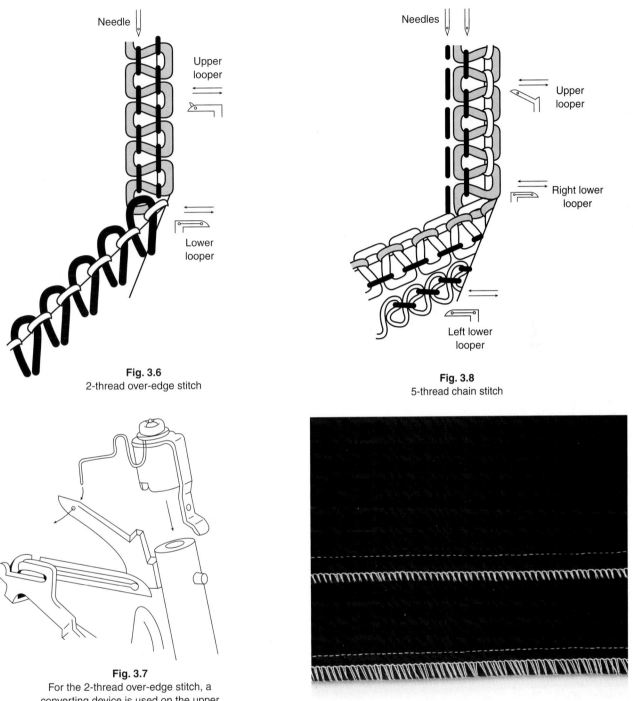

Needle ↓

Upper looper

Lower looper

Fig. 3.6
2-thread over-edge stitch

Needles ↓ ↓

Upper looper

Right lower looper

Left lower looper

Fig. 3.8
5-thread chain stitch

Fig. 3.7
For the 2-thread over-edge stitch, a
converting device is used on the upper
looper to fool it from being used.

Fig. 3.9

chain stitch along the side of a 3-thread overlock stitch.
The latter part of the stitch can be created wide or narrow on some machine models. It is a very stable stitch
and used frequently on woven and stable knit fabrics,
such as seams for home decorating and costuming.

This stitch can also be used with the upper looper
converter so that the stitch combines the 2-thread
needle/looper and 2-thread over-edge stitch as
shown in Fig. 3.9.

Chain Stitch

The chain stitch itself (Fig. 3.10) is very versatile, and in
most cases the tension does not have to be adjusted.
It can be stitched without the overlock portion for a
variety of applications. Seamstresses like it because
it is strong, but removes easily for fitting purposes.
Consumers also like the ease with which it is removed
when altering costumes used for a variety of different-
sized people.

Full of Tucks Pillow

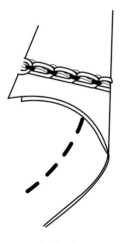

Fig. 3.10
The chain stitch

The stitch is formed with one needle and one looper and resembles a straight stitch on the right side of the fabric and a 3-ply stitch on the underside. The stitch has to be started on fabric, but can be stitched "on air" to create chains for tassels, fringe, belt and button loops, etc.

The chain stitch can also be made on the cover-

stitch section of the machine simply by removing one of the needles.

The chain stitch can be used in decorative applications, such as stitch tucks and pleats, revealing the looper side with decorative thread as shown in Fig. 3.11.

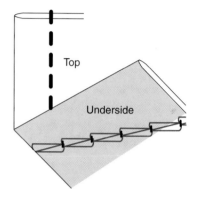

Fig. 3.11
Use decorative thread in the looper and
reveal that side for decorative purposes.

By increasing the looper and/or needle tensions, slight gathering can be achieved as shown in Fig. 3.12.

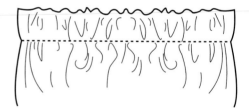

Fig. 3.12
Increase the looper and/or needle
tensions for slight gathering.

Chain-stitch shirring can take place if elastic thread is placed in the looper, as shown in Fig. 3.13. Refer to the elastic thread section on texturizing on page 22.

Fig. 3.13

Cover Stitch

The cover stitch (Fig. 3.14) is achieved with either two or three needles, which create two or three rows of stitching on the right side of the fabric, and the looper stitching on the underside. It is a functional stitch for hems, seams, elastic, binding and topstitching, but also serves well for decorative functions.

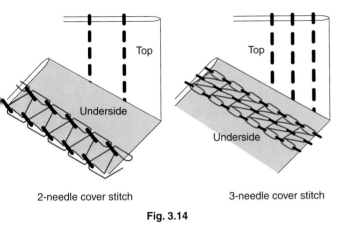

2-needle cover stitch   3-needle cover stitch

Fig. 3.14

Unlike other conventional overlock stitch functions, it is sewn on top of the fabric without the cutting blades. It has to be started on and completed on the fabric. For instance, an entire garment can be constructed first and the hem left for the finish work.

On some machines the two needles can be positioned to create a narrow or wide space between. Another variation of the cover stitch is the 3-needle stitch showing the looper stitches on the top and bottom of the fabric as shown in Fig. 3.15. This is commonly seen in ready-to-wear garments, particularly on better quality casual clothes.

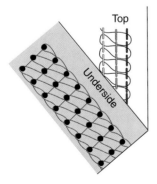

Fig. 3.15
3-needle cover-stitch variation shows
looper stitches on the top and the
bottom of the fabric.

Rolled Hems

For a rolled edge, you will use a very narrow pin-like stitch finger. As mentioned previously, this creates the

Majestic Pillow

Dainty Daisy Pillow

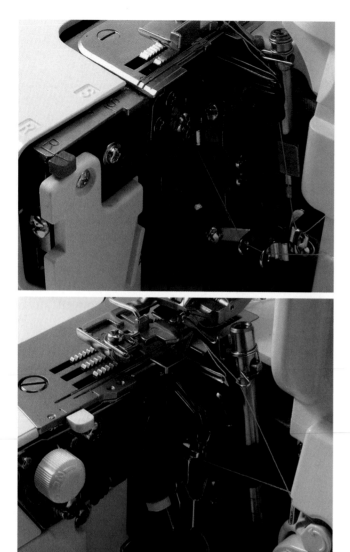

Fig. 3.16

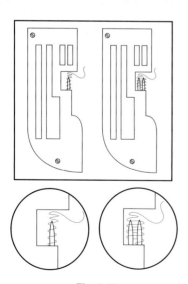

Fig. 3.17
A plate and a presser foot have to be replaced
on some machines to use the narrow stitch finger.

narrowest stitch-width space. When used with a tension adjustment, it encourages the fabric to roll to the underside. Most sergers now have this stitch finger built into the machine so all you have to do is move a lever to reveal it (Fig. 3.16). On older machines a plate and presser foot have to be replaced (Fig. 3.17).

Referring to your manual, use the right needle and tighten the lower looper tension. The upper looper thread should wrap around the edge to the underside of the fabric. The lower looper thread takes on a straight line of stitching next to the needle thread on the underside as shown in Fig. 3.18.

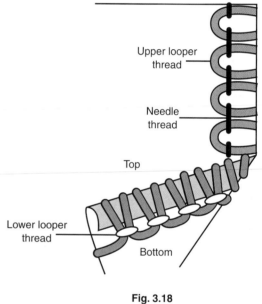

Fig. 3.18
Rolled-hem stitch

Most light- to medium-weight fabrics roll easily, while some are more stubborn. Grain lines also affect the roll. When roll-hemming scarves or napkins, serge a test piece on the crosswise and lengthwise grain of the fabric to determine if slight fine-tuning adjustments need to be done.

To avoid the "dog ears" on corners, particularly on napkins, about 1¹/₂" from each corner increase the cutting width slightly as you are tapering and serging off the fabric as shown in Fig. 3.19. Do the same thing when starting another side.

If you are having problems with fabric moving away when starting the corner again, try the following remedy. With a hand needle, stitch a 3"–4" length of knotted doubled thread once near the corner and hold it taut with your left hand as you feed the fabric through the right hand as shown in Fig. 3.20. This should keep the corner in place until you have serged enough length to release threaded needle.

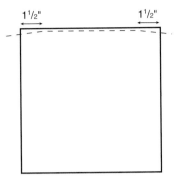

Fig. 3.19
About 1¹/₂" from corners, increase
cutting width slightly, tapering
and serging off fabric.

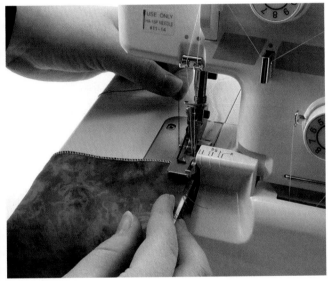

Fig. 3.20

For the best rolled hem, always trim some fabric to ensure that enough fabric is being rolled under. On stubborn, loosely woven or metallic fabrics, increase the cutting width to encourage a better roll. Prewashing fabric whenever possible will remove any sizing, which at times can work against a good roll. For the most stubborn fabrics, use a monofilament thread or Woolly Nylon type in the looper. The increase in tension that this thread creates will pull the roll nicely in most cases.

Lady of Spain Shawl

When all efforts have been exhausted and the fabric still will not roll, consider a narrow balanced stitch. It still could be very effective, particularly when used with a decorative thread.

The rolled hem can also include cords, fine wire or fish line to either enhance and strengthen the edge or decorate or create a definite and permanent "wave" to the edge. ✂

Flatlock Stitches

latlocking is joining two pieces of fabric with a serged seam. Then the seam is pulled apart until the two layers lie flat. Flatlocking can be used as a practical stitch, such as applying elastic or lace in lingerie, or as a decorative function. It can be stitched with either two or three threads. There are times where the upper looper thread hinders the appearance of a good flatlock in the 3-thread version. Therefore, I prefer the 2-thread application, which incorporates the use of the adapter device placed on the upper looper (see page 27).

In addition to being easier to pull flatter, it also creates less bulk and uses less thread.

When pulled flat, the looper thread will be on the top side of the fabric and the needle thread, which resembles a ladder, will be on the underside of the fabric (Fig. 3.21). Either side can be used, but we'll discuss the looper side first.

Flatlocked Skirt & Jacket Ensemble

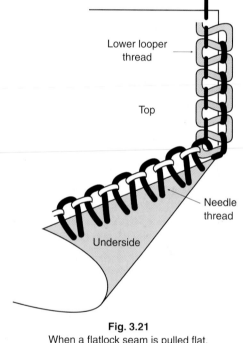

Fig. 3.21
When a flatlock seam is pulled flat, looper thread will be on the top and needle thread on the underside.

All versions can be stitched with the right or left needle and the narrow stitch finger.

3-Thread Flatlock Stitch

Always start the 3-thread flatlock stitch with a balanced stitch and work from there. Adjust the stitch length before adjusting tensions. Then loosen the needle tension dial down to a low setting (almost at 0 on some machines). Tighten the lower looper tension dial so the lower looper thread pulls into a straight line at the edge of the fabric. Loosen the upper looper thread slightly, only if necessary, to allow fabric to pull open flat. The needle thread should look like a V on the underside of the fabric as shown in Fig. 3.22.

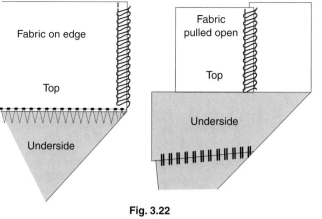

Fig. 3.22
3-thread flatlock stitch

2-Thread Flatlock Stitch

This stitch is actually a 2-thread over-edge stitch that you can also use for flatlocking. Since a 2-thread stitch does not lock or intersect at the seam line, the stitching will automatically lie flat as you gently pull it flat. Note the V on the underside as shown in Fig. 3.23.

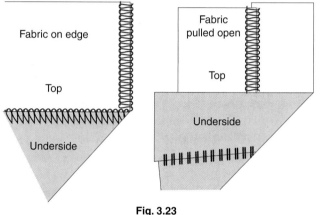

Fig. 3.23
2-thread flatlock stitch

When flatlocking, guide the edge of the fabric or fold so the stitches hang halfway off the fabric as shown in Fig. 3.24. This will allow the extra space the fabric requires to lie flat. Thicker fabrics will require more thread hanging off the edge, whereas thin fabrics will need less.

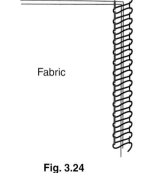

Fig. 3.24
Guide the edge of the fabric or fold when flatlocking so stitches hang halfway off the fabric.

The key to a successful project is to stitch evenly.

When flatlocking seams, you may want to use the left needle, as it will contain more fabric within the seam. On woven fabrics, fold the top layer on the seam line and then place it directly on the raw edge of the under fabric as shown in Fig. 3.25. This will ensure a safer seam.

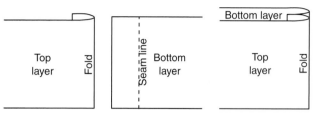

Fig. 3.25
Fold top layer of woven fabric on seam line and place directly on raw edge of under fabric.

Dare-to-Be-Different Set

For stress seams, press a ⁵/₈"-wide strip of fusible tricot on the inside of the seam directly over the flatlock section as shown in Fig. 3.26.

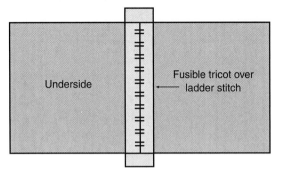

Fig. 3.26
Press 5/8"-wide fusible tricot strip on
inside of stress seam directly over
flatlock section.

Decorative thread is placed in either the upper looper for a 3-thread flatlock or lower looper for a 2-thread flatlock. Use serger thread in a blending color in the needle. The thicker decorative threads may look better in the left needle, but experiment, because there are no hard-and-fast rules in decorative work.

Doll Bed Coverlets

Flatlock Variations

There are many variations of flatlocking, such as adding beads, ribbons and cord as shown in Fig. 3.27. Though rarely used, a ³/₄" flatlock can be used. With the additional needle, the flatlock will be a little bulkier. To make this stitch look its best, tensions need to be precise or the stitch looks messy.

Fig. 3.27
Beads, ribbons and cord can be
added with flatlocking.

A very narrow flatlock with decorative thread in the upper looper will simulate soutache trim. This is a variation of the pintuck discussed in another section (page 38). Other decorative features include creating unique trims and pipings.

Reverse Flatlock

Reverse flatlock refers to the ladder side of the stitch. The technique is done in the same manner as above, except that the decorative thread is in the needle. In order for this thread to be visible on the top side, the fabric is placed right sides together before it is stitched. This ladder can be filled with contrasting decorative threads or ribbons and woven back and forth in a pattern with a yarn needle as shown in Fig. 3.28. When the weaving process is completed, it looks entirely different.

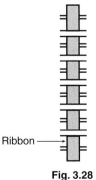

Ribbon

Fig. 3.28
The ladder side of the flatlock stitch
can be filled by weaving decorative
threads or ribbons through the stitches.

Serger Fagoting

This is the same technique as used for reverse flatlock, except the ladder and looper stitches fill a space between two pieces of fabric. In this case, thread the same decorative thread in the needle and lower looper of a 2-thread flatlock. Stitch so that there are more loopers hanging off the fabric than on, as shown in Fig. 3.29. Try to barely catch the two folds. The seam will have a space that resembles fagoting, which is traditionally done by hand or conventional sewing machine.

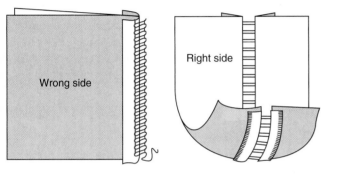

Fig. 3.29
For fagoting, stitch so more loopers hang off the fabric than on. When the seam is opened it will have a space that resembles fagoting.

Blanket Stitch

Another fun and decorative reversible stitch is the blanket stitch (Fig. 3.30). In this case, the decorative thread is in the left needle and wraps to the edge on both sides of the fabric. The looper threads then interlock on the edge of the fabric as shown in Fig. 3.31. This effect is achieved by loosening the needle tension while at the same time tightening the looper tensions significantly. If the decorative thread requires a looser tension, remove it from one or more of the thread guides. Some machines have an attachment to keep the thread completely from the tension guide.

Blanket Stitch Pillows

Fig. 3.31
Looper threads interlock on edge of fabric.

Although you can use either the right or left needle for this technique, some machines will not pull the left needle thread completely to the edge. You can help the process by threading the loopers with a stretchy thread, such as Woolly Nylon, Woolie Poly or Resilon. Adjust your machine for the longest and widest stitch to accommodate the thicker thread.

If the stitch rolls to the fabric top side, you can use tweezers or your fingernails and gently encourage or pull it to the edge as shown in Fig. 3.32.

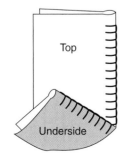

Fig. 3.30
Blanket stitch

Fig. 3.32

Fig. 3.33

Another method to encourage the thread to lie on the edge is to first serge over a water-soluble stabilizer and then pull the stitch to the edge using the stabilizer as shown in Fig. 3.33.

Wrap Stitch

In a wrap stitch, decorative thread is in the lower looper of a 2-thread setting using the converter. Tighten the needle tension until it pulls the looper thread from the front to the underside, completely wrapping the folded or finished edge as shown in Fig. 3.34. This is a great stitch for a reversible garment or a jacket with lapel-like features. Either the right or left needle may be used. ✀

Fig. 3.34

Serger Accessories

There are many serger accessories available to facilitate construction of your projects—both in accuracy and speed. All serger companies have accessories available, but the design may differ from one model to another. Consult your machine manufacturer for more detailed explanations. The following general information is applicable to all accessories.

Blind Hem Foot

The blind hem foot (Fig. 4.1) aids in serging nearly invisible woven fabric hems and stretchy hems in knitted fabrics. It is easy to use and provides perfect results because the hem is sewn and neatened in one smooth operation. The guide on the blind hem foot can be adjusted sideways to allow you to use one foot for different types of hems or for completely different 3-thread, right-needle sewing projects where an additional fabric guide may be useful.

Fig. 4.1

It provides a strong hem in curtains, drapes and slipcovers. The long fabric guide also aids in heirloom serging when making pintucks and attaching laces.

In hemming, the fabric is folded in the same manner as for conventional sewing machine applications. Unlike the fine "bites" of the sewing machine stitch, however, some serger needle thread will be visible, depending on the weight of the fabric. Because strength is imperative in home decor and in sport garments, such as knitted tops and variations of fleece and sweatshirt-type fabrics, some amount of needle thread should be visible on the right side of the item.

The stitch length should be set on the longest setting. Although elongated, the stitches will still be more closely spaced than sewing machine work.

Double fold fabric with the lower raw edge under and beyond the front extension of the foot. Place the fold against the extension as shown in Fig. 4.2. The hem will be stitched and trimmed in the same operation. Unlike the conventional sewing machine, where the needle can be moved to fine-tune the "bite," on a serger you move the extension to create more or less space for the needle to penetrate. Reduce needle tension as appropriate to the fabric to reduce or avoid puckering.

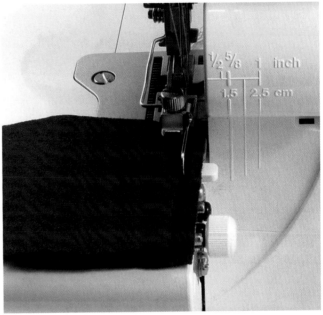

Fig. 4.2

Double Drapery Hem

Because curtain and drapery hems require more weight, double-fold the fabric. Place the double folds next to the extension and stitch through all layers. You will not be trimming fabric in this case.

Weighted Hem

For a more weighted hem, as in heavier drapery fabric, first stitch drapery weights on the raw edge. Drapery weights are actually metal beads covered with a lightweight fabric and can be purchased by the yard.

With the aid of a beading foot, first serge the weights on the raw edge as shown in Fig. 4.3 and then follow the double drapery hem concept.

Flatlock Hem

The flatlock blind hem is ideal for any type of fabric. Use decorative thread in the needle and take a wider needle bite. Reduce needle tension to allow for more thread to show. When stitching is completed, gently pull open to flatten the stitching.

Fig. 4.3

The stitching can then be left as the ladder stitch or woven with other decorative threads or yarns to bring attention to the hemmed area as shown in Fig. 4.4.

Pintucking

The blade on the blind hem foot can be used conveniently as a guide when serging without cutting. The serging results will be regular and guiding the fabric is very easy. It is therefore ideal for fine pintucks or lace insertions.

Antique Battenburg Lace Pillow

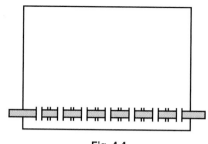

Fig. 4.4
The ladder side of the flatlock hem can be woven with decorative threads, yarn or ribbon.

Use the narrow stitch finger and set tensions for narrow seaming. Move the guide on the blind hem foot to the right so the needle catches the fabric. Fold the fabric where you want to sew a pintuck and press. Hold the folded fabric toward the guide of the blind hem foot while serging.

To ensure perfect spacing between pintucks, mark the fabric at spaced intervals and then pull a fabric thread at each mark as shown in Fig. 4.5. This will create a fine run in the fabric. Use the run to fold the fabric and then serge.

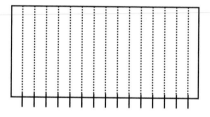

Fig. 4.5
Pull threads at marked intervals to ensure perfect spacing between pintucks.

Serging Lace to Lace

Engage the narrow stitch finger and reduce needle tension slightly. Move the guide to the right so the needle catches the heading of the lace.

To serge, place the lace right sides together and serge through both layers. Gently pull flat and the lace will be butted for a practically invisible flat-joining seam as shown in Fig. 4.6.

Use heirloom sewing threads such as fine cotton or rayon for a lightweight effect.

Cording Foot

Do not confuse the cording foot (Fig. 4.7) with the piping foot (Fig. 4.8). The cording foot has a guide for serging in special threads and yarn, fish line or shirring elastic while roll hemming. This easy-to-use foot speeds up techniques such as reinforced roll hems, serger trims and serger piping. It is essential for wedding and evening wear.

Fig. 4.6

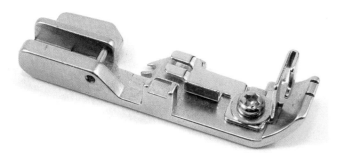

Fig. 4.7

Fig. 4.8

Wavy Edge With Fish Line

Attach the cording foot and set the overlock for roll hemming. Choose a lightweight fish line up to .7mm diameter. If you serge in a heavier nylon thread, the edge will be stiff and wavy.

Set the serger for roll hemming and place the spool of fish line on the spool holder for the left-hand needle thread. Place it through the guide on the support rod and through the guide near the sewing light. Take it under the foot, slip it into the rear guide and then into the front guide on the foot.

Pull the fish line out behind the presser foot before you start to serge. Serge over the fish line, leaving a generous tail at the end. Gently stretch the roll-hemmed edge to create a wavy effect.

A true bias will work the best on woven fabrics, while the greater stretch (crosswise) works well with knits.

Batik Two-Piece Outfit

Gathering With Cord

Prepare the serger for roll hemming and follow the directions for fish line.

Fold the fabric right sides together and gently press a crease. Serge along the folded edge without cutting into the fabric. When serging is completed, open the seam and pull on the cord until the desired gathering effect is achieved.

This is an effective way to gather on heavier weight fabrics where the differential and gathering foot isn't enough.

Shirring With Elastic Thread

Follow the same general directions as for cord and fish line. Pull elastic thread gently until the desired amount of shirring is achieved.

Serger Trims

You can create a wide variety of trims by using decorative threads serged over filler cords or yarns.

Set the machine with the narrow stitch finger. Use a narrow balanced setting for a wide, thicker trim or a rolled hem setting for a narrower version. Stitch length should be as close as possible without bunching the threads.

Fusing thread can be of benefit here when used in the lower looper on a narrow balanced setting. Sufficient fusing thread must be exposed to allow for proper fusing. Then couch in place on the sewing machine.

Serger Piping

Piping can easily be created by adding a simple seam-allowance heading to the above serger trim instructions.

Fold a piece of 1$\frac{1}{2}$"-wide bias-cut tricot fabric strip in half. Place the fold next to the blind-hem-foot guide and serge over yhe fold with decorative thread in either a roll hem or narrow balanced setting. The lightweight tricot reduces the bulk in seams.

Stretchy Trims and Piping

You can also make elasticized trims to add decorative details to garments that stretch, such as bathing suits and other sport-related garments.

Clear elastic is ideal for this purpose and is used as a base instead of tricot. Because it is so lightweight, it is important to serge through it to keep it from rolling. Use 1"-wide clear elastic for the piping and continue with the piping technique as described above.

Majestic Place Mat & Napkin

Keep the elastic taut in front and behind the presser foot while serging. Don't stretch it, as the serged stitch allows for the stretch factor.

As a trim, select an elastic that is wider than the trim. Then trim the elastic close to the serging stitch, taking care not to cut the stitches. Topstitch to the project on the sewing machine with monofilament thread.

For a double trim, serge one side of the elastic, then turn and serge the other side next to the needle line of the previous stitching.

An elasticator or elastic foot helps to keep narrow elastics in place. Keep the elasticator/elastic foot on a neutral setting.

Elasticator

The elasticator is probably the least-understood presser foot in the accessory line. Basic knowledge of stretch factors on various types of elastic is important to understand the fundamental use of the elasticator. The type of fabric and quality, along with the degree of stretch of individual types, will greatly influence the results. Generally speaking, a very soft and stretchy elastic, such as in lingerie, often requires less elastic. A firmer elastic, such as those used in swimsuits and action-wear, will require more elastic.

The elastic foot, or elasticator (Fig. 4.10) is used to easily guide and stretch narrow elastic during its application to the fabric. It can be adjusted to vary the amount of stretch as it is being serged. You do not have to stretch the elastic, as the foot does it for you. Unfortunately, there have not been explicit instructions that come with these feet, and there are no guides to let you know how many times the tension screw has to be turned. Check your elasticator presser foot for the width of elastic it will accommodate.

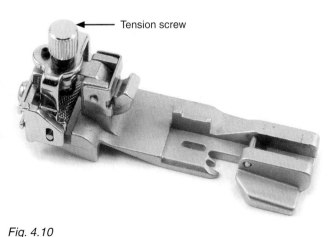
Tension screw

Fig. 4.10

Beaded Floral Sampler

The concept is simple and easy. If your elasticator does not have the necessary markings, loosen the roller pressure or tension screw to its minimum. The old rule "righty tighty, lefty loosey" applies. With a permanent marker, place a mark on the tension screw just above the very tiny, round, screwlike object directly below it. This will indicate a guiding point from which to start.

Now turn the tension screw one complete revolution. Continue turning until you have determined the number of turns it takes to reach maximum, or until the screw will not move any farther without forcing it. It takes about five to six turns or revolutions on most elasticators. Each elasticator has its own personality, so testing on each one is necessary. In addition, the pressure regulator on top of the machine may need adjusting to create greater stretch.

Make a test sample similar to the one you made for stitch width and length on pages 9 and 10. On a long strip of fabric approximately 3"–4" inches wide by 36" long, mark off the instructions, place the fabric under the presser foot and start serging at minimum pressure. Then turn the screw one complete revolution to the right as you approach the first mark. Continue following this technique until you have reached the final complete revolution to the right or maximum pressure.

Use this as a guideline (Fig. 4.11) for determining the various degrees of stretch in the types of elastic you might be using.

Fig. 4.11

Beaded Jewelry Bag

When you have determined how many times you need to turn the tension screw, it will be much easier to understand the system of stretching. For example, on a bathing suit application the front part of the leg elastic is usually stretched less than the back part. Knowing the number of turns or revolutions it takes to do either portion is of great benefit.

In addition to garment construction, the elasticator can also be applied to home decor sewing for items such as seat cushions, picnic table and bench covers, poolside furniture covers, pockets on tablecloths to hold eating utensils, ironing board covers, etc.

Piping Feet

There are different sizes of piping feet and some manufacturers offer more than one size. There is at least one for standard-size piping and a wider, grooved foot for larger piping for home decor. The serging technique is the same for both sizes. The groove under the foot accommodates the piping. The piping used can be purchased or made to customize a project.

Place the piping along the seam line between the two pieces of fabric, which are placed right sides together. Then serge the piping into the seam as shown in Fig. 4.12.

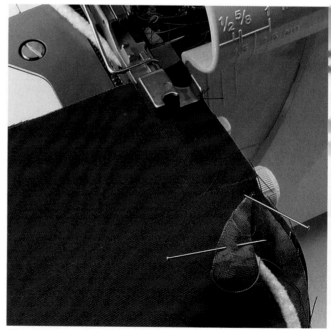

Fig. 4.12

Beading/Sequin Foot

The beading/sequin foot (Fig. 4.13) is a handy foot that acts as a shelf to hold the beads, thus making it easier to guide beads and sequins between the needle and the knives so they can be serged over. On some models you can use this foot when serging over wire or making trims. Some machines have an additional separate guide to attach to the machine that you thread the cord or beading through before it is stitched over.

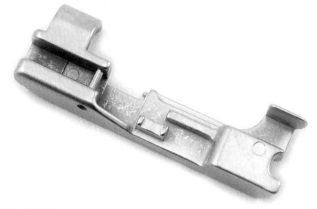

Fig. 4.13

Adjust the stitch length so the looper thread stitches between each bead rather than over it. Beads can be stitched to the edges of fabric or in the middle by flatlocking.

Gathering Foot

The gathering foot or attachment (Fig. 4.14) is used either to gather one piece of fabric or two pieces while gathering only one of the fabric layers as it is stitched to the flat layer.

When gathering a ruffle onto another piece of fabric, divide both pieces in quarter or eighth sections, depending on the amount to be gathered. In the case of insufficient gathering, hold onto the top layer with some resistance, but don't pull. This will encourage the bottom layer to catch up. ✂

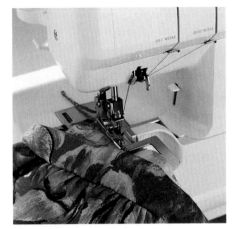

Fig. 4.14

Novelty Attachments

Every serger with cover stitch capabilities has a special presser foot for cover stitching and 2-thread chain stitching. There are several other novelty accessory feet available, most commonly in a clear-plastic version for greater visibility. Some available are:

- Bias tape foot
- Bias tape folder foot
- Hemming foot
- Cording and piping feet
- Corded pintuck foot
- Belt loops foot
- Flat fell seam foot
- Elastic foot
- Fagoting foot
- Topside lace application foot
- Underside lace application foot
- Raised pintuck foot

Serger Machines

Sergers are available today from a variety of companies as can be seen by those shown here.
Most companies have several models, so the consumer has more choices than ever before.

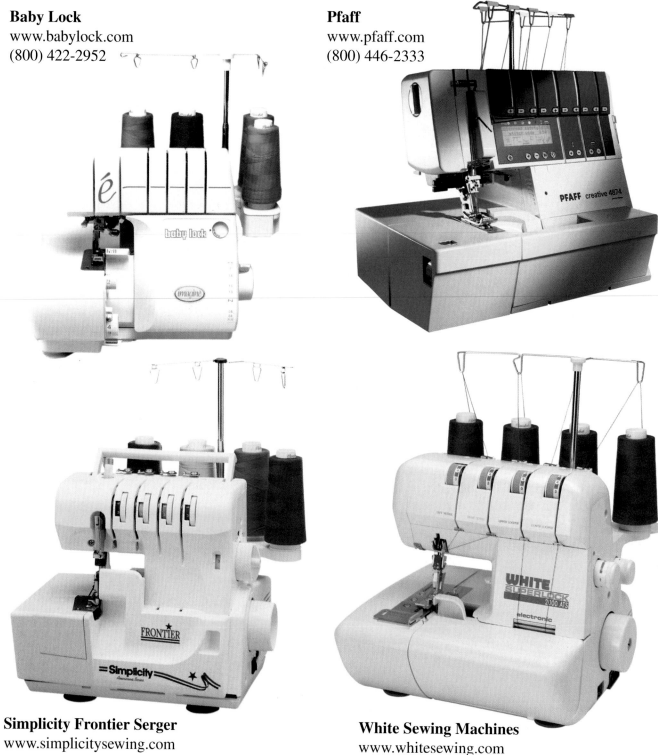

Baby Lock
www.babylock.com
(800) 422-2952

Pfaff
www.pfaff.com
(800) 446-2333

Simplicity Frontier Serger
www.simplicitysewing.com
(800) 335-0035

White Sewing Machines
www.whitesewing.com
(800) 446-2333

Elna
www.elnausa.com
(800) 848-3562

Janome America Inc.
www.janome.com
(800) 631-0183

Bernina of America
www.berninausa.com
(630) 978-2500

Brother International Corporation
www.brothersews.com
(908) 704-1700

Husqvarna Viking
www.husqvarnaviking.com
(800) 358-0001

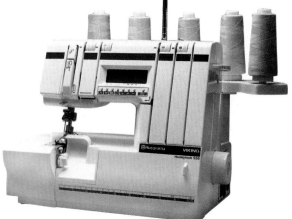

Heirloom Serging

By Agnes Mercik

Create a delicate ensemble, or any project of your choice, with heirloom serger methods.

Heirloom, or French sewing, consists of a variety of intermediate-level sewing techniques, which include gathering, puffing, pintucks, attaching pieces of edging and insertion laces, fine fabrics, entredeux, embroidered insertions and beadings to create pieces of fabric. The pattern is then placed on the fabric and cut for assembly.

These techniques are traditionally done by hand, although sewing machine and serger applications have increasingly become more popular because they save time.

Because gathering and puffing are widely used in heirloom work, the serger's differential and gathering feet and attachments are a tremendous asset. Ruffles can be gathered onto the main fabric in one operation.

Pintucks, sewn with double needles on the sewing machine, can be simulated on the serger with a simple rolled hem or narrow seam finish over a fold. French seams can also be simulated using the same setting. An alternate method would be to first serge the seam with a narrow balanced setting and then stitch on the sewing machine in a traditional way.

For seams that require more strength, use the 4-thread application, but engage the narrow stitch finger to reduce the width. This is also helpful when applying piecing techniques in quilt projects.

Patterns: Any basic pattern may be used. The fabric is made and the pattern is placed on the created fabric.

Fabrics: Fine Swiss batiste, linen and silks in a variety of weights are the most common fabrics associated with this type of work, but other natural fiber fabrics, such as chambray and quilting fabrics, work well, also.

Threads: Good all-purpose sewing/serging threads are the keys to fine sewing. For rolled hems, #60 cotton embroidery thread is nice for a delicate look.

Needles: Start every new project with a new sharp #70 or #80 needle. Microtex needles also work well on silk fabrics.

Fabric Preparation: It is very important that the fabric grain is straight. Clip the selvage and pull a thread across the width of the fabric. Then cut on the pulled thread line.

Pintucks: The pulled thread technique works well for spacing lines for pintucks. Mark fabric for desired spaces. Pull a thread and then use the pulled thread line as the fold to serge. A blind hem foot is helpful for this technique. Move the front extension of the presser foot to the depth of the pintuck and then place the fold against the extension.

Materials

- Commercial patterns of choice
- Fabrics and notions as recommended by pattern and as suggested above
- Basic sewing supplies and tools

Instructions

Pintucks

Step 1. Before creating pintucked fabric, it is necessary to estimate the amount of fabric required for the project. Measure your pattern piece and add approximately 2" in each direction as shown in Fig. 1.

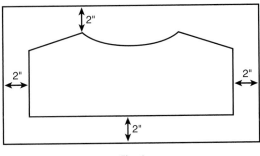

Fig. 1
Estimate size of fabric by adding
at least 2" in each direction
to pattern piece.

Step 2. After creating the pintucks, place the pattern on the newly created fabric and cut.

Gathering

Step 1. The projects shown incorporate gathered lace in many ways. You can gather by setting the differential and stitch length to maximum. Tighten the needle tensions as necessary. Or, you can use the gathering foot attachment.

Step 2. Place the fabric to be gathered against the feed dogs and the fabric to be gathered onto in the slot of the gathering foot or attachment. Follow your machine's instructions, as each will have a slightly different means of gathering. Also refer to Serger Accessories, page 37.

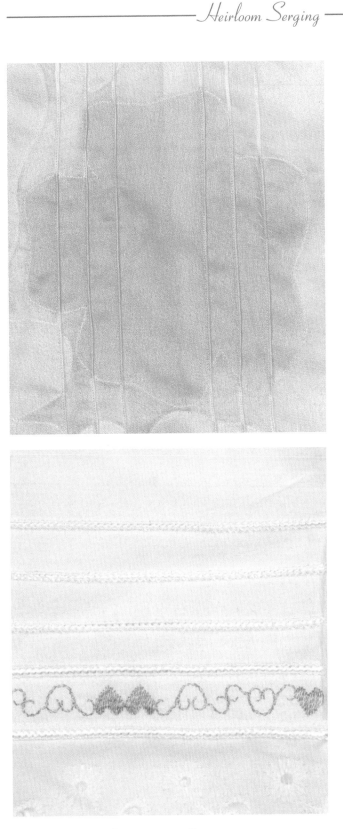

Soutache Pintucks

Step 1. Another type of pintuck is the soutache pintuck. It is just a slight variation from the traditional pintuck. Determine the desired spacing between pintucks. Pull threads or mark with a fabric-marking tool. Place the fold of the fabric against the blind hem

foot extension, adjust tension (see step 2 below) and serge over the fold without cutting as shown in Fig. 2.

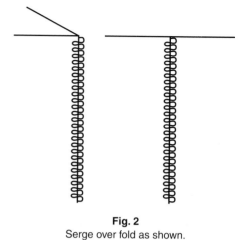

Fig. 2
Serge over fold as shown.

Step 2. Loosen needle tension slightly and then gently pull the tuck flat after serging. This is an easy version of flatlocking. Because the looper threads do not have far to go, the needle tension only requires a slight adjustment. Decorative thread in the looper could be of a finer nature or heavier. Designer 6 and Décor 6 were used for the models for a more pronounced look for white-on-white.

Serger Ribbons

Step 1. The decorative stitches on your sewing machine are excellent for making ribbons. Choose a nice single or multiple combination of decorative stitches. Stitch on approximately 2"-wide strips of fabric that have been backed with a lightweight fusible tricot interfacing.

Step 2. With decorative thread in the upper looper of a 3-thread narrow balanced stitch, serge on both sides of the decoratively stitched strips, These strips could be of any desired width. Two inches is just approximate.

Step 3. On the sewing machine, attach the strips to the garment by stitching along each serged edge. ✄

Heirloom Pillow

By Agnes Mercik

You'll be delighted with the delicate heirloom effect you can create when you make this pillow with your serger.

Project Specifications

Skill Level: Beginner

Heirloom Pillow Size: Approximately 14" x 9" (excluding ruffle)

Materials

- 1¹/₂ yards white Swiss batiste
- 10" strip of 2³/₄"-wide embroidery insertion
- Pillow form 14" x 9"
- ³/₄ yard 1¹/₄"-wide Swiss cotton edging lace
- 12" white zipper
- 1 spool blue #30 rayon embroidery thread and matching blue serger thread
- 4 spools white serger thread
- Basic sewing supplies and tools

Instructions

Step 1. From white batiste cut two pieces 12" x 10". Cut two 10" pieces of Swiss cotton edging lace. Place one piece of lace on each 10" piece of batiste as shown in Fig. 1.

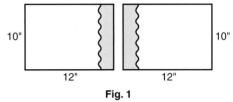

Fig. 1
Place lace on one side
of each batiste piece as shown.

Step 2. Place 2³/₄"-wide embroidery insertion right sides together on top of each piece of lace edging and serge both seams with a 3-thread narrow stitch.

Note: *You may want to jump ahead to Steps 5–7 and seam and edge-stitch the ruffles while machine is threaded in this mode. Insertion of zipper in pillow back, Step 13, could be done at this time, too.*

Step 3. Open the pillow top flat and press. Measure five intervals each side of embroidery insertion strip, top and bottom, as shown in Fig. 2. Carefully fold and press creases on these marks.

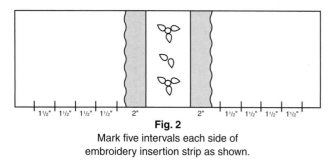

Fig. 2
Mark five intervals each side of
embroidery insertion strip as shown.

Step 4. To prepare serger for chain stitch, thread chain stitch looper with blue rayon embroidery thread and matching blue serger thread in the needle. Using the presser foot as a guide, serge along the pressed creases 1/2" from the fold, right side down so that the looper thread is highlighting the tuck as shown in

Fig. 3. The pleats should be folded away from the center embroidery panel.

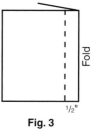

Fig. 3
Serge 1/2" from fold as shown.

Step 5. From white batiste cut two strips each 4¹/2" x 45" and 5¹/2" x 45".

Step 6. With machine set on 3-thread, narrow stitch, serge seams on short ends of each width, making two rings. Seams will be placed at the center of each short side of pillow.

Step 7. Edge-stitch on edge of each ring. Press 5/8" hem to wrong side.

Step 8. With right sides of fabric down, stitch the hem in the same way pleats were stitched in Step 4.

Step 9. Place narrow ruffle on top of wider ruffle. Machine-baste together on raw edges.

Step 10. Set machine for regular 4-thread construction function. With differential set at maximum, gather the basted edges handling both ruffles as one piece and leaving sufficient chain at the start and end of stitching. Check fit with pillow edges.

Note: *If too much or too little gathering, loosen the stitches at the chain ends so you have two long threads and two short threads. The short threads are the needle threads because they do not take up as much thread yardage as the looper threads. See Fig. 4. Pull the needle threads to adjust gathering.*

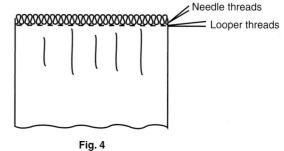

Fig. 4
Needle and looper threads.

Step 11. Match the seam ends of the ruffle to the centers of the short ends of pillow top. Distribute fullness evenly and pin. Serge around perimeter.

Step 12. Cut two pieces of Swiss batiste 10" x 10" for pillow back.

Step 13. Place 12" white zipper right sides together with one edge of one pillow back piece. Note that the zipper needs to be longer than the fabric at both ends as shown in Fig. 5. Extend the pull tab end longer, as the tab is more difficult to maneuver.

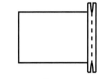

Fig. 5
Zipper is longer than seam at both ends.

Step 14. With piping or multipurpose foot, place zipper teeth in the groove of the foot and serge entire length of one side. Repeat from the other side, serging in the opposite direction.

Step 15. Make a fold in the fabric parallel to and

covering the zipper. This will be approximately a 1" fold. As in Step 4, chain-stitch right side down. Repeat on the other side of the zipper.

Step 16. Fold the fabric again to make a 1/2" pleat each side of zipper. Stitch again as in Step 4 as shown in Fig. 6.

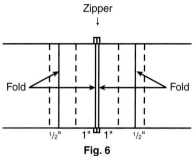

Fig. 6
Make pleats each side of zipper as shown.

Step 17. Place pillow top and pillow back right sides together and serge all four sides. Turn right side out and insert pillow form. ✄

Creating Diamonds

By Nancy Fiedler

Learn this fast-cut and fast-sew diamond method for use in the next two patterns and dozens of other designs of your choice.

All 60-degree diamond panels are created in the same manner. Any differences will be in the choice of fabrics, threads and the size of the diamonds. The panel is put together using a 2-thread flatlock stitch. However, if your serger does not have 2-thread capabilities, set up for a 3-thread flatlock.

The right side of the finished diamond panel can have either the loop or ladder side of the stitch showing. Always cut an extra strip of each color to test the thread, stitch and tension. As the choice of fabrics and threads will affect the finished stitch, it is important to make decisions regarding stitch length, loop or ladder size and tension setting to achieve the desired look.

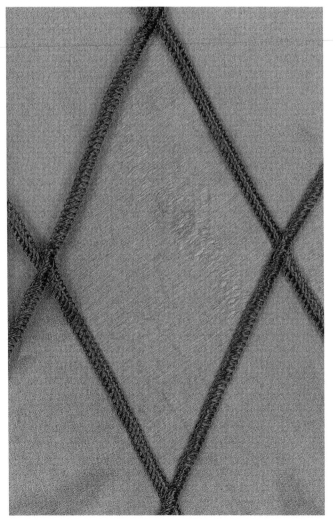

Materials

- Rotary cutter and mat
- 6" x 24" clear acrylic quilter's ruler that has a 60-degree angle marked
- Fine-point permanent marker
- Seam gauge
- Basic sewing supplies and tools

Instructions

Note: The numbers, measurements and fabric requirements for each project will be given with the project directions.

Cutting

Step 1. Cut fabric on the crosswise grain (selvage to selvage) from fabrics A and B. The total number of strips must be an even number.

Step 2. A start position for sewing the fabric together must be marked on the wrong side of each strip. To determine this start position, place four or six strips parallel to each other on the work surface, offsetting each by a few inches. Place the clear acrylic quilting ruler on the strips at a 60-degree angle. Arrange the strips to create the angle, then measure the distance from the selvage edge to the straight edge of the ruler. This is the number of inches that will be marked on each strip.

Sewing

Note: Sew all the flatlocked seams at 1/2" seam allowance. The knife will cut away 1/4". Be careful and be consistent in marking, cutting and pinning to assure alignment of the diamonds.

Step 1. Place one strip of color A and one strip of color B together, matching the edge of strip A with the mark on strip B. Flatlock the two pieces together with 1/2" seam allowance. When the seam is completed, gently pull the fabrics out to flatten the seam.

Step 2. Continue sewing strips together, offsetting and alternating colors until you have sewn all the strips together as shown in Fig. 1.

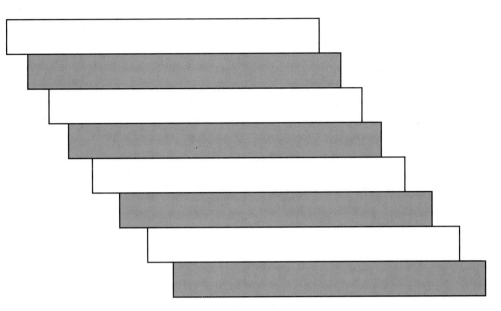

Fig. 1
Sew strips together, offsetting and
alternating colors as shown.

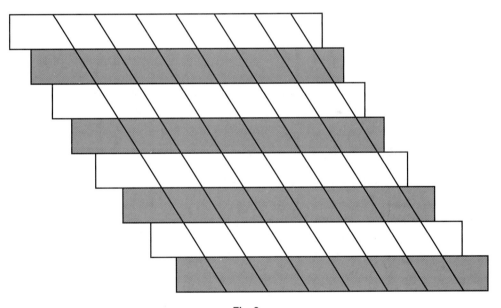

Fig. 2
Mark 60-degree angle lines as shown.

Step 3. Steam and press the panel. If the width of the strips and the number to be sewn together becomes too large to handle, create two or more identical panels. Keep the width of the panels no wider than 32"–36".

Marking & Cutting

Note: *Because the panels may be wider than the length of a quilter's ruler, it is easier to mark cutting lines with a fine-point marker and cut the strips with*

scissors. A permanent black marker shows up on most fabrics and the line will be cut off during the sewing process.

Step 1. Using the quilter's ruler, mark a 60-degree angle starting at the lower left corner of one panel. When all the lines are marked as shown in Fig. 2, cut the strips with scissors.

Step 2. Repeat for any additional panels until you have the number of strips needed according to calculations.

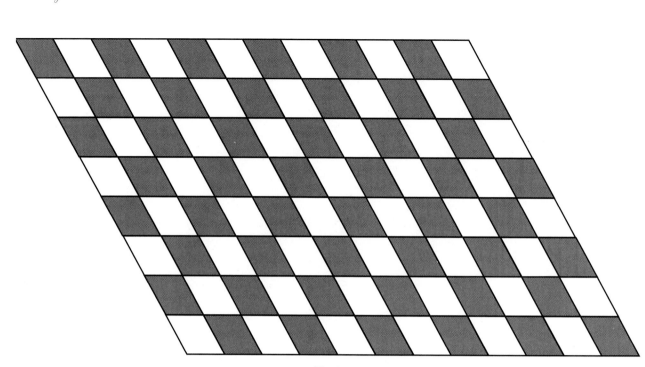

Fig. 3
Alternate strips as shown.

Sewing Again

Step 1. Place the new, angled strips in two piles. Pile 1 should have color A on top and pile 2 should have color B on top. Pin two strips together, one from each pile. Offset the seams $1/2$" so they intersect on the seam line. Measure and pin accurately.

Step 2. Using a $1/2$" seam allowance, serge the two pieces together, cutting off $1/4$" as you sew. Gently open the flatlock seam.

Step 3. Continue adding strips, alternating piles, until all strips are sewn together as shown in Fig. 3. Carefully steam and press the diamond panel. The diamonds are formed on the bias, so be careful not to distort the shape while pressing.

Pressing

Keep in mind the type of fabric and thread when pressing seams flat. Many decorative threads are rayon or nylon and must be pressed from the reverse side with a cool iron or press cloth. Some fabrics, such as fleece, manmade leather or suede, may not tolerate pressing with heat. Take time to flatten these seams and finger-press instead of pressing with an iron.

Reassembling

Step 1. Referring to Fig. 4, and starting at the corner indicated, cut through the center of the row of diamonds as shown. Move the top piece to the other end of the diamond panel and pin side A to side B as shown. Offset seams $1/2$". Use a $1/2$" seam allowance and serge the pieces together, cutting off $1/4$" as you sew. Gently open the flatlock seam.

Step 2. Referring to Fig. 5 (see page 56), locate the center horizontal row of diamonds. From this point, cut through the center of the vertical row of diamonds to the end of the panel. Move the piece to the opposite side of the diamond panel. Pin side A to side B, offsetting the seams $1/2$". Serge together with $1/2$" seam allowance and gently open the flatlock seam.

Step 3. Make a second cut, again referring to Fig. 5, and move the piece to the opposite side. Pin sides C and D together, offsetting the seams $1/2$". Serge to form a rectangle. Open the flatlock seam and press.

Calculation of Diamonds

Note: Create diamonds of any size in a panel of any dimension by using these calculations.

Step 1. The finished panel width divided by the finished width of a strip equals the number of strips to cut in each color. Example: If the finished width of the panel is 36", divide 36" by 3", which equals 12. Therefore, you will need twelve 3" strips each of color A and color B.

Step 2. The finished panel length divided by the finished width of a strip equals the number of diagonal strips to cut. Example: If the finished length of the panel is 30", divide 30" by 3", which equals ten 3" diagonal strips.

Step 3. After determining the number of strips, add 1" to the strip width for seam allowances. Example: Add 1"–3" finished strips for seam allowances.

Step 4. The number of strips in Steps 1 and 2 must always be an even number. If necessary, add a strip.

Step 5. For this example the panel size desired is 36" x 30". Cut twelve 4" strips of color A and twelve 4" strips of color B. Sew two panels using six strips of color A and six strips of color B in each panel.

Step 6. Cut ten 4" diagonal strips. In this example, there will be enough fabric to cut approximately 16 diagonal strips from 45"-wide fabric. The finished diamond panel will be longer if all the diagonal strips are sewn together. ✂

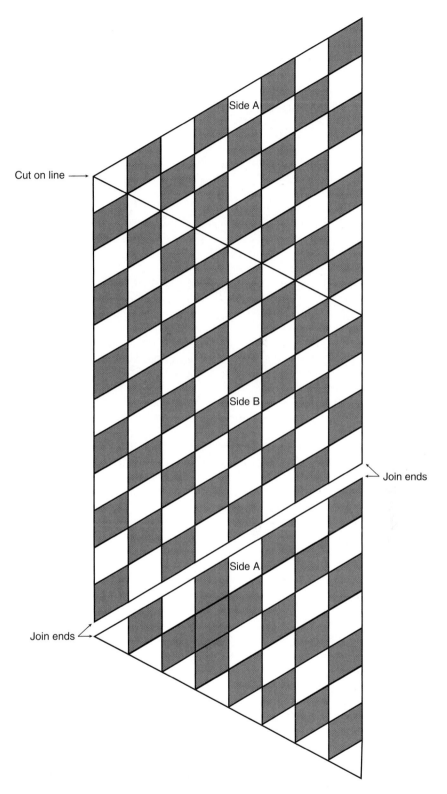

Fig. 4
Cut and move top piece to
lower position and sew.

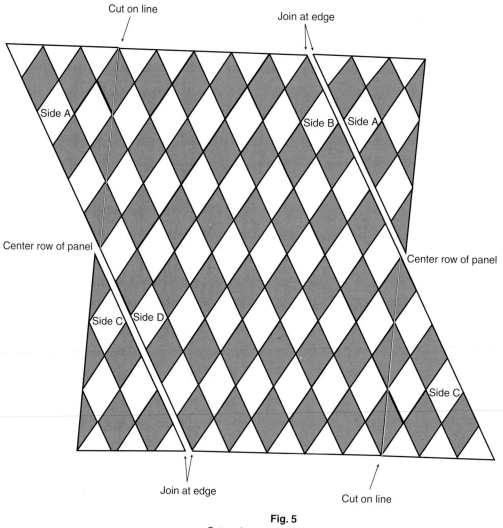

Cut on line

Join at edge

Side A

Side B   Side A

Center row of panel

Center row of panel

Side C Side D

Side C

Join at edge

Cut on line

Fig. 5
Cut and move sections as shown.

Flatlocked Diamond Blouse

By Nancy Fiedler

Whenever you create your own fabric, you know you will have a unique garment.

Project Specifications

Skill Level: Intermediate

Blouse Size: Any size

Note: *Rather than a self-facing, a better choice with a sheer fabric, to avoid the diamond pattern shadowing through the front, is a neutral-colored sewn-on front facing.*

Materials

- Commercial blouse pattern
- 1¼ yards 45"-wide organza for diamonds (color A)
- 2 yards color A for one sleeve, back, collar and cuff
- 1¼ yards 45"-wide organza for contrasting diamonds (color B)
- 1 yard color B for one sleeve and cuff
- Tulle for facing in amount suggested on pattern for interfacing
- 2 spools Madeira Décor 6 thread
- 4 cones serger thread to match
- 2 spools each Madeira Polyneon embroidery thread in colors to match each sleeve
- Buttons as suggested on pattern
- Rotary cutter and mat
- 6" x 24" clear acrylic quilter's ruler that has a 60-degree angle marked
- Pattern-tracing material
- Tailor's chalk
- Basic sewing supplies and tools

Instructions

Step 1. Cut eight 5"-wide strips across the width of fabrics A and B for a total of 16 strips.

Step 2. Mark 2½" from the selvage edge on the wrong side of each strip.

Step 3. Set serger for wide 2-thread flatlock. Thread lower looper with Madeira Décor 6 thread and thread the needle with serger thread. The same decorative effect can be achieved with a 3-thread flatlock. Place the Maderia Décor 6 in the upper looper and serger thread in the lower looper and needle. Test the stitch on two layers of the fabric and adjust the stitch length to achieve a satin stitch 2.5mm–3mm.

Step 4. Flatlock four strips of color A and four strips of color B together to make a 32" panel as in Creating Diamonds, Sewing, page 52. Repeat for a second identical panel.

Step 5. Cut the two panels into twelve 5" strips as in Creating Diamonds, Marking & Cutting, page 53.

Step 6. Sew the strips, wrong sides facing, as in Creating Diamonds, Sewing Again, page 54.

Step 7. Following instructions in Creating Diamonds, Reassembling, page 54, complete the fabric panel.

Step 8. Trace the blouse front pattern on pattern-tracing material, marking the center front line.

Step 9. Place fabric panel on large work surface, right side up. Find the center vertical row of diamonds of the panel.

Step 10. Place the left front pattern piece right side up on the fabric panel, staying to the left of the center of the panel. Place the center front line in the center of one row of diamonds. Place the center front line of the right front pattern piece in the mirror position, using this as a check before cutting. Cut out left front.

Step 11. Turn the cut piece right side down over the remainder of the panel, matching accurately all the flatlock seams and color diamonds. Cut out the right front piece.

Step 12. Cut out the remainder of the pattern pieces from the fabric purchased for the back, sleeves, etc. Construct the blouse according to pattern directions.

Chain Stitch Sleeve Option

Step 1. Before constructing the blouse, place the sleeve pieces wrong side up on a flat work surface. With tailor's chalk, mark a horizontal line across the widest part of each sleeve. Place the quilter's ruler at a 60-degree angle from this line and draw lines spaced 4" apart across the sleeve.

Step 2. Reverse the angle and draw lines in the opposite direction to form diamonds on the sleeves.

Step 3. Set up serger for chain stitch. Thread chain stitch looper and needle with Madeira Polyneon embroidery thread.

Step 4. Place fabric wrong side up under presser foot and sew a chain stitch on each drawn line to create diamond shapes on the sleeves. ✂

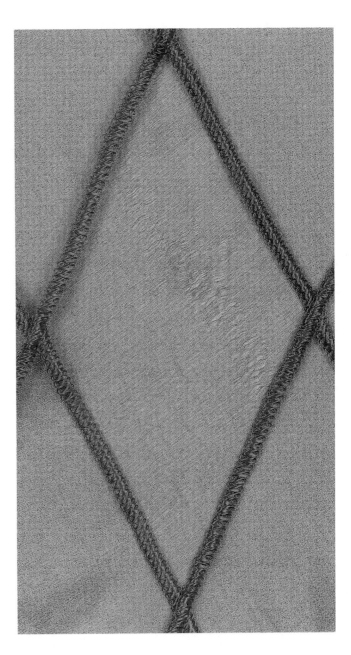

Flatlocked Diamond Fleece Pullover

By Nancy Fiedler

You'll love the ease of working with fleece—especially in fabric of your own design!

Project Specifications

Skill Level: Intermediate

Pullover Size: Any size

Materials

- Commercial pullover pattern (Butterick Pattern #3205 used for model)
- 1¹/₄ yards 60"-wide fleece in color A
- 1¹/₄ yards 60"-wide fleece in color B
- 1 yard 60"-wide fleece in color A or B for sleeves and collar
- A&E Signature variegated quilting thread that contrasts with fabric
- 4 cones serger thread to match quilting thread
- Notions as recommended by pattern
- Rotary cutter and mat
- 6" x 24" clear acrylic quilter's ruler with a 60-degree angle marked
- Basic sewing supplies and tools

Instructions

Note: The fleece panel was sewn with right sides together. The needle thread forms the ladder, which appears on the right side of the panel. Do not press the fleece with an iron. Careful pulling to flatten the flatlocked seam and pressure with fingers is adequate.

Step 1. Cut eight 5" strips each on the crosswise grain (selvage to selvage) from color A and color B for a total of 16 strips. Mark 2¹/₂" from the selvage edge on the wrong side of each strip.

Step 2. Set up serger for a wide 2-thread flatlock. Place serger thread in the lower looper and thread the needle with the variegated quilting thread. This same decorative effect can be achieved with a 3-thread flatlock. Place the variegated quilting thread in the needle and serger thread in the loopers. Test the stitch on two layers of the fabric, setting the stitch length to 5mm.

Step 3. Sew, right sides together, four strips of color A and four strips of color B to create a panel 32" wide as in Creating Diamonds, Sewing, page 52.

Step 4. With remaining strips create an identical panel.

Step 5. Cut the two panels into twenty 5" strips as in Creating Diamonds, Marking & Cutting, page 53.

Step 6. Sew the strips, right sides facing, as in Creating Diamonds, Sewing Again, page 54.

Step 7. Following instructions in Creating Diamonds, Reassembling, page 54, complete the fabric panel.

Step 8. Place the fabric panel on a large work surface right side up. Position the center front pattern piece fold line on the center vertical row of diamonds. Cut half of the front, stopping at the fold line. Fold the cut half over at the fold line and match the diamonds before cutting out the rest of the front. Repeat for the back.

Step 9. Cut out sleeves, collar and facings from remaining fabric. Construct the pullover according to pattern directions. ✂

Diamond Leather Purse

By Nancy Fiedler

Who would guess that you could create your own multicolored design in leather? It's easy with quick techniques using your serger!

Project Specifications

Skill Level: Beginner

Purse Size: Any size

Materials

Note: *Materials are adequate to create a diamond panel 36" x 45". If your purse pattern calls for more than a yard of fabric, you may need to make adjustments.*

- Commercial purse pattern
- 1³/₈ yards 45"-wide fake leather (A)
- 1³/₈ yards 45"-wide fake leather (B)

- 5–6 spools YLI silk #30 topstitch thread
- Matching serger thread
- Lining and notions as required by pattern
- Rotary cutter and mat
- 6" x 24" clear acrylic quilter's ruler that has a 60-degree angle marked
- Seam gauge
- Basic sewing supplies and tools

Instructions

Note: *The fake-leather panel was sewn right sides together. The needle thread forms the ladder, which appears on the right side of the panel. Do not press the fake leather with an iron. Carefully pull the seams apart and apply pressure with fingers to flatten the seam.*

Step 1. Cut twelve 4"-wide strips each from color A and color B fake leather, selvage to selvage. Mark 2¹/₂" from selvage edge on the wrong side of each strip.

Step 2. Set the serger for a wide 2-thread flatlock. Thread the lower looper with serger thread and thread the needle with the silk topstitch thread. The same decorative effect can be achieved with a 3-thread flatlock—serger thread in the loopers and topstitch thread in the needle. Test the stitch on two layers of the fabric and adjust the stitch length to 2.5mm–3mm.

Step 3. Right sides facing, sew six strips of color A and six strips of color B together to create a panel 36" wide as directed in Sewing, Steps 1 and 2, Creating Diamonds, page 52. Repeat to create a second identical panel.

Step 4. Cut the two panels into sixteen 4" strips and sew strips together as directed in Marking & Cutting and Sewing Again, Creating Diamonds, pages 53 and 54.

Step 5. Locate the center horizontal row of diamonds. Referring to Figs. 4 and 5 on pages 55 and 56, cut the panel to turn the diamonds on point.

Step 6. Lay out the pattern pieces, matching the rows of diamonds at the sides of the front and back pieces. Construct the purse according to pattern directions. ✂

Diamond Tote

By Nancy Fiedler

Use heavy upholstery fabric to design your own fabric and make a one-of-a-kind tote.

Specifications

Skill Level: Beginner

Tote Size: Any size

Materials

Note: *Materials are adequate to create a diamond panel 30" x 60". If your tote pattern calls for more than that amount of fabric, you may need to make adjustments.*

- Commercial tote pattern
- 1¼ yards 54"-wide upholstery fabric (A)
- 1¼ yards 54"-wide upholstery fabric (B)
- 1 spool Woolly Nylon
- Matching serger thread
- Lining and notions as required by pattern

- Rotary cutter and mat
- 6" x 24" clear acrylic quilters's ruler that has a 60-degree angle marked
- Seam gauge
- Basic sewing supplies and tools

Instructions

Note: *This tote was created from upholstery fabric sewn wrong sides together. Woolly Nylon was threaded into the looper to create the decorative effect on the fabric panel. Avoid high temperature settings on the iron when pressing, as heat may melt the thread and/or the fabric. Always press on the wrong side of the panel when using Woolly Nylon.*

Step 1. Cut ten 4" strips each from color A and color B upholstery fabric, selvage to selvage. Mark 2½" from selvage edge on the wrong side of each strip.

Step 2. Set the serger for a wide 2-thread flatlock. Thread the lower looper with Woolly Nylon and thread the needle with serger thread. The same decorative effect can be achieved with a 3-thread flatlock—Woolly Nylon in the upper looper and serger thread in the lower looper and needle. Test the stitch on two layers of fabric and adjust the stitch length to achieve a satin stitch .5mm–1mm wide.

Step 3. Wrong sides facing, sew five strips of color A and five strips of color B to create a panel 30" wide as directed in Sewing, Steps 1 and 2, Creating Diamonds, page 52. Repeat to create a second identical panel.

Step 4. Cut the two panels into 22 strips 4" wide and sew strips together as directed in Marking & Cutting and Sewing Again, Creating Diamonds, pages 53 and 54.

Step 5. Locate the center horizontal row of diamonds. Referring to Figs. 4 and 5 on pages 55 and 56, cut the panel to turn the diamonds on point.

Step 6. Lay out pattern pieces, matching the rows of diamonds at the sides of the front and back pieces. Construct the tote according to pattern directions. ✂

Beaded Jewelry Bag

By Naomi Baker

The serged pearl edging on this jewelry bag is unique and adds a very feminine finishing touch.

Project Specifications

Skill Level: Beginner

Jewelry Bag Size: Approximately 13$\frac{1}{2}$" x 13$\frac{1}{2}$" (open)

Materials

- 14" circle of satin or taffeta for bag
- 14" circle of matching cotton fabric for lining
- Two 10" circles of matching cotton lining fabric for jewelry pockets
- 1$\frac{3}{4}$ yards pearl beading
- 2 yards $\frac{1}{8}$"-wide white satin cord
- 1 spool all-purpose thread to match fabric
- 2 cones serger thread to match fabric
- 1 cone white buttonhole twist or similar weight thread
- Jewelry glue

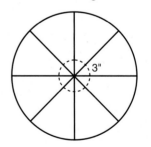

- Beading foot
- Basic sewing supplies and tools

Instructions

Step 1. On the right side of the 14" satin or taffeta circle, mark casing lines 1$\frac{1}{4}$" and 2" from edge. Sew two $\frac{1}{2}$" buttonholes opposite each other between casing lines as shown in Fig. 1.

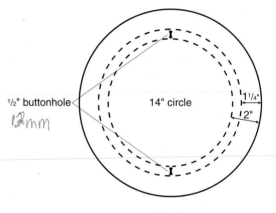

½" buttonhole

12mm

14" circle

1¼"

2"

Fig. 1
Mark casing lines and sew buttonholes
as shown on 14" fabric circle.

Step 2. Fold one 10" lining circle in eighths and lightly press for stitching lines. Mark a 3" circle in the center as shown in Fig. 2.

3"

Fig. 2
Fold 10" lining circle in eighths as shown
and lightly press. Draw 3" center circle.

Step 3. Place the 14" fabric and lining circles wrong sides together and straight-stitch $\frac{1}{4}$" from the outer edge and on the casing lines.

Step 4. Using the beading foot, with buttonhole twist in the upper looper and serger thread in the needle and lower looper, adjust the serger for a rolled edge. You may need to adjust the width of the stitch to allow for

3 thread narrow o/l

the beading. Slowly serge the beading to the edge of the right side of the 14" circles, allowing the beading to just meet at the beginning and the end. Glue the ends with jewelry glue to secure.

Step 5. Place the two 10" lining circles wrong sides together. Serge around the outer edges with rolled edge.

Step 6. Center the 10" circles on the lining side of the 14" circles. Straight-stitch on the wedge lines and on the 3" center circle as shown in Fig. 3.

Step 7. Cut the 1/8"-wide white satin cord in two equal lengths. Insert one cord through a buttonhole and back out through the same hole. Knot the ends. Repeat with the other cord, inserting in and out of the other buttonhole. Pull cords to draw up bag as shown in photo. ✂

Fig. 3
Center 10" circles on 14" circles and stitch as shown.

Dare-to-Be-Different Dress, Jacket & Purse

By Agnes Mercik

The challenge of this project is to create your own fabric. Use scraps to make the purse and learn the technique. Then let your imagination take over for the jacket, dress or garments of your choice.

Project Specifications

Skill Level: Intermediate

Dress & Jacket Size: Any size

Purse Size: Approximately 8^1/$_4$" x 9^3/$_4$"

Materials

- Commercial patterns for dress and jacket
- Rayon batik fabrics for dress and jacket as required by patterns, plus ^{1}/$_4$–^{1}/$_2$ yard extra of each to incorporate in fabric design
- ^{1}/$_4$–^{1}/$_2$ yard pieces of 4 or 5 additional coordinating rayon batiks and solids
- Lining and notions as required by patterns
- ^{3}/$_8$ yard coordinating lining fabric for purse
- ^{3}/$_8$ yard fusible tricot for purse
- 1 or more spools decorative thread
- 4 spools blending serger thread
- Weaving tool (crochet hook, needle, etc.)
- 6-strand embroidery floss in a variety of contrasting colors
- Seam sealant
- 1 (^{7}/$_8$") coordinating button for purse
- 1^1/$_4$ yards of 2 different ^{3}/$_8$"-wide decorative braid trims for purse handle
- Basic sewing supplies and tools

Instructions

Purse

Step 1. Set serger for 2- or 3-thread flatlock technique.

Step 2. Cut 12 assorted 5^1/$_2$" x 3^1/$_2$" rectangles of batik rayon prints and solids. Using the serger's longest stitch, flatlock the pieces together on the lengthwise grain as shown in Fig. 1. Either the left or right needle may be used, but the left needle provides more space for weaving.

Fig. 1
Flatlock pieces together as shown.

Step 3. With crochet hook, needle or other weaving tool, weave contrasting 6-strand embroidery floss under and over each flatlock ladder as shown in Fig. 2. Leave 1/2" tail at each end.

Fig. 2
Weave 6-strand embroidery floss over
and under flatlock ladders as shown.

Step 4. Press 5/8"-wide strips of fusible tricot over the wrong (looper) side of each seam.

Step 5. Cut two strips of rayon batik 2 1/2" by the length of the flatlocked strips.

Step 6. Set serger for 4-thread construction seam and serge the 2 1/2"-wide strips to each side of flatlocked section as shown in Fig. 3.

Fig. 3
Serge 2 1/2"-wide strips to each
side of flatlocked section.

Step 7. Use the pieced and serged purse panel as a pattern to cut a piece of fusible tricot the same size. Following manufacturer's instructions, fuse to the wrong side of the purse panel. Use purse panel again to cut lining from coordinating lining fabric. For a firmer purse, fusible tricot may be fused to the wrong side of lining if desired.

Step 8. From lining fabric cut a pocket 9 1/2" x 12". Fold long edge in half and serge. Turn right sides out and place the raw edges of the pocket on the raw edges of the lining. Edge-stitch the lower edge in place on the sewing machine.

Step 9. For an additional small inner pocket, cut another piece of lining fabric 4" x 8". Fold to a 4" x 4" square. Serge on three sides. Turn right side out and press lower raw edges in. Position as desired on larger pocket and edge-stitch three sides in place.

Step 10. Cut one strip of batik fabric 1³/₄" x 45" for purse handle and another 1³/₄" x 4" for button loop.

Step 11. Serge a length of chain 8"–9" long. Without cutting the chain, place it in the fold of the button loop strip, fabric wrong sides together as shown in Fig. 4. Serge the seam taking care not to catch the chain within the fabric strip. Turn the strip right side out by gently pulling the chain within the fold to the right side.

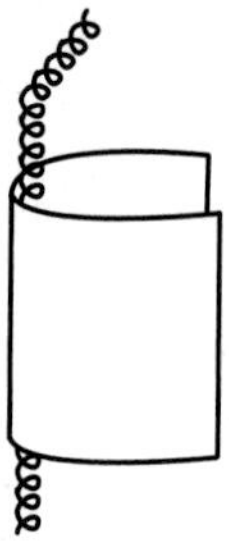

Fig. 4
Place chain within fold of
fabric strip as shown.

Step 12. Repeat for the purse handle by serging a chain about 50" long and serging it within the 1³/₄" x 45" batik strip. Turn right side out by pulling the chain.

Step 13. Braid the strip made in Step 12 with the two lengths of ³/₈"-wide decorative braid trims. Stay-stitch the braided ends on the sewing machine to prevent raveling.

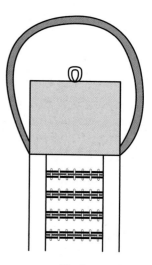

Step 14. Position button loop and braided purse handle on right side of purse panel, aligning raw edges as shown in Fig. 5. Place pocket lining on purse panel, right sides facing. Be sure pockets are positioned properly to be right side up. Serge one short side and both long sides. Turn right side out and edge-stitch the opening closed.

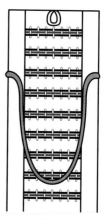

Fig. 5
Position button loop and
handle as shown.

Step 15. Press, fold and align sides to form purse and flap as shown in Fig. 6. Sew ⁷/₈" coordinating button on front of purse, matching button loop placement. Edge-stitch to close sides.

Fig. 6
Fold panel to form purse
and flap as shown.

Jacket

Step 1. With the flatlocking technique used to make fabric for the purse, plan and make the fabric panels from which to cut pieces as instructed on pattern directions.

Step 2. Construct jacket as instructed on pattern directions.

Dress

Step 1. The fabric for the bodice of the dress, sleeve hems and skirt hem were created by flatlocking pieces of the same fabric together. The dress bodice has nine flatlocked rows.

Step 2. Cut and construct dress as instructed on pattern directions. ✂

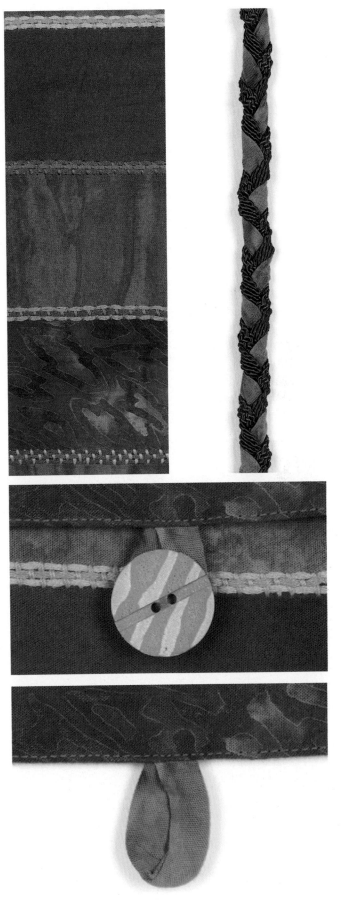

Prairie Points Purse

By Agnes Mercek

Make the purse and learn the prairie point technique, which can be applied to any garment.

Project Specifications

Skill Level: Intermediate

Vest Size: Any size

Purse Size: Approximately 10" x 8"

Note: *Materials are for purse only. If you choose to embellish a vest to match the purse, select a commercial vest pattern and follow instructions for materials and construction. Determine number of prairie points needed to trim and purchase fabrics accordingly.*

Materials

- $1/8$ yard each of four color-coordinated fabrics for background strips and handles
- $3/4$ yard print fabric for prairie points
- $3/8$ yard lining fabric
- $3/8$ yard fusible interfacing
- 1" x $3/4$" hook-and-loop tape
- 1 roll $1^1/2$"-wide tricot
- 1 spool decorative thread
- Clear nylon monofilament
- Beads (optional)
- Basic sewing supplies and tools

Instructions

Step 1. From $1/8$ yard of color-coordinated fabrics, cut five strips $2^1/2$" x 21" for background strips. Two strips will have to be cut from one color. Cut one strip each $1^1/2$" x 18" and $1^1/4$" x 18" for the handle. From print fabric cut five $2^1/2$"-wide strips across the width of the fabric for prairie points. Cut 1 strip 1" x 18" for the handle.

Step 2. Cut and press fusible interfacing to all strips except the five strips for prairie points.

Step 3. Set serger for 3-thread narrow balanced stitch with decorative thread in the upper looper. Serge-edge both long sides of each of the three handle strips.

Step 4. Make serger piping by folding a 30" length of $1^1/2$"-wide tricot in half lengthwise. Serge over the folded edge as shown in Fig. 1.

Step 5. Fold each $2^1/2$"-wide print prairie point strip in half lengthwise, wrong sides facing, and serge-edge over the fold as shown in Fig. 2. Cut each prairie point strip into 4" increments. Fold each as shown in Fig. 3.

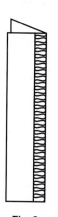

Fig. 1
Serge over folded edge of tricot strip.

Fig. 2
Serge-edge folded prairie point strip.

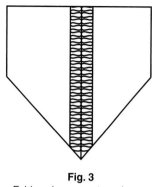

Fig. 3
Fold each segment as shown.

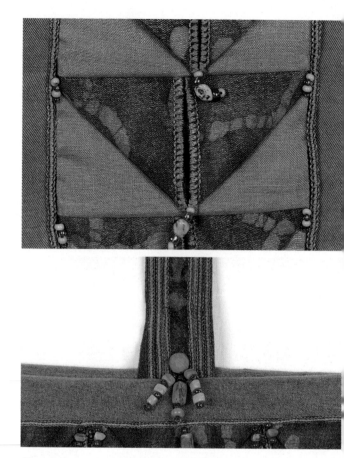

Step 6. Arrange 10 folded prairie points on four 2¹/₂" x 21" background strips as shown in Fig. 4, aligning raw edges. Serge the four strips together as shown in Fig. 5.

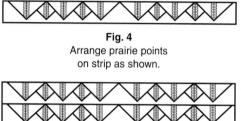

Fig. 4
Arrange prairie points
on strip as shown.

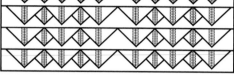

Fig. 5
Serge strips together as shown.

Step 7. Use the prairie point section as a pattern to cut two lining pieces from lining fabric.

Step 8. Sew the piping strip made in Step 4 to the top edge of the purse and then sew the remaining 2¹/₂" x 21" background strip to that same edge as shown in Fig. 6.

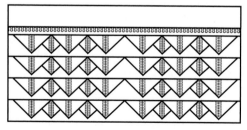

Fig. 6
Sew piping strip to top edge and
then add fifth strip as shown.

Step 9. Serge side and lower edge seams of lining together. Bring two short ends of prairie point section together to form front and back of purse. Center three prairie points along the lower front and back edges of purse, raw edges aligned. Serge side and lower edge seams of purse together.

Note: *If optional beading is desired, add before stitching side and bottom seams of purse.*

Step 10. Layer the three serged handle strips made in Step 3 and sew on sewing machine with clear nylon monofilament, stitching close to the serged edges of the strips.

Step 11. Fold the top fabric band to the inside of purse and stitch to first seam band.

Step 12. Position purse handle on purse centers back and front and stitch onto one of the strip seam allowances on the inside of the purse.

Step 13. Insert lining in purse, wrong sides facing, and hand-stitch to inside of top fabric band.

Step 14. Add any additional beads desired at handles and prairie points at lower edge of purse referring to photo for ideas.

Note: *The vest is a basic pattern with insert strips on the front and center back comprised of a variety of metallic and cotton blended fabrics. Use the same decorative thread on the prairie points. The strips are outlined on both sides with serger piping. Beads have been added for further enhancement and are optional.* ✄

Lady of Spain Shawl

By Anne van der Kley

Put on your dancing shoes, grab the castanets and make your own music as you start using your serger as a textile art tool.

Project Specifications

Skill Level: Intermediate

Shawl Size: Approximately 44" on straight-grain edges

Materials

- 1 length of supple silk jacquard or similar fabric, as long as the fabric is wide (if fabric is 44" wide, buy a 44" length)
- 6" of silk organza or other sheer fabric to contrast with jacquard
- 1 1/3 yards water-soluble stabilizer
- 3 spools of machine-embroidery thread to contrast, but harmonize with fabric (designer chose red, golden yellow and orange to use with her fabric selection)
- 1 spool heavy embellishment thread, such as YLI Pearl Crown Rayon or Madeira Décor
- All-purpose thread to match fabric for machine stitching
- Flower-head pins
- Beading needle
- Seed, bugle, glass and crystal beads as desired to complement fabrics
- Seam sealant
- Rotary tools
- Basic sewing supplies and tools

Instructions

Note: Be sure the silk you have selected is workable by testing to determine if it heat-marks or water-marks. If the silk water-marks, wash it by hand, air-drying it in the shade, lying flat. If it heat-marks, attach a non-stick cover to the sole of your iron and test again.

Scarf Construction

Step 1. Remove the selvages from both sides of the silk jacquard fabric square. Cut a 1 1/2"-wide strip each from one lengthwise edge and one cross-grain edge of the fabric square. Join the strips into one continuous length by stitching across short ends.

Step 2. Square up the fabric, trimming as necessary.

Fold on the diagonal and press a crease line, being careful not to stretch the bias edge. Open and cut on diagonal crease line. Cut a further 1 1/2"-wide strip from each straight-grain edge of one triangle.

Step 3. From the second triangle, cut one 1 1/2"-wide strip from one side of the fabric (either the lengthwise or crosswise grain.)

Step 4. Cut the silk organza into two 2 1/2"-wide strips across the width of the fabric.

Step 5. Thread serger for a balanced 3-thread narrow stitch with the three machine-embroidery threads.

Step 6. Place the longest 1 1/2"-wide strip on a flat work surface. Place the silk triangle on top of it, right sides facing along the bias edge.

Step 7. Pin with flower-head pins at right angles to the fabric and the flower head extending beyond the edges of the fabric.

Note: Pinning parallel to the fabric edge may cause stretching along the bias edge. If you do not feel comfortable with this method, baste the edges by hand or machine.

Step 8. Stitch the edges together, with the narrow strip next to the feed teeth of the serger. You will need only to trim a slight excess of threads. Set serger speed to a slow setting, stopping in advance of each flower-head pin and removing it before stitching.

Step 9. Carefully press the seam toward the fabric strip. Press the cut edge of the narrow strip to meet the edge of the stitching, creating a single fold. Press the folded edge toward the stitching line, encasing the stitching in a double fabric fold. Stitch together at your sewing machine with a shortened straight stitch.

Thread Fabric

Note: Some of the insertion embellishments on this scarf are made of fabrics of your own creation, called thread fabric.

Step 1. From its longest side, cut the water-soluble stabilizer into 1" strips. Raise the presser foot and

place the right-hand side of the stabilizer strip under the presser foot. Lower presser foot. Serge on the stabilizer strip, lengthwise, cutting a sliver off as you go. Run the chain off the end of the stabilizer for 2". Use the serger cutter to cut the chain tail.

Step 2. Turn the row of stitching so the stitching is on the left and stabilizer is to the right. Serge the next row. The left needle should just enter the outer edge of the previous row of stitching, covering a scant one-fourth of the stitching. The excess stabilizer will be trimmed off with this row of stitching.

Step 3. Adjust the width as necessary to the maximum width possible. Place a new strip of stabilizer under the presser foot. Stitch on the stabilizer, the length of the strip, again cutting a sliver off as you go, but joining the strips as you go. The left needle should just enter the outer edge of the previous row of stitching, covering a scant one-fourth of the stitching.

Step 4. Flip the stabilizer so the stitching is on the left and the stabilizer is coming from the underside, to the right. Serge on the stabilizer the length of the strip, trimming all excess.

Step 5. Continue in this manner until you have a piece of serger-made fabric four to six rows across. Make two more lengths as described. These will be for bows and flowers.

Step 6. Make another piece of thread fabric 1½" x 6". This is for the accept strip in the silk jacquard.

Step 7. When all of the thread fabric is completed, wash out the stabilizer. Soak and then rinse most of the excess out in a large container of cold water. Then rinse any residue out under cold running water. Dry thoroughly by placing on a flat surface out of direct sunlight. The fabric will spring to life when the stabilizer has been removed.

Rolled Hems

Step 1. Adjust serger for a 3-thread rolled hem with machine-embroidery threads in all positions.

Step 2. Stitch a dense rolled hem (0.5–1) down each straight-grain edge of the shawl, starting at the square corner and finishing at the shawl points. Repeat along each long edge of the three 1½"-wide strips cut in Steps 2 and 3 of Scarf Construction. Leave any thread chains intact. Cut one of the 1½"-wide strips into four 6" lengths.

Step 3. Stitch a rolled hem down both sides of the two

end. The organza band at the point of each side of the shawl will extend beyond the main body of the fabric, but will be generally aligned to the jacquard fabric strip.

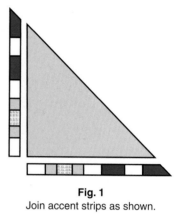

Fig. 1
Join accent strips as shown.

Step 5. Add the corner organza strip, butting to the main body of the fabric first and then to the jacquard strip as shown in Fig. 2. Repeat for the other side of the shawl.

silk organza strips cut in Step 4, Scarf Construction, to yield 2"-wide strips. Cross-cut the strips into four 10" lengths and one 12" length.

Step 4. Fold ends of silk organza segments back about $1/2$" to the wrong side. Stitch a rolled hem across each end. Be sure the rolled hem is worked from the right side of the fabric. With fine scissors, trim excess fabric back to the stitching line of the folded fabric. If the fabric is quite firm, it may not roll completely, showing some of the stitching from the lower looper. This will create a secondary decorative effect.

Accent Band

Step 1. Fold each of the 4" x 6" jacquard strips to the wrong side about $1/4$". Sandwich thread fabric between silk jacquard segments, matching the folded edges at both the front and the back. Secure with a row of machine stitching, using a shortened stitch length.

Step 2. Place edge-joining foot on sewing machine. Using machine-embroidery thread, wind a bobbin to closely match the dominant rolled hem color.

Step 3. Butt fabric edges together, following Fig. 1. Leave a 2"–3" space between the strips for bows and flowers and to tie the shawl. The spacing may vary depending on your fabric and strip dimensions.

Step 4. Stitch with a fine zigzag stitch 1.5 long and 2–2.5 wide, joining the edges invisibly. Tie off the ends and secure with seam sealant applied with the point of a pin. When the seam sealant is completely dry, trim the

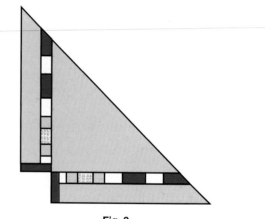

Fig. 2
Add corner strips and then jacquard strips as shown.

Thread Bows

Step 1. At one end of one thread fabric length, form a bow as shown in Fig. 3 that will fit into a fabric window.

Fig. 3
Form bow as shown.

Step 2. Apply seam sealant across the tails of the bow. Allow seam sealant to dry thoroughly and trim. Repeat for the remaining length of thread fabric.

Flowers

Step 1. Thread serger for a balanced 3-thread narrow stitch with the machine-embroidery threads in the needle and lower looper and the heavy embellishment thread in the upper looper. Increase the stitch length to approximately 3.

Step 2. Take remaining long strips of thread fabric and serge along each of the long sides.

Step 3. Form into four flowers with five petals as shown in Fig. 4, two to fit a fabric window and two for each tied end of the shawl.

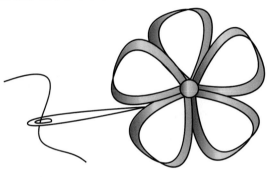

Fig. 4
Form flower as shown.

Step 4. Secure with a needle and thread.

Organza Bow

Step 1. Form a bow from the long strip of organza to fit at the lower point of the shawl. Secure the loose ends at the back of the shawl with a few hand stitches.

Step 2. Attach the bow between the ends of each band with hand stitches.

Embellishment

Step 1. Bead each accent corner and the shawl points as desired.

Step 2. Encrust each tip of the shawl with seed and bugle beads, stitching to both the front and back, or as desired.

Step 3. Create drops of glass or crystal beads at lower point if desired.

Step 4. Loop one end of shawl through the open window on the opposite side. Repeat on the other side. ✄

Sheer Delight Scarf

By Anne van der Kley

Add a hint of metallic thread to a beautiful silk fabric for some wonderful color and texture play.

Project Specifications

Skill Level: Beginner

Scarf Size: Approximately 50" x 6½" excluding tassels

Materials

- 1⅔ yards silk chiffon fabric (less than half the amount if you seam the lengths, or if you can purchase 60" width)
- 1 spool gold metallic thread
- 1 spool dark embroidery thread to blend with fabric
- 1 spool light embroidery thread to blend with fabric
- 1 reel ribbon floss to blend or contrast with threads and fabric
- Horizontal spool pin
- Tube turner
- Point turner
- Spray starch or fabric finish
- Seam sealant
- Hand needle and thread to match tassels
- Basic sewing supplies and tools

Instructions

Notes: *Test silk to see if it water-marks or heat-marks. If silk water-marks, wash it by hand and air-dry it flat. If silk heat-marks, use a non-stick cover on the sole of your iron. Starch or fabric finish will give silk a slight crispness to make it easier to sew.*

There may be very little variation from right to wrong side of silk chiffon. If you can't determine in five seconds, don't worry about it!

Scarf

Step 1. Cut silk into three strips 6" x 60", piecing if necessary.

Step 2. Set up serger for a 3-thread wide flatlock with gold metallic thread in the needle, dark embroidery thread in the upper looper and light embroidery thread in the lower looper. Adjust the stitch to a length of 1.0–1.5.

Step 3. Fold each strip in half lengthwise, wrong sides facing. Serge the raw edges of each strip together with a flatlock stitch as shown in Fig. 1. Turn each strip right

side out with a tube turner. Gently ease flatlock apart over the tube. Press the seam to the center of the fabric strip as shown in Fig. 2. The metallic thread will have formed a ladder and the embroidery thread a trellis. In this case the trellis will be showing.

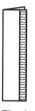

Fig. 1
Serge the raw edges of each strip together with a flatlock stitch.

Fig. 2
Turn right side out and press seam to center of strip.

Step 4. Serge the newly created fabric strips together, again using the flatlock stitch as shown in Fig. 3. Alternate the order of the ladder and trellis stitch as you prefer. Gently ease the flatlocked strips apart and press seam to center of fabric panel.

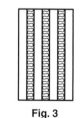

Fig. 3
Serge 2 strips side by side down center of fabric.

Step 5. Machine-stitch across each end with a shortened straight stitch as shown in Fig. 4. Be sure all threads are secure; trim both ends.

Step 6. Place fabric flat on a work surface, right side up. Bring the fabric to the front from both corners at one end, forming a point as shown in Fig. 5; press. Repeat on both ends.

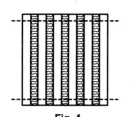

Fig. 4
Machine-stitch across each
end as shown.

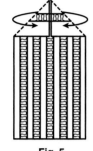

Fig. 5
Fold fabric as shown.

Step 7. Open the fabric out, folding right sides together, matching the pressed crease lines. Stitch along this line with a shortened machine stitch as shown in Fig. 6. Trim the seam and finish with a narrow serged hem as shown in Fig. 7. Turn to the right side, using a point turner.

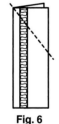

Fig. 6
Stitch along fold line as shown.

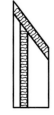

Fig. 7
Trim seam and serge.

Step 2. Place ribbon floss on the horizontal spool pin, thread feeding from the back. Run the serger with no fabric under the foot until you have about 5–10 yards of thread braid. Serge at a moderate speed rather than full speed.

Step 3. Cut the thread braid in two equal lengths. Apply seam sealant to the cut ends and allow to dry.

Step 4. Reset the serger, replacing the ribbon floss with metallic thread. Remove the horizontal spool pin from the upper looper thread spindle. Decrease the stitch length to about 1–1.5. Again, run the serger with no fabric under the foot until you have 15–20 yards of thread chain. Serge at a moderate speed.

Step 5. Cut thread chain into two equal lengths. Apply seam sealant to the cut ends and allow to dry.

Step 6. Take one thread chain and one thread braid and wind together over your hand in a figure 8, starting at your thumb and extending over your little finger. You will run out of thread braid before thread chain. This is intended. Repeat for second tassel.

Step 7. Use a loose thread to wind around the neck of the tassel as shown in Fig. 8. Tuck any loose ends into the tassel head.

Fig. 8
Wind loose thread around
neck of tassel.

Tassels

Step 1. Set up serger for 3-thread rolled hem, dark embroidery thread in needle position, ribbon floss in upper looper, light embroidery thread in lower looper. Attach the horizontal spool pin to the upper looper thread spindle. Increase the stitch length to approximately 4.

Step. 8. Run hand needle and thread through the tassel head enough times to be sure all thread chains/braids are caught. Stitch one tassel to the point at each end of the scarf. ✂

Double-Layer Chiffon Scarf

By Agnes Mercik

Layering two delicate fabrics will create lovely illusions when draping and tying this simple scarf.

Project Specifications

Skill Level: Beginner

Scarf Size: 13" x 44"

Materials

- ³/₈ yard print chiffon-type fabric
- ³/₈ yard solid-color chiffon-type fabric that coordinates with print
- Coordinating #40 rayon machine-embroidery thread
- 3 spools serger thread to match machine-embroidery thread
- Spray fabric adhesive
- Basic sewing supplies and tools

Instructions

Step 1. Remove selvages and straighten both fabrics on the grain line. Snip into the fabric and pull a thread to straighten. Cut on the pulled thread line.

Step 2. Lightly spray fabric adhesive on the wrong side of one of the fabrics. Place second piece wrong side to the sprayed side.

Step 3. Set machine on basic 3-thread rolled hem with the rayon embroidery thread in the upper looper. Place printed side of scarf up and the solid side against the feed dogs. Roll the hem on all four sides.

Notes: Always trim a slight amount of fabric when serging a rolled hem, as it assures sufficient fabric has been caught in the roll.

Use fine threads for fine fabrics.

If the fabric is lightweight and floats away from the initial cutting area, thread a hand needle with regular thread. Stitch one or two stitches leaving 3"–4" tail. Hold this thread tail while starting each new side as shown in Fig. 1. ✂

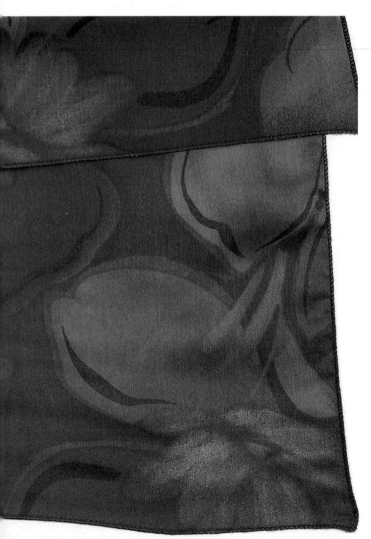

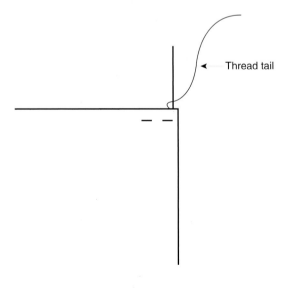

Fig. 1
Make 2 stitches with hand needle and thread as shown. Hold thread tail while starting a new side to hold fabric in place.

Little Miss Lace Collar

By Naomi Baker

Make this crisp little white collar in minutes to dress up a basic dress.
Use elastic thread to make quick, decorative button loops.

Project Specifications

Skill Level: Beginner

Lace Collar Size: Approximately 11" in diameter

Note: *Collar size and shape may be adjusted to match neckline of dress by matching collar neckline and shoulders to basic dress pattern.*

Materials

- 12" lace, Battenburg or eyelet doily (measure across shoulder if size needs to be adjusted)
- 3 cones matching serger thread
- 1 cone matching decorative thread
- 1 spool elastic thread
- 3 (³⁄₈") white ball buttons
- Scraps of water-soluble stabilizer
- Tapestry needle or loop turner

Instructions

Step 1. Cut front and back collar pieces from doily as directed on pattern. Cut along center fold of back for collar opening.

Step 2. With right sides of collar facing, match front and back shoulder seams. With a 3-thread balanced

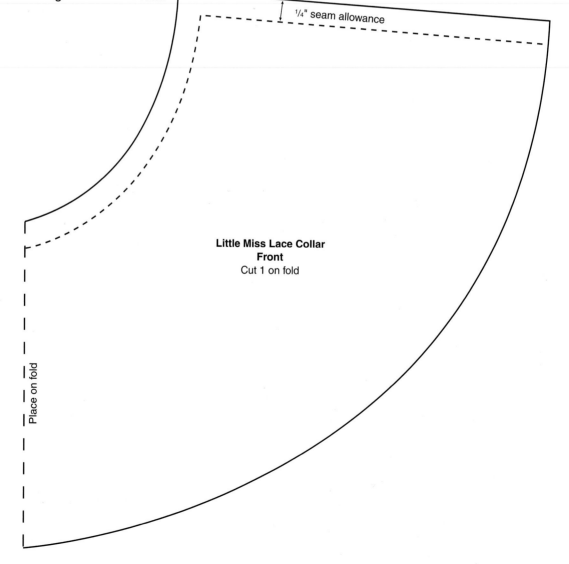

¼" seam allowance

Little Miss Lace Collar
Front
Cut 1 on fold

Place on fold

stitch and serger thread in needle and loopers, serge 1/4" shoulder seams.

Step 3. With decorative thread in the upper looper and elastic thread in the lower looper and a 3-thread short, medium-width stitch, adjust the tension so the upper looper wraps the fabric edge slightly. You may need to loosen the lower looper tension for the elastic to serge easily.

Step 4. When tension is adjusted correctly, serge the left center back of collar. If the lace or doily has open spaces, place a strip of water-soluble stabilizer along the edge to achieve even stitches in the spaces.

Step 5. Rethread lower looper with serger thread. Serge the right side of the back opening.

Step 6. Fold 1/8"–1/4" of neck edge to wrong side and serge. Pull thread chains to the wrong side with a tapestry needle or loop turner.

Step 7. Sew three evenly spaced buttons to right side of back opening.

Step 8. On left side of back opening, pull elastic thread out to form a loop opposite each button. Measure carefully, because once elastic is pulled it cannot be returned into the serging. ✄

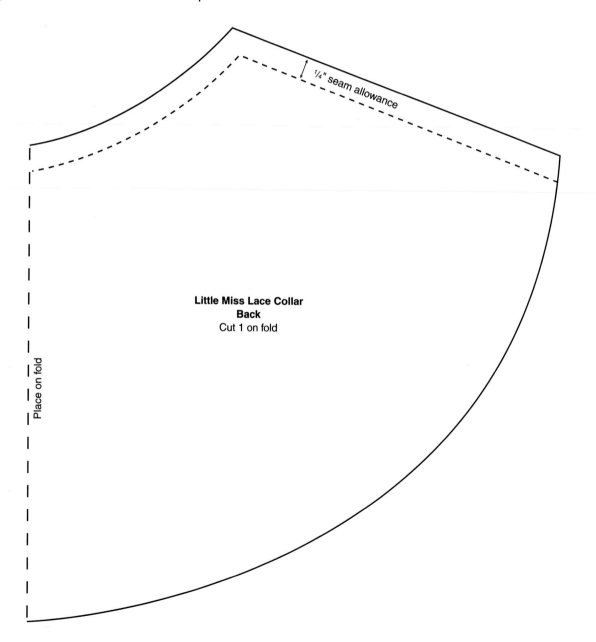

1/4" seam allowance

Little Miss Lace Collar
Back
Cut 1 on fold

Place on fold

Rosy Fleece Robe

By Carol Zentgraf

*What could be cozier than rose-hued fleece? Lettuce-leaf
the edges and add some pretty roses for a very feminine robe.*

Project Specifications

Skill Level: Beginner
Robe Size: Any size

Materials

- Unlined robe pattern designed for fleece
- Ombre fleece in yardage required by pattern plus
  1/4 yard for roses
- Scraps of green fleece for leaves
- Rotary-cutting tools, including decorative wave blade
- Permanent fabric glue
- Pattern paper
- Compass
- Tapestry needle
- 1 spool Woolly Nylon and 2 spools serger thread
  to coordinate with fleece
- All-purpose thread to blend with fleece
- Seam sealant
- Basic sewing supplies and tools

Instructions

Step 1. Place unfolded fleece right side up on work
surface. Arrange pattern pieces crosswise on fleece
to achieve the desired color effect. Cut out front, back,
pocket and belt pieces.

Step 2. For sleeve pieces, instead of cutting on fold,
use the half-sleeve pattern to cut two pieces, adding a
1/2" seam allowance to the center edge.

Step 3. Use rotary cutter with decorative blade to trim
sleeve center seam allowances. Overlap the seam
allowances with the upper layer toward the back; topstitch together 1/4" from the edge.

Step 4. Trim side and lower edges of pocket with rotary
cutter and decorative blade.

Step 5. Construct robe following pattern guide sheet.
Omit the center back loop.

Step 6. Using Woolly Nylon in the upper looper, finish
all edges of the robe and the belt with a rolled-edge
stitch. Pull the fabric slightly as you sew to create a
rippled or lettuce edge.

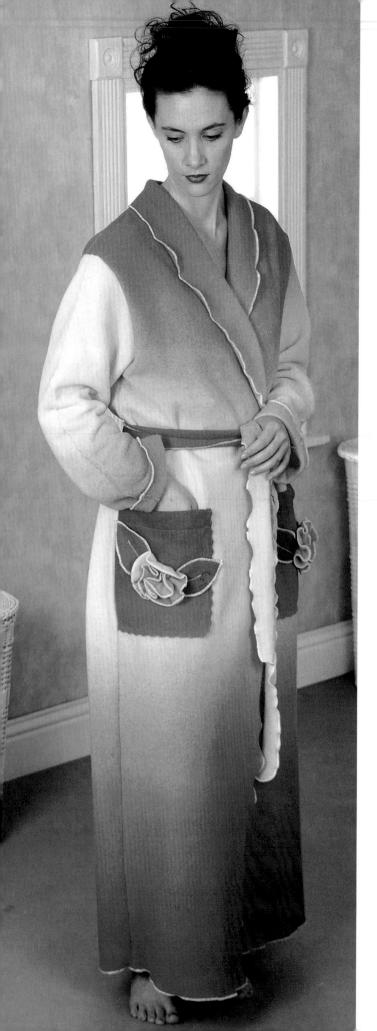

Step 7. To make belt loops, stitch off two 6" serger chains. Try the robe on and mark your waist at each side seam. Thread a tapestry needle with one serger chain. Stitching from the wrong side of robe, make a loop with the chain on the right side. Knot the ends together on the wrong side. Apply seam sealant to the thread ends.

Step 8. To make roses, use a compass to draw an 8" circle on pattern paper. Draw a spiral design in the circle as shown in Fig. 1. Cut two circles from fleece and then cut each fleece circle along the spiral line. Stitch one edge of each spiral with a rolled edge.

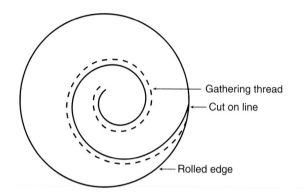

Gathering thread

Cut on line

Rolled edge

Fig. 1
Draw spiral design on 8" circle as shown.

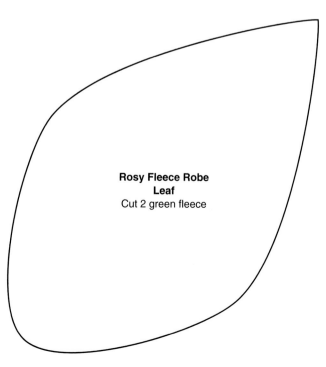

Rosy Fleece Robe
Leaf
Cut 2 green fleece

Step 9. Stitch a gathering thread along the opposite side of the spiral and pull up to gather; knot to secure. Beginning at the pointed end, wrap the gathered edges into a loose spiral to shape the rose. Use permanent fabric glue to hold the edges in place as you wrap.

Step 10. Glue a rose to the center of each pocket.

Step 11. Cut leaves as directed on pattern. Finish edges with rolled-edge stitch. Seal threads at leaf ends with seam sealant. Place leaves on pockets as shown in photo and glue with permanent fabric glue. ✂

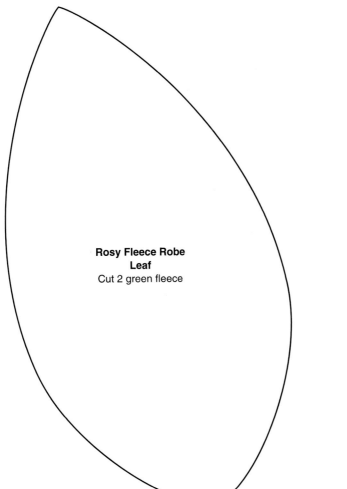

Rosy Fleece Robe
Leaf
Cut 2 green fleece

Flatlocked Oriental Tunic

By Carol Zentgraf

Creating your own fabric with serger techniques says, "One-of-a-kind!"

Project Specifications

Skill Level: Intermediate

Tunic Size: Any size

Materials

Note: *Model was made from Kwik Sew pattern #2989, small size, and required 1-yard cuts of three different fabrics. Adjust yardage according to pattern requirements.*

- Unlined tunic pattern
- 1–1$^{1}/_{2}$ yards of three different print fabrics
- $^{1}/_{4}$ yard coordinating solid fabric
- Notions as required by pattern
- Pattern tracing cloth
- Acrylic quilter's ruler
- Serger thread in color of choice
- Seam sealant
- Basic sewing supplies and tools

Instructions

Step 1. Trace one right front, one left front and one complete back on pattern tracing cloth. Referring to Fig. 1, draw cutting lines on each piece as shown. Label each piece. Cut each pattern piece apart on the drawn lines.

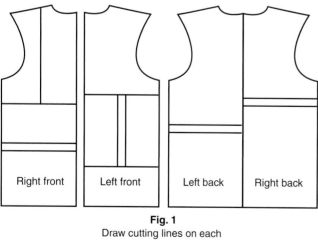

Fig. 1
Draw cutting lines on each
pattern piece as shown.

Step 2. Working with one pattern section at a time, such as right front, plan the fabric layout to achieve a pleasing balance of print and solid fabrics. Cut the pieces from selected fabrics, adding $^{1}/_{2}$" seam allowance to each piecing edge.

Step 3. Wrong sides facing, flatlock the pieces of each section together, working from the top down. Apply seam sealant to each intersection of threads and to all thread ends; press. Repeat for left front and back.

Step 4. Compare each piece to the original uncut pattern to check for accuracy. Trim edges if necessary.

Step 5. Cut collar and each sleeve from a different fabric that is pleasing with the layout of tunic fronts and back.

Step 6. Follow the pattern guide sheet to complete the tunic. ✄

Back side of Flatlocked seam.

Right side of Flatlocked seam.

T-shirt Twin Set

By Diana Cedolia

From two T-shirts, make a terrific duo using your serger for finishing and trim.

Project Specifications

Skill Level: Beginner

T-shirt Size: Any size

Materials

- 2 T-shirts, one a size larger than the other
- 1/2 yard coordinating cotton print fabric
- 2 different colors of Designer 6 thread that coordinate with fabric
- 4 cones of serger thread that blend with Designer 6 thread
- 1 spool all-purpose thread that coordinates with fabric
- 1 roll 1/2"-wide fusible web
- Rotary-cutting tools
- Water-soluble marker
- Press cloth
- Basic sewing supplies and tools

Instructions

Step 1. Fold and mark the center front of both T-shirts by lightly pressing with an iron.

Step 2. Cut on the marked center of the larger T-shirt only.

Step 3. Set serger for 3-thread overlock with the left needle.

Step 4. Measure the length of the center cut edge of the larger T-shirt and cut two strips of the cotton print fabric 3 1/2" wide and 1" longer than the cut edge.

Step 5. From cotton print fabric cut two strips 2" x 24" and one strip 3 1/2" x 40".

Step 6. With one 2" x 24" print fabric strip right side up, serge down both long edges with the Designer 6 thread.

Step 7. Cut the 2" x 24" serged strip into 2" squares. Serge the remaining two edges of each piece. This should yield 12 decoratively serged squares.

Step 8. Change the color of the Designer 6 thread and repeat the procedure with the other 2" x 24" strip.

Step 9. Change the serger setup to a 4-thread overlock with serger thread.

Step 10. Fold the strips cut in Step 4 right sides together lengthwise. Serge across one short end of each strip. Turn right side out and match the finished end to the neck edge. Mark each strip with a pin where the T-shirt hem meets it.

Step 11. Again, turn each strip right sides together and serge across the open end, keeping the needle on the line where the strip is marked with a pin. The strips should be exactly the same length as the cut edge of the T-shirt front. Turn right side out and press.

Step 12. Place a strip on the right side of one of the fronts. Keeping the strip on the top of the shirt, serge the strip to the T-shirt. Repeat with the other side.

Continued on page 107

Opulent Abstract Elegant Jacket

By Anne van der Kley

Embellish silk brocade with rich serger crazy patchwork for a contemporary look on a classic garment.

Project Specifications

Skill Level: Beginner
Jacket Size: Any size

Materials

- Park Bench Pattern Co., Audoban Park pattern #14
- Winter white silk brocade as required by pattern
- $1/2$ yard light beige silk brocade
- $3/4$ yard medium beige silk broadcloth
- $3/4$ yard fusible interfacing
- Cotton press cloth
- 2 YLI Natural Pearl Crown Rayon thread
- 4 serger threads to match fabric
- $1/4$"-wide fusible web
- Universal #80 needles or system to suit your serger
- Scrap of template material
- Seam sealant
- Rotary-cutting tools
- Tailor's ham for pressing (optional)
- Polyester thread to match white silk brocade
- Basic sewing supplies and tools

Instructions

Step 1. Cut front and back pattern pieces following pattern directions. Serge all edges with a balanced 3-thread narrow stitch to prevent silk from fraying.

Step 2. Cut two bands from light beige silk brocade $2/3$ of the collar width.

Step 3. Cut two bands from medium beige silk broadcloth $2/3$ of the cuff depth.

Step 4. Cut facing pieces from medium beige silk broadcloth. Fuse interfacing following manufacturer's instructions.

Step 5. Trace and cut trapezoid template.

Step 6. Serge all garment edges of the main body of the jacket with a rolled hem to prevent silk from fraying. Sew front and back of jacket together following pattern instructions. Press seams open.

Step 7. Join front and back facings with a 4-thread stitch for construction, following the pattern instructions. Serge to the main body of the jacket with a 4-thread stitch. Press well, rolling approximately $1/8$"–$1/4$" of the facing to the front of the jacket, creating a piping effect. Press well, preferably over a tailor's ham. Allow

each section of the garment to cool before pressing the next section.

Step 8. Reset serger for a balanced 3-thread narrow stitch with Pearl Crown Rayon thread in the upper looper. Lengthen the stitch to approximately 3½. Serge the decorative finish along the loose facing edge. Seal the thread chains close to the fabric edge with seam sealant. After the sealant dries, trim the excess thread chains.

Step 9. Using cotton press cloth, fuse 4"–6" lengths of ¼"-wide fusible web to hold the decoratively finished

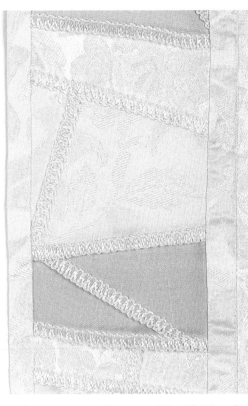

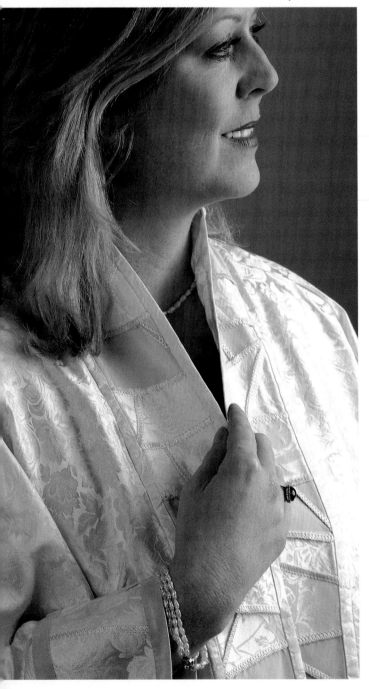

facing to the garment with no visible stitching line. You will need to apply the fusible web close to the decorative edge to ensure that the hem fits well. Because you can reposition the strips, this is not difficult. Let each section cool before fusing the next.

Step 10. After cutting out jacket pieces, you should have pieces of each fabric remaining. For the decorative front and collar band, square up a 6½" width of each and fold with wrong sides facing. Serge a 3-thread decorative edge at random across each piece as shown in Fig. 1; press flat. The sections will be slightly distorted because of the central seam. Seal the thread chains close to the fabric edges with seam sealant. When dry, trim thread chains close to fabric.

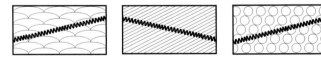

Fig. 1
Serge a 3-thread decorative edge
at random across each piece.

Step 11. Stack the fabrics on top of each other on the rotary-cutting mat as shown in Fig. 2. The number of layers you can cut will depend on the size of your cutting blade and the texture of your fabrics. Avoid too many layers or there will be distortion. Grain line is not critical.

Step 12. Cut the fabrics using the trapezoid template,

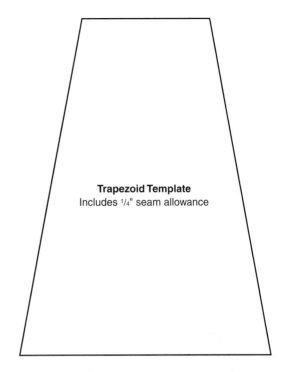

Trapezoid Template
Includes ¹/₄" seam allowance

flipping it between cuts to form wedges as shown in Fig. 3. Select the pieces you like best to join into panels.

patchwork flat. After you stitch 4 or 5 sections together, place them on the pattern piece to determine how much construction length is required.

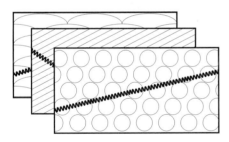

Fig. 2
Stack the fabrics as shown on rotary-cutting mat.

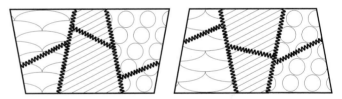

Fig. 4
Join wedges with decorative stitch.

Step 14. Create bands for cuffs by cutting wedge-shaped pieces from all three fabrics, but omit the fold-and-stitch step of Step 10.

Step 15. When panels are long enough, fuse interfacing to pieced sections and trim into rectangles the length of the collar and cuff pieces.

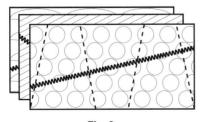

Fig. 3
Cut fabric in wedges with template as shown.

Step 13. Set your serger for a balanced 3-thread wide stitch with Pearl Crown Rayon thread in the upper looper. Lengthen the stitch to 3¹/₂–4. Join the wedges with decorative stitch as shown in Fig. 4. Press well to one side. Flip the wedges, stitching in the same direction each time. Press after each row to keep the crazy

Step 16. Reset serger for a balanced 4-thread stitch. Place the crazy-pieced fabrics in the center of the bands cut in Steps 2 and 3. Press well. The bands will be larger than the pattern pieces. Trim to size, allowing enough fabric to show on each side when it is joined to the garment. One fabric side will be wider than the other.

Step 17. Join to the garment, following pattern instructions, omitting the final row of machine stitching for both the sleeve bands and the collar bands. To create an elegant seam finish, fuse the band in position with short strips of ¹/₄"-wide fusible web. Have the garment professionally pressed for a fine finish. ✄

Puffed-Braid-Closure Vest

By Naomi Baker

This kind of frog, or braid closure, adds a wonderful finishing touch to any vest, jacket or sweater.

Project Specifications

Skill Level: Beginner

Vest Size: Any size

Materials

- Commercial V-neck vest pattern of choice
- Fabric as recommended by vest pattern
- 4 cones serger thread to match vest fabric
- 1 spool all-purpose thread to match vest fabric
- 2 strips 1" x 60" matching-color jersey or tricot cut on crosswise grain for puffed-braid closure
- 1 cone heavy rayon serger thread
- 1 cone matching woolly-type thread
- Seam sealant
- Beading foot, if available

Instructions

Step 1. Adjust vest pattern if necessary so that vest opening meets at center front with no overlap.

Step 2. Construct vest according to pattern instructions.

Step 3. Thread serger with serger thread in needles, heavy rayon in upper looper and woolly-type thread in lower looper. Adjust to a medium length and medium to wide stitch, tightening the lower looper slightly.

Step 4. Pull the 1" x 60" strip slightly so that it rolls into a tube. Place the tube into a beading foot or under the back and over the front of a regular presser foot between the needle and knives.

Step 5. Hold the fabric tube taut to avoid jamming when beginning to serge. Continue to hold the tube

taut and serge with the stitches forming around the tube. Repeat with second strip.

Step 6. Cut a 10½" strip and a 22" strip from the serged tubes, selecting the best sections. Use seam sealant at each cut end to prevent raveling. Form four decorative loops from the 10½"strip as shown in Fig. 1.

Step 7. With the 22" strip, make a ball button and three loops as shown in Fig. 2. Hand-tack the ends together on the wrong side.

Step 8. Hand-tack four-loop closure to right side of vest (as worn) and ball button and loop to left side. ✄

Fig. 1
Form 4 loops as shown.

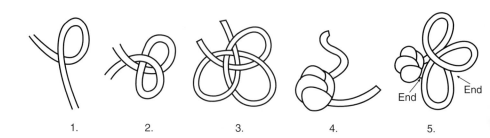

Fig. 2
Form ball button and 3 loops as shown.

Leather Beaded Vest

By Agnes Mercik

Use snakeskin appliqués, serger trims and seed beads to create a vest of many textures.

Project Specifications

Skill Level: Beginner

Vest Size: Any size

Materials

- Commercial vest pattern of your choice
- Suede-type fabric for vest in amount recommended on pattern
- Lining for vest as required by pattern
- Scraps of fake snakeskin and suede for appliqués
- Scraps of iron-on fabric stabilizer
- Seed beads in quantity and color of choice
- Clear nylon monofilament or metallic embroidery thread similar to decorative threads
- Variety of filler cords (baby or other knitting yarns, crochet cottons, topstitching threads or multiple threads held together all work well. Choose colors that closely match decorative threads)
- Variety of decorative threads that match filler cords
- Serger threads that match decorative threads
- Purchased or self-made buttons as required by pattern
- Fabric glue for self-made buttons
- Fabric glue stick
- All-purpose thread to match fabrics
- Cording or piping foot (optional)
- Press cloth with nonstick surface
- Basic sewing supplies and tools

Instructions

Step 1. Cut out vest and lining as instructed on pattern.

Note: Serger trim is used to cover the raw edges of the appliqué on this vest. Conventional sewing machine satin stitch, which would typically be used for appliqué, would not work well on natural or fake skin. An open zigzag could be used, but it would not be very attractive. Serger trim covers the raw edges attractively and adds texture and sparkle.

Step 2. Read Designer Note and Steps 1 and 2 of Zebra Vest, page 104, to make serger trim for leaves and stems.

Continued on page 107

Zebra Vest

By Agnes Mercik

Find a fabric that resembles animal skin or another effect that you desire.
Embellish the fabric design with serger trims for added texture and sparkle.

Project Specifications

Skill Level: Beginner

Vest Size: Any size

Materials

- Commercial vest pattern of your choice
- Fabric for vest in amount recommended on pattern plus 1/2 yard
- Iron-on fabric stabilizer in same amount required for vest

- Lining for vest as required by pattern
- Clear nylon monofilament or metallic embroidery thread similar to decorative threads
- Variety of filler cords (baby or other knitting yarns, crochet cottons, topstitching threads or multiple threads held together all work well. Choose colors that closely match decorative threads)
- Variety of decorative threads that match filler cords
- Serger threads that match decorative threads
- Purchased or self-made buttons as required by pattern
- Fabric glue for self-made buttons
- All-purpose thread to match fabrics
- Cording or piping foot (optional)
- Press cloth with nonstick surface
- Basic sewing supplies and tools

Instructions

Designer Note: *The serger applications for the Zebra Vest and the Leather Beaded Vest are the same. It's the thickness or thinness of the decorative thread used with a filler cord that makes them look different.*

Serger trims can be made in a variety of weights and textures. The basic technique is created through a very simple process of either a rolled hem or narrow balanced setting, depending on the type of decorative thread used. The 2-thread concept can also be used to minimize bulk.

The additional aid of a cording foot or piping foot will hold the filler cord in place and prevent it from wandering, though just holding the cord will also work with some effort and concentration

Step 1. Place decorative yarn/thread in upper looper of a 3-thread rolled hem, or lower looper of a 2-thread setting, and matching serger thread in the needle and lower looper.

Step 2. Start the rolled hem at a medium setting and gradually increase or decrease stitch length so filler cord is completely covered. Hold the filler cord from behind the presser foot to give it a good start. The thickness of the decorative thread used in the looper

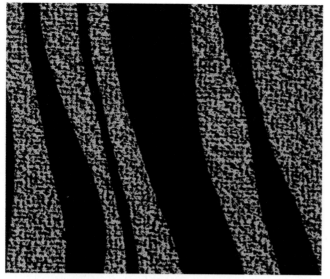

Fig. 1

Fig. 2

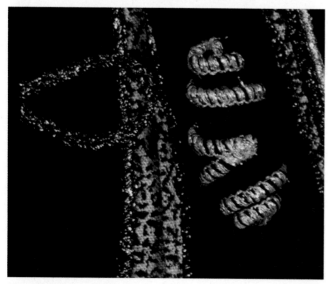

Vest button and loop opened.

will dictate whether the setting will be as a rolled hem or narrow balance. Because Woolly Nylon increases tensions by two or three numbers, try using it in the lower looper of a 3-thread application for stubborn situations. If the trim becomes too curly, start winding it around an empty spool to control it.

Step 3. Create embellished fabric before cutting out pattern pieces. The fabric will tell you where to embellish and how. A photo of the fabric selected for the Zebra Vest is shown in Fig. 1. A selection of metallic threads and yarns to bring out the black and gray were selected for embellishment, as shown in Fig. 2.

Step 4. Trace the pattern pieces on the fabric and then extend the embellishment several inches beyond the cutting lines.

Step 5. When you have created a sufficient amount of serger trim, back the fabric with the iron-on stabilizer.

Step 6. Using a sewing machine, couch the serger trims onto the desired design lines on the fabric with either clear nylon monofilament or metallic embroidery thread similar to decorative threads. A simple narrow zigzag set to the exact width of the trim works very well. Other stitch possibilities include the blanket stitch or other decorative stitches that highlight the trim.

Note: *To temporarily hold the trim in place, try using fusible thread in the lower looper when using a 3-thread narrow stitch. Then press it onto the garment using a press cloth with a nonstick finish. It is important that sufficient fusible thread be exposed for this to work well. Additional stitching is still required to secure the trim to the fabric.*

Step 7. Cut out and construct vest as instructed on pattern.

Step 8. To create your own interesting, matching toggle-type buttons, fuse two triangles of matching fabric and roll-edge the two long sides as shown in Fig. 3. Fabric-glue one surface and roll the triangle,

Fig. 3
Roll-edge two long sides of triangle.

starting from the wide end, to make a button as shown in Fig. 4.

Step 9. For button loops, simply use a length of serger trim long enough to fit around the button. Include the loop in the seam when sewing the lining to the vest. ✂

Fig. 4
Roll triangle starting at wide end
to create button as shown.

T-Shirt Twin Set

Continued from page 94

Step 13. Remove about 3" of the underarm seam starting at the hem edge of the sleeve. Cut in half the 3¹/₂" x 40" strip cut in Step 5. Press both strips in half lengthwise, wrong sides facing.

Step 14. Cut the hem from the sleeves close to the hem stitching. Place one of the pressed strips to the right side of the cut sleeve edge, right sides facing. Serge it to the sleeve, keeping the strip on the top. Repeat with the other sleeve. Press the seam toward the sleeve and topstitch the seam flat.

Step 15. Turn the T-shirt wrong side out and serge the underarm seam right sides together.

Step 16. Press the center front bands flat and topstitch the seam towards the T-shirt.

Step 17. Trim the tails on the decoratively edged squares to no more than ³/₄". Put ¹/₂"-wide fusible web around all four sides of each square, tucking the tails under to keep them out of the way.

Step 18. Referring to the photo for placement, arrange three of the squares on the cardigan T-shirt front. With a press cloth, fuse permanently in place.

Step 19. Referring to the photo for placement, arrange the remaining squares on the smaller T-shirt; fuse in place. ✂

Leather Beaded Vest

Continued from page 102

Step 3. Trace and cut fake snakeskin and suede leaves as directed on template. Referring to photo, arrange on pattern pieces (front and back) and secure with glue stick.

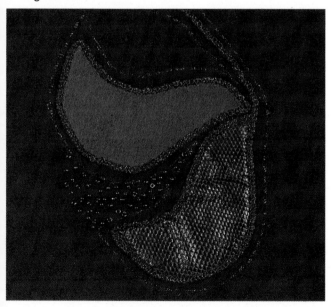

Step 4. Referring to photo, mark stem placement on vest.

Step 5. When you have created a sufficient amount of serger trim, back the design areas with iron-on fabric stabilizer.

Step 6. Follow Step 6 and its following Note, Zebra Vest, page 104, to couch the trim around appliqué and make the stems. Referring to the photo, hand-sew beads for embellishment using clear nylon monofilament. *Note: Project uses metallic thread and a chain stitch to quilt around design elements and ¹/₈" from each side of stems.*

Step 7. Create toggle buttons and loops if desired, as in Steps 8 and 9, Zebra Vest.

Step 8. Construct vest as instructed on pattern, adding button loops between vest and lining. ✂

Leather Beaded Vest
Cut 12
(reverse 6)

Seams Great

By Agnes Mercik

This garment is a variation of the Batik Two-Piece Outfit, page 114. A versatile pattern and a different serger technique will add variety to your wardrobe.

Project Specifications

Skill Level: Intermediate

Dress Size: Any size

Materials

Note: *See Designer Note, page 114.*

The design emphasis on this garment is the contrasting bound seams and the decorative appliqué.

- Lyla Messinger pattern LJ-723
- Fabric and notions as directed on pattern, plus 1/2 yard extra fabric for scrunching
- 1 yard contrasting fabric for bound seams and appliqué
- 1/2 yard paper-backed fusible tear-away stabilizer
- 1/2 yard fusible tricot
- Serger thread to match fabrics
- Elastic thread to blend or contrast with fabric
- Rayon embroidery thread to match contrasting appliqué fabric
- All-purpose thread to match serger threads and machine embroidery thread
- 2"-wide waistband elastic as designated by pattern
- Basic sewing supplies and tools

Instructions

Skirt

Step 1. Cut fabric as instructed on pattern.

Step 2. Serge-edge one vertical side of each skirt panel. Be consistent with the side that is serge-edged.

Step 3. Measure the vertical edge of each serge-edged skirt panel and cut a 1"-wide bias strip that length for each panel. Measure the hem width of each skirt panel and cut a 1"-wide bias strip for each. Serge one side of each bias strip as shown in Fig. 1.

Fig. 1
Serge-edge one side
of each bias strip.

Step 4. Serge the raw edge of a bias strip to the hem of each skirt panel, right sides together, as shown in Fig. 2. Fold the bias strip to the wrong side of the skirt, press and stitch in the ditch on the sewing machine as shown in Fig. 3.

Fig. 2
Serge raw edge of bias strip to skirt panel.

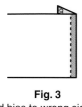
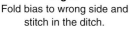

Fig. 3
Fold bias to wrong side and
stitch in the ditch.

Step 5. Repeat Step 4 on the serged-edge skirt seams.

Step 6. Place the bound seam of one skirt panel on top of the seam line of next panel and stitch in the ditch on the sewing machine. Continue until all panels are joined.

Step 7. Finish the waistband as directed on pattern, using 2"-wide waistband elastic.

Top

Step 1. Refer to Steps 2–6, Butterfly Wall Quilt, page 160, for directions for serger elastic scrunching technique and for leaf patterns. Use the garment fabric for scrunching and the contrasting fabric for the outer appliquéd part of the leaves. Make 35 leaf appliqués. Using this technique, complete the appliquéd leaf designs on the front and back pieces of the garment top. Refer to photos for placement.

Step 2. Follow pattern directions to complete the garment top, but repeat the bound seam technique on front and back center seams, sleeve seams and hems, and garment hem. ✂

Flatlocked Skirt & Jacket Ensemble

By Nancy Fiedler

Create your own custom fabric by joining three different fabrics with variegated thread and the flatlock stitch.

Project Specifications

Skill Level: Intermediate

Skirt & Jacket Size: Any size

Materials

Note: *Select light- to medium-weight linens that will drape nicely for the bias-cut skirt. Choose patterns with simple lines, and line both skirt and jacket to prevent stretching.*

- Patterns of choice for skirt and jacket (Butterick skirt 5154 and Butterick jacket 6938 were used for model)
- 2^1/$_4$ yards each of 52"–60"-wide linen in 3 coordinating colors (A, B and C)
- Additional ^{1}/$_4$ yard of 1 of the above colors for facing and waistband
- Lining fabric and notions as directed on pattern
- 1 spool Valdani Hand-Dyed Variegated quilting thread
- 4 cones serger thread
- Rotary-cutting tools
- Basic sewing supplies and tools

Instructions

Step 1. Using rotary-cutting tools, cut six 12"-wide strips across the width of each of the three linen fabrics.

Step 2. Set up the serger for a wide 2-thread flatlock, placing the variegated quilting thread in the lower looper and serger thread in the needle.

Step 3. With wrong sides facing, flatlock the strips together alternately as shown in Fig. 1. Gently pull each seam open after it is sewn. Press all seams when the panel is completed. Sew three identical panels of six strips each.

Step 4. Cut each panel into 3^1/$_2$" segments as shown in Fig. 2.

Step 5. Bring the short ends of one segment together,

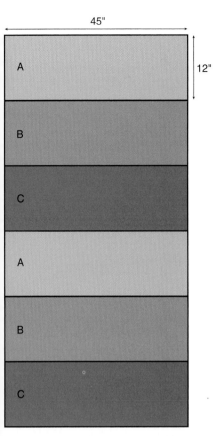

Fig. 1
Flatlock strips together as shown.

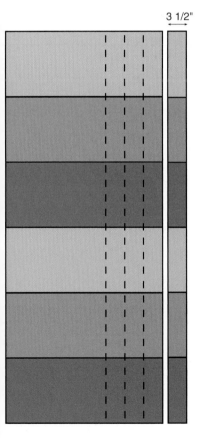

Fig. 2
Cut panel into 3 1/2" segments.

wrong sides facing. Flatlock the seam to form a ring as shown in Fig. 3. Cut the strip in the center of one B section as shown in Fig. 4.

Fig. 3
Bring short ends together to form ring.

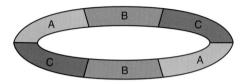

Fig. 4
Cut strip in center of B fabric as shown.

Step 6. Place an original strip cut in Step 4 together with the strip cut in Step 5, wrong sides facing, as shown in Fig. 5. Flatlock the strips together.

A	B	C	A	B	C
B	C	A	B	C	A	B

Fig. 5
Join original strip with cut strip as shown.

Step 7. Repeat Steps 5 and 6, alternating strips to create a fabric panel approximately 70" x 135" as shown in Fig. 6. Press all of the seams.

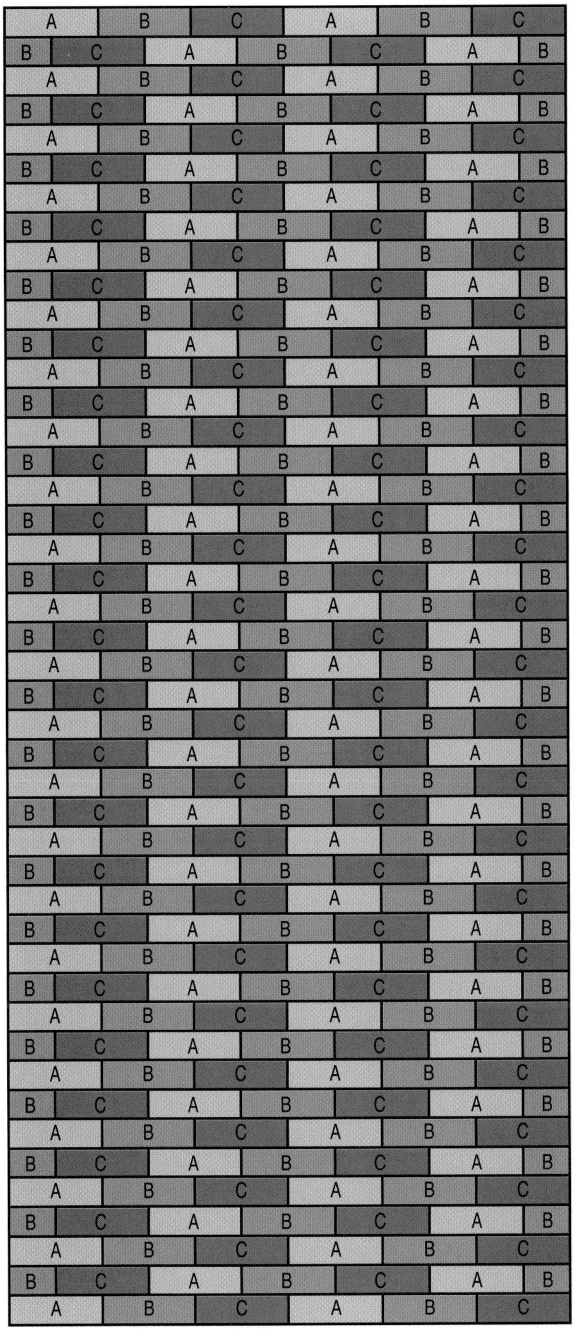

Fig. 6
Continue to alternate strips to form panel as shown.

Step 8. Draw a line on the front, back and sleeve jacket pattern pieces at a 45-degree angle to the grain line. Make duplicate pattern pieces for the right and left sides marking the bias grain lines.

Step 9. Place pattern pieces on fabric panel, single layer, using new line to place pieces on the bias. Cut facings and waistband from the extra 1/4 yard fabric piece.

Step 10. Place each piece on a flat work surface and hand-baste around the edges of each of the bias-cut pattern pieces. This will help stabilize the pieces and prevent stretching as the fabric is handled.

Step 11. Set up the serger for a 3-thread overlock and overlock all the edges of each piece.

Step 12. Construct the garments according to pattern directions. Hang the garments for 24 hours before hemming. ✂

Batik Two-Piece Outfit

By Agnes Mercik

This pattern and Seams Great, page 108, are two variations of one pattern and two serger methods—rolled edge seams and bound seams. Make both to expand your wardrobe!

Project Specifications

Skill Level: Intermediate

Dress Size: Any size

Materials

Designer Note: *I like to use rayon for garments. It drapes beautifully and launders easily. Rayon is a natural fiber made of wood fiber and cotton linters. It is wonderfully comfortable to wear. It has a right and wrong side, but either side may be used. Hang the garment overnight to relax the fibers before hemming or making buttonholes.*

This garment and Seams Great on page 108 are both made from the same pattern by Lyla Messinger.

- Lyla Messinger pattern LJ-723
- Fabric and notions as directed on pattern
- Serger thread to match fabrics
- All-purpose thread to match serger thread
- 2"-wide waistband elastic as designated by pattern
- Basic sewing supplies and tools

Instructions

Skirt

Step 1. Cut fabric as instructed on pattern.

Step 2. Serge-edge all vertical seams on skirt panels.

Step 3. Fold back and press the seam allowance on one side of each panel. Roll-edge over the fold carefully without trimming any fabric as shown in Fig. 1. Be consistent with the side that is roll-hemmed.

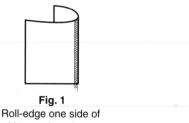

Fig. 1
Roll-edge one side of
skirt panel as shown.

Step 4. Roll-edge the hem edge of each skirt panel.

Step 5. Place the rolled-edge fold of one skirt panel over the seam line of the next panel and straight-stitch on the sewing machine, as shown in Fig. 2. Use the same color of thread used on the serger. Continue until all panels are joined.

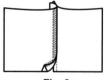

Fig. 2
Place rolled-edge fold over seam line
of next panel and stitch.

Step 6. Finish the waistband as directed on pattern, using 2"-wide skirt elastic.

Top

Step 1. Follow pattern directions to complete the garment top, which is asymmetrical and smocked on the sewing machine.

Step 2. Assemble top on serger. ✄

Suede Book Cover

By Agnes Mercik

Disguise any publication, from your phone directory to your journal, with a personalized, colorful cover.

Project Specifications

Skill Level: Beginner

Cover Size: 22" x 12½"

(Can be easily adapted to any size)

Materials

- 5 or 6 colors of suede fabric scraps
- 12½" x 17½" lining fabric
- 12½" x 22" woven fusible interfacing
- Variety of decorative threads to match suede fabrics
- Gold metallic decorative thread
- Serger threads to match decorative threads
- Press cloth with nonstick surface
- Spray fabric adhesive
- Rotary-cutting tools
- Basic sewing supplies and tools

Instructions

Step 1. Plan a decorative layout of choice for book cover on woven fusible interfacing and make patterns for each piece. The model includes matching 5" strips along each side, as shown in Fig. 1, which wrap to the back to hold the book cover.

Step 2. Cut suede pieces with rotary cutter. Pieces butt

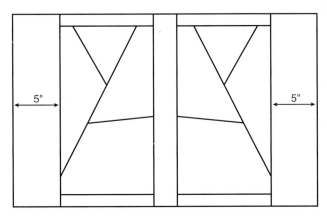

Fig. 1
Plan layout as shown.

up to each other exactly, so be careful to cut accurately.

Step 3. Arrange pieces on fusible side of woven interfacing. Using press cloth with nonstick surface, carefully press both sides of suede and interfacing.

Step 4. Thread cover stitch looper with decorative thread and use matching serger thread in the needle. On the interfacing side, cover each butted section by centering the presser foot over the two sections. The stitching lines will be visible and easily viewed through the interfacing. Change thread colors as design element. Refer to photo for ideas.

Step 5. Change to 2-thread chain stitch function with gold metallic thread in looper and matching serger thread in needle.

Step 6. Stitch each side of the cover stitch areas, being careful to stitch just alongside the area but not through the cover stitching.

Step 7. Center the lining fabric, wrong sides together, on the pieced section. Spray with fabric adhesive to secure layers.

Step 8. Mark lines about ⁵/₈" apart on flap areas and stitch (same function as Step 5) as shown in Fig. 2.

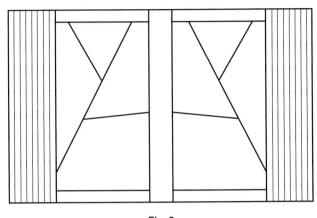

Fig. 2
Mark lines on flap areas as shown.

2³/₄"   2³/₄"

Fig. 3
Fold flaps to inside as shown.

Step 9. Change machine to basic 3-thread, left needle setup. With decorative thread in both loopers, edge-stitch both long inner flap areas. Fold flaps 2³/₄" to inside as shown in Fig. 3. Edge-stitch top and bottom edges of book cover, including flaps. ✂

Jungle Crayon Bag

By Agnes Mercik

This colorful, child's crayon bag utilizes machine embroidery and serger applications. Variegated thread color-blocks and highlights the primary color theme.

Project Specifications

Skill Level: Beginner

Crayon Bag Size: Approximately 17" x 16" folded

Materials

- 2 pieces jungle print 10" x 17"
- 1/2 yard red solid
- 7/8 yard royal blue solid
- 1 yard green solid
- 1/2 yard yellow solid
- 2 spools variegated Woolly Nylon
- 6" x 1" strip red hook-and-loop tape
- 1 spool blending serger thread
- Embroidery threads to contrast with fabrics.
- All-purpose threads to match fabrics
- 1 1/4 yards 1"-wide red webbing for handles
- Can of temporary spray adhesive
- Seam sealant
- Basic sewing supplies and tools

Instructions

Outer Bag

Step 1. From red solid fabric cut two pieces 17" x 14". From royal blue solid cut two pieces 17" x 17".

Step 2. Machine-embroider a 3" to 4" band on one 17" edge of each red piece with appropriate jungle animals as shown in photo.

Step 3. With variegated thread in both loopers and blending serger thread in left needle, serge top (17") edge of jungle print pieces and red pockets.

Step 4. Place three fabric layers together and spray with temporary spray adhesive as shown in Fig. 1. With right sides of each piece facing, sew all layers together along unserged 17" edges.

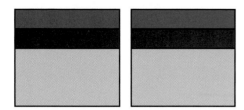

Fig. 1
Place outer pocket layers together as shown.

Inner Bag

Step 1. From red cut one piece 17" x 8". From royal blue solid cut one piece 17" x 12". From yellow solid cut one piece 17" x 20". From green solid cut one piece 17" x 32".

Step 2. Embellish both 17" edges of each strip with appropriate machine embroidery as shown in photo.

Step 3. Serge both 17" edges of yellow, red and blue pockets as in Step 3 above. Layer red and royal blue pieces. Mark 1" intervals on red fabric and stitch through both layers on marked lines as shown in Fig. 2.

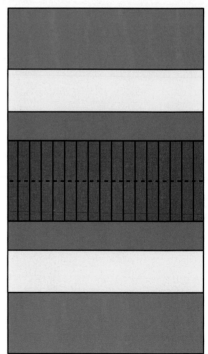

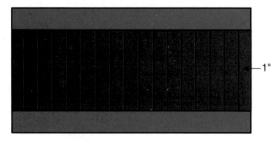

Fig. 2
Layer pockets and mark intervals
on red pocket as shown.

Step 4. Layer all four fabrics and spray with temporary adhesive as shown. With red thread stitch a horizontal line across the center of the red pocket to complete crayon pocket partitions as shown in Fig. 3.

Assembly

Step 1. Place inner and outer bag layers together, wrong sides facing. Spray with temporary adhesive.

Step 2. Serge around all outer edges with variegated thread in both loopers and blending serger thread in left needle.

Fig. 3
Stitch horizontal line across center of red pocket.

Continued on page 123

Sashiko Place Mat

By Diana Cedolia

Sashiko is a Japanese style of quilting with running stitches sewn by hand in various patterns. If you serge the running stitches you will save hours of time!

Project Specifications

Skill Level: Beginner
Place Mat Size: 18" x 12"

Materials

- ½ yard dark navy solid for Sashiko and backing
- ⅛ yard navy print for borders
- ½ yard fusible interfacing
- 4 cones navy polyester serger thread to match dark navy solid fabric
- 1 cone white polyester serger thread
- 6" strip of ½"-wide fusible web
- Rotary-cutting tools
- Clear cover stitch foot
- Basic sewing supplies and tools

Instructions

Step 1. From dark navy solid and fusible interfacing cut one rectangle each 12" x 18". Following manufacturer's instructions, fuse interfacing to backside of navy fabric.

Step 2. From navy print, cut two 2"-wide strips across the width of the fabric. Cut two pieces of fusible interfacing the same size and fuse to backside of fabric.

Step 3. Set up serger with white serger thread in needle and navy serger thread in looper. Set serger for chain stitch, with needle tension 3.0 and looper tension 9.0. Set the stitch length at 4.5. Use the clear cover stitch foot and set for slow speed.

Step 4. Tape the two pattern pieces together along the centerline with small pieces of tape. Do not put any tape on pattern lines.

Centerline

Shashiko Pattern
Enlarge 140% before cutting
Make 2 copies for complete pattern

Step 5. Center the paper pattern on the stabilizer side of 12" x 18" navy rectangle. Pin in place. With the

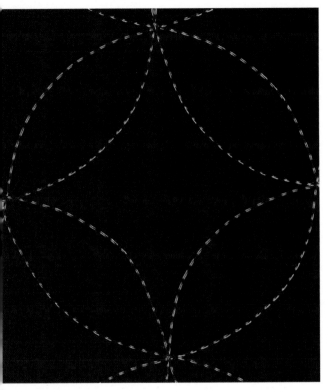

stabilizer side up, serge along all pattern lines. Do not pivot at ends of lines. Serge off the fabric before starting another line.

Step 6. Carefully tear away the paper pattern and press the rectangle. Trim to approximately 16" x 10".

Step 7. Convert the serger to 4-thread overlock using navy thread in all positions.

Step 8. Serge a 2" navy print strip to each short side of rectangle, right sides facing. Trim ends to match rectangle. Press seams toward strips. Serge 2" strips to long sides of rectangle and trim ends to match rectangle. Press seams toward strips.

Step 9. Place bordered place mat on navy solid fabric and cut same size for backing. Mark a 4" opening on one side at least 2" from any corner. Place right sides together; starting at one end of 4" opening serge all around perimeter. Wrap the fabric at corners for crisp, neat corners. Stop serging at other end of 4" marked opening. Raise presser foot and remove place mat.

Step 10. Turn place mat right side out through opening. Press the place mat. Place a strip of 1/2"-wide fusible web inside the 4" opening and press to fuse. ✂

Jungle Crayon Bag

Continued from page 120

Step 3. Place seam sealant at all corners. Allow to dry completely and then trim serger tail threads.

Step 4. Cut red webbing in two 20 1/2" lengths for handles. Stitch to both ends of outer bag front, as shown in Fig. 4.

Step 5. Cut hook-and-loop tape in 1" segments for fasteners. Place two fasteners between jungle print and red pockets, each side of outer bag. Center one fastener between red and blue pockets, each side of outer bag. ✂

Fig. 4
Stitch handles to bag front as shown.

Flatlocked Fringed Table Set

By Carol Zentgraf

Make matched table sets in a matter of minutes with this flatlocking technique.

Project Specifications

Skill Level: Beginner

Place Mat Size: 21" x 15"

Napkin Size: 18" x 18"

Coaster Size: 6" x 6"

Materials

Note: *Materials and instructions are for one place mat, one napkin and one coaster.*

- Loosely and evenly woven plaid cotton fabric: 15" x 21" for place mat, 18" x 18" for napkin and 6" x 6" for coaster
- 2 ($^7/_8$") buttons
- 2 (3") tassels
- Matching serger thread
- Basic sewing supplies and tools

Instructions

Step 1. Press under 1" along all edges of place mat, napkin and coaster.

Step 2. Follow flatlocking instructions on page 32 to stitch a row of flatlocking along each fold. Pull the edges flat.

Step 3. Ravel each edge to the stitching by beginning at an outer edge and removing the threads parallel to the edge. The threads of loosely woven fabrics will pull out easily. For more tightly woven fabrics, clip the fabric to the flatlocking at 2" intervals and then pull out the threads.

Step 4. For each place mat and coaster sew a button loosely to one corner, leaving a $^1/_4$" thread shank between the button and the fabric. Wrap the hanging loop of a tassel around the thread shank and tack the tassel and wrapped loop in place. ✄

Front side of serged edge.

Back side of serged edge.

Majestic Place Mat & Napkin

By Agnes Mercik

Use a few basic serger techniques and some decorative stitches to make this elegant table setting.

Project Specifications

Skill Level: Beginner
Place Mat Size: 21" x 14"
Napkin Size: 18" x 18"

Materials

- 2 pieces cotton print with gold metallic design 16" x 15" and 1 piece 2" x 7" for main portion of place mat and pocket binding
- 2 pieces coordinating cotton print with gold metallic design 7" x 15" and 1 piece 11" x 11" for pocket backing and motif
- 2 pieces third coordinating cotton print with gold metallic design 7" x 8" for pocket
- 18" x 18" square coordinating solid for napkin
- 6" x 6" and 7" x 8" lightweight fusible tricot
- 6" x 6" tear-away fabric stabilizer
- Thin fleece 16" x 15" and 7" x 15"

- 2 spools gold metallic embroidery thread
- Coordinating serger thread
- 1 package gold metallic elastic thread
- Can of spray fabric adhesive
- Basic sewing supplies and tools

Instructions

Step 1. Sandwich 16" x 15" piece of thin fleece between two layers of cotton print with gold metallic design for main portion of place mat. Align and spray layers together with spray fabric adhesive.

Step 2. Mark sections on place mat as shown in Fig. 1. Stitch on sewing machine using decorative stitches or on serger using chain stitch.

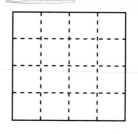

Fig. 1
Make grid on place mat as shown.

Step 3. With gold metallic elastic thread in looper and coordinating thread in needle, chain-stitch a grid design on the 11" x 11" square of coordinating print for pocket motif as shown in Fig 2. Stitch on wrong side of fabric on lengthwise grain, then on crosswise grain, using presser foot as a guide. Follow Steps 2–4, Majestic Pillow, page 128 for scrunching and reverse appliqué instructions to add motif to one pocket piece.

Fig. 2
Chain-stitch a grid on fabric square.

Step 4. Place 7" x 8" pocket pieces wrong sides together. Fold 2" x 7" pocket binding fabric in half lengthwise. Serge to right side of pocket top. Turn to *3 stitch overlock*

wrong side and slipstitch by hand or stitch in the ditch by machine.

Step 5. Place pocket on lower left corner of place mat, right sides together.

Step 6. Place one pocket backing piece, right sides together, on top of pocket and main portion of place mat. Place 7" x 15" piece of thin fleece on top of pocket backing. Place second pocket backing piece on reverse of place mat, right sides facing.

Step 7. Serge all six layers with four threads. Turn so all seams are inside for reversible effect; press.

Step 8. With decorative gold metallic embroidery thread in both loopers and serger thread in needle, serge all four edges of place mat. Use seam sealant at corners and trim threads when completely dry.

Step 9. With gold metallic embroidery thread, stitch a rolled hem around 18" x 18" napkin square. Monogram may be embroidered if desired. ✀

Majestic Pillow

By Agnes Mercik

The creation of gold metallic tassels and an interesting serger elastic fabric-scrunching effect are two additional techniques that make this pillow very special.

Project Specifications

Skill Level: Beginner
Pillow Size: 18" x 18"

Materials

- 1¹/₂ yards cotton print with gold metallic design
- Lightweight fusible tricot: 12" x 12", 19" x 19", and 2 pieces 12" x 19"
- 12" x 12" tear-away fabric stabilizer
- 18" zipper to match fabric
- 1 spool gold metallic embroidery thread
- 1 package gold metallic elastic thread
- Coordinating serger thread
- All-purpose thread to match fabric
- 4" piece of cardboard
- 14" x 14" pillow form
- Seam sealant (optional)
- Basic sewing supplies and tools

Instructions

Step 1. Cut a 20" x 20" square of cotton print with gold metallic design. With gold metallic elastic thread in the looper and coordinating serger thread in the needle, chain-stitch in diagonal rows across the entire square, using the presser foot as a guide for spacing as shown in Fig. 1. Stitch with the right side of the fabric toward the feed dogs so elastic thread will add texture to the surface.

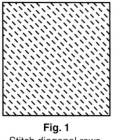

Fig. 1
Stitch diagonal rows
across fabric square.

Step 2. Steam-press the wrong side of stitched fabric lightly to scrunch. Fuse lightweight fusible tricot to wrong side of square to stabilize.

Step 3. Cut a 19" x 19" square of cotton print with gold metallic design for pillow top. Fuse lightweight fusible tricot to wrong side of square to stabilize. Fold square on both diagonals to find center and trace motifs on right side of square as shown in Fig. 2. Straight-stitch around the design lines to stabilize. Cut out the pattern shapes just inside the straight-stitch line.

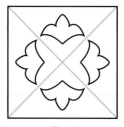

Fig. 2
Trace motifs on
square as shown, using
gray lines only as guides
for positioning.

Step 4. Place scrunched fabric square behind the cut-out area. Place tear-away fabric stabilizer behind the scrunched square. Satin-stitch the raw areas with gold metallic embroidery thread in reverse appliqué technique. Highlight the satin stitch by working a straight stitch around the outline. Decorative machine stitches may be added if desired as shown in photo. Remove fabric stabilizer.

Step 5. Cut two pieces of cotton print with gold metallic design 12" x 19" for pillow back. Fuse lightweight fusible tricot to wrong side of each piece.

Step 6. With 3–4-thread serged seam application, serge the zipper between two 19" edges of pillow back pieces using piping or multipurpose foot. It is necessary to extend the zipper with the tab end beyond the fabric edge, as shown in Fig. 3, to avoid tab contact with the presser foot.

Fig. 3
Zipper is longer than seam at both ends.

Step 7. Change machine function to chain stitch and place gold metallic embroidery thread in the looper and coordinating serger thread in the needle.

Step 8. Fold the fabric one inch on each side of zipper and bring folds to meet in the center of the coils as shown in Fig. 4. With right sides of fabric against the plate, serge folds to conceal zipper.

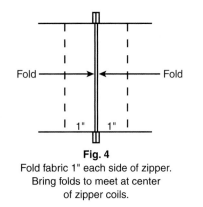

Fig. 4
Fold fabric 1" each side of zipper.
Bring folds to meet at center
of zipper coils.

Step 9. Place pillow front and back together, right sides facing. If you choose to make decorative corners as shown in the photo, trace the shape on each corner.

Stitch around perimeter of pillow and on traced line. Trim fabric from stitched corners.

Step 10. Turn pillow right side out and topstitch with chain stitch (machine threaded as in Step 7) approximately 2" from edge. Stitch with front of pillow against feed dogs. Repeat with two more rows using presser foot as a guide for spacing.

Note: When pivoting on corners, barely pierce the tip of the needle to hold the fabric corner in position. Turn the fabric and continue stitching until all four sides are completed.

Step 11. Wrap gold metallic elastic thread around 4" cardboard template until desired fullness for tassel is achieved. Slip a 4" length of gold metallic embroidery thread through the folds at the top of the template as shown in Fig. 5. Tie securely and remove threads from the cardboard. Wrap a 10" length of gold metallic embroidery thread about 1/2" from the tied end as shown in Fig. 6. Repeat for four tassels.

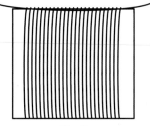

Fig. 5
Slip thread through
folds as shown.

Fig. 6
Wrap thread around tassel
$\frac{1}{2}$" below tied end.

– Cut

Fig. 7
Apply seam sealant to folds
before cutting.

Step 12. Cut the other folded end of each tassel. If raveling may be a problem, apply seam sealant along fold. Allow to dry thoroughly and then cut along the fold as shown in Fig. 7.

Step 13. Hand-stitch or pin a tassel to each corner of pillow. Insert pillow form and zip closure. ✄

Decorative Corner Pattern

Appliqué Motif

Blanket-Stitched Pillows

By Carol Zentgraf

Fleece is wonderful to work with! It comes in gorgeous colors, it's soft and user-friendly, and you'll enjoy developing these new techniques.

Project Specifications

Skill Level: Beginner
Square Pillow Size: 12" x 12"
Neck Roll Pillow Size: 5" x 14"
Flap Rectangle Pillow Size: 12" x 16"

Materials

- $3/4$ yard each of 1 fleece plaid and 3 coordinating solids
- 12" x 12" pillow form
- 5" x 14" neck roll pillow form
- 12" x 16" pillow form
- Water-soluble stabilizer
- Seam sealant
- Contrasting serger thread: two spools of Woolly Nylon and one spool of all-purpose
- All-purpose thread to match fabrics
- 9" length of $3/4$"-wide hook-and-loop tape
- Rotary-cutting tools including decorative blade
- Permanent fabric adhesive (optional)
- Basic sewing supplies and tools, and tailor's chalk

Instructions

Square Pillow

Step 1. From plaid fleece cut two squares 13" x 13" for pillow front and back. From a solid-color fleece cut four $2^1/2$" x 17" strips for flanges, four $3/4$" x 4" strips for corner ties and two tie panel flaps as shown in Fig. 1.

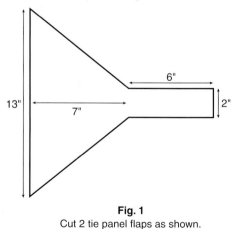

Fig. 1
Cut 2 tie panel flaps as shown.

Step 2. Cut 1"-wide strips of water-soluble stabilizer. Pin to the wrong side of fleece along the flange outer edges and the diagonal and tie edges of the flap panels.

Step 3. Thread the serger with Woolly Nylon in the

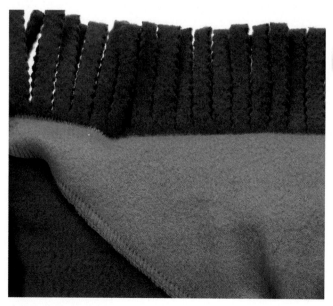

upper and lower loopers, and all-purpose thread in the needle. Set the needle tension to 0 and tighten the looper tensions almost all the way. Lengthen the stitch width and length as far as they will go. Test on a fleece scrap, adjusting the tensions as needed until both looper threads are on the fleece edge and the needle thread forms a blanket stitch.

Step 4. Holding the fleece taut, stitch along all stabilized edges. Also stitch one edge of each corner tie strip. Apply seam sealant to the thread ends.

Step 5. For the pillow front, baste the straight edges of the tie panels to opposite edges of one pillow panel on the right side. With right sides together, center and sew the flange strips to the edges of the front pillow panel, mitering the corners.

Step 6. Sew the pillow front and back panels together, leaving an opening for the pillow form. Insert the pillow form and close the opening with hand stitches.

Step 7. Tie the center ties into a loose overhand knot. Fold each corner of flange to the front and tie securely with a corner tie.

Neck Roll Pillow

Step 1. From one solid-color fleece, cut a 20" x 26" piece for the pillow cover. From a contrasting solid-color fleece, cut two 2¹/₂" x 21" strips for the center wrap outer bands. From the plaid fleece, cut one 5" x 21" strip for the center wrap and two 2" x 20" strips for the end ties.

Step 2. Follow Steps 2 and 3 for the square pillow to set up the serger, and to stabilize and stitch the fleece edges with a blanket stitch. Stitch both short edges of the pillow cover and one long edge of each solid center wrap strip.

Step 3. Set the serger for an overlock stitch. With right sides together and using a $1/4$" seam allowance, serge the pillow cover long edges, right sides together.

Step 4. Insert the pillow form in the center of the cover. Gather each end and tie with a plaid strip.

Step 5. For the center wrap, serge the unstitched edges of the solid-color side strips to the plaid center strip. Serge-finish the ends. Sew hook-and-loop tape to the wrap ends. Wrap around the pillow center, securing the ends in back.

Rectangle Flap Pillow

Step 1. From one solid-color fleece, cut two 18" x 22" pillow panels. From a contrasting solid-color fleece, cut a triangular flap that is 16" long at the base and 8" from the base to the point as shown in Fig. 2. From the plaid fleece, cut one 7" x 12" piece for the tassels.

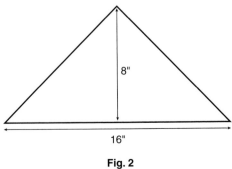

Fig. 2
Cut triangular flap as shown.

Step 2. Follow Steps 2 and 3 for the square pillow to set up the serger, and to stabilize stitch the flap diagonal edges with a blanket stitch.

Step 3. Pin the pillow panels wrong sides together with edges even. On the back panel, use tailor's chalk to mark a line 3" from the edge, along the side and lower edges.

Step 4. Center and pin the flap straight edge to the front panel, 3" from the upper edge. Sew in place using a zigzag stitch. Turn the panels over and sew the side and lower edges together along the marked line, leaving an opening for the pillow form. Insert the form and zigzag-stitch the opening closed.

Step 5. Use the rotary cutter with decorative blade to cut the pillow outer edges into $1/2$"-wide fringe strips, cutting to $1/2$" from the zigzag stitching.

Step 6. To make the tassels, fold the 7" x 12" plaid piece in half lengthwise. Cut fringe to 1" from the fold. Open flat with the fringe at the sides; cut two 2" x 7" strips from the end as shown in Fig. 3.

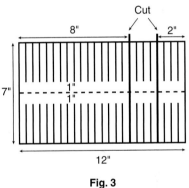

Fig. 3
Cut 2 strips 2" x 7" from ends.

Step 7. For large tassel, begin at one end and roll up loosely the 7" x 8" strip; for small tassels roll up the 2" x 7" strips. Fold each rolled-up strip in half to form a tassel. Use a fleece scrap to gather and tie tightly at the top of the fringe as shown in Fig. 4.

Step. 8. Tie the large tassel to the point of the flap, securing with permanent fabric adhesive if needed for stability. Tie the small tassels to the upper corners of the pillow. ✄

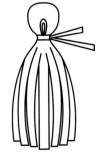

Fig. 4
Gather and tie tassel tightly as shown.

Dainty Daisy Pillow

By Agnes Mercik

Learn a variety of serger techniques as you construct this pillow sham in the traditional Rail Fence quilt design.

Project Specifications

Skill Level: Beginner
Pillow Sham Size: 18" x 18", including ruffles

Materials

- $5/8$ yard primary print fabric
- $1/8$ yard each of 2 coordinating prints
- $4^{1}/2$ yards $5/8$"-wide lace edging
- $3/4$ yard $5/8$"-wide edging or insertion lace for zipper area (optional)
- 14" zipper to match fabric
- Serger thread to match fabrics
- 14" x 14" pillow form
- Gathering foot or attachment
- Basic sewing supplies and tools

Instructions

Note: *This project can be stitched almost entirely in the cover-stitch mode, or with the traditional 3- or 4-thread serger stitch.*

Step 1. From the primary fabric and each of the coordinating prints cut one strip each $2^{1}/2$" x 30" inches. Serge the strips together with $5/8$"-wide lace edging sandwiched between strips as shown in Fig. 1.

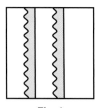

Fig. 1
Serge 3 strips together with lace
sandwiched between as shown.

Step 2. Cut piece into four $6^{1}/2$" segments as shown in Fig. 2. Arrange $6^{1}/2$" x $6^{1}/2$" squares as shown in Fig. 3 and serge together.

Step 3. Cut two 4" strips across the width of the primary fabric; piece together on two short ends to make one long strip. Serge $5/8$"-wide lace edging to strip, right sides together, rounding the ends as shown in Fig. 4.

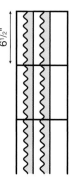

Fig. 2
Cut piece into $6^{1}/2$"
segments as shown.

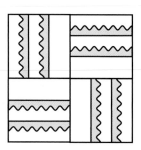

Fig. 3
Arrange squares as shown.

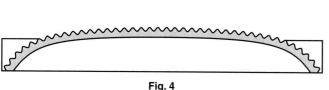

Fig. 4
Serge lace to fabric strip,
rounding ends as shown.

Step 4. Turn the lace-edged fabric to the wrong side and serge the hem with cover stitch, or topstitch on the sewing machine.

Step 5. Divide the ruffle and pillow top each into four sections and use as a guide to distribute the ruffles evenly. With gathering foot or attachment, serge the ruffle onto the pieced pillow top. Overlap the curved ends as shown in Fig. 5.

serger piecing technique. For sharper corners, serge the first seam, then fold the serged seam allowance downward and serge the second seam as shown in Fig. 7. Following this method, continue serging the next two sides.

Step 9. Insert 14" pillow form and zip closure. ✂

Fig. 5
Overlap curved ends as shown.

Fig. 6
Cover-stitch lace over zipper
area to conceal zipper coils.

Step 6. From the primary fabric cut two pieces $6^1/2$" x $12^1/2$" for the pillow sham back. Place the 14" zipper tape right side down on the $12^1/2$" edge of each strip and serge together.

Step 7. If desired, place the optional $^5/8$"-wide edging or insertion lace on top of the serged zipper area and cover-stitch the lace to the fabric concealing the zipper coils as shown in Fig. 6.

Step 8. Place pillow sham front to pillow sham back, right sides together, and serge using 3–4-thread

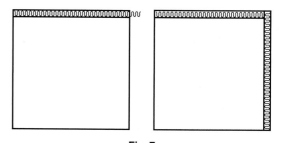

Fig. 7
At corner, fold serged seam allowance
downward and then serge second seam.

Full-of-Tucks Pillow

By Agnes Mercik

This pillow will teach you a surprising number of techniques, considering its small size.

Project Specifications

Skill Level: Beginner

Pillow Size: Approximately 9" x 14"

Materials

- Light green batik for center panel 14$\frac{1}{2}$" x 7" and two pieces each 6" x 19" for side-button areas
- 2 pieces purple batik for single-pleat areas 3" x 22" each, 1$\frac{1}{2}$" x 13" for piping and 4" x 6" for button covers
- 2 pieces dark teal batik 6$\frac{1}{2}$" x 3" each for center panel frames, 1$\frac{1}{2}$" x 44" for piping and 10" x 10" for pillow back
- 6 ($\frac{3}{4}$"–$\frac{7}{8}$") buttons for covering
- $\frac{1}{3}$ yard muslin for pillow lining and pillow form
- 1 package polyester fiberfill

- 2–4 spools #30 decorative rayon thread
- 2 spools polyester thread to blend with rayon thread (for needles)
- 4 cones serger thread for assembling project
- Rotary cutter, mat and acrylic quilter's ruler
- Seam sealant
- Water-soluble marker
- Basic sewing supplies and tools

Instructions

Note: The practical and decorative cover stitch and single chain stitch will be used to make two kinds of tucks in this project.

Step 1. Set up the serger in cover-stitch mode with new needles.

Step 2. Mark the top and bottom edge of the green

batik center panel for six wave pleats approximately 2" apart as shown in Fig. 1.

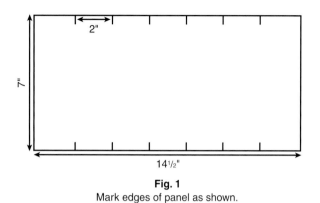

Fig. 1
Mark edges of panel as shown.

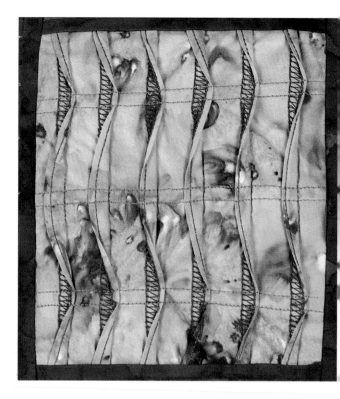

Step 3. Matching a top and bottom mark, decorative rayon thread in the looper, fold and 2-needle cover-stitch as shown in Fig. 2. Repeat for six pleats as shown in Fig. 3. The width of the pleats should be approximately ³/₈".

Pleat depth ³/₈"

Fig. 2
Fold and stitch as shown.

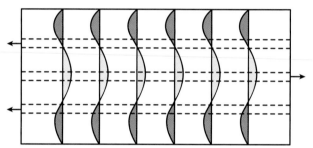

Fig. 4
Stitch back and forth across the pleated area as shown.

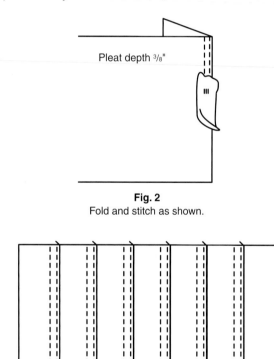

Fig. 3
Stitch 6 pleats as shown.

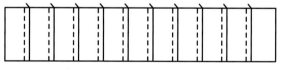

Fig. 5
Stitch single-pleat strips as shown.

purple batik single-pleat areas, mark, fold and stitch the 3" x 22" strips as in Steps 2 and 3 above and as shown in Fig. 5. Stitch with a chain stitch and contrasting thread color.

Step 4. Pulling the pleats in the direction of the stitching, stitch back and forth across the pleated area as shown in Fig. 4 to create wave tucks. Trim the piece to a 6¹/₂" x 6¹/₂" square, centering the pleats on the square.

Step 5. Convert serger to chain-stitch mode. For the

Step 6. Convert serger to basic 4-thread construction mode. Cut purple batik piping strip in two 6¹/₂" lengths. Fold in half lengthwise, wrong sides facing; press. Align raw edges with top and bottom of wave-tuck section. Place one dark teal batik 6¹/₂" x 3" strip face down over each piping strip, again aligning raw edges. Stitch through all layers.

Step 7. Cut dark teal piping strip in four equal pieces. Fold each in half lengthwise, wrong sides facing; press. Align raw edges with both long sides of each single-pleat strip and stitch.

Step 8. Stitch single-pleat sections to sides of center panel. Trim entire piece to 10" x 10".

Step 9. Place pillow top and dark teal batik back together, right sides facing. Stitch together along top edge as shown in Fig. 6. Using the pillow top/back as a pattern, cut two pieces from muslin the same size. Stitch one piece to the backside of pillow top as a lining.

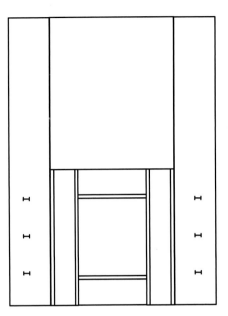

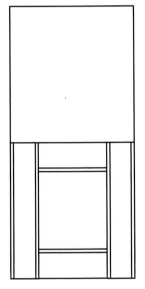

Fig. 6
Stitch pillow top and back together as shown.

Fig. 7
Sew button-area strips to pillow back and front as shown.

Step 10. Fold the 6" x 19" button-area panels in half lengthwise, wrong sides facing. Aligning raw edges, sew to each side of pillow front and back as shown in Fig. 7. Mark and stitch buttonholes to match button size, again referring to Fig. 7.

Step 11. Right sides facing, bring remaining two raw edges of pillow together and stitch.

Step 12. Fold the remaining piece of muslin cut in Step 9, bringing the two short ends together. Serge two raw edges. Turn right side out and stuff with polyester fiberfill. Serge final seam.

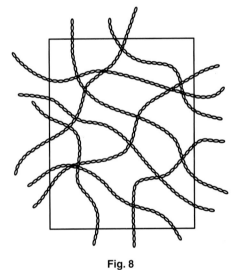

Fig. 8
Chain-stitch randomly over button-cover fabric as shown.

Step 13. For button covers, chain-stitch in a random pattern and contrasting thread over 4" x 6" purple button-cover fabric as shown in Fig. 8.

Step 14. Cover buttons following package directions. Sew in place to match buttonholes.

Step 15. Insert pillow and button to close. ✁

Flower-Power Pillow

By Carol Zentgraf

This pillow packs a powerful design punch with limited material, time and effort!

Project Specifications

Skill Level: Beginner

Pillow Size: 18" x 18"

Materials

- 2 navy plaid squares 19" x 19" for pillow front and back
- ¼ yard 28"-wide red interlock knit
- 3 (1") buttons: yellow, blue and white
- 1¾ yards ⅛"-wide red satin ribbon
- 18" x 18" pillow form
- Air-soluble marker
- Permanent fabric glue
- Serger thread: 1 spool each red and green Woolly Nylon, and 2 spools each red and green all-purpose
- All-purpose sewing thread to match fabrics
- Basic sewing supplies and tools

Instructions

Step 1. With air-soluble marker, draw flower stems on one pillow square, beginning at lower edge. Find center and draw one 14" perpendicular line. Mark an 11" line

4" to the left of center and a 9" line to the right of center. See Fig. 1.

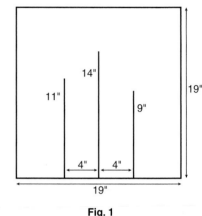

Fig. 1
Mark stem lines on pillow front as shown.

Step 2. Thread serger with green Woolly Nylon in upper looper and green serger thread in lower looper and needle. Fold the fabric on each marked stem line and flatlock the stems. Pull the stitches flat.

Step 3. From red interlock knit cut one strip 2" x 28" and two strips 2" x 14".

Step 4. Thread serger with red Woolly Nylon in upper

Double flower

Single flower

looper and red serger thread in lower looper and needle. Stitch a rolled edge on one long edge of each interlock knit strip, stretching the edge as you serge to create a "lettuce" effect.

Step 5. Sew a running stitch along the remaining edge of each knit strip. Pull the threads to gather tightly and knot the thread ends.

Step 6. Use the 28" strip for the center flower and the 14" strips for the outer flowers. Apply a $1/2$"-diameter circle of permanent fabric glue at the top of each stem and press the gathered edge of the knit strip into the adhe-

sive, overlapping the cut ends. For the center flower, wrap the gathered edge into a spiral, applying more glue as needed, again overlapping the ends of the strips.

Step 7. Sew a button to the center of each flower.

Step 8. Sew the pillow panels right sides together, using a $1/2$" seam allowance and leaving an opening for the pillow form. Turn right side out, insert form and close opening with hand stitches.

Step 9. Cut $1/8$"-wide red satin ribbon in four equal pieces. Tie each length into a bow around a pillow corner as shown in photo. ✄

Woven Fabric Ribbon Pillows

By Agnes Mercik

Roll-edge and embellish fabric strips to make these wonderful ribbonlike pillow panels.

Project Specifications

Skill Level: Beginner

Pillow Sizes: 14" x 14" and 12" x 16"

Materials

Note: *Fabric amounts are for one pillow. The color scheme of each pillow featured is slightly different. Plan each pillow individually, but coordinate with each other, if desired.*

- $5/8$ yard batik for borders, ribbons and backing
- $3/8$ yard each of three different contrasting or coordinating fabrics for ribbons
- $1^1/2$ yards fusible tricot
- 14" x 14" or 12" x 16" pillow form for pillow of choice
- 18" zipper for square pillow or 20" zipper for rectangular pillow (2"–4" longer than pillow size for serge application)
- 4 spools coordinating serger thread
- YLI Jeans Stitch decorative thread in 2 different colors for each pillow
- YLI Pearl Crown rayon thread in 2 different colors for each pillow
- Clear or smoky nylon monofilament (depending on fabric colors used)
- 6-strand cotton embroidery floss or other suitable ribbon, cord, knitting/crochet yarn in 2 different colors for each pillow
- Tapestry needle
- Serger with 4-thread overlock and rolled-hem functions
- 2-thread adapter for flatlocking technique (optional)
- Piping foot for zipper application
- Basic sewing supplies and tools

Instructions

Step 1. For each pillow cut four $1^1/4$"-wide strips each across the width of all four fabrics.

Step 2. For each square pillow cut two batik pieces $8^1/2$" x 16". For rectangular pillow cut two batik pieces 6" x 14".

Step 3. Cut one matching batik piece 13" x 17" for rectangular pillow front. Cut one matching batik piece 15" x 15" for square pillow.

Step 4. Following manufacturer's instructions, press fusible tricot to strips, pillow fronts and backs for added durability.

Step 5. With decorative thread in the upper looper, roll-edge two of the colors of $1^1/4$"-wide fabric strips. Trimming the fabric will ensure a nice rolled hem.

Decorative thread in the upper looper will require a slightly looser tension.

Optional: Place 2-thread adapter on upper looper to bypass this function and tighten the lower looper. Now the decorative thread will be in the lower looper.

Note: If the decorative thread is stubborn and will not roll properly, then create a narrow balanced stitch that will resemble a soutache trim on the edge of the fabric.

Step 6. On the other two colors of fabric strips, fold the strips in half right sides together and flatlock with left needle. Place decorative thread in the embroidery or topstitch needle.

Note: The 2-thread adapter simplifies adjusting tensions and creates a more durable and flatter flatlock.

This step may be easier to do before roll-hemming the edges.

Place Jeans Stitch decorative thread in the embroidery or topstitch needle and fold fabric right sides together. Serge so that half the stitch is on the fabric and half off. This will create more room for the fabric to lie flat by reducing the amount of the tuck or eliminating it entirely.

Step 7. Gently pull fabric flat, centering the ladder on top of the strip; press. Weave floss, ribbon, cord or yarn though the ladders, over and under the threads.

Repeat a second or third row as needed to fill the space. Interesting patterns can be achieved by varying the number of ladders and the colors of yarns woven.

Step 8. For square pillow, pin a 9" x 9" square of fusible tricot face up on a padded surface or board. Begin placing vertical fabric strips across the square in a pleasing color arrangement as shown in Fig. 1. For rectangular pillow use a 9" x 13" tricot base.

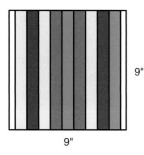

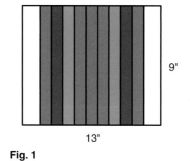

9"

9"

9"

13"

Fig. 1
Place vertical strips on square or rectangle as shown.

Step 9. Weave horizontal strips over and under vertical strips as shown in Fig. 2 until surface is covered. Press

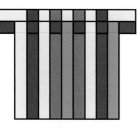

Fig. 2
Weave horizontal strips through vertical strips as shown.

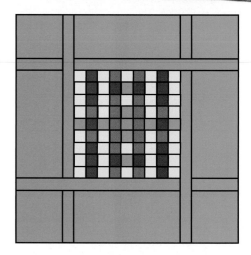

Fig. 3
Place additional strips around the edges as shown.

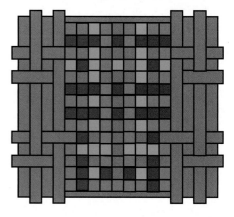

Fig. 4
Leave some ribbons with extra length as shown.

woven section to fuse. Place on 15" x 15" pillow square (straight or on point) or on 13" x 17" rectangular base. Place additional strips around the edges as shown in Fig. 3 to cover raw edges. Leave some ribbons with extra length to be incorporated into the side panels of the rectangular pillow as shown in Fig. 4. Edge-stitch with clear or smoky nylon monofilament.

Step 10. Place right side of zipper onto right side of one pillow back section, leaving zipper ends extended longer than the seam edge as shown in Fig. 5. With piping foot, place nylon zipper coil under the tunnel and serge the entire edge. Turn and repeat on the other side.

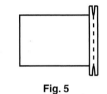

Fig. 5
Zipper is longer than seam at both ends.

Step 11. Press a ³/₄" pleat to cover zipper opening as shown in Fig. 6 and stitch on sewing machine. Before

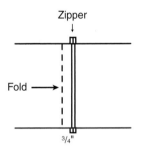

Fig. 6
Make a pleat to cover zipper as shown.

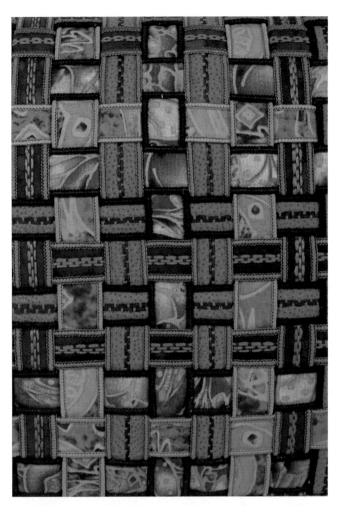

trimming ends of zipper, bar-tack on sewing machine to secure zipper ends. On tab end, pull the tab down a few inches before securing.

Step 12. Place front and back of pillow right sides together and serge all four sides. Before starting to serge each additional side, fold the serged seam on the seam line toward either the front or back of the pillow and then serge the seam. Continue on all four sides. This step will create a more pointed corner than simply serging on and off the fabric.

Step 13. Turn right side out and carefully push out the corners with a blunt object.

Note: Stitch a cord at each corner first, and then proceed with the above instructions. When the pillow is turned right side out, pull the cord to straighten out the corner. Trim the cord near the seam line and remove. ✄

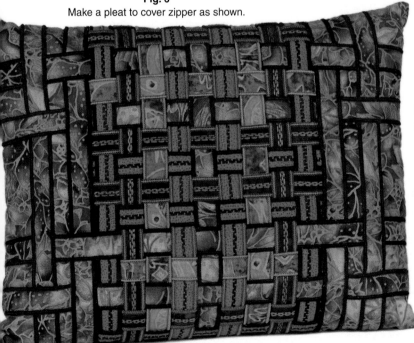

Decorator Cushion Trio

By Anne van der Kley

Learn some decorative techniques making these fabulous cushions that will translate into a myriad of ideas for more sewing adventures.

Project Specifications

Skill Level: Intermediate
Cushion Size: 18" x 18" including flange/borders

Materials

- ⅞ yard floral print on black background
- ⅞ yard black-and-cream plaid

- ⁷/₈ yard black-and-cream stripe
- ¹/₄ yard navy solid for inner narrow folded border
- ¹/₄ yard burgundy solid for outer narrow folded border
- 6 strips lightweight fusible interfacing 4" x 20¹/₂"
- Three 14" x 14" pillow forms
- 1¹/₂ yards heavyweight fusible interfacing
- 3 different colors of YLI Pearl Crown rayon or Madeira Décor to contrast or blend with fabrics

- ¹/₄"-wide fusible web
- 4 cones of serger thread to match fabrics
- All-purpose thread to match fabrics
- 9 (⁷/₈") buttons for back closures
- Variety of buttons to decorate cushion fronts
- Water-soluble glue stick
- Seam sealant
- Rotary-cutting tools
- Spray starch
- Basic sewing supplies and tools

Instructions

Note: Regardless of technique, throughout these projects the serger is set up with the same thread in the needle and lower looper. The only change of threads is to the upper looper, to introduce a thick embellishment thread. Each fabric has the same technique carrying through each cushion, with the fabrics moving one position each time. Practice the technique to be sure you like the stitching.

Step 1. From plaid and striped fabrics cut one rectangle each 6¹/₂" x 12¹/₂", 4¹/₂" x 12¹/₂" and 2¹/₂" x 12¹/₂" for center pieced section of pillow. From floral print cut one strip 2¹/₂" x 12¹/₂". From each fabric cut two rectangles each 4¹/₂" x 12¹/₂" and 4¹/₂" x 20¹/₂" for outer borders. From each fabric cut two rectangles each 14" x 20¹/₂" for pillow backs. From floral print fabric cut one rectangle 6¹/₂" x 23" and 4¹/₂" x 23" for thread-embellished panels.

Step 2. From navy solid cut four 1³/₄"-wide strips across the width of the fabric. From burgundy solid cut four 1¹/₂"-wide strips across the width of the fabric for narrow folded borders.

Double Edging

Note: Each cushion is embellished just a little differently. Although each cushion is essentially the same, the primary fabrics are rotated. Try out the trim techniques on scraps, then mix-and-match to your preference. No exact measurements have been given for any of the trim techniques, allowing you complete creative freedom.

Step 1. Thread the serger for a 3-thread wide stitch. Use serger thread to match your fabric in both the needle and lower looper. Place the heavy embellishment thread in the upper looper.

Step 2. Cut 1"-wide strips across the width of the fabric. Remove selvage. If the fabric is very soft, spray with spray starch and press well. Dry well.

Step 5. Seal with seam sealant on the ends of each of the thread chains closest to the fabric and a thin line across the raw fabric edge. Trim the excess chain and fabric once the sealant is completely dry.

Step 6. Tie strips in one or more knots and place on matching fabric backgrounds. Odd numbers are more aesthetically pleasing, as are offset knots.

Folded Stripes

Note: *This edging is created on striped fabric, working stripe both vertically and horizontally for visual interest and movement. It may also be worked on plaid fabric if you choose.*

Step 1. Set serger for 3-thread rolled hem. Use YLI Pearl Crown rayon or Madeira Décor thread in the upper looper. Lengthen the stitch to around 4. Loosen the tension on the upper looper until the stitch is rolling to the underside. Keep in mind that some cotton may not want to roll completely, but the underside of the strips will not be seen.

Step 2. Serge a variety of strips, both narrow and wide, and with the stripe going both horizontally and vertically. Apply seam sealant on the ends of each thread chain closest to the fabric and a thin line across the raw fabric edge. Trim excess chain and fabric once the sealant is completely dry.

Step 3. Fold the strips as shown in Fig. 2.

Note: *This trim makes a nice prairie point for any application.*

Thread Embellishment

Step 1. Cut 6$\frac{1}{2}$" x 23" floral panel into several pieces as shown in Fig. 3. Place right side up on rotary mat. Working systematically from one side to the other, overlap the fabric 1"–2" and rotary-cut in gentle curves as shown in Fig. 4.

Step 3. Place two strips wrong sides together. Serge a single edging on long sides of strips, chaining off at ends. Seal with seam sealant on the ends of each of the thread chains closest to the fabric and a thin line across the raw fabric edge. Trim the excess chain and fabric once the sealant is completely dry.

Step 4. Rethread serger with a contrasting color of YLI Pearl Crown or Madeira Décor. Reset serger for a narrow hem. Serge again as a second edging. The needle should just enter the outer edge of the previous row of stitching, covering about $\frac{1}{4}$ of the stitch as shown in Fig. 1. All stitching should be worked with the right side up.

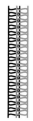

Fig. 1
Serge second row of stitches over first as shown.

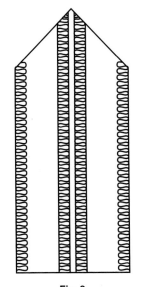

Fig. 2
Fold strips as shown.

Step 2. Set serger for a 2-thread rolled hem with YLI Pearl Crown rayon or Madeira Décor thread in the lower looper. You will have to use your converter/spacer, which will deactivate the upper looper of the serger. Lengthen the stitch to about 4. Loosen the tension on the lower looper until the stitch is rolling to the underside. Remember again, if the fabric does not want to roll completely it will not be seen from the underside.

Step 3. Align parallel edges as shown in Fig. 5. Stitch with a 2-thread rolled hem. Press flat when stitching is complete. Trim to 6$\frac{1}{2}$" x 12$\frac{1}{2}$".

Fig. 5
Align parallel edges as shown.

Step 4. Repeat with 4$\frac{1}{2}$" x 23" floral fabric, varying the curves and cuts for interest. Trim piece to 4$\frac{1}{2}$" x 12$\frac{1}{2}$".

Assembly

Step 1. Referring to the photo, arrange the 12$\frac{1}{2}$" strips for the center pieced sections of each pillow. Cut and arrange folded-stripe and double-edging embellishment according to photos or your own preference.

Step 2. Apply $\frac{1}{4}$" strips of fusible web behind loose embellishments. Fuse in place. Join the embellished

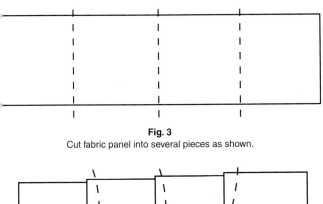

Fig. 3
Cut fabric panel into several pieces as shown.

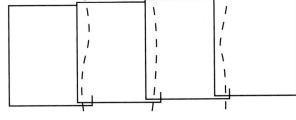

Fig. 4
Overlap fabric panels and rotary-cut curves as shown.

Step 5. Referring to photo for color placement, stitch 4½" x 12½" border pieces to two opposite sides of pillow centers. Press seams toward borders. Stitch 4½" x 20½" borders to top and bottom of pillows. Press seams toward borders.

Step 6. Fuse one 4" x 20½" strip of fusible interfacing to one 20½" edge of each pillow backing piece. Fold fabric over the facing and press.

Step 7. Staying 4½" away from outside edges, center and make three buttonholes to fit selected buttons. Buttonholes will be sewn through two fabric layers.

Step 8. Press heavyweight fusible interfacing to back of each pillow top. Trim even with top.

strips with a balanced 4-thread stitch. Trim to 12½" x 12½" square if necessary.

Step 3. Fold 1¾" navy solid strips and 1½" burgundy solid strips in half lengthwise, wrong sides together; press. Cut twelve 12½" segments from each color.

Step 4. Place a folded navy strip on a burgundy folded strip. Align raw edges with one raw edge of a pieced center section. Use glue stick to hold in place and machine-stitch; press well. Add another double navy/burgundy strip to opposite side of pieced section. Repeat with two remaining sides. Repeat for two remaining pillow centers.

Step 9. Place matching pillow back pieces on appropriate pillow tops, right sides facing. Overlap pillow back pieces, making sure the buttonhole section is closest to the cushion front.

Step 10. Serge around all edges with a balanced 4-thread stitch. Secure each corner by applying seam sealant, trimming thread chains when thoroughly dry. Turn cushion right side out; press.

Step 11. Measure out 1¼" from center panel and stitch around perimeter to create flange.

Step. 12. Stitch buttons to back to match buttonholes and decoratively to front as desired. Insert cushions. ✄

Antique Battenburg Lace Pillow

By Agnes Mercik

Use a simple flatlock stitch to join two layers of lace to trim this charming pillow top. Lace serged in the zipper application gives the back a fine, finished look, too.

Project Specifications

Skill Level: Beginner
Pillow Size: 15" x 15" excluding ruffle

Materials

- 1⅛ yards cream cotton fabric
- 1 yard 2½"-wide Battenburg edging lace
- 2¾ yards 1½"-wide Battenburg edging lace
- 4 yards 3½"-wide Battenburg edging lace
- 18" cream zipper
- 1 spool cream rayon embroidery thread
- 4 spools cream serger thread
- Glue stick (optional)
- Basic sewing supplies and tools

Instructions

Step 1. Cut 16" x 16" pillow top from cream cotton fabric. Fold in half and press lightly to mark. Make a fold 5" each side of center fold; press to mark.

Step 2. Cut two 16" pieces of 2½"-wide lace edging. Place one straight edge of one lace strip each side of center fold line as shown in Fig. 1. Machine-baste in place or secure with glue stick. Repeat for two remaining folds using four 16" pieces of 1½"-wide lace edging.

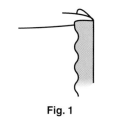

Fig. 1
Place lace strip each side of fold line.

Step 3. Set serger on 2-thread flatlock. Place cream rayon embroidery thread in lower looper and cream serger thread in needle. Flatlock all three layers, allowing looper threads to hang off fold slightly on each of the three marked lines as shown in Fig. 2.

Step 4. Cut two pieces 8¼" x 15½" from cream cotton fabric for pillow back. Cut two 15½" pieces of 1½"-wide lace edging. Place the straight side of lace along one 15½" edge of each pillow back piece. Machine-baste in place or use glue stick to secure.

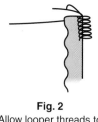

Fig. 2
Allow looper threads to hang off fold slightly.

Step 5. Place the zipper face down on top of lace, and with the cording or multipurpose foot, serge each side of the zipper as shown in Fig. 3.

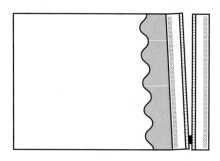

Fig. 3
Place zipper on top of lace and serge.

Step 6. Cut three 5½" strips across the width of the cream cotton fabric. Set serger for 2-thread rolled hem by changing needle position to the right. Roll-edge one long side of each fabric strip.

Step 7. Set serger with 3–4-thread serger construction stitch. Piece together the three ruffle strips on short ends to make a ring.

Step 8. Cut an equal length of 3½"-wide lace edging. Align the straight edge of the lace with the raw edge of the fabric ruffle. Machine-baste layers together.

Step 9. Set differential on maximum and longest stitch length. Gather the basted edge of the ruffle.

Note: You may have to use the gathering foot or attachment to gather multiple layers.

Step 10. Distribute the gathered ruffle evenly on the pillow top and serge-baste.

Step 11. Right sides together, place pillow front to

pillow back, making sure ruffles are strategically placed at the corners. Open zipper slightly before serging to allow for easy turning. Serge pieces together and turn right side out.

Note: *If corners are not sharp enough, serge a cord into each corner and then pull the cord to straighten the corner out as shown in Fig 4. Cut the cords at the seam line when all corners have been pulled out to your satisfaction.* ✂

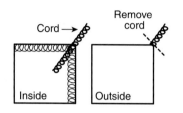

Fig. 4
Serge a cord in each corner and pull to straighten corner.

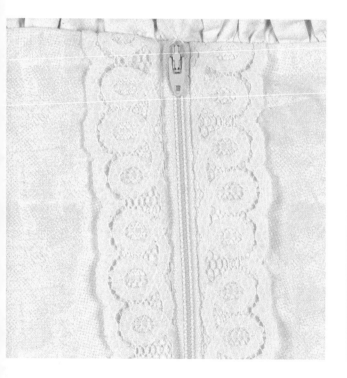

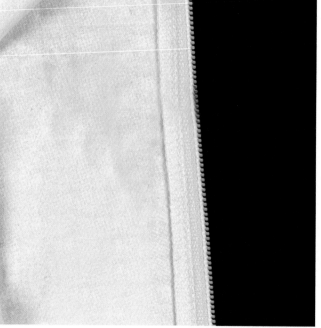

Doll Bed Coverlets & Pillows

By Agnes Mercik

Dolls and their accessories are hot items—and not just for little girls!

Project Specifications

Skill Level: Beginner

Coverlet Size: Fits 10" x 20" bed

Pillow Size: Approximately 4" x 8³/₄"

Note: *A 10" x 20" doll bed is standard. Adjust fabric pieces accordingly for other beds.*

Materials

For Bright Print Coverlet & Pillow

- Bright novelty print: 2 squares 4¹/₂" x 4¹/₂" for center panel, 2 strips 4¹/₂" x 40" for side ruffles, 1 strip 4¹/₂" x 20" for end ruffle and 9¹/₂" x 4¹/₂" for pillow backing

- 1 square each 4¹/₂" x 4¹/₂" and 1 rectangle each 3¹/₂" x 4¹/₂" of 3 bright coordinating prints for center panel and pillow

- Bright coordinating striped fabric: 2 strips 4¹/₂" x 20¹/₂"

- Backing 12" x 22"

- Thin batting or flannel 12" x 22"

- 2 yards ⁵/₈"-wide lightweight fusible tricot

- 4 cones matching serger thread

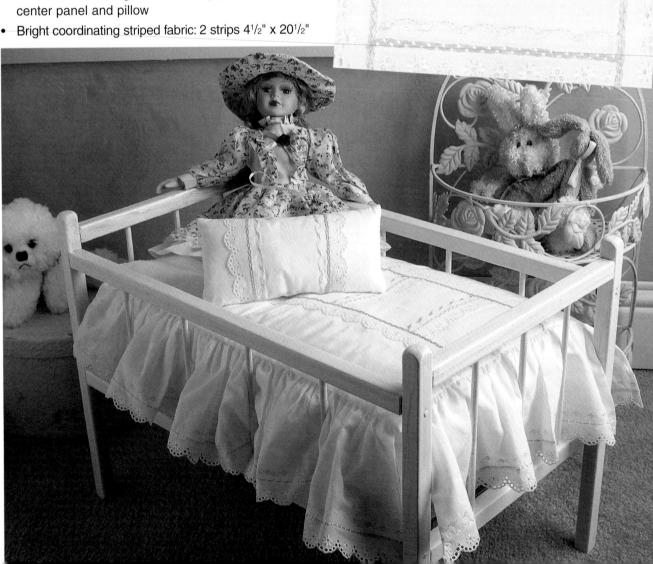

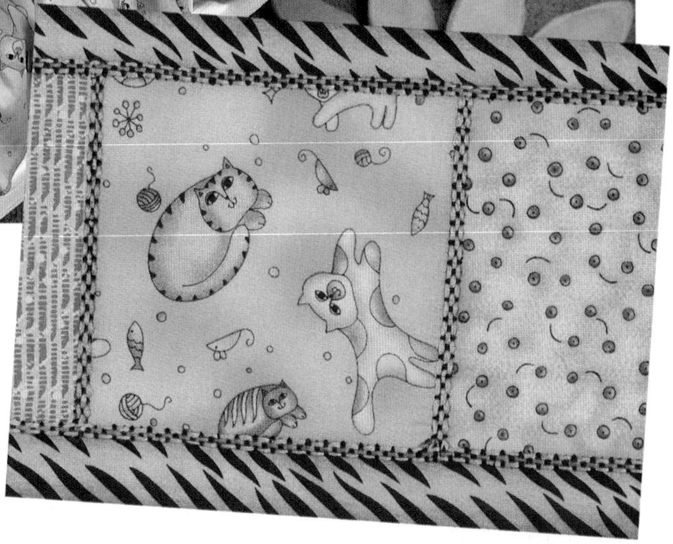

- Rotary-cutting tools
- Tapestry needle
- Decorative thread
- 1 or 2 skeins coordinating cotton or rayon embroidery floss, or other interesting thick yarns
- Polyester fiberfill
- Basic sewing supplies and tools

Instructions

Print Coverlet

Step 1. Prepare serger for 2-thread flatlock. Referring to photo for placement, alternate the two bright print and three coordinating print 4$\frac{1}{2}$" x 4$\frac{1}{2}$" squares. Flatlock wrong sides together for center strip. Gently pull out seams to flatten.

Step 2. With tapestry needle, weave floss or yarn through stitch ladders, going over and under each thread or creating your own weaving pattern. Leave at least 1" of floss extending at each end of each seam.

Step 3. Flatlock the two bright striped 4$\frac{1}{2}$" x 20$\frac{1}{2}$" strips to the center panel and repeat the weaving process.

Step 4. Fuse $\frac{5}{8}$"-wide tricot to back of all flatlocked and woven seams.

Step 5. Change serger settings to rolled hem, and with either 2- or 3-thread technique, roll edge of each of the three ruffle strips on one long and two short edges.

Step 6. Place coverlet top on backing fabric and batting or flannel, and trim to same size.

Step 7. Change serger setting to basic 4-thread seam and differential to a maximum setting and longest stitch length. Gather all three pieces of ruffle. Adjust to fit two long sides and one short end of coverlet. Place lining piece and batting or flannel on top and serge three ruffled edges.

Step 8. Turn right side out and serge remaining edge.

Print Pillow

Step 1. For pillow panel, flatlock 3$\frac{1}{2}$" x 4$\frac{1}{2}$" bright

Continued on page 174

Chili Peppers Mini Banner

By Agnes Mercik

It takes only a little chili pepper to make a big impact!

Project Specifications

Skill Level: Beginner

Banner Size: Approximately 9" x 7$^1/_4$" (excluding sleeve)

Materials

- Variety of bright red, green and neutral scraps
- 4 cones neutral serger thread
- Seam sealant
- Wooden spoon approximately 12" long
- Temporary spray adhesive
- Thin batting 9" x 7$^1/_4$"
- Backing 9" x 7$^1/_4$"
- Embroidery machine and supplies
- Rotary-cutting tools
- Basic sewing supplies and tools

Instructions

Step 1. Embroider a chili pepper motif on a neutral-colored fabric scrap. Trim to 4" x 9$^1/_2$"

Step 2. Serge a variety of scraps together in a crazy-patch design as shown in Fig. 1.

Step 3. Cut two strips 2$^1/_2$" x 9$^1/_2$" from crazy-patched fabrics. Serge to top and bottom of chili pepper panel.

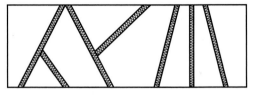

Fig. 1
Serge scraps together in crazy-patch design.

Press and trim to 9" x 7$^1/_4$".

Step 4. Spray both sides of batting with adhesive and carefully layer between pieced panel and backing.

Step 5. From green scraps cut two pieces 4$^1/_2$" x 5$^1/_2$" for hanging sleeve. Right sides facing, stitch along both 4$^1/_2$" sides. Turn right side out and press. Bring raw edges together, fold and press. Center on upper edge of banner backing, aligning raw edges; pin.

Step 6. Cut and piece together, if necessary, enough 2$^1/_2$"-wide green strips to make a 40" length of binding. Fold in half lengthwise, wrong sides facing. Bind edges of mini banner, catching sleeve in binding.

Step 7. Fold sleeve upward for hanging. With hand stitches, tack to upper edge of banner for stability. Insert spoon for hanging. ✁

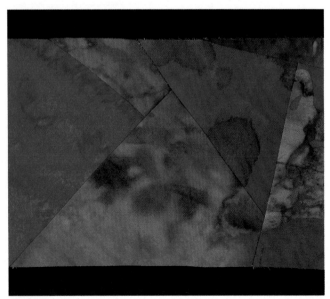

Right side

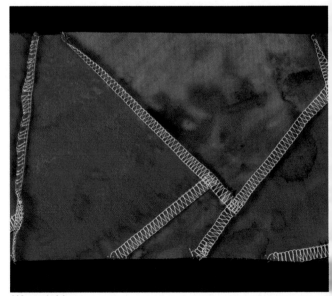

Wrong side

Butterfly Wall Quilt

By Agnes Mercik

The serger elastic scrunching technique adds interesting dimension to the appliqué shapes in this quilt, and the very narrow frames accentuate each block.

Project Specifications

Skill Level: Beginner

Quilt Size: 29$\frac{1}{2}$" x 37"

Materials

- 1$\frac{1}{4}$ yards off-white fabric for block backgrounds
- $\frac{3}{4}$ yard batik for sashing and borders
- $\frac{3}{4}$ yard coordinating batik for narrow frames and binding
- Variety of $\frac{1}{8}$–$\frac{1}{4}$ yard coordinating batik pieces for appliqué
- Colored elastic threads to blend or contrast with appliqué batiks
- Variety of coordinating rayon embroidery threads (#30 or #40) to blend or contrast with appliqué batiks
- Serger threads to match embroidery threads
- All-purpose threads to match fabrics
- 1 yard paper-backed fusible tear-away stabilizer
- 1 yard lightweight fusible tricot
- Coordinating beads for embellishment (optional)
- Backing 34" x 41"
- Thin batting 34" x 41"
- Basic sewing supplies and tools

Instructions

Step 1. From off-white background fabric cut the following rectangles: 26" x 9$\frac{1}{2}$" (block A); 13$\frac{1}{2}$" x 10$\frac{1}{2}$" (block B); 13$\frac{1}{2}$" x 6$\frac{1}{2}$" (block C); 7$\frac{1}{2}$" x 23" (block D); 17$\frac{1}{2}$" x 8$\frac{1}{2}$" (block E).

Step 2. Referring to photo, select fabrics for each block. To scrunch the batik centers (area within dashed lines on templates), estimate the cut fabric size by measuring motif and multiplying by 4.

Step 3. With blending or contrasting elastic thread in the looper and coordinating thread in the needle, chain-stitch a grid design on each square to be scrunched as shown in Fig. 1. Stitch on the wrong side of the fabric on the lengthwise grain and then on the crosswise grain, using the presser foot as a guide.

Step 4. Steam-press the wrong side of the stitched fabric lightly to scrunch. Fuse lightweight fusible tricot to the wrong side of the square to stabilize.

Fig. 1
Chain-stitch a grid on each square as shown.

Step 5. Trace the appliqué motifs on paper-backed fusible tear-away stabilizer. Cut out leaving roughly $\frac{1}{4}$" margin around traced solid lines. Following manufacturer's instructions, fuse to selected appliqué fabrics. Cut out on solid traced line, remove paper and fuse to block background. Cut out the center sections (dashed lines) through all layers.

Step 6. Place scrunched fabric behind cut-out areas and straight-stitch in place. Satin-stitch all raw edges; add decorative outline or buttonhole stitch outside satin stitch if desired. Repeat for all blocks.

Step 7. From narrow-frame batik fabric cut $\frac{3}{4}$"-wide strips to match the appropriate length and width of blocks or joined blocks. Align raw edges of strips with raw edges of block(s) and stitch in place. Stitch to the bottom of block A, right side of block B, left side of block C, left side of block D and top of block E.

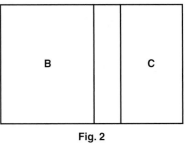

Fig. 2
Join blocks B and C
with sashing.

Step 8. From sashing batik cut one strip 2" x 13$\frac{1}{2}$". Sew between blocks B and C as shown in Fig. 2. Add a narrow frame strip across the bottom of the B-C unit. Cut another sashing strip 2" x 17$\frac{1}{2}$" and join the B-C

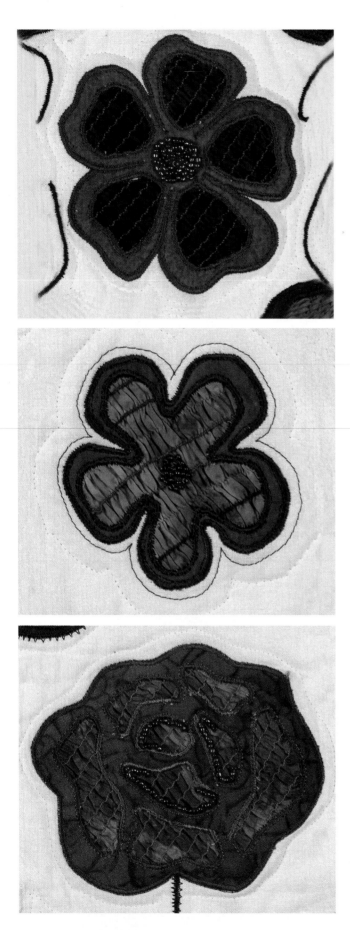

unit to E as shown in Fig. 3. Add a narrow frame strip to the right side of the B-C-E unit.

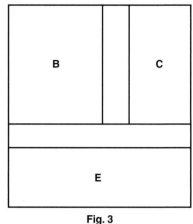

Fig. 3
Join the B-C unit and sashing with E as shown.

Step 9. From sashing batik cut one strip 2" x 23". Sew between block D and the B-C-E unit as shown in Fig. 4. Add narrow frame strips to the top and bottom edges of the B-C-E-D unit.

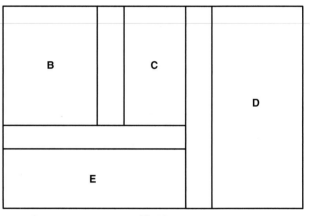

Fig. 4
Add sashing and block D to the B-C-E unit.

Step 10. From sashing batik cut one strip 2" x 26" and add to the top of the B-C-D-E unit. Add block A to the top of the quilt as shown in Fig. 5. Add a narrow frame strip to the top of the quilt.

Step 11. From border/sashing batik cut two strips $2\frac{1}{2}$" x 26" and serge to top and bottom of quilt. Add a narrow frame strip to the two sides of the quilt.

Step 12. From border/sashing batik cut two strips $2\frac{1}{2}$" x $37\frac{1}{2}$" and stitch to sides of quilt.

Step 13. Baste quilt layers for quilting. Quilt and embellish with beads and decorative threads as desired.

Step 14. From narrow frame/binding batik prepare 4 yards of $3\frac{1}{2}$"-wide binding. Fold the binding

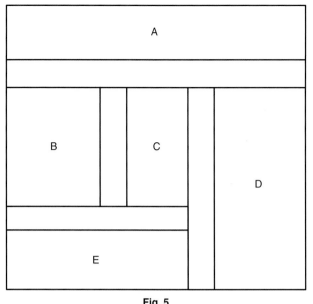

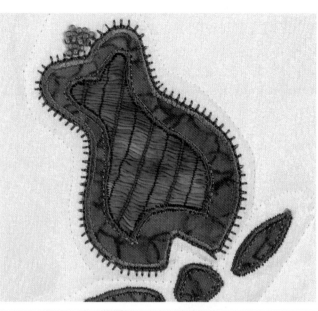

Fig. 5
Add block A to the top as shown.

engthwise, wrong sides together. Serge the raw edges
o the quilt border. Bring the folded edge to the back
f the quilt and slipstitch by hand or quilt in the ditch
by machine. ✂

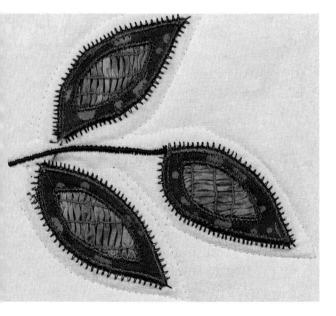

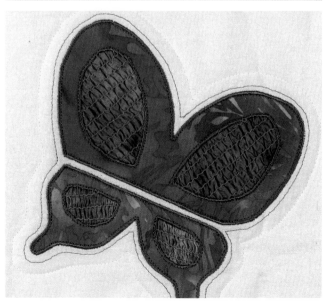

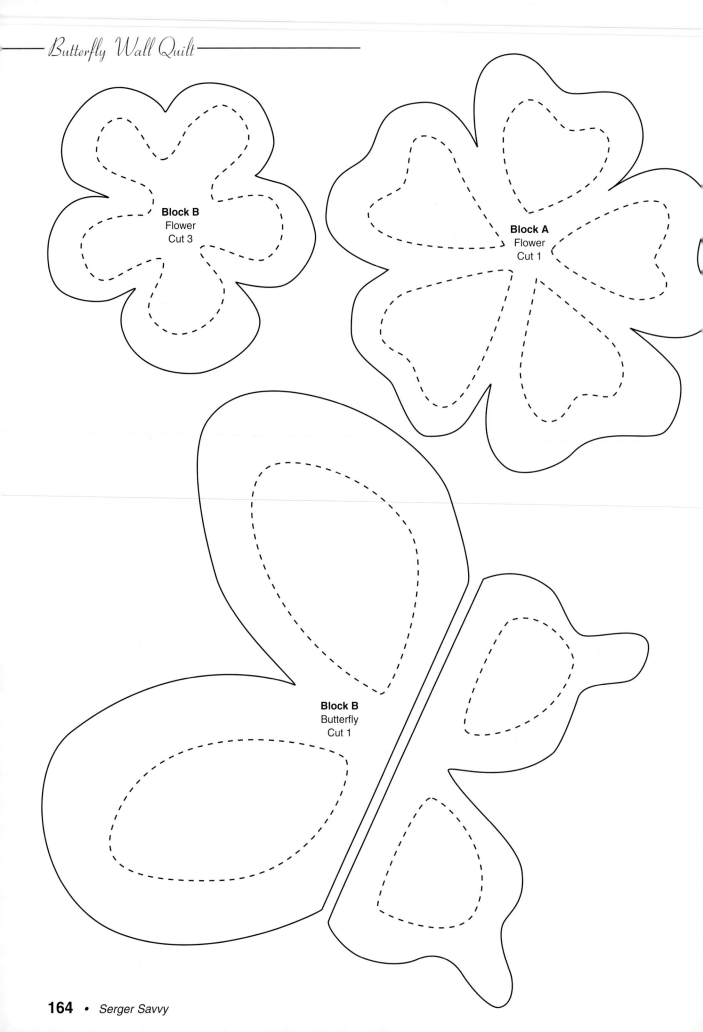

Block B
Flower
Cut 3

Block A
Flower
Cut 1

Block B
Butterfly
Cut 1

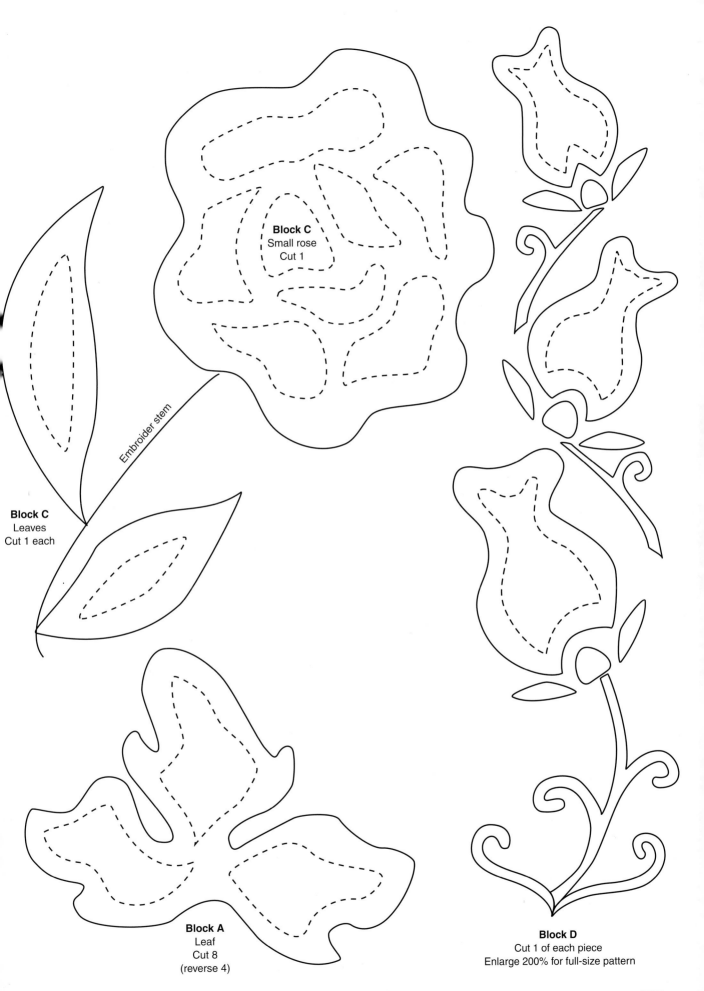

Block C
Small rose
Cut 1

Embroider stem

Block C
Leaves
Cut 1 each

Block A
Leaf
Cut 8
(reverse 4)

Block D
Cut 1 of each piece
Enlarge 200% for full-size pattern

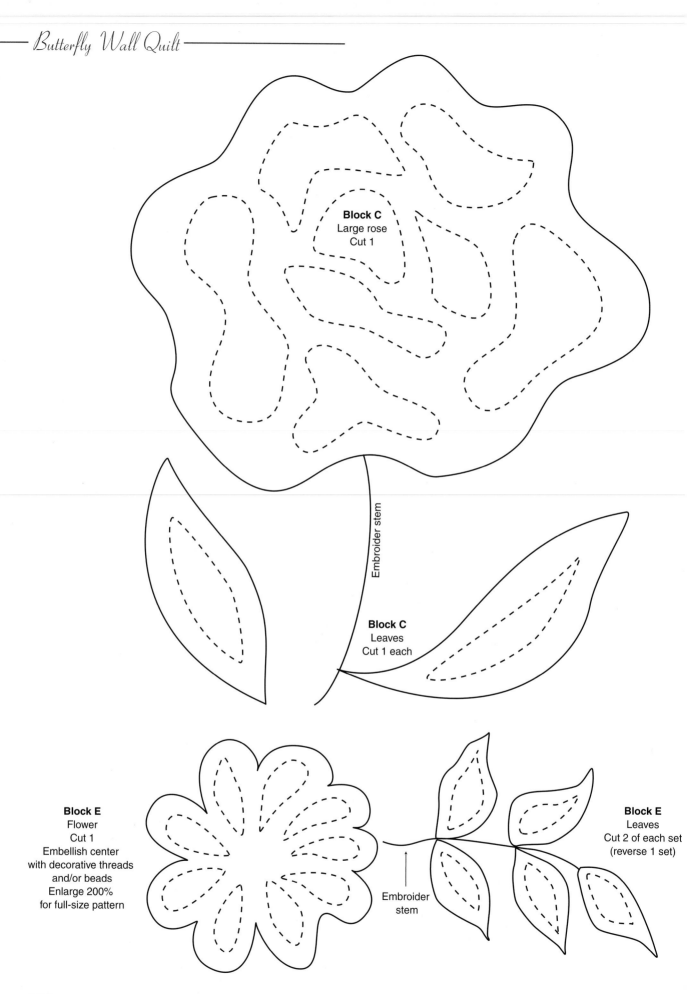

Block C
Large rose
Cut 1

Embroider stem

Block C
Leaves
Cut 1 each

Block E
Flower
Cut 1
Embellish center
with decorative threads
and/or beads
Enlarge 200%
for full-size pattern

Embroider
stem

Block E
Leaves
Cut 2 of each set
(reverse 1 set)

Beaded Floral Sampler

By Agnes Mercik

Learn and apply four different appliqué techniques when you make this embellished wall quilt.

Project Specifications

Skill Level: Intermediate

Quilt Size: 30½" x 33½"

Materials

- 1 yard cream background fabric
- ½ yard multicolored batik for sashing and borders
- ¼ yard lighter coordinating batik for narrow borders
- ⅓ yard darker coordinating batik for binding
- Wide variety of batik scraps in coordinating, contrasting and green shades for appliqué
- ½ yard very fine fusible tricot
- 1 yard fusible transfer web
- ½ yard paper-backed fusible tear-away stabilizer
- Water-soluble stabilizer
- Clear and smoky nylon monofilament
- Wide variety of rayon, cotton, poly and metallic decorative threads
- 2-ply wool/acrylic thread in coordinating colors
- Thick rayon, cotton and metallic-type threads
- 6-strand embroidery floss in matching and contrasting colors
- 4-strand rayon or silk floss
- Matching or contrasting elastic threads
- Matching all-purpose threads
- Temporary spray adhesive
- Variety of beads as desired for embellishment
- Backing 35" x 39"
- Thin batting 35" x 39"
- Open-toe embroidery foot
- Open-toe appliqué foot
- Tapestry needle
- Basic sewing supplies and tools

Instructions

Contemporary Tulips

Note: *This block is based on the Mola, an interesting and colorful technique incorporating both traditional and reverse appliqué. It is typically associated with the Indian women of the Kuna tribe living on the San Blas Islands, just off the Atlantic coast of Panama.*

The traditional Mola starts with two to four layers of different-colored fabrics placed in an order where parts of the various layers are cut away to reveal a section of the color beneath.

The contemporary machine Mola technique is very interesting when used in a nontraditional way. It is ideal for quilting, and fashion garments and accessories where unusual interest or rich, bold effects are desired.

Step 1. From cream background fabric cut one rectangle 14½" x 14".

Step 2. Trace the outline of the tulip motif onto the paper side of the fusible transfer web. Draw another line approximately ³⁄₈" outside the first line as shown in Fig. 1.

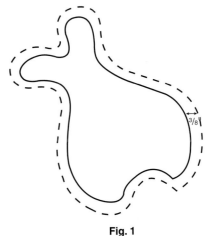

³⁄₈"

Fig. 1
Draw another line approximately ³⁄₈"
outside the first line as shown.

Note: *Prior to cutting any fabric, spray the motifs with sizing to prevent fraying while handling.*

Step 3. Place the traced tulip motif, fusible side down, to the wrong side of the background rectangle. With fine, sharp scissors, cut out the entire motif along the inner line, leaving the ³⁄₈" outer edge in place.

Step 4. Trace the next inner piece of the tulip, also adding the ³⁄₈" seam allowance on the paper-backed fusible web. Fuse to the wrong side of the second layer of fabric. Trim away the center design area and along the ³⁄₈" outer line.

Step 5. Remove the paper backing from the top layer and with right side to wrong side, center and fuse the

next layer to the first under the motif opening.

Step 6. Remove the paper backing from the back of the second layer and with right side to wrong side use a bottom layer of fabic that is large enough to cover the cutaway area to the second layer.

Step 7. With nylon monofilament, stitch all cut edges through all layers using a very narrow blanket stitch, approximately 1/2–1mm wide and 1 1/2–2mm long.

Step 8. For the stems and three leaf areas, treat as usual fusible appliqué. Trace pieces on fusible transfer web, cut out leaving roughly 1/4" margin around traced lines. Following manufacturer's instructions, fuse to selected fabrics. Cut out on traced lines and fuse to background.

Step 9. With matching or contrasting thread satin-stitch or buttonhole-stitch around shapes. Additional machine stitching and beading may be used to embellish flowers, stems and leaves.

Elasti-Quations

Note: Elastic thread can be used either in the bobbin or looper of a serger chain stitch to create interesting effects for appliqué motifs.

Elastic thread comes in many weights, colors and stretch characteristics. Choose the thread weight in relation to the fabric weight or the amount you want to shirr. This technique is not applicable to heavy fabric types.

Fabric weight, finish and dyes all play a part in the shirring equation. A rule of thumb in selecting fabric is to purchase two to four times more than the pattern or motif to be used. Testing is imperative.

Needle thread will show slightly, so choose a thread that will either match exactly or blend well. Decide whether or not you want to highlight the elastic thread on the right side of the motif or on the underside for a more subtle form of shirring.

Step 1. From cream background fabric cut one rectangle 10 1/2" x 14".

Step 2. Review the instructions for scrunching and appliquéing in Butterfly Wall Quilt, page 160, Steps 2–6. Repeat for flowers and leaves.

Step 3. Highlight the satin stitching with a contrasting thread and a straight stitch alongside the satin stitch, or blanket-stitch, directly over the satin stitch.

Step 4. Trace stems on background fabric. Cover

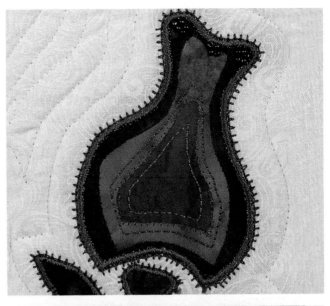

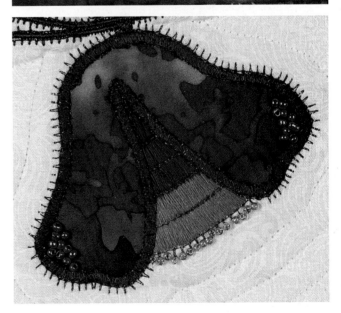

with satin stitch and blanket-stitch directly over the satin stitch.

Step 5. Embellish with beads as desired.

Upside-Down Appliqué

Note: Upside-down appliqué is another nontraditional approach to finishing edges of motifs. The decorative threads are used in the bobbin instead of the needle. With this technique, any thicker threads and yarns can be used that would not normally work in a needle. When using heavier and bulkier threads, lengthen the stitch length to allow the threads to lie flat.

Step 1. From cream background fabric cut one rectangle 10½" x 14".

Step 2. Trace, cut and fuse two of each appliqué motif on selected fabrics. Cut out on traced lines.

Step 3. Referring to photo, position and mark placement of the motifs on the background fabric. On the right side of the fabric, straight-stitch or zigzag with a very narrow stitch (approximately 1.5mm long and 1–1.5mm wide) along the edge of the large flower motifs.

Step 4. Place a heavy decorative thread in the bobbin, fine-tune the length, width and tension on scrap fabric. Thicker threads usually require less tension and slightly longer and wider stitch lengths as the zigzag fills in more quickly than with thin threads.

Step 5. On the wrong side of the background fabric, zigzag to cover the previous stitching line with decorative bobbin thread.

Step 6. Add more stitching on the right side of the fabric wherever the motifs seem to need more definition.

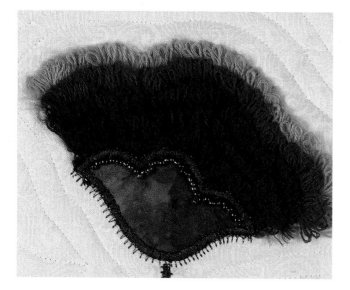

Step 7. The outer parts of the leaves are handled in the same manner as the flowers. The centers are placed on top of the larger leaf shape and satin-stitched as traditional machine appliqué.

Step 8. Embellish with beads as desired.

Wool Appliqué

Note: This technique simulates traditional machine appliqué, the difference being the thread. Wool and acrylic thread used for this project is often in a 2-ply version and can be stitched with a #90 or #100 topstitch or embroidery needle. There is also a thicker version, but it can only be used on the bobbin or looper of an overlock machine. Occasionally you may have to tighten the needle tension slightly. Testing is recommended.

Step 1. From cream background fabric cut one rectangle 14½" x 14".

Step 2. Trace, cut and fuse appliqué motifs on selected fabrics. Cut out on traced lines.

Step 3. Fuse flower A and fuse and stitch leaves and flowers C and D to the background fabric. The centers of flowers C and D are placed directly over the bottom layer of the flower and stitched. Transfer dashed lines for flower A and flower B to background fabric,

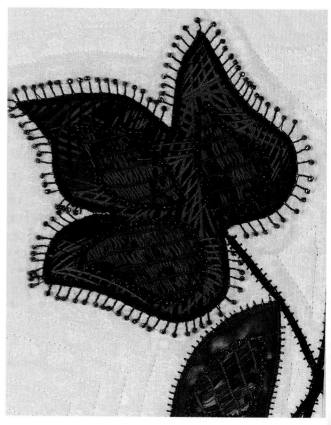

Step 4. To complete the fringed flower A, zigzag with the widest satin stitch your machine can stitch on the dashed lines indicated. To gain as much width to the fringe as possible, lower the needle tension almost to 0. This will carry the needle thread underneath to a greater distance.

Step 5. Along one edge of the wide satin stitch, stitch a narrow satin stitch or close straight stitch. Complete each row following this two-step procedure. Shade the thread colors used for a natural look.

Step 6. When all rows are completed, cut the bobbin thread of the wide satin stitch carefully with a pair of very sharp embroidery scissors. From the right side, lift the satin stitch carefully away from the edge with a tapestry needle. This will create the fringe.

Step 7. Satin-stitch the base of flower A after the fringing is complete.

Step 8. The center of flower B has rows of satin stitches between the dashed lines with a reversible straight stitch between each row. After satin stitching is complete, fuse and stitch the fabric flower piece.

Step 9. Trace stems and stitch as in Elasti-Quations, Step 4.

Step 10. Embellish with beads as desired.

Assembly

Step 1. From multicolored batik cut two strips 2½" x 14" and one strip 2½" x 26½" for sashing. From lighter

Wool Appliqué
Enlarge pattern 200%

coordinating batik cut two strips 1¼" x 14" and one strip 1½" x 26½". Fold narrow strips in half lengthwise, wrong sides together. Sew one narrow strip to one side of each wide strip, aligning raw edges.

Step 2. Join blocks with sashing as shown in Fig. 2. Press narrow strips toward blocks.

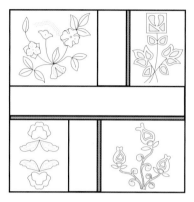

Fig. 2
Join blocks with sashing as shown.

Step 3. From multicolored batik cut two strips each 2¾" x 29½" and 2¾" x 31". From lighter coordinating batik cut two strips each 1¼" x 29½" and 1¼" x 31". Fold narrow strips in half lengthwise, wrong sides together. Sew one narrow strip to one side of each wide strip, aligning raw edges.

Step 4. Sew two strips to opposite sides of quilt, narrow border strips toward the blocks. Press narrow border strips toward blocks. Sew longer strips to top and bottom of quilt in same manner.

Step 5. Sandwich quilt top, batting and backing, using temporary spray adhesive to secure the layers together. Echo-quilt by machine around the appliqué shapes. Trim layers even with top.

Step 6. From darker coordinating batik, cut and join enough 2½"-wide strips to make 4 yards of binding. Fold the binding lengthwise, wrong sides together. Serge the raw edges to the quilt border. Bring the folded edge to the back of the quilt and slipstitch by hand or quilt in the ditch by machine. ✄

Upside-Down Appliqué
Repeat design and flip upside-down
Enlarge pattern 133% before cutting

Elasti-Quations
Enlarge 133%

Contemporary Tulips
Enlarge pattern 200%

Doll Bed Coverlets & Pillows

Continued from page 157

coordinating rectangles together on long edges as in Steps 1 and 2.

Step 2. Place panel on pillow backing and trim to same size. Serge on all sides, leaving a 3" opening for turning. Turn right side out, stuff with polyester fiberfill and close opening with hand stitches.

White Coverlet & Pillow

This coverlet and pillow pattern may be varied in many ways. The white model in the photo has a slightly longer ruffle and white solid fabric is substituted for the prints. It also requires 5½ yards of 1" eyelet edging. Construction is the same, but before flatlocking each seam, place the straight edge of the eyelet edging on the raw edge of fabric. Then place the second fabric over the lace and continue to flatlock in the same manner as above. A pastel floss or yarn woven in the ladder adds a delicate highlight. Machine embroidery will also enhance the project. Choose colors and designs that will show off the embroidery, rather than take away from it. This project is simple enough to be constructed by a young girl as a beginner sewing project. ✁

Special Thanks

We would like to thank the talented sewing designers whose work is featured in this collection.

Naomi Baker
Beaded Jewelry Bag, 66
Little Miss Lace Collar, 86
Puffed-Braid Closure Vest, 100

Diana Cedolia
T-shirt Twin Set, 94
Sashiko Place Mat, 121

Nancy Fiedler
Creating Diamonds, 52
Flatlocked Diamond Blouse, 57
Flatlocked Diamond Fleece
    Pullover, 60
Diamond Leather Purse, 62
Diamond Tote, 64
Flatlocked Skirt & Jacket
    Ensemble, 110

Agnes Mercik
Heirloom Serging, 46

Heirloom Pillow, 49
Prairie Points Purse, 72
Double-Layer Chiffon Scarf, 84
Dare-to-Be-Different Dress,
    Jacket & Purse, 68
Leather Beaded Vest, 102
Zebra Vest, 104
Seams Great, 108
Batik Two-Piece Outfit, 114
Suede Book Cover, 116
Jungle Crayon Bag, 118
Majestic Place Mat & Napkin, 126
Majestic Pillow, 128
Dainty Daisy Pillow, 136
Full-of-Tucks Pillow, 139
Woven Fabric Ribbon Pillows, 144
Antique Battenburg Lace
    Pillow, 153
Doll Bed Coverlets & Pillows, 156
Chili Peppers Mini Banner, 158

Butterfly Wall Quilt, 160
Beaded Floral Sampler, 167

Anne van der Kley
Lady of Spain Shawl, 75
Sheer Delight Scarf, 81
Opulent Abstract Elegant
    Jacket, 96
Decorator Cushion Trio, 148

Carol Zentgraf
Rosy Fleece Robe, 89
Flatlocked Oriental Tunic, 92
Flatlocked Fringe Table
    Set, 124
Blanket-Stitched Pillows, 132
Flower-Power Pillow, 142

We add a special thank you to Agnes Mercik for writing the informational material on sergers and to Nancy Fiedler for introducing her special technique for creating diamonds. We also thank Meredith Yoder, Lori Bender, Louise Phillips and Florine Golden for sharing their serger expertise with us.

Fabrics & Supplies

Page 57: Flatlocked Diamond Blouse—Madeira Décor 6 thread, Madeira Polyneon embroidery thread

Page 60: Flatlocked Diamond Fleece Pullover—Butterick Pattern #3205 and A&E Signature variegated quilting thread

Page 62: Diamond Leather Purse—YLI silk #30 thread

Page 64: Diamond Tote—YLI Woolly Nylon

Page 75: Lady of Spain Shawl —YLI Pearl Crown Rayon or Madeira Décor embellishment thread

Page 89: Rosy Fleece Robe—YLI Woolly Nylon

Page 92: Flatlocked Oriental Tunic—Kwik Sew pattern #2989

Page 94: T-Shirt Twin Set—Designer 6 thread

Page 96: Opulent Abstract Elegant Jacket— YLI Natural Pearl Crown Rayon thread

Page 108: Seams Great—Lyla Messinger pattern LJ-72?

Page 110: Flatlocked Skirt & Jacket Ensemble—Butterick skirt pattern #5254, Butterick jacket pattern #6938, and Valdani Hand-Dyed variegated quilting thread

Page 114: Batik Two-Piece Outfit—Lyla Messinger pattern LJ-723

Page 118: Jungle Crayon Bag—YLI Woolly Nylon

Page 132: Blanket-Stitched Pillows—YLI Woolly Nylon

Page 142: Flower-Power Pillow—YLI Woolly Nylon

Page 144: Woven Fabric Ribbon Pillows—YLI Jeans Stitch thread, YLI Pearl Crown rayon thread

Page 148: Decorator Cushion Trio—YLI Pearl Crown rayon or Madeira Décor

Metric Conversion Charts

Metric Conversions

U.S. Measurement		Multiplied by		Metric Measurement
yards	x	.9144	=	meters (m)
yards	x	91.44	=	centimeters (cm)
inches	x	2.54	=	centimeters (cm)
inches	x	25.40	=	millimeters (mm)
inches	x	.0254	=	meters (m)

Metric Measurement		Multiplied by		U.S. Measurement
centimeters	x	.3937	=	inches
meters	x	1.0936	=	yards

Standard Equivalents

U.S. Measurement		Metric Measurement		
1/8 inch	=	3.20 mm	=	0.32 cm
1/4 inch	=	6.35 mm	=	0.635 cm
3/8 inch	=	9.50 mm	=	0.95 cm
1/2 inch	=	12.70 mm	=	1.27 cm
5/8 inch	=	15.90 mm	=	1.59 cm
3/4 inch	=	19.10 mm	=	1.91 cm
7/8 inch	=	22.20 mm	=	2.22 cm
1 inch	=	25.40 mm	=	2.54 cm
1/8 yard	=	11.43 cm	=	0.11 m
1/4 yard	=	22.86 cm	=	0.23 m
3/8 yard	=	34.29 cm	=	0.34 m
1/2 yard	=	45.72 cm	=	0.46 m
5/8 yard	=	57.15 cm	=	0.57 m
3/4 yard	=	68.58 cm	=	0.69 m
7/8 yard	=	80.00 cm	=	0.80 m
1 yard	=	91.44 cm	=	0.91 m

U.S. Measurement		Metric Measurement		
1 1/8 yard	=	102.87 cm	=	1.03 m
1 1/4 yard	=	114.30 cm	=	1.14 m
1 3/8 yard	=	125.73 cm	=	1.26 m
1 1/2 yard	=	137.16 cm	=	1.37 m
1 5/8 yard	=	148.59 cm	=	1.49 m
1 3/4 yard	=	160.02 cm	=	1.60 m
1 7/8 yard	=	171.44 cm	=	1.71 m
2 yards	=	182.88 cm	=	1.83 m
2 1/8 yards	=	194.31 cm	=	1.94 m
2 1/4 yards	=	205.74 cm	=	2.06 m
2 3/8 yards	=	217.17 cm	=	2.17 m
2 1/2 yards	=	228.60 cm	=	2.29 m
2 5/8 yards	=	240.03 cm	=	2.40 m
2 3/4 yards	=	251.46 cm	=	2.51 m
2 7/8 yards	=	262.88 cm	=	2.63 m
3 yards	=	274.32 cm	=	2.74 m
3 1/8 yards	=	285.75 cm	=	2.86 m
3 1/4 yards	=	297.18 cm	=	2.97 m
3 3/8 yards	=	308.61 cm	=	3.09 m
3 1/2 yards	=	320.04 cm	=	3.20 m
3 5/8 yards	=	331.47 cm	=	3.31 m
3 3/4 yards	=	342.90 cm	=	3.43 m
3 7/8 yards	=	354.32 cm	=	3.54 m
4 yards	=	365.76 cm	=	3.66 m
4 1/8 yards	=	377.19 cm	=	3.77 m
4 1/4 yards	=	388.62 cm	=	3.89 m
4 3/8 yards	=	400.05 cm	=	4.00 m
4 1/2 yards	=	411.48 cm	=	4.11 m
4 5/8 yards	=	422.91 cm	=	4.23 m
4 3/4 yards	=	434.34 cm	=	4.34 m
4 7/8 yards	=	445.76 cm	=	4.46 m
5 yards	=	457.20 cm	=	4.57 m